THE RYRIE STUDY BIBLE

The New Testament

The Ryrie Study Bible:

THE NEW TESTAMENT

Charles Caldwell Ryrie, TH.D., PH.D.

MOODY PRESS
CHICAGO, ILLINOIS

THE RYRIE STUDY BIBLE: THE NEW TESTAMENT
Published by Pillar Books for Moody Press

Second printing, February 1977
ISBN: 0-8024-7432-2
Library of Congress Catalogue Card Number: 76-17518
Copyright © 1976 by Moody Bible Institute of Chicago
All Rights Reserved
Printed in the United States of America

Moody Press
820 North LaSalle Street
Chicago, Illinois 60610, U.S.A.

To the Reader

THE BIBLE is the greatest of all books; to study it is the noblest of all pursuits; to understand it, the highest of all goals. The Ryrie Study Bible is especially designed to help you achieve that goal.

Every time you read this Bible, whether seriously or casually, be sure to look at the notes at the bottom of the page. These are designed to help you understand and illuminate the verses you are reading. The notes provide a variety of helps: some furnish historical or archeological background; others translate or interpret the text more clearly; some define words and doctrines; and many refer you to other passages which relate to the same subject.

When you wish to study a book of the Bible more systematically, then you will want to read the Introduction to that book, which will give you information about the author, background, and contents. A unique feature of this Bible is the outline of each book printed at the end of each Introduction and also interspersed throughout the text. In this way you can readily see as you are reading through a book exactly where you are in the development of the ideas of that book by simply referring to the complete outline in the Introduction. The Introductions will start you on the right track; the outlines will keep you on the track; and the notes will illuminate the track.

In addition, you will find at the back of the Bible an index of the principal subjects treated in the notes. For example, if you want to study the doctrine of Christ, you will find in that index a list of references to notes where various aspects of that subject are mentioned. There is also a Harmony of the Gospels for use when you want to locate the several accounts of any event in the Gospels.

Useful as helps can be, the most important thing is to read the Bible itself. This is God's Word to you. I pray that these notes will serve to make it clearer and more personally meaningful.

Charles Caldwell Ryrie, TH.D., PH.D.

The New Testament

THE NAME given to the second half of the English Bible is "the New Testament," which comes from the Greek phrase "the New Covenant." The word *covenant* meant an arrangement made by one party which the other party involved could accept or reject but could not alter. The Old Testament records God's dealings with Israel on the basis of the covenant given through Moses at Mt. Sinai, while the New Testament describes the new arrangement of God with men through Christ and on the basis of the new covenant (see Ex. 24:1–8; Luke 22:14–20; 2 Cor. 3:6–11). The Old Covenant revealed the holiness of God in the righteous standard of the law and promised a coming Redeemer; the New Covenant shows the holiness of God in His righteous Son. The New Testament, then, contains those writings which reveal the content of this New Covenant.

The message of the New Testament centers around (1) the Person who gave Himself for the remission of sins (Matt. 26:28) and (2) the people (the church) who have received His salvation. Thus the central theme of the New Testament is salvation. The Gospels introduce the Savior. The book called the Acts of the Apostles describes the spread of the good news about His salvation through a large part of the Mediterranean world of the first century A.D. The epistles give details of the blessings of that salvation, and the Revelation previews the culmination of salvation.

The Arrangement of the Books of the New Testament
The New Testament includes 27 books written by nine different authors (unless Paul wrote Hebrews, then only eight), over about 50 years' time. These books fall naturally into four divisions:

1) The Four Gospels. These describe the life and ministry of Jesus Christ. Although they were actually written later than many other books of the New Testament, it was only natural that in the order of the books a priority position should be given to these accounts of Jesus' ministry.

2) The book of Acts. This is the history of the beginning of the church and the spread of Christianity throughout the Greco-Roman world.

3) The 21 letters (Romans through Jude). Since archeological discoveries have shown that letter-writing was a common means of communication in the first Christian centuries, it is not surprising to find that most of the books of the New Testament were letters. The apostle Paul, the great missionary and theologian of the early church, wrote 13 or 14 of these letters. They were addressed to churches and to individuals, and they teach Christian doctrine in a formal way (as in Romans), as well as in its application to life situations (as in 1 Corinthians and Philemon).

4) The Revelation. The last book describes the ultimate triumph of Jesus Christ and His people in the future.

The Order of the Books of the New Testament The order of the books of the New Testament is a logical one. First come the Gospels, which record the life of Christ; then the Acts, which gives the history of the spread of Christianity; then the letters, which show the development of the doctrines of the church along with its problems; and finally the vision of the second coming of Christ in the Revelation.

However, the order of the writing of the books was approximately like this:

James	A.D. 45–50
Galatians	49
1 and 2 Thessalonians	51
Mark	50's
1 Corinthians	56
2 Corinthians	57
Romans	58
Luke	60
Colossians, Ephesians, Philippians, Philemon	61
Acts	61
Matthew	60's
1 Timothy	63
1 Peter	63
Titus	65
2 Timothy	66
2 Peter	66
Hebrews	64–68
Jude	70–80
John	85–90
1, 2, 3 John	90
Revelation	90's

The Collection of the Books   After they were written, the individual books were not immediately gathered together into the canon or collection of 27 which comprise the New Testament. Groups of books like Paul's letters and the Gospels were preserved at first by the churches or people to whom they were sent, and gradually all 27 books were collected and formally acknowledged by the church as a whole.

This process took about 350 years. In the second century the circulation of books that promoted heresy gave strong impetus to the distinguishing of valid scripture from other Christian literature. Certain tests were applied to determine which books should be included. 1) Was the book written or backed by an apostle? 2) Were its contents of a spiritual nature? 3) Did it give evidence of being inspired by God? 4) Was it widely received by the churches?

Not all of the 27 books that were eventually recognized as canonical were accepted by all the churches in the early centuries, but this does not mean that those that were not immediately or universally accepted were spurious. Letters addressed to individuals (Philemon, 2 and 3 John) would not have been circulated as widely as those sent to churches. The books most disputed were James, Jude, 2 Peter, 2 and 3 John, and Philemon, but ultimately these were included and the canon was certified at the Council of Carthage in A.D. 397.

Although no original copy of any of the writings which comprise the New Testament has survived, there exist more than 4,500 Greek manuscripts of all or part of the text, plus some 8,000 Latin manuscripts and at least 1,000 other versions into which the original books were translated. Careful study and comparison of these many copies has given us an accurate and trustworthy New Testament.

Introduction to the Gospels

What Are the Gospels? Gospel means "good news." Thus the Gospels are so called because they record the good news that a way of salvation has been opened to all mankind through the death and resurrection of Jesus Christ (Mark 1:1; 1 Cor. 15:3–4).

Biography as we know it was unknown when the Gospels were written, and they are not really biographies as we understand that literary form. They were written that people might know who Jesus was and believe on Him (John 20:31).

Why Did the Gospels Need to Be Written? The rapid spread of Christianity precipitated the need for written accounts of the life of Christ. Too, as major figures in the stories, and eyewitnesses also, began to die there was an increasing need for written accounts of what they had seen. These written Gospels were used to evangelize, to catechize new converts, and probably as part of early Christian worship (Luke 1:1–4). In the Introduction to each Gospel we shall try to show its distinctive quality.

Why Four Gospels? Although there were numerous other gospels written, only four were deemed worthy to be included in the New Testament. These other gospels were written later and are of doubtful reliability, and although they contain some of the information that is in the four canonical Gospels, they also add much that is obviously fanciful and legendary (like the story of Jesus' condemning a boy to die because he had knocked Him down, as reported in an apocryphal Gnostic writing known as 1 Infancy, 19: 22–24). Too, they often tried to bolster some heretical or sectarian viewpoint.

The early church did distinguish these apocryphal gospels from the true ones and regarded the apocryphal ones as of much lesser importance. One of the reasons was that the Four Gospels were written by apostles or by their close associates. Later church councils confirmed their authenticity and included only the four in the canon or collection of books recognized as inspired and authoritative.

The Four Gospels were written to the great groups of the

first century. Matthew was written for the Jews; Mark for the Romans; Luke for the Gentiles; and John for the Christian church.

What Are the Synoptic Gospels? Matthew, Mark, and Luke present much similar material about the life of Christ, as even a quick examination of a harmony of His life will show. They have a more or less common view of His activities and teachings, and of the chronology of events. Therefore they are called the Synoptic Gospels (from synopsis = a viewing together). For example, all but 31 verses in Mark have parallels in either Matthew or Luke. On the other hand, much of the material in John's Gospel is unique, since its organization is according to long discourses, and it cannot be grouped with the other three. The differences in the four supplement each other without contradiction, and the similarities complement each other, so that the result is a fourfold record of the redemptive ministry of Jesus Christ.

INTRODUCTION TO
THE GOSPEL ACCORDING TO
Matthew

AUTHOR: Matthew   DATE: 60's

The Author   Matthew, who was surnamed Levi (Mark 2:14), was a Jewish tax-collector (a publican) for the Roman government (9:9). Because he collaborated with the Romans, who were hated by the Jews as overlords of their country, Matthew (and all publicans) was despised by fellow Jews. Nevertheless, Matthew responded to Christ's simple call to follow Him. After the account of the banquet he gave for his colleagues so they too could meet Jesus, he is not mentioned again except in the list of the Twelve (Matt. 10:3; see also Acts 1:13). Tradition says that he preached in Palestine for a dozen years after the resurrection of Christ and then went to other lands, but there is no certainty of this.

The Distinctive Approach of Matthew   Matthew was written to Jews to answer their questions about Jesus of Nazareth who claimed to be their Messiah. Was He in fact the Messiah predicted in the Old Testament? If He was, why did He fail to establish the promised kingdom? Will it ever be established, and what is God's purpose in the meantime? Thus, in the Gospel, Jesus is often spoken of as the Son of David and the one who fulfills the Old Testament prophecies of Messiah; and the kingdom of heaven is the subject of much of His recorded teaching.

Matthew is also characterized by its inclusion of those outside of Judaism. The closing verses record the commission to go into all the world, and only in Matthew does the word church appear in the Gospels (16:18; 18:17). Jesus is also designated as the Son of Abraham (1:1), and in

1

Abraham "shall all families of the earth be blessed" (Gen. (12:3).

The Date Although the Gospel has been dated in the 80's or 90's, the fact that the destruction of Jerusalem in A.D. 70 is viewed as an event yet future in 24:2 seems to require an earlier date. Some feel that this was the first of the Gospels to be written (about 50), while others think it was not the first and that it was written in the 60's.

The Contents Important sections in Matthew include the Sermon on the Mount (chapters 5–7) with the Beatitudes (5:3–12) and the Lord's Prayer (6:9–13), the parables of the kingdom (chapter 13), and the Olivet Discourse concerning future events (chapters 24–25). The theme of the book is Christ the King, and the outline reflects that theme.

OUTLINE OF THE GOSPEL OF MATTHEW

I The Person of the King, 1:1–4:25
  A His Background, 1:1–17
  B His Birth, 1:18–2:23
    1 The announcement of the birth, 1:18–25
    2 The adoration of the baby, 2:1–12
    3 The advancement of the boy, 2:13–23
  C His Baptism, 3:1–17
  D His Temptation, 4:1–11
  E His Inauguration, 4:12–25
II The Preaching of the King, 5:1–7:29
  A The Picture of Kingdom Life, 5:1–16
  B The Precepts for Kingdom Life, 5:17–48
    1 The law of Moses, 5:17–20
    2 The law of murder, 5:21–22
    3 The law of reconciliation, 5:23–26
    4 The law of adultery, 5:27–30
    5 The law of divorce, 5:31–32
    6 The law of oaths, 5:33–37
    7 The law of nonresistance, 5:38–42
    8 The law of love, 5:43–48
  C The Practice of Kingdom Life, 6:1–7:12
    1 In relation to almsgiving, 6:1–4
    2 In relation to prayer, 6:5–15
    3 In relation to fasting, 6:16–18
    4 In relation to money, 6:19–24
    5 In relation to anxiety, 6:25–34
    6 In relation to judging, 7:1–5
    7 In relation to prudence, 7:6
    8 In relation to prayer, 7:7–11
    9 In relation to others, 7:12

THE GOSPEL ACCORDING TO
Matthew

I THE PERSON OF THE KING, 1:1–4:25

A His Background, 1:1–17

1 The book of the generation of Jesus Christ, the son of David, the son of Abraham.

2 Abraham begat Isaac; and Isaac begat Jacob; and Jacob begat Judas and his brethren;

3 And Judas begat Phār'es and Zara of Thamar; and Phares begat Esrom; and Esrom begat Aram;

4 And Aram begat Amin'adab; and Aminadab begat Nāas'son; and Naasson begat Salmon;

5 And Salmon begat Bō'oz of Rā'chab; and Booz begat Obed of Ruth; and Obed begat Jesse;

6 And Jesse begat David the king; and David the king begat Solomon of her *that had been the wife* of Ūrī'as;

7 And Solomon begat Rōbō'am; and Roboam begat Abī'a; and Abia begat Asa;

8 And Asa begat Jos'aphat; and Josaphat begat Joram; and Joram begat Ōzī'as;

1:1 *Jesus Christ.* The name "Jesus" is Greek (and Latin) for the Hebrew "Joshua." It means "the Lord is salvation." "Christ" is Greek for the Hebrew *Meshiah*, meaning "Messiah" or "anointed one." *Son of David* was a highly popular Messianic title of the times. The genealogy here is traced through Joseph, Jesus' legal (though not natural) father, and it establishes His claim and right to the throne of David (1:6). The genealogy in Luke 3:23–38 is evidently that of Mary, though some believe it also is Joseph's by assuming that Matthan (Matt. 1:15)

9 And Ōzĭ'as begat Jō'atham; and Joatham begat Ā'chaz; and Achaz begat Ezēkī'as;

10 And Ezēkī'as begat Manas'sēs; and Manasses begat Amon; and Amon begat Josias;

11 And Josias begat Jechōnī'as and his brethren, about the time they were carried away to Babylon:

12 And after they were brought to Babylon, Jechōnī'as begat Salā'thiel; and Salathiel begat Zorob'abel;

13 And Zorob'abel begat Abī'ud; and Abiud begat Ēlī'-akim; and Eliakim begat Ā'zor;

14 And Ā'zor begat Sadoc; and Sadoc begat Ā'chim; and Achim begat Ēlī'ud;

15 And Ēlī'ud begat Eleā'zar; and Eleazar begat Mat'-than; and Matthan begat Jacob;

16 And Jacob begat Joseph the husband of Mary, of whom was born Jesus, who is called Christ.

17 So all the generations from Abraham to David *are* fourteen generations; and from David until the carrying away into Babylon *are* fourteen generations; and from the carrying away into Babylon unto Christ *are* fourteen generations.

B His Birth, 1:18–2:23

1 *The announcement of the birth*, 1:18–25

18 ¶ Now the birth of Jesus Christ was on this wise: When as his mother Mary was espoused to Joseph, before they came together, she was found with child of the Holy Ghost.

19 Then Joseph her husband, being a just *man*, and not

and Matthat (Luke 3:24) were the same person and Jacob and Heli were brothers (one being Joseph's father and the other his uncle). See note at Luke 3:23.

1:11 *Jechonias.* The N.T. form of Jeconiah, who was Jehoiachin, king of Judah, and who was taken into captivity by Nebuchadnezzar in 597 B.C. Jeremiah contracted "Jeconiah" to "Coniah" (Jer. 22:24,28; 37:1). A curse was pronounced on Coniah that none of his seed would prosper sitting on the throne of David. Had our Lord been the natural son of Joseph, He could not have prospered on the throne of David because of this curse. But since He came through Mary's lineage, He was not affected by this curse.

1:16 *of whom.* The word is feminine singular, indicating clearly that Jesus was born of Mary only and not of Mary and Joseph. It is one of the strongest evidences for the virgin birth.

1:19 *her husband.* Although Joseph and Mary were not yet married at this time, so sacred was the period of engagement or

willing to make her a publick example, was minded to put her away privily.

20 But while he thought on these things, behold, the angel of the Lord appeared unto him in a dream, saying, Joseph, thou son of David, fear not to take unto thee Mary thy wife: for that which is conceived in her is of the Holy Ghost.

21 And she shall bring forth a son, and thou shalt call his name JESUS: for he shall save his people from their sins.

22 Now all this was done, that it might be fulfilled which was spoken of the Lord by the prophet, saying,

23 Behold, a virgin shall be with child, and shall bring forth a son, and they shall call his name Emmanuel, which being interpreted is, God with us.

24 Then Joseph being raised from sleep did as the angel of the Lord had bidden him, and took unto him his wife:

25 And knew her not till she had brought forth her first-born son: and he called his name JESUS.

2 *The adoration of the baby,* 2:1–12

2 Now when Jesus was born in Bethlehem of Judæa in the days of Herod the king, behold, there came wise men from the east to Jerusalem,

2 Saying, Where is he that is born King of the Jews? for we have seen his star in the east, and are come to worship him.

3 When Herod the king had heard *these things,* he was troubled, and all Jerusalem with him.

4 And when he had gathered all the chief priests and scribes of the people together, he demanded of them where Christ should be born.

betrothal that they were by custom considered as if married (Gen. 29:21; Deut. 22:23–30). That is why Joseph's only recourse seemed to be to "put her away," which meant to give her a bill of divorcement, that is, a certificate saying in effect, "This woman is not my wife; I am not her husband" (see Hos. 2:2).

2:1 *Bethlehem.* The town is five miles S. of Jerusalem. *Herod the king.* This was Herod the Great, whose family, though nominally Jewish, were in reality Edomite, and who was king, with Roman help, from 40–4 B.C. He built the temple in Jerusalem which Christ knew. *wise men.* These magi from the east were experts in the study of the stars. Tradition says that there were three and that they were kings.

2:4 *scribes.* Scribes, who belonged mainly to the party of the

5 And they said unto him, In Bethlehem of Judæa: for thus it is written by the prophet,

6 And thou Bethlehem, *in* the land of Juda, art not the least among the princes of Juda: for out of these shall come a Governor, that shall rule my people Israel.

7 Then Herod, when he had privily called the wise men, enquired of them diligently what time the star appeared.

8 And he sent them to Bethlehem, and said, Go and search diligently for the young child; and when ye have found *him*, bring me word again, that I may come and worship him also.

9 When they had heard the king, they departed; and, lo, the star, which they saw in the east, went before them, till it came and stood over where the young child was.

10 When they saw the star, they rejoiced with exceeding great joy.

11 ¶ And when they were come into the house, they saw the young child with Mary his mother, and fell down, and worshipped him: and when they had opened their treasures, they presented unto him gifts; gold, and frankincense, and myrrh.

12 And being warned of God in a dream that they should not return to Herod, they departed into their own country another way.

3 *The advancement of the boy*, 2:13-23

13 And when they were departed, behold, the angel of the Lord appeareth to Joseph in a dream, saying, Arise, and take the young child and his mother, and flee into

---

Pharisees, functioned as members of a highly honored profession. They were professional students and defenders of the law, gathering around them pupils whom they instructed in the law. They were also referred to as lawyers because they were entrusted with the administration of the law as judges in the Sanhedrin (Matt. 22:35).

2:6 *a Governor*. See Micah 5:2. An earthly king, though a supernatural one, is meant.

2:11 *into the house . . . the young child*. These words need not indicate that the wise men came sometime after the birth of Christ. The family would naturally have moved into a house as quickly as possible after Jesus was born, and "young child" can mean a newborn (John 16:21). *gold, and frankincense, and myrrh*. These were gifts worthy of a king. The early church fathers understood the gold to be symbolic of Christ's deity; the frankincense, of His purity; and the myrrh, of His death (since it was used for embalming).

Egypt, and be thou there until I bring thee word: for Herod will seek the young child to destroy him.

14 When he arose, he took the young child and his mother by night, and departed into Egypt:

15 And was there until the death of Herod: that it might be fulfilled which was spoken of the Lord by the prophet, saying, Out of Egypt have I called my son.

16 ¶ Then Herod, when he saw that he was mocked of the wise men, was exceeding wroth, and sent forth, and slew all the children that were in Bethlehem, and in all the coasts thereof, from two years old and under, according to the time which he had diligently enquired of the wise men.

17 Then was fulfilled that which was spoken by Jeremy the prophet, saying,

18 In Rama was there a voice heard, lamentation, and weeping, and great mourning, Rachel weeping *for* her children, and would not be comforted, because they are not.

19 ¶ But when Herod was dead, behold, an angel of the Lord appeareth in a dream to Joseph in Egypt,

20 Saying, Arise, and take the young child and his mother, and go into the land of Israel: for they are dead which sought the young child's life.

21 And he arose, and took the young child and his mother, and came into the land of Israel.

22 But when he heard that Archelā'us did reign in Judæa in the room of his father Herod, he was afraid to go thither: notwithstanding, being warned of God in a dream, he turned aside into the parts of Galilee:

23 And he came and dwelt in a city called Nazareth: that it might be fulfilled which was spoken by the prophets, He shall be called a Nazarene.

2:15 See Hosea 11:1.
2:17–18 A quotation of Jer. 31:15, which depicts the wailing at the time of Israel's exile. That calamity and Herod's new atrocity are viewed as part of the same picture. Since Matthew was writing to those with Jewish background, he used more quotations from the O.T. than the other Gospel writers (there are 93 in Matthew, 49 in Mark, 80 in Luke, and 33 in John).
2:22 *Archelaus.* On the death of Herod the Great the Romans divided his kingdom among his sons: Archelaus (Judah and Samaria), Antipas (Galilee and and Perea), Philip (NE. Palestine). Archelaus was a bloody king and, worse in the eyes of Rome, ineffective. He was removed by Caesar Augustus in A.D. 6 and banished to Gaul.
2:23 *He shall be called a Nazarene.* Probably a synonym for "contemptible" or "despised" since Nazareth was a most unlikely place for the residence of the Messiah (Isa. 53:3; Ps. 22:6).

C His Baptism, 3:1–17

3 In those days came John the Baptist, preaching in the wilderness of Judæa,

2 And saying, Repent ye: for the kingdom of heaven is at hand.

3 For this is he that was spoken of by the prophet Ēsā′as, saying, The voice of one crying in the wilderness, Prepare ye the way of the Lord, make his paths straight.

4 And the same John had his raiment of camel's hair, and a leathern girdle about his loins; and his meat was locusts and wild honey.

5 Then went out to him Jerusalem, and all Judæa, and all the region round about Jordan,

6 And were baptized of him in Jordan, confessing their sins.

7 ¶ But when he saw many of the Pharisees and Sadducees come to his baptism, he said unto them, O generation of vipers, who hath warned you to flee from the wrath to come?

3:1 *the wilderness of Judea.* A barren wasteland extending along the W. shore of the Dead Sea.

3:2 *Repent ye.* Repentance is a change of mind that bears fruit in a changed life (see v. 8). *kingdom of heaven.* This is the rule of heaven over the earth. The Jewish people of Christ's day were looking for this Messianic or Davidic kingdom to be established on the earth, and this is what John proclaimed as "at hand." The rejection of Christ by the people delayed the establishment of the kingdom until the second coming of Christ (Matt. 25:31). Today heaven rules through the professing church (Matt. 13).

3:7 *Pharisees.* The Pharisees were the most influential of the Jewish sects at the time of Christ. Though holding orthodox doctrines, their zeal for the Mosaic law led them to a degenerate though strict outward observance of both the law and their equally authoritative interpretations of it. They knew the Scriptures (Matt. 23:2), tithed (Luke 18:12), fasted (Matt. 9:14), prayed (Mark 12:40); but they were hypocritical (Matt. 23:15), self-righteous (Luke 18:9), and the foremost persecutors of the Lord (Matt. 9:3). *Sadducees.* The Sadducees, whose membership came largely from the priesthood and upper classes, were the anti-supernaturalists of Christ's day. They denied the tuth of bodily resurrection, of future punishment and reward, and of the existence of angels (Acts 23:8). Though they upheld the written law of Moses, they were opposed to the oral tradition observed by the Pharisees. They were the party of the high-priestly families of Jerusalem with direct interests in the apparatus of temple worship, and were generally collaborators with the Roman rulers. They opposed Christ as

8 Bring forth therefore fruits meet for repentance:

9 And think not to say within yourselves, We have Abraham to *our* father: for I say unto you, that God is able of these stones to raise up children unto Abraham.

10 And now also the axe is laid unto the root of the trees: therefore every tree which bringeth not forth good fruit is hewn down, and cast into the fire.

11 I indeed baptize you with water unto repentance: but he that cometh after me is mightier than I, whose shoes I am not worthy to bear: he shall baptize you with the Holy Ghost, and *with* fire:

12 Whose fan *is* in his hand, and he will throughly purge his floor, and gather his wheat into the garner; but he will burn up the chaff with unquenchable fire.

13 ¶ Then cometh Jesus from Galilee to Jordan unto John, to be baptized of him.

14 But John forbad him, saying, I have need to be baptized of thee, and comest thou to me?

15 And Jesus answering said unto him, Suffer *it to be so* now: for thus it becometh us to fulfil all righteousness. Then he suffered him.

16 And Jesus, when he was baptized, went up straightway out of the water: and, lo, the heavens were opened unto

vigorously as the Pharisees and were condemned by Him as severely though not so frequently (Matt. 16:1–4, 6).

3:9 *We have Abraham to our father.* The common teaching of that day said that the Jews participated in the merits of Abraham, which made their prayers acceptable, helped in war, expiated sins, appeased the wrath of God, and assured a share in God's eternal kingdom. No wonder the people were startled when John and Jesus preached the necessity of personal repentance.

3:11 *baptize.* Baptism is an identification. John's baptism was a sign of an individual's acknowledgment of his need of repentance for the remission of his sins. When Jesus was baptized by John (v. 15) He identified Himself with John's message of righteousness (though being sinless, He Himself needed no cleansing from sin). The baptism with the Holy Spirit, predicted here, identifies members of the body of Christ with Christ, the risen Head of that body (1 Cor. 12:13). Christian baptism is identification with the Christian message and the Christian group. *with fire.* Probably a reference to the judgments associated with the return of Christ (v. 12; Mal. 3:1–5; 4:1–3).

3:12 *Whose fan is in his hand.* A wooden shovel used for tossing grain against the wind after threshing so that the lighter chaff would be blown away, leaving the grain to settle in a pile.

3:16–17 This is the first clear expression of the concept of the

him, and he saw the Spirit of God descending like a dove, and lighting upon him:

17 And lo a voice from heaven, saying, This is my beloved Son, in whom I am well pleased.

D His Temptation, 4:1–11

4 Then was Jesus led up of the Spirit into the wilderness to be tempted of the devil.

2 And when he had fasted forty days and forty nights, he was afterward an hungred.

3 And when the tempter came to him, he said, If thou be the Son of God, command that these stones be made bread.

4 But he answered and said, It is written, Man shall not live by bread alone, but by every word that proceedeth out of the mouth of God.

5 Then the devil taketh him up into the holy city, and setteth him on a pinnacle of the temple,

6 And saith unto him, If thou be the Son of God, cast thyself down: for it is written, He shall give his angels charge concerning thee: and in *their* hands they shall bear thee up, lest at any time thou dash thy foot against a stone.

7 Jesus said unto him, It is written again, Thou shalt not tempt the Lord thy God.

8 Again, the devil taketh him up into an exceeding high mountain, and sheweth him all the kingdoms of the world, and the glory of them;

9 And saith unto him, All these things will I give thee, if thou wilt fall down and worship me.

10 Then saith Jesus unto him, Get thee hence, Satan:

Trinity. The descent of the Spirit upon Christ was for special power at the beginning of His public ministry.

4:1 Satan's intention in the temptation was to make Christ sin so as to thwart the whole purpose of God for man's redemption by disqualifying the Savior. God's purpose (note that the Spirit led Jesus into the test) was to prove His Son to be sinless and thus a worthy Savior. It is clear that He was actually tempted; it is equally clear that He was sinless (2 Cor. 5:21). See note at Heb. 4:15.

4:4 See Deut. 8:3.

4:6 Satan also quotes the Bible (in this instance, Ps. 91:11–12), though not accurately, for he omitted a phrase which was not suited to his purpose.

4:7 See Deut. 6:16.

4:9 *will I give thee.* Satan, as prince of this world, was within his rights to make this offer (John 12:31; see note at 1 John 2:15).

4:10 See Deut. 6:13; 10:20.

for it is written, Thou shalt worship the Lord thy God, and him only shalt thou serve.

11 Then the devil leaveth him, and, behold, angels came and ministered unto him.

E His Inauguration, 4:12–25

12 ¶ Now when Jesus had heard that John was cast into prison, he departed into Galilee;

13 And leaving Nazareth, he came and dwelt in Caper′naum, which is upon the sea coast, in the borders of Zabū′lon and Neph′thalim:

14 That it might be fulfilled which was spoken by Ēsǎ′as the prophet, saying,

15 The land of Zabū′lon, and the land of Neph′thalim, *by* the way of the sea, beyond Jordan, Galilee of the Gentiles;

16 The people which sat in darkness saw great light; and to them which sat in the region and shadow of death light is sprung up.

17 ¶ From that time Jesus began to preach, and to say, Repent: for the kingdom of heaven is at hand.

18 ¶ And Jesus, walking by the sea of Galilee, saw two brethren, Simon called Peter, and Andrew his brother, casting a net into the sea: for they were fishers.

19 And he saith unto them, Follow me, and I will make you fishers of men.

20 And they straightway left *their* nets, and followed him.

21 And going on from thence, he saw other two brethren, James *the son* of Zebedee, and John his brother, in a ship with Zebedee their father, mending their nets; and he called them.

4:13 *leaving Nazareth*. According to Luke 4:16–30 this was because of what had happened there.

4:14 See Isa. 9:1–2; 42:6–7.

4:19 *Follow me*. This was their call to service and is illustrative of the directness, profundity, and power of Christ's commands ("Go ye . . . ," 28:19; "love one another," John 13:34).

4:21 *James the son of Zebedee*. This is the apostle James, the brother of John, who was martyred under Herod Agrippa I (Acts 12:2). Other men named James in the N.T. are: James the son of Alphaeus, "the less" (Mark 15:40), also one of the twelve (Matt. 10:3); James, the half-brother of Christ and writer of the epistle of James; James, the father or, less probably, brother of the apostle Judas, to be distinguished from Judas Iscariot (Luke 6:16; Acts 1:13).

22 And they immediately left the ship and their father, and followed him.

23 ¶ And Jesus went about all Galilee, teaching in their synagogues, and preaching the gospel of the kingdom, and healing all manner of sickness and all manner of disease among the people.

24 And his fame went throughout all Syria: and they brought unto him all sick people that were taken with divers diseases and torments, and those which were possessed with devils, and those which were lunatick, and those that had the palsy; and he healed them.

25 And there followed him great multitudes of people from Galilee, and *from* Decapolis, and *from* Jerusalem, and *from* Judæa, and *from* beyond Jordan.

II THE PREACHING OF THE KING, 5:1–7:29

A The Picture of Kingdom Life, 5:1–16

5 And seeing the multitudes, he went up into a mountain: and when he was set, his disciples came unto him:

2 And he opened his mouth, and taught them, saying,

4:23 *the gospel of the kingdom*. This is the good news that the presence of the King caused the rule of God on the earth (in fulfillment of many O.T. prophecies) to be "at hand." Prerequisites for entrance into the kingdom included repentance (Matt. 4:17), righteousness (Matt. 5:20), childlike faith (Matt. 18:3), or, in summary, being born again (John 3:3). Because the people rejected these requirements, Christ taught that His earthly reign would not immediately come (Luke 19:11). However, this gospel of the kingdom will be preached again during the tribulation period (Matt. 24:14) just prior to the return of Christ to establish His kingdom on earth (Matt. 25:31,34).

4:25 *Decapolis*. A district, originally containing ten cities, S. of the Sea of Galilee, mainly to the E. of the Jordan river.

5:1 *into a mountain*. Chapters 5–7 contain the widely known and loved Sermon on the Mount. It is one of 5 big discourses by Christ found in Matthew, the others being 9:35–10:42; 13:1–52; 17:24–18:35; and 23:1–25:46. The Sermon on the Mount does not present the way of salvation but the way of righteous living for those who are in God's family, contrasting the new Way with the old of the scribes and the Pharisees. For the Jews of Christ's day it was a detailed explanation of "repent" (3:2; 4:17). It was also an elaboration of the spirit of the law (5:17, 21–22, 27–28). For all of us it is a detailed revelation of the righteousness of God, and its principles are applicable to the children of God today.

3 Blessed *are* the poor in spirit: for theirs is the kingdom of heaven.

4 Blessed *are* they that mourn: for they shall be comforted.

5 Blessed *are* the meek: for they shall inherit the earth.

6 Blessed *are* they which do hunger and thirst after righteousness: for they shall be filled.

7 Blessed *are* the merciful: for they shall obtain mercy.

8 Blessed *are* the pure in heart: for they shall see God.

9 Blessed *are* the peacemakers: for they shall be called the children of God.

10 Blessed *are* they which are persecuted for righteousness' sake: for theirs is the kingdom of heaven.

11 Blessed are ye, when *men* shall revile you, and persecute *you*, and shall say all manner of evil against you falsely, for my sake.

12 Rejoice, and be exceeding glad: for great *is* your reward in heaven: for so persecuted they the prophets which were before you.

13 ¶ Ye are the salt of the earth: but if the salt have lost his savour, wherewith shall it be salted? it is thenceforth good for nothing, but to be cast out, and to be trodden under foot of men.

14 Ye are the light of the world. A city that is set on an hill cannot be hid.

15 Neither do men light a candle, and put it under a bushel, but on a candlestick; and it giveth light unto all that are in the house.

16 Let your light so shine before men, that they may see your good works, and glorify your Father which is in heaven.

B The Precepts for Kingdom Life, 5:17–48

1 *The law of Moses*, 5:17–20

17 ¶ Think not that I am come to destroy the law, or the prophets: I am not come to destroy, but to fulfil.

18 For verily I say unto you, Till heaven and earth pass, one jot or one tittle shall in no wise pass from the law, till all be fulfilled.

5:3–12 The Beatitudes (*blessed* means happy) describe the inner condition of a follower of Christ and promise him blessings in the future.

5:13 *salt* is a preservative from corruption, and it loses its savor by adulteration. So the disciples are to be the indispensable preservative of the world, and its light (v. 14).

5:18 *jot or tittle*. The jot is the smallest Hebrew letter, *yodh*,

19 Whosoever therefore shall break one of these least commandments, and shall teach men so, he shall be called the least in the kingdom of heaven: but whosoever shall do and teach *them*, the same shall be called great in the kingdom of heaven.

20 For I say unto you, That except your righteousness shall exceed *the righteousness* of the scribes and Pharisees, ye shall in no case enter into the kingdom of heaven.

2 *The law of murder,* 5:21–22

21 ¶ Ye have heard that it was said by them of old time, Thou shalt not kill; and whosoever shall kill shall be in danger of the judgment:

22 But I say unto you, That whosoever is angry with his brother without a cause shall be in danger of the judgment: and whosoever shall say to his brother, Rā'ca, shall be in danger of the council: but whosoever shall say, Thou fool, shall be in danger of hell fire.

3 *The law of reconciliation,* 5:23–26

23 Therefore if thou bring thy gift to the altar, and there rememberest that thy brother hath ought against thee;

24 Leave there thy gift before the altar, and go thy way; first be reconciled to thy brother, and then come and offer thy gift.

25 Agree with thine adversary quickly, whiles thou art in the way with him; lest at any time the adversary deliver thee to the judge, and the judge deliver thee to the officer, and thou be cast into prison.

26 Verily I say unto thee, Thou shalt by no means come out thence, till thou hast paid the uttermost farthing.

which looks like an apostrophe ('). A tittle is a very small extension or protrusion on several Hebrew letters which distinguish those letters from similar ones that do not have the extension. The Lord's point is that every letter of every word of the O.T. is vital and will be fulfilled.

5:20 *your righteousness.* We may understand this as "your practice of religion."

5:22 *Raca.* Probably means "empty-head." *hell fire.* The word translated "hell" is *geenna,* or Gehenna, a place in the valley of Hinnom where human sacrifices were offered (Jer. 7:31) and where the continuous burning of rubbish made it an apt illustration of the lake of fire (Mark 9:44; Jas. 3:6; Rev. 20:14).

5:26 *uttermost farthing.* We would say, "last penny."

4 *The law of adultery*, 5:27–30

27 ¶ Ye have heard that it was said by them of old time,
Thou shalt not commit adultery:

28 But I say unto you, That whosoever looketh on a
woman to lust after her hath committed adultery with her
already in his heart.

29 And if thy right eye offend thee, pluck it out, and cast
it from thee: for it is profitable for thee that one of thy
members should perish, and not *that* thy whole body should
be cast into hell.

30 And if thy right hand offend thee, cut it off, and cast
it from thee: for it is profitable for thee that one of thy
members should perish, and not *that* thy whole body
should be cast into hell.

5 *The law of divorce*, 5:31–32

31 It hath been said, Whosoever shall put away his wife,
let him give her a writing of divorcement:

32 But I say unto you, That whosoever shall put away
his wife, saving for the cause of fornication, causeth her to
commit adultery: and whosoever shall marry her that is
divorced committeth adultery.

6 *The law of oaths*, 5:33–37

33 ¶ Again, ye have heard that it hath been said by them
of old time, Thou shalt not forswear thyself, but shalt perform unto the Lord thine oaths:

5:28 The desire itself is sinful, and wrong desire leads to a sinful
act.

5:29–30 This is strong language used to emphasize the comparison; i.e., sin is so dangerous because it leads to eternal condemnation that it would be better to lose hands or eyes
temporarily than life eternally.

5:32 *saving for the cause of fornication.* See Matt. 19:3–9; Mark
10:2–12; Luke 16:18; and 1 Cor. 7:10–11 for Jesus' teaching
on divorce. It is disallowed except for fornication, which may
mean (1) adultery, or (2) unfaithfulness during the period
of betrothal (see Matt. 1:19), or (3) marriage between near
relatives (Lev. 18; Acts 15:29).

5:33 *forswear thyself.* This means "not perjure." Oaths taken in
the name of the Lord were binding, and perjury was strongly
condemned in the law (Ex. 20:7; Lev. 19:12; Deut. 19:16–
19). Every oath contained an affirmation or promise and an
appeal to God as omniscient and punisher of falsehoods which
made the oath binding. Thus we find phrases like "as the Lord
liveth" (1 Sam. 14:39). The emphasis on the sanctity of oaths
led to the feeling that ordinary phrasing might not be truthful;

34 But I say unto you, Swear not at all; neither by heaven; for it is God's throne:

35 Nor by the earth; for it is his footstool: neither by Jerusalem; for it is the city of the great King.

36 Neither shalt thou swear by thy head, because thou canst not make one hair white or black.

37 But let your communication be, Yea, yea; Nay, nay: for whatsoever is more than these cometh of evil.

7 *The law of nonresistance*, 5:38–42

38 ¶ Ye have heard that it hath been said, An eye for an eye, and a tooth for a tooth:

39 But I say unto you, That ye resist not evil: but whosoever shall smite thee on thy right cheek, turn to him the other also.

40 And if any man will sue thee at the law, and take away thy coat, let him have *thy* cloke also.

41 And whosoever shall compel thee to go a mile, go with him twain.

42 Give to him that asketh thee, and from him that would borrow of thee turn not thou away.

8 *The law of love*, 5:43–48

43 ¶ Ye have heard that it hath been said, Thou shalt love thy neighbour, and hate thine enemy.

44 But I say unto you, Love your enemies, bless them that curse you, do good to them that hate you, and pray for them which despitefully use you, and persecute you;

45 That ye may be the children of your Father which is in heaven: for he maketh his sun to rise on the evil and on the good, and sendeth rain on the just and on the unjust.

46 For if ye love them which love you, what reward have ye? do not even the publicans the same?

47 And if ye salute your brethren only, what do ye more *than others?* do not even the publicans so?

48 Be ye therefore perfect, even as your Father which is in heaven is perfect.

that is why the Lord said (Matt. 5:37), Say and mean yes or no, but do not equivocate.

5:38 See Ex. 21:24. The *lex talionis* (law of retaliation) did provide for the ending of feuds, but Christ showed another way to do the same (Matt. 5:39–42).

5:43 See Lev. 19:16–18.

5:44 A new teaching, found nowhere in the O.T.

5:48 *perfect.* Not necessarily without sin, but mature and complete in the likeness of God.

C The Practice of Kingdom Life, 6:1–7:12

1 *In relation to almsgiving, 6:1–4*

6 Take heed that ye do not your alms before men, to be seen of them: otherwise ye have no reward of your Father which is in heaven.

2 Therefore when thou doest *thine* alms, do not sound a trumpet before thee, as the hypocrites do in the synagogues and in the streets, that they may have glory of men. Verily I say unto you, They have their reward.

3 But when thou doest alms, let not thy left hand know what thy right hand doeth:

4 That thine alms may be in secret: and thy Father which seeth in secret himself shall reward thee openly.

2 *In relation to prayer, 6:5–15*

5 ¶ And when thou prayest, thou shalt not be as the hypocrites *are*: for they love to pray standing in the synagogues and in the corners of the streets, that they may be seen of men. Verily I say unto you, They have their reward.

6 But thou, when thou prayest, enter into thy closet, and when thou hast shut thy door, pray to thy Father which is in secret; and thy Father which seeth in secret shall reward thee openly.

7 But when ye pray, use not vain repetitions, as the heathen *do*: for they think that they shall be heard for their much speaking.

8 Be not yet therefore like unto them: for your Father knoweth what things ye have need of, before ye ask him.

9 After this manner therefore pray ye: Our Father which art in heaven, Hallowed be thy name.

10 Thy kingdom come. Thy will be done in earth, as *it is* in heaven.

11 Give us this day our daily bread.

6:1–18 Christ discusses 3 Pharisaic practices of piety; almsgiving, prayer, and fasting.

6:1 *alms*. Any righteous act.

6:4 *That thine alms may be in secret*. Jewish tradition says that there was in the temple a "chamber of secrets" into which the devout used to put their gifts in secret so that the poor could receive support therefrom in secret.

6:9 *After this manner*. The Lord's Prayer is a model for our prayers. It begins with adoration of God (v. 9), acknowledges subjection to His will (v. 10), asks petitions of Him (vv. 11–13a), and ends with an ascription of praise (v. 13b, though this may have been added later).

6:11 *bread*. This means all necessary food.

12 And forgive us our debts, as we forgive our debtors.

13 And lead us not into temptation, but deliver us from evil: For thine is the kingdom, and the power, and the glory, for ever. Amen.

14 For if ye forgive men their trespasses, your heavenly Father will also forgive you:

15 But if ye forgive not men their trespasses, neither will your Father forgive your trespasses.

3 *In relation to fasting*, 6:16–18

16 ¶ Moreover when ye fast, be not, as the hypocrites, of a sad countenance: for they disfigure their faces, that they may appear unto men to fast. Verily I say unto you, They have their reward.

17 But thou, when thou fastest, anoint thine head, and wash thy face;

18 That thou appear not unto men to fast, but unto thy Father which is in secret: and thy Father, which seeth in secret, shall reward thee openly.

4 *In relation to money*, 6:19–24

19 ¶ Lay not up for yourselves treasures upon earth, where moth and rust doth corrupt, and where thieves break through and steal:

20 But lay up for yourselves treasures in heaven, where neither moth nor rust doth corrupt, and where thieves do not break through nor steal:

21 For where your treasure is, there will your heart be also.

22 The light of the body is the eye: if therefore thine eye be single, thy whole body shall be full of light.

23 But if thine eye be evil, thy whole body shall be full of darkness. If therefore the light that is in thee be darkness, how great *is* that darkness!

24 ¶ No man can serve two masters: for either he will hate the one, and love the other; or else he will hold to the

---

6:12 *our debts*. These are obligations incurred; i.e., sins of omission and commission. Forgiveness means cancellation of these debts or obligations.

6:14–15 Notice that the only point the Lord emphasizes from the prayer is the necessity for forgiving one another. Forgiveness with the Father depends on forgiveness among the members of the family of God. This is the forgiveness of fellowship within the family of God, not the forgiveness that leads to salvation.

6:24 *mammon*=money.

one, and despise the other. Ye cannot serve God and mam'mon.

5 In relation to anxiety, 6:25–34

25 Therefore I say unto you, Take no thought for your life, what ye shall eat, or what ye shall drink; nor yet for your body, what ye shall put on. Is not the life more than meat, and the body than raiment?

26 Behold the fowls of the air: for they sow not, neither do they reap, nor gather into barns; yet your heavenly Father feedeth them. Are ye not much better than they?

27 Which of you by taking thought can add one cubit unto his stature?

28 And why take ye thought for raiment? Consider the lilies of the field, how they grow; they toil not, neither do they spin:

29 And yet I say unto you, That even Solomon in all his glory was not arrayed like one of these.

30 Wherefore, if God so clothe the grass of the field, which to day is, and to morrow is cast into the oven, *shall he* not much more *clothe* you, O ye of little faith?

31 Therefore take no thought, saying, What shall we eat? or, What shall we drink? or, Wherewithal shall we be clothed?

32 (For after all these things do the Gentiles seek:) for your heavenly Father knoweth that ye have need of all these things.

33 But seek ye first the kingdom of God, and his righteousness; and all these things shall be added unto you.

34 Take therefore no thought for the morrow: for the morrow shall take thought for the things of itself. Sufficient unto the day *is* the evil thereof.

6 In relation to judging, 7:1–5

7 Judge not, that ye be not judged.

2 For with what judgment ye judge, ye shall be

6:25 *take no thought*=be not anxious.

6:26 *your heavenly Father feedeth them.* God feeds the birds not by miraculous supply of food but through natural processes involving the earth and the birds' use of their faculties. Likewise, the child of God, though sometimes the recipient of a miracle, is usually cared for by normal means.

6:27 *cubit.* About 18 inches.

6:34 *evil*=trouble. Let each day's trouble be enough for that day. (This saying is like a proverb).

7:1 *Judge not.* This does not mean that one is never to judge another, for v. 5 indicates that when one's own life is pure he

judged: and with what measure ye mete, it shall be measured to you again.

3 And why beholdest thou the mote that is in thy brother's eye, but considerest not the beam that is in thine own eye?

4 Or how wilt thou say to thy brother, Let me pull out the mote out of thine eye; and, behold, a beam *is* in thine own eye?

5 Thou hypocrite, first cast out the beam out of thine own eye; and then shalt thou see clearly to cast out the mote out of thy brother's eye.

7 *In relation to prudence*, 7:6

6 ¶ Give not that which is holy unto the dogs, neither cast ye your pearls before swine, lest they trample them under their feet, and turn again and rend you.

8 *In relation to prayer*, 7:7–11

7 ¶ Ask, and it shall be given you; seek, and ye shall find; knock, and it shall be opened unto you:

8 For every one that asketh receiveth; and he that seeketh findeth; and to him that knocketh it shall be opened.

9 Or what man is there of you, whom if his son ask bread, will he give him a stone?

10 Or if he ask a fish, will he give him a serpent?

11 If ye then, being evil, know how to give good gifts unto your children, how much more shall your Father which is in heaven give good things to them that ask him?

9 *In relation to others*, 7:12

12 Therefore all things whatsoever ye would that men should do to you, do ye even so to them: for this is the law and the prophets.

D The Proof of Kingdom Life, 7:13–29

13 ¶ Enter ye in at the strait gate: for wide *is* the gate,

should cast the mote out of the brother's eye. It does mean, however, that a follower of Christ is not to be censorious.
7:3 *mote*. A very small dry particle; a speck.
7:6 The disciples were expected to make moral distinctions and not allow those who reject the invitation of Christ to treat precious things as cheap.
7:12 The well-known Golden Rule. It was also taught by the great Jewish rabbis, such as Rabbi Hillel.
7:13–29 In these verses notice the two ways (13–14), two trees (15–20), two professions (21–23), and two builders (24–29).

and broad *is* the way, that leadeth to destruction, and many
there be which go in thereat:

14 Because strait *is* the gate, and narrow *is* the way,
which leadeth unto life, and few there be that find it.

15 ¶ Beware of false prophets, which come to you in
sheep's clothing, but inwardly they are ravening wolves.

16 Ye shall know them by their fruits. Do men gather
grapes of thorns, or figs of thistles?

17 Even so every good tree bringeth forth good fruit;
but a corrupt tree bringeth forth evil fruit.

18 A good tree cannot bring forth evil fruit, neither *can*
a corrupt tree bring forth good fruit.

19 Every tree that bringeth not forth good fruit is hewn
down, and cast into the fire.

20 Wherefore by their fruits ye shall know them.

21 ¶ Not every one that saith unto me, Lord, Lord,
shall enter into the kingdom of heaven; but he that doeth
the will of my Father which is in heaven.

22 Many will say to me in that day, Lord, Lord, have
we not prophesied in thy name? and in thy name have cast
out devils? and in thy name done many wonderful works?

23 And then will I profess unto them, I never knew
you: depart from me, ye that work iniquity.

24 ¶ Therefore whosoever heareth these sayings of
mine, and doeth them, I will liken him unto a wise man,
which built his house upon a rock:

25 And the rain descended, and the floods came, and
the winds blew, and beat upon that house; and it fell not:
for it was founded upon a rock.

26 And every one that heareth these sayings of mine,
and doeth them not, shall be likened unto a foolish man,
which built his house upon the sand:

27 And the rain descended, and the floods came, and
the winds blew, and beat upon that house; and it fell: and
great was the fall of it.

The "two ways" was a common method of teaching in Judaism
and Greco-Roman philosophy.

7:21 Obedience to the will of God comes first.

7:22 *devils.* Lit., demons. There is only one devil (Satan) but
there are many demons. The demons are those angels who
sinned with Satan by following him when he revolted against
God. Some are confined (2 Pet. 2:4), but many are active in
the world (Matt. 12:43–45). They seek to thwart the purposes of God (Eph. 6:11–12); they promote their own system
of doctrine (1 Tim. 4:1); they can inflict diseases (Matt. 9:33)
and possess the bodies of men and animals (Matt. 4:24; Mark
5:13).

28 And it came to pass, when Jesus had ended these sayings, the people were astonished at his doctrine:

29 For he taught them as *one* having authority, and not as the scribes.

III THE PROOF OF THE KING, 8:1–9:38

A Exhibit #1: Power, 8:1–34

1 *Power over defilement,* 8:1–4

8 When he was come down from the mountain, great multitudes followed him.

2 And, behold, there came a leper and worshipped him, saying, Lord, if thou wilt, thou canst make me clean.

3 And Jesus put forth *his* hand, and touched him, saying, I will; be thou clean. And immediately his leprosy was cleansed.

4 And Jesus saith unto him, See thou tell no man; but go thy way, shew thyself to the priest, and offer the gift that Moses commanded, for a testimony unto them.

2 *Power over distance,* 8:5–13

5 ¶ And when Jesus was entered into Caper'naum, there came unto him a centurion, beseeching him,

6 And saying, Lord, my servant lieth at home sick of the palsy, grievously tormented.

7 And Jesus saith unto him, I will come and heal him.

8 The centurion answered and said, Lord, I am not worthy that thou shouldest come under my roof: but speak the word only, and my servant shall be healed.

9 For I am a man under authority, having soldiers under me: and I say to this *man,* Go, and he goeth; and to another, Come, and he cometh; and to my servant, Do this, and he doeth *it.*

10 When Jesus heard *it,* he marvelled, and said to them that followed, Verily I say unto you, I have not found so great faith, no, not in Israel.

11 And I say unto you, That many shall come from the

7:29 The scribes had to rely on tradition for authority; Christ's authority was His own. It disturbed the Pharisees that He had no "credentials" as an official teacher in their system.

8:2 *a leper.* See note at Luke 5:12.

8:4 *the gift that Moses commanded.* See Lev. 14:4–32.

8:5 *centurion.* A Roman army officer who commanded 100 men.

8:9 *a man under authority.* If a lesser officer can give orders, certainly Christ, who possesses all authority, can.

8:11 Gentiles will be included in the blessings of the millennial

east and west, and shall sit down with Abraham, and Isaac, and Jacob, in the kingdom of heaven.

12 But the children of the kingdom shall be cast out into outer darkness: there shall be weeping and gnashing of teeth.

13 And Jesus said unto the centurion, Go thy way; and as thou hast believed, so be it done unto thee. And his servant was healed in the selfsame hour.

3 Power over disease, 8:14–17

14 ¶ And when Jesus was come into Peter's house, he saw his wife's mother laid, and sick of a fever.

15 And he touched her hand, and the fever left her: and she arose, and ministered unto them.

16 ¶ When the even was come, they brought unto him many that were possessed with devils: and he cast out the spirits with *his* word, and healed all that were sick:

17 That it might be fulfilled which was spoken by Esaías the prophet, saying, Himself took our infirmities, and bare *our* sicknesses.

4 Power over disciples, 8:18–22

18 ¶ Now when Jesus saw great multitudes about him, he gave commandment to depart unto the other side.

19 And a certain scribe came, and said unto him, Master, I will follow thee whithersoever thou goest.

20 And Jesus saith unto him, The foxes have holes, and the birds of the air *have* nests; but the Son of man hath not where to lay *his* head.

21 And another of his disciples said unto him, Lord, suffer me first to go and bury my father.

22 But Jesus said unto him, Follow me; and let the dead bury their dead.

reign of Christ on this earth.
8:12 *children*=sons, *heirs*=Jews.
8:14 *his wife's mother.* Notice that Peter was married (see 1 Cor. 9:5).
8:15 *ministered*=served food.
8:17 See Isa. 53:4.
8:20 *Son of man.* The title Son of God is Jesus' divine name (Matt. 8:29); the Son of David, His Jewish name (Matt. 9:27); but Son of Man, the name that linked Him to the earth and to His mission. It was His favorite designation of Himself (used over 80 times) and was based on Dan. 7:13–14. It emphasizes: (1) the lowliness and humanity of His person (Matt. 8:20); (2) His suffering and death (Luke 19:10); and (3) His future reign as King (Matt. 24:27).

5 Power over the deep, 8:23-27

23 ¶And when he was entered into a ship, his disciples followed him.

24 And, behold, there arose a great tempest in the sea, insomuch that the ship was covered with the waves: but he was asleep.

25 And his disciples came to *him*, and awoke him, saying, Lord, save us: we perish.

26 And he saith unto them, Why are ye fearful, O ye of little faith? Then he arose, and rebuked the winds and the sea; and there was a great calm.

27 But the men marvelled, saying, What manner of man is this, that even the winds and the sea obey him!

6 Power over demons, 8:28-34

28 ¶ And when he was come to the other side into the country of the Ger'gesēnes, there met him two possessed with devils, coming out of the tombs, exceeding fierce, so that no man might pass by that way.

29 And, behold, they cried out, saying, What have we to do with thee, Jesus, thou Son of God? art thou come hither to torment us before the time?

30 And there was a good way off from them an herd of many swine feeding.

31 So the devils besought him, saying, If thou cast us out, suffer us to go away into the herd of swine.

32 And he said unto them, Go. And when they were come out, they went into the herd of swine: and, behold, the whole herd of swine ran violently down a steep place into the sea, and perished in the waters.

33 And they that kept them fled, and went their ways into the city, and told every thing, and what was befallen to the possessed of the devils.

34 And, behold, the whole city came out to meet Jesus: and when they saw him, they besought *him* that he would depart out of their coasts.

B Exhibit #2: Pardon, 9:1-17

1 Pardon of a palsied man, 9:1-8

9 And he entered into a ship, and passed over, and came into his own city.

2 And, behold, they brought to him a man sick of the

8:28 *Gergesenes.* Gadarenes, on the eastern shore of the Lake of Galilee.

9:1 *his own city.* Capernaum.

9:2 *sick of the palsy.* A paralytic. *thy sins be forgiven thee.* This

palsy, lying on a bed: and Jesus seeing their faith said unto the sick of the palsy; Son, be of good cheer; thy sins be forgiven thee.

3 And, behold, certain of the scribes said within themselves, This *man* blasphemeth.

4 And Jesus knowing their thoughts said, Wherefore think ye evil in your hearts?

5 For whether is easier, to say, *Thy* sins be forgiven thee; or to say, Arise, and walk?

6 But that ye may know that the Son of man hath power on earth to forgive sins, (then saith he to the sick of the palsy,) Arise, take up thy bed, and go unto thine house.

7 And he arose, and departed to his house.

8 But when the multitudes saw *it*, they marvelled, and glorified God, which had given such power unto men.

2 *Pardon of a publican*, 9:9–13

9 ¶ And as Jesus passed forth from thence, he saw a man, named Matthew, sitting at the receipt of custom: and he saith unto him, Follow me. And he arose, and followed him.

10 ¶ And it came to pass, as Jesus sat at meat in the house, behold, many publicans and sinners came and sat down with him and his disciples.

11 And when the Pharisees saw *it*, they said unto his disciples, Why eateth your Master with publicans and sinners?

12 But when Jesus heard *that*, he said unto them, They that be whole need not a physician, but they that are sick.

13 But go ye and learn what *that* meaneth, I will have mercy, and not sacrifice: for I am not come to call the righteous, but sinners to repentance.

may indicate that the man's sickness was the direct result of sin. Some Jews speculated that such was always the case, but see John 9:2 and note at Phil. 2:30.

9:5 Of course it is easier to *say* "Thy sins be forgiven," since the veracity of the statement cannot be tested so easily as "Arise." By making the statement Christ was taking to Himself a prerogative of God who alone can forgive sins.

9:10 *publicans and sinners*. Publicans were tax-collectors for the Romans, and they had a bad reputation for extortion and malpractice. They were subcontractors employed by a contractor or tax farmer who in turn was responsible to contractors in Rome. "Sinners" were those whose daily occupations rendered them ceremonially unclean and not, in Pharisaic eyes, to be consorted with.

9:13 See Hos. 6:6.

3 Problem concerning fasting, 9:14–17

14 ¶ Then came to him the disciples of John, saying, Why do we and the Pharisees fast oft, but thy disciples fast not?

15 And Jesus said unto them, Can the children of the bridechamber mourn, as long as the bridegroom is with them? but the days will come, when the bridegroom shall be taken from them, and then shall they fast.

16 No man putteth a piece of new cloth unto an old garment, for that which is put in to fill it up taketh from the garment, and the rent is made worse.

17 Neither do men put new wine into old bottles: else the bottles break, and the wine runneth out, and the bottles perish: but they put new wine into new bottles, and both are preserved.

C Exhibit #3: Power, 9:18–38

1 Power over death, 9:18–26

18 ¶ While he spake these things unto them, behold, there came a certain ruler, and worshipped him, saying, My daughter is even now dead: but come and lay thy hand upon her, and she shall live.

19 And Jesus arose, and followed him, and so did his disciples.

20 ¶ And, behold, a woman, which was diseased with an issue of blood twelve years, came behind him, and touched the hem of his garment:

21 For she said within herself, If I may but touch his garment, I shall be whole.

22 But Jesus turned him about, and when he saw her, he said, Daughter, be of good comfort; thy faith hath made thee whole. And the woman was made whole from that hour.

9:14 The Pharisees fasted twice a week—conspicuous piety. John's followers were probably fasting in mourning for him. The truly required public fasts were only 3 in number: the Day of Atonement; the day before Purim; and the 9th of Ab, commemorating the fall of Jerusalem.

9:16–17 The old and new cannot be combined. See note at Luke 5:37.

9:20 *an issue of blood.* I.e., suffering from hemorrhage. *the hem of his garment.* Probably the fringes or tassels at the corners of Christ's mantle. These were religious reminders to the wearer to observe the commandments (Num. 15:37–39).

23 And when Jesus came into the ruler's house, and saw the minstrels and the people making a noise,

24 He said unto them, Give place: for the maid is not dead, but sleepeth. And they laughed him to scorn.

25 But when the people were put forth, he went in, and took her by the hand, and the maid arose.

26 And the fame hereof went abroad into all that land.

2 *Power over darkness*, 9:27–31

27 ¶ And when Jesus departed thence, two blind men followed him, crying, and saying, *Thou* Son of David, have mercy on us.

28 And when he was come into the house, the blind men came to him: and Jesus saith unto them, Believe ye that I am able to do this? They said unto him, Yea, Lord.

29 Then touched he their eyes, saying, According to your faith be it unto you.

30 And their eyes were opened; and Jesus straitly charged them, saying, See *that* no man know *it*.

31 But they, when they were departed, spread abroad his fame in all that country.

3 *Power over dumbness*, 9:32–34

32 ¶ As they went out, behold, they brought to him a dumb man possessed with a devil.

33 And when the devil was cast out, the dumb spake: and the multitudes marvelled, saying, It was never so seen in Israel.

34 But the Pharisees said, He casteth out devils through the prince of the devils.

4 *Power over disease*, 9:35

35 And Jesus went about all the cities and villages, teaching in their synagogues, and preaching the gospel of the kingdom, and healing every sickness and every disease among the people.

5 *Pity on the people*, 9:36–38

36 ¶ But when he saw the multitudes, he was moved with compassion on them, because they fainted, and were scattered abroad, as sheep having no shepherd.

37 Then saith he unto his disciples, The harvest truly *is* plenteous, but the labourers *are* few;

38 Pray ye therefore the Lord of the harvest, that he will send forth labourers into his harvest.

9:23 *minstrels*. It was customary, even among the very poor, to hire two or more flute-players at times of mourning.

IV THE PROGRAM OF THE KING, 10:1–16:12

A The Program Announced, 10:1–11:1

10 And when he had called unto *him* his twelve disciples, he gave them power *against* unclean spirits, to cast them out, and to heal all manner of sickness and all manner of disease.

2 Now the names of the twelve apostles are these; The first, Simon, who is called Peter, and Andrew his brother; James *the son* of Zebedee, and John his brother;

3 Philip, and Bartholomew; Thomas, and Matthew the publican; James *the son* of Alphæ'us, and Lebbæ'us, whose surname was Thaddæ'us;

4 Simon the Cā'naanīte, and Judas Iscariot, who also betrayed him.

5 These twelve Jesus sent forth, and commanded them, saying, Go not into the way of the Gentiles, and into *any* city of the Samaritans enter ye not:

6 But go rather to the lost sheep of the house of Israel.

7 And as ye go, preach, saying, The kingdom of heaven is at hand.

8 Heal the sick, cleanse the lepers, raise the dead, cast out devils: freely ye have received, freely give.

9 Provide neither gold, nor silver, nor brass in your purses,

10 Nor scrip for *your* journey, neither two coats, neither shoes, nor yet staves: for the workman is worthy of his meat.

10:1 *disciples.* A disciple is one who is taught by another; he is a learner. In the Gospels the word is used frequently of disciples of Moses (John 9:28), of John the Baptist (John 3:25), and of Christ. Judas is an example of an unsaved disciple of Christ and there were others who deserted Him as well (John 6:66). The word is used in Acts as a synonym for believer, but it does not appear at all in the rest of the N.T.

10:2 *apostles.* The word "apostle" means "one sent forth" as an ambassador who bears a message and who represents the one who sent him. The qualifications included: (1) seeing the Lord and being an eyewitness to His resurrection (Acts 1:22; 1 Cor. 9:1); (2) being invested with miraculous sign-gifts (Acts 5:15–16; Heb. 2:3–4); (3) being chosen by the Lord or the Holy Spirit (Matt. 10:1–2; Acts 1:26).

10:4 *Canaanite.* In Luke 6:15 and Acts 1:13 Simon is called "Zelotes" (the Zealot) (the equivalent Greek term for Canaanite, or, more accurately, Canaanaean, a resident of Cana). He likely belonged, before following the Lord, to the extremist party of Zealots who advocated the overthrow of Rome by force.

10:10 *Nor scrip for your journey.* They are to travel light; perhaps

11 And into whatsoever city or town ye shall enter, enquire who in it is worthy; and there abide till ye go thence.

12 And when ye come into an house, salute it.

13 And if the house be worthy, let your peace come upon it: but if it be not worthy, let your peace return to you.

14 And whosoever shall not receive you, nor hear your words, when ye depart out of that house or city, shake off the dust of your feet.

15 Verily I say unto you, It shall be more tolerable for the land of Sodom and Gōmor'rha in the day of judgment, than for that city.

16 ¶ Behold, I send you forth as sheep in the midst of wolves: be ye therefore wise as serpents, and harmless as doves.

17 But beware of men: for they will deliver you up to the councils, and they will scourge you in their synagogues;

18 And ye shall be brought before governors and kings for my sake, for a testimony against them and the Gentiles.

19 But when they deliver you up, take no thought how or what ye shall speak: for it shall be given you in that same hour what ye shall speak.

20 For it is not ye that speak, but the Spirit of your Father which speaketh in you.

21 And the brother shall deliver up the brother to death, and the father the child: and the children shall rise up against *their* parents, and cause them to be put to death.

22 And ye shall be hated of all *men* for my name's sake: but he that endureth to the end shall be saved.

23 But when they persecute you in this city, flee ye into another: for verily I say unto you, Ye shall not have gone over the cities of Israel, till the Son of man be come.

24 The disciple is not above *his* master, nor the servant above his lord.

25 It is enough for the disciple that he be as his master,

---

it was a quick journey. They could count on traditional hospitality at the hands of many devout Jewish householders. Notice the change of instructions later in Luke 22:36.

10:17 *councils*=local courts. *scourge*=flog, with a bastinado, a painful punishment.

10:21–23 These verses are a prediction of persecution in the tribulation days and at the second coming of Christ (Matt. 24:9–14). Such unnatural acts against members of one's family have taken place under totalitarian regimes in the past.

10:25 *Beelzebub.* Means "lord of flies," a guardian deity of the Ekronites (2 Kings 1:2), but used by the Jews as an epithet for Satan. The name may have been a mocking Hebrew altera-

and the servant as his lord. If they have called the master of the house Bēel'zebub, how much more *shall they call* them of his household?

26 Fear them not therefore: for there is nothing covered, that shall not be revealed; and hid, that shall not be known.

27 What I tell you in darkness, *that* speak ye in light: and what ye hear in the ear, *that* preach ye upon the housetops.

28 And fear not them which kill the body, but are not able to kill the soul: but rather fear him which is able to destroy both soul and body in hell.

29 Are not two sparrows sold for a farthing? and one of them shall not fall on the ground without your Father.

30 But the very hairs of your head are all numbered.

31 Fear ye not therefore, ye are of more value than many sparrows.

32 Whosoever therefore shall confess me before men, him will I confess also before my Father which is in heaven.

33 But whosoever shall deny me before men, him will I also deny before my Father which is in heaven.

34 Think not that I am come to send peace on earth: I came not to send peace, but a sword.

35 For I am come to set a man at variance against his father, and the daughter against her mother, and the daughter in law against her mother in law.

36 And a man's foes *shall be* they of his own household.

37 He that loveth father or mother more than me is not worthy of me: and he that loveth son or daughter more than me is not worthy of me.

38 And he that taketh not his cross, and followeth after me, is not worthy of me.

tion of Baal-zebul, a local arch-demon of N. Palestine and Syria. For Jesus' enemies to allege that He was possessed by Beelzebub was the worst kind of blasphemy (Mark 3:22).

10:28 *him.* I.e., God, not Satan.

10:29 *a farthing.* This small copper coin is called in the Greek of this verse *assarion.* Its value was 1/16 of a denarius, the basic unit in Roman coinage, a silver coin worth about 20 cents. One denarius was the day's wage of a rural worker. *without your Father.* Without His knowledge.

10:34 Christ's mission involves tension, persecution, death. The gospel divides families (Mic. 7:6). The world will experience peace only when the King returns again to rule (Isa. 2:4).

10:38 *cross.* This first reference to a cross needed no explanation, for the Jews had seen thousands of their countrymen crucified by the Romans. Allegiance even to death is demanded of Christ's followers.

39 He that findeth his life shall lose it: and he that loseth his life for my sake shall find it.

40 ¶ He that receiveth you receiveth me, and he that receiveth me receiveth him that sent me.

41 He that receiveth a prophet in the name of a prophet shall receive a prophet's reward; and he that receiveth a righteous man in the name of a righteous man shall receive a righteous man's reward.

42 And whosoever shall give to drink unto one of these little ones a cup of cold *water* only in the name of a disciple, verily I say unto you, he shall in no wise lose his reward.

B The Program Attested, 11:2–12:50

1 *By comforting John's disciples*, 11:2–19

11 And it came to pass, when Jesus had made an end of commanding his twelve disciples, he departed thence to teach and to preach in their cities.

2 Now when John had heard in the prison the works of Christ, he sent two of his disciples,

3 And said unto him, Art thou he that should come, or do we look for another?

4 Jesus answered and said unto them, Go and shew John again those things which ye do hear and see:

5 The blind receive their sight, and the lame walk, the lepers are cleansed, and the deaf hear, the dead are raised up, and the poor have the gospel preached to them.

6 And blessed is *he*, whosoever shall not be offended in me.

7 ¶ And as they departed, Jesus began to say unto the multitudes concerning John, What went ye out into the wilderness to see? A reed shaken with the wind?

8 But what went ye out for to see? A man clothed in soft raiment? behold, they that wear soft *clothing* are in kings' houses.

9 But what went ye out for to see? A prophet? yea, I say unto you, and more than a prophet.

10 For this is *he*, of whom it is written, Behold, I send my messenger before thy face, which shall prepare thy way before thee.

10:41 *in the name of*=because he is.

11:6 *whosoever shall not be offended in me.* I.e., he who can in full faith acknowledge and accept my "mighty work" as evidence of my Messiahship.

11:7–8 These are rhetorical questions expecting negative answers.

11:10 See Isa. 40:3; Mal. 3:1. *which*=who.

11 Verily I say unto you, Among them that are born of women there hath not risen a greater than John the Baptist: notwithstanding he that is least in the kingdom of heaven is greater than he.

12 And from the days of John the Baptist until now the kingdom of heaven suffereth violence, and the violent take it by force.

13 For all the prophets and the law prophesied until John.

14 And if ye will receive *it*, this is Ēlī'as, which was for to come.

15 He that hath ears to hear, let him hear.

16 ¶ But whereunto shall I liken this generation? It is like unto children sitting in the markets, and calling unto their fellows,

17 And saying, We have piped unto you, and ye have not danced; we have mourned unto you, and ye have not lamented.

18 For John came neither eating nor drinking, and they say, He hath a devil.

19 The Son of man came eating and drinking, and they say, Behold a man gluttonous, and a winebibber, a friend of publicans and sinners. But wisdom is justified of her children.

2 *By condemning the cities*, 11:20–24

20 ¶Then began he to upbraid the cities wherein most of his mighty works were done, because they repented not:

21 Woe unto thee, Chōrā'zin! woe unto thee, Bethsā'-ida! for if the mighty works, which were done in you, had been done in Tyre and Sidon, they would have repented long ago in sackcloth and ashes.

11:11 *is greater than he*. The greatness of John the Baptist in the old dispensation before the cross fades in comparison with the high position every believer has today since the cross, the resurrection, and the descent of the Spirit.

11:12 This verse means that since John began preaching the response had been a violent one, whether by vicious opponents or enthusiastic supporters.

11:14 *this is Elias*. Jesus is saying that if the Jews had received Him, they would also have understood that John fulfilled the O.T. prediction of the coming of Elijah before the day of the Lord (Mal. 4:5; see Matt. 17:12).

11:19 One can always find a reason to carp at prophets rather than repent at their urging. *Children* means "works" or "deeds."

11:21 *Chorazin* was about 2½ miles N. of Capernaum. *Bethsaida*

22 But I say unto you, It shall be more tolerable for
Tyre and Sidon at the day of judgment, than for you.

23 And thou, Caper'naum, which art exalted unto
heaven, shalt be brought down to hell: for if the mighty
works, which have been done in thee, had been done in
Sodom, it would have remained until this day.

24 But I say unto you, That it shall be more tolerable for
the land of Sodom in the day of judgment, than for thee.

3 By calling all to Himself, 11:25–30

25 ¶ At that time Jesus answered and said, I thank thee,
O Father, Lord of heaven and earth, because thou hast hid
these things from the wise and prudent, and hast revealed
them unto babes.

26 Even so, Father: for so it seemed good in thy sight.

27 All things are delivered unto me of my Father: and
no man knoweth the Son, but the Father; neither knoweth
any man the Father, save the Son, and *he* to whomsoever
the Son will reveal *him*.

28 ¶ Come unto me, all *ye* that labour and are heavy
laden, and I will give you rest.

29 Take my yoke upon you, and learn of me; for I am
meek and lowly in heart: and ye shall find rest unto your
souls.

30 For my yoke *is* easy, and my burden is light.

4 By controversies over the Sabbath, 12:1–13

12 At that time Jesus went on the sabbath day through
the corn; and his disciples were an hungred, and
began to pluck the ears of corn, and to eat.

2 But when the Pharisees saw *it*, they said unto him,
Behold, thy disciples do that which is not lawful to do
upon the sabbath day.

3 But he said unto them, Have ye not read what David

is at the N. end of the Sea of Galilee. *Tyre and Sidon* were
pagan cities in Phoenicia.
11:28–30 This great invitation, extended to all, is threefold: (1)
to come and receive salvation; (2) to learn in discipleship; and
(3) to serve in yoke with the Lord. The yoke involves instruction under discipline. Yet, in contrast to the teaching of the
scribes, His yoke is easier. Through the ages these verses have
been among the most beloved in the N.T.
12:2 *not lawful to do upon the sabbath day.* It was lawful for
persons to pick grain from another's field to satisfy a hunger
(Deut. 23:25) but not to work on the Sabbath (Ex. 20:10).
The latter was the charge of the Pharisees.
12:3 *what David did.* See 1 Sam. 21:1–6.

did, when he was an hungred, and they that were with him;

4 How he entered into the house of God, and did eat the shewbread, which was not lawful for him to eat, neither for them which were with him, but only for the priests?

5 Or have ye not read in the law, how that on the sabbath days the priests in the temple profane the sabbath, and are blameless?

6 But I say unto you, That in this place is *one* greater than the temple.

7 But if ye had known what *this* meaneth, I will have mercy, and not sacrifice, ye would not have condemned the guiltless.

8 For the Son of man is Lord even of the sabbath day.

9 And when he was departed thence, he went into their synagogue:

10 ¶ And, behold, there was a man which had *his* hand withered. And they asked him, saying, Is it lawful to heal on the sabbath days? that they might accuse him.

11 And he said unto them, What man shall there be among you, that shall have one sheep, and if it fall into a pit on the sabbath day, will he not lay hold on it, and lift *it* out?

12 How much then is a man better than a sheep? Wherefore it is lawful to do well on the sabbath days.

13 Then saith he to the man, Stretch forth thine hand. And he stretched *it* forth; and it was restored whole, like as the other.

5 By condemnation of the Pharisees (the unpardonable sin), 12:14–37

14 ¶ Then the Pharisees went out, and held a council against him, how they might destroy him.

15 But when Jesus knew *it*, he withdrew himself from thence: and great multitudes followed him, and he healed them all;

16 And charged them that they should not make him known:

12:4 *the shewbread.* Better, bread of the Presence. Twelve cakes, made of fine flour, were placed in the Holy Place in the tabernacle each day on the table which stood opposite the candlestick. The old bread was eaten by the priests. It was this bread that David requested of Ahimelech, the priest, for himself and his men.

12:6 *one.* Better, something; i.e., the kingdom of God.

12:16 *they should not make him known.* Many were drawn to Christ because of His reputation as a healer, which may have

17 That it might be fulfilled which was spoken by Ēsà'as the prophet, saying,

18 Behold my servant, whom I have chosen; my beloved, in whom my soul is well pleased: I will put my spirit upon him, and he shall shew judgment to the Gentiles.

19 He shall not strive, nor cry; neither shall any man hear his voice in the streets.

20 A bruised reed shall he not break, and smoking flax shall he not quench, till he send forth judgment unto victory.

21 And in his name shall the Gentiles trust.

22 ¶ Then was brought unto him one possessed with a devil, blind, and dumb: and he healed him, insomuch that the blind and dumb both spake and saw.

23 And all the people were amazed, and said, Is not this the son of David?

24 But when the Pharisees heard *it*, they said, This *fellow* doth not cast out devils, but by Bēel'zebub the prince of the devils.

25 And Jesus knew their thoughts, and said unto them, Every kingdom divided against itself is brought to desolation; and every city or house divided against itself shall not stand:

26 And if Satan cast out Satan, he is divided against himself; how shall then his kingdom stand?

27 And if I by Bēel'zebub cast out devils, by whom do your children cast *them* out? therefore they shall be your judges.

28 But if I cast out devils by the Spirit of God, then the kingdom of God is come unto you.

29 Or else how can one enter into a strong man's house, and spoil his goods, except he first bind the strong man? and then he will spoil his house.

30 He that is not with me is against me; and he that gathereth not with me scattereth abroad.

31 ¶ Wherefore I say unto you, All manner of sin and blasphemy shall be forgiven unto men: but the blasphemy *against* the *Holy* Ghost shall not be forgiven unto men.

been diverting attention from His primary role as Messiah.

12:18–21 See Isa. 42:1–4. Here is one of Matthew's descriptive gems, highlighting the graciousness and gentleness of Jesus' ministry.

12:31 *blasphemy against the Holy Ghost*. Blasphemy consists in attributing to Satan (v. 24) what is God's work through the Holy Spirit (v. 28), though technically, according to the scribes, blasphemy involved the direct and explicit use of the divine

32 And whosoever speaketh a word against the Son of man, it shall be forgiven him: but whosoever speaketh against the Holy Ghost, it shall not be forgiven him, neither in this world, neither in the *world* to come.

33 Either make the tree good, and his fruit good; or else make the tree corrupt, and his fruit corrupt: for the tree is known by *his* fruit.

34 O generation of vipers, how can ye, being evil, speak good things? for out of the abundance of the heart the mouth speaketh.

35 A good man out of the good treasure of the heart bringeth forth good things: and an evil man out of the evil treasure bringeth forth evil things.

36 But I say unto you, That every idle word that men shall speak, they shall give account thereof in the day of judgment.

37 For by thy words thou shalt be justified, and by thy words thou shalt be condemned.

6 *By certain signs*, 12:38–45

38 ¶ Then certain of the scribes and of the Pharisees answered, saying, Master, we would see a sign from thee.

39 But he answered and said unto them, An evil and adulterous generation seeketh after a sign; and there shall no sign be given to it, but the sign of the prophet Jonas:

40 For as Jonas was three days and three nights in the whale's belly; so shall the Son of man be three days and three nights in the heart of the earth.

41 The men of Nin'evēh shall rise in judgment with

---

name. To Jesus it was the reviling of God by attributing the Spirit's work to Satan. The special circumstances involved in this blasphemy cannot be duplicated today.

12:36 *idle*=careless because of its worthlessness.

12:39 *adulterous*. The nation was unfaithful in its vows to the Lord. *the sign of the prophet Jonas*. In Matt. 16:4 and Luke 11:29–32 the sign is the warning of judgment to come (Jonah 1:2; 3:4). Here the sign is related to the death and resurrection of the Son of man.

12:40 *three days and three nights*. This phrase does not necessarily require that 72 hours elapse between Christ's death and resurrection, for the Jews reckoned part of a day to be as a whole day. Thus this prophecy can be properly fulfilled if the crucifixion occurred on Friday. However, the statement does require an historical Jonah who was actually swallowed by a great fish.

12:41 *a greater*. The Greek word is neuter here and in v. 42 and refers to the kingdom of God.

this generation, and shall condemn it: because they repented at the preaching of Jonas; and, behold, a greater
than Jonas *is* here.

42 The queen of the south shall rise up in the judgment
with this generation, and shall condemn it: for she came
from the uttermost parts of the earth to hear the wisdom
of Solomon; and, behold, a greater than Solomon *is* here.

43 When the unclean spirit is gone out of a man, he
walketh through dry places, seeking rest, and findeth none.

44 Then he saith, I will return into my house from
whence I came out; and when he is come, he findeth *it*
empty, swept, and garnished.

45 Then goeth he, and taketh with himself seven other
spirits more wicked than himself, and they enter in and
dwell there: and the last *state* of that man is worse than
the first. Even so shall it be also unto this wicked generation.

7 *By changed relationships,* 12:46–50

46 ¶ While he yet talked to the people, behold, *his*
mother and his brethren stood without, desiring to speak
with him.

47 Then one said unto him, Behold, thy mother and
thy brethren stand without, desiring to speak with thee.

48 But he answered and said unto him that told him,
Who is my mother? and who are my brethren?

49 And he stretched forth his hand toward his disciples,
and said, Behold my mother and my brethren!

50 For whosoever shall do the will of my Father which
is in heaven, the same is my brother, and sister, and mother.

C The Program Altered, 13:1–52

1 *The sower,* 13:1–23

13 The same day went Jesus out of the house, and sat
by the sea side.

2 And great multitudes were gathered together unto
him, so that he went into a ship, and sat; and the whole
multitude stood on the shore.

3 And he spake many things unto them in parables,
saying, Behold, a sower went forth to sow;

12:43 *unclean spirit*=a demon. See note at Matt. 7:22.
12:50 This means that the spiritual relation between Christ and
believers is closer than the closest of blood ties. Obedience to
God takes precedence over responsibilities to family.
13:3 *parables.* A parable is a figure of speech in which a moral or
spiritual truth is illustrated from an analogy drawn from every-

4 And when he sowed, some *seeds* fell by the way side, and the fowls came and devoured them up:

5 Some fell upon stony places, where they had not much earth: and forthwith they sprung up, because they had no deepness of earth:

6 And when the sun was up, they were scorched; and because they had no root, they withered away.

7 And some fell among thorns; and the thorns sprung up, and choked them:

8 But other fell into good ground, and brought forth fruit, some an hundredfold, some sixtyfold, some thirty-fold.

9 Who hath ears to hear, let him hear.

10 And the disciples came, and said unto him, Why speakest thou unto them in parables?

11 He answered and said unto them, Because it is given unto you to know the mysteries of the kingdom of heaven, but to them it is not given.

12 For whosoever hath, to him shall be given, and he shall have more abundance: but whosoever hath not, from him shall be taken away even that he hath.

13 Therefore speak I to them in parables: because they seeing see not; and hearing they hear not, neither do they understand.

14 And in them is fulfilled the prophecy of Ésáʹas, which saith, By hearing ye shall hear, and shall not under-stand; and seeing ye shall see, and shall not perceive:

15 For this people's heart is waxed gross, and *their* ears are dull of hearing, and their eyes they have closed; lest at any time they should see with *their* eyes, and hear with *their* ears, and should understand with *their* heart, and should be converted, and I should heal them.

16 But blessed *are* your eyes, for they see: and your ears, for they hear.

17 For verily I say unto you, That many prophets and righteous *men* have desired to see *those things* which ye see, and have not seen *them*; and to hear *those things* which ye hear, and have not heard *them*.

18 ¶ Hear ye therefore the parable of the sower.

19 When any one heareth the word of the kingdom,

day experiences. These parables present truths about the king-dom in this present day. These truths are called "mysteries" (v. 11) because they were not revealed in the O.T. and they are revealed by Christ only to those who are properly related to Him (vv. 11–13 and Mark 4:11–12).
13:14 See Isa. 6:9–10.

and understandeth *it* not, then cometh the wicked *one*, and catcheth away that which was sown in his heart. This is he which received seed by the way side.

20 But he that received the seed into stony places, the same is he that heareth the word, and anon with joy receiveth it;

21 Yet hath he not root in himself, but dureth for a while: for when tribulation or persecution ariseth because of the word, by and by he is offended.

22 He also that received seed among the thorns is he that heareth the word; and the care of this world, and the deceitfulness of riches, choke the word, and he becometh unfruitful.

23 But he that received seed into the good ground is he that heareth the word, and understandeth *it*; which also beareth fruit, and bringeth forth, some an hundredfold, some sixty, some thirty.

2 *The wheat and the tares*, 13:24–30

24 ¶ Another parable put he forth unto them, saying, The kingdom of heaven is likened unto a man which sowed good seed in his field:

25 But while men slept, his enemy came and sowed tares among the wheat, and went his way.

26 But when the blade was sprung up, and brought forth fruit, then appeared the tares also.

27 So the servants of the householder came and said unto him, Sir, didst not thou sow good seed in thy field? from whence then hath it tares?

28 He said unto them, An enemy hath done this. The servants said unto him, Wilt thou then that we go and gather them up?

29 But he said, Nay; lest while ye gather up the tares, ye root up also the wheat with them.

30 Let both grow together until the harvest: and in the time of harvest I will say to the reapers, Gather ye together first the tares, and bind them in bundles to burn them: but gather the wheat into my barn.

3 *The mustard seed*, 13:31–32

31 ¶ Another parable put he forth unto them, saying,

13:25 *tares*. Weeds, in this case probably darnel, which in the blade resembles wheat but which can be distinguished from wheat when fully ripe.
13:31 See note at Luke 13:19.

The kingdom of heaven is like to a grain of mustard seed, which a man took, and sowed in his field:

32 Which indeed is the least of all seeds: but when it is grown, it is the greatest among herbs, and becometh a tree, so that the birds of the air come and lodge in the branches thereof.

4 *The leaven*, 13:33

33 ¶ Another parable spake he unto them; The kingdom of heaven is like unto leaven, which a woman took, and hid in three measures of meal, till the whole was leavened.

5 *The wheat and the tares*, 13:34-43

34 All these things spake Jesus unto the multitude in parables; and without a parable spake he not unto them:

35 That it might be fulfilled which was spoken by the prophet, saying, I will open my mouth in parables; I will utter things which have been kept secret from the foundation of the world.

36 Then Jesus sent the multitude away, and went into the house: and his disciples came unto him, saying, Declare unto us the parable of the tares of the field.

37 He answered and said unto them, He that soweth the good seed is the Son of man;

38 The field is the world; the good seed are the children of the kingdom; but the tares are the children of the wicked *one*;

39 The enemy that sowed them is the devil; the harvest is the end of the world; and the reapers are the angels.

40 As therefore the tares are gathered and burned in the fire; so shall it be in the end of this world.

41 The Son of man shall send forth his angels, and they shall gather out of his kingdom all things that offend, and them which do iniquity;

42 And shall cast them into a furnace of fire: there shall be wailing and gnashing of teeth.

43 Then shall the righteous shine forth as the sun

13:33 *leaven*. Since leaven is everywhere else in the Bible regarded as typifying the presence of impurity or evil, some understand it here to indicate the presence of evil within Christendom (Ex. 12:15; Lev. 2:11; Matt. 16:6; 1 Cor. 5:6-9; Gal. 5:9; 1 Tim. 4:1, Jude 12). Others regard the meaning of leaven in this parable in a good sense, as indicating the growth of the kindom of heaven by means of the penetrating power of the gospel.

13:35 See Ps. 78:2-3.

in the kingdom of their Father. Who hath ears to hear, let him hear.

6 *The hid treasure*, 13:44

44 ¶ Again, the kingdom of heaven is like unto treasure hid in a field; the which when a man hath found, he hideth, and for joy thereof goeth and selleth all that he hath, and buyeth that field.

7 *The pearl of great price*, 13:45–46

45 ¶ Again, the kingdom of heaven is like unto a merchant man, seeking goodly pearls:
46 Who, when he had found one pearl of great price, went and sold all that he had, and bought it.

8 *The dragnet*, 13:47–50

47 ¶ Again, the kingdom of heaven is like unto a net, that was cast into the sea, and gathered of every kind:
48 Which, when it was full, they drew to shore, and sat down, and gathered the good into vessels, but cast the bad away.
49 So shall it be at the end of the world: the angels shall come forth, and sever the wicked from among the just,
50 And shall cast them into the furnace of fire: there shall be wailing and gnashing of teeth.

9 *The householder*, 13:51–52

51 Jesus saith unto them, Have ye understood all these things? They say unto him, Yea, Lord.
52 Then said he unto them, Therefore every scribe *which is* instructed unto the kingdom of heaven is like unto a man *that is* an householder, which bringeth forth out of his treasure *things* new and old.

D The Program Attacked, 13:53–16:12

1 *Attack by His townspeople*, 13:53–58

53 ¶ And it came to pass, *that* when Jesus had finished these parables, he departed thence.

13:44–45 The parables of the treasure and pearl indicate the incomparable value of the kingdom, which will cause a man to do everything possible to possess it. Another possible interpretation equates the man with Christ (as in v. 37) who sacrifices His all to purchase His people.

54 And when he was come into his own country, he taught them in their synagogue, insomuch that they were astonished, and said, Whence hath this *man* this wisdom, and *these* mighty works?

55 Is not this the carpenter's son? is not his mother called Mary? and his brethren, James, and Joses, and Simon, and Judas?

56 And his sisters, are they not all with us? Whence then hath this *man* all these things?

57 And they were offended in him. But Jesus said unto them, A prophet is not without honour, save in his own country, and in his own house.

58 And he did not many mighty works there because of their unbelief.

2 Attack by Herod and followed by miracles (5000 fed and Jesus walking on water), 14:1-36

14 At that time Herod the te'trarch heard of the fame of Jesus,

2 And said unto his servants, This is John the Baptist; he is risen from the dead; and therefore mighty works do shew forth themselves in him.

3 ¶ For Herod had laid hold on John, and bound him, and put *him* in prison for Hero'dias' sake, his brother Philip's wife.

4 For John said unto him, It is not lawful for thee to have her.

5 And when he would have put him to death, he feared the multitude, because they counted him as a prophet.

6 But when Herod's birthday was kept, the daughter of Hero'dias danced before them, and pleased Herod.

7 Whereupon he promised with an oath to give her whatsoever she would ask.

13:55 *his brethren*. These were the sons of Joseph and Mary born subsequent to the birth of Jesus from Mary alone. To understand them as sons of Joseph by a former marriage or cousins of Jesus is contrary to the natural sense of "brethren."

13:57 *were offended in him*. Better, took offense at Him.

14:1 *Herod the tetrarch*. Herod Antipas, who ruled his territories 4 B.C.–A.D. 39, son of Herod the Great and brother of Archelaus (see Matt. 2:1,22).

14:3 *Herodias*. The wife of Herod's half-brother Philip, her uncle, who had been persuaded to leave her husband and marry Herod Antipas, thus committing incest (Lev. 18:16). John condemned him for this, and Antipas knew that John spoke the truth. See Mark 6:20.

8 And she, being before instructed of her mother, said, Give me here John Baptist's head in a charger.

9 And the king was sorry: nevertheless for the oath's sake, and them which sat with him at meat, he commanded *it* to be given *her*.

10 And he sent, and beheaded John in the prison.

11 And his head was brought in a charger, and given to the damsel: and she brought *it* to her mother.

12 And his disciples came, and took up the body, and buried it, and went and told Jesus.

13 ¶ When Jesus heard *of it*, he departed thence by ship into a desert place apart: and when the people had heard *thereof*, they followed him on foot out of the cities.

14 And Jesus went forth, and saw a great multitude, and was moved with compassion toward them, and he healed their sick.

15 ¶And when it was evening, his disciples came to him, saying, This is a desert place, and the time is now past; send the multitude away, that they may go into the villages, and buy themselves victuals.

16 But Jesus said unto them, They need not depart; give ye them to eat.

17 And they say unto him, We have here but five loaves, and two fishes.

18 He said, Bring them hither to me.

19 And he commanded the multitude to sit down on the grass, and took the five loaves, and the two fishes, and looking up to heaven, he blessed, and brake, and gave the loaves to *his* disciples, and the disciples to the multitude.

20 And they did all eat, and were filled: and they took up of the fragments that remained twelve baskets full.

21 And they that had eaten were about five thousand men, beside women and children.

22 ¶ And straightway Jesus constrained his disciples to get into a ship, and to go before him unto the other side, while he sent the multitudes away.

23 And when he had sent the multitudes away, he

14:8 *charger*=platter.

14:15 *when it was evening*. The Hebrew day, that is, the interval between dawn and darkness, was divided into three parts: morning, noon, and evening (Ps. 55:17). The Jews distinguished two evenings in the day: the first was about 3 P.M., and the second, at sundown (see Ex. 12:6, lit., "between the evenings.") In this verse the first evening is meant; in v. 23, the second.

14:20 *were filled*=were satisfied.

went up into a mountain apart to pray: and when the evening was come, he was there alone.

24 But the ship was now in the midst of the sea, tossed with waves: for the wind was contrary.

25 And in the fourth watch of the night Jesus went unto them, walking on the sea.

26 And when the disciples saw him walking on the sea, they were troubled, saying, It is a spirit; and they cried out for fear.

27 But straightway Jesus spake unto them, saying, Be of good cheer; it is I; be not afraid.

28 And Peter answered him and said, Lord, if it be thou, bid me come unto thee on the water.

29 And he said, Come. And when Peter was come down out of the ship, he walked on the water, to go to Jesus.

30 But when he saw the wind boisterous, he was afraid; and beginning to sink, he cried, saying, Lord, save me.

31 And immediately Jesus stretched forth *his* hand, and caught him, and said unto him, O thou of little faith, wherefore didst thou doubt?

32 And when they were come into the ship, the wind ceased.

33 Then they that were in the ship came and worshipped him, saying, Of a truth thou art the Son of God.

34 ¶ And when they were gone over, they came into the land of Gennes'aret.

35 And when the men of that place had knowledge of him, they sent out into all that country round about, and brought unto him all that were diseased;

36 And besought him that they might only touch the hem of his garment: and as many as touched were made perfectly whole.

3 *Attack by the scribes and Pharisees and followed by miracles (Syrophenician woman's daughter healed and 4000 fed), 15:1–39*

15 Then came to Jesus scribes and Pharisees, which were of Jerusalem, saying,

2 Why do thy disciples transgress the tradition of the

14:25 *fourth watch*=3–6 a.m.
14:26 *spirit*, or "ghost."
14:34 *land of Gennesaret*. NW. of the Sea of Galilee.
15:2 The written law did not require this (Lev. 22:1–16), only traditional interpretation and expansion of it. Only priests need make an ablution before eating to cleanse themselves from anything unclean. Christ accuses them of also expanding

elders? for they wash not their hands when they eat bread.

3 But he answered and said unto them, Why do ye also transgress the commandment of God by your tradition?

4 For God commanded, saying, Honour thy father and mother: and, He that curseth father or mother, let him die the death.

5 But ye say, Whosoever shall say to *his* father or *his* mother, *It is* a gift, by whatsoever thou mightest be profited by me;

6 And honour not his father or his mother, *he shall be free*. Thus have ye made the commandment of God of none effect by your tradition.

7 *Ye* hypocrites, well did Ésaías prophesy of you, saying,

8 This people draweth nigh unto me with their mouth, and honoureth me with *their* lips; but their heart is far from me.

9 But in vain they do worship me, teaching *for* doctrines the commandments of men.

10 ¶ And he called the multitude, and said unto them, Hear, and understand:

11 Not that which goeth into the mouth defileth a man; but that which cometh out of the mouth, this defileth a man.

12 Then came his disciples, and said unto him, Knowest thou that the Pharisees were offended, after they heard this saying?

13 But he answered and said, Every plant, which my heavenly Father hath not planted, shall be rooted up.

14 Let them alone: they be blind leaders of the blind. And if the blind lead the blind, both shall fall into the ditch.

15 Then answered Peter and said unto him, Declare unto us this parable.

16 And Jesus said, Are ye also yet without understanding?

17 Do not ye yet understand, that whatsoever entereth in at the mouth goeth into the belly, and is cast out into the draught?

18 But those things which proceed out of the mouth come forth from the heart; and they defile the man.

19 For out of the heart proceed evil thoughts, murders,

(and negating) the commandment (or law) about honoring parents (vv. 4–6).
15:7 See Isa. 29:13.
15:15 *this parable*. The reference is to v. 11.
15:17 *draught*=the drain or latrine.

adulteries, fornications, thefts, false witness, blasphemies:

20 These are *the things* which defile a man: but to eat with unwashen hands defileth not a man.

21 ¶ Then Jesus went thence, and departed into the coasts of Tyre and Sidon.

22 And, behold, a woman of Cā'naan came out of the same coasts, and cried unto him, saying, Have mercy on me, O Lord, *thou* Son of David; my daughter is grievously vexed with a devil.

23 But he answered her not a word. And his disciples came and besought him, saying, Send her away; for she crieth after us.

24 But he answered and said, I am not sent but unto the lost sheep of the house of Israel.

25 Then came she and worshipped him, saying, Lord, help me.

26 But he answered and said, It is not meet to take the children's bread, and to cast *it* to dogs.

27 And she said, Truth, Lord: yet the dogs eat of the crumbs which fall from their masters' table.

28 Then Jesus answered and said unto her, O woman, great *is* thy faith: be it unto thee even as thou wilt. And her daughter was made whole from that very hour.

29 And Jesus departed from thence, and came nigh unto the sea of Galilee; and went up into a mountain, and sat down there.

30 And great multitudes came unto him, having with them *those that were* lame, blind, dumb, maimed, and many others, and cast them down at Jesus' feet; and he healed them:

31 Insomuch that the multitude wondered, when they saw the dumb to speak, the maimed to be whole, the lame to walk, and the blind to see: and they glorified the God of Israel.

32 ¶ Then Jesus called his disciples *unto him*, and said, I have compassion on the multitude, because they continue with me now three days, and have nothing to eat: and I will not send them away fasting, lest they faint in the way.

33 And his disciples say unto him, Whence should we

15:22 *a devil*. Better, demon.
15:25 *worshipped*=knelt down before Him.
15:26 *meet*=right. *to dogs*. Children ("the lost sheep of the house of Israel") must be fed before dogs. This Gentile woman, like the centurion, showed great faith (v. 28) and was rewarded for it.

have so much bread in the wilderness, as to fill so great
a multitude?

34 And Jesus saith unto them, How many loaves have
ye? And they said, Seven, and a few little fishes.

35 And he commanded the multitude to sit down on
the ground.

36 And he took the seven loaves and the fishes, and
gave thanks, and brake *them*, and gave to his disciples, and
the disciples to the multitude.

37 And they did all eat, and were filled: and they took
up of the broken *meat* that was left seven baskets full.

38 And they that did eat were four thousand men, beside women and children.

39 And he sent away the multitude, and took ship, and
came into the coasts of Mag'dala.

4 *Attack by the Pharisees and Sadducees*, 16:1–12

16 The Pharisees also with the Sadducees came, and
tempting desired him that he would shew them a
sign from heaven.

2 He answered and said unto them, When it is evening,
ye say, *It will be* fair weather: for the sky is red.

3 And in the morning, *It will be* foul weather to day:
for the sky is red and lowring. O *ye* hypocrites, ye can
discern the face of the sky; but can ye not *discern* the signs
of the times?

4 A wicked and adulterous generation seeketh after a
sign; and there shall no sign be given unto it, but the
sign of the prophet Jonas. And he left them, and departed.

5 And when his disciples were come to the other side,
they had forgotten to take bread.

6 ¶ Then Jesus said unto them, Take heed and beware
of the leaven of the Pharisees and of the Sadducees.

7 And they reasoned among themselves, saying, *It is*
because we have taken no bread.

8 *Which* when Jesus perceived, he said unto them, O
ye of little faith, why reason ye among yourselves, because
ye have brought no bread?

9 Do ye not yet understand, neither remember the five
loaves of the five thousand, and how many baskets ye took
up?

10 Neither the seven loaves of the four thousand, and
how many baskets ye took up?

16:4 See note at Matt. 12:39.
16:8 *reason ye among yourselves because*=Are you arguing over
the fact that you have no bread?

11 How is it that ye do not understand that I spake *it* not to you concerning bread, that ye should beware of the leaven of the Pharisees and of the Sadducees?

12 Then understood they how that he bade *them* not beware of the leaven of bread, but of the doctrine of the Pharisees and of the Sadducees.

V THE PEDAGOGY OF THE KING, 16:13–20:28

A Concerning His Church
(Peter's Confession of Faith), 16:13–20

13 ¶ When Jesus came into the coasts of Cæsarea Phĭlip′pī, he asked his disciples, saying, Whom do men say that I the Son of man am?

14 And they said, Some *say that thou art* John the Baptist: some, Ēlĭ′as; and others, Jĕrĕmĭ′as, or one of the prophets.

15 He saith unto them, But whom say ye that I am?

16 And Simon Peter answered and said, Thou art the Christ, the Son of the living God.

17 And Jesus answered and said unto him, Blessed art thou, Simon Bar-jō′na: for flesh and blood hath not revealed *it* unto thee, but my Father which is in heaven.

18 And I say also unto thee, That thou art Peter, and upon this rock I will build my church; and the gates of hell shall not prevail against it.

19 And I will give unto thee the keys of the kingdom

16:13 *coasts*=region. This Caesarea was in Herod Philip's tetrarchy, about 25 miles N. of the Sea of Galilee.

16:14 *Elias*=Elijah. *Jeremias*=Jeremiah. Some must have seen resemblances between Christ's teachings and those of these two great prophets.

16:17 *Blessed art thou* because he had received this insight through divine revelation, and not through human influences.

16:18 *upon this rock*. While the name Peter (Greek: *Petros*) means rock or rock-man, in the next phrase Christ used *petra* ("upon this rock"), a feminine form meaning "rock," not a name. Christ is indulging in a play on words. He does not say "upon you, Peter" or "upon your successors," but "upon this rock"—upon this divine revelation and profession of faith in Christ. *I will build* shows that the formation of the church was still in the future. It did begin on the day of Pentecost (Acts 2). The word "church" appears in the Gospels only here and in 18:17.

16:19 *the keys*. The authority to open the doors of Christendom was given to Peter, who used that authority for Jews on the

of heaven: and whatsoever thou shalt bind on earth shall
be bound in heaven: and whatsoever thou shalt loose on
earth shall be loosed in heaven.

20 Then charged he his disciples that they should tell
no man that he was Jesus the Christ.

B Concerning His Death, 16:21–28

21 ¶ From that time forth began Jesus to shew unto his
disciples, how that he must go unto Jerusalem, and suffer
many things of the elders and chief priests and scribes, and
be killed, and be raised again the third day.

22 Then Peter took him, and began to rebuke him, saying, Be it far from thee, Lord: this shall not be unto thee.

23 But he turned, and said unto Peter, Get thee behind
me, Satan: thou art an offence unto me: for thou savourest
not the things that be of God, but those that be of men.

24 ¶ Then said Jesus unto his disciples, If any *man* will
come after me, let him deny himself, and take up his cross,
and follow me.

25 For whosoever will save his life shall lose it: and
whosoever will lose his life for my sake shall find it.

26 For what is a man profited, if he shall gain the whole
world, and lose his own soul? or what shall a man give in
exchange for his soul?

day of Pentecost and for Gentiles in the house of Cornelius
(Acts 10). *shall be bound . . . shall be loosed.* Lit., shall
have been bound . . . shall have been loosed. Heaven, not the
apostles, initiates all binding and loosing, while the apostles
announce these things. In John 20:22–23 sins are in view;
here, things (i.e., practices), since the word "whatsoever" is
neuter. An example of the apostles' binding practices on people
is in Acts 15:20.

16:21 This is Matthew's first prediction of the Passion (see also
17:22; 20:18). Notice the number of specific details in this
prediction.

16:23 *Satan.* Peter is sharply rebuked for aligning himself with
Satan's plan to deter Jesus from fulfilling His mission. The
harshness of the rebuke stems from Christ's fierce realism about
the principal purpose of His coming to earth, and that was to
die. *an offence*=a stumbling-block or "rock of offence" (Rom.
9:33), perhaps a further play on the word "rock" in v. 18.
thou savourest not=thou thinketh not.

16:24–28 This passage is on discipleship. Verses 13–20 are on
Messiahship; vv. 21–23 are on the atonement; 17:1–8 concern
eschatology. These four together deal with the foundational
truths of N.T. theology.

16:24 *cross.* See note at 10:38.

27 For the Son of man shall come in the glory of his Father with his angels; and then he shall reward every man according to his works.

28 Verily I say unto you, There be some standing here, which shall not taste of death, till they see the Son of man coming in his kingdom.

C Concerning His Glory (the Transfiguration), 17:1–21

17 And after six days Jesus taketh Peter, James, and John his brother, and bringeth them up into an high mountain apart,

2 And was transfigured before them: and his face did shine as the sun, and his raiment was white as the light.

3 And, behold, there appeared unto them Moses and Ēlī'as talking with him.

4 Then answered Peter, and said unto Jesus, Lord, it is good for us to be here: if thou wilt, let us make here three tabernacles; one for thee, and one for Moses, and one for Ēlī'as.

5 While he yet spake, behold, a bright cloud overshadowed them: and behold a voice out of the cloud, which said, This is my beloved Son, in whom I am well pleased; hear ye him.

6 And when the disciples heard *it*, they fell on their face, and were sore afraid.

7 And Jesus came and touched them, and said, Arise, and be not afraid.

8 And when they had lifted up their eyes, they saw no man, save Jesus only.

9 And as they came down from the mountain, Jesus charged them, saying, Tell the vision to no man, until the Son of man be risen again from the dead.

16:28 *see the Son of man coming in his kingdom*. This was fulfilled when the disciples witnessed the transfiguration (17:1–8), which was, in miniature, a preview of the kingdom with the Lord appearing in a state of glory (Dan. 7:9–14).

17:1 *after six days*. Luke's "about eight days" includes the termini as well as the interval. *Peter, James, and John*. These men comprised the inner circle of the disciples.

17:2 *transfigured*. Lit., transformed. The transfiguration gave the three disciples a preview of Jesus' future exaltation and the coming kingdom. The Lord was seen in His body of glory; Moses and Elijah illustrated those whom Christ will bring with Him (either through death or translation, 1 Thess. 4:13–18); and the disciples represented those who will behold His coming (Rev. 1:7).

17:4 *tabernacles*=booths or shelters, for temporary residence.

10 And his disciples asked him, saying, Why then say the scribes that Ēlī'as must first come?

11 And Jesus answered and said unto them, Ēlī'as truly shall first come, and restore all things.

12 But I say unto you, That Ēlī'as is come already, and they knew him not, but have done unto him whatsoever they listed. Likewise shall also the Son of man suffer of them.

13 Then the disciples understood that he spake unto them of John the Baptist.

14 ¶ And when they were come to the multitude, there came to him a *certain* man, kneeling down to him, and saying,

15 Lord, have mercy on my son: for he is lunatick, and sore vexed: for ofttimes he falleth into the fire, and oft into the water.

16 And I brought him to thy disciples, and they could not cure him.

17 Then Jesus answered and said, O faithless and perverse generation, how long shall I be with you? how long shall I suffer you? bring him hither to me.

18 And Jesus rebuked the devil; and he departed out of him: and the child was cured from that very hour.

19 Then came the disciples to Jesus apart, and said, Why could not we cast him out?

20 And Jesus said unto them, Because of your unbelief: for verily I say unto you, If ye have faith as a grain of mustard seed, ye shall say unto this mountain, Remove hence to yonder place; and it shall remove; and nothing shall be impossible unto you.

21 Howbeit this kind goeth not out but by prayer and fasting.

D Concerning His Betrayal, 17:22–23

22 ¶ And while they abode in Galilee, Jesus said unto

17:10 *scribes.* I.e., the accredited expounders of Hebrew scriptures.
17:11–12 The sequence of thought is as follows (1) Elijah is coming as the restorer (Mal. 4:5); (2) he is come, unrecognized, in the person of John the Baptist, and killed; (3) the Son of man faces a like fate. The disciples seem to grasp only the first two points.
17:15 *lunatic.* I.e., an epileptic.
17:20 *nothing shall be impossible.* Of course, the will of God governs all things, including this promise.
17:21 Many manuscripts omit this verse.
17:22 *betrayed,* or delivered.

them, The Son of man shall be betrayed into the hands of men:

23 And they shall kill him, and the third day he shall be raised again. And they were exceeding sorry.

E Concerning Taxes, 17:24–27

24 ¶ And when they were come to Caper'naum, they that received tribute *money* came to Peter, and said, Doth not your master pay tribute?

25 He saith, Yes. And when he was come into the house, Jesus prevented him, saying, What thinkest thou, Simon? of whom do the kings of the earth take custom or tribute? of their own children, or of strangers?

26 Peter saith unto him, Of strangers. Jesus saith unto him, Then are the children free.

27 Notwithstanding, lest we should offend them, go thou to the sea, and cast an hook, and take up the fish that first cometh up; and when thou hast opened his mouth, thou shalt find a piece of money: that take, and give unto them for me and thee.

F Concerning Humility, 18:1–35

1 *Illustrated in childlike faith*, 18:1–6

18 At the same time came the disciples unto Jesus, saying, Who is the greatest in the kingdom of heaven?

2 And Jesus called a little child unto him, and set him in the midst of them,

3 And said, Verily I say unto you, Except ye be converted, and become as little children, ye shall not enter into the kingdom of heaven.

4 Whosoever therefore shall humble himself as this little child, the same is greatest in the kingdom of heaven.

17:24–27 This assessment of a half-shekel (2 drachmas) was collected annually for the support of the temple. Jesus anticipated (=*prevented*, v. 25) Peter's confusion by trying to show him that members of the royal family are exempt from toll. Thus, Jesus, the Son of God, was not personally obligated to pay for the support of God's house. Nevertheless, to avoid offense, He would pay. The miraculously caught fish yielded a shekel which was equal to two half-shekels, sufficient for Jesus and Peter.

18:3 *be converted*=turn, an active and voluntary turning from sin.

18:4 *humble himself.* The sense is, whoever humbles himself until he becomes as this little child exhibiting trust, openness,

5 And whoso shall receive one such little child in my name receiveth me.

6 But whoso shall offend one of these little ones which believe in me, it were better for him that a millstone were hanged about his neck, and *that* he were drowned in the depth of the sea.

2 *Illustrated in concern for the lost*, 18:7–14

7 ¶ Woe unto the world because of offences! for it must needs be that offences come; but woe to that man by whom the offence cometh!

8 Wherefore if thy hand or thy foot offend thee, cut them off, and cast *them* from thee: it is better for thee to enter into life halt or maimed, rather than having two hands or two feet to be cast into everlasting fire.

9 And if thine eye offend thee, pluck it out, and cast *it* from thee: it is better for thee to enter into life with one eye, rather than having two eyes to be cast into hell fire.

10 Take heed that ye despise not one of these little ones; for I say unto you, That in heaven their angels do always behold the face of my Father which is in heaven.

11 For the Son of man is come to save that which was lost.

12 How think ye? if a man have an hundred sheep, and one of them be gone astray, doth he not leave the ninety and nine, and goeth into the mountains, and seeketh that which is gone astray?

13 And if so be that he find it, verily I say unto you, he rejoiceth more of that *sheep*, than of the ninety and nine which went not astray.

14 Even so it is not the will of your Father which is in heaven, that one of these little ones should perish.

3 *Illustrated in church discipline*, 18:15–20

15 ¶ Moreover if thy brother shall trespass against thee,

and eagerness to learn. These are the childlike qualities that constitute greatness.

18:6 *offend*=cause to stumble or lead into sin. Offences (v. 7) are occasions for stumbling or temptations to sin. *millstone*. The milling of grain was was done by grinding it between 2 stones, each about 18 inches in diameter and 3 or 4 inches thick. The upper millstone was turned by a donkey walking in a circle.

18:8 *cut them off*. See note at Matt. 5:29–30.

18:10 *their angels*. Apparently children have guardian angels (Ps. 91:11; Acts 12:15). *behold the face*=are in the immediate presence.

go and tell him his fault between thee and him alone: if he shall hear thee, thou hast gained thy brother.

16 But if he will not hear *thee, then* take with thee one or two more, that in the mouth of two or three witnesses every word may be established.

17 And if he shall neglect to hear them, tell *it* unto the church: but if he neglect to hear the church, let him be unto thee as an heathen man and a publican.

18 Verily I say unto you, Whatsoever ye shall bind on earth shall be bound in heaven: and whatsoever ye shall loose on earth shall be loosed in heaven.

19 Again I say unto you, That if two of you shall agree on earth as touching any thing that they shall ask, it shall be done for them of my Father which is in heaven.

20 For where two or three are gathered together in my name, there am I in the midst of them.

4 *Illustrated in continual forgiveness,* 18:21–35

21 ¶ Then came Peter to him, and said, Lord, how oft shall my brother sin against me, and I forgive him? till seven times?

22 Jesus saith unto him, I say not unto thee, Until seven times: but, Until seventy times seven.

23 ¶ Therefore is the kingdom of heaven likened unto a certain king, which would take account of his servants.

24 And when he had begun to reckon, one was brought unto him, which owed him ten thousand talents.

25 But forasmuch as he had not to pay, his lord commanded him to be sold, and his wife, and children, and all that he had, and payment to be made.

26 The servant therefore fell down, and worshipped him, saying, Lord, have patience with me, and I will pay thee all.

27 Then the lord of that servant was moved with compassion, and loosed him, and forgave him the debt.

18:16 *two or three witnesses.* An ancient law (Deut. 19:15) for the purpose of reconciliation.

18:17 *neglect*=refuse. *church.* Here and 16:18 are the only mention of church in the Gospels. A local congregation is meant here; in 16:18 all the followers of Christ.

18:18 See notes at Matt. 16:19 and John 20:23.

18:21 *till seven times?* The rabbis said to forgive 3 times, so Peter thought he was being exceptionally worthy by suggesting 7 times!

18:24 *talents.* A talent was a measure of weight varying in size from about 58–80 lb. It was used for precious metals but was never coined. A talent of silver was worth $1,000–$1,500.

28 But the same servant went out, and found one of his fellowservants, which owed him an hundred pence: and he laid hands on him, and took *him* by the throat, saying, Pay me that thou owest.

29 And his fellowservant fell down at his feet, and besought him, saying, Have patience with me, and I will pay thee all.

30 And he would not: but went and cast him into prison, till he should pay the debt.

31 So when his fellowservants saw what was done, they were very sorry, and came and told unto their lord all that was done.

32 Then his lord, after that he had called him, said unto him, O thou wicked servant, I forgave thee all that debt, because thou desiredst me:

33 Shouldest not thou also have had compassion on thy fellowservant, even as I had pity on thee?

34 And his lord was wroth, and delivered him to the tormentors, till he should pay all that was due unto him.

35 So likewise shall my heavenly Father do also unto you, if ye from your hearts forgive not every one his brother their trespasses.

G Concerning Human Problems, 19:1–26

1 *Physical problems,* 19:1–2

19 And it came to pass, *that* when Jesus had finished these sayings, he departed from Galilee, and came into the coasts of Judæa beyond Jordan;

2 And great multitudes followed him; and he healed them there.

2 *Divorce and remarriage,* 19:3–12

3 ¶ The Pharisees also came unto him, tempting him, and saying unto him, Is it lawful for a man to put away his wife for every cause?

4 And he answered and said unto them, Have ye not

18:28 *an hundred pence.* About $20, a trifling sum in comparison.
19:1 *coasts*=regions. *beyond Jordan*=Perea, not part of Judea but within the tetrarchy of Herod Antipas.
19:3 *tempting him.* I.e., testing Him. *for every cause?* The rabbis were divided on what were legitimate grounds for divorce. The followers of Shammai held that a man could not divorce his wife unless he found her guilty of sexual immorality. The followers of Hillel were more lax, allowing divorce for many, including trivial, reasons.
19:4–5 See Gen. 1:27; 2:23–24. Rather than aligning Himself

read, that he which made *them* at the beginning made them
male and female,

5 And said, For this cause shall a man leave father and
mother, and shall cleave to his wife: and they twain shall
be one flesh?

6 Wherefore they are no more twain, but one flesh.
What therefore God hath joined together, let not man put
asunder.

7 They say unto him, Why did Moses then command to
give a writing of divorcement, and to put her away?

8 He saith unto them, Moses because of the hardness of
your hearts suffered you to put away your wives: but from
the beginning it was not so.

9 And I say unto you, Whosoever shall put away his
wife, except *it be* for fornication, and shall marry another,
committeth adultery: and whoso marrieth her which is
put away doth commit adultery.

10 ¶ His disciples say unto him, If the case of the man
be so with *his* wife, it is not good to marry.

11 But he said unto them, All *men* cannot receive this
saying, save *they* to whom it is given.

12 For there are some eunuchs, which were so born from
their mother's womb: and there are some eunuchs, which
were made eunuchs of men: and there be eunuchs, which
have made themselves eunuchs for the kingdom of heaven's
sake. He that is able to receive *it*, let him receive *it*.

3 *Children*, 19:13–15

13 ¶ Then were there brought unto him little children,

with either rabbinical position, Jesus cites the purpose of God
in creation that husband and wife should be one flesh (the
oneness of kinship or fellowship with the body as the medium
causing marriage to be the deepest corporeal and spiritual
unity).

19:7 *a writing of divorcement*. See note at Matt. 5:32.

19:8 *suffered*=permitted. Moses made a concession with regard
to God's intention that marriage be lifelong and monogamous
(Deut. 24:1–4).

19:10 *it is not good to marry*. The disciples seemed to have understood that Christ was teaching a very restricted meaning to
"fornication" and that He disallowed divorce of married persons (see note at Matt. 5:32). In turn, Christ acknowledges
that the saying "it is not good to marry" is valid in some cases,
and these are enumerated in v. 12—those congenitally incapable, those made incapable, and those who wish to devote themselves more completely to the service of God (1 Cor. 7:7, 8,
26, 32–35). Celibacy is a lively option.

that he should put *his* hands on them, and pray: and the disciples rebuked them.

14 But Jesus said, Suffer little children, and forbid them not, to come unto me: for of such is the kingdom of heaven.

15 And he laid *his* hands on them, and departed thence.

4 *Wealth*, 19:16–26

16 ¶ And, behold, one came and said unto him, Good Master, what good thing shall I do, that I may have eternal life?

17 And he said unto him, Why callest thou me good? *there is* none good but one, *that is*, God: but if thou wilt enter into life, keep the commandments.

18 He saith unto him, Which? Jesus said, Thou shalt do no murder, Thou shalt not commit adultery, Thou shalt not steal, Thou shalt not bear false witness,

19 Honour thy father and *thy* mother: and, Thou shalt love thy neighbour as thyself.

20 The young man saith unto him, All these things have I kept from my youth up: what lack I yet?

21 Jesus said unto him, If thou wilt be perfect, go *and* sell that thou hast, and give to the poor, and thou shalt have treasure in heaven: and come *and* follow me.

22 But when the young man heard that saying, he went away sorrowful: for he had great possessions.

23 ¶ Then said Jesus unto his disciples, Verily I say unto you, That a rich man shall hardly enter into the kingdom of heaven.

24 And again I say unto you, It is easier for a camel to

19:14 *Suffer*=permit.

19:16 Jews of the time believed that performing some one act would guarantee salvation.

19:21 *perfect*=complete, i.e., genuinely pleasing to God: *go and sell*. The man was being asked to prove his claim to have kept the commandments, especially the one that says "thou shalt love thy neighbor as thyself." His unwillingness to do so belied his claim of v. 20 and showed him up as a sinner in need of salvation.

19:23 *a rich man shall hardly enter*=it will be hard for a rich man to enter.

19:24 *needle*. This means a sewing needle. In this proverbial expression, Christ does not say that a rich man could not be saved (v. 26), but only that it is more difficult, since such a person seldom senses his personal need as readily as a poorer man does.

go through the eye of a needle, than for a rich man to enter into the kingdom of God.

25 When his disciples heard *it*, they were exceedingly amazed, saying, Who then can be saved?

26 But Jesus beheld *them*, and said unto them, With men this is impossible; but with God all things are possible.

H Concerning the Kingdom, 19:27–20:28

1 *Rewards in the kingdom*, 19:27–30

27 ¶ Then answered Peter and said unto him, Behold, we have forsaken all, and followed thee; what shall we have therefore?

28 And Jesus said unto them, Verily I say unto you, That ye which have followed me, in the regeneration when the Son of man shall sit in the throne of his glory, ye also shall sit upon twelve thrones, judging the twelve tribes of Israel.

29 And every one that hath forsaken houses, or brethren, or sisters, or father, or mother, or wife, or children, or lands, for my name's sake, shall receive an hundredfold, and shall inherit everlasting life.

30 But many *that are* first shall be last; and the last *shall be* first.

2 *Recognition in the kingdom*, 20:1–16

20 For the kingdom of heaven is like unto a man *that is* an householder, which went out early in the morning to hire labourers into his vineyard.

2 And when he had agreed with the labourers for a penny a day, he sent them into his vineyard.

3 And he went out about the third hour, and saw others standing idle in the marketplace.

4 And said unto them; Go ye also into the vineyard, and whatsoever is right I will give you. And they went their way.

19:27 In his mind Peter must have been thinking, "Well, we disciples certainly don't have any such hindrances of wealth!"
19:28 *in the regeneration*=in the New Age, the millennium, when the earth will be made new. The only other use of the word "regeneration" in the N.T. speaks of people being made new (Tit. 3:5). *in the throne of his glory*, see Matt. 25:31.
20:1–16 The subject is the reward of willingness to serve, whether one comes early or late. Christ is not teaching economics.
20:2 *a penny a day*. A denarius, about 20¢, but a good and normal wage for a rural worker. Additional workers were hired at about 9 a.m., noon, 3 p.m., and 5 p.m.

5 Again he went out about the sixth and ninth hour, and did likewise.

6 And about the eleventh hour he went out, and found others standing idle, and saith unto them, Why stand ye here all the day idle?

7 They say unto him, Because no man hath hired us. He saith unto them, Go ye also into the vineyard; and whatsoever is right, *that* shall ye receive.

8 So when even was come, the lord of the vineyard saith unto his steward, Call the labourers, and give them *their* hire, beginning from the last unto the first.

9 And when they came that *were hired* about the eleventh hour, they received every man a penny.

10 But when the first came, they supposed that they should have received more; and they likewise received every man a penny.

11 And when they had received *it*, they murmured against the goodman of the house,

12 Saying, These last have wrought *but* one hour, and thou hast made them equal unto us, which have borne the burden and heat of the day.

13 But he answered one of them, and said, Friend, I do thee no wrong: didst not thou agree with me for a penny?

14 Take *that* thine *is*, and go thy way: I will give unto this last, even as unto thee.

15 Is it not lawful for me to do what I will with mine own? Is thine eye evil, because I am good?

16 So the last shall be first, and the first last: for many be called, but few chosen.

3 *Rank in the kingdom,* 20:17–28

17 ¶ And Jesus going up to Jerusalem took the twelve disciples apart in the way, and said unto them,

18 Behold, we go up to Jerusalem; and the Son of man shall be betrayed unto the chief priests and unto the scribes, and they shall condemn him to death,

19 And shall deliver him to the Gentiles to mock, and to scourge, and to crucify *him*: and the third day he shall rise again.

20 ¶ Then came to him the mother of Zebedee's children with her sons, worshipping *him*, and desiring a certain thing of him.

21 And he said unto her, What wilt thou? She saith unto

20:14 *I will give.* This is the point of the parable: God's grace and generosity know no bounds, and man's ideas of merit and earned rewards are irrelevant.

him, Grant that these my two sons may sit, the one on thy right hand, and the other on the left, in thy kingdom.

22 But Jesus answered and said, Ye know not what ye ask. Are ye able to drink of the cup that I shall drink of, and to be baptized with the baptism that I am baptized with? They say unto him, We are able.

23 And he saith unto them, Ye shall drink indeed of my cup, and be baptized with the baptism that I am baptized with: but to sit on my right hand, and on my left, is not mine to give, but *it shall be given to them* for whom it is prepared of my Father.

24 And when the ten heard *it*, they were moved with indignation against the two brethren.

25 But Jesus called them *unto him*, and said, Ye know that the princes of the Gentiles exercise dominion over them, and they that are great exercise authority upon them.

26 But it shall not be so among you: but whosoever will be great among you, let him be your minister;

27 And whosoever will be chief among you, let him be your servant:

28 Even as the Son of man came not to be ministered unto, but to minister, and to give his life a ransom for many.

VI THE PRESENTATION OF THE KING,
20:29–23:39

A The Power of the King, 20:29–34

29 And as they departed from Jericho, a great multitude followed him.

20:22 *the cup that I shall drink of.* I.e., the cup of suffering. *with the baptism that I am baptized with.* I.e., go with me into the deep waters of suffering and death. *We are able.* James, of course, was the first of the apostles to be martyred (Acts 12:2).

20:26 *minister*=servant.

20:27 *servant*=slave.

20:28 *ransom for many.* The word "for" undebatably means "in the place of" many. Christ here clearly interprets the meaning of His sacrifice as a substitution for sinners.

20:29–34 The difference in this account (which speaks of 2 blind men and of the miracle being done as Jesus left Jericho) and the accounts in Mark 10:46–52 and Luke 18:35–43 (which mention only 1 blind man and the miracle performed as they entered Jericho) are explained thus: (1) there were actually 2 men involved, but Bartimaeus, being more aggressive, takes the place of prominence; and (2) the men pled with Jesus

30 ¶ And, behold, two blind men sitting by the way side, when they heard that Jesus passed by, cried out, saying, Have mercy on us, O Lord, *thou* Son of David.

31 And the multitude rebuked them, because they should hold their peace: but they cried the more, saying, Have mercy on us, O Lord, *thou* Son of David.

32 And Jesus stood still, and called them, and said, What will ye that I shall do unto you?

33 They say unto him, Lord, that our eyes may be opened.

34 So Jesus had compassion *on them*, and touched their eyes: and immediately their eyes received sight, and they followed him.

B The Presentation of the King, 21:1–11

21 And when they drew nigh unto Jerusalem, and were come to Beth'phaġē, unto the mount of Olives, then sent Jesus two disciples,

2 Saying unto them, Go into the village over against you, and straightway ye shall find an ass tied, and a colt with her: loose *them*, and bring *them* unto me.

3 And if any *man* say ought unto you, ye shall say, The Lord hath need of them; and straightway he will send them.

4 All this was done, that it might be fulfilled which was spoken by the prophet, saying,

5 Tell ye the daughter of Sion, Behold, thy King cometh unto thee, meek, and sitting upon an ass, and a colt the foal of an ass.

6 And the disciples went, and did as Jesus commanded them,

7 And brought the ass, and the colt, and put on them their clothes, and they set *him* thereon.

8 And a very great multitude spread their garments in the way; others cut down branches from the trees, and strawed *them* in the way.

9 And the multitudes that went before, and that fol-

as He entered Jericho but were not healed until He was leaving. It is also possible that the healing took place after Jesus left old Jericho and was nearing new Jericho.
20:30 *son of David*. The specific Messianic title (Ps. 72; Isa. 9:7).
21:1 *Bethphage*. A village ½ mile E. of Jerusalem, on the S. side of the Mount of Olives.
21:3 *he will send them*. I.e., the owner will.
21:4 See Zech. 9:9.
21:8 *strawed*=strewed.
21:9 *Hosanna*=save now. The acclamation is a quotation based

lowed, cried, saying, Hosanna to the Son of David: Blessed
is he that cometh in the name of the Lord; Hosanna in the
highest.

10 And when he was come into Jerusalem, all the city
was moved, saying, Who is this?

11 And the multitude said, This is Jesus the prophet of
Nazareth of Galilee.

C The Purification by the King, 21:12–17

12 ¶ And Jesus went into the temple of God, and cast
out all them that sold and bought in the temple, and
overthrew the tables of the moneychangers, and the seats
of them that sold doves,

13 And said unto them, It is written, My house shall be
called the house of prayer; but ye have made it a den of
thieves.

14 And the blind and the lame came to him in the
temple; and he healed them.

15 And when the chief priests and scribes saw the
wonderful things that he did, and the children crying in
the temple, and saying, Hosanna to the Son of David; they
were sore displeased,

16 And said unto him, Hearest thou what these say?
And Jesus saith unto them, Yea; have ye never read, Out
of the mouth of babes and sucklings thou hast perfected
praise?

17 ¶ And he left them, and went out of the city into
Bethany; and he lodged there.

D The Cursing of the Fig Tree, 21:18–22

18 Now in the morning as he returned into the city, he
hungered.

upon Ps. 118:25–27, sung at the Feast of Tabernacles. The
crowd wanted salvation from the oppression of Rome, not the
spiritual salvation which Christ offered.
21:12 *moneychangers.* Ordinary coinage had to be exchanged into
ancient Hebrew or Tyrian shekels, which were of standard
weight and without blemish, as an offering to God.
21:13 Jesus here combines parts of 2 O.T. verses, Isa. 56:7 and
Jer. 7:11.
21:14 *in the temple.* Doubtless at the gate or in the temple court,
for *the blind and the lame* were not permitted into the temple
(2 Sam. 5:8).
21:16 Jesus is apparently quoting Ps. 8:2, though *perfected praise*
comes from the Septuagint version of the Psalm and may be
translated "provided thyself with praise."
21:18 *in the morning.* I.e., on Monday of Holy Week.

19 And when he saw a fig tree in the way, he came to it, and found nothing thereon, but leaves only, and said unto it, Let no fruit grow on thee henceforward for ever. And presently the fig tree withered away.

20 And when the disciples saw *it*, they marvelled, saying, How soon is the fig tree withered away!

21 Jesus answered and said unto them, Verily I say unto you, If ye have faith, and doubt not, ye shall not only do this *which is done* to the fig tree, but also if ye shall say unto this mountain, Be thou removed, and be thou cast into the sea; it shall be done.

22 And all things, whatsoever ye shall ask in prayer, believing, ye shall receive.

E The Challenge to the King, 21:23–27

23 ¶ And when he was come into the temple, the chief priests and the elders of the people came unto him as he was teaching, and said, By what authority doest thou these things? and who gave thee this authority?

24 And Jesus answered and said unto them, I also will ask you one thing, which if ye tell me, I in like wise will tell you by what authority I do these things.

25 The baptism of John, whence was it? from heaven, or of men? And they reasoned with themselves, saying, If we shall say, From heaven; he will say unto us, Why did ye not then believe him?

26 But if we shall say, Of men; we fear the people; for all hold John as a prophet.

27 And they answered Jesus, and said, We cannot tell. And he said unto them, Neither tell I you by what authority I do these things.

F The Parables of the King, 21:28–22:14

1 *The rebellion of the nation*, 21:28–32

28 ¶ But what think ye? A *certain* man had two sons; and he came to the first, and said, Son, go work to day in my vineyard.

21:19 *in the way*. along or beside the road.   *but leaves only*. normally the fruit and leaves appear at the same time. The curse on the tree is illustrative of the rejection of Israel, a nation unfruitful despite every advantage.

21:23 This begins Tuesday of Holy Week.

21:23–27 In effect Jesus refuses to accept their claim to a right to examine Him.

21:25 *whence was it?* Christ placed these men on the horns of a dilemma by asking them what test they applied in the case of John.

29 He answered and said, I will not: but afterward he repented, and went.

30 And he came to the second, and said likewise. And he answered and said, I go, sir: and went not.

31 Whether of them twain did the will of *his* father? They say unto him, The first. Jesus saith unto them, Verily I say unto you, That the publicans and the harlots go into the kingdom of God before you.

32 For John came unto you in the way of righteousness, and ye believed him not: but the publicans and the harlots believed him: and ye, when ye had seen *it*, repented not afterward, that ye might believe him.

2 *The retribution on the nation*, 21:33–46

33 ¶ Hear another parable: There was a certain householder, which planted a vineyard, and hedged it round about, and digged a winepress in it, and built a tower, and let it out to husbandmen, and went into a far country:

34 And when the time of the fruit drew near, he sent his servants to the husbandmen, that they might receive the fruits of it.

35 And the husbandmen took his servants, and beat one, and killed another, and stoned another.

36 Again, he sent other servants more than the first: and they did unto them likewise.

37 But last of all he sent unto them his son, saying, They will reverence my son.

38 But when the husbandmen saw the son, they said among themselves, This is the heir; come, let us kill him, and let us seize on his inheritance.

39 And they caught him, and cast *him* out of the vineyard, and slew *him*.

40 When the lord therefore of the vineyard cometh, what will he do unto those husbandmen?

41 They say unto him, He will miserably destroy those wicked men, and will let out *his* vineyard unto other husbandmen, which shall render him the fruits in their seasons.

42 Jesus saith unto them, Did ye never read in the scriptures, The stone which the builders rejected, the same is become the head of the corner: this is the Lord's doing, and it is marvellous in our eyes?

21:34 *husbandmen*. Better, tenants (also vv. 35, 40).
21:42 See Ps. 118:22–23. The cornerstone figure was popular with N.T. writers (Acts 4:11; Eph. 2:20; 1 Pet. 2:7).

43 Therefore say I unto you, The kingdom of God shall be taken from you, and given to a nation bringing forth the fruits thereof.

44 And whosoever shall fall on this stone shall be broken: but on whomsoever it shall fall, it will grind him to powder.

45 And when the chief priests and Pharisees had heard his parables, they perceived that he spake of them.

46 But when they sought to lay hands on him, they feared the multitude, because they took him for a prophet.

3 *The rejection of the nation,* 22:1–14

22 And Jesus answered and spake unto them again by parables, and said,

2 The kingdom of heaven is like unto a certain king, which made a marriage for his son,

3 And sent forth his servants to call them that were bidden to the wedding: and they would not come.

4 Again, he sent forth other servants, saying, Tell them which are bidden, Behold, I have prepared my dinner: my oxen and *my* fatlings *are* killed, and all things *are* ready: come unto the marriage.

5 But they made light of *it,* and went their ways, one to his farm, another to his merchandise:

6 And the remnant took his servants, and entreated *them* spitefully, and slew *them.*

7 But when the king heard *thereof,* he was wroth: and he sent forth his armies, and destroyed those murderers, and burned up their city.

8 Then saith he to his servants, The wedding is ready, but they which were bidden were not worthy.

9 Go ye therefore into the highways, and as many as ye shall find, bid to the marriage.

10 So those servants went out into the highways, and gathered together all as many as they found, both bad and good: and the wedding was furnished with guests.

11 ¶ And when the king came in to see the guests, he saw there a man which had not on a wedding garment:

12 And he saith unto him, Friend, how camest thou in

21:43 *taken from you and given to a nation.* I.e., taken from the Jews and given the church (1 Pet. 2:9).

22:7 *and burned up their city.* A prediction of the destruction of Jerusalem in A.D. 70.

22:9 *highways.* Better, broad places or plazas.

22:12 *not having a wedding garment.* This assumes that the guests would have been supplied with robes by the king's servants,

hither not having a wedding garment? And he was speechless.

13 Then said the king to the servants, Bind him hand and foot, and take him away, and cast *him* into outer darkness; there shall be weeping and gnashing of teeth.

14 For many are called, but few *are* chosen.

G The Pronouncements of the King, 22:15–23:39

1 *In answer to the Herodians,* 22:15–22

15 ¶ Then went the Pharisees, and took counsel how they might entangle him in *his* talk.

16 And they sent out unto him their disciples with the Herō'dians, saying, Master, we know that thou art true, and teachest the way of God in truth, neither carest thou for any *man*: for thou regardest not the person of men.

17 Tell us therefore, What thinkest thou? Is it lawful to give tribute unto Cæsar, or not?

18 But Jesus perceived their wickedness, and said, Why tempt ye me, *ye* hypocrites?

19 Shew me the tribute money. And they brought unto him a penny.

20 And he saith unto them, Whose *is* this image and superscription?

since all the guests came in a hurry and most were unsuitably attired.

22:14 An ancient proverb, used 3 times in the apocryphal 4 Esdras. Here it indicates that there is a general call of God to sinners inviting them to receive His salvation, and there is also a specific election that brings some to God. At the same time, man is held responsible for his rejecting Christ whether it be because of indifference (v. 5), rebellion (v. 6), or self-righteousness (v. 12).

22:16 *Herodians.* They were a Jewish party who favored the Herodian dynasty, the party of peace at any price and of appeasers to Rome. *person.* I.e., position.

22:17 *Is it lawful.* I.e., is it in accordance with the Torah, the sacred law? *to give tribute to Caesar.* The tribute was a poll tax imposed by Rome on every Jew. The burning question in the minds of many Jews of that day was simply this: If God gave the land of Israel to the Hebrews, and if God meant them to live there, and if He received their sacrifices and offerings in acknowledgment of His relationship to them, how could they pay tribute to any other power, king, god, or anything? If Christ said that they should, then they could charge Him with disloyalty to Judaism; if He said no, then they could denounce Him to the Romans.

21 They say unto him, Cæsar's. Then saith he unto them, Render therefore unto Cæsar the things which are Cæsar's; and unto God the things that are God's.

22 When they had heard *these words*, they marvelled, and left him, and went their way.

2 *In answer to the Sadducees*, 22:23–33

23 ¶ The same day came to him the Sadducees, which say that there is no resurrection, and asked him,

24 Saying, Master, Moses said, If a man die, having no children, his brother shall marry his wife, and raise up seed unto his brother.

25 Now there were with us seven brethren: and the first, when he had married a wife, deceased, and, having no issue, left his wife unto his brother:

26 Likewise the second also, and the third, unto the seventh.

27 And last of all the woman died also.

28 Therefore in the resurrection whose wife shall she be of the seven? for they all had her.

29 Jesus answered and said unto them, Ye do err, not knowing the scriptures, nor the power of God.

30 For in the resurrection they neither marry, nor are given in marriage, but are as the angels of God in heaven.

31 But as touching the resurrection of the dead, have ye not read that which was spoken unto you by God, saying,

32 I am the God of Abraham, and the God of Isaac, and the God of Jacob? God is not the God of the dead, but of the living.

33 And when the multitude heard *this*, they were astonished at his doctrine.

22:21 Christ recognized the distinction between political and spiritual responsibilities. Caesar gets taxes and a certain amount of poltical obedience; God gets worship, obedience, service, and the dedication of one's whole life.

22:24 *seed*=children. See Deut. 25:5–6; Gen. 38:8. The object of such a marriage law was to perpetuate the line of the dead brother and to keep his property within the family.

22:30 *as the angels of God*. Christ's argument is: In the resurrection men do not marry, women are not given in marriage, in fact there is no married state in that life. Thus the whole case cited is irrelevant and immaterial. So they are like angels, who are neither male or female.

22:32 See Ex. 3:6. There is life after death, and it is rooted in the character of God.

22:33 *doctrine*=teaching.

3 *In answer to the Pharisees,* 22:34–40

34 ¶ But when the Pharisees had heard that he had put the Sadducees to silence, they were gathered together.

35 Then one of them, *which was* a lawyer, asked *him a question,* tempting him, and saying,

36 Master, which *is* the great commandment in the law?

37 Jesus said unto him, Thou shalt love the Lord thy God with all thy heart, and with all thy soul, and with all thy mind.

38 This is the first and great commandment.

39 And the second *is* like unto it, Thou shalt love thy neighbour as thyself.

40 On these two commandments hang all the law and the prophets.

4 *In questioning the Pharisees,* 22:41–46

41 ¶ While the Pharisees were gathered together, Jesus asked them,

42 Saying, What think ye of Christ? whose son is he? They say unto him, *The Son* of David.

43 He saith unto them, How then doth David in spirit call him Lord, saying,

44 The LORD said unto my Lord, Sit thou on my right hand, till I make thine enemies thy footstool?

45 If David then call him Lord, how is he his son?

46 And no man was able to answer him a word, neither durst any *man* from that day forth ask him any more *questions.*

5 *Concerning the Pharisees,* 23:1–36

23 Then spake Jesus to the multitude, and to his disciples,

22:35 *lawyer*=scribe. *tempting him.* Better, to test Him.
22:36 Earlier, O.T. attempts to answer this question are found in Isa. 33:15; Amos 5:4; Mic. 6:8; Hab. 2:4.
22:37 Christ quotes Deut. 6:5, part of the Shema, used by all Jews in their daily prayers.
22:39–40 See Lev. 19:18. Christ was the first to combine these two texts into a summary of the law.
22:43 *in spirit.* I.e., inspired by the Spirit.
22:44 *The Lord said unto my Lord.* Christ was trying to make the Pharisees see that the Son of David was also the Lord of David (Ps. 110:1); i.e., the Messiah was both human and divine. *make thine enemies thy footstool.* I.e., put your enemies under your feet, in subjection to you.

2 Saying, The scribes and the Pharisees sit in Moses' seat:

3 All therefore whatsoever they bid you observe, *that* observe and do; but do not ye after their works: for they say, and do not.

4 For they bind heavy burdens and grievous to be borne, and lay *them* on men's shoulders; but they *themselves* will not move them with one of their fingers.

5 But all their works they do for to be seen of men: they make broad their phylacteries, and enlarge the borders of their garments,

6 And love the uppermost rooms at feasts, and the chief seats in the synagogues,

7 And greetings in the markets, and to be called of men, Rabbi, Rabbi.

8 But be not ye called Rabbi: for one is your Master, *even* Christ; and all ye are brethren.

9 And call no *man* your father upon the earth: for one is your Father, which is in heaven.

10 Neither be ye called masters: for one is your Master, *even* Christ.

11 But he that is greatest among you shall be your servant.

12 And whosoever shall exalt himself shall be abased; and he that shall humble himself shall be exalted.

13 ¶ But woe unto you, scribes and Pharisees, hypocrites! for ye shut up the kingdom of heaven against men: for ye neither go in *yourselves*, neither suffer ye them that are entering to go in.

14 Woe unto you, scribes and Pharisees, hypocrites! for

23:5 *phylacteries*. A phylactery was a square leathern box which contained four strips of parchment on which were written Deut. 11:13-21, Deut. 6:4-9, Ex. 13:11-16, and Ex. 13:1-10. During prayer one was worn on the forehead between the eyebrows and another on the left arm close to the elbow. They were held in place by leather bands, which the Pharisees made broad to attract more attention to themselves. The custom was based on Ex. 13:9, 16; Deut. 6:8; 11:18, though phylacteries had only begun to be used by the ultra-pious in Christ's day. Christ criticizes not the custom but the spirit that corrupted it.

23:5 *enlarge the borders of their garments*. A hem or fringe on a garment was placed there in accordance with Num. 15:38, but the Pharisees made theirs very wide.

23:13-33 This passage is often called "the seven woes," each beginning with the same phrase. (There are 8 if v. 14, which is omitted in many manuscripts, is included).

23:14 *devour widows' houses*. They used their position as jurists

ye devour widows' houses, and for a pretence make long
prayer: therefore ye shall receive the greater damnation.

15 Woe unto you, scribes and Pharisees, hypocrites! for
ye compass sea and land to make one proselyte, and when
he is made, ye make him twofold more the child of hell
than yourselves.

16 Woe unto you, ye blind guides, which say, Whosoever shall swear by the temple, it is nothing; but whosoever
shall swear by the gold of the temple, he is a debtor!

17 Ye fools and blind: for whether is greater, the gold,
or the temple that sanctifieth the gold?

18 And, Whosoever shall swear by the altar, it is nothing; but whosoever sweareth by the gift that is upon it, he
is guilty.

19 Ye fools and blind: for whether is greater, the gift,
or the altar that sanctifieth the gift?

20 Whoso therefore shall swear by the altar, sweareth
by it, and by all things thereon.

21 And whoso shall swear by the temple, sweareth by it,
and by him that dwelleth therein.

22 And he that shall swear by heaven, sweareth by the
throne of God, and by him that sitteth thereon.

23 Woe unto you, scribes and Pharisees, hypocrites! for
ye pay tithe of mint and anise and cummin, and have
omitted the weightier *matters* of the law, judgment, mercy,
and faith: these ought ye to have done, and not to leave
the other undone.

24 Ye blind guides, which strain at a gnat, and swallow
a camel.

to adjust claims against wealthy widows or to get them to
bestow on them their estates.   *damnation*=condemnation.

23:15 *proselyte*. Proselytes were converts from paganism to Judaism.

23:16 *swear*. Here Christ argues with the Pharisees on their own
grounds. *he is a debtor*. I.e., his oath is binding. See Matt.
5:33–37.

23:17 *whether*=which, also in v. 19.

23:18 *guilty*. I.e., under obligation, guilty if he fails to carry out
his oath.

23:21 *him*=God.

23:23 *pay tithe*. The tithing of various herbs was based on Lev.
27:30. Though tithing of grain, fruit, wine, and oil was demanded (see also Num. 18:12; Deut. 14:22–23), the scribes
had expanded the items required to be tithed to include even
the smallest of herbs. *anise*=dill; *cummin*=a seed resembling
the caraway. *and not to leave the other undone*. I.e., without
leaving undone the proper normal tithing.

23:24 *strain at*=strain out. This misprint in the King James

25 Woe unto you, scribes and Pharisees, hypocrites! for ye make clean the outside of the cup and of the platter, but within they are full of extortion and excess.

26 *Thou* blind Pharisee, cleanse first that *which is* within the cup and platter, that the outside of them may be clean also.

27 Woe unto you, scribes and Pharisees, hypocrites! for ye are like unto whited sepulchres, which indeed appear beautiful outward, but are within full of dead *men's* bones, and of all uncleanness.

28 Even so ye also outwardly appear righteous unto men, but within ye are full of hypocrisy and iniquity.

29 Woe unto you, scribes and Pharisees, hypocrites! because ye build the tombs of the prophets, and garnish the sepulchres of the righteous,

30 And say, If we had been in the days of our fathers, we would not have been partakers with them in the blood of the prophets.

31 Wherefore ye be witnesses unto yourselves, that ye are the children of them which killed the prophets.

32 Fill ye up then the measure of your fathers.

33 *Ye* serpents, *ye* generation of vipers, how can ye escape the damnation of hell?

34 ¶ Wherefore, behold, I send unto you prophets, and wise men, and scribes: and *some* of them ye shall kill and crucify; and *some* of them shall ye scourge in your synagogues, and persecute *them* from city to city:

35 That upon you may come all the righteous blood shed upon the earth, from the blood of righteous Abel unto

Version has never been corrected.

23:25 *excess*=greed.

23:27 *whited sepulchres.* The outsides of tombs were often white-washed and made attractive and plainly seen, while inside were death and decay.

23:30 *in the blood*=in the death.

23:31 The idea is: "like father, like son."

23:32 *the measure.* I.e., add to the iniquity of your fathers and bring down divine judgment on yourselves.

23:34 The last part of the verse refers to the apostles (see Matt. 10:17, 23).

23:35 *Zacharias son of Barachias.* This murder is recorded in 2 Chron. 24:20–22. Barachias was likely the father of Zacharias, while the famous Jehoiada was his grandfather. This is not the prophet Zechariah (though his father was also named Barachias). Since Abel's death is recorded in Genesis, and since 2 Chronicles is the last book in the Hebrew Bible, Christ was saying, in effect, "from the first to the last murder in the Bible." See Luke 11:51.

the blood of Zachari′as son of Barachi′as, whom ye slew between the temple and the altar.

36 Verily I say unto you, All these things shall come upon this generation.

6 Concerning Jerusalem, 23:37–39

37 O Jerusalem, Jerusalem, *thou* that killest the prophets, and stonest them which are sent unto thee, how often would I have gathered thy children together, even as a hen gathereth her chickens under *her* wings, and ye would not!

38 Behold, your house is left unto you desolate.

39 For I say unto you, Ye shall not see me henceforth, till ye shall say, Blessed *is* he that cometh in the name of the Lord.

VII THE PREDICTIONS OF THE KING, 24:1–25:46

A The Destruction of the Temple, 24:1–2

24 And Jesus went out, and departed from the temple: and his disciples came to *him* for to shew him the buildings of the temple.

2 And Jesus said unto them, See ye not all these things? verily I say unto you, There shall not be left here one stone upon another, that shall not be thrown down.

B The Disciples' Questions, 24:3

3 ¶ And as he sat upon the mount of Olives, the disciples came unto him privately, saying, Tell us, when shall these

---

23:38 *your house*=the temple and the city of Jerusalem.

23:39 *Ye shall not see me henceforth*. I.e., I will no longer teach publicly. *till ye shall say*. At the second coming of Christ Israel will recognize and welcome their rejected Messiah (Zech. 12:10).

24:1 *the buildings of the temple*. Herod the Great began the building of the temple in 20 B.C., and it was still unfinished in A.D. 64 when the Romans destroyed the city. The stones, 10–12 feet in length, would have been plainly visible.

24:3 *the mount of Olives*, just E. of Jerusalem across the Kidron Valley. In this discourse Jesus answered two of the three questions the disciples asked. He does not answer *"when shall these things be?"*. He answers *"what shall be the sign of thy coming?"* in vv. 29–31 and He speaks of the signs of the end of the age in vv. 4–28. Verses 4–14 list characteristics of the first half of the tribulation period while vv. 15–28 deal with the second half.

things be? and what *shall be* the sign of thy coming, and of the end of the world?

C The Signs of the End of the Age, 24:4–28

4 And Jesus answered and said unto them, Take heed that no man deceive you.

5 For many shall come in my name, saying, I am Christ; and shall deceive many.

6 And ye shall hear of wars and rumours of wars: see that ye be not troubled: for all *these things* must come to pass, but the end is not yet.

7 For nation shall rise against nation, and kingdom against kingdom: and there shall be famines, and pestilences, and earthquakes, in divers places.

8 All these *are* the beginning of sorrows.

9 Then shall they deliver you up to be afflicted, and shall kill you: and ye shall be hated of all nations for my name's sake.

10 And then shall many be offended, and shall betray one another, and shall hate one another.

11 And many false prophets shall rise, and shall deceive many.

12 And because iniquity shall abound, the love of many shall wax cold.

13 But he that shall endure unto the end, the same shall be saved.

14 And this gospel of the kingdom shall be preached in all the world for a witness unto all nations; and then shall the end come.

15 When ye therefore shall see the abomination of desolation, spoken of by Daniel the prophet, stand in the holy place, (whoso readeth, let him understand:)

16 Then let them which be in Judæa flee into the mountains:

24:6–7 See the same judgments outlined in Rev. 6:1–8.

24:9 *for my name's sake.* I.e., because they are His followers.

24:14 *this gospel of the kingdom.* This is the good news that will be preached during the tribulation days concerning the coming of Messiah and the setting up of His kingdom.

24:15 *abomination of desolation.* This is the man of sin (2 Thess. 2:4), the Antichrist, who at this mid-point in the tribulation breaks his covenant which he made at the beginning of the tribulation with the Jewish people (Dan. 9:27), and demands that they and the world worship him. Those who resist will be persecuted and many will be martyred; that is the reason for the urgency of the instructions in vv. 16–22.

17 Let him which is on the housetop not come down to take any thing out of his house:

18 Neither let him which is in the field return back to take his clothes.

19 And woe unto them that are with child, and to them that give suck in those days!

20 But pray ye that your flight be not in the winter, neither on the sabbath day:

21 For then shall be great tribulation, such as was not since the beginning of the world to this time, no, nor ever shall be.

22 And except those days should be shortened, there should no flesh be saved: but for the elect's sake those days shall be shortened.

23 Then if any man shall say unto you, Lo, here *is* Christ, or there; believe *it* not.

24 For there shall arise false Christs, and false prophets, and shall shew great signs and wonders; insomuch that, if *it were* possible, they shall deceive the very elect.

25 Behold, I have told you before.

26 Wherefore if they shall say unto you, Behold, he is in the desert; go not forth: behold, *he is* in the secret chambers; believe *it* not.

27 For as the lightning cometh out of the east, and shineth even unto the west; so shall also the coming of the Son of man be.

28 For wheresoever the carcase is, there will the eagles be gathered together.

D The Sign of His Coming, 24:29–31

29 ¶ Immediately after the tribulation of those days shall the sun be darkened, and the moon shall not give her light, and the stars shall fall from heaven, and the powers of the heavens shall be shaken:

30 And then shall appear the sign of the Son of man in heaven: and then shall all the tribes of the earth mourn,

---

24:22 *no flesh*=no human being. *the elect's sake*=those redeemed during the tribulation days. The elect of this age (the church) will have been translated before that time begins.

24:25 *before*=in advance. This is a warning as well as a prediction.

24:28 *eagles*=vultures.

24:29 *the sun . . . darkened*. These astral phenomena which will accompany the return of the Son of man are foretold in Isa. 13:9–10 and Joel 2:31, 3:15.

24:30 *the sign*. Some think this is the lightning of v. 27; others,

and they shall see the Son of man coming in the clouds of heaven with power and great glory.

31 And he shall send his angels with a great sound of a trumpet, and they shall gather together his elect from the four winds, from one end of heaven to the other.

E The Illustrations, 24:32–25:46

1 *The fig tree*, 24:32–35

32 Now learn a parable of the fig tree; When his branch is yet tender, and putteth forth leaves, ye know that summer *is* nigh:

33 So likewise ye, when ye shall see all these things, know that it is near, *even* at the doors.

34 Verily I say unto you, This generation shall not pass, till all these things be fulfilled.

35 Heaven and earth shall pass away, but my words shall not pass away.

2 *The days of Noah*, 24:36–39

36 ¶ But of that day and hour knoweth no *man*, no, not the angels of heaven, but my Father only.

37 But as the days of Nō′ē *were*, so shall also the coming of the Son of man be.

38 For as in the days that were before the flood they were eating and drinking, marrying and giving in marriage, until the day that Nō′ē entered into the ark,

39 And knew not until the flood came, and took them all away; so shall also the coming of the Son of man be.

3 *The two*, 24:40–41

40 Then shall two be in the field; the one shall be taken, and the other left.

41 Two *women shall be* grinding at the mill; the one shall be taken, and the other left.

the Shekinah or glory of Christ; still others leave it unspecified. At any rate, *the Son of man* Himself will come visibly (Rev. 1:7). There seems to be no reason for not taking this part of Jesus' teaching as plainly as other parts.

24:33 *all these things*=the signs described in vv. 4–28.

24:34 *This generation.* The generation living when Jesus spoke these words did not live to see "all these things" come to pass. However, the Greek word can mean "race" or "family," which makes good sense here; i.e., the Jewish race will be preserved in spite of terrible persecution until the Lord comes.

24:37 *Noe*=Noah.

4 The faithful householder, 24:42–44

42 ¶ Watch therefore: for ye know not what hour your Lord doth come.

43 But know this, that if the goodman of the house had known in what watch the thief would come, he would have watched, and would not have suffered his house to be broken up.

44 Therefore be ye also ready: for in such an hour as ye think not the Son of man cometh.

5 The wise servant, 24:45–51

45 Who then is a faithful and wise servant, whom his lord hath made ruler over his houhehold, to give them meat in due season?

46 Blessed *is* that servant, whom his lord when he cometh shall find so doing.

47 Verily I say unto you, That he shall make him ruler over all his goods.

48 But and if that evil servant shall say in his heart, My lord delayeth his coming;

49 And shall begin to smite *his* fellowservants, and to eat and drink with the drunken;

50 The lord of that servant shall come in a day when he looketh not for *him*, and in an hour that he is not aware of,

51 And shall cut him asunder, and appoint *him* his portion with the hypocrites: there shall be weeping and gnashing of teeth.

6 The ten virgins, 25:1–13

25 Then shall the kingdom of heaven be likened unto ten virgins, which took their lamps, and went forth to meet the bridegroom.

2 And five of them were wise, and five *were* foolish.

24:45 *his lord* = his master.

25:1–13 The story clearly teaches watchfulness (v. 13); i.e., only those who are prepared for His coming will enter the kingdom.

25:1 *to meet the bridegroom.* There were two phases to Jewish weddings. First the bridegroom went to the bride's home to obtain his bride and observe certain religious ceremonies. Then he took his bride to his own home for a resumption of the festivities. Christ will take His bride, the church, to heaven before the tribulation period begins; then He will return with His bride at His second coming to the marriage supper on earth. The virgins represent the professing Jewish remnant on earth at His return.

3 They that *were* foolish took their lamps, and took no oil with them:

4 But the wise took oil in their vessels with their lamps.

5 While the bridegroom tarried, they all slumbered and slept.

6 And at midnight there was a cry made, Behold, the bridegroom cometh; go ye out to meet him.

7 Then all those virgins arose, and trimmed their lamps.

8 And the foolish said unto the wise, Give us of your oil; for our lamps are gone out.

9 But the wise answered, saying, *Not so*; lest there be not enough for us and you: but go ye rather to them that sell, and buy for yourselves.

10 And while they went to buy, the bridegroom came; and they that were ready went in with him to the marriage: and the door was shut.

11 Afterward came also the other virgins, saying, Lord, Lord, open to us.

12 But he answered and said, Verily I say unto you, I know you not.

13 Watch therefore, for ye know neither the day nor the hour wherein the Son of man cometh.

7 *The talents*, 25:14–30

14 ¶ For *the kingdom of heaven is* as a man travelling into a far country, *who* called his own servants, and delivered unto them his goods.

15 And unto one he gave five talents, to another two, and to another one; to every man according to his several ability; and straightway took his journey.

16 Then he that had received the five talents went and traded with the same, and made *them* other five talents.

17 And likewise he that *had received* two, he also gained other two.

18 But he that had received one went and digged in the earth, and hid his lord's money.

19 After a long time the lord of those servants cometh, and reckoneth with them.

20 And so he that had received five talents came and brought other five talents, saying, Lord, thou deliveredst unto me five talents: behold, I have gained beside them five talents more.

25:14–30 The contrast here is between those who make use of God's gifts and those who do not.

25:15 *talents*. See note at 18:24. These were silver (the word "money" in v. 18 means silver).

21 His lord said unto him, Well done, *thou* good and faithful servant: thou hast been faithful over a few things, I will make thee ruler over many things: enter thou into the joy of thy lord.

22 He also that had received two talents came and said, Lord, thou deliveredst unto me two talents: behold, I have gained two other talents beside them.

23 His lord said unto him, Well done, good and faithful servant; thou hast been faithful over a few things, I will make thee ruler over many things: enter thou into the joy of thy lord.

24 Then he which had received the one talent came and said, Lord, I knew thee that thou art an hard man, reaping where thou hast not sown, and gathering where thou hast not strawed:

25 And I was afraid, and went and hid thy talent in the earth: lo, *there* thou hast *that is* thine.

26 His lord answered and said unto him, *Thou* wicked and slothful servant, thou knewest that I reap where I sowed not, and gather where I have not strawed:

27 Thou oughtest therefore to have put my money to the exchangers, and *then* at my coming I should have received mine own with usury.

28 Take therefore the talent from him, and give *it* unto him which hath ten talents.

29 For unto every one that hath shall be given, and he shall have abundance: but from him that hath not shall be taken away even that which he hath.

30 And cast ye the unprofitable servant into outer darkness: there shall be weeping and gnashing of teeth.

8 *The judgment of Gentiles,* 25:31–46

31 ¶ When the Son of man shall come in his glory, and all the holy angels with him, then shall he sit upon the throne of his glory:

32 And before him shall be gathered all nations: and he

25:21, 23, 26 Two of the men received the same reward, indicating that faithfulness in the use of the different abilities given to each of us is what is required. The third is condemned for his sloth and indifference.

25:24 *strawed*=winnowed.

25:27 *usury*=interest.

25:30 *unprofitable*=useless.

25:32 *all nations.* Lit., all Gentiles. This is a judgment of those Gentiles who survive the tribulation and whose heart relation to God is evidenced by their treatment of the Jews (Christ's

shall separate them one from another, as a shepherd divideth *his* sheep from the goats:

33 And he shall set the sheep on his right hand, but the goats on the left.

34 Then shall the King say unto them on his right hand, Come, ye blessed of my Father, inherit the kingdom prepared for you from the foundation of the world:

35 For I was an hungred, and ye gave me meat: I was thirsty, and ye gave me drink: I was a stranger, and ye took me in:

36 Naked, and ye clothed me: I was sick, and ye visited me: I was in prison, and ye came unto me.

37 Then shall the righteous answer him, saying, Lord, when saw we thee an hungred, and fed *thee*? or thirsty, and gave *thee* drink?

38 When saw we thee a stranger, and took *thee* in? or naked, and clothed *thee*?

39 Or when saw we thee sick, or in prison, and came unto thee?

40 And the King shall answer and say unto them, Verily I say unto you, Inasmuch as ye have done *it* unto one of the least of these my brethren, ye have done *it* unto me.

41 Then shall he say also unto them on the left hand, Depart from me, ye cursed, into everlasting fire, prepared for the devil and his angels:

42 For I was an hungred, and ye gave me no meat: I was thirsty, and ye gave me no drink:

43 I was a stranger, and ye took me not in: naked, and ye clothed me not: sick, and in prison, and ye visited me not.

44 Then shall they also answer him, saying, Lord, when saw we thee an hungred, or athirst, or a stranger, or naked, or sick, or in prison, and did not minister unto thee?

45 Then shall he answer them, saying, Verily I say unto you, Inasmuch as ye did *it* not to one of the least of these, ye did *it* not to me.

46 And these shall go away into everlasting punishment: but the righteous into life eternal.

brethren, v. 40) especially during that time. Surviving Jews will also be judged at this same time (Ezek. 20:33–38).

25:33 *on his right hand*=the place of honor.

25:37 *when.* They are unconscious of their goodness, in contrast to the ostentation of the Pharisees. In v. 40 we see the opposite, the unconscious neglect of duty.

VIII THE PASSION OF THE KING, 26:1–27:66

A The Preparation, 26:1–16

26 And it came to pass, when Jesus had finished all these sayings, he said unto his disciples,

2 Ye know that after two days is *the feast* of the passover, and the Son of man is betrayed to be crucified.

3 Then assembled together the chief priests, and the scribes, and the elders of the people, unto the palace of the high priest, who was called Cáï'aphas.

4 And consulted that they might take Jesus by subtilty, and kill *him*.

5 But they said, Not on the feast *day*, lest there be an uproar among the people.

6 ¶ Now when Jesus was in Bethany, in the house of Simon the leper,

7 There came unto him a woman having an alabaster box of very precious ointment, and poured it on his head, as he sat *at meat*.

8 But when his disciples saw *it*, they had indignation, saying, To what purpose *is* this waste?

9 For this ointment might have been sold for much, and given to the poor.

10 When Jesus understood *it*, he said unto them, Why trouble ye the woman? for she hath wrought a good work upon me.

11 For ye have the poor always with you; but me ye have not always.

26:2 *after two days*=two days from now. The events recorded in 26:1–16 occurred on Wednesday. *is betrayed*=will be delivered. *passover*. This was the ancient Jewish festival commemorating the deliverance from Egypt. It was followed immediately by the seven days' Feast of Unleavened Bread, and the entire festival was often called "Passover." See note at Acts 2:1.

26:3 *Caiaphas*, high priest A.D. 18–36 and son-in-law and successor of Annas.

26:6 *Simon the leper*. Nothing more of him is known. Perhaps Christ had healed him.

26:7 *very precious ointment*. Mark (14:5) says it was worth 300 denarii (about $60.) *as he sat at meat*=as He reclined at the table.

26:11 *For ye have the poor always with you*. This should not be understood callously. Christ says, in effect, that there will be other opportunities to do good to the poor, but not another opportunity to do what had just been done to Him.

12 For in that she hath poured this ointment on my body, she did *it* for my burial.

13 Verily I say unto you, Wheresoever this gospel shall be preached in the whole world, *there* shall also this, that this woman hath done, be told for a memorial of her.

14 ¶ Then one of the twelve, called Judas Iscariot, went unto the chief priests,

15 And said *unto them*, What will ye give me, and I will deliver him unto you? And they covenanted with him for thirty pieces of silver.

16 And from that time he sought opportunity to betray him.

B The Passover, 26:17–30

17 ¶ Now the first *day* of the *feast of* unleavened bread the disciples came to Jesus, saying unto him, Where wilt thou that we prepare for thee to eat the passover?

18 And he said, Go into the city to such a man, and say unto him, The Master saith, My time is at hand; I will keep the passover at thy house with my disciples.

19 And the disciples did as Jesus had appointed them; and they made ready the passover.

20 Now when the even was come, he sat down with the twelve.

21 And as they did eat, he said, Verily I say unto you, that one of you shall betray me.

22 And they were exceeding sorrowful, and began every one of them to say unto him, Lord, is it I?

23 And he answered and said, He that dippeth *his* hand with me in the dish, the same shall betray me.

26:12 *she did it for my burial.* Though the disciples ignored Christ's many predictions of His approaching death, apparently the woman believed them (16:21; 17:22; 20:18). John identifies her with Mary (John 12:3).

26:15 *thirty pieces of silver.* Assuming a silver shekel was meant, Judas's price was a mere $30.

26:17 *eat the passover.* I.e., the passover lamb (Ex. 12:3–10), meaning the whole sacred meal.

26:18 *My time* (of death) *is at hand.*

26:20 *he sat down with the twelve.* The order of events that night was: eating the Passover; washing the disciples' feet (John 13:1–20); identifying Judas as the betrayer (Matt. 26:21–25), after which he left (John 13:30); the institution of the Lord's Supper (Matt. 26:26–29); messages in the Upper Room (John 14) and on the way to Gethsemane (John 15–16); Christ's great prayer for His people (John 17); the betrayal and arrest in Gethsemane (Matt. 26:36–56).

24 The Son of man goeth as it is written of him: but woe unto that man by whom the Son of man is betrayed! it had been good for that man if he had not been born.

25 Then Judas, which betrayed him, answered and said, Master, is it I? He said unto him, Thou hast said.

26 ¶ And as they were eating, Jesus took bread, and blessed *it*, and brake *it*, and gave *it* to the disciples, and said, Take, eat; this is my body.

27 And he took the cup, and gave thanks, and gave *it* to them, saying, Drink ye all of it;

28 For this is my blood of the new testament, which is shed for many for the remission of sins.

29 But I say unto you, I will not drink henceforth of this fruit of the vine, until that day when I drink it new with you in my Father's kingdom.

30 And when they had sung an hymn, they went out into the mount of Olives.

C The Betrayal, 26:31–56

31 Then saith Jesus unto them, All ye shall be offended because of me this night: for it is written, I will smite the shepherd, and the sheep of the flock shall be scattered abroad.

32 But after I am risen again, I will go before you into Galilee.

33 Peter answered and said unto him, Though all *men* shall be offended because of thee, *yet* will I never be offended.

34 Jesus said unto him, Verily I say unto thee, That this night, before the cock crow, thou shalt deny me thrice.

35 Peter said unto him, Though I should die with thee, yet will I not deny thee. Likewise also said all the disciples.

26:25 *Thou hast said.* I.e., You have said it, meaning Yes.

26:27 *Drink ye all of it*=drink it, all of you.

26:28 *the new testament.* The new testament or new covenant is God's new arrangement with men based on the death of Christ. See introduction to the New Testament.

26:29 *until the day that I drink it new with you in my Father's kingdom.* The disciples' attention is directed toward their eventual reunion in the future millennial kingdom with its joy and fellowship.

26:30 *hymn.* Probably all or part of Ps. 113–118, the traditional Passover Hallel.

26:31 *All ye shall be offended.* All the disciples will "take offense at me" ("stumble" or "fall away" because of me) before the night is over (v. 56), not only Peter. See Zech. 13:7.

36 ¶ Then cometh Jesus with them unto a place called Gethsemane, and saith unto the disciples, Sit ye here, while I go and pray yonder.

37 And he took with him Peter and the two sons of Zebedee, and began to be sorrowful and very heavy.

38 Then saith he unto them, My soul is exceeding sorrowful, even unto death: tarry ye here, and watch with me.

39 And he went a little farther, and fell on his face, and prayed, saying, O my Father, if it be possible, let this cup pass from me: nevertheless not as I will, but as thou *wilt*.

40 And he cometh unto the disciples, and findeth them asleep, and saith unto Peter, What, could ye not watch with me one hour?

41 Watch and pray, that ye enter not into temptation: the spirit indeed *is* willing, but the flesh *is* weak.

42 He went away again the second time, and prayed, saying, O my Father, if this cup may not pass away from me, except I drink it, thy will be done.

43 And he came and found them asleep again: for their eyes were heavy.

44 And he left them, and went away again, and prayed the third time, saying the same words.

45 Then cometh he to his disciples, and saith unto them, Sleep on now, and take *your* rest: behold, the hour is at hand, and the Son of man is betrayed into the hands of sinners.

46 Rise, let us be going: behold, he is at hand that doth betray me.

47 ¶ And while he yet spake, lo, Judas, one of the twelve, came, and with him a great multitude with swords and staves, from the chief priests and elders of the people.

48 Now he that betrayed him gave them a sign, saying, Whomsoever I shall kiss, that same is he: hold him fast.

26:36 *Gethsemane.* The name means "oil press." It was a garden, doubtless containing olive trees, on the side of the Mount of Olives.

26:37 *the two sons of Zebedee.* I.e., James and John.

26:38 *watch*=stay awake, be alert. So also in vv. 40, 41.

26:39 *this cup.* The cup was all the suffering involved in the sinless Son of God taking upon Himself the sin of mankind including the necessary, though temporary, separation from God (27:46). He naturally shrank from this, though He willingly submitted to it.

26:45 *Sleep on now, and take your rest.* Better, Are you still sleeping and taking your rest?

26:47 *staves*=clubs.

49 And forthwith he came to Jesus, and said, Hail, master; and kissed him.

50 And Jesus said unto him, Friend, wherefore art thou come? Then came they, and laid hands on Jesus, and took him.

51 And, behold, one of them which were with Jesus stretched out *his* hand, and drew his sword, and struck a servant of the high priest's, and smote off his ear.

52 Then said Jesus unto him, Put up again thy sword into his place: for all they that take the sword shall perish with the sword.

53 Thinkest thou that I cannot now pray to my Father, and he shall presently give me more than twelve legions of angels?

54 But how then shall the scriptures be fulfilled, that thus it must be?

55 In that same hour said Jesus to the multitudes, Are ye come out as against a thief with swords and staves for to take me? I sat daily with you teaching in the temple, and ye laid no hold on me.

56 But all this was done, that the scriptures of the prophets might be fulfilled. Then all the disciples forsook him, and fled.

D The Hearings, 26:57–27:26

1 *Before the high priest*, 26:57–75

57 ¶ And they that had laid hold on Jesus led *him* away to Ca'iaphas the high priest, where the scribes and the elders were assembled.

58 But Peter followed him afar off unto the high priest's palace, and went in, and sat with the servants, to see the end.

59 Now the chief priests, and elders, and all the council, sought false witness against Jesus, to put him to death;

60 But found none: yea, though many false witnesses

26:50 *Friend*=comrade or companion.

26:51 *one of them*. This was Peter (John 18:10).

26:53 *twelve legions*. Christ meant simply a huge army, not an exact number. A Roman legion varied in number from 3000 to 6000.

26:57 The order of Jesus' trials was as follows: (1) a hearing before Annas (John 18:12–14, 19–23); (2) the trial before Caiaphas and the Sanhedrin (Matt. 26:57–68; 27:1); (3) the first appearance before Pilate (Matt. 27:2, 11–14); (4) an appearance before Herod (Luke 23:6–12); (5) a second trial before Pilate (Matt. 27:15–26).

came, *yet* found they none. At the last came two false witnesses,

61 And said, This *fellow* said, I am able to destroy the temple of God, and to build it in three days.

62 And the high priest arose, and said unto him, Answerest thou nothing? what *is it which* these witness against thee?

63 But Jesus held his peace. And the high priest answered and said unto him, I adjure thee by the living God, that thou tell us whether thou be the Christ, the Son of God.

64 Jesus saith unto him, Thou hast said: nevertheless I say unto you, Hereafter shall ye see the Son of man sitting on the right hand of power, and coming in the clouds of heaven.

65 Then the high priest rent his clothes, saying, He hath spoken blasphemy; what further need have we of witnesses? behold, now ye have heard his blasphemy.

66 What think ye? They answered and said, He is guilty of death.

67 Then did they spit in his face, and buffeted him; and others smote *him* with the palms of their hands,

68 Saying, Prophesy unto us, thou Christ, Who is he that smote thee?

69 ¶ Now Peter sat without in the palace: and a damsel came unto him, saying, Thou also wast with Jesus of Galilee.

70 But he denied before *them* all, saying, I know not what thou sayest.

71 And when he was gone out into the porch, another *maid* saw him, and said unto them that were there, This *fellow* was also with Jesus of Nazareth.

26:58 *palace.* Better, courtyard.
26:60 *two false witnesses.* To establish a charge, two witnesses were required under Jewish law, and their testimony had to be in agreement.
26:61 *destroy the temple.* A garbled version of 24:2.
26:63 *Jesus held his peace.* See Isa. 53:7. *I adjure thee*=I command thee.
26:64 *Thou hast said.* Supply *it*, meaning "Yes." See v. 25.
26:65 *the high priest rent his clothes.* An action expressive of grief obligatory on hearing blasphemy.
26:66 *He is guilty of death.* I.e., He deserves to die.
26:67 *spit.* See Isa. 50:6. *buffeted.* See Isa. 52:14.
26:68 *Prophesy unto us.* Having blindfolded Him, they suggest He name His taunters (Luke 22:64).
26:69 *without in the palace*=outside in the courtyard.

72 And again he denied with an oath, I do not know the man.

73 And after a while came unto *him* they that stood by, and said to Peter, Surely thou also art *one* of them; for thy speech bewrayeth thee.

74 Then began he to curse and to swear, *saying*, I know not the man. And immediately the cock crew.

75 And Peter remembered the word of Jesus, which said unto him, Before the cock crow, thou shalt deny me thrice. And he went out, and wept bitterly.

2 *Before the Sanhedrin*, 27:1-10

27 When the morning was come, all the chief priests and elders of the people took counsel against Jesus to put him to death:

2 And when they had bound him, they led *him* away, and delivered him to Pontius Pilate the governor.

3 ¶ Then Judas, which had betrayed him, when he saw that he was condemned, repented himself, and brought again the thirty pieces of silver to the chief priests and elders,

4 Saying, I have sinned in that I have betrayed the innocent blood. And they said, What *is that* to us? see thou *to that*.

5 And he cast down the pieces of silver in the temple, and departed, and went and hanged himself.

6 And the chief priests took the silver pieces, and said, It is not lawful for to put them into the treasury, because it is the price of blood.

7 And they took counsel, and bought with them the potter's field, to bury strangers in.

26:73 *speech*=accent. Galilean pronunciation differed from Judean. *bewrayeth*=betrayeth.

26:74 *to curse*. Peter began to call down a curse on himself if he were lying.

27:2 *Pontius Pilate*. See note at Mark 15:1. His headquarters were in the city Herod built in honor of Caesar Augustus, Caesarea, on the Mediterranean. He had a palace in Jerusalem and was in the city at Passover time, when crowds would be huge and trouble always possible.

27:3-10 Compare Acts 1:16-19.

27:3 *when he saw that he was condemned*. Perhaps Judas had only wanted to force Jesus to "do something" to confound His enemies, not to get Him condemned.

27:6 *the price of blood*. I.e., "blood money" and thus impure and defiling to the temple.

27:7 *potter's field*. A field where potters dug clay for making

8 Wherefore that field was called, The field of blood, unto this day.

9 Then was fulfilled that which was spoken by Jeremy the prophet, saying, And they took the thirty pieces of silver, the price of him that was valued, whom they of the children of Israel did value;

10 And gave them for the potter's field, as the Lord appointed me.

3 Before Pilate, 27:11-26

11 And Jesus stood before the governor: and the governor asked him, saying, Art thou the King of the Jews? And Jesus said unto him, Thou sayest.

12 And when he was accused of the chief priests and elders, he answered nothing.

13 Then said Pilate unto him, Hearest thou not how many things they witness against thee?

14 And he answered him to never a word; insomuch that the governor marvelled greatly.

15 Now at *that* feast the governor was wont to release unto the people a prisoner, whom they would.

16 And they had then a notable prisoner, called Barabbas.

17 Therefore when they were gathered together, Pilate said unto them, Whom will ye that I release unto you? Barabbas, or Jesus which is called Christ?

18 For he knew that for envy they had delivered him.

19 ¶ When he was set down on the judgment seat, his wife sent unto him, saying, Have thou nothing to do with that just man: for I have suffered many things this day in a dream because of him.

20 But the chief priests and elders persuaded the multitude that they should ask Barabbas, and destroy Jesus.

21 The governor answered and said unto them, Whether

pottery vessels. It may have been full of holes so as to make it easy to bury people there who had no family tombs.

27:9 *spoken by Jeremy.* These words are found in Zech. 11:12-13 with allusions to Jer. 18:1-4; 19:1-3. They are ascribed to Jeremiah since at that time the books of the prophets were headed by Jeremiah, not Isaiah as now, and the quotation is identified by the name of the first book of the group rather than by the name of the specific book within the group. Similarly in Luke 24:44 "psalms" includes all the books known as the "Writings" because it is the first book of the group.

27:15 *was wont*=was accustomed. *whom they would.* I.e., whomever the people wished freed.

27:21 *Whether of the twain*=which of the two.

of the twain will ye that I release unto you? They said, Barabbas.

22 Pilate saith unto them, What shall I do then with Jesus which is called Christ? *They* all say unto him, Let him be crucified.

23 And the governor said, Why, what evil hath he done? But they cried out the more, saying, Let him be crucified.

24 ¶ When Pilate saw that he could prevail nothing, but *that* rather a tumult was made, he took water, and washed *his* hands before the multitude, saying, I am innocent of the blood of this just person: see ye *to it*.

25 Then answered all the people, and said, His blood *be* on us, and on our children.

26 ¶ Then released he Barabbas unto them: and when he had scourged Jesus, he delivered *him* to be crucified.

E The Crucifixion, 27:27–66

1 *The preliminaries*, 27:27–44

27 Then the soldiers of the governor took Jesus into the common hall, and gathered unto him the whole band *of soldiers*.

28 And they stripped him, and put on him a scarlet robe.

29 ¶ And when they had platted a crown of thorns, they put *it* upon his head, and a reed in his right hand: and they bowed the knee before him, and mocked him, saying, Hail, King of the Jews!

30 And they spit upon him, and took the reed, and smote him on the head.

27:24 *and washed his hands before the multitude*. A Jewish custom which when used legitimately (though not so in Pilate's case) was a symbol of absolution of an innocent man from implication in a wrongful death. *this just person*. Pilate found no political or military threat to Rome in Christ, and this was his only concern.

27:25 *all the people*. I.e., all those present, which was only a fractional part of the nation. Some of the leaders opposed the crucifixion (Luke 23:51). See also Luke 23:34; Acts 5:28; 1 Cor. 2:8.

27:26 *scourged*. Better, flogged by means of a leather whip that had pieces of bone or metal imbedded in its thongs. It was used by the Romans on murderers and traitors only.

27:27 *the common hall*=praetorium, Pilate's residence in Jerusalem. This was probably in the Castle of Antonia, near the temple, though it may have been located near Herod's palace. *band of soldiers*=a cohort, one-tenth of a legion, about 400–600 men.

31 And after that they had mocked him, they took the robe off from him, and put his own raiment on him, and led him away to crucify *him*.

32 And as they came out, they found a man of Cȳrē'nē, Simon by name: him they compelled to bear his cross.

33 And when they were come unto a place called Golgotha, that is to say, a place of a skull,

34 ¶ They gave him vinegar to drink mingled with gall: and when he had tasted *thereof*, he would not drink.

35 And they crucified him, and parted his garments, casting lots: that it might be fulfilled which was spoken by the prophet, They parted my garments among them, and upon my vesture did they cast lots.

36 And sitting down they watched him there;

37 And set up over his head his accusation written, THIS IS JESUS RHE KING OF THE JEWS.

38 Then were there two thieves crucified with him, one on the right hand, and another on the left.

39 ¶ And they that passed by reviled him, wagging their heads,

40 And saying, Thou that destroyest the temple, and

27:31 *to crucify him*. A painful and slow means of execution which the Romans adopted from the Phoenicians. The victim died after 2 or 3 days, of thirst, exhaustion, and exposure. The hands were nailed to the crossbeam, which was then hoisted up and affixed to the upright, to which the feet were then nailed. A peg, astride which the victim sat, supported the main weight of the body. Death was sometimes hastened by breaking the legs, but not in Christ's case (John 19:33).

27:32 *Cyrene*. The capital of Cyrenaica in N. Africa. Many Jews lived there. *to bear his cross*. The crossbeam was carried to the place of execution usually by the victim, but Jesus was too weakened by the tortures that had already been inflicted on Him.

27:33 *Golgotha*. Aramaic for "skull," indicating either that the place of crucifixion looked like a skull or that it was a place of execution where skulls accumulated. Its site is uncertain.

27:34 *vinegar*. Lit., wine mixed with gall, a drink given to victims to deaden their pain. Jesus refused it, preferring to meet His death with all His faculties unimpaired.

27:35 *parted*=divided. What the victim had on him were spoils for his executioners. The quotation is from Ps. 22:18.

27:37 *over his head*. To the soldiers the charge would be insurrection. His cross was in the traditional shape pictured in Christian art, with room over the crossbeam for this sign.

27:39 *wagging their heads*. A Near Eastern gesture of scorn.

27:40 See 26:61.

buildest *it* in three days, save thyself. If thou be the Son of God, come down from the cross.

41 Likewise also the chief priests mocking *him*, with the scribes and elders, said,

42 He saved others; himself he cannot save. If he be the King of Israel, let him now come down from the cross, and we will believe him.

43 He trusted in God; let him deliver him now, if he will have him: for he said, I am the Son of God.

44 The thieves also, which were crucified with him, cast the same in his teeth.

2 *The death,* 27:45–56

45 Now from the sixth hour there was darkness over all the land unto the ninth hour.

46 And about the ninth hour Jesus cried with a loud voice, saying, Eli, Eli, la′ma sabach′thani? that is to say, My God, my God, why hast thou forsaken me?

47 Some of them that stood there, when they heard *that,* said, This *man* calleth for Ēlī′as.

48 And straightway one of them ran, and took a spunge, and filled *it* with vinegar, and put *it* on a reed, and gave him to drink.

49 The rest said, Let be, let us see whether Ēlī′as will come to save him.

50 ¶ Jesus, when he had cried again with a loud voice, yielded up the ghost.

51 And, behold, the veil of the temple was rent in twain from the top to the bottom; and the earth did quake, and the rocks rent;

27:42 See 12:38; 16:1.
27:45 *sixth . . . unto the ninth hour,* from noon to 3 p.m.
27:46 *Eli, Eli, lama sabachthani,* quoting Ps. 22:1 in its Aramaic form, except that *Eloi* (Mark 15:34) has been reconverted to Hebrew *Eli.* This cry may reflect the desertion Jesus felt as He was bearing the sins of the world (2 Cor. 5:21).
27:47 *Elias.* Some listeners make a poor guess as to what Christ is saying and hear "Elias" (Elijah) for "Eli."
27:48 *vinegar*=cheap wine. *put it on a reed.* To raise it to His lips.
27:50 *the ghost.* Lit., His spirit. Christ was not killed by anyone nor was He overcome by natural processes; He released His spirit (John 10:18).
27:51 *veil.* I.e., the curtain separating the Holy of Holies from the rest of the temple (Ex. 26:37; 38:18; Heb. 9:3). *from the top to the bottom,* showing that God did it, not man.

52 And the graves were opened; and many bodies of the saints which slept arose,

53 And came out of the graves after his resurrection, and went into the holy city, and appeared unto many.

54 Now when the centurion, and they that were with him, watching Jesus, saw the earthquake, and those things that were done, they feared greatly, saying, Truly this was the Son of God.

55 And many women were there beholding afar off, which followed Jesus from Galilee, ministering unto him:

56 Among which was Mary Magdalene, and Mary the mother of James and Joses, and the mother of Zebedee's children.

3 The burial, 27:57–66

57 When the even was come, there came a rich man of Arimathæ'a, named Joseph, who also himself was Jesus' disciple:

58 He went to Pilate, and begged the body of Jesus. Then Pilate commanded the body to be delivered.

59 And when Joseph had taken the body, he wrapped it in a clean linen cloth,

60 And laid it in his own new tomb, which he had hewn out in the rock: and he rolled a great stone to the door of the sepulchre, and departed.

61 And there was Mary Magdalene, and the other Mary, sitting over against the sepulchre.

62 ¶ Now the next day, that followed the day of the preparation, the chief priests and Pharisees came together unto Pilate,

63 Saying, Sir, we remember that that deceiver said, while he was yet alive, After three days I will rise again.

64 Command therefore that the sepulchre be made sure until the third day, lest his disciples come by night, and

---

It signified that the new and living way was now open into the presence of God (Heb. 10:20; Eph. 2:11–22). One probable result of this supernatural tearing of the veil is recorded in Acts 6:7b.

27:52–53 *out of the graves*. These people may have been restored to earthly bodies to die again, or resurrected with glorified bodies.

27:57 *Arimathea*. A town N. of Lydda.

27:60 *to the door*. I.e., against the opening of the tomb, hewn out of rock. See Isa. 53:9.

27:62 *the next day*=the day before the Sabbath.

27:64 *error*. Better, deception.

steal him away, and say unto the people, He is risen from the dead: so the last error shall be worse than the first.

65 Pilate said unto them, Ye have a watch: go your way, make *it* as sure as ye can.

66 So they went, and made the sepulchre sure, sealing the stone, and setting a watch.

IX THE POWER OF THE KING, 28:1-20

A The Conquest, 28:1-10

28 In the end of the sabbath, as it began to dawn toward the first *day* of the week, came Mary Magdalene and the other Mary to see the sepulchre.

2 And, behold, there was a great earthquake: for the angel of the Lord descended from heaven, and came and rolled back the stone from the door, and sat upon it.

3 His countenance was like lightning, and his raiment white as snow:

4 And for fear of him the keepers did shake, and became as dead *men*.

5 And the angel answered and said unto the women, Fear not ye: for I know that ye seek Jesus, which was crucified.

6 He is not here: for he is risen, as he said. Come, see the place where the Lord lay.

7 And go quickly, and tell his disciples that he is risen from the dead; and, behold, he goeth before you into Galilee; there shall ye see him: lo, I have told you.

8 And they departed quickly from the sepulchre with fear and great joy; and did run to bring his disciples word.

9 ¶ And as they went to tell his disciples, behold, Jesus met them, saying, All hail. And they came and held him by the feet, and worshipped him.

10 Then said Jesus unto them, Be not afraid: go tell my

27:65 *Ye have a watch*=Take a guard.
27:66 *sealing the stone*. This was likely done by connecting the stone to the tomb with a cord and wax so that any tampering could easily be detected.
28:1 *In the end of the sabbath*=After the Sabbath. It was now Sunday morning, and the work of preparing Christ's body for permanent burial could be done.
28:4 *keepers*=guards.
28:6 *he is risen*. This simple statement of fact is the basis of our Christian faith. *as he said*. See Matt. 16:21; 17:23; 20:19.
28:10 *that they*=to.

brethren that they go into Galilee, and there shall they see me.

B The Conspiracy, 28:11–15

11 ¶ Now when they were going, behold, some of the watch came into the city, and shewed unto the chief priests all the things that were done.

12 And when they were assembled with the elders, and had taken counsel, they gave large money unto the soldiers,

13 Saying, Say ye, His disciples came by night, and stole him *away* while we slept.

14 And if this come to the governor's ears, we will persuade him, and secure you.

15 So they took the money, and did as they were taught: and this saying is commonly reported among the Jews until this day.

C The Commission, 28:16–20

16 ¶ Then the eleven disciples went away into Galilee, into a mountain where Jesus had appointed them.

17 And when they saw him, they worshipped him: but some doubted.

18 And Jesus came and spake unto them, saying, All power is given unto me in heaven and in earth.

19 ¶ Go ye therefore, and teach all nations, baptizing them in the name of the Father, and of the Son, and of the Holy Ghost:

28:13 *while we slept.* How would sleeping people know what happened? Would it be likely that all the soldiers were sleeping at the same time? Why would Roman soldiers risk incriminating themselves even for a large bribe? The story was self-contradictory!

28:14 *secure*=protect, shield.

28:16 *appointed*=commanded, see 26:32; 28:7.

28:18 *All power.* Better, all authority. The Great Commission which follows is based upon and backed by the authority of the risen and exalted Lord who promises to be ever-present with His people.

28:19 *teach all nations*=make disciples of all nations. This is the one command in the Commission. It is surrounded by three participles: go (lit., going), *baptizing* and *teaching* (v. 20). This is the missionary task of the church. *in the name of the Father, and of the Son, and of the Holy Ghost* (better, Spirit). Here is unsophisticated evidence for the trinity of God: one God (*the name*) who subsists in three (Father, Son and Holy Spirit). Each of the three is distinguished from the others; each possesses all the divine attributes; yet the three

20 Teaching them to observe all things whatsoever I have commanded you: and, lo, I am with you alway, *even* unto the end of the world. Amen.

are one. This is a mystery which nothing illustrates well. The sun, sunlight, and the power of the sun may come close to a suitable illustration of the Trinity.

28:20 *end of the world*=end of the age. The personal and empowering presence of the One whom we have seen so vividly portrayed in this Gospel is promised to His followers. In His power the commission can be performed.

INTRODUCTION TO
THE GOSPEL ACCORDING TO
Mark

AUTHOR: Mark DATE: 50's

The Author John Mark was the son of Mary, who was a woman of wealth and position in Jerusalem (Acts 12:12). Barnabas was his cousin (Col. 4:10). Mark was a close friend (and possibly a convert) of the apostle Peter (1 Pet. 5:13). He had the rare privilege of accompanying Paul and Barnabas on the first missionary journey, but he failed to stay with them through the entire trip. Because of this, Paul refused to take him on the second journey, so he went with Barnabas to Cyprus (Acts 15:38–40) About a dozen years later he was again with Paul (Col. 4:10; Philem. 24), and just before Paul's execution he sent for Mark (2 Tim. 4:11). His biography proves that one failure in life does not mean the end of usefulness.

The Distinctive Approach of Mark (1) Mark wrote for Gentile readers in general and Roman readers in particular. For this reason the genealogy of Christ is not included (for it would have meant little to Gentiles), the Sermon on the Mount is not reported, and the condemnations of the Jewish sects receive little attention. As a further indication of his Gentile readership, Mark felt it necessary to interpret Aramaic words (5:41; 7:34; 15:22), and he used Latin words not found in the other Gospels ("executioner," 6:27; "farthing," 12:42). (2) There are only about 63 quotations or allusions from the Old Testament in Mark as compared with about 128 in Matthew and between 90 and 100 in Luke. (3) This Gospel emphasizes what Jesus did rather than what He said. It is a book of action (the word "straightway" occurs more than 40 times).

Mark and Peter It is generally agreed that Mark received much of the information in his Gospel from Peter. With

Peter's apostolic authority behind the Gospel, there was never any challenge to its inclusion in the canon of Scripture.

The Date   If one denies the phenomenon of predictive prophecy, then the book must be dated after A.D. 70 because of 13:2, but since our Lord could predict the future, this late date is unnecessary. In fact, if Acts must be dated about 61, and if Luke, the companion volume, preceded it, then Mark must be even earlier, since Luke apparently utilized Mark in writing his Gospel. This points to a date in the 50's for Mark. However, many scholars understand that Mark was not written until after Peter died (sometime after 67 but before 70).

The Contents   The theme of the book is Christ the Servant. The key verse is 10:45, which divides the Gospel in two major divisions: the service of the Servant (1:1–10:52) and the sacrifice of the Servant (11:1–16:20).

OUTLINE OF THE GOSPEL OF MARK

I The Service of the Servant, 1:1–10:52
  A His Preparation, 1:1–13
    1 By the ministry of John the Baptist, 1:2–8
    2 By His baptism, 1:9–11
    3 By His temptation, 1:12–13
  B His Preaching, 1:14–20
  C His Power, 1:21–3:12
    1 Over a demon, 1:21–28
    2 Over disease, 1:29–39
    3 Over leprosy, 1:40–45
    4 Over paralysis, 2:1–12
    5 Over a publican, 2:13–20
    6 Over the old religion, 2:21–22
    7 Over the Sabbath, 2:23–28
    8 Over deformity, 3:1–6
    9 Over demons, 3:7–12
  D His Personnel, 3:13–35
    1 The call of the twelve, 3:13–21
    2 The condemnation of rejectors, 3:22–30
    3 The call to be in Jesus' spiritual family, 3:31–35
  E His Parables, 4:1–34
    1 The sower, 4:1–20
    2 The lamp, 4:21–25
    3 The seed growing gradually, 4:26–29
    4 The mustard seed, 4:30–34
  F His Prerogatives, 4:35–9:1

THE GOSPEL ACCORDING TO

Mark

I THE SERVICE OF THE SERVANT, 1:1–10:52

A His Preparation, 1:1–13

1 *By the ministry of John the Baptist,* 1:2–8

1 The beginning of the gospel of Jesus Christ, the Son of God;

2 As it is written in the prophets, Behold, I send my messenger before thy face, which shall prepare thy way before thee.

3 The voice of one crying in the wilderness, Prepare ye the way of the Lord, make his paths straight.

4 John did baptize in the wilderness, and preach the baptism of repentance for the remission of sins.

1:1 *The beginning of the gospel.* Here begins the good news—i.e., that Jesus Christ is the Savior.

1:2 *in the prophets.* See Isa. 40:3; Mal. 3:1.

1:4 *baptism of repentance for the remission of sins.* The Jews practiced self-immersion as a form of baptism, but John immersed others as a witness to their repentance. Christian baptism is performed in the name of the Trinity as a witness to

5 And there went out unto him all the land of Judæa, and they of Jerusalem, and were all baptized of him in the river of Jordan, confessing their sins.

6 And John was clothed with camel's hair, and with a girdle of a skin about his loins; and he did eat locusts and wild honey;

7 And preached, saying, There cometh one mightier than I after me, the latchet of whose shoes I am not worthy to stoop down and unloose.

8 I indeed have baptized you with water: but he shall baptize you with the Holy Ghost.

2 *By His baptism*, 1:9–11

9 And it came to pass in those days, that Jesus came from Nazareth of Galilee, and was baptized of John in Jordan.

10 And straightway coming up out of the water, he saw the heavens opened, and the Spirit like a dove descending upon him:

11 And there came a voice from heaven, *saying*, Thou art my beloved Son, in whom I am well pleased.

3 *By His temptation*, 1:12–13

12 And immediately the Spirit driveth him into the wilderness.

13 And he was there in the wilderness forty days, tempted of Satan; and was with the wild beasts; and the angels ministered unto him.

B His Preaching, 1:14–20

14 Now after that John was put in prison, Jesus came into Galilee, preaching the gospel of the kingdom of God,

15 And saying, The time is fulfilled, and the kingdom of God is at hand: repent ye, and believe the gospel.

one's faith in Christ. Some who followed John and who later believed in Christ were rebaptized (Acts 19:5).

1:7 *latchet*=thong of the sandal, which was usually loosened by a slave as a guest entered a home.

1:8 See note at Matt. 3:11.

1:10 See note at Matt. 3:16–17.

1:12 *the spirit driveth him*. Though *spirit* is not capitalized, this is a reference to the Holy Spirit. *driveth* reflects Mark's forceful style (the other Gospel writers used "led").

1:14 Between the temptation and the imprisonment of John occurred the events recorded in John 1:19–4:54. How John came to be imprisoned is told in Mark 6:17–20.

1:15 *the kingdom of God is at hand*. The rule of the Messiah on

16 Now as he walked by the sea of Galilee, he saw Simon and Andrew his brother casting a net into the sea: for they were fishers.

17 And Jesus said unto them, Come ye after me, and I will make you to become fishers of men.

18 And straightway they forsook their nets, and followed him.

19 And when he had gone a little farther thence, he saw James the *son* of Zebedee, and John his brother, who also were in the ship mending their nets.

20 And straightway he called them: and they left their father Zebedee in the ship with the hired servants, and went after him.

C His Power, 1:21–3:12

1 *Over a demon*, 1:21–28

21 And they went into Caper'naum; and straightway on the sabbath day he entered into the synagogue, and taught.

22 And they were astonished at his doctrine: for he taught them as one that had authority, and not as the scribes.

23 And there was in their synagogue a man with an unclean spirit; and he cried out,

24 Saying, Let *us* alone; what have we to do with thee, thou Jesus of Nazareth? art thou come to destroy us? I know thee who thou art, the Holy One of God.

25 And Jesus rebuked him, saying, Hold thy peace, and come out of him.

26 And when the unclean spirit had torn him, and cried with a loud voice, he came out of him.

earth, promised in the Old Testament and earnestly longed for by the Jewish people, was near, for the Messiah had now come. However, instead of accepting Him, the people rejected Him, and the fulfillment of the kingdom promises had to be delayed until God's purpose in saving Jews and Gentiles and forming His church was completed. Then Christ will return and set up God's kingdom on this earth (Acts 15:14–16; Rev. 19:15).

1:21 *Capernaum.* Situated on the NW. shore of the Sea of Galilee, this was an important town on the caravan route to Damascus. It was the site of a customs station (2:14), had a Roman garrison (Matt. 8:5–13), and was the home of Peter, Andrew, James, and John.

1:22 *authority.* Jesus' teaching was based on His own personal authority in contrast to that of the scribes, whose manner of teaching was to quote the authoritative statements of the scribes who had gone before.

27 And they were all amazed, insomuch that they questioned among themselves, saying, What thing is this? what new doctrine *is* this? for with authority commandeth he even the unclean spirits, and they do obey him.

28 And immediately his fame spread abroad throughout all the region round about Galilee.

2 Over disease, 1:29–39

29 And forthwith, when they were come out of the synagogue, they entered into the house of Simon and Andrew, with James and John.

30 But Simon's wife's mother lay sick of a fever, and anon they tell him of her.

31 And he came and took her by the hand, and lifted her up; and immediately the fever left her, and she ministered unto them.

32 And at even, when the sun did set, they brought unto him all that were diseased, and them that were possessed with devils.

33 And all the city was gathered together at the door.

34 And he healed many that were sick of divers diseases, and cast out many devils; and suffered not the devils to speak, because they knew him.

35 And in the morning, rising up a great while before day, he went out, and departed into a solitary place, and there prayed.

36 And Simon and they that were with him followed after him.

37 And when they had found him, they said unto him, All *men* seek for thee.

38 And he said unto them, Let us go into the next towns, that I may preach there also: for therefore came I forth.

39 And he preached in their synagogues throughout all Galilee, and cast out devils.

3 Over leprosy, 1:40–45

40 And there came a leper to him, beseeching him, and kneeling down to him, and saying unto him, If thou wilt, thou canst make me clean.

1:32 *when the sun did set, they brought unto him.* Burdens could not be carried on the Sabbath (v. 21), but the next day, when they could, began at sundown.

1:38 *therefore came I forth.* I.e., that is why I left Capernaum.

1:40 *leper.* See note at Luke 5:12. The laws concerning leprosy are in Lev. 13–14.

41 And Jesus, moved with compassion, put forth *his* hand, and touched him, and saith unto him, I will; be thou clean.

42 And as soon as he had spoken, immediately the leprosy departed from him, and he was cleansed.

43 And he straitly charged him, and forthwith sent him away;

44 And saith unto him, See thou say nothing to any man: but go thy way, shew thyself to the priest, and offer for thy cleansing those things which Moses commanded, for a testimony unto them.

45 But he went out, and began to publish *it* much, and to blaze abroad the matter, insomuch that Jesus could no more openly enter into the city, but was without in desert places: and they came to him from every quarter.

4 *Over paralysis*, 2:1–12

2 And again he entered into Caper'naum after *some* days; and it was noised that he was in the house.

2 And straightway many were gathered together, insomuch that there was no room to receive *them*, no, not so much as about the door: and he preached the word unto them.

3 And they come unto him, bringing one sick of the palsy, which was borne of four.

4 And when they could not come nigh unto him for the press, they uncovered the roof where he was: and when they had broken *it* up, they let down the bed wherein the sick of the palsy lay.

5 When Jesus saw their faith, he said unto the sick of the palsy, Son, thy sins be forgiven thee.

6 But there were certain of the scribes sitting there, and reasoning in their hearts,

7 Why doth this *man* thus speak blasphemies? who can forgive sins but God only?

8 And immediately when Jesus perceived in his spirit that they so reasoned within themselves, he said unto them, Why reason ye these things in your hearts?

9 Whether is it easier to say to the sick of the palsy, *Thy*

1:44 *say nothing to any man.* Jesus did not want people coming to Him merely to receive physical benefits. The result of the leper's failure to obey is seen in v. 45.
2:3 *sick of the palsy.* Lit., a paralytic.
2:5 See note at Matt. 9:2.
2:8 *in his spirit*=intuitively.

sins be forgiven thee; or to say, Arise, and take up thy bed, and walk?

10 But that ye may know that the Son of man hath power on earth to forgive sins, (he saith to the sick of the palsy,)

11 I say unto thee, Arise, and take up thy bed, and go thy way into thine house.

12 And immediately he arose, took up the bed, and went forth before them all; insomuch that they were all amazed, and glorified God, saying, We never saw it on this fashion.

5 *Over a publican*, 2:13–20

13 And he went forth again by the sea side; and all the multitude resorted unto him, and he taught them.

14 And as he passed by, he saw Levi the *son* of Alphæ'us sitting at the receipt of custom, and said unto him, Follow me. And he arose and followed him.

15 And it came to pass, that, as Jesus sat at meat in his house, many publicans and sinners sat also together with Jesus and his disciples: for there were many, and they followed him.

16 And when the scribes and Pharisees saw him eat with publicans and sinners, they said unto his disciples, How is it that he eateth and drinketh with publicans and sinners?

17 When Jesus heard *it*, he saith unto them, They that are whole have no need of the physician, but they that are sick: I came not to call the righteous, but sinners to repentance.

18 And the disciples of John and of the Pharisees used to fast: and they come and say unto him, Why do the disciples of John and of the Pharisees fast, but thy disciples fast not?

19 And Jesus said unto them, Can the children of the bridechamber fast, while the bridegroom is with them? as long as they have the bridegroom with them, they cannot fast.

2:10 *the Son of man.* A favorite title of Christ in Mark, used 14 times. See note on Matt. 8:20 for its significance.

2:12 *We never saw it on this fashion.* I.e., we never saw anything like this!

2:15 *publicans*=tax-collectors.

2:18 Jesus' disciples did not fast because it was incompatible with the joy they had being with Him. On the Jews' fasting see note at Matt. 9:14. The N.T. church did not fast regularly as a prescribed rite, though it was done on occasion (Acts 13:2–3; 14:23; 2 Cor. 6:5; 11:27). Whenever practiced, it is never to be done ostentatiously (Matt. 6:16–18).

20 But the days will come, when the bridegroom shall be taken away from them, and then shall they fast in those days.

6 Over the old religion, 2:21–22

21 No man also seweth a piece of new cloth on an old garment: else the new piece that filled it up taketh away from the old, and the rent is made worse.

22 And no man putteth new wine into old bottles: else the new wine doth burst the bottles, and the wine is spilled, and the bottles will be marred: but new wine must be put into new bottles.

7 Over the Sabbath, 2:23–28

23 And it came to pass, that he went through the corn fields on the sabbath day; and his disciples began, as they went, to pluck the ears of corn.

24 And the Pharisees said unto him, Behold, why do they on the sabbath day that which is not lawful?

25 And he said unto them, Have ye never read what David did, when he had need, and was an hungred, he, and they that were with him?

26 How he went into the house of God in the days of Abī′athar the high priest, and did eat the shewbread, which is not lawful to eat but for the priests, and gave also to them which were with him?

27 And he said unto them, The sabbath was made for man, and not man for the sabbath:

28 Therefore the Son of man is Lord also of the sabbath.

8 Over deformity, 3:1–6

3 And he entered again into the synagogue; and there was a man there which had a withered hand.

2 And they watched him, whether he would heal him on the sabbath day; that they might accuse him.

3 And he saith unto the man which had the withered hand, Stand forth.

2:22 *bottles.* Lit., wineskins. See note at Luke 5:37.
2:23 *corn fields.* Not fields of U.S. "corn" but fields of grain such as barley or wheat.
2:25 *what David did.* See 1 Sam. 21:1–6. See note at Matt. 12:2.
3:2 *on the sabbath.* Rabbinic tradition, not the law, forbade practicing medicine on the Sabbath unless the person were on the verge of death. Christ's critics were simply determined somehow to stop His activities.

4 And he saith unto them, Is it lawful to do good on the sabbath days, or to do evil? to save life, or to kill? But they held their peace.

5 And when he had looked round about on them with anger, being grieved for the hardness of their hearts, he saith unto the man, Stretch forth thine hand. And he stretched *it* out: and his hand was restored whole as the other.

6 And the Pharisees went forth, and straightway took counsel with the Hero'dians against him, how they might destroy him.

9 *Over demons,* 3:7–12

7 But Jesus withdrew himself with his disciples to the sea: and a great multitude from Galilee followed him, and from Judæa,

8 And from Jerusalem, and from Īdūmǣ'a, and *from* beyond Jordan; and they about Tyre and Sidon, a great multitude, when they had heard what great things he did, came unto him.

9 And he spake to his disciples, that a small ship should wait on him because of the multitude, lest they should throng him.

10 For he had healed many; insomuch that they pressed upon him for to touch him, as many as had plagues.

11 And unclean spirits, when they saw him, fell down before him, and cried, saying, Thou art the Son of God.

12 And he straitly charged them that they should not make him known.

D His Personnel, 3:13–35

1 *The call of the twelve,* 3:13–21

13 And he goeth up into a mountain, and calleth *unto him* whom he would: and they came unto him.

14 And he ordained twelve, that they should be with him, and that he might send them forth to preach,

15 And to have power to heal sicknesses, and to cast out devils:

16 And Simon he surnamed Peter;

3:4 Christ's argument is: To be able to do good and refuse to do it is evil; not to heal this man was to do evil.

3:6 *Pharisees.* See note at Matt. 3:7. *Herodians.* See note at Matt. 22:16.

3:8 *Idumaea*=the successor of the country of Edom, which in the time of Christ included the region around Hebron.

3:16–19 There are 4 lists of the apostles given in the N.T.

17 And James the *son* of Zebedee, and John the brother of James; and he surnamed them Bōanergēs, which is, The sons of thunder:

18 And Andrew, and Philip, and Bartholomew, and Matthew, and Thomas, and James the *son* of Alphǣus, and Thaddǣus, and Simon the Cā'naanīte,

19 And Judas Iscariot, which also betrayed him: and they went into an house.

20 And the multitude cometh together again, so that they could not so much as eat bread.

21 And when his friends heard *of it*, they went out to lay hold on him: for they said, He is beside himself.

2 *The condemnation of rejectors*, 3:22-30

22 ¶ And the scribes which came down from Jerusalem said, He hath Bēel'zebub, and by the prince of the devils casteth he out devils.

23 And he called them *unto him*, and said unto them in parables, How can Satan cast out Satan?

24 And if a kingdom be divided against itself, that kingdom cannot stand.

25 And if a house be divided against itself, that house cannot stand.

26 And if Satan rise up against himself, and be divided, he cannot stand, but hath an end.

27 No man can enter into a strong man's house, and spoil his goods, except he will first bind the strong man; and then he will spoil his house.

28 Verily I say unto you, All sins shall be forgiven unto the sons of men, and blasphemies wherewith soever they shall blaspheme:

29 But he that shall blaspheme against the Holy Ghost hath never forgiveness, but is in danger of eternal damnation:

30 Because they said, He hath an unclean spirit.

(Matt. 10:1-4; Luke 6:13-16; Acts 1:13 are the others). Thaddaeus (Matt. 10:3; Mark 3:18) is apparently the same as Judas the son or brother of James (Thaddaeus may represent a corruption of *Yaddai*, a form of Judas).

3:17 *The sons of thunder*. Probably indicating the fiery zeal and energy of James and John.

3:21 *to lay hold on him*. I.e., to take Him away with them that He might rest.

3:22 *Beelzebub*. See note at Matt. 10:25.

3:29 *blaspheme against the Holy Ghost*. See note at Matt. 12:31.

3 *The call to be in Jesus' spiritual family,* 3:31–35

31 ¶ There came then his brethren and his mother, and, standing without, sent unto him, calling him.

32 And the multitude sat about him, and they said unto him, Behold, thy mother and thy brethren without seek for thee.

33 And he answered them, saying, Who is my mother, or my brethren?

34 And he looked round about on them which sat about him, and said, Behold my mother and my brethren!

35 For whosoever shall do the will of God, the same is my brother, and my sister, and mother.

E His Parables, 4:1–34

1 *The sower,* 4:1–20

4 And he began again to teach by the sea side: and there was gathered unto him a great multitude, so that he entered into a ship, and sat in the sea; and the whole multitude was by the sea on the land.

2 And he taught them many things by parables, and said unto them in his doctrine,

3 Hearken; Behold, there went out a sower to sow:

4 And it came to pass, as he sowed, some fell by the way side, and the fowls of the air came and devoured it up.

5 And some fell on stony ground, where it had not much earth; and immediately it sprang up, because it had no depth of earth:

6 But when the sun was up, it was scorched; and because it had no root, it withered away.

7 And some fell among thorns, and the thorns grew up, and choked it, and it yielded no fruit.

8 And other fell on good ground, and did yield fruit

3:35 Those who belong to God's family are closer than His natural family.

4:2 *parables.* A parable is a short discourse that makes a comparison; it is usually designed to inculcate a single truth. However, some parables, like those of the wheat and the tares, are given detailed interpretations. Also the Greek word "parable" is used in Luke 4:23 of what we would normally call a proverb. Parables were told by Christ for opposite effects: to make the truth more engaging and clear to those who heard (Luke 15:3) and to make the truth obscure to those who lacked spiritual perception (Mark 4:11–12).

4:5–8 Jesus wanted the people to examine their hearts' responses to His message. Though some of the soils proved barren, nevertheless how great the harvest.

that sprang up and increased; and brought forth, some thirty, and some sixty, and some an hundred.

9 And he said unto them, He that hath ears to hear, let him hear.

10 And when he was alone, they that were about him with the twelve asked of him the parable.

11 And he said unto them, Unto you it is given to know the mystery of the kingdom of God: but unto them that are without, all *these* things are done in parables:

12 That seeing they may see, and not perceive; and hearing they may hear, and not understand; lest at any time they should be converted, and *their* sins should be forgiven them.

13 And he said unto them, Know ye not this parable? and how then will ye know all parables?

14 ¶ The sower soweth the word.

15 And these are they by the way side, where the word is sown; but when they have heard, Satan cometh immediately, and taketh away the word that was sown in their hearts.

16 And these are they likewise which are sown on stony ground; who, when they have heard the word, immediately receive it with gladness;

17 And have no root in themselves, and so endure but for a time: afterward, when affliction or persecution ariseth for the word's sake, immediately they are offended.

18 And these are they which are sown among thorns; such as hear the word,

19 And the cares of this world, and the deceitfulness of riches, and the lusts of other things entering in, choke the word, and it becometh unfruitful.

20 And these are they which are sown on good ground; such as hear the word, and receive *it*, and bring forth fruit, some thirtyfold, some sixty, and some an hundred.

2 The lamp, 4:21–25

21 ¶ And he said unto them, Is a candle brought to be

4:11 *the mystery.* Just as in pagan mystery religions the initiate was instructed in the teaching of the cult which was not revealed to outsiders, so the purpose of parables was to instruct the disciples without revealing truths to *them that are without.* Parables test the spiritual responsiveness of those who hear them.

4:19 *lusts of other things.* I.e., desire for things other than the gospel.

4:21 *candle.* Better, lamp.

put under a bushel, or under a bed? and not to be set on a candlestick?

22 For there is nothing hid, which shall not be manifested; neither was any thing kept secret, but that it should come abroad.

23 If any man have ears to hear, let him hear.

24 And he said unto them, Take heed what ye hear: with what measure ye mete, it shall be measured to you: and unto you that hear shall more be given.

25 For he that hath, to him shall be given: and he that hath not, from him shall be taken even that which he hath.

3 The seed growing gradually, 4:26–29

26 ¶ And he said, So is the kingdom of God, as if a man should cast seed into the ground;

27 And should sleep, and rise night and day, and the seed should spring and grow up, he knoweth not how.

28 For the earth bringeth forth fruit of herself; first the blade, then the ear, after that the full corn in the ear.

29 But when the fruit is brought forth, immediately he putteth in the sickle, because the harvest is come.

4 The mustard seed, 4:30–34

30 ¶ And he said, Whereunto shall we liken the kingdom of God? or with what comparison shall we compare it?

31 It is like a grain of mustard seed, which, when it is sown in the earth, is less than all the seeds that be in the earth:

32 But when it is sown, it groweth up, and becometh greater than all herbs, and shooteth out great branches; so that the fowls of the air may lodge under the shadow of it.

33 And with many such parables spake he the word unto them, as they were able to hear it.

34 But without a parable spake he not unto them: and when they were alone, he expounded all things to his disciples.

4:26–29 The Word of God when sown in men's hearts produces fruit slowly but surely (see 1 Pet. 1:23–25).

4:31 a grain of mustard seed. Though one of the smallest seeds and an herb, the mustard plant grows to a height of 10 or 12 feet. It pictures the phenomenally rapid spread of Christianity from a minute beginning.

F His Prerogatives, 4:35—9:1

1 *Over the storm*, 4:35—41

35 And the same day, when the even was come, he saith unto them, Let us pass over unto the other side.

36 And when they had sent away the multitude, they took him even as he was in the ship. And there were also with him other little ships.

37 And there arose a great storm of wind, and the waves beat into the ship, so that it was now full.

38 And he was in the hinder part of the ship, asleep on a pillow: and they awake him, and say unto him, Master, carest thou not that we perish?

39 And he arose, and rebuked the wind, and said unto the sea, Peace, be still. And the wind ceased, and there was a great calm.

40 And he said unto them, Why are ye so fearful? how is it that ye have no faith?

41 And they feared exceedingly, and said one to another, What manner of man is this, that even the wind and the sea obey him?

2 *Over demons*, 5:1—20

5 And they came over unto the other side of the sea, into the country of the Gad'arēnes.

2 And when he was come out of the ship, immediately there met him out of the tombs a man with an unclean spirit,

3 Who had *his* dwelling among the tombs; and no man could bind him, no, not with chains:

4 Because that he had been often bound with fetters and chains, and the chains had been plucked asunder by him, and the fetters broken in pieces: neither could any *man* tame him.

5 And always, night and day, he was in the mountains, and in the tombs, crying, and cutting himself with stones.

6 But when he saw Jesus afar off, he ran and worshipped him,

7 And cried with a loud voice, and said, What have I

4:41 *And they feared exceedingly.* The disciples were rebuked in v. 40 for being fearful, which literally means "cowardly." In v. 41 the word *fear* is different, meaning reverential, respectful awe for the Lord. In exclaiming *What manner of man is this,* they acknowledge that He is greater than they thought.

5:7 *What have I to do with thee.* We would today say instead: What have you to do with me? *Jesus, thou Son of the most*

to do with thee, Jesus, *thou* Son of the most high God? I
adjure thee by God, that thou torment me not.

8 For he said unto him, Come out of the man, *thou*
unclean spirit.

9 And he asked him, What *is* thy name? And he answered, saying, My name *is* Legion: for we are many.

10 And he besought him much that he would not send
them away out of the country.

11 Now there was there nigh unto the mountains a great
herd of swine feeding.

12 And all the devils besought him, saying, Send us
into the swine, that we may enter into them.

13 And forthwith Jesus gave them leave. And the unclean spirits went out, and entered into the swine: and
the herd ran violently down a steep place into the sea,
(they were about two thousand;) and were choked in the
sea.

14 And they that fed the swine fled, and told *it* in the
city, and in the country. And they went out to see what it
was that was done.

15 And they come to Jesus, and see him that was possessed with the devil, and had the legion, sitting, and
clothed, and in his right mind: and they were afraid.

16 And they that saw *it* told them how it befell to him
that was possessed with the devil, and *also* concerning the
swine.

17 And they began to pray him to depart out of their
coasts.

18 And when he was come into the ship, he that had
been possessed with the devil prayed him that he might be
with him.

19 Howbeit Jesus suffered him not, but saith unto him,
Go home to thy friends, and tell them how great things
the Lord hath done for thee, and hath had compassion on
thee.

20 And he departed, and began to publish in Decapolis
how great things Jesus had done for him: and all *men* did
marvel.

high God. Though apparently his first encounter with Jesus,
this man knew who He was, such knowledge coming to him
from the demons who dwelt in him.

5:8 *For he said.* Better, For He (Christ) had said.

5:9 *Legion.* The largest unit of the Roman army, then 5000–6000
strong, indicating that many demons possessed the man (see
Luke 8:2 and Matt. 12:45).

5:17 *coasts*=neighborhood, region.

5:20 *Decapolis,* the region SE. of the Sea of Galilee, in which

3 *Over sickness and death,* 5:21-43

21 And when Jesus was passed over again by ship unto the other side, much people gathered unto him: and he was nigh unto the sea.

22 And, behold, there cometh one of the rulers of the synagogue, Jaï′rus by name; and when he saw him, he fell at his feet,

23 And besought him greatly, saying, My little daughter lieth at the point of death: *I pray thee,* come and lay thy hands on her, that she may be healed; and she shall live.

24 And *Jesus* went with him; and much people followed him, and thronged him.

25 And a certain woman, which had an issue of blood twelve years,

26 And had suffered many things of many physicians, and had spent all that she had, and was nothing bettered, but rather grew worse,

27 When she had heard of Jesus, came in the press behind, and touched his garment.

28 For she said, If I may touch but his clothes, I shall be whole.

29 And straightway the fountain of her blood was dried up; and she felt in *her* body that she was healed of that plague.

30 And Jesus, immediately knowing in himself that virtue had gone out of him, turned him about in the press, and said, Who touched my clothes?

31 And his disciples said unto him, Thou seest the multitude thronging thee, and sayest thou, Who touched me?

32 And he looked round about to see her that had done this thing.

33 But the woman fearing and trembling, knowing what was done in her, came and fell down before him, and told him all the truth.

34 And he said unto her, Daughter, thy faith hath made thee whole; go in peace, and be whole of thy plague.

35 While he yet spake, there came from the ruler of the

were located 10 cities which were Greek in organization and culture.

5:22 *one of the rulers of the synagogue.* Jairus was an elder in the synagogue at Capernaum which Jesus attended.

5:25 *an issue of blood.* I.e., a chronic hemorrhage.

5:30 *virtue.* Lit., power.

5:34 *thy faith hath made thee whole.* I.e., your faith has made possible your recovery.

synagogue's *house certain* which said, Thy daughter is dead: why troublest thou the Master any further?

36 As soon as Jesus heard the word that was spoken, he saith unto the ruler of the synagogue, Be not afraid, only believe.

37 And he suffered no man to follow him, save Peter, and James, and John the brother of James.

38 And he cometh to the house of the ruler of the synagogue, and seeth the tumult, and them that wept and wailed greatly.

39 And when he was come in, he saith unto them, Why make ye this ado, and weep? the damsel is not dead, but sleepeth.

40 And they laughed him to scorn. But when he had put them all out, he taketh the father and the mother of the damsel, and them that were with him, and entereth in where the damsel was lying.

41 And he took the damsel by the hand, and said unto her, Tal'itha cū'mī; which is, being interpreted, Damsel, I say unto thee, arise.

42 And straightway the damsel arose, and walked; for she was *of the age* of twelve years. And they were astonished with a great astonishment.

43 And he charged them straitly that no man should know it; and commanded that something should be given her to eat.

4 Rejected by His townspeople, 6:1–6

6 And he went out from thence, and came into his own country; and his disciples follow him.

2 And when the sabbath day was come, he began to teach in the synagogue: and many hearing *him* were astonished, saying, From whence hath this *man* these things? and what wisdom *is* this which is given unto him, that even such mighty works are wrought by his hands?

3 Is not this the carpenter, the son of Mary, the brother

5:36 *only believe*. Lit., just keep on believing! There are no limits, Christ says, to what faith in the power of God can do.

5:38 *them that wept and wailed greatly*. These were professional mourners hired by the family.

5:39 *sleepeth*. The girl had been pronounced dead (Luke 8:55). Christ's reference to death as sleep was intended to suggest that her condition was temporary and that she would come back to life again.

6:1 *his own country*. Lit., His native place; i.e., Nazareth.

6:3 *brother of*. The four half-brothers and two or more half-sisters were children of Joseph and Mary who were born after

of James, and Joses, and of Juda, and Simon? and are not his sisters here with us? And they were offended at him.

4 But Jesus said unto them, A prophet is not without honour, but in his own country, and among his own kin, and in his own house.

5 And he could there do no mighty work, save that he laid his hands upon a few sick folk, and healed *them*.

6 And he marvelled because of their unbelief. And he went round about the villages, teaching.

5 *In commissioning the twelve*, 6:7–13

7 ¶ And he called *unto him* the twelve, and began to send them forth by two and two; and gave them power over unclean spirits;

8 And commanded them that they should take nothing for *their* journey, save a staff only; no scrip, no bread, no money in *their* purse:

9 But *be* shod with sandals; and not put on two coats.

10 And he said unto them, In what place soever ye enter into an house, there abide till ye depart from that place.

11 And whosoever shall not receive you, nor hear you, when ye depart thence, shake off the dust under your feet for a testimony against them. Verily I say unto you, It shall be more tolerable for Sodom and Gōmor'rha in the day of judgment, than for that city.

12 And they went out, and preached that men should repent.

13 And they cast out many devils, and anointed with oil many that were sick, and healed *them*.

6 *As affecting Herod, who killed John the Baptist*, 6:14–29

14 And king Herod heard *of him*; (for his name was spread abroad:) and he said, That John the Baptist was

the birth of Jesus (Matt. 1:25). James became the leader of the church in Jerusalem and author of the Epistle of James. Jude wrote the letter that bears his name. *They were offended.* I.e., they took offense—something stood in the way of their believing in Him.

6:8 *scrip*=wallet for small articles or provisions. *purse*=belt.

6:11 *shake off the dust*. An action symbolical of a complete break in fellowship and a renunciation of all further responsibility. See Acts 13:51; 18:6.

6:14 *king Herod*. Herod Antipas, tetrarch of Galilee and Perea 4 B.C.–A.D. 39. Officially he was not a king, but this title for him was popularly used.

risen from the dead, and therefore mighty works do shew forth themselves in him.

15 Others said, That it is Elī'as. And others said, That it is a prophet, or as one of the prophets.

16 But when Herod heard *thereof*, he said, It is John, whom I beheaded: he is risen from the dead.

17 For Herod himself had sent forth and laid hold upon John, and bound him in prison for Herō'dias' sake, his brother Philip's wife: for he had married her.

18 For John had said unto Herod, It is not lawful for thee to have thy brother's wife.

19 Therefore Herō'dias had a quarrel against him, and would have killed him; but she could not:

20 For Herod feared John, knowing that he was a just man and an holy, and observed him; and when he heard him, he did many things, and heard him gladly.

21 And when a convenient day was come, that Herod on his birthday made a supper to his lords, high captains, and chief *estates* of Galilee;

22 And when the daughter of the said Herō'dias came in, and danced, and pleased Herod and them that sat with him, the king said unto the damsel, Ask of me whatsoever thou wilt, and I will give *it* thee.

23 And he sware unto her, Whatsoever thou shalt ask of me, I will give *it* thee, unto the half of my kingdom.

24 And she went forth, and said unto her mother, What shall I ask? And she said, The head of John the Baptist.

25 And she came in straightway with haste unto the king, and asked, saying, I will that thou give me by and by in a charger the head of John the Baptist.

26 And the king was exceeding sorry; *yet* for his oath's sake, and for their sakes which sat with him, he would not reject her.

27 And immediately the king sent an executioner, and commanded his head to be brought: and he went and beheaded him in the prison,

28 And brought his head in a charger, and gave it to the damsel: and the damsel gave it to her mother.

6:15 *Elias*=Elijah.
6:17 *Philip*. Herod's brother but not the same Philip mentioned in Luke 3:1. Herodias, who was married to Herod Philip, left him to live with another uncle, Herod Antipas.
6:18 *not lawful*. See Mark 10:11; Lev. 18:16.
6:25 *by and by in a charger*. Lit., at once on a dish (or platter).
6:26 *for his oath's sake*. In the ancient Near East an oath was considered to be irrevocable.

29 And when his disciples heard *of it*, they came and took up his corpse, and laid it in a tomb.

7 *In feeding 5000 men,* 6:30–44

30 And the apostles gathered themselves together unto Jesus, and told him all things, both what they had done, and what they had taught.

31 And he said unto them, Come ye yourselves apart into a desert place, and rest a while: for there were many coming and going, and they had no leisure so much as to eat.

32 And they departed into a desert place by ship privately.

33 And the people saw them departing, and many knew him, and ran afoot thither out of all cities, and outwent them, and came together unto him.

34 And Jesus, when he came out, saw much people, and was moved with compassion toward them, because they were as sheep not having a shepherd: and he began to teach them many things.

35 And when the day was now far spent, his disciples came unto him, and said, This is a desert place, and now the time *is* far passed:

36 Send them away, that they may go into the country round about, and into the villages, and buy themselves bread: for they have nothing to eat.

37 He answered and said unto them, Give ye them to eat. And they say unto him, Shall we go and buy two hundred pennyworth of bread, and give them to eat?

38 He saith unto them, How many loaves have ye? go and see. And when they knew, they say, Five, and two fishes.

39 And he commanded them to make all sit down by companies upon the green grass.

40 And they sat down in ranks, by hundreds, and by fifties.

41 And when he had taken the five loaves and the two fishes, he looked up to heaven, and blessed, and brake the loaves, and gave *them* to his disciples to set before them; and the two fishes divided he among them all.

42 And they did all eat, and were filled.

43 And they took up twelve baskets full of the fragments, and of the fishes.

6:34 *a shepherd.* See Num. 27:17; 1 Kings 22:17; Ezek. 34.5.

6:37 *two hundred pennyworth.* For *penny,* read always denarius (plural: denarii), the basic Roman silver coin much used in Palestine, worth about 20 cents.

44 And they that did eat of the loaves were about five thousand men.

8 *In walking on water,* 6:45–52

45 And straightway he constrained his disciples to get into the ship, and to go to the other side before unto Bethsā'ida, while he sent away the people.

46 And when he had sent them away, he departed into a mountain to pray.

47 And when even was come, the ship was in the midst of the sea, and he alone on the land.

48 And he saw them toiling in rowing; for the wind was contrary unto them: and about the fourth watch of the night he cometh unto them, walking upon the sea, and would have passed by them.

49 But when they saw him walking upon the sea, they supposed it had been a spirit, and cried out:

50 For they all saw him, and were troubled. And immediately he talked with them, and saith unto them, Be of good cheer: it is I; be not afraid.

51 And he went up unto them into the ship; and the wind ceased: and they were sore amazed in themselves beyond measure, and wondered.

52 For they considered not *the miracle* of the loaves: for their heart was hardened.

9 *Over sickness,* 6:53–56

53 And when they had passed over, they came into the land of Gennes'aret, and drew to the shore.

54 And when they were come out of the ship, straightway they knew him,

55 And ran through that whole region round about, and began to carry about in beds those that were sick, where they heard he was.

56 And whithersoever he entered, into villages, or cities, or country, they laid the sick in the streets, and besought

6:44 *five thousand men.* The count did not include women and children.
6:45 *before.* I.e., before him. *Bethsaida.* About 2 miles N. of the Sea of Galilee.
6:48 *the fourth watch.* From 3 to 6 a.m.
6:49 *troubled*=terrified.
6:52 *considered not*=did not understand. *their heart was hardened.* I.e., they were "dull-witted," not understanding the truth concerning the deity of Christ which His miracles were continually demonstrating.
6:53 *land of Gennesaret,* on the NE. shore of the Sea of Galilee.

him that they might touch if it were but the border of his garment: and as many as touched him were made whole.

10 *Over the Pharisees' traditions,* 7:1–23

7 Then came together unto him the Pharisees, and certain of the scribes, which came from Jerusalem.

2 And when they saw some of his disciples eat bread with defiled, that is to say, with unwashen, hands, they found fault.

3 For the Pharisees, and all the Jews, except they wash *their* hands oft, eat not, holding the tradition of the elders,

4 And *when they come* from the market, except they wash, they eat not. And many other things there be, which they have received to hold, *as* the washing of cups, and pots, brasen vessels, and of tables.

5 Then the Pharisees and scribes asked him, Why walk not thy disciples according to the tradition of the elders, but eat bread with unwashen hands?

6 He answered and said unto them, Well hath Ēsa͞i'as prophesied of you hypocrites, as it is written, This people honoureth me with *their* lips, but their heart is far from me.

7 Howbeit in vain do they worship me, teaching *for* doctrines the commandments of men.

8 For laying aside the commandment of God, ye hold the tradition of men, *as* the washing of pots and cups: and many other such like things ye do.

9 And he said unto them, Full well ye reject the commandment of God, that ye may keep your own tradition.

10 For Moses said, Honour thy father and thy mother; and, Whoso curseth father or mother, let him die the death:

7:1 *scribes.* See note at Matt. 2:4.

7:3 *the tradition of the elders* was the unwritten body of commands and teachings of honored rabbis of the past; it was the authoritative source of scribal teachings.

7:5 *unwashen hands.* This does not mean dirty hands but hands not washed according to the rules of the elders, and therefore not free of defilement.

7:6 *Esaias prophesied.* Isa. 29:13.

7:8 Christ is here criticizing the reinterpretation and debasement of the law by the scribes and Pharisees who viewed oral tradition as more authoritative than the written law of the O.T. He then illustrates the point in vv. 9–13.

7:10 *Moses said.* See Ex. 20:12; Deut. 5:16. For *whoso curseth* see Ex. 21:17.

11 But ye say, If a man shall say to his father or mother, *It is* Corban, that is to say, a gift, by whatsoever thou mightest be profited by me; *he shall be free.*

12 And ye suffer him no more to do ought for his father or his mother;

13 Making the word of God of none effect through your tradition, which ye have delivered: and many such like things do ye.

14 ¶ And when he had called all the people *unto him,* he said unto them, Hearken unto me every one *of you,* and understand:

15 There is nothing from without a man, that entering into him can defile him: but the things which come out of him, those are they that defile the man.

16 If any man have ears to hear, let him hear.

17 And when he was entered into the house from the people, his disciples asked him concerning the parable.

18 And he saith unto them, Are ye so without understanding also? Do ye not perceive, that whatsoever thing from without entereth into the man, *it* cannot defile him;

19 Because it entereth not into his heart, but into the belly, and goeth out into the draught, purging all meats?

20 And he said, That which cometh out of the man, that defileth the man.

21 For from within, out of the heart of men, proceed evil thoughts, adulteries, fornications, murders,

22 Thefts, covetousness, wickedness, deceit, lasciviousness, an evil eye, blasphemy, pride, foolishness:

23 All these evil things come from within, and defile the man.

11 *Over a Syrophenician woman,* 7:24–30

24 ¶ And from thence he arose, and went into the borders of Tyre and Sidon, and entered into an house,

---

7:11 *Corban.* The transliteration of a Hebrew word meaning a "gift." The word was used to refer to something devoted to God by a vow which was inviolable. If a son declared that the amount needed to support his parents was Corban, the scribes said that he was exempt from his duty to care for his parents as prescribed in the law. Evidently, too, he was not really obliged to devote that sum to the temple.

7:18 *it cannot defile him.* Foods declared to be "unclean" are specified in Lev. 11. Jesus is here not abrogating the law but making the point that sin comes from the heart of the man who disobeys God. Thus the defilement that came to a Jew who ate "unclean" food was caused not by the food itself but by the rebellious heart that acted in disobedience to God.

and would have no man know *it*: but he could not be hid.

25 For a *certain* woman, whose young daughter had an unclean spirit, heard of him, and came and fell at his feet:

26 The woman was a Greek, a Sўrōphēnic′ian by nation; and she besought him that he would cast forth the devil out of her daughter.

27 But Jesus said unto her, Let the children first be filled: for it is not meet to take the children's bread, and to cast *it* unto the dogs.

28 And she answered and said unto him, Yes, Lord: yet the dogs under the table eat of the children's crumbs.

29 And he said unto her, For this saying go thy way; the devil is gone out of thy daughter.

30 And when she was come to her house, she found the devil gone out, and her daughter laid upon the bed.

12 *Over a deaf mute*, 7:31–37

31 ¶ And again, departing from the coasts of Tyre and Sidon, he came unto the sea of Galilee, through the midst of the coasts of Dĕ·căp′o·lĭs.

32 And they bring unto him one that was deaf, and had an impediment in his speech; and they beseech him to put his hand upon him.

33 And he took him aside from the multitude, and put his fingers into his ears, and he spit, and touched his tongue;

34 And looking up to heaven, he sighed, and saith unto him, Ĕph′pha·tha, that is, Be opened.

35 And straightway his ears were opened, and the string of his tongue was loosed, and he spake plain.

36 And he charged them that they should tell no man: but the more he charged them, so much the more a great deal they published *it*;

37 And were beyond measure astonished, saying, He hath done all things well: he maketh both the deaf to hear, and the dumb to speak.

13 *In feeding 4000*, 8:1–9

8 In those days the multitude being very great, and having nothing to eat, Jesus called his disciples *unto him*, and saith unto them,

7:26 *Syrophenician.* By birth this Gentile woman was a Syrian of the region of Phoenicia.

7:27 *the dogs.* See note at Matt. 15:26.

7:30 This miracle was performed at a distance without any vocal command from Christ.

7:35 *string*=the bond which kept him tongue-tied.

2 I have compassion on the multitude, because they have now been with me three days, and have nothing to eat:

3 And if I send them away fasting to their own houses, they will faint by the way: for divers of them came from far.

4 And his disciples answered him, From whence can a man satisfy these *men* with bread here in the wilderness?

5 And he asked them, How many loaves have ye? And they said, Seven.

6 And he commanded the people to sit down on the ground: and he took the seven loaves, and gave thanks, and brake, and gave to his disciples to set before *them*; and they did set *them* before the people.

7 And they had a few small fishes: and he blessed, and commanded to set *them* also before *them*.

8 So they did eat, and were filled: and they took up of the broken *meat* that was left seven baskets.

9 And they that had eaten were about four thousand: and he sent them away.

14 *In condemning the Pharisees,* 8:10–13

10 ¶ And straightway he entered into a ship with his disciples, and came into the parts of Dalmanū'tha.

11 And the Pharisees came forth, and began to question with him, seeking of him a sign from heaven, tempting him.

12 And he sighed deeply in his spirit, and saith, Why doth this generation seek after a sign? verily I say unto you, There shall no sign be given unto this generation.

13 And he left them, and entering into the ship again departed to the other side.

15 *In His teaching on leaven,* 8:14–21

14 ¶ Now *the disciples* had forgotten to take bread, neither had they in the ship with them more than one loaf.

8:3 *divers*=some.
8:8 *broken meat*=fragments. *seven baskets.* The word *basket* denotes larger baskets than the word used of the twelve baskets in which the leftovers were collected from the feeding of the 5,000 (6:43). The larger basket was the kind used to let Paul down over the wall of Damascus (Acts 9:25).
8:10 *Dalmanutha.* An unknown location.
8:11 *a sign from heaven.* The Pharisees wanted some startling miracle or celestial portent which would prove that Jesus was the Messiah. They did not believe He could provide such a sign.

15 And he charged them, saying, Take heed, beware of the leaven of the Pharisees, and of the leaven of Herod.

16 And they reasoned among themselves, saying, It is because we have no bread.

17 And when Jesus knew it, he saith unto them, Why reason ye, because ye have no bread? perceive ye not yet, neither understand? have ye your heart yet hardened?

18 Having eyes, see ye not? and having ears, hear ye not? and do ye not remember?

19 When I brake the five loaves among five thousand, how many baskets full of fragments took ye up? They say unto him, Twelve.

20 And when the seven among four thousand, how many baskets full of fragments took ye up? And they said, Seven.

21 And he said unto them, How is it that ye do not understand?

16 *Over blindness,* 8:22–26

22 ¶ And he cometh to Bethsā'ida; and they bring a blind man unto him, and besought him to touch him.

23 And he took the blind man by the hand, and led him out of the town; and when he had spit on his eyes, and put his hands upon him, he asked him if he saw ought.

24 And he looked up, and said, I see men as trees, walking.

25 After that he put *his* hands again upon his eyes, and made him look up: and he was restored, and saw every man clearly.

26 And he sent him away to his house, saying, Neither go into the town, nor tell *it* to any in the town.

17 *Over Peter,* 8:27–33

27 ¶ And Jesus went-out, and his disciples, into the towns of Cæsarea Phĭlip'pī: and by the way he asked his disciples, saying unto them, Whom do men say that I am?

28 And they answered, John the Baptist: but some *say,* Elī'as; and others, One of the prophets.

8:15 *the leaven of the Pharisees* was hypocrisy (Luke 12:1) and *the leaven of Herod* was secularism and worldliness.
8:17 *reason ye, because.* See note at Matt. 16:8.
8:25 This miracle was performed in stages.
8:27 *Caesarea Philippi.* A city about 25 miles N. of the Sea of Galilee built by Herod Philip in honor of Caesar Augustus. *by the way*=on the way.
8:27–30 See notes on Matt. 16:13, 14.

29 And he saith unto them, But whom say ye that I am? And Peter answereth and saith unto him, Thou art the Christ.

30 And he charged them that they should tell no man of him.

31 And he began to teach them, that the Son of man must suffer many things, and be rejected of the elders, and of the chief priests, and scribes, and be killed, and after three days rise again.

32 And he spake that saying openly. And Peter took him, and began to rebuke him.

33 But when he had turned about and looked on his disciples, he rebuked Peter, saying, Get thee behind me, Satan: for thou savourest not the things that be of God, but the things that be of men.

18 *Over the lives of His disciples,* 8:34–9:1

34 ¶ And when he had called the people *unto him* with his disciples also, he said unto them, Whosoever will come after me, let him deny himself, and take up his cross, and follow me.

35 For whosoever will save his life shall lose it; but whosoever shall lose his life for my sake and the gospel's, the same shall save it.

36 For what shall it profit a man, if he shall gain the whole world, and lose his own soul?

37 Or what shall a man give in exchange for his soul?

38 Whosoever therefore shall be ashamed of me and of my words in this adulterous and sinful generation; of him also shall the Son of man be ashamed, when he cometh in the glory of his Father with the holy angels.

9 And he said unto them, Verily I say unto you, That there be some of them that stand here, which shall

---

8:31 *the Son of man must suffer.* Christ is expanding for the disciples the concept of Son of man who in Daniel's vision (7:13–14) and in the apocryphal book of Enoch was not expected to suffer and die; the thought was unthinkable, and Peter says so (v. 32).

8:33 *Get thee behind me, Satan.* Peter was being used by Satan to try to dissuade Christ from going to the cross.

8:34 *take up his cross.* See notes on Matt. 10:38 and Luke 9:23.

8:35 The verse means: Whoever would save his life (by renouncing the gospel and thus avoiding the risk of martyrdom) will lose it (eternally because he has not believed the gospel): but whoever will lose his life (as a martyr) will save it (i.e., will prove that he is a follower of Christ and an heir of eternal life).

not taste of death, till they have seen the kingdom of God come with power.

G His Previews, 9:2–50

1 *Of His glory,* 9:2–29

2 ¶ And after six days Jesus taketh *with him* Peter, and James, and John, and leadeth them up into an high mountain apart by themselves: and he was transfigured before them.

3 And his raiment became shining, exceeding white as snow; so as no fuller on earth can white them.

4 And there appeared unto them Elī'as with Moses: and they were talking with Jesus.

5 And Peter answered and said to Jesus, Master, it is good for us to be here: and let us make three tabernacles; one for thee, and one for Moses, and one for Elī'as.

6 For he wist not what to say; for they were sore afraid.

7 And there was a cloud that overshadowed them: and a voice came out of the cloud, saying, This is my beloved Son: hear him.

8 And suddenly, when they had looked round about, they saw no man any more, save Jesus only with themselves.

9 And as they came down from the mountain, he charged them that they should tell no man what things they had seen, till the Son of man were risen from the dead.

10 And they kept that saying with themselves, questioning one with another what the rising from the dead should mean.

9:1 *till they have seen the kingdom of God come with power.* See note at Matt. 16:28.

9:2 *after six days.* Luke 9:28 says "about eight days" which includes the termini as well as the interval of six full days. *into an high mountain*: either Mt. Tabor, 10 miles SW. of the Sea of Galilee or Mt. Hermon, 40 miles NE. of the Sea of Galilee. *transfigured*=transformed.

9:3 *fuller.* One who cleans clothes.

9:4 *Elias.* Elijah's return was expected (Mal. 4:5–6). *talking with Jesus.* Luke tells what they were talking about (9:31).

9:5 *and let us make three tabernacles.* Lit., booths of intertwined branches. Peter thought they would be there a while so they might as well get settled down! His suggestion also implied that he viewed Jesus, Moses, and Elijah as all three being on an equality. God's answer was to remove Moses and Elijah from view (v. 8) and declare the uniqueness of His Son (v. 7).

9:10 *the rising from the dead.* I.e., Christ's resurrection from the dead, not resurrection in general.

11 ¶ And they asked him, saying, Why say the scribes that Ēlī′as must first come?

12 And he answered and told them, Ēlī′as verily cometh first, and restoreth all things; and how it is written of the Son of man, that he must suffer many things, and be set at nought.

13 But I say unto you, That Ēlī′as is indeed come, and they have done unto him whatsoever they listed, as it is written of him.

14 ¶ And when he came to *his* disciples, he saw a great multitude about them, and the scribes questioning with them.

15 And straightway all the people, when they beheld him, were greatly amazed, and running to *him* saluted him.

16 And he asked the scribes, What question ye with them?

17 And one of the multitude answered and said, Master, I have brought unto thee my son, which hath a dumb spirit;

18 And wheresoever he taketh him, he teareth him: and he foameth, and gnasheth with his teeth, and pineth away: and I spake to thy disciples that they should cast him out; and they could not.

19 He answereth him, and saith, O faithless generation, how long shall I be with you? how long shall I suffer you? bring him unto me.

20 And they brought him unto him: and when he saw him, straightway the spirit tare him; and he fell on the ground, and wallowed foaming.

21 And he asked his father, How long is it ago since this came unto him? And he said, Of a child.

22 And ofttimes it hath cast him into the fire, and into

9:11–13 The progression of thought is this: If Elijah is to come before the last day and "turn the hearts" (Mal. 4:5–6), why should the Son of Man have to die? Christ replies that they are correct about Elijah but that their concept of the Son of Man was deficient since it did not include the thought of His suffering and death (Ps. 22:6; Isa. 53). Then Christ adds (v. 13) that Elijah has come, unrecognized, in John the Baptist. See also the note on Matt. 17:11–12.

9:16 *question ye*=are you arguing about.

9:17 *a dumb spirit*. A demon caused the boy's dumbness and deafness (v. 25). Other effects were similar to epilepsy.

9:18 *pineth away*=becomes rigid; lit., dries up.

the waters, to destroy him: but if thou canst do any thing, have compassion on us, and help us.

23 Jesus said unto him, If thou canst believe, all things *are* possible to him that believeth.

24 And straightway the father of the child cried out, and said with tears, Lord, I believe; help thou mine unbelief.

25 When Jesus saw that the people came running together, he rebuked the foul spirit, saying unto him, *Thou* dumb and deaf spirit, I charge thee, come out of him, and enter no more into him.

26 And *the spirit* cried, and rent him sore, and came out of him: and he was as one dead; insomuch that many said, He is dead.

27 But Jesus took him by the hand, and lifted him up; and he arose.

28 And when he was come into the house, his disciples asked him privately, Why could not we cast him out?

29 And he said unto them, This kind can come forth by nothing, but by prayer and fasting.

2 *Of His death*, 9:30–32

30 ¶ And they departed thence, and passed through Galilee; and he would not that any man should know *it*.

31 For he taught his disciples, and said unto them, The Son of man is delivered into the hands of men, and they shall kill him; and after that he is killed, he shall rise the third day.

32 But they understood not that saying, and were afraid to ask him.

3 *Of rewards*, 9:33–41

33 ¶ And he came to Caper'naum: and being in the house he asked them, What was it that ye disputed among yourselves by the way?

34 But they held their peace: for by the way they had disputed among themselves, who *should be* the greatest.

35 And he sat down, and called the twelve, and saith

9:23 *all things are possible*. Seen note on Matt. 17:20.

9:24 *help thou my unbelief*. The man cries for help for his own weak faith.

9:29 *This kind*. I.e., this kind of demon can be conquered only by prayer *and fasting*. Some manuscripts omit these words.

9:31 *they shall kill him*. This is the second prediction of His death (8:31).

9:32 *and were afraid to ask him*. Perhaps because of the rebuke to Peter (8:32–33).

unto them, If any man desire to be first, *the same* shall be last of all, and servant of all.

36 And he took a child, and set him in the midst of them: and when he had taken him in his arms, he said unto them,

37 Whosoever shall receive one of such children in my name, receiveth me: and whosoever shall receive me, receiveth not me, but him that sent me.

38 ¶ And John answered him, saying, Master, we saw one casting out devils in thy name, and he followeth not us: and we forbad him, because he followeth not us.

39 But Jesus said, Forbid him not: for there is no man which shall do a miracle in my name, that can lightly speak evil of me.

40 For he that is not against us is on our part.

41 For whosoever shall give you a cup of water to drink in my name, because ye belong to Christ, verily I say unto you, he shall not lose his reward.

4 *Of hell,* 9:42–50

42 And whosoever shall offend one of *these* little ones that believe in me, it is better for him that a millstone were hanged about his neck, and he were cast into the sea.

43 And if thy hand offend thee, cut it off: it is better for thee to enter into life maimed, than having two hands to go into hell, into the fire that never shall be quenched:

44 Where their worm dieth not, and the fire is not quenched.

45 And if thy foot offend thee, cut it off: it is better for thee to enter halt into life, than having two feet to be cast into hell, into the fire that never shall be quenched:

46 Where their worm dieth not, and the fire is not quenched.

47 And if thine eye offend thee, pluck it out: it is better for thee to enter into the kingdom of God with one eye, than having two eyes to be cast into hell fire:

48 Where their worm dieth not, and the fire is not quenched.

49 For every one shall be salted with fire, and every sacrifice shall be salted with salt.

9:38 *devils.* Lit., demons.
9:42 *whosoever shall offend*=whoever causes . . . to fall into sin. So also with *offend*=causes you to sin in vv. 43, 45, 47.
9:49 *salted with fire.* Everyone who enters hell will be preserved, as salt preserves, through an eternity of torment. The last half of this verse is not in better manuscripts.

50 Salt *is* good: but if the salt have lost his saltness, wherewith will ye season it? Have salt in yourselves, and have peace one with another.

H His Preaching in Perea, 10:1-52

10 And he arose from thence, and cometh into the coasts of Judæa by the farther side of Jordan: and the people resort unto him again; and, as he was wont, he taught them again.

1 *Concerning divorce*, 10:2-12

2 ¶ And the Pharisees came to him, and asked him, Is it lawful for a man to put away *his* wife? tempting him.

3 And he answered and said unto them, What did Moses command you?

4 And they said, Moses suffered to write a bill of divorcement, and to put *her* away.

5 And Jesus answered and said unto them, For the hardness of your heart he wrote you this precept.

6 But from the beginning of the creation God made them male and female.

7 For this cause shall a man leave his father and mother, and cleave to his wife;

8 And they twain shall be one flesh: so then they are no more twain, but one flesh.

9 What therefore God hath joined together, let not man put asunder.

10 And in the house his disciples asked him again of the same *matter*.

11 And he saith unto them, Whosoever shall put away his wife, and marry another, committeth adultery against her.

12 And if a woman shall put away her husband, and be married to another, she committeth adultery.

2 *Concerning children*, 10:13-16

13 ¶ And they brought young children to him, that he

9:50 *Have salt in yourselves.* Christ's followers are to be permeated with this preserving power, which will influence the world for good.

10:1 *coasts*=region. For *by* read "and."

10:4 See Deut. 24:1-4. *suffered*=permitted.

10:6 *male and female.* See Gen. 2:21-25; it presupposes and enjoins monogamy. The Mosaic law concerning divorce was a concession to God's original purpose.

10:11-12 See notes at Matt. 5:32 and 19:4-5.

should touch them: and *his* disciples rebuked those that
brought *them*.

14 But when Jesus saw *it*, he was much displeased, and
said unto them, Suffer the little children to come unto me,
and forbid them not: for of such is the kingdom of God.

15 Verily I say unto you, Whosoever shall not receive
the kingdom of God as a little child, he shall not enter
therein.

16 And he took them up in his arms, put *his* hands upon
them, and blessed them.

3 *Concerning eternal life*, 10:17–31

17 ¶ And when he was gone forth into the way, there
came one running, and kneeled to him, and asked him,
Good Master, what shall I do that I may inherit eternal
life?

18 And Jesus said unto him, Why callest thou me good?
there is none good but one, *that is*, God.

19 Thou knowest the commandments, Do not commit
adultery, Do not kill, Do not steal, Do not bear false witness, Defraud not, Honour thy father and mother.

20 And he answered and said unto him, Master, all
these have I observed from my youth.

21 Then Jesus beholding him loved him, and said unto
him, One thing thou lackest: go thy way, sell whatsoever
thou hast, and give to the poor, and thou shalt have
treasure in heaven: and come, take up the cross, and follow
me.

22 And he was sad at that saying, and went away grieved:
for he had great possessions.

23 ¶ And Jesus looked round about, and saith unto his
disciples, How hardly shall they that have riches enter into
the kingdom of God!

24 And the disciples were astonished at his words. But
Jesus answereth again, and saith unto them, Children, how
hard is it for them that trust in riches to enter into the
kingdom of God!

25 It is easier for a camel to go through the eye of a

10:14 *Suffer*=allow. *for of such is the kingdom of God*. In order
to enter the kingdom we must come to Christ in childlike faith.

10:18 *Why callest thou me good?* "Good" was a designation reserved in the absolute sense for God; thus Jesus was reacting
to being addressed thus by someone who had no insight into
His divine nature.

10:21 Christ was trying to show the man that in reality his love
of money violated the law and made him a sinner.

10:25 *eye of a needle*. See note on Matt. 19:24.

needle, than for a rich man to enter into the kingdom of God.

26 And they were astonished out of measure, saying among themselves, Who then can be saved?

27 And Jesus looking upon them saith, With men *it is* impossible, but not with God: for with God all things are possible.

28 ¶ Then Peter began to say unto him, Lo, we have left all, and have followed thee.

29 And Jesus answered and said, Verily I say unto you, There is no man that hath left house, or brethren, or sisters, or father, or mother, or wife, or children, or lands, for my sake, and the gospel's,

30 But he shall receive an hundredfold now in this time, houses, and brethren, and sisters, and mothers, and children, and lands, with persecutions; and in the world to come eternal life.

31 But many *that are* first shall be last; and the last first.

4 Concerning His own death and resurrection, 10:32–34

32 ¶ And they were in the way going up to Jerusalem; and Jesus went before them: and they were amazed; and as they followed, they were afraid. And he took again the twelve, and began to tell them what things should happen unto him,

33 *Saying,* Behold, we go up to Jerusalem; and the Son of man shall be delivered unto the chief priests, and unto the scribes; and they shall condemn him to death, and shall deliver him to the Gentiles:

34 And they shall mock him, and shall scourge him, and shall spit upon him, and shall kill him: and the third day he shall rise again.

5 Concerning ambition, 10:35–45

35 ¶ And James and John, the sons of Zebedee, come unto him, saying, Master, we would that thou shouldest do for us whatsoever we shall desire.

10:26 *out of measure*=utterly.

10:27 *with God all things are possible.* This was also taught in the O.T. (Gen. 18:14; Job 42:2).

10:32 *going up.* Jerusalem is 2593 feet above sea level; their probable route was down the Jordan Valley, below sea level, then up to Jerusalem. *amazed.* At Jesus' determination to push on to Jerusalem.

10:33–34 This is the third Passion announcement (8:31; 9:31).

36 And he said unto them, What would ye that I should do for you?

37 They said unto him, Grant unto us that we may sit, one on thy right hand, and the other on thy left hand, in thy glory.

38 But Jesus said unto them, Ye know not what ye ask: can ye drink of the cup that I drink of? and be baptized with the baptism that I am baptized with?

39 And they said unto him, We can. And Jesus said unto them, Ye shall indeed drink of the cup that I drink of; and with the baptism that I am baptized withal shall ye be baptized:

40 But to sit on my right hand and on my left hand is not mine to give; but *it shall be given to them* for whom it is prepared.

41 And when the ten heard *it*, they began to be much displeased with James and John.

42 But Jesus called them *to him*, and saith unto them, Ye know that they which are accounted to rule over the Gentiles exercise lordship over them; and their great ones exercise authority upon them.

43 But so shall it not be among you: but whosoever will be great among you, shall be your minister:

44 And whosoever of you will be the chiefest, shall be servant of all.

45 For even the Son of man came not to be ministered unto, but to minister, and to give his life a ransom for many.

6 *To blind Bartimaeus,* 10:46–52

46 ¶ And they came to Jericho: and as he went out of Jericho with his disciples and a great number of people, blind Bartīmǣ'us, the son of Timǣ'us, sat by the highway side begging.

47 And when he heard that it was Jesus of Nazareth, he began to cry out, and say, Jesus, *thou* Son of David, have mercy on me.

48 And many charged him that he should hold his

10:37 *in thy glory.* I.e., in the Messianic kingdom (see Matt. 20:21).

10:38 *the cup . . . the baptism.* Figures of speech for Christ's coming sufferings (see Mark 14:36 and Luke 12:50).

10:39 James did die as a martyr (Acts 12:2) and John suffered exile (Rev. 1:9).

10:46–52 For a comparison of the different accounts of this miracle, see the note at Matt. 30:29–34.

peace: but he cried the more a great deal, *Thou* Son of David, have mercy on me.

49 And Jesus stood still, and commanded him to be called. And they call the blind man, saying unto him, Be of good comfort, rise; he calleth thee.

50 And he, casting away his garment, rose, and came to Jesus.

51 And Jesus answered and said unto him, What wilt thou that I should do unto thee? The blind man said unto him, Lord, that I might receive my sight.

52 And Jesus said unto him, Go thy way; thy faith hath made thee whole. And immediately he received his sight, and followed Jesus in the way.

II THE SACRIFICE OF THE SERVANT, 11:1–15:47

A Triumphal Entry into Jerusalem on Sunday, 11:1–11

11 And when they came nigh to Jerusalem, unto Beth'-phagē and Bethany, at the mount of Olives, he sendeth forth two of his disciples,

2 And saith unto them, Go your way into the village over against you: and as soon as ye be entered into it, ye shall find a colt tied, whereon never man sat; loose him, and bring *him*.

3 And if any man say unto you, Why do ye this? say ye that the Lord hath need of him; and straightway he will send him hither.

4 And they went their way, and found the colt tied by the door without in a place where two ways met; and they loose him.

5 And certain of them that stood there said unto them, What do ye, loosing the colt?

6 And they said unto them even as Jesus had commanded: and they let them go.

7 And they brought the colt to Jesus, and cast their garments on him; and he sat upon him.

8 And many spread their garments in the way: and others cut down branches off the trees, and strawed *them* in the way.

10:52 *thy faith hath made thee whole.* Cf. 5:34.
11:2 *the village over against you.* Bethphage, on the S. side of the Mount of Olives.
11:3 *and straightway he will send him hither.* Better, and will send him back here immediately.

9 And they that went before, and they that followed, cried, saying, Hosanna; Blessed *is* he that cometh in the name of the Lord:

10 Blessed *be* the kingdom of our father David, that cometh in the name of the Lord: Hosanna in the highest.

11 And Jesus entered into Jerusalem, and into the temple: and when he had looked round about upon all things, and now the eventide was come, he went out unto Bethany with the twelve.

B Cursing of the Fig Tree and Cleansing of the Temple on Monday, 11:12–19

12 ¶ And on the morrow, when they were come from Bethany, he was hungry:

13 And seeing a fig tree afar off having leaves, he came, if haply he might find any thing thereon: and when he came to it, he found nothing but leaves; for the time of figs was not *yet*.

14 And Jesus answered and said unto it, No man eat fruit of thee hereafter for ever. And his disciples heard *it*.

15 ¶ And they come to Jerusalem: and Jesus went into the temple, and began to cast out them that sold and bought in the temple, and overthrew the tables of the moneychangers, and the seats of them that sold doves;

16 And would not suffer that any man should carry *any* vessel through the temple.

17 And he taught, saying unto them, Is it not written, My house shall be called of all nations the house of prayer? but ye have made it a den of thieves.

18 And the scribes and chief priests heard *it*, and sought how they might destroy him: for they feared him, because all the people was astonished at his doctrine.

19 And when even was come, he went out of the city.

11:9 *Hosanna*=Save now! This was the fulfillment of Zech. 9:9. In a few days the same crowd who hailed Him on this occasion would desert Him.

11:10 *kingdom of our father David*. I.e., the Messianic kingdom.

11:13 *fig tree*. See note on Matt. 21:19.

11:15 *cast out them that sold and bought in the temple*. This is the second time Christ purged the temple (See John 2:13–17, which occurred at the beginning of His ministry). The animals, guaranteed to be without blemish, were sold for sacrificial purposes, and Greek and Roman coinage was changed into the standard-weight half-shekel required for the temple tax. The merchants were guilty of secular profanation of the temple and excess profiteering.

11:17 See Isa. 56:7 and Jer. 7:11.

C Teaching on Tuesday, 11:20–13:37

1 *Concerning faith,* 11:20–26

20 ¶ And in the morning, as they passed by, they saw the fig tree dried up from the roots.

21 And Peter calling to remembrance saith unto him, Master, behold, the fig tree which thou cursedst is withered away.

22 And Jesus answering saith unto them, Have faith in God.

23 For verily I say unto you, That whosoever shall say unto this mountain, Be thou removed, and be thou cast into the sea; and shall not doubt in his heart, but shall believe that those things which he saith shall come to pass; he shall have whatsoever he saith.

24 Therefore I say unto you, What things soever ye desire, when ye pray, believe that ye receive *them,* and ye shall have *them.*

25 And when ye stand praying, forgive, if ye have ought against any: that your Father also which is in heaven may forgive you your trespasses.

26 But if ye do not forgive, neither will your Father which is in heaven forgive your trespasses.

2 *Concerning His authority,* 11:27–33

27 ¶ And they come again to Jerusalem: and as he was walking in the temple, there come to him the chief priests, and the scribes, and the elders,

28 And say unto him, By what authority doest thou these things? and who gave thee this authority to do these things?

29 And Jesus answered and said unto them, I will also ask of you one question, and answer me, and I will tell you by what authority I do these things.

30 The baptism of John, was *it* from heaven, or of men? answer me.

31 And they reasoned with themselves, saying, If we shall say, From heaven; he will say, Why then did ye not believe him?

11:24 *What things soever.* This is qualified by Christ in His teaching (Matt. 6:10) and in His own life (Mark 14:36).
11:25 *stand praying.* In ancient worship this was the normal position of prayer.
11:28 *these things.* I.e., the cleansing of the temple (vv. 15–18).
11:30 *answer me.* Christ placed these Jewish leaders on the horns of a dilemma, for whichever answer they gave would have condemned them.

32 But if we shall say, Of men; they feared the people: for all *men* counted John, that he was a prophet indeed.

33 And they answered and said unto Jesus, We cannot tell. And Jesus answering saith unto them, Neither do I tell you by what authority I do these things.

3 Concerning the Jewish nation, 12:1–12

12 And he began to speak unto them by parables. A *certain* man planted a vineyard, and set an hedge about *it*, and digged *a place for* the winefat, and built a tower, and let it out to husbandmen, and went into a far country.

2 And at the season he sent to the husbandmen a servant, that he might receive from the husbandmen of the fruit of the vineyard.

3 And they caught *him*, and beat him, and sent *him* away empty.

4 And again he sent unto them another servant; and at him they cast stones, and wounded *him* in the head, and sent *him* away shamefully handled.

5 And again he sent another; and him they killed, and many others; beating some, and killing some.

6 Having yet therefore one son, his well-beloved, he sent him also last unto them, saying, They will reverence my son.

7 But those husbandmen said among themselves, This is the heir; come, let us kill him, and the inheritance shall be ours.

8 And they took him, and killed *him*, and cast *him* out of the vineyard.

9 What shall therefore the lord of the vineyard do? he will come and destroy the husbandmen, and will give the vineyard unto others.

10 And have ye not read this scripture; The stone which the builders rejected is become the head of the corner:

11 This was the Lord's doing, and it is marvellous in our eyes?

12:1–12 This parable, which was addressed to the obdurate religious leaders of Israel, illustrates God's dealings with that people. The man (v. 1) is God. The vineyard (v. 1) is Israel. The servants are the O.T. prophets and John the Baptist (vv. 2–5). The son is Jesus (vv. 6–8), whom they killed. The prediction of the destruction of the husbandman (v. 9) was fulfilled when Jerusalem was destroyed in A.D. 70.

12:10 *The stone*. See Ps. 118:22–23 and the use of the cornerstone figure in Acts 4:11; 1 Pet. 2:6–7.

12 And they sought to lay hold on him, but feared the people: for they knew that he had spoken the parable against them: and they left him, and went their way.

4 Concerning taxes, 12:13–17

13 ¶ And they send unto him certain of the Pharisees and of the Herō'dians, to catch him in *his* words.

14 And when they were come, they say unto him, Master, we know that thou art true, and carest for no man: for thou regardest not the person of men, but teachest the way of God in truth: Is it lawful to give tribute to Cæsar, or not?

15 Shall we give, or shall we not give? But he, knowing their hypocrisy, said unto them, Why tempt ye me? bring me a penny, that I may see *it*.

16 And they brought *it*. And he saith unto them, Whose *is* this image and superscription? And they said unto him, Cæsar's.

17 And Jesus answering said unto them, Render to Cæsar the things that are Cæsar's, and to God the things that are God's. And they marvelled at him.

5 Concerning resurrection, 12:18–27

18 ¶ Then come unto him the Sadducees, which say there is no resurrection; and they asked him, saying,

19 Master, Moses wrote unto us, If a man's brother die, and leave *his* wife *behind him*, and leave no children, that his brother should take his wife, and raise up seed unto his brother.

20 Now there were seven brethren: and the first took a wife, and dying left no seed.

21 And the second took her, and died, neither left he any seed: and the third likewise.

22 And the seven had her, and left no seed: last of all the woman died also.

23 In the resurrection therefore, when they shall rise, whose wife shall she be of them? for the seven had her to wife.

24 And Jesus answering said unto them, Do ye not

12:14 *carest for no man*. I.e., you're no sycophant, you "play up" to no one. Their opening remark employs flattery. *tribute to Cæsar*. See note at Matt. 22:17.

12:15 *a penny*. Lit., a denarius. See note at Mark 6:37.

12:18 *Sadducees*. See note at Matt. 3:7.

12:19 See Deut. 25:5.

therefore err, because ye know not the scriptures, neither the power of God?

25 For when they shall rise from the dead, they neither marry, nor are given in marriage; but are as the angels which are in heaven.

26 And as touching the dead, that they rise: have ye not read in the book of Moses, how in the bush God spake unto him, saying, I *am* the God of Abraham, and the God of Isaac, and the God of Jacob?

27 He is not the God of the dead, but the God of the living: ye therefore do greatly err.

6 Concerning the greatest commandments, 12:28-34

28 ¶ And one of the scribes came, and having heard them reasoning together, and perceiving that he had answered them well, asked him, Which is the first commandment of all?

29 And Jesus answered him, The first of all the commandments *is*, Hear, O Israel; The Lord our God is one Lord:

30 And thou shalt love the Lord thy God with all thy heart, and with all thy soul, and with all thy mind, and with all thy strength: this *is* the first commandment.

31 And the second *is* like, *namely* this, Thou shalt love thy neighbour as thyself. There is none other commandment greater than these.

32 And the scribe said unto him, Well, Master, thou hast said the truth: for there is one God; and there is none other but he:

33 And to love him with all the heart, and with all the understanding, and with all the soul, and with all the strength, and to love *his* neighbour as himself, is more than all whole burnt offerings and sacrifices.

34 And when Jesus saw that he answered discreetly, he said unto him, Thou art not far from the kingdom of God. And no man after that durst ask him *any question*.

12:25 *as the angels*. I.e., in the resurrection state there will be no need for conjugal union nor for the reproduction of children.

12:26 See Ex. 3:6. When God spoke to Moses, He was still associated with the patriarchs who had "died" many years before. Thus there is life after death.

12:29 See Deut. 6:4.

12:31 See Lev. 19:18.

12:32 *Well, Master, thou hast said the truth: for.* Better, You are right, Master; you have truly said that . . .

12:33 So taught the prophets (Isa. 1:11-17; Mic. 6:6-8).

12:34 *discreetly*. I.e., with intelligence, understandingly.

7 *Concerning His deity*, 12:35-37

35 ¶ And Jesus answered and said, while he taught in the temple, How say the scribes that Christ is the Son of David?

36 For David himself said by the Holy Ghost, The LORD said to my Lord, Sit thou on my right hand, till I make thine enemies thy footstool.

37 David therefore himself calleth him Lord; and whence is he *then* his son? And the common people heard him gladly.

8 *Concerning pride*, 12:38-40

38 ¶ And he said unto them in his doctrine, Beware of the scribes, which love to go in long clothing, and *love* salutations in the marketplaces,

39 And the chief seats in the synagogues, and the uppermost rooms at feasts:

40 Which devour widows' houses, and for a pretence make long prayers: these shall receive greater damnation.

9 *Concerning giving*, 12:41-44

41 ¶ And Jesus sat over against the treasury, and beheld how the people cast money into the treasury: and many that were rich cast in much.

42 And there came a certain poor widow, and she threw in two mites, which make a farthing.

43 And he called *unto him* his disciples, and saith unto them, Verily I say unto you, That this poor widow hath cast more in, than all they which have cast into the treasury:

44 For all *they* did cast in of their abundance; but she of her want did cast in all that she had, *even* all her living.

10 *Concerning the future*, 13:1-37

13 And as he went out of the temple, one of his disciples saith unto him, Master, see what manner of stones and what buildings *are here!*

12:35 See note at Matt. 22:24.
12:38 *doctrine*=teaching. *long clothing*. The long flowing robe of a dignitary or wealthy man.
12:39 *chief seats*=seats in the front row. *uppermost rooms*=seats or couches of honor at banquets.
12:40 *devour widows' houses*. See note at Matt. 23:14.
12:41 *treasury*. A chest located in the temple area, designed to receive coins dropped in a spout.
12:42 *two mites*. A mite was the smallest of copper coins, worth one-eighth of a cent.
13:1 See note at Matt. 24:1.

2 And Jesus answering said unto him, Seest thou these great buildings? there shall not be left one stone upon another, that shall not be thrown down.

3 And as he sat upon the mount of Olives over against the temple, Peter and James and John and Andrew asked him privately,

4 Tell us, when shall these things be? and what *shall be* the sign when all these things shall be fulfilled?

5 And Jesus answering them began to say, Take heed lest any *man* deceive you:

6 For many shall come in my name, saying, I am *Christ*; and shall deceive many.

7 And when ye shall hear of wars and rumours of wars, be ye not troubled: for *such things* must needs be; but the end *shall* not *be* yet.

8 For nation shall rise against nation, and kingdom against kingdom: and there shall be earthquakes in divers places, and there shall be famines and troubles: these *are* the beginnings of sorrows.

9 ¶ But take heed to yourselves: for they shall deliver you up to councils; and in the synagogues ye shall be beaten: and ye shall be brought before rulers and kings for my sake, for a testimony against them.

10 And the gospel must first be published among all nations.

11 But when they shall lead *you*, and deliver you up, take no thought beforehand what ye shall speak, neither do ye premeditate: but whatsoever shall be given you in that hour, that speak ye: for it is not ye that speak, but the Holy Ghost.

12 Now the brother shall betray the brother to death, and the father the son; and children shall rise up against *their* parents, and shall cause them to be put to death.

13 And ye shall be hated of all *men* for my name's sake: but he that shall endure unto the end, the same shall be saved.

13:4 *when shall these things be?* There is a double perspective in Christ's answer: some of the events described were to be fulfilled in the destruction of Jerusalem in A.D. 70 and some are yet to be fulfilled during the tribulation days that precede His second coming.

13:7 *needs be*=take place.

13:9 *synagogues*. They were used as places of assembly and as courtrooms. Floggings were therefore administered in them (2 Cor. 11:24). These predictions began to be fulfilled in the book of Acts (see Acts 4:5ff.; 5:27ff.; 12:1ff.; 24:1ff.; 25:1ff.).

13:11 *deliver you up*. I.e., denounce you to the authorities.

13:13 *endure*. I.e., remain loyal.

14 ¶ But when ye shall see the abomination of desolation, spoken of by Daniel the prophet, standing where it ought not, (let him that readeth understand,) then let them that be in Judæa flee to the mountains:

15 And let him that is on the housetop not go down into the house, neither enter *therein*, to take any thing out of his house:

16 And let him that is in the field not turn back again for to take up his garment.

17 But woe to them that are with child, and to them that give suck in those days!

18 And pray ye that your flight be not in the winter.

19 For *in* those days shall be affliction, such as was not from the beginning of the creation which God created unto this time, neither shall be.

20 And except that the Lord had shortened those days, no flesh should be saved: but for the elect's sake, whom he hath chosen, he hath shortened the days.

21 And then if any man shall say to you, Lo, here *is* Christ; or, lo, *he is* there; believe *him* not:

22 For false Christs and false prophets shall rise, and shall shew signs and wonders, to seduce, if *it were* possible, even the elect.

23 But take ye heed: behold, I have foretold you all things.

24 ¶ But in those days, after that tribulation, the sun shall be darkened, and the moon shall not give her light,

25 And the stars of heaven shall fall, and the powers that are in heaven shall be shaken.

26 And then shall they see the Son of man coming in the clouds with great power and glory.

27 And then shall he send his angels, and shall gather together his elect from the four winds, from the uttermost part of the earth to the uttermost part of heaven.

28 Now learn a parable of the fig tree; When her branch is yet tender, and putteth forth leaves, ye know that summer is near:

29 So ye in like manner, when ye shall see these things

13:14 *abomination of desolation*. See note at Matt. 24:15.

13:20 *the elect's sake*. This refers to the elect (saved) remnant of Israel during the tribulation days. At the second coming these people will be gathered to Palestine (v. 27).

13:23 This is the third warning to be prepared; the others are in v. 5 and v. 9.

13:28 *a parable*. I.e., the lesson of the fig tree teaches. *is yet*= becomes.

13:29 *it*=He, the Son of man.

come to pass, know that it is nigh, *even* at the doors.

30 Verily I say unto you, that this generation shall not pass, till all these things be done.

31 Heaven and earth shall pass away: but my words shall not pass away.

32 ¶ But of that day and *that* hour knoweth no man, no, not the angels which are in heaven, neither the Son, but the Father.

33 Take ye heed, watch and pray: for ye know not when the time is.

34 *For the Son of man is* as a man taking a far journey, who left his house, and gave authority to his servants, and to every man his work, and commanded the porter to watch.

35 Watch ye therefore: for ye know not when the master of the house cometh, at even, or at midnight, or at the cockcrowing, or in the morning:

36 Lest coming suddenly he find you sleeping.

37 And what I say unto you I say unto all, Watch.

D Anointing by Mary and
Agreement to Betray by Judas on Wednesday, 14:1–11

14 After two days was *the feast of* the passover, and of unleavened bread: and the chief priests and the scribes sought how they might take him by craft, and put *him* to death.

2 But they said, Not on the feast *day*, lest there be an uproar of the people.

3 ¶ And being in Bethany in the house of Simon the leper, as he sat at meat, there came a woman having an alabaster box of ointment of spikenard very precious; and she brake the box, and poured *it* on his head.

13:30 *this generation*. See note at Matt. 24:34.

13:32 *neither the Son*. In His humanity, Jesus did not know. See note at Phil. 2:7 on the self-limitation of Christ.

13:33 A fourth and final warning of this chapter.

14:1 *the feast of the passover*. One of Israel's three great yearly festivals (the other two were Pentecost and Tabernacles) commemorating their deliverance from Egypt on the night when God "passed over" the homes of the Israelites in the slaughter of the firstborn. It was celebrated on the 14th of Nisan (March–April) and was followed immediately by the Feast of Unleavened Bread, which continued from the 15th to the 21st. See Ex. 12.

14:3 *a woman*. This was Mary of Bethany (John 12:3). *spikenard*. A costly aromatic anointing oil extracted from an East Indian plant.

4 And there were some that had indignation within themselves, and said, Why was this waste of the ointment made?

5 For it might have been sold for more than three hundred pence, and have been given to the poor. And they murmured against her.

6 And Jesus said, Let her alone; why trouble ye her? she hath wrought a good work on me.

7 For ye have the poor with you always, and whensoever ye will ye may do them good: but me ye have not always.

8 She hath done what she could: she is come aforehand to anoint my body to the burying.

9 Verily I say unto you, Wheresoever this gospel shall be preached throughout the whole world, *this* also that she hath done shall be spoken of for a memorial of her.

10 ¶ And Judas Iscariot, one of the twelve, went unto the chief priests, to betray him unto them.

11 And when they heard *it*, they were glad, and promised to give him money. And he sought how he might conveniently betray him.

12 ¶ And the first day of unleavened bread, when they killed the passover, his disciples said unto him, Where wilt thou that we go and prepare that thou mayest eat the passover?

E Supper and Betrayal on Thursday, 14:12–52

1 *Preparation for the Last Supper*, 14:12–16

13 And he sendeth forth two of his disciples, and saith unto them, Go ye into the city, and there shall meet you a man bearing a pitcher of water: follow him.

14:4 *Why was this waste.* It was Judas who instigated the murmuring (John 12:4–6).

14:5 *three hundred pence* = 300 denarii. The value was roughly $60, though in purchasing power it was equivalent to 300 days' wages.

14:7 *the poor.* See note at Matt. 26:11.

14:10–11 Judas' motive in betraying Jesus was, in part, avarice (Matt. 26:15), though it may also have been related to his bitterness at the failure of Jesus to be a Messiah in the political sense. Ultimately, however, Judas' act was inspired by Satan (John 12:6; 13:2, 27).

14:11 *conveniently.* I.e., in the absence of the multitude (Luke 22:6).

14:12 *killed the passover.* I.e., the passover lamb.

14:13 *a man bearing a pitcher of water.* Since women usually performed this task, they would easily notice a man carrying water.

14 And wheresoever he shall go in, say ye to the good-man of the house, The Master saith, Where is the guest-chamber, where I shall eat the passover with my disciples?

15 And he will shew you a large upper room furnished *and* prepared: there make ready for us.

16 And his disciples went forth, and came into the city, and found as he had said unto them: and they made ready the passover.

2 *Partaking of the Last Supper,* 14:17–21

17 And in the evening he cometh with the twelve.

18 And as they sat and did eat, Jesus said, Verily I say unto you, One of you which eateth with me shall betray me.

19 And they began to be sorrowful, and to say unto him one by one, *Is* it I? and another *said, Is* it I?

20 And he answered and said unto them, *It is* one of the twelve, that dippeth with me in the dish.

21 The Son of man indeed goeth, as it is written of him: but woe to that man by whom the Son of man is betrayed! good were it for that man if he had never been born.

3 *Institution of the Lord's Supper,* 14:22–25

22 ¶ And as they did eat, Jesus took bread, and blessed, and brake *it,* and gave to them, and said, Take, eat: this is my body.

23 And he took the cup, and when he had given thanks, he gave *it* to them: and they all drank of it.

24 And he said unto them, This is my blood of the new testament, which is shed for many.

25 Verily I say unto you, I will drink no more of the fruit of the vine, until that day that I drink it new in the kingdom of God.

4 *Walk to Gethsemane,* 14:26–31

26 ¶ And when they had sung an hymn, they went out into the mount of Olives.

14:21 See Ps. 22 and Isa. 53.
14:24 *new testament*=new covenant. See Introduction to the New Testament. *shed*=poured out.
14:25 *until that day.* See note at Matt. 26:29.
14:26 *an hymn.* This would have been a portion of Ps. 115–118, traditional at this season.

27 And Jesus saith unto them, All ye shall be offended because of me this night: for it is written, I will smite the shepherd, and the sheep shall be scattered.

28 But after that I am risen, I will go before you into Galilee.

29 But Peter said unto him, Although all shall be offended, yet *will* not I.

30 And Jesus saith unto him, Verily I say unto thee, That this day, *even* in this night, before the cock crow twice, thou shalt deny me thrice.

31 But he spake the more vehemently, If I should die with thee, I will not deny thee in any wise. Likewise also said they all.

5 *Prayer in Gethsemane*, 14:32–42

32 And they came to a place which was named Gethsemane: and he saith to his disciples, Sit ye here, while I shall pray.

33 And he taketh with him Peter and James and John, and began to be sore amazed, and to be very heavy;

34 And saith unto them, My soul is exceeding sorrowful unto death: tarry ye here, and watch.

35 And he went forward a little, and fell on the ground, and prayed that, if it were possible, the hour might pass from him.

36 And he said, Abba, Father, all things *are* possible unto thee; take away this cup from me: nevertheless not what I will, but what thou wilt.

37 And he cometh, and findeth them sleeping, and saith unto Peter, Simon, sleepest thou? couldest not thou watch one hour?

38 Watch ye and pray, lest ye enter into temptation. The spirit truly *is* ready, but the flesh *is* weak.

39 And again he went away, and prayed, and spake the same words.

40 And when he returned, he found them asleep again, (for their eyes were heavy,) neither wist they what to answer him.

41 And he cometh the third time, and saith unto them,

14:27 *be offended.* Lit., be caused to stumble; i.e., you will fall away.
14:31 *should*=must.
14:32 *Gethsemane.* See note at Matt. 26:36.
14:35 *if it were possible.* I.e., if in accordance with God's will.
14:36 *this cup.* See note at Matt. 26:39.
14:41 *Sleep on now, and take your rest.* Some understand this as

Sleep on now, and take *your* rest: it is enough, the hour is come; behold, the Son of man is betrayed into the hands of sinners.

42 Rise up, let us go; lo, he that betrayeth me is at hand.

6 *Betrayal and arrest in Gethsemane*, 14:43–52

43 ¶ And immediately, while he yet spake, cometh Judas, one of the twelve, and with him a great multitude with swords and staves, from the chief priests and the scribes and the elders.

44 And he that betrayed him had given them a token, saying, Whomsoever I shall kiss, that same is he; take him, and lead *him* away safely.

45 And as soon as he was come, he goeth straightway to him, and saith, Master, master; and kissed him.

46 ¶ And they laid their hands on him, and took him.

47 And one of them that stood by drew a sword, and smote a servant of the high priest, and cut off his ear.

48 And Jesus answered and said unto them, Are ye come out, as against a thief, with swords and *with* staves to take me?

49 I was daily with you in the temple teaching, and ye took me not: but the scriptures must be fulfilled.

50 And they all forsook him, and fled.

51 And there followed him a certain young man, having a linen cloth cast about *his* naked *body*; and the young men laid hold on him:

52 And he left the linen cloth, and fled from them naked.

F Trials and Crucifixion on Friday, 14:53–15:47

1 *Christ before Caiaphas*, 14:53–65

53 ¶ And they led Jesus away to the high priest: and with him were assembled all the chief priests and the elders and the scribes.

54 And Peter followed him afar off, even into the palace

a statement of reproach; others translate it as a question: are you still sleeping . . . ?
14:44 *a token*. Lit., a signal.
14:47 *one of them*. This was Peter (John 18:10).
14:53 *to the high priest*. This is the examination before Caiaphas and the Sanhedrin. See note at Matt. 26:57 on the order of Jesus' trials.
14:54 *palace*. Better, courtyard.

of the high priest: and he sat with the servants, and warmed himself at the fire.

55 And the chief priests and all the council sought for witness against Jesus to put him to death; and found none.

56 For many bare false witness against him, but their witness agreed not together.

57 And there arose certain, and bare false witness against him, saying, •

58 We heard him say, I will destroy this temple that is made with hands, and within three days I will build another made without hands.

59 But neither so did their witness agree together.

60 And the high priest stood up in the midst, and asked Jesus, saying, Answerest thou nothing? what *is it which* these witness against thee?

61 But he held his peace, and answered nothing. Again the high priest asked him, and said unto him, Art thou the Christ, the Son of the Blessed?

62 And Jesus said, I am: and ye shall see the Son of man sitting on the right hand of power, and coming in the clouds of heaven.

63 Then the high priest rent his clothes, and saith, What need we any further witnesses?

64 Ye have heard the blasphemy: what think ye? And they all condemned him to be guilty of death.

65 And some began to spit on him, and to cover his face, and to buffet him, and to say unto him, Prophesy: and the servants did strike him with the palms of their hands.

14:56 In Jewish law it required two agreeing witnesses to establish a charge (Deut. 19:15).

14:58 This seems to be a mixed-up version of 13:2.

14:60 The high priest invites Christ to incriminate Himself.

14:61 *held his peace.* Defense seemed irrelevant to Christ.

14:62 *I am.* Christ affirms that He is the Messiah and assures His judges that He is also the coming judge of all mankind. *right hand of power* is the right hand of God.

14:63 *rent his clothes.* The proper gesture for the high priest acting as judge to make upon hearing blasphemy.

14:64 *the blasphemy.* The members of the council understood clearly that in Christ's answer (v. 62) He claimed to be equal with God. Since they viewed Him as a mere man, this was blasphemy in their minds, and the penalty was death (Lev. 24:16).

14:65 *spit on Him.* See Isa. 50:6. *Prophecy.* This was said in mockery. Perhaps: Tell us who is hitting you (as each blow is given).

2 Peter's denial of Jesus, 14:66-72

66 ¶ And as Peter was beneath in the palace, there cometh one of the maids of the high priest:

67 And when she saw Peter warming himself, she looked upon him, and said, And thou also wast with Jesus of Nazareth.

68 But he denied, saying, I know not, neither understand I what thou sayest. And he went out into the porch; and the cock crew.

69 And a maid saw him again, and began to say to them that stood by, This is *one* of them.

70 And he denied it again. And a little after, they that stood by said again to Peter, Surely thou art *one* of them: for thou art a Galilæan, and thy speech agreeth *thereto*.

71 But he began to curse and to swear, *saying*, I know not this man of whom ye speak.

72 And the second time the cock crew. And Peter called to mind the word that Jesus said unto him, Before the cock crow twice, thou shalt deny me thrice. And when he thought thereon, he wept.

3 Christ before Pilate, 15:1-15

15 And straightway in the morning the chief priests held a consultation with the elders and scribes and the whole council, and bound Jesus, and carried *him* away, and delivered *him* to Pilate.

2 And Pilate asked him, Art thou the King of the Jews? And he answering said unto him, Thou sayest *it*.

14:68 *porch.* Better, gateway or forecourt.

14:70 *thy speech agreeth.* Galileans spoke a dialect form of Aramaic, with pronunciation differences.

15:1 *in the morning.* See note at Luke 22:66. *Pilate.* Pilate was the Roman prefect or governor of Judea (usually referred to as procurator), to which position he was appointed by Tiberius in A.D. 26. He was in charge of the army of occupation, kept the taxes flowing to Rome, had the power of life and death over his subjects, appointed the high priests, and decided cases involving capital punishment. He was a capricious, weak governor who let personal and political considerations outweigh his vague feeling that justice was not being done in Jesus' case. He did not want another report to get to Rome that he had offended Jewish customs or could not control a situation— charges made to Tiberius earlier.

15:2 *King of the Jews.* The Jews knew that Pilate would be concerned only with a charge of a political nature which this was. *Thou sayest it.* This was an affirmative answer, which accord-

3 And the chief priests accused him of many things:
but he answered nothing.

4 And Pilate asked him again, saying, Answerest thou
nothing? behold how many things they witness against
thee.

5 But Jesus yet answered nothing; so that Pilate marvelled.

6 Now at *that* feast he released unto them one prisoner,
whomsoever they desired.

7 And there was *one* named Barabbas, *which lay* bound
with them that had made insurrection with him, who had
committed murder in the insurrection.

8 And the multitude crying aloud began to desire *him
to do* as he had ever done unto them.

9 But Pilate answered them, saying, Will ye that I release unto you the King of the Jews?

10 For he knew that the chief priests had delivered him
for envy.

11 But the chief priests moved the people, that he should
rather release Barabbas unto them.

12 And Pilate answered and said again unto them, What
will ye then that I shall do *unto him* whom ye call the King
of the Jews?

13 And they cried out again, Crucify him.

14 Then Pilate said unto them, Why, what evil hath he
done? And they cried out the more exceedingly, Crucify
him.

15 ¶ And *so* Pilate, willing to content the people, released Barabbas unto them, and delivered Jesus, when he
had scourged *him*, to be crucified.

4 *Abuse by the soldiers,* 15:16–20

16 And the soldiers led him away into the hall, called
Prætor′ium; and they call together the whole band.

17 And they clothed him with purple, and platted a
crown of thorns, and put it about his *head*,

18 And began to salute him, Hail, King of the Jews!

19 And they smote him on the head with a reed, and
did spit upon him, and bowing *their* knees worshipped him.

ing to John 18:34–38 was accompanied by an explanation as
to what kind of king Jesus claimed to be.

15:6 *at that feast.* I.e., at Passover.

15:15 *scourged.* See note at Matt. 27:26. *crucified.* See note at
Matt. 27:31.

15:16 *Praetorium.* The residence of the governor, perhaps in the
fortress of Antonia, where the Roman troops were quartered.
whole band=company or battalion.

20 And when they had mocked him, they took off the purple from him, and put his own clothes on him, and led him out to crucify him.

5 Crucifixion of Jesus, 15:21–32

21 And they compel one Simon a Cȳrē′nian, who passed by, coming out of the country, the father of Alexander and Rufus, to bear his cross.

22 And they bring him unto the place Golgotha, which is, being interpreted, The place of a skull.

23 And they gave him to drink wine mingled with myrrh: but he received *it* not.

24 And when they had crucified him, they parted his garments, casting lots upon them, what every man should take.

25 And it was the third hour, and they crucified him.

26 And the superscription of his accusation was written over, THE KING OF THE JEWS.

27 And with him they crucify two thieves; the one on his right hand, and the other on his left.

28 And the scripture was fulfilled, which saith, And he was numbered with the transgressors.

29 And they that passed by railed on him, wagging their heads, and saying, Ah, thou that destroyest the temple, and buildest *it* in three days,

30 Save thyself, and come down from the cross.

31 Likewise also the chief priests mocking said among themselves with the scribes, He saved others; himself he cannot save.

32 Let Christ the King of Israel descend now from the cross, that we may see and believe. And they that were crucified with him reviled him.

6 Death of Jesus, 15:33–41

33 And when the sixth hour was come, there was darkness over the whole land until the ninth hour.

15:21 *Simon a Cyrenian.* Cyrene was a port in N. Africa where there was a Jewish community. *coming out of the country.* I.e., coming from the country into the city, probably as another pilgrim to Jerusalem at Passover.
15:22 *Golgotha.* See note at Matt. 27:33.
15:23 *wine mingled with myrrh.* I.e., as a sedative.
15:24 *they parted his garments.* The garments were customarily given to the executioners. See Ps. 22:18.
15:25 *it was the third hour* = 9 a.m.
15:28 The quotation is from Isa. 53:12.
15:32 *Let Christ.* I.e., Let the false (to them) Christ.

34 And at the ninth hour Jesus cried with a loud voice, saying, Ē′lōī, Eloi, la′ma sabach′thani? which is, being interpreted, My God, my God, why hast thou forsaken me?

35 And some of them that stood by, when they heard it, said, Behold, he calleth Ēlī′as.

36 And one ran and filled a spunge full of vinegar, and put it on a reed, and gave him to drink, saying, Let alone; let us see whether Ēlī′as will come to take him down.

37 And Jesus cried with a loud voice, and gave up the ghost.

38 And the veil of the temple was rent in twain from the top to the bottom.

39 ¶ And when the centurion, which stood over against him, saw that he so cried out, and gave up the ghost, he said, Truly this man was the Son of God.

40 There were also women looking on afar off: among whom was Mary Magdalene, and Mary the mother of James the less and of Joses, and Salome;

41 (Who also, when he was in Galilee, followed him, and ministered unto him;) and many other women which came up with him unto Jerusalem.

7 Burial of Jesus, 15:42–47

42 ¶ And now when the even was come, because it was the preparation, that is, the day before the sabbath,

43 Joseph of Arimathæ′a, an honourable counsellor, which also waited for the kingdom of God, came, and went in boldly unto Pilate, and craved the body of Jesus.

44 And Pilate marvelled if he were already dead: and calling unto him the centurion, he asked him whether he had been any while dead.

15:34 why hast thou forsaken me? See note at Matt. 27:46.
15:35 Elias. See note at Matt. 27:47.
15:36 Let alone=wait now! See Ps. 69:21.
15:37 cried with a loud voice. Better, uttered a great shout. gave up the ghost=expired.
15:38 the veil. See note at Matt. 27:51.
15:40 A list of trustworthy witnesses (the apostles having fled) is given. They appear again in 16:1.
15:43 Joseph. See Matt. 27:57; Luke 23:50; and John 19:38. craved=asked for.
15:44 marvelled if he were already dead. Pilate wondered, since several days' of agony on a cross before death came was common. Christ's death after 6 hours was very quick. centurion. I.e., he had been in charge of the crucifixion. had been any while dead=was already dead.

45 And when he knew *it* of the centurion, he gave the body to Joseph.

46 And he bought fine linen, and took him down, and wrapped him in the linen, and laid him in a sepulchre which was hewn out of a rock, and rolled a stone unto the door of the sepulchre.

47 And Mary Magdalene and Mary *the mother* of Joses beheld where he was laid.

III THE SUCCESS OF THE SERVANT, 16:1–20

A His Resurrection, 16:1–8

16 And when the sabbath was past, Mary Magdalene, and Mary the *mother* of James, and Salome, had bought sweet spices, that they might come and anoint him.

2 And very early in the morning the first *day* of the week, they came unto the sepulchre at the rising of the sun.

3 And they said among themselves, Who shall roll us away the stone from the door of the sepulchre?

4 And when they looked, they saw that the stone was rolled away: for it was very great.

5 And entering into the sepulchre, they saw a young man sitting on the right side, clothed in a long white garment; and they were affrighted.

6 And he saith unto them, Be not affrighted: Ye seek Jesus of Nazareth, which was crucified: he is risen; he is not here: behold the place where they laid him.

7 But go your way, tell his disciples and Peter that he goeth before you into Galilee: there shall ye see him, as he said unto you.

8 And they went out quickly, and fled from the sepulchre; for they trembled and were amazed: neither said they any thing to any *man;* for they were afraid.

15:46 *wrapped him in the linen.* The linen was wrapped around the body in strips (John 19:40). *sepulchre.* See Isa. 53:9.

16:1 *when the sabbath was past.* Work could now be done to prepare the body for permanent burial.

16:3 *the stone.* See note at Luke 24:2.

16:5 *a young man.* Evidently the angel who rolled away the stone (Matt. 28:2). *affrighted.* Lit., utterly amazed or astonished.

16:6 *he is risen.* This simple statement of fact is the foundation of the Christian faith.

B His Appearances, 16:9–18

9 ¶ Now when *Jesus* was risen early the first *day* of the week, he appeared first to Mary Magdalene, out of whom he had cast seven devils.

10 *And* she went and told them that had been with him, as they mourned and wept.

11 And they, when they had heard that he was alive, and had been seen of her, believed not.

12 ¶ After that he appeared in another form unto two of them, as they walked, and went into the country.

13 And they went and told *it* unto the residue: neither believed they them.

14 ¶ Afterward he appeared unto the eleven as they sat at meat, and upbraided them with their unbelief and hardness of heart, because they believed not them which had seen him after he was risen.

15 And he said unto them, Go ye into all the world, and preach the gospel to every creature.

16 He that believeth and is baptized shall be saved; but he that believeth not shall be damned.

17 And these signs shall follow them that believe; In my name shall they cast out devils; they shall speak with new tongues;

18 They shall take up serpents; and if they drink any deadly thing, it shall not hurt them; they shall lay hands on the sick, and they shall recover.

C His Ascension, 16:19–20

19 ¶ So then after the Lord had spoken unto them, he was received up into heaven, and sat on the right hand of God.

20 And they went forth, and preached every where, the Lord working with *them*, and confirming the word with signs following. Amen.

16:9–20 These verses do not appear in the two most truthworthy manuscripts of the N.T., though they are part of many other manuscripts and versions. If they are not a part of the genuine text of Mark, the abrupt ending at verse 8 is probably because the original closing verses were lost. Because of the doubtful genuineness of verses 9–20 it would be unwise to build any doctrine or base any experience on them (especially vv. 16–18).

16:16 *baptized.* This may be a reference to the baptism of the Holy Spirit (1 Cor. 12:13). Water baptism does not save (see notes at Acts 2:38; 1 Pet. 3:21).

INTRODUCTION TO
THE GOSPEL ACCORDING TO
Luke

AUTHOR: Luke   DATE: 60

The Author Luke, the "beloved physician" (Col. 4:14), close friend and companion of Paul, was probably the only Gentile author of any part of the New Testament. We know nothing about his early life or conversion except that he was not an eyewitness of the life of Jesus Christ (1:2). Though a physician by profession, he was primarily an evangelist, writing this Gospel and the book of Acts and accompanying Paul in missionary work (see the Introduction to Acts). He was with Paul at the time of his martyrdom (2 Tim. 4:11), but of his later life we have no certain facts.

Luke's Methodology In his prologue, Luke states that his own work was stimulated by the work of others (1:1), that he consulted eyewitnesses (1:2), and that he sifted and arranged the information (1:3) under the guidance of the Holy Spirit to instruct Theophilus in the historical reliability of the faith (1:4). This is a carefully researched and documented writing.

The Distinctive Approach of Luke Though specifically dedicated to Theophilus, the Gospel is slanted toward all Gentiles. (1) The author displays an unusual interest in medical matters (4:38; 7:15; 8:55; 14:2; 18:25; 22:50). (2) Much attention is given to the recounting of the events surrounding the birth of Christ. Only Luke records the annunciation to Zacharias and Mary, the songs of Elizabeth and Mary, the birth and childhood of John the Baptist, the birth of Jesus, the visit of the shepherds, the circumcision, presentation in the temple, details of Christ's childhood, and the inner thoughts of Mary. (3) Luke shows an uncommon interest in individuals in the accounts of Zacchaeus

(19:1–10) and the penitent thief (23:39–43) and in the parables of the Prodigal Son (15:11–32) and the penitent publican (18:9–14). It is Luke who gives us the story of the Good Samaritan (10:29–37) and the one thankful ex-leper (17:11–19). (4) There is in this Gospel a special emphasis on prayer (3:21; 5:16; 6:12; 9:18, 28–29; 10:21; 11:1; 22:39–46; 23:34, 46). (5) A prominent place given to women is another distinctive feature of this Gospel (chapters 1, 2; 7:11–17, 36–8:1–3; 10:38–42; 21:1–4; 23:27–31, 49). (6) The writer also shows an interest in poverty and wealth (1:52–53; 4:16–22; 6:20, 24–25; 12:13–21; 14:12–13; 16:19–31). (7) The book preserves for us four beautiful hymns: the Magnificat of Mary (1:46–55), the Benedictus of Zechariah (1:67–79), the Gloria in Excelsis of the angels (2:14), and the Nunc Dimittis of Simeon (2:29–32). This is a Gospel of the compassionate Son of Man offering His salvation to the whole world (19:10).

The Date Since the conclusion of Acts brings Paul to Rome, and since the Gospel of Luke was written before Acts (Acts 1:1), Luke's Gospel was probably written about 60 A.D., possibly in Caesarea during Paul's two-year imprisonment there (Acts 24:27).

The Contents The theme of Luke's Gospel is Christ, the Son of Man, and it narrates many of those events which demonstrated Christ's humanity (see "The Distinctive Approach of Luke" for a listing of favorite passages).

OUTLINE OF THE GOSPEL OF LUKE

THE GOSPEL ACCORDING TO
Luke

I PREFACE: THE METHOD
AND PURPOSE OF WRITING, 1:1–4

1 Forasmuch as many have taken in hand to set forth in order a declaration of those things which are most surely believed among us,

2 Even as they delivered them unto us, which from the beginning were eyewitnesses, and ministers of the word;

3 It seemed good to me also, having had perfect understanding of all things from the very first, to write unto thee in order, most excellent Thēoph'ilus.

4 That thou mightest know the certainty of those things, wherein thou hast been instructed.

II THE IDENTIFICATION OF THE SON OF MAN WITH MEN, 1:5–4:13

A The Announcement of the Birth of John the Baptist, 1:5–25

5 ¶ There was in the days of Herod, the king of Judæa, a certain priest named Zacharī'as, of the course of Abī'a: and his wife *was* of the daughters of Aaron, and her name *was* Elisabeth.

6 And they were both righteous before God, walking in all the commandments and ordinances of the Lord blameless.

7 And they had no child, because that Elisabeth was barren, and they both were *now* well stricken in years.

8 And it came to pass, that while he executed the priest's office before God in the order of his course,

9 According to the custom of the priest's office, his lot was to burn incense when he went into the temple of the Lord.

10 And the whole multitude of the people were praying without at the time of incense.

1:3 *from the very first* of the Gospel story, the birth of John the Baptist. The word is translated the same way in Acts 26:5 (though in some instances it means "from above," John 3:31; Jas. 1:17). *most excellent Theophilus.* His name means "dear to God," or "friend of God." He is unknown otherwise, but the form of the address shows that he was a person of high rank.

1:5 *Herod.* This was Herod the Great. See note at Matt. 2:1. *the course of Abia* (Abijah). Work in the temple was divided among "divisions" of priests, each division or "course" named for its leader (1 Chron. 24:10). *daughters of Aaron.* Elizabeth, like Zacharias, was of a priestly family.

1:6 *they were both righteous before God.* In a godless age this couple lived lives that were fully pleasing to God, yet they were without the blessing of children.

1:9 *his lot.* The privilege of burning incense was permitted only once in the lifetime of any priest.

11 And there appeared unto him an angel of the Lord standing on the right side of the altar of incense.

12 And when Zacharî'as saw *him*, he was troubled, and fear fell upon him.

13 But the angel said unto him, Fear not, Zacharî'as: for thy prayer is heard; and thy wife Elisabeth shall bear thee a son, and thou shalt call his name John.

14 And thou shalt have joy and gladness; and many shall rejoice at his birth.

15 For he shall be great in the sight of the Lord, and shall drink neither wine nor strong drink; and he shall be filled with the Holy Ghost, even from his mother's womb.

16 And many of the children of Israel shall he turn to the Lord their God.

17 And he shall go before him in the spirit and power of Elî'as, to turn the hearts of the fathers to the children, and the disobedient to the wisdom of the just; to make ready a people prepared for the Lord.

18 And Zacharî'as said unto the angel, Whereby shall I know this? for I am an old man, and my wife well stricken in years.

19 And the angel answering said unto him, I am Gabriel, that stand in the presence of God; and am sent to speak unto thee, and to show thee these glad tidings.

20 And, behold, thou shalt be dumb, and not able to speak, until the day that these things shall be performed, because thou believest not my words, which shall be fulfilled in their season.

21 And the people waited for Zacharî'as, and marvelled that he tarried so long in the temple.

22 And when he came out, he could not speak unto them: and they perceived that he had seen a vision in the temple: for he beckoned unto them, and remained speechless.

23 And it came to pass, that, as soon as the days of his

1:11 *an angel*. This was Gabriel, according to v. 19.

1:17 *in the spirit and power of Elias*. Elijah was the stern prophet who rebuked the idolatrous King Ahab (1 Kings 21:17-24). He preached repentance, as John the Baptist would also do (Luke 3:8). See notes at Matt. 11:14; 17:11-12.

1:19 *Gabriel*. The angel's name means "man of God," and his ministry involves making special announcements concerning God's plans (Dan. 8:16; 9:21). He and Michael, the archangel, are the only angels named in the Bible.

1:21 *marvelled that he tarried so long*. The people probably wondered if Zacharias had died.

1:23 *he departed to his own house*. After serving in his course

ministration were accomplished, he departed to his own house.

24 And after those days his wife Elisabeth conceived, and hid herself five months, saying,

25 Thus hath the Lord dealt with me in the days wherein he looked on *me*, to take away my reproach among men.

B The Announcement of the Birth of the Son of Man, 1:26–56

26 And in the sixth month the angel Gabriel was sent from God unto a city of Galilee, named Nazareth,

27 To a virgin espoused to a man whose name was Joseph, of the house of David; and the virgin's name *was* Mary.

28 And the angel came in unto her, and said, Hail, *thou that art* highly favoured, the Lord *is* with thee: blessed *art* thou among women.

29 And when she saw *him*, she was troubled at his saying, and cast in her mind what manner of salutation this should be.

30 And the angel said unto her, Fear not, Mary: for thou hast found favour with God.

31 And, behold, thou shalt conceive in thy womb, and bring forth a son, and shalt call his name JESUS.

32 He shall be great, and shall be called the Son of the Highest: and the Lord God shall give unto him the throne of his father David:

33 And he shall reign over the house of Jacob for ever; and of his kingdom there shall be no end.

34 Then said Mary unto the angel, How shall this be, seeing I know not a man?

---

for a limited time, Zacharias was free to return to his home which was in the hill country, probably not far from Jerusalem (1:39).

1:27 *a virgin espoused.* According to Jewish law, espousal or engagement was as binding as marriage. See note at Matt. 1:19.

1:28 *highly favoured*=filled with grace. The word is used in the N.T. elsewhere only in Eph. 1:6, where all believers in Christ also are said to be filled with grace.

1:31 *Jesus.* The name means "the Lord is salvation." See note at Matt. 1:1.

1:32 *his father David.* See 3:31 and note at Matt. 1:1.

1:33 *he shall reign.* Jesus is the Davidic Messiah, and though He reigns always, the ultimate fulfillment of this promise in relation to the *house of Jacob* begins in the millennial kingdom. See 2 Sam. 7:16.

35 And the angel answered and said unto her, The Holy Ghost shall come upon thee, and the power of the Highest shall overshadow thee: therefore also that holy thing which shall be born of thee shall be called the Son of God.

36 And, behold, thy cousin Elisabeth, she hath also conceived a son in her old age: and this is the sixth month with her, who was called barren.

37 For with God nothing shall be impossible.

38 And Mary said, Behold the handmaid of the Lord; be it unto me according to thy word. And the angel departed from her.

39 And Mary arose in those days, and went into the hill country with haste, into a city of Juda;

40 And entered into the house of Zacharī'as, and saluted Elisabeth.

41 And it came to pass, that, when Elisabeth heard the salutation of Mary, the babe leaped in her womb; and Elisabeth was filled with the Holy Ghost:

42 And she spake out with a loud voice, and said, Blessed *art* thou among women, and blessed *is* the fruit of thy womb.

43 And whence *is* this to me, that the mother of my Lord should come to me?

44 For, lo, as soon as the voice of thy salutation sounded in mine ears, the babe leaped in my womb for joy.

45 And blessed *is* she that believed: for there shall be a performance of those things which were told her from the Lord.

46 And Mary said, My soul doth magnify the Lord,

47 And my spirit hath rejoiced in God my Saviour.

48 For he hath regarded the low estate of his handmaiden: for, behold, from henceforth all generations shall call me blessed.

1:35 *The Holy Ghost shall come upon thee.* The means of the incarnation was accomplished by this creative act of the Holy Spirit in the body of Mary. The virgin birth was a special miracle performed by the Third Person of the Trinity, the Holy Spirit, whereby the Second Person of the Trinity, the eternal Son of God, took to Himself a genuine, though sinless, human nature and was born as a man without surrendering in any particular His deity.

1:38 *handmaid*=bondmaid or female slave.

1:46–56 are called "the Magnificat" from the first word of the Latin translation. There are 15 discernible quotations from the O.T. in this poem. This shows how much the O.T. was known and loved in the home in which Jesus was reared.

49 For he that is mighty hath done to me great things; and holy *is* his name.

50 And his mercy *is* on them that fear him from generation to generation.

51 He hath shewed strength with his arm; he hath scattered the proud in the imagination of their hearts.

52 He hath put down the mighty from *their* seats, and exalted them of low degree.

53 He hath filled the hungry with good things; and the rich he hath sent empty away.

54 He hath holpen his servant Israel, in remembrance of *his* mercy;

55 As he spake to our fathers, to Abraham, and to his seed for ever.

56 And Mary abode with her about three months, and returned to her own house.

C The Advent of John the Baptist, 1:57–80

57 Now Elisabeth's full time came that she should be delivered; and she brought forth a son.

58 And her neighbours and her cousins heard how the Lord had shewed great mercy upon her; and they rejoiced with her.

59 And it came to pass, that on the eighth day they came to circumcise the child; and they called him Zachari'as, after the name of his father.

60 And his mother answered and said, Not *so*; but he shall be called John.

61 And they said unto her, There is none of thy kindred that is called by this name.

62 And they made signs to his father, how he would have him called.

63 And he asked for a writing table, and wrote, saying, His name is John. And they marvelled all.

64 And his mouth was opened immediately, and his tongue *loosed*, and he spake, and praised God.

65 And fear came on all that dwelt round about them: and all these sayings were noised abroad throughout all the hill country of Judæa.

66 And all they that heard *them* laid *them* up in their hearts, saying, What manner of child shall this be! And the hand of the Lord was with him.

1:59 *to circumcise the child*. This ritual act was done 8 days after birth, and the name was given at this time.

1:60 *John*=God is gracious.

67 And his father Zachari'as was filled with the Holy Ghost, and prophesied, saying,

68 Blessed *be* the Lord God of Israel; for he hath visited and redeemed his people,

69 And hath raised up an horn of salvation for us in the house of his servant David;

70 As he spake by the mouth of his holy prophets, which have been since the world began:

71 That we should be saved from our enemies, and from the hand of all that hate us;

72 To perform the mercy *promised* to our fathers, and to remember his holy covenant;

73 The oath which he sware to our father Abraham,

74 That he would grant unto us, that we being delivered out of the hand of our enemies might serve him without fear,

75 In holiness and righteousness before him, all the days of our life.

76 And thou, child, shalt be called the prophet of the Highest: for thou shalt go before the face of the Lord to prepare his ways;

77 To give knowledge of salvation unto his people by the remission of their sins,

78 Through the tender mercy of our God; whereby the dayspring from on high hath visited us,

79 To give light to them that sit in darkness and *in* the shadow of death, to guide our feet into the way of peace.

80 And the child grew, and waxed strong in spirit, and was in the deserts till the day of his shewing unto Israel.

D The Advent of the Son of Man, 2:1–20

2 And it came to pass in those days, that there went out a decree from Cæsar Augustus, that all the world should be taxed.

2 (*And* this taxing was first made when Cyre'nius was governor of Syria.)

1:69 *horn of salvation.* Horn is often used as a metaphor for power (2 Sam. 22:3); thus this phrase means "a powerful Savior."

1:73 *The oath.* The covenant which God made with Abraham, recorded in Gen. 22:16–18.

1:78 dayspring=sunrising. See Mal. 4:2.

2:1 *Caesar Augustus* reigned from 27 B.C. to A.D. 14. *should be taxed.* This was an enrolling, numbering, or census of all the Roman world.

2:2 *Cyrenius was governor of Syria.* Apparently he was governor

3 And all went to be taxed, every one into his own city.

4 And Joseph also went up from Galilee, out of the city of Nazareth, into Judæa, unto the city of David, which is called Bethlehem; (because he was of the house and lineage of David:)

5 To be taxed with Mary his espoused wife, being great with child.

6 And so it was, that, while they were there, the days were accomplished that she should be delivered.

7 And she brought forth her firstborn son, and wrapped him in swaddling clothes, and laid him in a manger; because there was no room for them in the inn.

8 And there were in the same country shepherds abiding in the field, keeping watch over their flock by night.

9 And, lo, the angel of the Lord came upon them, and the glory of the Lord shone round about them: and they were sore afraid.

10 And the angel said unto them, Fear not: for, behold, I bring you good tidings of great joy, which shall be to all people.

11 For unto you is born this day in the city of David a Saviour, which is Christ the Lord.

12 And this *shall be* a sign unto you; Ye shall find the babe wrapped in swaddling clothes, lying in a manger.

13 And suddenly there was with the angel a multitude of the heavenly host praising God, and saying,

14 Glory to God in the highest, and on earth peace, good will toward men.

15 And it came to pass, as the angels were gone away from them into heaven, the shepherds said one to another, Let us now go even unto Bethlehem, and see this thing

of Syria twice: from 4 B.C. to A.D. 1, when this census was taken, and again in A.D. 6.

2:4 *Bethlehem.* This fulfilled the prophecy of Mic. 5:2.

2:7 *swadddling clothes* were cloths wrapped around an infant in the Near East in Bible times. *manger.* A feeding trough for animals in a stall or stable. Tradition says that Jesus was born in a cave, in which case the manger may have been cut out of the rock walls.

2:11 Notice the three titles given to Jesus in the angel's announcement: *Saviour, Christ* (Messiah, anointed One), and *Lord* (Yahweh or God). He was both God and man.

2:14 *good will toward men.* More accurately the phrase reads, "among men with whom He is pleased." The peace promised is not given universally to men who possess good will toward God but individually to men who are the recipients of His favor and grace.

which is come to pass, which the Lord hath made known unto us.

16 And they came with haste, and found Mary, and Joseph, and the babe lying in a manger.

17 And when they had seen *it*, they made known abroad the saying which was told them concerning this child.

18 And all they that heard *it* wondered at those things which were told them by the shepherds.

19 But Mary kept all these things, and pondered *them* in her heart.

20 And the shepherds returned, glorifying and praising God for all the things that they had heard and seen, as it was told unto them.

E The Adoration of the Babe, 2:21–38

21 And when eight days were accomplished for the circumcising of the child, his name was called JESUS, which was so named of the angel before he was conceived in the womb.

22 And when the days of her purification according to the law of Moses were accomplished, they brought him to Jerusalem, to present *him* to the Lord;

23 (As it is written in the law of the Lord, Every male that openeth the womb shall be called holy to the Lord;)

24 And to offer a sacrifice according to that which is said in the law of the Lord, A pair of turtledoves, or two young pigeons.

25 And, behold, there was a man in Jerusalem, whose name *was* Simeon; and the same man *was* just and devout, waiting for the consolation of Israel: and the Holy Ghost was upon him.

26 And it was revealed unto him by the Holy Ghost, that he should not see death, before he had seen the Lord's Christ.

27 And he came by the Spirit into the temple: and when the parents brought in the child Jesus, to do for him after the custom of the law,

2:21 *for the circumcising* in accord with Lev. 12:3.

2:22 *the days of her purification.* According to the Mosaic law the mother of a male child was unclean for 7 days. On the eighth day the boy was circumcised but she remained unclean for 33 more days, after which she presented a burnt offering and a sin offering for her cleansing (Lev. 12:4–6).

2:24 *A pair of turtledoves.* This shows the poverty of Christ's family, since they could not afford a lamb for the offering.

2:25 *Simeon.* All we know of Simeon is what Luke tells us here. *the consolation of Israel* is the promised Messiah.

28 Then took he him up in his arms, and blessed God, and said,

29 Lord, now lettest thou thy servant depart in peace, according to thy word:

30 For mine eyes have seen thy salvation,

31 Which thou hast prepared before the face of all people;

32 A light to lighten the Gentiles, and the glory of thy people Israel.

33 And Joseph and his mother marvelled at those things which were spoken of him.

34 And Simeon blessed them, and said unto Mary his mother, Behold, this *child* is set for the fall and rising again of many in Israel; and for a sign which shall be spoken against;

35 (Yea, a sword shall pierce through thy own soul also,) that the thoughts of many hearts may be revealed.

36 And there was one Anna, a prophetess, the daughter of Phanü'el, of the tribe of Aser: she was of a great age, and had lived with an husband seven years from her virginity;

37 And she *was* a widow of about fourscore and four years, which departed not from the temple, but served God with fastings and prayers night and day.

38 And she coming in that instant gave thanks likewise unto the Lord, and spake of him to all them that looked for redemption in Jerusalem.

F The Advancement of the Boy, 2:39–52

39 And when they had performed all things according to the law of the Lord, they returned into Galilee, to their own city Nazareth.

40 And the child grew, and waxed strong in spirit, filled with wisdom: and the grace of God was upon him.

41 Now his parents went to Jerusalem every year at the feast of the passover.

42 And when he was twelve years old, they went up to Jerusalem after the custom of the feast.

2:32 Christ's salvation was offered to Gentile and Jew alike.

2:35 *a sword*. This refers to the agony which Mary would have to bear.

2:37 *a widow of about fourscore and four years*. This may mean that Anna was a widow for 84 years after 7 years of marriage (making her over 100), or it may mean that she was 84 years old.

2:42 *he was twelve years old*. At 13 a Jewish boy became a "son

43 And when they had fulfilled the days, as they returned, the child Jesus tarried behind in Jerusalem; and Joseph and his mother knew not *of it*.

44 But they, supposing him to have been in the company, went a day's journey; and they sought him among *their* kinsfolk and acquaintance.

45 And when they found him not, they turned back again to Jerusalem, seeking him.

46 And it came to pass, that after three days they found him in the temple, sitting in the midst of the doctors, both hearing them, and asking them questions.

47 And all that heard him were astonished at his understanding and answers.

48 And when they saw him, they were amazed: and his mother said unto him, Son, why hast thou thus dealt with us? behold, thy father and I have sought thee sorrowing.

49 And he said unto them, How is it that ye sought me? wist ye not that I must be about my Father's business?

50 And they understood not the saying which he spake unto them.

51 And he went down with them, and came to Nazareth, and was subject unto them: but his mother kept all these sayings in her heart.

52 And Jesus increased in wisdom and stature, and in favour with God and man.

G The Baptism of the Son of Man, 3:1–22

3 Now in the fifteenth year of the reign of Tĭbē′rius Cæsar, Pontius Pilate being governor of Judæa, and Herod being tē′trarch of Galilee, and his brother Philip

of the commandment" and a full member of the religious community. This age was often anticipated by one or two years in the matter of going to the temple.

2:48 *thy father*. As Mary's husband, Joseph was Jesus' legal, though not natural, father.

2:49 *wist ye not*=knew ye not.

2:51 *came to Nazareth*. A veil is drawn over the life of Jesus until the beginning of His public ministry 18 years later.

3:1 *Tiberius Caesar* was the adopted son of Augustus Caesar (2:1) and reigned from A.D. 14–37. *Pilate*. See note at Mark 15:1. *Herod*. The son of Herod the Great (Matt. 2:1) ruled over Galilee (*tetrarch*=ruler of one quarter of a given territory). *Philip*. Another son of Herod the Great, he ruled over Ituraea, NE. of Galilee and E. of Mt. Hermon. *Abilene*. A little kingdom on the E. slope of the Lebanon mountains, NE. of Damascus.

tetrarch of Ītūræ'a and of the region of Trachōnī'tis, and Lȳsā'nias the tetrarch of Abilē'nē,

2 Annas and Cáī'aphas being the high priests, the word of God came unto John the son of Zacharī'as in the wilderness.

3 And he came into all the country about Jordan, preaching the baptism of repentance for the remission of sins;

4 As it is written in the book of the words of Ēsáī'as the prophet, saying, The voice of one crying in the wilderness, Prepare ye the way of the Lord, make his paths straight.

5 Every valley shall be filled, and every mountain and hill shall be brought low; and the crooked shall be made straight, and the rough ways *shall be* made smooth;

6 And all flesh shall see the salvation of God.

7 Then said he to the multitude that came forth to be baptized of him, O generation of vipers, who hath warned you to flee from the wrath to come?

8 Bring forth therefore fruits worthy of repentance, and begin not to say within yourselves, We have Abraham to *our* father: for I say unto you, That God is able of these stones to raise up children unto Abraham.

9 And now also the axe is laid unto the root of the trees: every tree therefore which bringeth not forth good fruit is hewn down, and cast into the fire.

10 And the people asked him, saying, What shall we do then?

11 He answereth and saith unto them, He that hath two coats, let him impart to him that hath none; and he that hath meat, let him do likewise.

12 Then came also publicans to be baptized, and said unto him, Master, what shall we do?

13 And he said unto them, Exact no more than that which is appointed you.

3:2 *Annas and Caiaphas.* Caiaphas was the ruling high priest (A.D. 18–36). Annas, high priest, A.D. 6–15, continued to exercise weighty influence (John 18:13; Acts 4:6).

3:4 See Isa. 40:3–5.

3:8 This meaning of this is: Do not trust in your religious ancestry, however good it may be. You must personally have a right relation with God.

3:9 *the axe is laid unto the root of the trees.* Just as unproductive trees are cut down, so the unfruitful nation of Israel could expect judgment.

3:11 *meat*=food in general.

3:12 *publicans*=tax-collectors. See notes at Matt. 9:10 and Luke 19:2.

14 And the soldiers likewise demanded of him, saying, And what shall we do? And he said unto them, Do violence to no man, neither accuse *any* falsely; and be content with your wages.

15 And as the people were in expectation, and all men mused in their hearts of John, whether he were the Christ, or not;

16 John answered, saying unto *them* all, I indeed baptize you with water; but one mightier than I cometh, the latchet of whose shoes I am not worthy to unloose: he shall baptize you with the Holy Ghost and with fire:

17 Whose fan *is* in his hand, and he will throughly purge his floor, and will gather the wheat into his garner; but the chaff he will burn with fire unquenchable.

18 And many other things in his exhortation preached he unto the people.

19 But Herod the tē'trarch, being reproved by him for Herō'dias his brother Philip's wife, and for all the evils which Herod had done,

20 Added yet this above all, that he shut up John in prison.

21 Now when all the people were baptized, it came to pass, that Jesus also being baptized, and praying, the heaven was opened,

22 And the Holy Ghost descended in a bodily shape like a dove upon him, and a voice came from heaven, which said, Thou art my beloved Son; in thee I am well pleased.

H The Genealogy of the Son of Man, 3:23–38

23 And Jesus himself began to be about thirty years of age, being (as was supposed) the son of Joseph, which was *the son* of Heli,

3:14 *soldiers* were often brutal to civilians and practiced extortion. *Do violence to no man* means "do not 'shake down' anyone" and has the same meaning as the modern idiom.
3:15 *in expectation* of the Messiah's coming.
3:16 *baptize.* See note at Matt. 3:11. *latchet*=shoelace. *with the Holy Ghost and with fire.* The baptism with the Holy Spirit occurred on the day of Pentecost, and the baptism with fire is a reference to the judgments accompanying the second coming of Christ.
3:19 *Herodias.* See note at Matt. 14:3.
3:22 *like a dove.* The dove was used as a symbol for all kinds of virtues in those days (see Matt. 10:16). All persons of the Trinity were present at Christ's baptism.
3:23 *son of Heli.* Joseph was Jacob's son by birth (Matt. 1:16)

24 Which was *the son* of Matthat, which was *the son* of Levi, which was *the son* of Mel'chī, which was *the son* of Janna, which was *the son* of Josếph,

25 Which was *the son* of Mattathī'as, which was *the son* of Amos, which was *the son* of Nā'um, which was *the son* of Esli, which was *the son* of Nag'gē,

26 Which was *the son* of Mā'ath, which was *the son* of Mattathī'as, which was *the son* of Sem'eī, which was *the son* of Joseph, which was *the son* of Juda,

27 Which was *the son* of Joanna, which was *the son* of Rhesa, which was *the son* of Zorob'abel, which was *the son* of Salā'thiel, which was *the son* of Neri,

28 Which was *the son* of Mel'chī, which was *the son* of Addi, which was *the son* of Cosam, which was *the son* of Elmŏ'dam, which was *the son* of Er,

29 Which was *the son* of Jŏ'sē, which was *the son* of Eliē'zer, which was *the son* of Jorim, which was *the son* of Matthat, which was *the son* of Levi,

30 Which was *the son* of Simeon, which was *the son* of Juda, which was *the son* of Joseph, which was *the son* of Jonan, which was *the son* of Ēlī'akim,

31 Which was *the son* of Mel'ea, which was *the son* of Menan, which was *the son* of Mat'tatha, which was *the son* of Nathan, which was *the son* of David,

32 Which was *the son* of Jesse, which was *the son* of Obed, which was *the son* of Bŏ'oz, which was *the son* of Salmon, which was *the son* of Nāas'son,

33 Which was *the son* of Amin'adab, which was *the son* of Aram, which was *the son* of Esrom, which was *the son* of Phār'ēs, which was *the son* of Juda,

34 Which was *the son* of Jacob, which was *the son* of Isaac, which was *the son* of Abraham, which was *the son* of Thara, which was *the son* of Nā'chor,

35 Which was *the son* of Sār'uch, which was *the son* of Rā'gâu, which was *the son* of Phā'lec, which was *the son* of Heber, which was *the son* of Sala,

36 Which was *the son* of Cāī'nan, which was *the son* of Arphax'ad, which was *the son* of Sem, which was *the son* of Nŏ'ē, which was *the son* of Lā'mech,

37 Which was *the son* of Mathū'sala, which was *the son* of Enoch, which was *the son* of Jared, which was *the son* of Mal'eléèl, which was *the son* of Cāī'nan,

38 Which was *the son* of Ē'nos, which was *the son* of

and Heli's son by marriage. This is apparently the genealogy of Jesus through His mother, Mary. See note at Matt. 1:1.

Seth, which was *the son* of Adam, which was *the son* of God.

I The Temptation of the Son of Man, 4:1–13

4 And Jesus being full of the Holy Ghost returned from Jordan, and was led by the Spirit into the wilderness,

2 Being forty days tempted of the devil. And in those days he did eat nothing: and when they were ended, he afterward hungered.

3 And the devil said unto him, If thou be the Son of God, command this stone that it be made bread.

4 And Jesus answered him, saying, It is written, That man shall not live by bread alone, but by every word of God.

5 And the devil, taking him up into an high mountain, shewed unto him all the kingdoms of the world in a moment of time.

6 And the devil said unto him, All this power will I give thee, and the glory of them: for that is delivered unto me; and to whomsoever I will I give it.

7 If thou therefore wilt worship me, all shall be thine.

8 And Jesus answered and said unto him, Get thee behind me, Satan: for it is written, Thou shalt worship the Lord thy God, and him only shalt thou serve.

9 And he brought him to Jerusalem, and set him on a pinnacle of the temple, and said unto him, If thou be the Son of God, cast thyself down from hence:

10 For it is written, He shall give his angels charge over thee, to keep thee:

11 And in *their* hands they shall bear thee up, lest at any time thou dash thy foot against a stone.

4:1 *the wilderness.* The traditional site of the temptation is NW. of the Dead Sea.

4:2 *tempted of the devil.* See note at Matt. 4:1.

4:3 *If thou be the Son of God.* The particular Greek construction used here indicates that the devil did not doubt that Jesus was the Son of God.

4:4 See Deut. 8:3.

4:8 See Deut. 6:13; 10:20.

4:9 *pinnacle of the temple.* One of the battlements or towers that overlooked the courtyard of the temple. If Jesus had cast Himself off and landed unharmed among the crowds below, He surely would have been acclaimed Messiah.

4:10 See Ps. 91:11–12. Satan omits from the quotation the phrase "in all thy ways" in an attempt to apply the promise to something which was contrary to God's will.

12 And Jesus answering said unto him, It is said, Thou shalt not tempt the Lord thy God.

13 And when the devil had ended all the temptation, he departed from him for a season.

III THE MINISTRY OF THE SON OF MAN TO MEN, 4:14–9:50

A The Announcement of His Ministry, 4:14–30

14 ¶ And Jesus returned in the power of the Spirit into Galilee: and there went out a fame of him through all the region round about.

15 And he taught in their synagogues, being glorified of all.

16 ¶ And he came to Nazareth, where he had been brought up: and, as his custom was, he went into the synagogue on the sabbath day, and stood up for to read.

17 And there was delivered unto him the book of the prophet Ēsā'as. And when he had opened the book, he found the place where it was written,

18 The Spirit of the Lord is upon me, because he hath anointed me to preach the gospel to the poor; he hath sent me to heal the brokenhearted, to preach deliverance to the captives, and recovering of sight to the blind, to set at liberty them that are bruised,

19 To preach the acceptable year of the Lord.

20 And he closed the book, and he gave it again to the minister, and sat down. And the eyes of all them that were in the synagogue were fastened on him.

21 And he began to say unto them, This day is this scripture fulfilled in your ears.

22 And all bare him witness, and wondered at the gracious words which proceeded out of his mouth. And they said, Is not this Joseph's son?

23 And he said unto them, Ye will surely say unto me

4:12 See Deut. 6:16. The temptations were designed to offer Christ the glory of ruling without the suffering of dying for sin.

4:17 book. More correctly, the scroll.

4:18 See Isa. 61:1–2a. Christ stopped reading in the middle of 61:2 since at His first coming He preached only the "acceptable year of the Lord" (v. 19), the "day of vengeance of our God" (Isa. 61:2b) being reserved for His second coming. Long suffering and the cross are connected with His first coming; judgment and a crown, with His second.

4:20 the minister. This was the attendant who had charge of the scrolls of Scriptures.

this proverb, Physician, heal thyself: whatsoever we have heard done in Caper′naum, do also here in thy country.

24 And he said, Verily I say unto you, No prophet is accepted in his own country.

25 But I tell you of a truth, many widows were in Israel in the days of Ēlī′as, when the heaven was shut up three years and six months, when great famine was throughout all the land;

26 But unto none of them was Ēlī′as sent, save unto Sarep′ta, *a city* of Sidon, unto a woman *that was* a widow.

27 And many lepers were in Israel in the time of Elisē′us the prophet; and none of them was cleansed, saving Nā′aman the Syrian.

28 And all they in the synagogue, when they heard these things, were filled with wrath,

29 And rose up, and thrust him out of the city, and led him unto the brow of the hill whereon their city was built, that they might cast him down headlong.

30 But he passing through the midst of them went his way,

B The Authority of His Ministry, 4:31–6:11

1 *Over demons,* 4:31–37

31 And came down to Caper′naum, a city of Galilee, and taught them on the sabbath days.

32 And they were astonished at his doctrine: for his word was with power.

33 ¶ And in the synagogue there was a man, which had a spirit of an unclean devil, and cried out with a loud voice,

34 Saying, Let *us* alone; what have we to do with thee, *thou* Jesus of Nazareth? art thou come to destroy us? I know thee who thou art; the Holy One of God.

35 And Jesus rebuked him, saying, Hold thy peace, and come out of him. And when the devil had thrown him in the midst, he came out of him, and hurt him not.

36 And they were all amazed, and spake among them-

4:25–26 The story is in 1 Kings 17:8–24.

4:27 *Naaman the Syrian.* The story is in 2 Kings 5:1–14.

4:30 *passing through the midst of them.* These words do not necessarily imply a miraculous deliverance. Rather, His commanding presence and righteousness had power to thwart the crowd's plan.

4:31 *Capernaum.* A city on the shore of the Lake of Galilee, about 25 miles NE. of Nazareth. Jesus carried on an extensive ministry there.

4:36 *devil=demon.* See note at Matt. 7:22.

selves, saying, What a word *is* this! for with authority and power he commandeth the unclean spirits, and they come out.

37 And the fame of him went out into every place of the country round about.

2 *Over disease,* 4:38–44

38 ¶ And he arose out of the synagogue, and entered into Simon's house. And Simon's wife's mother was taken with a great fever; and they besought him for her.

39 And he stood over her, and rebuked the fever; and it left her: and immediately she arose and ministered unto them.

40 ¶ Now when the sun was setting, all they that had any sick with divers diseases brought them unto him; and he laid his hands on every one of them, and healed them.

41 And devils also came out of many, crying out, and saying, Thou art Christ the Son of God. And he rebuking *them* suffered them not to speak: for they knew that he was Christ.

42 And when it was day, he departed and went into a desert place: and the people sought him, and came unto him, and stayed him, that he should not depart from them.

43 And he said unto them, I must preach the kingdom of God to other cities also: for therefore am I sent.

44 And he preached in the synagogues of Galilee.

3 *Over the disciples,* 5:1–11

5 And it came to pass, that, as the people pressed upon him to hear the word of God, he stood by the lake of Gennes'aret,

2 And saw two ships standing by the lake: but the fishermen were gone out of them, and were washing *their* nets.

3 And he entered into one of the ships, which was Simon's, and prayed him that he would thrust out a little from the land. And he sat down, and taught the people out of the ship.

4 Now when he had left speaking, he said unto Simon, Launch out into the deep, and let down your nets for a draught.

4:38 *a great fever.* Only Luke, the physician, recorded this fact.
5:1 *the lake of Gennesaret*=the Lake of Galilee.
5:4 *draught*=catch.

5 And Simon answering said unto him, Master, we have toiled all the night, and have taken nothing: nevertheless at thy word I will let down the net.

6 And when they had this done, they inclosed a great multitude of fishes: and their net brake.

7 And they beckoned unto *their* partners, which were in the other ship, that they should come and help them. And they came, and filled both the ships, so that they began to sink.

8 When Simon Peter saw *it*, he fell down at Jesus' knees, saying, Depart from me; for I am a sinful man, O Lord.

9 For he was astonished, and all that were with him, at the draught of the fishes which they had taken:

10 And so *was* also James, and John, the sons of Zebedee, which were partners with Simon. And Jesus said unto Simon, Fear not; from henceforth thou shalt catch men.

11 And when they had brought their ships to land, they forsook all, and followed him.

4 Over defilement (a leper healed), 5:12–16

12 ¶ And it came to pass, when he was in a certain city, behold a man full of leprosy: who seeing Jesus fell on *his* face, and besought him, saying, Lord, if thou wilt, thou canst make me clean.

13 And he put forth *his* hand, and touched him, saying, I will: be thou clean. And immediately the leprosy departed from him.

14 And he charged him to tell no man: but go, and shew thyself to the priest, and offer for thy cleansing, according as Moses commanded, for a testimony unto them.

15 But so much the more went there a fame abroad of him: and great multitudes came together to hear, and to be healed by him of their infirmities.

16 ¶ And he withdrew himself into the wilderness, and prayed.

5:8 The miracle demonstrated to Peter his own sinfulness and Jesus' deity.

5:12 *leprosy*. See Lev. 13 for 7 forms of this skin disease, generally regarded not to be the leprosy we know today. A leper was ceremonially unclean, had to live outside of the towns, and had to cry "unclean." Ps. 51:5 seems to use leprosy as an illustration of sin.

5:16 *prayed*. See Introduction, "The Distinctive Approach of Luke."

5 Over defectiveness (a paralytic healed), 5:17–26

17 And it came to pass on a certain day, as he was teaching, that there were Pharisees and doctors of the law sitting by, which were come out of every town of Galilee, and Judæa, and Jerusalem: and the power of the Lord was *present* to heal them.

18 ¶ And, behold, men brought in a bed a man which was taken with a palsy: and they sought *means* to bring him in, and to lay *him* before him.

19 And when they could not find by what *way* they might bring him in because of the multitude, they went upon the housetop, and let him down through the tiling with *his* couch into the midst before Jesus.

20 And when he saw their faith, he said unto him, Man, thy sins are forgiven thee.

21 And the scribes and the Pharisees began to reason, saying, Who is this which speaketh blasphemies? Who can forgive sins, but God alone?

22 But when Jesus perceived their thoughts, he answering said unto them, What reason ye in your hearts?

23 Whether is easier, to say, Thy sins be forgiven thee; or to say, Rise up and walk?

24 But that ye may know that the Son of man hath power upon earth to forgive sins, (he said unto the sick of the palsy,) I say unto thee, Arise, and take up thy couch, and go into thine house.

25 And immediately he rose up before them, and took up that whereon he lay, and departed to his own house, glorifying God.

26 And they were all amazed, and they glorified God, and were filled with fear, saying, We have seen strange things to day.

6 Over the despised
(the call of Matthew and parables), 5:27–39

27 ¶ And after these things he went forth, and saw a publican, named Levi, sitting at the receipt of custom: and he said unto him, Follow me.

5:17 Only Luke mentions the presence of religious leaders from all parts of the land, listening critically to the claims of Jesus.
5:20 *Man, thy sins are forgiven thee.* The Lord began with the man's greater problem, his spiritual need, rather than his physical one. Jesus' statement was considered blasphemy, since it was clearly understood to be a claim of being equal with God. See notes at Matt. 9:2 and 9:5.
5:27 *publican*=tax-collector. *Levi.* This is Matthew. See Introduction to Matthew and note at Matt. 9:10.

28 And he left all, rose up, and followed him.

29 And Levi made him a great feast in his own house: and there was a great company of publicans and of others that sat down with them.

30 But their scribes and Pharisees murmured against his disciples, saying, Why do ye eat and drink with publicans and sinners?

31 And Jesus answering said unto them, They that are whole need not a physician; but they that are sick.

32 I came not to call the righteous, but sinners to repentance.

33 ¶ And they said unto him, Why do the disciples of John fast often, and make prayers, and likewise *the disciples* of the Pharisees; but thine eat and drink?

34 And he said unto them, Can ye make the children of the bridechamber fast, while the bridegroom is with them?

35 But the days will come, when the bridegroom shall be taken away from them, and then shall they fast in those days.

36 ¶ And he spake also a parable unto them; No man putteth a piece of a new garment upon an old; if otherwise, then both the new maketh a rent, and the piece that was *taken* out of the new agreeth not with the old.

37 And no man putteth new wine into old bottles; else the new wine will burst the bottles, and be spilled, and the bottles shall perish.

38 But new wine must be put into new bottles; and both are preserved.

39 No man also having drunk old *wine* straightway desireth new: for he saith, The old is better.

7 Over days, 6:1-5

6 And it came to pass on the second sabbath after the first, that he went through the corn fields; and his disciples plucked the ears of corn, and did eat, rubbing *them* in *their* hands.

2 And certain of the Pharisees said unto them, Why do ye that which is not lawful to do on the sabbath days?

5:37 *bottles.* Not glass containers but skins used as sacks for liquid. If filled with new wine, old skins lost elasticity and burst when it fermented. The point is that the new teaching of the grace of Christ cannot be contained within the old forms of the law (John 1:17).

6:2 *not lawful to do on the sabbath days.* Jesus was being charged with working on the Sabbath, though it was lawful to pick grain from another's field to satisfy hunger (Deut. 23:25).

3 And Jesus answering them said, Have ye not read so much as this, what David did, when himself was an hungred, and they which were with him;

4 How he went into the house of God, and did take and eat the shewbread, and gave also to them that were with him; which it is not lawful to eat but for the priests alone?

5 And he said unto them, That the Son of man is Lord also of the sabbath.

8 *Over deformity*, 6:6–11

6 And it came to pass also on another sabbath, that he entered into the synagogue and taught: and there was a man whose right hand was withered.

7 And the scribes and Pharisees watched him, whether he would heal on the sabbath day; that they might find an accusation against him.

8 But he knew their thoughts, and said to the man which had the withered hand, Rise up, and stand forth in the midst. And he arose and stood forth.

9 Then said Jesus unto them, I will ask you one thing; Is it lawful on the sabbath days to do good, or to do evil? to save life, or to destroy *it*?

10 And looking round about upon them all, he said unto the man, Stretch forth thy hand. And he did so: and his hand was restored whole as the other.

11 And they were filled with madness; and communed one with another what they might do to Jesus.

C The Associates of His Ministry, 6:12–49

1 *The call of the disciples*, 6:12–16

12 And it came to pass in those days, that he went out into a mountain to pray, and continued all night in prayer to God.

6:3 *what David did*. See 1 Sam. 21:1–6. To the Pharisees' objections Jesus quoted an O.T. example of the spirit of the law taking priority over the letter of the law. See note at Matt. 12:1.

6:5 *Lord also of the sabbath*. Not only had Christ claimed deity (5:20), but now He claimed sovereignty over the Sabbath day and its laws, and He asserted His right to interpret its laws without reference to the traditions of the Pharisees.

6:7 *an accusation against him*. To heal on the Sabbath would have been a violation, according to the traditions of the Pharisees, of the prohibition against work on that day; but not to heal, as Christ tried to point out to the Pharisees, would have been to do evil and to destroy life (v. 9). To heal and therefore to do a good work would be no violation of Sabbath laws.

13 ¶ And when it was day, he called *unto him* his disciples: and of them he chose twelve, whom also he named apostles;

14 Simon, (whom he also named Peter,) and Andrew his brother, James and John, Philip and Bartholomew,

15 Matthew and Thomas, James the *son* of Alphæ'us, and Simon called Zēlō'tēs,

16 And Judas *the brother* of James, and Judas Iscariot, which also was the traitor.

2 *The characteristics of disciples* (The Great Sermon), 6:17–49

17 ¶ And he came down with them, and stood in the plain, and the company of his disciples, and a great multitude of people out of all Judæa and Jerusalem, and from the sea coast of Tyre and Sidon, which came to hear him, and to be healed of their diseases;

18 And they that were vexed with unclean spirits: and they were healed.

19 And the whole multitude sought to touch him: for there went virtue out of him, and healed *them* all.

20 ¶ And he lifted up his eyes on his disciples, and said, Blessed *be ye* poor: for yours is the kingdom of God.

21 Blessed *are ye* that hunger now: for ye shall be filled. Blessed *are ye* that weep now: for ye shall laugh.

22 Blessed are ye, when men shall hate you, and when they shall separate you *from their company*, and shall reproach *you*, and cast out your name as evil, for the Son of man's sake.

23 Rejoice ye in that day, and leap for joy: for, behold, your reward *is* great in heaven: for in the like manner did their fathers unto the prophets.

24 But woe unto you that are rich! for ye have received your consolation.

25 Woe unto you that are full! for ye shall hunger. Woe unto you that laugh now! for ye shall mourn and weep.

26 Woe unto you, when all men shall speak well of you! for so did their fathers to the false prophets.

6:13 *apostles*. See note at Matt. 10:2.
6:17–26 This may be Luke's account of the same occasion and teaching recorded in Matt. 5–7 (the Sermon on the Mount), or it may simply be similar teaching given on a different occasion.
6:19 *virtue*=power.

27 ¶ But I say unto you which hear, Love your enemies, do good to them which hate you,

28 Bless them that curse you, and pray for them which despitefully use you.

29 And unto him that smiteth thee on the *one* cheek offer also the other; and him that taketh away thy cloke forbid not *to take thy* coat also.

30 Give to every man that asketh of thee; and of him that taketh away thy goods ask *them* not again.

31 And as ye would that men should do to you, do ye also to them likewise.

32 For if ye love them which love you, what thank have ye? for sinners also love those that love them.

33 And if ye do good to them which do good to you, what thank have ye? for sinners also do even the same.

34 And if ye lend *to them* of whom ye hope to receive, what thank have ye? for sinners also lend to sinners, to receive as much again.

35 But love ye your enemies, and do good, and lend, hoping for nothing again; and your reward shall be great, and ye shall be the children of the Highest: for he is kind unto the unthankful and *to* the evil.

36 Be ye therefore merciful, as your Father also is merciful.

37 Judge not, and ye shall not be judged: condemn not, and ye shall not be condemned: forgive, and ye shall be forgiven:

38 Give, and it shall be given unto you; good measure, pressed down, and shaken together, and running over, shall men give into your bosom. For with the same measure that ye mete withal it shall be measured to you again.

39 And he spake a parable unto them, Can the blind lead the blind? shall they not both fall into the ditch?

40 The disciple is not above his master: but every one that is perfect shall be as his master.

41 And why beholdest thou the mote that is in thy brother's eye, but perceivest not the beam that is in thine own eye?

42 Either how canst thou say to thy brother, Brother, let me pull out the mote that is in thine eye, when thou

---

6:38 *pressed down, and shaken together, and running over.* The imagery is of a measure of grain filled to the brim and running over the edge. Our liberality should be like that.

6:41 *mote . . . beam.* A mote is something tiny like a bit of sawdust, while a beam, of course, is large. Perhaps Jesus was drawing on His experience as a carpenter.

thyself beholdest not the beam that is in thine own eye?
Thou hypocrite, cast out first the beam out of thine own
eye, and then shalt thou see clearly to pull out the mote
that is in thy brother's eye.

43 For a good tree bringeth not forth corrupt fruit;
neither doth a corrupt tree bring forth good fruit.

44 For every tree is known by his own fruit. For of
thorns men do not gather figs, nor of a bramble bush
gather they grapes.

45 A good man out of the good treasure of his heart
bringeth forth that which is good; and an evil man out of
the evil treasure of his heart bringeth forth that which is
evil: for of the abundance of the heart his mouth speaketh.

46 ¶ And why call ye me, Lord, Lord, and do not the
things which I say?

47 Whosoever cometh to me, and heareth my sayings,
and doeth them, I will shew you to whom he is like:

48 He is like a man which built an house, and digged
deep, and laid the foundation on a rock: and when the
flood arose, the stream beat vehemently upon that house,
and could not shake it: for it was founded upon a rock.

49 But he that heareth, and doeth not, is like a man
that without a foundation built an house upon the earth;
against which the stream did beat vehemently, and immediately it fell; and the ruin of that house was great.

D The Activities of His Ministry, 7:1–9:50

1 *Ministry in sickness,* 7:1–10

7 Now when he had ended all his sayings in the audience of the people, he entered into Caper'naum.

2 And a certain centurion's servant, who was dear unto
him, was sick, and ready to die.

3 And when he heard of Jesus, he sent unto him the
elders of the Jews, beseeching him that he would come and
heal his servant.

4 And when they came to Jesus, they besought him instantly, saying, That he was worthy for whom he should
do this:

5 For he loveth our nation, and he hath built us a
synagogue.

7:2 *centurion.* Here was an atypical Roman officer who loved
his servant and the Jewish people.
7:5 *synagogue.* A Jewish house of worship first established during
the Babylonian captivity but also used after the temple was
rebuilt by groups of Jews wherever they settled. The service
included prescribed readings and prayer and a sermon (4:20).

6 Then Jesus went with them. And when he was now not far from the house, the centurion sent friends to him, saying unto him, Lord, trouble not thyself: for I am not worthy that thou shouldest enter under my roof:

7 Wherefore neither thought I myself worthy to come unto thee: but say in a word, and my servant shall be healed.

8 For I also am a man set under authority, having under me soldiers, and I say unto one, Go, and he goeth; and to another, Come, and he cometh; and to my servant, Do this, and he doeth *it*.

9 When Jesus heard these things, he marvelled at him, and turned him about, and said unto the people that followed him, I say unto you, I have not found so great faith, no, not in Israel.

10 And they that were sent, returning to the house, found the servant whole that had been sick.

2 *Ministry in death,* 7:11–17

11 ¶ And it came to pass the day after, that he went into a city called Nā′in; and many of his disciples went with him, and much people.

12 Now when he came nigh to the gate of the city, behold, there was a dead man carried out, the only son of his mother, and she was a widow: and much people of the city was with her.

13 And when the Lord saw her, he had compassion on her, and said unto her, Weep not.

14 And he came and touched the bier: and they that bare *him* stood still. And he said, Young man, I say unto thee, Arise.

15 And he that was dead sat up, and began to speak. And he delivered him to his mother.

16 And there came a fear on all: and they glorified God, saying, That a great prophet is risen up among us; and, That God hath visited his people.

17 And this rumour of him went forth throughout all Judæa, and throughout all the region round about.

Any competent teacher might be asked to speak (Acts 13:15). Ruins of a later synagogue can be seen in Capernaum today.

7:9 *so great faith.* This pagan's faith was a welcome contrast to the unbelief of the Jews.

7:11 *Nain.* About 10 miles SE. of Nazareth.

7:15 *And he that was dead sat up.* This is one of three resurrections recorded in the Gospels that Christ effected, the others being Jairus' daughter (Mark 5:41) and Lazarus (John 11:44).

3 *Ministry in doubt,* 7:18–35

18 And the disciples of John shewed him of all these things.

19 ¶ And John calling *unto him* two of his disciples sent *them* to Jesus, saying, Art thou he that should come? or look we for another?

20 When the men were come unto him, they said, John Baptist hath sent us unto thee, saying, Art thou he that should come? or look we for another?

21 And in that same hour he cured many of *their* infirmities and plagues, and of evil spirits; and unto many *that were* blind he gave sight.

22 Then Jesus answering said unto them, Go your way, and tell John what things ye have seen and heard; how that the blind see, the lame walk, the lepers are cleansed, the deaf hear, the dead are raised, to the poor the gospel is preached.

23 And blessed is *he*, whosoever shall not be offended in me.

24 ¶ And when the messengers of John were departed, he began to speak unto the people concerning John, What went ye out into the wilderness for to see? A reed shaken with the wind?

25 But what went ye out for to see? A man clothed in soft raiment? Behold, they which are gorgeously apparelled, and live delicately, are in kings' courts.

26 But what went ye out for to see? A prophet? Yea, I say unto you, and much more than a prophet.

27 This is *he*, of whom it is written, Behold, I send my messenger before thy face, which shall prepare thy way before thee.

28 For I say unto you, Among those that are born of women there is not a greater prophet than John the Baptist: but he that is least in the kingdom of God is greater than he.

29 And all the people that heard *him*, and the publicans, justified God, being baptized with the baptism of John.

7:22 *tell John what things ye have seen and heard.* These were things that the O.T. predicted the Messiah would do. Jesus had done them; therefore, the men had their answer.

7:24–25 John the Baptist was not like a reed that bends in whatever direction the wind blows; he was a man of conviction. Neither was he given to soft living.

7:28 *is greater than he.* See note at Matt. 11:11.

7:29 *justified God.* I.e., agreed that God's way was right.

30 But the Pharisees and lawyers rejected the counsel of God against themselves, being not baptized of him.

31 ¶ And the Lord said, Whereunto then shall I liken the men of this generation? and to what are they like?

32 They are like unto children sitting in the market-place, and calling one to another, and saying, We have piped unto you, and ye have not danced; we have mourned to you, and ye have not wept.

33 For John the Baptist came neither eating bread nor drinking wine; and ye say, He hath a devil.

34 The Son of man is come eating and drinking; and ye say, Behold a gluttonous man, and a winebibber, a friend of publicans and sinners!

35 But wisdom is justified of all her children.

4 Ministry to sinners, 7:36–50

36 ¶ And one of the Pharisees desired him that he would eat with him. And he went into the Pharisee's house, and sat down to meat.

37 And, behold, a woman in the city, which was a sinner, when she knew that Jesus sat at meat in the Pharisee's house, brought an alabaster box of ointment,

38 And stood at his feet behind him weeping, and began to wash his feet with tears, and did wipe them with the hairs of her head, and kissed his feet, and anointed them with the ointment.

39 Now when the Pharisee which had bidden him saw it, he spake within himself, saying, This man, if he were a prophet, would have known who and what manner of woman this is that toucheth him: for she is a sinner.

40 And Jesus answering said unto him, Simon, I have somewhat to say unto thee. And he saith, Master, say on.

41 There was a certain creditor which had two debtors: the one owed five hundred pence, and the other fifty.

42 And when they had nothing to pay, he frankly forgave them both. Tell me therefore, which of them will love him most?

43 Simon answered and said, I suppose that he, to

7:36–50 This is not the same as a similar incident which occurred in Bethany of Judea during the last week of Christ's life (Matt. 26:6–31; Mark 14:3–9; John 12:1–8).

7:37 an alabaster box of ointment. A long-necked flask of fine translucent material, used for storing perfume.

7:41 pence. Better, denarii (singular: denarius), a Roman silver coin, worth about 20 cents, a day's wage for ordinary workers.

whom he forgave most. And he said unto him, Thou hast rightly judged.

44 And he turned to the woman, and said unto Simon, Seest thou this woman? I entered into thine house, thou gavest me no water for my feet: but she hath washed my feet with tears, and wiped *them* with the hairs of her head.

45 Thou gavest me no kiss: but this woman since the time I came in hath not ceased to kiss my feet.

46 My head with oil thou didst not anoint: but this woman hath anointed my feet with ointment.

47 Wherefore I say unto thee, Her sins, which are many, are forgiven; for she loved much: but to whom little is forgiven, *the same* loveth little.

48 And he said unto her, Thy sins are forgiven.

49 And they that sat at meat with him began to say within themselves, Who is this that forgiveth sins also?

50 And he said to the woman, Thy faith hath saved thee; go in peace.

5 *Ministry financed*, 8:1-3

8 And it came to pass afterward, that he went throughout every city and village, preaching and shewing the glad tidings of the kingdom of God: and the twelve *were* with him,

2 And certain women, which had been healed of evil spirits and infirmities, Mary called Magdalene, out of whom went seven devils,

3 And Joanna the wife of Chū'za Herod's steward, and Susanna, and many others, which ministered unto him of their substance.

6 *Ministry illustrated through parables*, 8:4-21

4 ¶And when much people were gathered together, and were come to him out of every city, he spake by a parable:

5 A sower went out to sow his seed: and as he sowed,

8:2 *Mary called Magdalene.* Magdala is a small town between Capernaum and Tiberius. Other Marys in the N.T. are: (1) the mother of Jesus (1:27); (2) the mother of James and wife of Cleophas-Alphaeus (6:15; John 19:25)—these two Marys were evidently cousins; (3) the sister of Martha and Lazarus (Luke 10:39); (4) the mother of John Mark (Acts 12:12); (5) a Christian woman in Rome (Rom. 16:6).

8:3 *Herod's steward.* A position of some rank involving the management of Herod's income and expenditures. *ministered unto him of their substance.* These women helped finance Christ's ministry.

some fell by the way side; and it was trodden down, and the fowls of the air devoured it.

6 And some fell upon a rock; and as soon as it was sprung up, it withered away, because it lacked moisture.

7 And some fell among thorns; and the thorns sprang up with it, and choked it.

8 And other fell on good ground, and sprang up, and bare fruit an hundredfold. And when he had said these things, he cried, He that hath ears to hear, let him hear.

9 And his disciples asked him, saying, What might this parable be?

10 And he said, Unto you it is given to know the mysteries of the kingdom of God: but to others in parables; that seeing they might not see, and hearing they might not understand.

11 Now the parable is this: The seed is the word of God.

12 Those by the way side are they that hear; then cometh the devil, and taketh away the word out of their hearts, lest they should believe and be saved.

13 They on the rock *are they*, which, when they hear, receive the word with joy; and these have no root, which for a while believe, and in time of temptation fall away.

14 And that which fell among thorns are they, which, when they have heard, go forth, and are choked with cares and riches and pleasures of *this* life, and bring no fruit to perfection.

15 But that on the good ground are they, which in an honest and good heart, having heard the word, keep *it*, and bring forth fruit with patience.

16 ¶ No man, when he hath lighted a candle, covereth it with a vessel, or putteth *it* under a bed; but setteth *it* on a candlestick, that they which enter in may see the light.

17 For nothing is secret, that shall not be made manifest; neither *any thing* hid, that shall not be known and come abroad.

18 Take heed therefore how ye hear: for whosoever hath, to him shall be given; and whosoever hath not, from him shall be taken even that which he seemeth to have.

19 ¶ Then came to him *his* mother and his brethren, and could not come at him for the press.

8:6 *upon a rock*. On rocky soil or on thin soil covering rock. Palestine is a stony country.

8:16 *a candle*. Lit., a lamp, which was a small clay dish in which olive oil and a wick were placed. It gave a feeble light at best (when placed on a lampstand).

20 And it was told him *by certain* which said, Thy mother and thy brethren stand without, desiring to see thee.

21 And he answered and said unto them, My mother and my brethren are these which hear the word of God, and do it.

7 *Ministry in storms*, 8:22–25

22 ¶ Now it came to pass on a certain day, that he went into a ship with his disciples: and he said unto them, Let us go over unto the other side of the lake. And they launched forth.

23 But as they sailed he fell asleep: and there came down a storm of wind on the lake; and they were filled *with water*, and were in jeopardy.

24 And they came to him, and awoke him, saying, Master, master, we perish. Then he arose, and rebuked the wind and the raging of the water: and they ceased, and there was a calm.

25 And he said unto them, Where is your faith? And they being afraid wondered, saying one to another, What manner of man is this! for he commandeth even the winds and water, and they obey him.

8 *Ministry over demons*, 8:26–39

26 ¶ And they arrived at the country of the Gad'arēnes, which is over against Galilee.

27 And when he went forth to land, there met him out of the city a certain man, which had devils long time, and ware no clothes, neither abode in *any* house, but in the tombs.

28 When he saw Jesus, he cried out, and fell down before him, and with a loud voice said, What have I to do with thee, Jesus, *thou* Son of God most high? I beseech thee, torment me not.

29 (For he had commanded the unclean spirit to come out of the man. For oftentimes it had caught him: and he was kept bound with chains and in fetters; and he brake the bands, and was driven of the devil into the wilderness.)

30 And Jesus asked him, saying, What is thy name?

8:21 *My mother and my brethren.* Those who belong to God's family are closer to Christ than those related to Him by natural birth.
8:28 *Gadarenes.* On the E. shore of the Lake of Galilee.
8:30 *Legion.* See note at Mark 5:9.

And he said, Legion: because many devils were entered into him.

31 And they besought him that he would not command them to go out into the deep.

32 And there was there an herd of many swine feeding on the mountain: and they besought him that he would suffer them to enter into them. And he suffered them.

33 Then went the devils out of the man, and entered into the swine: and the herd ran violently down a steep place into the lake, and were choked.

34 When they that fed *them* saw what was done, they fled, and went and told *it* in the city and in the country.

35 Then they went out to see what was done; and came to Jesus, and found the man, out of whom the devils were departed, sitting at the feet of Jesus, clothed, and in his right mind: and they were afraid.

36 They also which saw *it* told them by what means he that was possessed of the devils was healed.

37 ¶ Then the whole multitude of the country of the Gad'arēnes round about besought him to depart from them; for they were taken with great fear: and he went up into the ship, and returned back again.

38 Now the man out of whom the devils were departed besought him that he might be with him: but Jesus sent him away, saying,

39 Return to thine own house, and shew how great things God hath done unto thee. And he went his way, and published throughout the whole city how great things Jesus had done unto him.

9 *Ministry in death and despair*, 8:40–56

40 And it came to pass, that, when Jesus was returned, the people *gladly* received him: for they were all waiting for him.

41 ¶ And, behold, there came a man named Jāī'rus, and he was a ruler of the synagogue: and he fell down at Jesus' feet, and besought him that he would come into his house:

42 For he had one only daughter, about twelve years of age, and she lay a dying. But as he went the people thronged him.

43 ¶ And a woman having an issue of blood twelve years, which had spent all her living upon physicians, neither could be healed of any,

8:31 *the deep*. Lit., the abyss, the place to which all evil spirits will ultimately be consigned (Rev. 9:1; 20:1, 3).
8:43 Luke makes clear that this chronic hemorrhage was an incurable condition.

44 Came behind *him*, and touched the border of his garment: and immediately her issue of blood stanched.

45 And Jesus said, Who touched me? When all denied, Peter and they that were with him said, Master, the multitude throng thee and press *thee*, and sayest thou, Who touched me?

46 And Jesus said, Somebody hath touched me: for I perceive that virtue is gone out of me.

47 And when the woman saw that she was not hid, she came trembling, and falling down before him, she declared unto him before all the people for what cause she had touched him, and how she was healed immediately.

48 And he said unto her, Daughter, be of good comfort: thy faith hath made thee whole; go in peace.

49 ¶ While he yet spake, there cometh one from the ruler of the synagogue's *house*, saying to him, Thy daughter is dead; trouble not the Master.

50 But when Jesus heard *it*, he answered him, saying, Fear not: believe only, and she shall be made whole.

51 And when he came into the house, he suffered no man to go in, save Peter, and James, and John, and the father and the mother of the maiden.

52 And all wept, and bewailed her: but he said, Weep not; she is not dead, but sleepeth.

53 And they laughed him to scorn, knowing that she was dead.

54 And he put them all out, and took her by the hand, and called, saying, Maid, arise.

55 And her spirit came again, and she arose straightway: and he commanded to give her meat.

56 And her parents were astonished: but he charged them that they should tell no man what was done.

10 *Ministry through the disciples*, 9:1–9

9 Then he called his twelve disciples together, and gave them power and authority over all devils, and to cure diseases.

2 And he sent them to preach the kingdom of God, and to heal the sick.

8:44 *the border of his garment*. This was a tassel which a rabbi wore on his outer garment. The garment was draped over the back so that the tassel of one corner hung between the shoulder blades.

8:46 *virtue*. Lit., power.

8:52 *she is not dead, but sleepeth*. The mourners looked on death as irreversible, so Christ called it sleep since (though the girl was actually dead) she would be awakened to life once again.

3 And he said unto them, Take nothing for *your* journey, neither staves, nor scrip, neither bread, neither money; neither have two coats apiece.

4 And whatsoever house ye enter into, there abide, and thence depart.

5 And whosoever will not receive you, when ye go out of that city, shake off the very dust from your feet for a testimony against them.

6 And they departed, and went through the towns, preaching the gospel, and healing every where.

7 ¶ Now Herod the te'trarch heard of all that was done by him: and he was perplexed, because that it was said of some, that John was risen from the dead;

8 And of some, that Ēlī'as had appeared; and of others, that one of the old prophets was risen again.

9 And Herod said, John have I beheaded: but who is this, of whom I hear such things? And he desired to see him.

11 *Ministry to physical needs*, 9:10–17

10 ¶ And the apostles, when they were returned, told him all that they had done. And he took them, and went aside privately into a desert place belonging to the city called Bethsā'ida.

11 And the people, when they knew *it*, followed him: and he received them, and spake unto them of the kingdom of God, and healed them that had need of healing.

12 And when the day began to wear away, then came the twelve, and said unto him, Send the multitude away, that they may go into the towns and country round about, and lodge, and get victuals: for we are here in a desert place.

13 But he said unto them, Give ye them to eat. And they said, We have no more but five loaves and two fishes; except we should go and buy meat for all this people.

14 For they were about five thousand men. And he said

9:3 See Luke 22:35–36 for a change of orders. See note at Matt. 10:19.

9:5 *shake off the very dust*. See note at Mark 6:11.

9:7 *Herod the tetrarch*. Herod Antipas, tetrarch of Galilee and Perea 4 B.C.–A.D. 39.

9:10 *into a desert place*. This does not mean a barren place but uninhabited. Bethsaida was a small town on the N. shore of the Lake of Galilee.

9:13 *loaves . . . fishes*. The loaves were round cakes (like biscuits) and the fish were small smoked or pickled fish, typical food of the poor in Palestine.

to his disciples, Make them sit down by fifties in a company.

15 And they did so, and made them all sit down.

16 Then he took the five loaves and the two fishes, and looking up to heaven, he blessed them, and brake, and gave to the disciples to set before the multitude.

17 And they did eat, and were all filled: and there was taken up of fragments that remained to them twelve baskets.

12 *Ministry of prediction*, 9:18–50

18 ¶ And it came to pass, as he was alone praying, his disciples were with him: and he asked them, saying, Whom say the people that I am?

19 They answering said, John the Baptist; but some *say*, Ēlī'as; and others *say*, that one of the old prophets is risen again.

20 He said unto them, But whom say ye that I am? Peter answering said, The Christ of God.

21 And he straitly charged them, and commanded *them* to tell no man that thing;

22 Saying, The Son of man must suffer many things, and be rejected of the elders and chief priests and scribes, and be slain, and be raised the third day.

23 ¶ And he said to *them* all, If any *man* will come after me, let him deny himself, and take up his cross daily, and follow me.

24 For whosoever will save his life shall lose it: but whosoever will lose his life for my sake, the same shall save it.

25 For what is a man advantaged, if he gain the whole world, and lose himself, or be cast away?

26 For whosoever shall be ashamed of me and of my words, of him shall the Son of man be ashamed, when he shall come in his own glory, and *in his* Father's, and of the holy angels.

27 But I tell you of a truth, there be some standing here, which shall not taste of death, till they see the kingdom of God.

28 ¶ And it came to pass about an eight days after these

9:18–21 See notes at Matt. 16:13, 14.
9:23 *cross*. This is the first mention of a cross in Luke. The cross was well known as an instrument of death, so it represents here the death or separation from the old life that must mark a disciple (Rom. 8:13). See note at Matt. 10:38.
9:27–36 See notes at Matt. 16:28; 17:1, 2, 4; Mark 9:5.

sayings, he took Peter and John and James, and went up into a mountain to pray.

29 And as he prayed, the fashion of his countenance was altered, and his raiment *was* white *and* glistering.

30 And, behold, there talked with him two men, which were Moses and Ēli′as:

31 Who appeared in glory, and spake of his decease which he should accomplish at Jerusalem.

32 But Peter and they that were with him were heavy with sleep: and when they were awake, they saw his glory, and the two men that stood with him.

33 And it came to pass, as they departed from him, Peter said unto Jesus, Master, it is good for us to be here: and let us make three tabernacles; one for thee, and one for Moses, and one for Ēli′as: not knowing what he said.

34 While he thus spake, there came a cloud, and overshadowed them: and they feared as they entered into the cloud.

35 And there came a voice out of the cloud, saying, This is my beloved Son: hear him.

36 And when the voice was past, Jesus was found alone. And they kept *it* close, and told no man in those days any of those things which they had seen.

37 ¶ And it came to pass, that on the next day, when they were come down from the hill, much people met him.

38 And, behold, a man of the company cried out, saying, Master, I beseech thee, look upon my son: for he is mine only child.

39 And, lo, a spirit taketh him, and he suddenly crieth out; and it teareth him that he foameth again, and bruising him hardly departeth from him.

40 And I besought thy disciples to cast him out; and they could not.

41 And Jesus answering said, O faithless and perverse generation, how long shall I be with you, and suffer you? Bring thy son hither.

42 And as he was yet a coming, the devil threw him down, and tare *him*. And Jesus rebuked the unclean spirit, and healed the child, and delivered him again to his father.

43 ¶ And they were all amazed at the mighty power of God. But while they wondered every one at all things which Jesus did, he said unto his disciples,

44 Let these sayings sink down into your ears: for the Son of man shall be delivered into the hands of men.

9:40 *they could not.* The reason was that the disciples failed to pray (Mark 9:29).

45 But they understood not this saying, and it was hid from them, that they perceived it not: and they feared to ask him of that saying.

46 ¶ Then there arose a reasoning among them, which of them should be greatest.

47 And Jesus, perceiving the thought of their heart, took a child, and set him by him,

48 And said unto them, Whosoever shall receive this child in my name receiveth me: and whosoever shall receive me receiveth him that sent me: for he that is least among you all, the same shall be great.

49 ¶ And John answered and said, Master, we saw one casting out devils in thy name; and we forbad him, because he followeth not with us.

50 And Jesus said unto him, Forbid *him* not: for he that is not against us is for us.

IV THE REPUDIATION OF THE SON OF MAN BY MEN, 9:51–19:27

A Rejection by Samaritans, 9:51–56

51 ¶ And it came to pass, when the time was come that he should be received up, he stedfastly set his face to go to Jerusalem,

52 And sent messengers before his face: and they went, and entered into a village of the Samaritans, to make ready for him.

53 And they did not receive him, because his face was as though he would go to Jerusalem.

54 And when his disciples James and John saw *this*, they said, Lord, wilt thou that we command fire to come down from heaven, and consume them, even as Ēlī′as did?

55 But he turned, and rebuked them, and said, Ye know not what manner of spirit ye are of.

56 For the Son of man is not come to destroy men's lives, but to save *them*. And they went to another village.

B Rejection by Worldly Men, 9:57–62

57 ¶ And it came to pass, that, as they went in the way, a certain *man* said unto him, Lord, I will follow thee whithersoever thou goest.

9:49 *devils*=demons.
9:50 *he that is not against us is for us.* This is the test by which others are tried. In 11:23 is a test by which one tries himself.
9:54 *as Elias did.* See 2 Kings 1:10–12.

58 And Jesus said unto him, Foxes have holes, and birds
of the air *have* nests; but the Son of man hath not where
to lay *his* head.

59 And he said unto another, Follow me. But he said,
Lord, suffer me first to go and bury my father.

60 Jesus said unto him, Let the dead bury their dead:
but go thou and preach the kingdom of God.

61 And another also said, Lord, I will follow thee; but
let me first go bid them farewell, which are at home at
my house.

62 And Jesus said unto him, No man, having put his
hand to the plough, and looking back, is fit for the kingdom of God.

C Commissioning of the Seventy, 10:1–24

10 After these things the Lord appointed other seventy
also, and sent them two and two before his face
into every city and place, whither he himself would come.

2 Therefore said he unto them, The harvest truly *is*
great, but the labourers *are* few: pray ye therefore the Lord
of the harvest, that he would send forth labourers into his
harvest.

3 Go your ways: behold, I send you forth as lambs
among wolves.

4 Carry neither purse, nor scrip, nor shoes: and salute
no man by the way.

5 And into whatsoever house ye enter, first say, Peace
be to this house.

6 And if the son of peace be there, your peace shall rest
upon it: if not, it shall turn to you again.

7 And in the same house remain, eating and drinking

9:58 *Son of man.* For the meaning of this title see note at Matt.
8:20.

9:59 *bury my father.* The father had not died; the speaker meant
that he was obligated to care for him until he died.

9:60 *Let the dead bury their dead.* I.e., let those who are
spiritually dead bury those who die physically. The claims of
the kingdom are paramount.

9:62 *looking back.* This will make the furrow crooked.

10:1 *seventy.* Only Luke records this mission. The fact that 70
people could be sent out shows that Jesus must have had a large
following.

10:4 *salute no man by the way.* The urgency of the mission did
not allow for the usual elaborate ceremonial greetings.

10:6 *the son of peace.* A Hebrew idiom meaning "a peaceful
man."

such things as they give: for the labourer is worthy of his hire. Go not from house to house.

8 And into whatsoever city ye enter, and they receive you, eat such things as are set before you:

9 And heal the sick that are therein, and say unto them, The kingdom of God is come nigh unto you.

10 But into whatsoever city ye enter, and they receive you not, go your ways out into the streets of the same, and say,

11 Even the very dust of your city, which cleaveth on us, we do wipe off against you: notwithstanding be ye sure of this, that the kingdom of God is come nigh unto you.

12 But I say unto you, that it shall be more tolerable in that day for Sodom, than for that city.

13 Woe unto thee, Chōrā'zin! woe unto thee, Bethsā'ida! for if the mighty works had been done in Tyre and Sidon, which have been done in you, they had a great while ago repented, sitting in sackcloth and ashes.

14 But it shall be more tolerable for Tyre and Sidon at the judgment, than for you.

15 And thou, Caper'naum, which art exalted to heaven, shalt be thrust down to hell.

16 He that heareth you heareth me; and he that despiseth you despiseth me; and he that despiseth me despiseth him that sent me.

17 ¶ And the seventy returned again with joy, saying, Lord, even the devils are subject unto us through thy name.

18 And he said unto them, I beheld Satan as lightning fall from heaven.

19 Behold, I give unto you power to tread on serpents and scorpions, and over all the power of the enemy: and nothing shall by any means hurt you.

20 Notwithstanding in this rejoice not, that the spirits are subject unto you; but rather rejoice, because your names are written in heaven.

21 ¶ In that hour Jesus rejoiced in spirit, and said, I thank thee, O Father, Lord of heaven and earth, that thou hast hid these things from the wise and prudent, and hast revealed them unto babes: even so, Father; for so it seemed good in thy sight.

22 All things are delivered to me of my Father: and no

10:12 *in that day.* I.e., the day of judgment. The judgment on Sodom is recorded in Gen. 19.

10:18 *Satan . . . fall from heaven.* The power of Satan was broken, and the success of the seventy over demons was proof of it (v. 17).

man knoweth who the Son is, but the Father; and who the Father is, but the Son, and *he* to whom the Son will reveal *him*.

23 ¶ And he turned him unto *his* disciples, and said privately, Blessed *are* the eyes which see the things that ye see:

24 For I tell you, that many prophets and kings have desired to see those things which ye see, and have not seen *them*; and to hear those things which ye hear, and have not heard *them*.

D Rejection by a Lawyer
(Parable of the Good Samaritan), 10:25-37

25 ¶ And, behold, a certain lawyer stood up, and tempted him, saying, Master, what shall I do to inherit eternal life?

26 He said unto him, What is written in the law? how readest thou?

27 And he answering said, Thou shalt love the Lord thy God with all thy heart, and with all thy soul, and with all thy strength, and with all thy mind; and thy neighbour as thyself.

28 And he said unto him, Thou hast answered right: this do, and thou shalt live.

29 But he, willing to justify himself, said unto Jesus, And who is my neighbour?

30 And Jesus answering said, A certain *man* went down from Jerusalem to Jericho, and fell among thieves, which stripped him of his raiment, and wounded *him*, and departed, leaving *him* half dead.

31 And by chance there came down a certain priest that way: and when he saw him, he passed by on the other side.

32 And likewise a Levite, when he was at the place, came and looked *on him*, and passed by on the other side.

33 But a certain Samaritan, as he journeyed, came

10:25 *a certain lawyer.* I.e., a scribe. See note at Matt. 2:4.

10:27 See Deut. 6:5; Lev. 19:18.

10:30 *went down from Jerusalem to Jericho.* The steeply descending road winds through rocky places that easily hide robbers.

10:33 *a certain Samaritan.* The Samaritans were descendants of colonists whom the Assyrian kings planted in Palestine after the fall of the Northern Kingdom in 721 B.C. They were despised by the Jews because of their mixed Gentile blood and their different worship, which centered at Mt. Gerizim (John 4:20-22).

where he was: and when he saw him, he had compassion on *him,*

34 And went to *him,* and bound up his wounds, pouring in oil and wine, and set him on his own beast, and brought him to an inn, and took care of him.

35 And on the morrow when he departed, he took out two pence, and gave *them* to the host, and said unto him, Take care of him; and whatsoever thou spendest more, when I come again, I will repay thee.

36 Which now of these three, thinkest thou, was neighbour unto him that fell among the thieves?

37 And he said, He that shewed mercy on him. Then said Jesus unto him, Go, and do thou likewise.

E Reception at Bethany, 10:38–42

38 ¶ Now it came to pass, as they went, that he entered into a certain village: and a certain woman named Martha received him into her house.

39 And she had a sister called Mary, which also sat at Jesus' feet, and heard his word.

40 But Martha was cumbered about much serving, and came to him, and said, Lord, dost thou not care that my sister hath left me to serve alone? bid her therefore that she help me.

41 And Jesus answered and said unto her, Martha, Martha, thou art careful and troubled about many things:

42 But one thing is needful: and Mary hath chosen that good part, which shall not be taken away from her.

F Instruction on Prayer, 11:1–13

11 And it came to pass, that, as he was praying in a certain place, when he ceased, one of his disciples said unto him, Lord, teach us to pray, as John also taught his disciples.

2 And he said unto them, When ye pray, say, Our Father which art in heaven, Hallowed be thy name. Thy kingdom come. Thy will be done, as in heaven, so in earth.

10:38 *a certain village.* I.e., Bethany (John 12:1).
10:40 *cumbered*=distracted.
10:41 *thou art careful*=you are anxious.
10:42 *one thing is needful.* One simple dish for the meal is all that is necessary, rather than the elaborate preparations Martha had made.
11:1 *teach us to pray.* It was customary for famous rabbis to compose special prayers.
11:2–4 See notes at Matt. 6:9, 11, 12.

3 Give us day by day our daily bread.

4 And forgive us our sins; for we also forgive every one that is indebted to us. And lead us not into temptation; but deliver us from evil.

5 And he said unto them, Which of you shall have a friend, and shall go unto him at midnight, and say unto him, Friend, lend me three loaves;

6 For a friend of mine in his journey is come to me, and I have nothing to set before him?

7 And he from within shall answer and say, Trouble me not: the door is now shut, and my children are with me in bed; I cannot rise and give thee.

8 I say unto you, Though he will not rise and give him, because he is his friend, yet because of his importunity he will rise and give him as many as he needeth.

9 And I say unto you, Ask, and it shall be given you; seek, and ye shall find; knock, and it shall be opened unto you.

10 For every one that asketh receiveth; and he that seeketh findeth; and to him that knocketh it shall be opened.

11 If a son shall ask bread of any of you that is a father, will he give him a stone? or if *he ask* a fish, will he for a fish give him a serpent?

12 Or if he shall ask an egg, will he offer him a scorpion?

13 If ye then, being evil, know how to give good gifts unto your children: how much more shall *your* heavenly Father give the Holy Spirit to them that ask him?

G Rejection by the Nation, 11:14–36

14 ¶ And he was casting out a devil, and it was dumb. And it came to pass, when the devil was gone out, the dumb spake; and the people wondered.

15 But some of them said, He casteth out devils through Bēel'zebub the chief of the devils.

16 And others, tempting *him*, sought of him a sign from heaven.

17 But he, knowing their thoughts, said unto them, Every kingdom divided against itself is brought to desolation; and a house *divided* against a house falleth.

18 If Satan also be divided against himself, how shall

11:8 *importunity*=persistence.
11:13 *give the Holy Spirit.* Since the day of Pentecost the gift of the Spirit is given to all believers (Acts 10:45; Rom. 8:9).
11:15 *Beelzebub.* See note at Matt. 10:25.

his kingdom stand? because ye say that I cast out devils through Bēel'zebub.

19 And if I by Bēel'zebub cast out devils, by whom do your sons cast *them* out? therefore shall they be your judges.

20 But if I with the finger of God cast out devils, no doubt the kingdom of God is come upon you.

21 When a strong man armed keepeth his palace, his goods are in peace:

22 But when a stronger than he shall come upon him, and overcome him, he taketh from him all his armour wherein he trusted, and divideth his spoils.

23 He that is not with me is against me: and he that gathereth not with me scattereth.

24 When the unclean spirit is gone out of a man, he walketh through dry places, seeking rest; and finding none, he saith, I will return unto my house whence I came out.

25 And when he cometh, he findeth *it* swept and garnished.

26 Then goeth he, and taketh *to him* seven other spirits more wicked than himself; and they enter in, and dwell there: and the last *state* of that man is worse than the first.

27 ¶ And it came to pass, as he spake these things, a certain woman of the company lifted up her voice, and said unto him, Blessed *is* the womb that bare thee, and the paps which thou hast sucked.

28 But he said, Yea rather, blessed *are* they that hear the word of God, and keep it.

29 ¶ And when the people were gathered thick together, he began to say, This is an evil generation: they seek a sign; and there shall no sign be given it, but the sign of Jonas the prophet.

30 For as Jonas was a sign unto the Nin'evītes, so shall also the Son of man be to this generation.

31 The queen of the south shall rise up in the judgment with the men of this generation, and condemn them: for she came from the utmost parts of the earth to hear the wisdom of Solomon; and, behold, a greater than Solomon *is* here.

11:21–22 The *strong man* (v. 21) is Satan; the *stronger* (v. 22) is Christ (4:18).

11:24 *my house*=the life of the person the demon indwelt.

11:26 *worse.* See 2 Pet. 2:20–21. Notice also that some demons are more wicked than others.

11:30 *Jonas was a sign* of judgment. See note at Matt. 12:39. To look at Jonah was to see the sign because of the appearance of his skin due to the effects of being in the fish's belly.

32 The men of Nin'evē shall rise up in the judgment with this generation, and shall condemn it: for they repented at the preaching of Jonas; and, behold, a greater than Jonas *is* here.

33 No man, when he hath lighted a candle, putteth *it* in a secret place, neither under a bushel, but on a candlestick, that they which come in may see the light.

34 The light of the body is the eye: therefore when thine eye is single, thy whole body also is full of light; but when *thine eye* is evil, thy body also *is* full of darkness.

35 Take heed therefore that the light which is in thee be not darkness.

36 If thy whole body therefore *be* full of light, having no part dark, the whole shall be full of light, as when the bright shining of a candle doth give thee light.

H Rejection by Pharisees and Lawyers, 11:37–54

37 ¶ And as he spake, a certain Pharisee besought him to dine with him: and he went in, and sat down to meat.

38 And when the Pharisee saw *it*, he marvelled that he had not first washed before dinner.

39 And the Lord said unto him, Now do ye Pharisees make clean the outside of the cup and the platter; but your inward part is full of ravening and wickedness.

40 *Ye* fools, did not he that made that which is without make that which is within also?

41 But rather give alms of such things as ye have; and, behold, all things are clean unto you.

42 But woe unto you, Pharisees! for ye tithe mint and rue and all manner of herbs, and pass over judgment and the love of God: these ought ye to have done, and not to leave the other undone.

43 Woe unto you, Pharisees! for ye love the uppermost seats in the synagogues, and greetings in the markets.

44 Woe unto you, scribes and Pharisees, hypocrites! for

11:32 *they repented.* See Jon. 3:5–9; 4:11.

11:37 *and sat down to meat.* Christ often used dinner invitations as opportunities to reach people (Luke 5:29; 7:36; 14:1, 19:5; John 2:1–12; 12:1–2).

11:42 *ye tithe.* See note at Matt. 23:23.

11:43 *the uppermost seats.* The front seats were usually reserved for the most important members.

11:44 *graves which appear not*=graves which are not seen. To step on a grave, even without knowing it, defiled a man (Num. 19:16). Jesus says that the Pharisees cause men to break the law and defile themselves.

ye are as graves which appear not, and the men that walk over *them* are not aware *of them*.

45 ¶ Then answered one of the lawyers, and said unto him, Master, thus saying thou reproachest us also.

46 And he said, Woe unto you also, *ye* lawyers! for ye lade men with burdens grievous to be borne, and ye yourselves touch not the burdens with one of your fingers.

47 Woe unto you! for ye build the sepulchres of the prophets, and your fathers killed them.

48 Truly ye bear witness that ye allow the deeds of your fathers: for they indeed killed them, and ye build their sepulchres.

49 Therefore also said the wisdom of God, I will send them prophets and apostles, and *some* of them they shall slay and persecute:

50 That the blood of all the prophets, which was shed from the foundation of the world, may be required of this generation;

51 From the blood of Abel unto the blood of Zacharī'as, which perished between the altar and the temple: verily I say unto you, It shall be required of this generation.

52 Woe unto you, lawyers! for ye have taken away the key of knowledge: ye entered not in yourselves, and them that were entering in ye hindered.

53 And as he said these things unto them, the scribes and the Pharisees began to urge *him* vehemently, and to provoke him to speak of many things:

54 Laying wait for him, and seeking to catch something out of his mouth, that they might accuse him.

I Instruction in the Light of Rejection, 12:1–19:27

1 Concerning hypocrisy, 12:1–12

12 In the mean time, when there were gathered together an innumerable multitude of people, insomuch that they trode one upon another, he began to say unto his disciples first of all, Beware ye of the leaven of the Pharisees, which is hypocrisy.

2 For there is nothing covered, that shall not be revealed; neither hid, that shall not be known.

3 Therefore whatsoever ye have spoken in darkness shall be heard in the light; and that which ye have spoken in the ear in closets shall be proclaimed upon the housetops.

4 And I say unto you my friends, Be not afraid of them that kill the body, and after that have no more that they can do.

11:51 *unto the blood of Zacharias.* See note at Matt. 23:35.

5 But I will forewarn you whom ye shall fear: Fear him, which after he hath killed hath power to cast into hell; yea, I say unto you, Fear him.

6 Are not five sparrows sold for two farthings, and not one of them is forgotten before God?

7 But even the very hairs of your head are all numbered. Fear not therefore: ye are of more value than many sparrows.

8 Also I say unto you, Whosoever shall confess me before men, him shall the Son of man also confess before the angels of God:

9 But he that denieth me before men shall be denied before the angels of God.

10 And whosoever shall speak a word against the Son of man, it shall be forgiven him: but unto him that blasphemeth against the Holy Ghost it shall not be forgiven.

11 And when they bring you unto the synagogues, and *unto* magistrates, and powers, take ye no thought how or what thing ye shall answer, or what ye shall say:

12 For the Holy Ghost shall teach you in the same hour what ye ought to say.

2 *Concerning coveteousness,* 12:13–34

13 ¶ And one of the company said unto him, Master, speak to my brother, that he divide the inheritance with me.

14 And he said unto him, Man, who made me a judge or a divider over you?

15 And he said unto them, Take heed, and beware of covetousness: for a man's life consisteth not in the abundance of the things which he possesseth.

16 And he spake a parable unto them, saying, The ground of a certain rich man brought forth plentifully:

17 And he thought within himself, saying, What shall I do, because I have no room where to bestow my fruits?

18 And he said, This will I do: I will pull down my

12:5 *Fear him.* I.e., God, who alone has the power to cast into hell (Rev. 20:10).

12:6 *five sparrows.* Sparrows were so cheap that although they sold two for a cent (Matt. 10:29), a fifth one was thrown in for the price of four. Yet the infinite God is concerned for each one.

12:10 *blasphemeth against the Holy Ghost.* See note at Matt. 12:31.

12:14 *who made me a judge?* Christ refused to assume the position of judge in this secular matter.

barns, and build greater; and there will I bestow all my fruits and my goods.

19 And I will say to my soul, Soul, thou hast much goods laid up for many years; take thine ease, eat, drink, *and* be merry.

20 But God said unto him, *Thou* fool, this night thy soul shall be required of thee: then whose shall those things be, which thou hast provided?

21 So *is* he that layeth up treasure for himself, and is not rich toward God.

22 ¶ And he said unto his disciples, Therefore I say unto you, Take no thought for your life, what ye shall eat; neither for the body, what ye shall put on.

23 The life is more than meat, and the body *is more* than raiment.

24 Consider the ravens: for they neither sow nor reap; which neither have storehouse nor barn; and God feedeth them: how much more are ye better than the fowls?

25 And which of you with taking thought can add to his stature one cubit?

26 If ye then be not able to do that thing which is least, why take ye thought for the rest?

27 Consider the lilies how they grow: they toil not, they spin not; and yet I say unto you, that Solomon in all his glory was not arrayed like one of these.

28 If then God so clothe the grass, which is to day in the field, and to morrow is cast into the oven; how much more *will he clothe* you, O ye of little faith?

29 And seek not ye what ye shall eat, or what ye shall drink, neither be ye of doubtful mind.

30 For all these things do the nations of the world seek after: and your Father knoweth that ye have need of these things.

31 ¶ But rather seek ye the kingdom of God; and all these things shall be added unto you.

32 Fear not, little flock; for it is your Father's good pleasure to give you the kingdom.

33 Sell that ye have, and give alms; provide yourselves bags which wax not old, a treasure in the heavens that faileth not, where no thief approacheth, neither moth corrupteth.

12:19–20 Man proposes; God disposes.
12:27 *lilies.* Probably anemones.
12:33 *Sell that ye have.* This is the way to lay up treasure in heaven. *which wax not old*=which do not become old.

34 For where your treasure is, there will your heart be also.

3 *Concerning faithfulness*, 12:35–48

35 Let your loins be girded about, and *your* lights burning;

36 And ye yourselves like unto men that wait for their lord, when he will return from the wedding; that when he cometh and knocketh, they may open unto him immediately.

37 Blessed *are* those servants, whom the lord when he cometh shall find watching: verily I say unto you, that he shall gird himself, and make them to sit down to meat, and will come forth and serve them.

38 And if he shall come in the second watch, or come in the third watch, and find *them* so, blessed are those servants.

39 And this know, that if the goodman of the house had known what hour the thief would come, he would have watched, and not have suffered his house to be broken through.

40 Be ye therefore ready also: for the Son of man cometh at an hour when ye think not.

41 ¶ Then Peter said unto him, Lord, speakest thou this parable unto us, or even to all?

42 And the Lord said, Who then is that faithful and wise steward, whom *his* lord shall make ruler over his household, to give *them their* portion of meat in due season?

43 Blessed *is* that servant, whom his lord when he cometh shall find so doing.

44 Of a truth I say unto you, that he will make him ruler over all that he hath.

45 But and if that servant say in his heart, My lord delayeth his coming; and shall begin to beat the men-

---

12:35 *let your loins be girded.* The long, flowing outer robe had to be tucked into a belt before traveling or working. The idea is: "be ready."

12:36 *when he will return from the wedding.* The groom first had supper with his friends, then went to the house of his bride to claim her, then returned to his own house. Although it might be quite late he expected his servants to be waiting and ready for him (the second watch was from 9 p.m. to midnight, v. 38). There is no place for slothful ease in the life of a believer while waiting for the return of the Lord.

12:39 *the goodman*=the master.

12:42 *portion of meat*=portion of food.

servants and maidens, and to eat and drink, and to be drunken;

46 The lord of that servant will come in a day when he looketh not for *him*, and at an hour when he is not aware, and will cut him in sunder, and will appoint him his portion with the unbelievers.

47 And that servant, which knew his lord's will, and prepared not *himself*, neither did according to his will, shall be beaten with many *stripes*.

48 But he that knew not, and did commit things worthy of stripes, shall be beaten with few *stripes*. For unto whomsoever much is given, of him shall be much required: and to whom men have committed much, of him they will ask the more.

4 Concerning division and signs, 12:49–59

49 ¶ I am come to send fire on the earth; and what will I, if it be already kindled?

50 But I have a baptism to be baptized with; and how am I straitened till it be accomplished!

51 Suppose ye that I am come to give peace on earth? I tell you, Nay; but rather division:

52 For from henceforth there shall be five in one house divided, three against two, and two against three.

53 The father shall be divided against the son, and the son against the father; the mother against the daughter, and the daughter against the mother; the mother in law against her daughter in law, and the daughter in law against her mother in law.

54 ¶ And he said also to the people, When ye see a cloud rise out of the west, straightway ye say, There cometh a shower; and so it is.

55 And when *ye see* the south wind blow, ye say, There will be heat; and it cometh to pass.

56 Ye hypocrites, ye can discern the face of the sky and of the earth; but how is it that ye do not discern this time?

57 Yea, and why even of yourselves judge ye not what is right?

58 ¶ When thou goest with thine adversary to the magistrate, *as thou art* in the way, give diligence that thou mayest be delivered from him; lest he hale thee to the

---

12:49 *fire*=judgment. *and what will I, if it be already kindled?*
Better, I wish it were already kindled.
12:50 *baptism*=His death.

judge, and the judge deliver thee to the officer, and the officer cast thee into prison.

59 I tell thee, thou shalt not depart thence, till thou hast paid the very last mite.

5 *Concerning repentance*, 13:1–9

13 There were present at that season some that told him of the Galilæans, whose blood Pilate had mingled with their sacrifices.

2 And Jesus answering said unto them, Suppose ye that these Galilæans were sinners above all the Galilæans, because they suffered such things?

3 I tell you, Nay: but, except ye repent, ye shall all likewise perish.

4 Or those eighteen, upon whom the tower in Siloam fell, and slew them, think ye that they were sinners above all men that dwelt in Jerusalem?

5 I tell you, Nay: but, except ye repent, ye shall all likewise perish.

6 ¶ He spake also this parable; A certain *man* had a fig tree planted in his vineyard; and he came and sought fruit thereon, and found none.

7 Then said he unto the dresser of his vineyard, Behold, these three years I come seeking fruit on this fig tree, and find none: cut it down; why cumbereth it the ground?

8 And he answering said unto him, Lord, let it alone this year also, till I shall dig about it, and dung *it*:

9 And if it bear fruit, *well*: and if not, *then* after that thou shalt cut it down.

6 *Concerning hypocrisy*, 13:10–17

10 And he was teaching in one of the synagogues on the sabbath.

11 ¶ And, behold, there was a woman which had a spirit

12:59 *mite*. The smallest of copper coins, worth one-eighth of a cent (see 21:2).

13:1 Though there is no other record of this incident, apparently some Galileans were slain by Pilate's soldiers while offering sacrifices at the temple, so that their blood and the blood of the sacrifices were mixed. The point Christ makes is that this did not happen to them because they were worse sinners than other Galileans, but that all need to repent (vv. 2–3).

13:6 *a fig tree*. The fruitless fig tree was symbolic of the Jewish people.

13:8–9 God's judgment is sure, and His patience is great.

of infirmity eighteen years, and was bowed together, and could in no wise lift up *herself*.

12 And when Jesus saw her, he called *her to him*, and said unto her, Woman, thou art loosed from thine infirmity.

13 And he laid *his* hands on her: and immediately she was made straight, and glorified God.

14 And the ruler of the synagogue answered with indignation, because that Jesus had healed on the sabbath day, and said unto the people, There are six days in which men ought to work: in them therefore come and be healed, and not on the sabbath day.

15 The Lord then answered him, and said, *Thou* hypocrite, doth not each one of you on the sabbath loose his ox or *his* ass from the stall, and lead *him* away to watering?

16 And ought not this woman, being a daughter of Abraham, whom Satan hath bound, lo, these eighteen years, be loosed from this bond on the sabbath day?

17 And when he had said these things, all his adversaries were ashamed: and all the people rejoiced for all the glorious things that were done by him.

7 *Concerning the kingdom*, 13:18–35

18 ¶ Then said he, Unto what is the kingdom of God like? and whereunto shall I resemble it?

19 It is like a grain of mustard seed, which a man took, and cast into his garden; and it grew, and waxed a great tree; and the fowls of the air lodged in the branches of it.

20 And again he said, Whereunto shall I liken the kingdom of God?

21 It is like leaven, which a woman took and hid in three measures of meal, till the whole was leavened.

22 And he went through the cities and villages, teaching, and journeying toward Jerusalem.

23 Then said one unto him, Lord, are there few that be saved? And he said unto them,

24 ¶ Strive to enter in at the strait gate: for many, I say unto you, will seek to enter in, and shall not be able.

13:16 *ought not this woman . . . be loosed*. Her healing was obligatory especially since animals could be watered on the Sabbath (v. 15).

13:19 *mustard seed*. From the smallest of seeds the mustard plant grows in one season to a shrub the size of a small tree.

13:21 *leaven*. See note at Matt. 13:33.

13:24 *strait gate*. This is Christ Himself, and there is no other way to heaven (John 14:6).

25 When once the master of the house is risen up, and
hath shut to the door, and ye begin to stand without, and
to knock at the door, saying, Lord, Lord, open unto us;
and he shall answer and say unto you, I know you not
whence ye are:

26 Then shall ye begin to say, We have eaten and drunk
in thy presence, and thou hast taught in our streets.

27 But he shall say, I tell you, I know you not whence
ye are; depart from me, all *ye* workers of iniquity.

28 There shall be weeping and gnashing of teeth, when
ye shall see Abraham, and Isaac, and Jacob, and all the
prophets, in the kingdom of God, and you *yourselves* thrust
out.

29 And they shall come from the east, and *from* the
west, and from the north, and *from* the south, and shall sit
down in the kingdom of God.

30 And, behold, there are last which shall be first, and
there are first which shall be last.

31 ¶ The same day there came certain of the Pharisees,
saying unto him, Get thee out, and depart hence: for
Herod will kill thee.

32 And he said unto them, Go ye, and tell that fox,
Behold, I cast out devils, and I do cures to day and to
morrow, and the third *day* I shall be perfected.

33 Nevertheless I must walk to day, and to morrow,
and the *day* following: for it cannot be that a prophet
perish out of Jerusalem.

34 O Jerusalem, Jerusalem, which killest the prophets,
and stonest them that are sent unto thee; how often would
I have gathered thy children together, as a hen *doth gather*
her brood under *her* wings, and ye would not!

35 Behold, your house is left unto you desolate: and
verily I say unto you, Ye shall not see me, until *the time*
come when ye shall say, Blessed *is* he that cometh in the
name of the Lord.

8 *Concerning inflexible people,* 14:1–6

14 And it came to pass, as he went into the house of
one of the chief Pharisees to eat bread on the
sabbath day, that they watched him.

13:32 *that* fox. Herod Antipas is described as a fox, known for
its use of cunning deceit to achieve its aims.

13:35 *your house is left unto you desolate.* This was fulfilled
when the temple was destroyed in A.D. 70 and the Jews expelled
under Hadrian in A.D. 135. *Blessed is He that cometh.* See
Ps. 118:26. This will be fulfilled at the second coming of Christ.

2 And, behold, there was a certain man before him which had the dropsy.

3 And Jesus answering spake unto the lawyers and Pharisees, saying, Is it lawful to heal on the sabbath day?

4 And they held their peace. And he took *him*, and healed him, and let him go;

5 And answered them, saying, Which of you shall have an ass or an ox fallen into a pit, and will not straightway pull him out on the sabbath day?

6 And they could not answer him again to these things.

9 *Concerning inflated people*, 14:7–11

7 ¶ And he put forth a parable to those which were bidden, when he marked how they chose out the chief rooms; saying unto them,

8 When thou art bidden of any *man* to a wedding, sit not down in the highest room; lest a more honourable man than thou be bidden of him;

9 And he that bade thee and him come and say to thee, Give this man place; and thou begin with shame to take the lowest room.

10 But when thou art bidden, go and sit down in the lowest room; that when he that bade thee cometh, he may say unto thee, Friend, go up higher: then shalt thou have worship in the presence of them that sit at meat with thee.

11 For whosoever exalteth himself shall be abased; and he that humbleth himself shall be exalted.

10 *Concerning invited people*, 14:12–14

12 ¶ Then said he also to him that bade him, When thou makest a dinner or a supper, call not thy friends, nor thy brethren, neither thy kinsmen, nor *thy* rich neighbours; lest they also bid thee again, and a recompence be made thee.

13 But when thou makest a feast, call the poor, the maimed, the lame, the blind:

14 And thou shalt be blessed; for they cannot recompense thee: for thou shalt be recompensed at the resurrection of the just.

14:2 *dropsy.* A swelling of the body due to retention of excessive liquid.
14:7 *chief rooms.* I.e., chief places or best seats.
14:10 *worship.* Better, honor or glory.
14:11 Humility is the path to promotion in the kingdom of God.

11 *Concerning indifferent people,* 14:15–24

15 ¶ And when one of them that sat at meat with him heard these things, he said unto him, Blessed *is* he that shall eat bread in the kingdom of God.

16 Then said he unto him, A certain man made a great supper, and bade many:

17 And sent his servant at supper time to say to them that were bidden, Come; for all things are now ready.

18 And they all with one *consent* began to make excuse. The first said unto him, I have bought a piece of ground, and I must needs go and see it: I pray thee have me excused.

19 And another said, I have bought five yoke of oxen, and I go to prove them: I pray thee have me excused.

20 And another said, I have married a wife, and therefore I cannot come.

21 So that servant came, and shewed his lord these things. Then the master of the house being angry said to his servant, Go out quickly into the streets and lanes of the city, and bring in hither the poor, and the maimed, and the halt, and the blind.

22 And the servant said, Lord, it is done as thou hast commanded, and yet there is room.

23 And the lord said unto the servant, Go out into the highways and hedges, and compel *them* to come in, that my house may be filled.

24 For I say unto you, That none of those men which were bidden shall taste of my supper.

12 *Concerning indulgent people,* 14:25–35

25 ¶ And there went great multitudes with him: and he turned, and said unto them,

26 If any *man* come to me, and hate not his father, and mother, and wife, and children, and brethren, and sisters, yea, and his own life also, he cannot be my disciple.

14:15 *Blessed is he* . . . A seemingly pious remark made for the purpose of dulling the point of Christ's teaching.

14:18–20 Excuses, excuses!

14:21 *halt*=lame.

14:25–33 The parable that precedes in vv. 16–24 expresses the open, compelling invitation to come to Christ in salvation. The teaching of vv. 25–33 cautions His followers to consider carefully the cost of full commitment to Christ in a life of service.

14:26 *hate.* This saying does not justify malice or ill will toward one's family, but it means that devotion to family must take second place to one's devotion to Christ.

27 And whosoever doth not bear his cross, and come after me, cannot be my disciple.

28 For which of you, intending to build a tower, sitteth not down first, and counteth the cost, whether he have *sufficient* to finish *it*?

29 Lest haply, after he hath laid the foundation, and is not able to finish *it*, all that behold *it* begin to mock him,

30 Saying, This man began to build, and was not able to finish.

31 Or what king, going to make war against another king, sitteth not down first, and consulteth whether he be able with ten thousand to meet him that cometh against him with twenty thousand?

32 Or else, while the other is yet a great way off, he sendeth an ambassage, and desireth conditions of peace.

33 So likewise, whosoever he be of you that forsaketh not all that he hath, he cannot be my disciple.

34 ¶ Salt *is* good: but if the salt have lost his savour, wherewith shall it be seasoned?

35 It is neither fit for the land, nor yet for the dunghill; *but* men cast it out. He that hath ears to hear, let him hear.

13 *Concerning God's love for sinners,* 15:1–32

15 Then drew near unto him all the publicans and sinners for to hear him.

2 And the Pharisees and scribes murmured, saying, This man receiveth sinners, and eateth with them.

3 ¶ And he spake this parable unto them, saying,

4 What man of you, having an hundred sheep, if he lose one of them, doth not leave the ninety and nine in the wilderness, and go after that which is lost, until he find it?

5 And when he hath found *it*, he layeth *it* on his shoulders, rejoicing.

6 And when he cometh home, he calleth together *his* friends and neighbours, saying unto them, Rejoice with me; for I have found my sheep which was lost.

7 I say unto you, that likewise joy shall be in heaven over one sinner that repenteth, more than over ninety and nine just persons, which need no repentance.

14:32 *an ambassage*=a delegation.
14:34 *salt*. See note at Matt. 5:13.
15:2 *This man receiveth sinners*. Since the Pharisees disdained publicans and sinners, Christ spoke these three parables to show God's interest in them.
15:4 *lose*. Eight times in this chapter the lostness of man is emphasized (vv. 4 [twice], 6, 8, 9, 17, 24, 32).

8 ¶ Either what woman having ten pieces of silver, if she lose one piece, doth not light a candle, and sweep the house, and seek diligently till she find *it?*

9 And when she hath found *it,* she calleth *her* friends and *her* neighbours together, saying, Rejoice with me; for I have found the piece which I had lost.

10 Likewise, I say unto you, there is joy in the presence of the angels of God over one sinner that repenteth.

11 ¶ And he said, A certain man had two sons:

12 And the younger of them said to *his* father, Father, give me the portion of goods that falleth *to me.* And he divided unto them *his* living.

13 And not many days after the younger son gathered all together, and took his journey into a far country, and there wasted his substance with riotous living.

14 And when he had spent all, there arose a mighty famine in that land; and he began to be in want.

15 And he went and joined himself to a citizen of that country; and he sent him into his fields to feed swine.

16 And he would fain have filled his belly with the husks that the swine did eat: and no man gave unto him.

17 And when he came to himself, he said, How many hired servants of my father's have bread enough and to spare, and I perish with hunger!

18 I will arise and go to my father, and will say unto him, Father, I have sinned against heaven, and before thee,

19 And am no more worthy to be called thy son: make me as one of thy hired servants.

20 And he arose, and came to his father. But when he was yet a great way off, his father saw him, and had compassion, and ran, and fell on his neck, and kissed him.

21 And the son said unto him, Father, I have sinned against heaven, and in thy sight, and am no more worthy to be called thy son.

22 But the father said to his servants, Bring forth the best robe, and put *it* on him; and put a ring on his hand, and shoes on *his* feet:

23 And bring hither the fatted calf, and kill *it;* and let us eat, and be merry:

24 For this my son was dead, and is alive again; he was lost, and is found. And they began to be merry.

15:8 *what woman.* The second parable using a woman shows that many women followed Christ and heard Him teach.

15:15 *to feed swine.* The lowest possible humiliation for a Jew!

15:18 *I have sinned.* Acknowledging one's personal responsibility for sin is the first step toward reconciliation.

25 Now his elder son was in the field: and as he came and drew nigh to the house, he heard musick and dancing.

26 And he called one of the servants, and asked what these things meant.

27 And he said unto him, Thy brother is come; and thy father hath killed the fatted calf, because he hath received him safe and sound.

28 And he was angry, and would not go in: therefore came his father out, and intreated him.

29 And he answering said to *his* father, Lo, these many years do I serve thee, neither transgressed I at any time thy commandment: and yet thou never gavest me a kid, that I might make merry with my friends:

30 But as soon as this thy son was come, which hath devoured thy living with harlots, thou hast killed for him the fatted calf.

31 And he said unto him, Son, thou art ever with me, and all that I have is thine.

32 It was meet that we should make merry, and be glad: for this thy brother was dead, and is alive again; and was lost, and is found.

14 *Concerning wealth*, 16:1–31

16 And he said also unto his disciples, There was a certain rich man, which had a steward; and the same was accused unto him that he had wasted his goods.

2 And he called him, and said unto him, How is it that I hear this of thee? give an account of thy stewardship; for thou mayest be no longer steward.

3 Then the steward said within himself, What shall I do? for my lord taketh away from me the stewardship: I cannot dig; to beg I am ashamed.

4 I am resolved what to do, that, when I am put out of the stewardship, they may receive me into their houses.

5 So he called every one of his lord's debtors *unto him,* and said unto the first, How much owest thou unto my lord?

6 And he said, An hundred measures of oil. And he said unto him, Take thy bill, and sit down quickly, and write fifty.

7 Then said he to another, And how much owest thou? And he said, An hundred measures of wheat. And he said unto him, Take thy bill, and write fourscore.

15:28 *And he was angry.* The elder son's attitude is the same as the Pharisees' (v. 2; 18:11–12). The words reflect self-righteousness.

8 And the lord commended the unjust steward, because he had done wisely: for the children of this world are in their generation wiser than the children of light.

9 And I say unto you, Make to yourselves friends of the mam'mon of unrighteousness; that, when ye fail, they may receive you into everlasting habitations.

10 He that is faithful in that which is least is faithful also in much: and he that is unjust in the least is unjust also in much.

11 If therefore ye have not been faithful in the unrighteous mam'mon, who will commit to your trust the true *riches?*

12 And if ye have not been faithful in that which is another man's, who shall give you that which is your own?

13 ¶ No servant can serve two masters: for either he will hate the one, and love the other; or else he will hold to the one, and despise the other. Ye cannot serve God and mam'mon.

14 And the Pharisees also, who were covetous, heard all these things: and they derided him.

15 And he said unto them, Ye are they which justify yourselves before men; but God knoweth your hearts: for that which is highly esteemed among men is abomination in the sight of God.

16 The law and the prophets *were* until John: since that time the kingdom of God is preached, and every man presseth into it.

17 And it is easier for heaven and earth to pass, than one tittle of the law to fail.

18 Whosoever putteth away his wife, and marrieth another, committeth adultery: and whosoever marrieth her that is put away from *her* husband committeth adultery.

16:8 *the lord.* I.e., the lord of the steward. *done wisely.* What is commended is the ingenuity, not the dishonesty, of the steward in using his present opportunities to prepare for the future. Likewise, the believer should use what he has in this life in the service of God in order to assure rewards in heaven (v. 9).

16:9 *mammon*=money or property.

16:11 *the true riches.* I.e., spiritual responsibilities.

16:12 Unfaithfulness in managing another's goods proves one unworthy to be given much of his own.

16:16 *every man presseth into it.* Men were crowding to enter the kingdom.

16:17 *tittle.* See note at Matt. 5:18.

16:18 *putteth away*=divorces. See notes at Matt. 5:32; 19:10.

19 ¶ There was a certain rich man, which was clothed in purple and fine linen, and fared sumptuously every day:

20 And there was a certain beggar named Lazarus, which was laid at his gate, full of sores,

21 And desiring to be fed with the crumbs which fell from the rich man's table: moreover the dogs came and licked his sores.

22 And it came to pass, that the beggar died, and was carried by the angels into Abraham's bosom: the rich man also died, and was buried;

23 And in hell he lift up his eyes, being in torments, and seeth Abraham afar off, and Lazarus in his bosom.

24 And he cried and said, Father Abraham, have mercy on me, and send Lazarus, that he may dip the tip of his finger in water, and cool my tongue; for I am tormented in this flame.

25 But Abraham said, Son, remember that thou in thy lifetime receivedst thy good things, and likewise Lazarus evil things: but now he is comforted, and thou art tormented.

26 And beside all this, between us and you there is a great gulf fixed: so that they which would pass from hence to you cannot; neither can they pass to us, that *would come* from thence.

27 Then he said, I pray thee therefore, father, that thou wouldest send him to my father's house:

28 For I have five brethren; that he may testify unto them, lest they also come into this place of torment.

29 Abraham saith unto him, They have Moses and the prophets; let them hear them.

30 And he said, Nay, father Abraham: but if one went unto them from the dead, they will repent.

16:19 *rich man.* His name is not given. Dives, which is sometimes said to be his name, is simply the Latin for "rich man." *fared sumptuously.* Lit., was merry every day. Life was one continual party for him.

16:22 *Abraham's bosom.* This is figurative speech for paradise, or the presence of God (Luke 23:43; 2 Cor. 12:4).

16:23 *in hell.* Lit., in hades. The unseen world in general, but specifically here the abode of the unsaved dead between death and judgment at the great white throne (Rev. 20:11–15). See note at Eph. 4:9. In this saying the Lord taught: (1) conscious existence after death; (2) the reality and torment of hell; (3) no second chance after death; and (4) the impossibility of the dead communicating with the living (v. 26). The two men in this story illustrate two different lives, two different deaths, and two different destinies.

31 And he said unto him, If they hear not Moses and the prophets, neither will they be persuaded, though one rose from the dead.

15 *Concerning forgiveness*, 17:1–6

17 Then said he unto the disciples, It is impossible but that offences will come: but woe *unto him*, through whom they come!

2 It were better for him that a millstone were hanged about his neck, and he cast into the sea, than that he should offend one of these little ones.

3 ¶ Take heed to yourselves: If thy brother trespass against thee, rebuke him; and if he repent, forgive him.

4 And if he trespass against thee seven times in a day, and seven times in a day turn again to thee, saying, I repent; thou shalt forgive him.

5 And the apostles said unto the Lord, Increase our faith.

6 And the Lord said, If ye had faith as a grain of mustard seed, ye might say unto this sycamine tree, Be thou plucked up by the root, and be thou planted in the sea; and it should obey you.

16 *Concerning service*, 17:7–10

7 But which of you, having a servant plowing or feeding cattle, will say unto him by and by, when he is come from the field, Go and sit down to meat?

8 And will not rather say unto him, Make ready wherewith I may sup, and gird thyself, and serve me, till I have eaten and drunken; and afterward thou shalt eat and drink?

9 Doth he thank that servant because he did the things that were commanded him? I trow not.

10 So likewise ye, when ye shall have done all those things which are commanded you, say. We are unprofitable servants: we have done that which was our duty to do.

17 *Concerning gratitude*, 17:11–19

11 ¶ And it came to pass, as he went to Jerusalem, that he passed through the midst of Samaria and Galilee.

17:2 *a millstone.* See note at Matt. 18:6. *offend*=cause to stumble or lead into sin.

17:6 *sycamine tree.* A tree of the mulberry family whose roots were regarded as being particularly strong, making it virtually impossible to uproot.

17:9 *I trow not*=I think or suppose not.

12 And as he entered into a certain village, there met him ten men that were lepers, which stood afar off:

13 And they lifted up *their* voices, and said, Jesus, Master, have mercy on us.

14 And when he saw *them*, he said unto them, Go shew yourselves unto the priests. And it came to pass, that, as they went, they were cleansed.

15 And one of them, when he saw that he was healed, turned back, and with a loud voice glorified God,

16 And fell down on *his* face at his feet, giving him thanks: and he was a Samaritan.

17 And Jesus answering said, Were there not ten cleansed? but where *are* the nine?

18 There are not found that returned to give glory to God, save this stranger.

19 And he said unto him, Arise, go thy way: thy faith hath made thee whole.

18 *Concerning the kingdom*, 17:20–37

20 ¶ And when he was demanded of the Pharisees, when the kingdom of God should come, he answered them and said, The kingdom of God cometh not with observation:

21 Neither shall they say, Lo here! or, lo there! for, behold, the kingdom of God is within you.

22 And he said unto the disciples, The days will come, when ye shall desire to see one of the days of the Son of man, and ye shall not see *it*.

23 And they shall say to you, See here; or, see there: go not after *them*, nor follow *them*.

24 For as the lightning, that lighteneth out of the one *part* under heaven, shineth unto the other *part* under heaven; so shall also the Son of man be in his day.

25 But first must he suffer many things, and be rejected of this generation.

17:12 *lepers*. See note at Luke 5:12.

17:14 *Go shew yourselves unto the priests*. The priest must certify the cleansing of a leper (Lev. 14:1–32). The men exhibited faith by starting on their way to the priest before being cleansed.

17:20 *with observation*=with outward show, like a political coup.

17:21 *the kingdom of God is within you*. Better, among you. The necessary elements of the kingdom were there assembled and present and needed only to be recognized. It cannot mean "within you," for the kingdom certainly was completely unconnected with the Pharisees to whom Jesus was speaking (v. 20).

26 And as it was in the days of Nō′ē, so shall it be also in the days of the Son of man.

27 They did eat, they drank, they married wives, they were given in marriage, until the day that Nō′ē, entered into the ark, and the flood came, and destroyed them all.

28 Likewise also as it was in the days of Lot; they did eat, they drank, they bought, they sold, they planted, they builded;

29 But the same day that Lot went out of Sodom it rained fire and brimstone from heaven, and destroyed *them* all.

30 Even thus shall it be in the day when the Son of man is revealed.

31 In that day, he which shall be upon the housetop, and his stuff in the house, let him not come down to take it away: and he that is in the field, let him likewise not return back.

32 Remember Lot's wife.

33 Whosoever shall seek to save his life shall lose it; and whosoever shall lose his life shall preserve it.

34 I tell you, in that night there shall be two *men* in one bed; the one shall be taken, and the other shall be left.

35 Two *women* shall be grinding together; the one shall be taken, and the other left.

36 Two *men* shall be in the field; the one shall be taken, and the other left.

37 And they answered and said unto him, Where, Lord? And he said unto them, Wheresoever the body *is*, thither will the eagles be gathered together.

19 *Concerning prayer*, 18:1–14

18 And he spake a parable unto them *to this end*, that men ought always to pray, and not to faint;

17:26–27 *in the days of Noe*=Noah. See Gen. 6. The things of v. 27 are not wrong; the people were unprepared for the judgment of the flood because they did not heed God's warnings through Noah.

17:28 *in the days of Lot*. See Gen. 19.

17:30 *Even thus shall it be*. Until the time of Christ's return, people will be prosperous and feel secure and unprepared for His return (as in the days of Noah and Lot).

17:32 *Lot's wife*. See Gen. 19:26.

17:37 *body*=corpse. *eagles*=vultures. A reference to the carnage of Armageddon (Rev. 19:17–19).

18:1 *always to pray and not to faint. always*=in every circumstance. *faint*=lose heart or be discouraged because answers do not come immediately.

2 Saying, There was in a city a judge, which feared not God, neither regarded man:

3 And there was a widow in that city; and she came unto him, saying, Avenge me of mine adversary.

4 And he would not for a while: but afterward he said within himself, Though I fear not God, nor regard man;

5 Yet because this widow troubleth me, I will avenge her, lest by her continual coming she weary me.

6 And the Lord said, Hear what the unjust judge saith.

7 And shall not God avenge his own elect, which cry day and night unto him, though he bear long with them?

8 I tell you that he will avenge them speedily. Nevertheless when the Son of man cometh, shall he find faith on the earth?

9 And he spake this parable unto certain which trusted in themselves that they were righteous, and despised others:

10 Two men went up into the temple to pray; the one a Pharisee, and the other a publican.

11 The Pharisee stood and prayed thus with himself, God, I thank thee, that I am not as other men *are*, extortioners, unjust, adulterers, or even as this publican.

12 I fast twice in the week, I give tithes of all that I possess.

13 And the publican, standing afar off, would not lift up so much as *his* eyes unto heaven, but smote upon his breast, saying, God be merciful to me a sinner.

14 I tell you, this man went down to his house justified *rather* than the other: for every one that exalteth himself shall be abased; and he that humbleth himself shall be exalted.

20 *Concerning entrance into the kingdom,* 18:15–30

15 And they brought unto him also infants, that he

18:8 *speedily.* Not necessarily immediately, but quickly when the answer begins to come. For other uses of the term see Rom. 16:20; Rev. 1:1. *shall he find faith on the earth?* This does not augur for improved spiritual conditions in the world before Christ's return.

18:12 *I fast.* See note at Matt. 9:14. *I give tithes.* See note at Matt. 23:23.

18:13 *God be merciful.* Lit., God be propitiated or satisfied. Now Christ is the propitiation or satisfaction for our sins (1 John 2:1).

18:14 The Pharisee saw God operating only on a merit system, and thus a God who could be put in man's debt through good works. The publican saw God operating on a mercy system, and thus a God in whom he could place his trust.

would touch them: but when *his* disciples saw *it*, they rebuked them.

16 But Jesus called them *unto him*, and said, Suffer little children to come unto me, and forbid them not: for of such is the kingdom of God.

17 Verily I say unto you, Whosoever shall not receive the kingdom of God as a little child shall in no wise enter therein.

18 And a certain ruler asked him, saying, Good Master, what shall I do to inherit eternal life?

19 And Jesus said unto him, Why callest thou me good? none *is* good, save one, *that is*, God.

20 Thou knowest the commandments, Do not commit adultery, Do not kill, Do not steal, Do not bear false witness, Honour thy father and thy mother.

21 And he said, All these have I kept from my youth up.

22 Now when Jesus heard these things, he said unto him, Yet lackest thou one thing: sell all that thou hast, and distribute unto the poor, and thou shalt have treasure in heaven: and come, follow me.

23 And when he heard this, he was very sorrowful: for he was very rich.

24 And when Jesus saw that he was very sorrowful, he said, How hardly shall they that have riches enter into the kingdom of God!

25 For it is easier for a camel to go through a needle's eye, than for a rich man to enter into the kingdom of God.

26 And they that heard *it* said, Who then can be saved?

27 And he said, The things which are impossible with men are possible with God.

28 Then Peter said, Lo, we have left all, and followed thee.

29 And he said unto them, Verily I say unto you, There is no man that hath left house, or parents, or brethren, or wife, or children, for the kingdom of God's sake,

30 Who shall not receive manifold more in this present time, and in the world to come life everlasting.

21 *Concerning His death,* 18:31–34

31 ¶ Then he took *unto him* the twelve, and said unto them, Behold, we go up to Jerusalem, and all things that

---

18:22 *Yet lackest thou one thing.* Apparently the man had kept the laws of v. 20, but Jesus saw his attachment to material things. Rather than admit this, the man turned his back on Christ's help.
18:25 *needle's eye.* See note at Matt. 19:24.

are written by the prophets concerning the Son of man
shall be accomplished.

32 For he shall be delivered unto the Gentiles, and shall
be mocked, and spitefully entreated, and spitted on:

33 And they shall scourge *him*, and put him to death:
and the third day he shall rise again.

34 And they understood none of these things: and this
saying was hid from them, neither knew they the things
which were spoken.

22 *Concerning salvation,* 18:35–19:10

35 ¶ And it came to pass, that as he was come nigh unto
Jericho, a certain blind man sat by the way side begging:

36 And hearing the multitude pass by, he asked what
it meant.

37 And they told him, that Jesus of Nazareth passeth by.

38 And he cried, saying, Jesus, *thou* Son of David, have
mercy on me.

39 And they which went before rebuked him, that he
should hold his peace: but he cried so much the more,
Thou Son of David, have mercy on me.

40 And Jesus stood, and commanded him to be brought
unto him: and when he was come near, he asked him,

41 Saying, What wilt thou that I shall do unto thee?
And he said, Lord, that I may receive my sight.

42 And Jesus said unto him, Receive thy sight: thy faith
hath saved thee.

43 And immediately he received his sight, and followed
him, glorifying God: and all the people, when they saw *it*,
gave praise unto God.

19 And *Jesus* entered and passed through Jericho.

2 And, behold, *there was* a man named Zacchæ´-
us, which was the chief among the publicans, and he was
rich.

3 And he sought to see Jesus who he was; and could not
for the press, because he was little of stature.

4 And he ran before, and climbed up into a sycomore

18:32 *spitefully entreated*=insulted.

18:35 *a certain blind man*. Concerning the differences in the
accounts in the Gospels see note at Matt. 20:29–34.

19:2 *publicans*. These were tax-collectors for the Romans. They
generally had a bad reputation, since the system was open to
abuse and extortion was common. The expression "chief
among the publicans" implies that Zacchaeus was responsible
for all the taxes of Jericho and had collectors under him.

tree to see him: for he was to pass that way.

5 And when Jesus came to the place, he looked up, and saw him, and said unto him, Zacchæus, make haste, and come down; for to day I must abide at thy house.

6 And he made haste, and came down, and received him joyfully.

7 And when they saw it, they all murmured, saying, That he was gone to be guest with a man that is a sinner.

8 And Zacchæus stood, and said unto the Lord; Behold, Lord, the half of my goods I give to the poor; and if I have taken any thing from any man by false accusation, I restore him fourfold.

9 And Jesus said unto him, This day is salvation come to this house, forsomuch as he also is a son of Abraham.

10 For the Son of man is come to seek and to save that which was lost.

23 Concerning faithfulness, 19:11-27

11 And as they heard these things, he added and spake a parable, because he was nigh to Jerusalem, and because they thought that the kingdom of God should immediately appear.

12 He said therefore, A certain nobleman went into a far country to receive for himself a kingdom, and to return.

13 And he called his ten servants, and delivered them ten pounds, and said unto them, Occupy till I come.

14 But his citizens hated him, and sent a message after him, saying, We will not have this man to reign over us.

15 And it came to pass, that when he was returned, having received the kingdom, then he commanded these servants to be called unto him, to whom he had given the money, that he might know how much every man had gained by trading.

19:8 This is Zacchaeus' declaration of what he intended to do from then on, now that his life had been changed by meeting Christ.

19:11 *because they thought.* The disciples still could not understand why they should not expect the triumph of the Messianic kingdom immediately (and without the cross).

19:13 *pounds.* A pound was a measure of money worth 100 drachmas or denarii. Notice that each servant received the same amount (in contrast to the parable of the talents in which each received according to his ability, Matt. 25:15). The pounds represent the equal opportunity of life itself; the talents, the different gifts God gives each individual. *Occupy*=trade.

16 Then came the first, saying, Lord, thy pound hath gained ten pounds.

17 And he said unto him, Well, thou good servant: because thou hast been faithful in a very little, have thou authority over ten cities.

18 And the second came, saying, Lord, thy pound hath gained five pounds.

19 And he said likewise to him, Be thou also over five cities.

20 And another came, saying, Lord, behold, *here is* thy pound, which I have kept laid up in a napkin:

. 21 For I feared thee, because thou art an austere man: thou takest up that thou layedst not down, and reapest that thou didst not sow.

22 And he saith unto him, Out of thine own mouth will I judge thee, *thou* wicked servant. Thou knewest that I was an austere man, taking up that I laid not down, and reaping that I did not sow:

23 Wherefore then gavest not thou my money into the bank, that at my coming I might have required mine own with usury?

24 And he said unto them that stood by, Take from him the pound, and give *it* to him that hath ten pounds.

25 (And they said unto him, Lord, he hath ten pounds.)

26 For I say unto you, That unto every one which hath shall be given; and from him that hath not, even that he hath shall be taken away from him.

27 But those mine enemies, which would not that I should reign over them, bring hither, and slay *them* before me.

V THE CONDEMNATION OF THE SON OF MAN FOR MEN, 19:28–23:56

A Sunday, 19:28–44

28 ¶ And when he had thus spoken, he went before, ascending up to Jerusalem.

29 And it came to pass, when he was come nigh to Beth'phagé and Bethany, at the mount called *the mount* of Olives, he sent two of his disciples,

19:23 *usury*. This means normal interest, not excessive interest (though that is the meaning of the word today).
19:29 *Bethphage*. Its site is unknown though it was near *Bethany* which was on the SE. side of the Mount of Olives.

30 Saying, Go ye into the village over against *you*; in the which at your entering ye shall find a colt tied, whereon yet never man sat: loose him, and bring *him hither*.

31 And if any man ask you, Why do ye loose *him?* thus shall ye say unto him, Because the Lord hath need of him.

32 And they that were sent went their way, and found even as he had said unto them.

33 And as they were loosing the colt, the owners thereof said unto them, Why loose ye the colt?

34 And they said, The Lord hath need of him.

35 And they brought him to Jesus: and they cast their garments upon the colt, and they set Jesus thereon.

36 And as he went, they spread their clothes in the way.

37 And when he was come nigh, even now at the descent of the mount of Olives, the whole multitude of the disciples began to rejoice and praise God with a loud voice for all the mighty works that they had seen;

38 Saying, Blessed *be* the King that cometh in the name of the Lord: peace in heaven, and glory in the highest.

39 And some of the Pharisees from among the multitude said unto him, Master, rebuke thy disciples.

40 And he answered and said unto them, I tell you that, if these should hold their peace, the stones would immediately cry out.

41 ¶ And when he was come near, he beheld the city, and wept over it,

42 Saying, If thou hadst known, even thou, at least in this thy day, the things *which belong* unto thy peace! but now they are hid from thine eyes.

43 For the days shall come upon thee, that thine enemies shall cast a trench about thee, and compass thee round, and keep thee in on every side,

44 And shall lay thee even with the ground, and thy children within thee; and they shall not leave in thee one stone upon another; because thou knewest not the time of thy visitation.

B Monday, 19:45–48

45 And he went into the temple, and began to cast out them that sold therein, and them that bought;

19:38 This quotation from Ps. 118:26 was sung as the pilgrims made their way into Jerusalem.
19:43 *thine enemies*=the Romans under Titus in A.D. 70.
19:45 *to cast out*. See note at Mark 11:15.

46 Saying unto them, It is written, My house is the house of prayer: but ye have made it a den of thieves.

47 And he taught daily in the temple. But the chief priests and the scribes and the chief of the people sought to destroy him,

48 And could not find what they might do: for all the people were very attentive to hear him.

C Tuesday, 20:1—21:38

1 *Authority requested*, 20:1-8

20 And it came to pass, *that* on one of those days, as he taught the people in the temple, and preached the gospel, the chief priests and the scribes came upon *him* with the elders,

2 And spake unto him, saying, Tell us, by what authority doest thou these things? or who is he that gave thee this authority?

3 And he answered and said unto them, I will also ask you one thing; and answer me:

4 The baptism of John, was it from heaven, or of men?

5 And they reasoned with themselves, saying, If we shall say, From heaven; he will say, Why then believed ye him not?

6 But and if we say, Of men; all the people will stone us: for they be persuaded that John was a prophet.

7 And they answered, that they could not tell whence *it was*.

8 And Jesus said unto them, Neither tell I you by what authority I do these things.

2 *Authority revealed*, 20:9-18

9 Then began he to speak to the people this parable; A certain man planted a vineyard, and let it forth to husbandmen, and went into a far country for a long time.

10 And at the season he sent a servant to the husbandmen, that they should give him of the fruit of the vineyard: but the husbandmen beat him, and sent *him* away empty.

20:1-8 See note at Mark 11:30.
20:9 *a vineyard*. The parable explains God's dealings with Israel (see Isa. 5:1-7 for a similar story). The O.T. prophets are called servants (vv. 10-12); Jesus Himself is the beloved son (v. 13).

11 And again he sent another servant: and they beat him also, and entreated *him* shamefully, and sent *him* away empty.

12 And again he sent a third: and they wounded him also, and cast *him* out.

13 Then said the lord of the vineyard, What shall I do? I will send my beloved son: it may be they will reverence *him* when they see him.

14 But when the husbandmen saw him, they reasoned among themselves, saying, This is the heir: come, let us kill him, that the inheritance may be ours.

15 So they cast him out of the vineyard, and killed *him*. What therefore shall the lord of the vineyard do unto them?

16 He shall come and destroy these husbandmen, and shall give the vineyard to others. And when they heard *it*, they said, God forbid.

17 And he beheld them, and said, What is this then that is written, The stone which the builders rejected, the same is become the head of the corner?

18 Whosoever shall fall upon that stone shall be broken; but on whomsoever it shall fall, it will grind him to powder.

3 *Authority resisted,* 20:19–40

19 ¶ And the chief priests and the scribes the same hour sought to lay hands on him; and they feared the people: for they perceived that he had spoken this parable against them.

20 And they watched *him*, and sent forth spies, which should feign themselves just men, that they might take hold of his words, that so they might deliver him unto the power and authority of the governor.

21 And they asked him, saying, Master, we know that thou sayest and teachest rightly, neither acceptest thou the person *of any*, but teachest the way of God truly:

22 Is it lawful for us to give tribute unto Cæsar, or no?

23 But he perceived their craftiness, and said unto them, Why tempt ye me?

24 Shew me a penny. Whose image and superscription hath it? They answered and said, Cæsar's.

25 And he said unto them, Render therefore unto

20:17 See Ps. 118:22.
20:24 *a penny.* Better, denarius, a Roman silver coin, bearing Caesar's image. See notes at Matt. 22:17, 21.

Cæsar the things which be Cæsar's, and unto God the things which be God's.

26 And they could not take hold of his words before the people: and they marvelled at his answer, and held their peace.

27 ¶ Then came to *him* certain of the Sadducees, which deny that there is any resurrection; and they asked him,

28 Saying, Master, Moses wrote unto us, If any man's brother die, having a wife, and he die without children, that his brother should take his wife, and raise up seed unto his brother.

29 There were therefore seven brethren: and the first took a wife, and died without children.

30 And the second took her to wife, and he died childless.

31 And the third took her; and in like manner the seven also: and they left no children, and died.

32 Last of all the woman died also.

33 Therefore in the resurrection whose wife of them is she? for seven had her to wife.

34 And Jesus answering said unto them, The children of this world marry, and are given in marriage:

35 But they which shall be accounted worthy to obtain that world, and the resurrection from the dead, neither marry, nor are given in marriage:

36 Neither can they die any more: for they are equal unto the angels; and are the children of God, being the children of the resurrection.

37 Now that the dead are raised, even Moses shewed at the bush, when he calleth the Lord the God of Abraham, and the God of Isaac, and the God of Jacob.

38 For he is not a God of the dead, but of the living: for all live unto him.

39 ¶ Then certain of the scribes answering said, Master, thou hast well said.

20:25 A follower of Christ has dual citizenship and responsibility. Of course, God's due takes precedence over Caesar's when there is conflict between them.

20:28 See Deut. 25:5–10. According to the law, if a man died without an heir, any unmarried brother of his was obliged to marry the man's widow.

20:36 *equal to the angels.* I.e., in the resurrection state there is no procreation. See note at Matt. 22:30.

20:37 See Ex. 3:6. There is life after death, for God acknowledged a continuing relationship with Abraham, Issac, and Jacob, though they died long before.

40 And after that they durst not ask him any *question at all.*

4 *Authority reiterated,* 20:41–21:4

41 And he said unto them, How say they that Christ is David's son?

42 And David himself saith in the book of Psalms, The Lᴏʀᴅ said unto my Lord, Sit thou on my right hand.

43 Till I make thine enemies thy footstool.

44 David therefore calleth him Lord, how is he then his son?

45 ¶ Then in the audience of all the people he said unto his disciples,

46 Beware of the scribes, which desire to walk in long robes, and love greetings in the markets, and the highest seats in the synagogues, and the chief rooms at feasts;

47 Which devour widows' houses, and for a shew make long prayers: the same shall receive greater damnation.

21 And he looked up, and saw the rich men casting their gifts into the treasury.

2 And he saw also a certain poor widow casting in thither two mites.

3 And he said, Of a truth I say unto you, that this poor widow hath cast in more than they all:

4 For all these have of their abundance cast in unto the offerings of God: but she of her penury hath cast in all the living that she had.

5 *The apocalyptic discourse,* 21:5–38

5 ¶ And as some spake of the temple, how it was adorned with goodly stones and gifts, he said,

6 *As for* these things which ye behold, the days will come, in the which there shall not be left one stone upon another, that shall not be thrown down.

7 And they asked him, saying, Master, but when shall these things be? and what sign *will there be* when these things shall come to pass?

20:44 *how is he then his son?* See note at Matt. 22:44.

21:1 *treasury.* These were chests in the court of the temple where gifts were deposited.

21:2 *mites.* See note at Luke 12:59.

21:7 *when shall these things be?* There is a double perspective in Christ's answer: the destruction of Jerusalem in A.ᴅ. 70 and the

8 And he said, Take heed that ye be not deceived: for many shall come in my name, saying, I am *Christ*; and the time draweth near: go ye not therefore after them.

9 But when ye shall hear of wars and commotions, be not terrified: for these things must first come to pass; but the end *is* not by and by.

10 Then said he unto them, Nation shall rise against nation, and kingdom against kingdom:

11 And great earthquakes shall be in divers places, and famines, and pestilences; and fearful sights and great signs shall there be from heaven.

12 But before all these, they shall lay their hands on you, and persecute *you*, delivering *you* up to the synagogues, and into prisons, being brought before kings and rulers for my name's sake.

13 And it shall turn to you for a testimony.

14 Settle *it* therefore in your hearts, not to meditate before what ye shall answer:

15 For I will give you a mouth and wisdom, which all your adversaries shall not be able to gainsay nor resist.

16 And ye shall be betrayed both by parents, and brethren, and kinsfolks, and friends; and *some* of you shall they cause to be put to death.

17 And ye shall be hated of all *men* for my name's sake.

18 But there shall not an hair of your head perish.

19 In your patience possess ye your souls.

20 And when ye shall see Jerusalem compassed with armies, then know that the desolation thereof is nigh.

21 Then let them which are in Judæa flee to the mountains; and let them which are in the midst of it depart out; and let not them that are in the countries enter thereinto.

22 For these be the days of vengeance, that all things which are written may be fulfilled.

23 But woe unto them that are with child, and to them that give suck, in those days! for there shall be great distress in the land, and wrath upon this people.

24 And they shall fall by the edge of the sword, and shall be led away captive into all nations: and Jerusalem

tribulation days just prior to His second coming. Verses 8–19 and 25–28 relate particularly to the latter while vv. 20–24 refer to the former.

21:24 *the times of the Gentiles.* The period of Gentile domination of Jerusalem, which began probably under Nebuchadnezzar (587 B.C.) though certainly in A.D. 70, and which continues into the tribulation days (Rev. 11:2 where the same word is used).

shall be trodden down of the Gentiles, until the times of the Gentiles be fulfilled.

25 ¶ And there shall be signs in the sun, and in the moon, and in the stars; and upon the earth distress of nations, with perplexity; the sea and the waves roaring;

26 Men's hearts failing them for fear, and for looking after those things which are coming on the earth: for the powers of heaven shall be shaken.

27 And then shall they see the Son of man coming in a cloud with power and great glory.

28 And when these things begin to come to pass, then look up, and lift up your heads; for your redemption draweth nigh.

29 And he spake to them a parable; Behold the fig tree, and all the trees;

30 When they now shoot forth, ye see and know of your own selves that summer is now nigh at hand.

31 So likewise ye, when ye see these things come to pass, know ye that the kingdom of God is nigh at hand.

32 Verily I say unto you, This generation shall not pass away, till all be fulfilled.

33 Heaven and earth shall pass away: but my words shall not pass away.

34 ¶ And take heed to yourselves, lest at any time your hearts be overcharged with surfeiting, and drunkenness, and cares of this life, and so that day come upon you unawares.

35 For as a snare shall it come on all them that dwell on the face of the whole earth.

36 Watch ye therefore, and pray always, that ye may be accounted worthy to escape all these things that shall come to pass, and to stand before the Son of man.

37 And in the day time he was teaching in the temple; and at night he went out, and abode in the mount that is called the mount of Olives.

38 And all the people came early in the morning to him in the temple, for to hear him.

D Wednesday, 22:1–6

22 Now the feast of unleavened bread drew nigh, which is called the Passover.

21:32 this generation. See note at Matt. 24:34.
21:34 surfeiting=dissipation or excesses.
22:1 Passover. See Ex. 12:1–28 and Lev. 23:5–6 and note at Matt. 26:2.

2 And the chief priests and scribes sought how they might kill him; for they feared the people.

3 ¶ Then entered Satan into Judas surnamed Iscariot, being of the number of the twelve.

4 And he went his way, and communed with the chief priests and captains, how he might betray him unto them.

5 And they were glad, and covenanted to give him money.

6 And he promised, and sought opportunity to betray him unto them in the absence of the multitude.

E Thursday, 22:7–53

1 *The Lord's Supper*, 22:7–38

7 ¶ Then came the day of unleavened bread, when the passover must be killed.

8 And he sent Peter and John, saying, Go and prepare us the passover, that we may eat.

9 And they said unto him, Where wilt thou that we prepare?

10 And he said unto them, Behold, when ye are entered into the city, there shall a man meet you, bearing a pitcher of water; follow him into the house where he entereth in.

11 And ye shall say unto the goodman of the house, The Master saith unto thee, Where is the guestchamber, where I shall eat the passover with my disciples?

12 And he shall shew you a large upper room furnished: there make ready.

13 And they went, and found as he had said unto them: and they made ready the passover.

14 And when the hour was come, he sat down, and the twelve apostles with him.

15 And he said unto them, With desire I have desired to eat this passover with you before I suffer:

16 For I say unto you, I will not any more eat thereof, until it be fulfilled in the kingdom of God.

22:3 *Then entered Satan into Judas.* Satan did this twice (see John 13:27).

22:7 *the passover must be killed*=the passover lamb must be killed.

22:10 *a man . . . bearing a pitcher of water.* He would be easily identifiable, since women usually performed this task.

22:15 *With desire I have desired.* A Hebrew idiom meaning "with great desire."

22:16 *until it be fulfilled in the kingdom of God.* See note at Matt. 26:29.

17 And he took the cup, and gave thanks, and said, Take this, and divide *it* among yourselves:

18 For I say unto you, I will not drink of the fruit of the vine, until the kingdom of God shall come.

19 ¶ And he took bread, and gave thanks, and brake *it*, and gave unto them, saying, This is my body which is given for you: this do in remembrance of me.

20 Likewise also the cup after supper, saying, This cup *is* the new testament in my blood, which is shed for you.

21 ¶ But, behold, the hand of him that betrayeth me *is* with me on the table.

22 And truly the Son of man goeth, as it was determined: but woe unto that man by whom he is betrayed!

23 And they began to enquire among themselves, which of them it was that should do this thing.

24 ¶ And there was also a strife among them, which of them should be accounted the greatest.

25 And he said unto them, The kings of the Gentiles exercise lordship over them; and they that exercise authority upon them are called benefactors.

26 But ye *shall* not *be* so: but he that is greatest among you, let him be as the younger; and he that is chief, as he that doth serve.

27 For whether *is* greater, he that sitteth at meat, or he that serveth? *is* not he that sitteth at meat? but I am among you as he that serveth.

28 Ye are they which have continued with me in my temptations.

29 And I appoint unto you a kingdom, as my Father hath appointed unto me;

30 That ye may eat and drink at my table in my kingdom, and sit on thrones judging the twelve tribes of Israel.

31 ¶ And the Lord said, Simon, Simon, behold, Satan hath desired *to have* you, that he may sift *you* as wheat:

32 But I have prayed for thee, that thy faith fail not: and when thou art converted, strengthen thy brethren.

22:19 *This is my body.* The bread remains bread but represents His body. It is an illustration, like "I am the door" (John 10:7).

22:20 *the new testament.* See note at Matt. 26:28.

22:25 *benefactors.* A favorite title used by the Greek kings of Egypt and Syria.

22:30 See note at Matt. 19:28.

22:32 *I have prayed for thee.* This is an illustration of Heb. 7:25. *when thou art converted.* I.e., when you have turned back again to me.

33 And he said unto him, Lord, I am ready to go with thee, both into prison, and to death.

34 And he said, I tell thee, Peter, the cock shall not crow this day, before that thou shalt thrice deny that thou knowest me.

35 And he said unto them, When I sent you without purse, and scrip, and shoes, lacked ye any thing? And they said, Nothing.

36 Then said he unto them, But now, he that hath a purse, let him take *it*, and likewise *his* scrip: and he that hath no sword, let him sell his garment, and buy one.

37 For I say unto you, that this that is written must yet be accomplished in me, And he was reckoned among the transgressors: for the things concerning me have an end.

38 And they said, Lord, behold, here *are* two swords. And he said unto them, It is enough.

2 *The garden of Gethsemane*, 22:39–46

39 ¶ And he came out, and went, as he was wont, to the mount of Olives; and his disciples also followed him.

40 And when he was at the place, he said unto them, Pray that ye enter not into temptation.

41 And he was withdrawn from them about a stone's cast, and kneeled down, and prayed,

42 Saying, Father, if thou be willing, remove this cup from me: nevertheless not my will, but thine, be done.

43 And there appeared an angel unto him from heaven, strengthening him.

44 And being in an agony he prayed more earnestly: and his sweat was as it were great drops of blood falling down to the ground.

45 And when he rose up from prayer, and was come to his disciples, he found them sleeping for sorrow,

46 And said unto them, Why sleep ye? rise and pray, lest ye enter into temptation.

3 *The arrest*, 22:47–53

47 ¶ And while he yet spake, behold a multitude, and he that was called Judas, one of the twelve, went before them, and drew near unto Jesus to kiss him.

22:35 See Luke 9:3.
22:37 See Isa. 53:12.
22:42 *this cup*. See note at Matt. 26:39.
22:43–44 These verses are not in certain important manuscripts.

48 But Jesus said unto him, Judas, betrayest thou the Son of man with a kiss?

49 When they which were about him saw what would follow, they said unto him, Lord, shall we smite with the sword?

50 ¶ And one of them smote the servant of the high priest, and cut off his right ear.

51 And Jesus answered and said, Suffer ye thus far. And he touched his ear, and healed him.

52 Then Jesus said unto the chief priests, and captains of the temple, and the elders, which were come to him, Be ye come out, as against a thief, with swords and staves?

53 When I was daily with you in the temple, ye stretched forth no hands against me: but this is your hour, and the power of darkness.

F Friday, 22:54–23:55

1 *Peter's denial*, 22:54–62

54 ¶ Then took they him, and led *him*, and brought him into the high priest's house. And Peter followed afar off.

55 And when they had kindled a fire in the midst of the hall, and were set down together, Peter sat down among them.

56 But a certain maid beheld him as he sat by the fire, and earnestly looked upon him, and said, This man was also with him.

57 And he denied him, saying, Woman, I know him not.

58 And after a little while another saw him, and said, Thou art also of them. And Peter said, Man, I am not.

59 And about the space of one hour after another confidently affirmed, saying, Of a truth this *fellow* also was with him: for he is a Galilæan.

60 And Peter said, Man, I know not what thou sayest. And immediately, while he yet spake, the cock crew.

61 And the Lord turned, and looked upon Peter. And Peter remembered the word of the Lord, how he had said unto him, Before the cock crow, thou shalt deny me thrice.

62 And Peter went out, and wept bitterly.

22:50 *one of them*. This was Peter (John 18:10).
22:55 *in the midst of the hall*. The house was built around a court.
22:59 *he is a Galilaean*. See note at Mark 14:70.
22:61 *cock crow*. This was a Roman division of time marking the end of the third watch at 3 a.m.

2 *Christ derided, beaten*, 22:63–65

63 ¶ And the men that held Jesus mocked him, and smote *him*.

64 And when they had blindfolded him, they struck him on the face, and asked him, saying, Prophesy, who is it that smote thee?

65 And many other things blasphemously spake they against him.

3 *Christ before the Sanhedrin*, 22:66–71

66 ¶ And as soon as it was day, the elders of the people and the chief priests and the scribes came together, and led him into their council, saying,

67 Art thou the Christ? tell us. And he said unto them, If I tell you, ye will not believe:

68 And if I also ask *you*, ye will not answer me, nor let *me* go.

69 Hereafter shall the Son of man sit on the right hand of the power of God.

70 Then said they all, Art thou then the Son of God? And he said unto them, Ye say that I am.

71 And they said, What need we any further witness? for we ourselves have heard of his own mouth.

4 *Christ before Pilate*, 23:1–5

23 And the whole multitude of them arose, and led him unto Pilate.

2 And they began to accuse him, saying, We found this *fellow* perverting the nation, and forbidding to give tribute to Cæsar, saying that he himself is Christ a King.

3 And Pilate asked him, saying, Art thou the King of the Jews? And he answered him and said, Thou sayest *it*.

4 Then said Pilate to the chief priests and *to* the people, I find no fault in this man.

5 And they were the more fierce, saying, He stirreth up

22:66 *as soon as it was day.* Matthew (26:57–58) and Mark (14:53, 55) mention a preliminary hearing held at night, but the Sanhedrin (70 or 72 elders and teachers of the nation) could not legally convene at night, so this verdict was made official as soon as it was day. However, the Sanhedrin had no power to carry out a capital sentence, so the case had to be remanded to Pilate, the senior representative of the Roman government in Judea.

23:2 *Christ a King.* The charge against Jesus made before Pilate was political—a rival "king." Insurrection against Rome was implied. The Jews knew that blasphemy would not be regarded by Rome as sufficient ground for the death penalty.

the people, teaching throughout all Jewry, beginning from Galilee to this place.

5 Christ before Herod, 23:6–12

6 When Pilate heard of Galilee, he asked whether the man were a Galilæan.

7 And as soon as he knew that he belonged unto Herod's jurisdiction, he sent him to Herod, who himself also was at Jerusalem at that time.

8 ¶ And when Herod saw Jesus, he was exceeding glad: for he was desirous to see him of a long *season*, because he had heard many things of him; and he hoped to have seen some miracle done by him.

9 Then he questioned with him in many words; but he answered him nothing.

10 And the chief priests and scribes stood and vehemently accused him.

11 And Herod with his men of war set him at nought, and mocked *him*, and arrayed him in a gorgeous robe, and sent him again to Pilate.

12 ¶ And the same day Pilate and Herod were made friends together: for before they were at enmity between themselves.

6 Christ again before Pilate, 23:13–25

13 ¶ And Pilate, when he had called together the chief priests and the rulers and the people,

14 Said unto them, Ye have brought this man unto me, as one that perverteth the people: and, behold, I, having examined *him* before you, have found no fault in this man touching those things whereof ye accuse him:

15 No, nor yet Herod: for I sent you to him; and, lo, nothing worthy of death is done unto him.

16 I will therefore chastise him, and release *him*.

17 (For of necessity he must release one unto them at the feast.)

18 And they cried out all at once, saying, Away with this *man*, and release unto us Barabbas:

23:7 *he sent him to Herod.* Pilate was not required to send Jesus to Herod Antipas but did so hoping to find a way out of his own dilemma and perhaps also as a diplomatic gesture (see v.12).

23:11 *sent him again to Pilate.* To Herod the whole matter seemed to be a joke, since he treated the incident as an occasion for amusement and then returned Jesus to Pilate.

23:15 *unto him.* Lit., by Him.

23:17 See John 18:39.

19 (Who for a certain sedition made in the city, and for murder, was cast into prison.)

20 Pilate therefore, willing to release Jesus, spake again to them.

21 But they cried, saying, Crucify *him*, crucify him.

22 And he said unto them the third time, Why, what evil hath he done? I have found no cause of death in him: I will therefore chastise him, and let *him* go.

23 And they were instant with loud voices, requiring that he might be crucified. And the voices of them and of the chief priests prevailed.

24 And Pilate gave sentence that it should be as they required.

25 And he released unto them him that for sedition and murder was cast into prison, whom they had desired; but he delivered Jesus to their will.

7 *The crucifixion,* 23:26–49

26 And as they led him away, they laid hold upon one Simon, a Cȳrē′nian, coming out of the country, and on him they laid the cross, that he might bear *it* after Jesus.

27 ¶ And there followed him a great company of people, and of women, which also bewailed and lamented him.

28 But Jesus turning unto them said, Daughters of Jerusalem, weep not for me, but weep for yourselves, and for your children.

29 For, behold, the days are coming, in the which they shall say, Blessed *are* the barren, and the wombs that never bare, and the paps which never gave suck.

30 Then shall they begin to say to the mountains, Fall on us; and to the hills, Cover us.

31 For if they do these things in a green tree, what shall be done in the dry?

32 And there were also two other, malefactors, led with him to be put to death.

23:22 *I will therefore chastise him.* This was done by scourging (Mark 15:15), i.e., whipping (see note at Matt. 27:26).

23:26 *a Cyrenian.* See note at Matt. 27:32.

23:28 *weep for yourselves, and for your children.* The Lord foresaw the destruction of Jerusalem with its attendant miseries in A.D. 70.

23:29 See Luke 21:23.

23:30 See Hos. 10:8; Rev. 6:16.

23:31 The meaning is this: If such injustice can be done to an innocent man as was being done then to Jesus, what will befall the Jews in time of war?

33 And when they were come to the place, which is called Calvary, there they crucified him, and the malefactors, one on the right hand, and the other on the left.

34 ¶ Then said Jesus, Father, forgive them; for they know not what they do. And they parted his raiment, and cast lots.

35 And the people stood beholding. And the rulers also with them derided *him*, saying, He saved others; let him save himself, if he be Christ, the chosen of God.

36 And the soldiers also mocked him, coming to him, and offering him vinegar,

37 And saying, If thou be the king of the Jews, save thyself.

38 And a superscription also was written over him in letters of Greek, and Latin, and Hebrew, THIS IS THE KING OF THE JEWS.

39 ¶ And one of the malefactors which were hanged railed on him, saying, If thou be Christ, save thyself and us.

40 But the other answering rebuked him, saying, Dost not thou fear God, seeing thou art in the same condemnation?

41 And we indeed justly; for we receive the due reward of our deeds: but this man hath done nothing amiss.

42 And he said unto Jesus, Lord, remember me when thou comest into thy kingdom.

43 And Jesus said unto him, Verily I say unto thee, To day shalt thou be with me in paradise.

44 And it was about the sixth hour, and there was a darkness over all the earth until the ninth hour.

45 And the sun was darkened, and the veil of the temple was rent in the midst.

46 ¶ And when Jesus had cried with a loud voice, he said, Father, into thy hands I commend my spirit: and having said thus, he gave up the ghost.

47 Now when the centurion saw what was done, he glorified God, saying, Certainly this was a righteous man.

23:33 *Calvary*=the skull. See note at Matt. 27:33.
23:34 *parted his raiment*. See Ps. 22:18 and note at Matt. 27:35.
23:38 *a superscription*. See note at Matt. 27:37.
23:39 *malefactors*=criminals.
23:42 *when thou comest into thy kingdom*. Seeing Jesus dying on a cross but believing that He would come into His kingdom shows the amazing faith of the thief.
23:43 *paradise*. Heaven, the abode of God (Luke 16:22; 2 Cor. 12:4).
23:44 *the sixth hour*=noon.
23:45 *the veil of the temple*. See note at Matt. 27:51.

48 And all the people that came together to that sight, beholding the things which were done, smote their breasts, and returned.

49 And all his acquaintance, and the women that followed him from Galilee, stood afar off, beholding these things.

8 *The burial*, 23:50–55

50 ¶ And, behold, *there was* a man named Joseph, a counsellor; *and he was* a good man, and a just:

51 (The same had not consented to the counsel and deed of them;) *he was* of Arimathǽ'a, a city of the Jews: who also himself waited for the kingdom of God.

52 This *man* went unto Pilate, and begged the body of Jesus.

53 And he took it down, and wrapped it in linen, and laid it in a sepulchre that was hewn in stone, wherein never man before was laid.

54 And that day was the preparation, and the sabbath drew on.

55 And the women also, which came with him from Galilee, followed after, and beheld the sepulchre, and how his body was laid.

G Saturday, 23:56

56 And they returned, and prepared spices and ointments; and rested the sabbath day according to the commandment.

VI THE VINDICATION OF THE SON OF MAN BEFORE MEN, 24:1–53

A The Victor over Death, 24:1–12

24 Now upon the first *day* of the week, very early in the morning, they came unto the sepulchre, bringing the spices which they had prepared, and certain *others* with them.

23:50 *a counsellor.* I.e., a member of the Sanhedrin.
23:51 *Arimathaea.* A town N. of Lydda.
23:53 *wrapped it.* The word means "wrap by winding tightly" the linen around the body. See also Isa. 53.9.
23:54 *And that day was the preparation.* Friday, the day Jesus died, was the time of the preparation for the Sabbath, which began Friday at sunset.
23:56 *according to the commandment.* I.e., not to work on the Sabbath (Ex. 20:10).

2 And they found the stone rolled away from the sepulchre.

3 And they entered in, and found not the body of the Lord Jesus.

4 And it came to pass, as they were much perplexed thereabout, behold, two men stood by them in shining garments:

5 And as they were afraid, and bowed down *their* faces to the earth, they said unto them, Why seek ye the living among the dead?

6 He is not here, but is risen: remember how he spake unto you when he was yet in Galilee,

7 Saying, The Son of man must be delivered into the hands of sinful men, and be crucified, and the third day rise again.

8 And they remembered his words,

9 And returned from the sepulchre, and told all these things unto the eleven, and to all the rest.

10 It was Mary Magdalene, and Joanna, and Mary *the mother* of James, and other *women that were* with them, which told these things unto the apostles.

11 And their words seemed to them as idle tales, and they believed them not.

12 Then arose Peter, and ran unto the sepulchre; and stooping down, he beheld the linen clothes laid by themselves, and departed, wondering in himself at that which was come to pass.

B The Fulfiller of the Prophecies
(the Emmaus Disciples), 24:13–35

13 ¶ And, behold, two of them went that same day to a village called Emmā′us, which was from Jerusalem *about* threescore furlongs.

24:2 *the stone rolled away.* A circular stone like a solid wheel rolled in front of the entrance to the tomb-cave to keep out intruders.

24:6–7 *remember.* See 9:31; 18:31–34.

24:12 *the linen clothes.* The wide bandage-like strips that were wound around the body (23:53). *laid by themselves.* Despite the absence of the body, the clothes retained the same position they had when it was there. If someone had stolen the body but left the clothes, he would have had to unwrap it and the clothes would not have been in this position. See John 20:6–7.

24:13 *two of them.* One is identified as Cleopas (v. 18); the other may have been his wife (v. 32: "our heart"). Many identify Cleopas as the person mentioned in John 19:25, in which case his wife's name was Mary. *Emmaus.* About 19 miles W. of Jerusalem.

14 And they talked together of all these things which had happened.

15 And it came to pass, that, while they communed *together* and reasoned, Jesus himself drew near, and went with them.

16 But their eyes were holden that they should not know him.

17 And he said unto them, What manner of communications *are* these that ye have one to another, as ye walk, and are sad?

18 And the one of them, whose name was Clē'opas, answering said unto him, Art thou only a stranger in Jerusalem, and hast not known the things which are come to pass there in these days?

19 And he said unto them, What things? And they said unto him, Concerning Jesus of Nazareth, which was a prophet mighty in deed and word before God and all the people:

20 And how the chief priests and our rulers delivered him to be condemned to death, and have crucified him.

21 But we trusted that it had been he which should have redeemed Israel: and beside all this, to day is the third day since these things were done.

22 Yea, and certain women also of our company made us astonished, which were early at the sepulchre;

23 And when they found not his body, they came, saying, that they had also seen a vision of angels, which said that he was alive.

24 And certain of them which were with us went to the sepulchre, and found *it* even so as the women had said: but him they saw not.

25 Then he said unto them, O fools, and slow of heart to believe all that the prophets have spoken:

26 Ought not Christ to have suffered these things, and to enter into his glory?

27 And beginning at Moses and all the prophets, he expounded unto them in all the scriptures the things concerning himself.

28 And they drew nigh unto the village, whither they went: and he made as though he would have gone further.

29 But they constrained him, saying, Abide with us: for it is toward evening, and the day is far spent. And he went in to tarry with them.

24:27 *in all the scriptures.* E.g., passages like Ps. 16; 22; Isa. 53.
24:29 *constrained*=urged.

30 And it came to pass, as he sat at meat with them, he took bread, and blessed *it*, and brake, and gave to them.

31 And their eyes were opened, and they knew him; and he vanished out of their sight.

32 And they said one to another, Did not our heart burn within us, while he talked with us by the way, and while he opened to us the scriptures?

33 And they rose up the same hour, and returned to Jerusalem, and found the eleven gathered together, and them that were with them,

34 Saying, The Lord is risen indeed, and hath appeared to Simon.

35 And they told what things *were done* in the way, and how he was known of them in breaking of bread.

C The Pattern of Resurrection Life, 24:36–43

36 ¶ And as they thus spake, Jesus himself stood in the midst of them, and saith unto them, Peace *be* unto you.

37 But they were terrified and affrighted, and supposed that they had seen a spirit.

38 And he said unto them, Why are ye troubled? and why do thoughts arise in your hearts?

39 Behold my hands and my feet, that it is I myself: handle me, and see; for a spirit hath not flesh and bones, as ye see me have.

40 And when he had thus spoken, he shewed them *his* hands and *his* feet.

41 And while they yet believed not for joy, and wondered, he said unto them, Have ye here any meat?

42 And they gave him a piece of a broiled fish, and of an honeycomb.

43 And he took *it*, and did eat before them.

24:30 *he took bread.* Christ's assumption of the position as host, and perhaps something in His gestures, made them recognize Him in His true identity.

24:31 *he vanished out of their sight.* Lit., He became invisible.

24:34 *appeared to Simon.* There is no other record of this except the mention in 1 Cor. 15:5.

24:39 The evidences that Jesus' appearance was not as a ghost are: (1) the scars on His hands and feet; (2) tangibleness in being able to be handled; and (3) ability to eat (v. 43; Acts 10:41). *handle me.* The same word is used in 1 John 1:1.

24:41 *meat*=food.

24:42 *and of an honeycomb.* These words are not in the best texts.

D The Head of the Church, 24:44–48

44 And he said unto them, These *are* the words which I spake unto you, while I was yet with you, that all things must be fulfilled, which were written in the law of Moses, and *in* the prophets, and *in* the psalms, concerning me.

45 Then opened he their understanding, that they might understand the scriptures,

46 And said unto them, Thus it is written, and thus it behooved Christ to suffer, and to rise from the dead the third day:

47 And that repentance and remission of sins should be preached in his name among all nations, beginning at Jerusalem.

48 And ye are witnesses of these things.

E The Giver of the Holy Spirit, 24:49

49 ¶ And, behold, I send the promise of my Father upon you: but tarry ye in the city of Jerusalem, until ye be endued with power from on high.

F The Ascended Lord, 24:50–53

50 ¶ And he led them out as far as to Bethany, and he lifted up his hands, and blessed them.

51 And it came to pass, while he blessed them, he was parted from them, and carried up into heaven.

52 And they worshipped him, and returned to Jerusalem with great joy:

53 And were continually in the temple, praising and blessing God. Amen.

24:44 This was a common Jewish division of the O.T. The *prophets* included most of the historical books, and the *psalms* included the writings.

24:49 *the promise of my Father*=the coming of the Holy Spirit on the day of Pentecost.

24:50 *as far as to Bethany*=toward Bethany.

24:51 Luke gives more details of the ascension of Christ in his other book; see Acts 1:9.

INTRODUCTION TO
THE GOSPEL ACCORDING TO
John

AUTHOR: The Apostle John   DATE: 85–90

The Author *The writer of this Gospel is identified in the book only as "the disciple whom Jesus loved" (21:20, 24). He obviously was a Palestinian Jew who was an eyewitness of the events of Christ's life, for he displays a knowledge of Jewish customs (7:37–39; 18:28) and of the land of Palestine (1:44, 46; 5:2), and he includes the details of an eyewitness (2:6; 13:26; 21:8, 11). Eliminating the other disciples that belonged to the "inner circle" (because James had been martyred before this time (Acts 12:1–5), and because Peter is named in close association with the disciple whom Jesus loved, (13:23–24; 20:2–10), one concludes that John was the author. Whether this was the apostle John or a different John (the Elder) is discussed in the Introduction to 1 John.*

John the apostle was the son of Zebedee and Salome and the older brother of James. He was a Galilean who apparently came from a fairly well-to-do home (Mark 15:40–41). Though often painted centuries later as an effeminate person, his real character was such that he was known as a "son of thunder" (Mark 3:17). He played a leading role in the work of the early church in Jerusalem (Acts 3:1; 8:14; Gal. 2:9). Later he went to Ephesus and for an unknown reason was exiled to the island of Patmos (Rev. 1:9).

The Distinctive Approach of John *This is the most theological of the Four Gospels in that it deals with the nature of the person of Christ and the meaning of faith in Him. John's presentation of Christ as the divine Son of God is seen in the titles given Him in the book: "the Word was God" (1:1), "the Lamb of God" (1:29), "the Messiah" (1:41), "the Son of God" and "the King of Israel" (1:49), the "Saviour of the world" (4:42), "Lord and God" (20:28). His deity is also asserted in the series of "I am . . ." claims* in the Gospel (6:35; 8:12; 10:7, 9, 11, 14; 11:25; 14:6; 15:1, 5). In other "I am" statements not followed by a complement, Christ made implicit and explicit claim to be the I AM–Yahweh of the O.T. (4:24, 26; 8:24, 28, 58; 13:19). This is the strongest kind of claim to deity that Jesus could have made.

The structure and style of the Gospel are different from the synoptics. It contains no parables, only seven miracles (five of which are not recorded elsewhere), and many personal interviews. The author emphasizes the physical actuality of Jesus' hunger, thirst, weariness, pain, and death as a defense against the Gnostic denial of Jesus' true human nature.

The Date Though John used to be dated by some extreme critics in the middle of the second century, the discovery of the Rylands papyrus fragment (a few verses from John 18 dated about A.D. 135) forced an earlier date. Several decades would have been required between the original writing of the Gospel and its being copied and circulated as far as the Egyptian hinterland where the fragment was found. The Gospel was apparently being circulated between 89 and 90, though it may have been written from Ephesus earlier (a pre-70 date has been suggested on the basis of 5:2 which may indicate that Jerusalem had not yet been destroyed). Discoveries at Qumran have attested to the genuineness of the Jewish background and thought patterns seen in the book.

The Contents John's statement of purpose is clearly spelled out in 20:20–21. The Gospel is sometimes called The Book of the Seven Signs, since the author chose seven sign-miracles to reveal the person and mission of Jesus. These are: (1) the turning of water into wine (2:1–11); (2) the cure of the nobleman's son (4:46–54); (3) the cure of the paralytic (5:1–18); (4) the feeding of the multitude (6:6–13); (5) the walking on the water (6:16–21); (6) the giving of sight to the blind (9:1–7); and (7) the raising of Lazarus (11:1–45). Other important themes in the book include teaching on the Holy Spirit (14:26; 15:26; 16:7–14), Satan and the world (8:44; 12:31; 17:15), the Logos (1:1–14), and the new birth (3:1–12).

OUTLINE OF THE GOSPEL OF JOHN

I Incarnation of the Son of God, 1:1–18
II Presentation of the Son of God, 1:19–4:54

THE GOSPEL ACCORDING TO

John

I INCARNATION OF THE SON OF GOD, 1:1–18

1 In the beginning was the Word, and the Word was with God, and the Word was God.

2 The same was in the beginning with God.

3 All things were made by him; and without him was not any thing made that was made.

4 In him was life; and the life was the light of men.

1:1 *in the beginning.* Before time began, Christ was already in existence with God. This is what is meant by the term "the pre-existent Christ." See Gen. 1:1 and 1 John 1:1. *Word* (Greek: *logos*). *Logos* means word, thought, concept, and the expressions thereof. In the O.T. the concept conveyed activity and revelation, and the word or wisdom of God is often personified (Ps. 33:6; Prov. 8). In the Targums (Aramaic paraphrases of the O.T.) it was a designation of God. To the Greek mind it expressed the ideas of reason and creative control. Revelation is the keynote idea in the *logos* concept. Here it is applied to Jesus, who is all that God is and the expression of Him (1:1, 14). In this verse the Word (Christ) is said to be *with God* (i.e., in communion with and yet distinct from God) and to be *God* (i.e., identical in essence with God).

1:3 *made by him.* Christ was active in the work of creation (Col. 1:16).

1:4–5 *life . . . light.* These are two words especially associated with John (8:12; 9:5, 11:25; 14:6). "Light" in John implies

5 And the light shineth in darkness; and the darkness comprehended it not.

6 ¶ There was a man sent from God, whose name *was* John.

7 The same came for a witness, to bear witness of the Light, that all *men* through him might believe.

8 He was not that Light, but *was sent* to bear witness of that Light.

9 *That* was the true Light, which lighteth every man that cometh into the world.

10 He was in the world, and the world was made by him, and the world knew him not.

11 He came unto his own, and his own received him not.

12 But as many as received him, to them gave he power to become the sons of God, *even* to them that believe on his name:

13 Which were born, not of blood, nor of the will of the flesh, nor of the will of man, but of God.

14 And the Word was made flesh, and dwelt among us,

revelation which reveals the "life" that is in Christ and which brings into judgment those who refuse it (3:19). "Life" denotes salvation, deliverance, based on Christ's atonement. *the darkness comprehended it not.* I.e., the darkness did not overcome the light.

1:6 *John* (the Baptist). His role, it is made clear in v. 8, was simply as a witness to the Light.

1:9 *which lighteth every man.* This does not mean that every man is redeemed automatically, for redemption comes through faith in the Savior (1:12). But that light is available to all men.

1:10 *knew him not.* The world did not recognize Christ.

1:11 *He came unto his own* (things—the world which He made), *and his own* (people—the Jews) *received him not.*

1:12 *sons* of God. Lit., children of God. *even to them who believe on his name.* An explanation of what it means to "receive" Him.

1:13 The new birth is something supernatural and therefore completely distinct from natural birth. It is *not of blood* (lit., bloods), i.e., contains no human element; nor does it lie within the scope of human achievement (it is not *of the will of the flesh* or *man*).

1:14 *the Word was made flesh.* Jesus Christ was a unique person, for He was God from all eternity and He joined Himself to sinless humanity in the incarnation. The God-man possessed all the attributes of deity (Phil. 2:6) and the attributes common to humanity (apart from sin), and He will exist forever as the God-man in His resurrected body (Acts 1:11; Rev. 5:6). Only the God-man can be an adequate Savior; for He must be human in order to be able to suffer and die, and He must be

(and we beheld his glory, the glory as of the only begotten of the Father,) full of grace and truth.

15 ¶ John bare witness of him, and cried, saying, This was he of whom I spake, He that cometh after me is preferred before me: for he was before me.

16 And of his fulness have all we received, and grace for grace.

17 For the law was given by Moses, *but* grace and truth came by Jesus Christ.

18 No man hath seen God at any time; the only begotten Son, which is in the bosom of the Father, he hath declared *him*.

II PRESENTATION OF THE SON OF GOD,
1:19–4:54

A By John the Baptizer, 1:19–34

19 ¶ And this is the record of John, when the Jews sent priests and Levites from Jerusalem to ask him, Who art thou?

20 And he confessed, and denied not; but confessed, I am not the Christ.

21 And they asked him, What then? Art thou Elī′as?

God to make that death effective as a payment for sin. The use of the word *flesh* contradicts the Gnostic teaching that pure deity could not be united with flesh which was regarded as evil. *glory*. In the O.T., glory expressed the splendor of a divine manifestation and attested the divine presence. Here it means the visible manifestation of God in Christ.

1:16 *grace for grace*. I.e., grace piled upon grace in the experiences of the Christian life.

1:17 *grace*. Though grace was manifest in the O.T. (Gen. 6:8; Ex. 34:6; Jer. 31:3), it was a candle compared with the brightness of grace that appeared at the incarnation (Tit. 2:11). Grace is the unmerited favor of God and is related to our salvation, justification, election, faith, and spiritual gifts (Eph. 1:7; Rom. 3:24; 11:5–6; Eph. 2:8–9; Rom. 12:6).

1:18 *No man hath seen God at any time*. I.e., since God is Spirit (John 4:24), no man has ever seen the essence of God, the Spirit-being. Yet He assumed visible form which man saw in O.T. times (Gen. 32:30; Ex. 24:9–10; Judg. 13:22; Isa. 6:1; Dan. 7:9) and in Jesus men could see God (John 14:8–9). Christ gives life (v. 12); He reveals (vv. 14, 18); He gives grace and truth (vv. 16–17).

1:19 *the Jews*. I.e., probably the chief priests.

1:21 *Elias*=Elijah. See Mal. 4:5. He was supposed to return to earth before the time of judgment (see note at Matt. 11:14).

And he saith, I am not. Art thou that prophet? And he answered, No.

22 Then said they unto him, Who art thou? that we may give an answer to them that sent us. What sayest thou of thyself?

23 He said, I *am* the voice of one crying in the wilderness, Make straight the way of the Lord, as said the prophet Ēsā'as.

24 And they which were sent were of the Pharisees.

25 And they asked him, and said unto him, Why baptizest thou then, if thou be not that Christ, nor Ēli'as, neither that prophet?

26 John answered them, saying, I baptize with water: but there standeth one among you, whom ye know not;

27 He it is, who coming after me is preferred before me, whose shoe's latchet I am not worthy to unloose.

28 These things were done in Bethab'ara beyond Jordan, where John was baptizing.

29 ¶ The next day John seeth Jesus coming unto him, and saith, Behold the Lamb of God, which taketh away the sin of the world.

30 This is he of whom I said, After me cometh a man which is preferred before me: for he was before me.

31 And I knew him not: but that he should be made manifest to Israel, therefore am I come baptizing with water.

32 And John bare record, saying, I saw the Spirit descending from heaven like a dove, and it abode upon him.

33 And I knew him not: but he that sent me to baptize with water, the same said unto me, Upon whom thou shalt see the Spirit descending, and remaining on him, the same is he which baptizeth with the Holy Ghost.

34 And I saw, and bare record that this is the Son of God.

that prophet. The prophecy referred to (Deut. 18:15) is of Christ, though the Jews did not understand it correctly, since they distinguished Christ and the prophet in v. 25 (Acts 3:22–23).

1:23 Quoted from Isa. 40:3.

1:24 *Pharisees.* See note at Matt. 3:7.

1:25 They seem to be saying: Since you have no authority, what are you doing baptizing and thus gathering followers?

1:29 *Lamb.* History (the Passover lamb, Ex. 12:3) and prophecy (the Messiah, Isa. 53:7) are linked in this metaphor. *the sin of the world,* no longer just the sins of Israel (Isa. 53:4–12; 1 John 2:2).

1:32 *record*=witness, here and in v. 34.

B To John's Disciples, 1:35–51

35 ¶ Again the next day after John stood, and two of his disciples;

36 And looking upon Jesus as he walked, he saith, Behold the Lamb of God!

37 And the two disciples heard him speak, and they followed Jesus.

38 Then Jesus turned, and saw them following, and saith unto them, What seek ye? They said unto him, Rabbi, (which is to say, being interpreted, Master,) where dwellest thou?

39 He saith unto them, Come and see. They came and saw where he dwelt, and abode with him that day: for it was about the tenth hour.

40 One of the two which heard John *speak*, and followed him, was Andrew, Simon Peter's brother.

41 He first findeth his own brother Simon, and saith unto him, We have found the Messias, which is, being interpreted, the Christ.

42 And he brought him to Jesus. And when Jesus beheld him, he said, Thou art Simon the son of Jona: thou shalt be called Cēʹphas, which is by interpretation, A stone.

43 ¶ The day following Jesus would go forth into Galilee, and findeth Philip, and saith unto him, Follow me.

44 Now Philip was of Bethsāʹida, the city of Andrew and Peter.

45 Philip findeth Nathanael, and saith unto him, We have found him, of whom Moses in the law, and the prophets, did write, Jesus of Nazareth, the son of Joseph.

46 And Nathanael said unto him, Can there any good thing come out of Nazareth? Philip saith unto him, Come and see.

47 Jesus saw Nathanael coming to him, and saith of him, Behold an Israelite indeed, in whom is no guile!

48 Nathanael saith unto him, Whence knowest thou me? Jesus answered and said unto him, Before that Philip called thee, when thou wast under the fig tree, I saw thee.

1:39 *the tenth hour.* 10 a.m. by Roman time; 4 p.m. by Jewish time.

1:41 *Messias*=Messiah. See note at Matt. 1:1.

1:46 *Nazareth.* The town possessed a negative reputation at this period (see 7:52).

1:48 *when thou wast under the fig tree, I saw thee.* Though bodily removed from Philip, the omnipresent Lord was with him under the fig tree.

49 Nathanael answered and saith unto him, Rabbi, thou art the Son of God, thou art the King of Israel.

50 Jesus answered and said unto him, Because I said unto thee, I saw thee under the fig tree, believest thou? thou shalt see greater things than these.

51 And he saith unto him, Verily, verily, I say unto you, Hereafter ye shall see heaven open, and the angels of God ascending and descending upon the Son of man.

C At a Wedding In Cana, 2:1-11

2 And the third day there was a marriage in Cana of Galilee; and the mother of Jesus was there:

2 And both Jesus was called, and his disciples, to the marriage.

3 And when they wanted wine, the mother of Jesus saith unto him, They have no wine.

4 Jesus saith unto her, Woman, what have I to do with thee? mine hour is not yet come.

5 His mother saith unto the servants, Whatsoever he saith unto you, do it.

6 And there were set there six waterpots of stone, after the manner of the purifying of the Jews, containing two or three firkins apiece.

7 Jesus saith unto them, Fill the waterpots with water. And they filled them up to the brim.

8 And he saith unto them, Draw out now, and bear unto the governor of the feast. And they bare it.

9 When the ruler of the feast had tasted the water that was made wine, and knew not whence it was: (but the

---

1:49 *Son of God*. A Messianic title for the One in whom the true destiny of Israel is to be fulfilled; also a claim of deity (5:18). The title *King of Israel* stated the Jewish political Messianic hope.

1:50 *greater things*. I.e., greater proofs of who I am as revealed in the seven great "signs" that comprise chapters 2-12.

1:51 *heaven open*. A symbol of the fellowship open to followers of Christ. *Son of man*. See note at Matt. 8:20. Notice the titles given to Jesus in chapter 1: *Logos* (v. 1), God (v. 1), Creator (v. 3), Light (v. 7), only begotten Son (v. 18), Lamb of God (vv. 29, 36), Son of God (vv. 39, 49), Messiah (v. 41), King of Israel (v. 49), and Son of man (v. 51).

2:4 *Woman, what have I to do with thee?* "Woman" was a term of respectful address (see 19:26). Christ's remark means: "that concerns you, leave me alone." The *hour* (He continues) for manifesting myself as Messiah has *not yet come* (see 8:20).

2:6 *firkin*=about 9 gallons.

2:8 *the governor of the feast*=the steward or headwaiter.

servants which drew the water knew;) the governor of the feast called the bridegroom,

10 And saith unto him, Every man at the beginning doth set forth good wine; and when men have well drunk, then that which is worse: *but* thou hast kept the good wine until now.

11 This beginning of miracles did Jesus in Cana of Galilee, and manifested forth his glory; and his disciples believed on him.

D At the Temple in Jerusalem, 2:12–25

12 ¶ After this he went down to Caper'naum, he, and his mother, and his brethren, and his disciples: and they continued there not many days.

13 ¶ And the Jews' passover was at hand, and Jesus went up to Jerusalem,

14 And found in the temple those that sold oxen and sheep and doves, and the changers of money sitting:

15 And when he had made a scourge of small cords, he drove them all out of the temple, and the sheep, and the oxen; and poured out the changers' money, and overthrew the tables;

16 And said unto them that sold doves, Take these things hence; make not my Father's house an house of merchandise.

17 And his disciples remembered that it was written, The zeal of thine house hath eaten me up.

18 ¶ Then answered the Jews and said unto him, What sign shewest thou unto us, seeing that thou doest these things?

19 Jesus answered and said unto them, Destroy this temple, and in three days I will raise it up.

2:11 *beginning of miracles.* Lit., beginning of the signs. The miracles of Jesus are called signs by John in order to draw attention to the significance of the miracles rather than to the miracles themselves. They revealed something about the person or work of Christ (here His glory), and their purpose was to encourage faith in His followers. For the specific signs in this book see Introduction, "The Contents."

2:13 *passover.* See note at Mark 14:1.

2:14 The many pilgrims that came to Jerusalem for Passover brought a variety of currency and no animals for sacrifice. The outer courts of the temple became a noisy market for changing money and selling animals.

2:17 See Ps. 69:9. Christ was jealous for the holiness of God's house. Their defiling it was the crime of the money-changers.

2:19 *in three days I will raise it up.* This cryptic expression is ex-

20 Then said the Jews, Forty and six years was this temple in building, and wilt thou rear it up in three days?

21 But he spake of the temple of his body.

22 When therefore he was risen from the dead, his disciples remembered that he had said this unto them; and they believed the scripture, and the word which Jesus had said.

23 ¶ Now when he was in Jerusalem at the passover, in the feast *day*, many believed in his name, when they saw the miracles which he did.

24 But Jesus did not commit himself unto them, because he knew all *men*,

25 And needed not that any should testify of man: for he knew what was in man.

E To Nicodemus, 3:1–21

3 There was a man of the Pharisees, named Nicodemus, a ruler of the Jews:

2 The same came to Jesus by night, and said unto him, Rabbi, we know that thou art a teacher come from God: for no man can do these miracles that thou doest, except God be with him.

3 Jesus answered and said unto him, Verily, verily, I say unto thee, Except a man be born again, he cannot see the kingdom of God.

4 Nicodemus saith unto him, How can a man be born when he is old? can he enter the second time into his mother's womb, and be born?

5 Jesus answered, Verily, verily, I say unto thee, Except

plained in v. 21, after a verse which states that the Jews characteristically misunderstood Him.

3:1 *Nicodemus, a ruler of the Jews*. He was a member of the Sanhedrin (see note at Luke 22:66). He perfectly represents aristocratic, well-intentioned but unenlightened Judaism of his day. For additional activities of Nicodemus see John 7:50–51 and 19:39.

3:3 *be born again*. Lit., be born from above (as in 3:31; 19:11, 23). The word also means "again" (Gal. 4:9). Both ideas (really merged in John's Gospel) may be combined in the translation "be born anew." The new birth or regeneration (Tit. 3:5) is the act of God which gives eternal life to the one who believes in Christ. As a result, he becomes a member of God's family (1 Pet. 1:23) with a new capacity and desire to please his heavenly Father (2 Cor. 5:17).

3:5 *born of water and of the Spirit*. Various interpretations have been suggested for the meaning here of "water": (1) It refers to baptism as a requirement for salvation. However, this would contradict many other N.T. passages (Eph. 2:8–9). (2) It

a man be born of water and *of* the Spirit, he cannot enter
into the kingdom of God.

6 That which is born of the flesh is flesh; and that which
is born of the Spirit is spirit.

7 Marvel not that I said unto thee, Ye must be born
again.

8 The wind bloweth where it listeth, and thou hearest
the sound thereof, but canst not tell whence it cometh,
and whither it goeth: so is every one that is born of the
Spirit.

9 Nicodemus answered and said unto him, How can
these things be?

10 Jesus answered and said unto him, Art thou a master
of Israel, and knowest not these things?

11 Verily, verily, I say unto thee, We speak that we do
know, and testify that we have seen; and ye receive not our
witness.

12 If I have told you earthly things, and ye believe not,
how shall ye believe, if I tell you *of* heavenly things?

13 And no man hath ascended up to heaven, but he
that came down from heaven, *even* the Son of man which
is in heaven.

14 ¶ And as Moses lifted up the serpent in the wilderness, even so must the Son of man be lifted up:

15 That whosoever believeth in him should not perish,
but have eternal life.

16 ¶ For God so loved the world, that he gave his only
begotten Son, that whosoever believeth in him should not
perish, but have everlasting life.

stands for the act of repentance which John the Baptist's baptism signified. (3) It refers to natural birth; thus it means
"except a man be born the first time by water and the second
time by the Spirit . . ." (4) It means the Word of God as in
John 15:3. (5) It is a synonym for the Holy Spirit and may be
translated "by water even the Spirit." One point is perfectly
clear: the new birth is from God through the Spirit.

3:8 *wind*. The Greek word, *pneuma*, means both *wind* and *spirit*.
listeth=wills.

3:10 *a master of Israel*. Lit., the teacher of Israel.

3:11 *witness, or testimony*. The witness theme is found throughout John (3:31-36; 5:31-47; 8:12-20).

3:13 *which is in heaven*. Some texts omit these words.

3:14 *Moses*. The reference is to Num. 21:5-9.

3:16 *everlasting life*. Better, eternal life, a new quality of life, not
an everlasting "this-life." Here begins another major theme of
John: Redemption and Judgment. It reappears at 5:22; 8:15;
9:39; 12:47. Here the emphasis is on the fact that men judge

17 For God sent not his Son into the world to condemn the world; but that the world through him might be saved.

18 ¶ He that believeth on him is not condemned: but he that believeth not is condemned already, because he hath not believed in the name of the only begotten Son of God.

19 And this is the condemnation, that light is come into the world, and men loved darkness rather than light, because their deeds were evil.

20 For every one that doeth evil hateth the light, neither cometh to the light, lest his deeds should be reproved.

21 But he that doeth truth cometh to the light, that his deeds may be made manifest, that they are wrought in God.

F By John the Baptizer, 3:22–36

22 ¶ After these things came Jesus and his disciples into the land of Judæa; and there he tarried with them, and baptized.

23 ¶And John also was baptizing in Ænon near to Salim, because there was much water there: and they came, and were baptized.

24 For John was not yet cast into prison.

25 ¶ Then there arose a question between *some* of John's disciples and the Jews about purifying.

26 And they came unto John, and said unto him, Rabbi, he that was with thee beyond Jordan, to whom thou barest witness, behold, the same baptizeth, and all *men* come to him.

27 John answered and said, A man can receive nothing, except it be given him from heaven.

28 Ye yourselves bear me witness, that I said, I am not the Christ, but that I am sent before him.

29 He that hath the bride is the bridegroom: but the friend of the bridegroom, which standeth and heareth him, rejoiceth greatly because of the bridegroom's voice: this my joy therefore is fulfilled.

30 He must increase, but I *must* decrease.

themselves. The acquitted are those who have believed in Him; the condemned, those who have rejected Him.

3:21 *truth*. I.e., what is true or right.

3:23 *Aenon . . . Salim*. Though not positively identified, they are thought to be in Samaria.

3:29 *the friend of the bridegroom*. As the bridegroom Christ must occupy the prominent place, though John the Baptist's place as the friend was unique, and he vicariously participated in the joy of the bridegroom.

31 He that cometh from above is above all: he that is
of the earth is earthly, and speaketh of the earth: he that
cometh from heaven is above all.

32 And what he hath seen and heard, that he testifieth;
and no man receiveth his testimony.

33 He that hath received his testimony hath set to his
seal that God is true.

34 For he whom God hath sent speaketh the words of
God: for God giveth not the Spirit by measure *unto him*.

35 The Father loveth the Son, and hath given all things
into his hand.

36 He that believeth on the Son hath everlasting life:
and he that believeth not the Son shall not see life; but the
wrath of God abideth on him.

G · To the Samaritan Woman, 4:1–42

4 When therefore the Lord knew how the Pharisees had
heard that Jesus made and baptized more disciples than
John,

2 (Though Jesus himself baptized not, but his disciples,)

3 He left Judæa, and departed again into Galilee.

4 And he must needs go through Samaria.

5 Then cometh he to a city of Samaria, which is called
Sy̆'char, near to the parcel of ground that Jacob gave to his
son Joseph.

6 Now Jacob's well was there. Jesus therefore, being
wearied with *his* journey, sat thus on the well: *and* it was
about the sixth hour.

7 There cometh a woman of Samaria to draw water:
Jesus saith unto her, Give me to drink.

8 (For his disciples were gone away unto the city to buy
meat.)

9 Then saith the woman of Samaria unto him, How is

3:31 This verse picks up where 3:13 left off. *He that cometh* is
   again the Son of man.

3:34 *by measure*=in a limited way.

4:1–3 The meaning is this: When the Lord knew that the
   Pharisees had heard that He was making and baptizing more
   disciples than John (though actually Jesus' disciples did the
   baptizing, not Jesus Himself), He determined to leave the area
   and go into Galilee to avoid any trouble with the Pharisees.

4:6 *the sixth hour*. 6 p.m. by Roman time and 12 noon by Jewish.
   The latter, at the sun's zenith, seems indicated.

4:9 *a woman of Samaria*. On the Samaritans, see note at Luke
   10:33.

it that thou, being a Jew, askest drink of me, which am a woman of Samaria? for the Jews have no dealings with the Samaritans.

10 Jesus answered and said unto her, If thou knewest the gift of God, and who it is that saith to thee, Give me to drink; thou wouldest have asked of him, and he would have given thee living water.

11 The woman saith unto him, Sir, thou hast nothing to draw with, and the well is deep: from whence then hast thou that living water?

12 Art thou greater than our father Jacob, which gave us the well, and drank thereof himself, and his children, and his cattle?

13 Jesus answered and said unto her, Whosoever drinketh of this water shall thirst again:

14 But whosoever drinketh of the water that I shall give him shall never thirst; but the water that I shall give him shall be in him a well of water springing up into everlasting life.

15 The woman saith unto him, Sir, give me this water, that I thirst not, neither come hither to draw.

16 Jesus saith unto her, Go, call thy husband, and come hither.

17 The woman answered and said, I have no husband. Jesus said unto her, Thou hast well said, I have no husband:

18 For thou hast had five husbands; and he whom thou now hast is not thy husband: in that saidst thou truly.

19 The woman saith unto him, Sir, I perceive that thou art a prophet.

20 Our fathers worshipped in this mountain; and ye say, that in Jerusalem is the place where men ought to worship.

21 Jesus saith unto her, Woman, believe me, the hour cometh, when ye shall neither in this mountain, nor yet at Jerusalem, worship the Father.

4:10 *living water*=new life through the Spirit (see Jer. 2:13; Zech. 14:8; John 7:37–39). Salvation is a gift from Jesus Christ, the Son of God and Messiah. Notice that Christ asked the woman to receive Him and His gift without any prerequisite change in her life. After she believed, and because she believed, she would then clean up her life.

4:20 *in this mountain*. On Mt. Gerizim the Samaritans had built a temple to rival the one in Jerusalem, from which they had long been separated politically and religiously.

22 Ye worship ye know not what: we know what we worship: for salvation is of the Jews.

23 But the hour cometh, and now is, when the true worshippers shall worship the Father in spirit and in truth: for the Father seeketh such to worship him.

24 God *is* a Spirit: and they that worship him must worship *him* in spirit and in truth.

25 The woman saith unto him, I know that Messias cometh, which is called Christ: when he is come, he will tell us all things.

26 Jesus saith unto her, I that speak unto thee am *he.*

27 ¶ And upon this came his disciples, and marvelled that he talked with the woman: yet no man said, What seekest thou? or, Why talkest thou with her?

28 The woman then left her waterpot, and went her way into the city, and saith to the men,

29 Come, see a man, which told me all things that ever I did: is not this the Christ?

30 Then they went out of the city, and came unto him.

31 ¶ In the mean while his disciples prayed him, saying, Master, eat.

32 But he said unto them, I have meat to eat that ye know not of.

33 Therefore said the disciples one to another, Hath any man brought him *ought* to eat ?

34 Jesus saith unto them, My meat is to do the will of him that sent me, and to finish his work.

35 Say not ye, There are yet four months, and *then* cometh harvest? behold, I say unto you, Lift up your eyes, and look on the fields; for they are white already to harvest.

36 And he that reapeth receiveth wages, and gathereth fruit unto life eternal: that both he that soweth and he that reapeth may rejoice together.

4:22 *salvation is of the Jews.* The Savior was a Jew and the Jews were the first messengers of the good news.

4:24 *God is a Spirit.* Better, God is Spirit. This describes His nature. *must worship him in spirit and in truth.* The English word "worship" was originally spelled "worthship" and means to acknowledge the worth of the object worshiped. We should acknowledge God's worth *in spirit* (in contrast to material ways) *and in truth* (in contrast to falsehood).

4:25 The Samaritans also believed in a coming Messiah.

4:32 *meat*=food, as also in vv. 8 and 34. The latter verse explains what His food was.

4:35 *they are white already.* The mission fields, Christ says, are ripe and waiting for harvesters.

37 And herein is that saying true, One soweth, and another reapeth.

38 I sent you to reap that whereon ye bestowed no labour: other men laboured, and ye are entered into their labours.

39 ¶ And many of the Samaritans of that city believed on him for the saying of the woman, which testified, He told me all that ever I did.

40 So when the Samaritans were come unto him, they besought him that he would tarry with them: and he abode there two days.

41 And many more believed because of his own word;

42 And said unto the woman, Now we believe, not because of thy saying: for we have heard *him* ourselves, and know that this is indeed the Christ, the Saviour of the world.

H To an Official of Capernaum, 4:43–54

43 ¶ Now after two days he departed thence, and went into Galilee.

44 For Jesus himself testified, that a prophet hath no honour in his own country.

45 Then when he was come into Galilee, the Galilæans received him, having seen all the things that he did at Jerusalem at the feast: for they also went unto the feast.

46 So Jesus came again into Cana of Galilee, where he made the water wine. And there was a certain nobleman, whose son was sick at Caper'naum.

47 When he heard that Jesus was come out of Judæa into Galilee, he went unto him, and besought him that he would come down, and heal his son: for he was at the point of death.

48 Then said Jesus unto him, Except ye see signs and wonders, ye will not believe.

49 The nobleman saith unto him, Sir, come down ere my child die.

50 Jesus saith unto him, Go thy way; thy son liveth. And the man believed the word that Jesus had spoken unto him, and he went his way.

51 And as he was now going down, his servants met him, and told *him*, saying, Thy son liveth.

52 Then enquired he of them the hour when he began to amend. And they said unto him, Yesterday at the seventh hour the fever left him.

4:46 *nobleman*. Lit., king's officer, probably a centurion.
4:52 *amend*=get better.

53 So the father knew that *it was* at the same hour, in the which Jesus said unto him, Thy son liveth: and himself believed, and his whole house.

54 This *is* again the second miracle *that* Jesus did, when he was come out of Judæa into Galilee.

III. CONFRONTATION WITH THE SON OF GOD, 5:1–12:50

A At a Feast in Jerusalem, 5:1–47

1 *The miraculous sign,* 5:1–9

5 After this there was a feast of the Jews; and Jesus went up to Jerusalem.

2 Now there is at Jerusalem by the sheep *market* a pool, which is called in the Hebrew tongue Bethesda, having five porches.

3 In these lay a great multitude of impotent folk, of blind, halt, withered, waiting for the moving of the water.

4 For an angel went down at a certain season into the pool, and troubled the water: whosoever then first after the troubling of the water stepped in was made whole of whatsoever disease he had.

5 And a certain man was there, which had an infirmity thirty and eight years.

6 When Jesus saw him lie, and knew that he had been now a long time *in that case,* he saith unto him, Wilt thou be made whole?

7 The impotent man answered him, Sir, I have no man, when the water is troubled, to put me into the pool: but while I am coming, another steppeth down before me.

8 Jesus saith unto him, Rise, take up thy bed, and walk.

9 And immediately the man was made whole, and took up his bed, and walked: and on the same day was the sabbath.

2 *The reaction,* 5:10–18

10 ¶ The Jews therefore said unto him that was cured, It is the sabbath day: it is not lawful for thee to carry *thy* bed.

5:2 *the sheep market*=the sheep gate (Neh. 3:1; 12:39). *five porches.* I.e., colonnades or cloisters to shelter the sick.
5:3 *waiting for the moving of the water.* This phrase and all of v. 4 are not found in some Greek manuscripts.
5:8 *bed*=pallet, the bed of the very poor.
5:10 *it is not lawful for thee to carry thy bed.* Carrying furniture

11 He answered them, He that made me whole, the same said unto me, Take up thy bed, and walk.

12 Then asked they him, What man is that which said unto thee, Take up thy bed, and walk?

13 And he that was healed wist not who it was: for Jesus had conveyed himself away, a multitude being in *that* place.

14 Afterward Jesus findeth him in the temple, and said unto him, Behold, thou art made whole: sin no more, lest a worse thing come unto thee.

15 The man departed, and told the Jews that it was Jesus, which had made him whole.

16 And therefore did the Jews persecute Jesus, and sought to slay him, because he had done these things on the sabbath day.

17 ¶ But Jesus answered them, My Father worketh hitherto, and I work.

18 Therefore the Jews sought the more to kill him, because he not only had broken the sabbath, but said also that God was his Father, making himself equal with God.

3 *The discourse*, 5:19–47

19 Then answered Jesus and said unto them, Verily, verily, I say unto you, The Son can do nothing of himself, but what he seeth the Father do: for what things soever he doeth, these also doeth the Son likewise.

20 For the Father loveth the Son, and sheweth him all things that himself doeth: and he will shew him greater works than these, that ye may marvel.

21 For as the Father raiseth up the dead, and quickeneth *them*; even so the Son quickeneth whom he will.

22 For the Father judgeth no man, but hath committed all judgment unto the Son:

23 That all *men* should honour the Son, even as they

on the Sabbath was one of the kinds of work which the rabbis taught that the Fourth Commandment prohibited.

5:15 *the Jews.* I.e., the Jewish authorities, here as in vv. 10, 16, 18.

5:17–47 In this important Christological passage Jesus asserts His authority, which he bases on His special relation to the Father. The Jews were perfectly aware that Jesus was claiming full deity—equality with God (v. 18).

5:21–27 Christ's authority is seen in the spheres of resurrection (v. 21, 25, 26) and judgment (v. 22–23, 27). God will make Christ the judge in order that the Son may be honored. Those who believe will escape judgment (v. 24).

honour the Father. He that honoureth not the Son honoureth not the Father which hath sent him.

24 Verily, verily, I say unto you, He that heareth my
word, and believeth on him that sent me, hath everlasting
life, and shall not come into condemnation; but is passed
from death unto life.

25 Verily, verily, I say unto you, The hour is coming,
and now is, when the dead shall hear the voice of the Son
of God: and they that hear shall live.

26 For as the Father hath life in himself; so hath he
given to the Son to have life in himself;

27 And hath given him authority to execute judgment
also, because he is the Son of man.

28 Marvel not at this: for the hour is coming, in the
which all that are in the graves shall hear his voice,

29 And shall come forth; they that have done good,
unto the resurrection of life; and they that have done evil,
unto the resurrection of damnation.

30 I can of mine own self do nothing: as I hear, I judge:
and my judgment is just; because I seek not mine own
will, but the will of the Father which hath sent me.

31 If I bear witness of myself, my witness is not true.

32 ¶ There is another that beareth witness of me; and
I know that the witness which he witnesseth of me is true.

33 Ye sent unto John, and he bare witness unto the
truth.

34 But I receive not testimony from man: but these
things I say, that ye might be saved.

35 He was a burning and a shining light: and ye were
willing for a season to rejoice in his light.

36 ¶ But I have greater witness than *that* of John: for
the works which the Father hath given me to finish, the
same works that I do, bear witness of me, that the Father
hath sent me.

37 And the Father himself, which hath sent me, hath
borne witness of me. Ye have neither heard his voice at
any time, nor seen his shape.

38 And ye have not his word abiding in you: for whom
he hath sent, him ye believe not.

5:31 Here Christ acquiesces to the arguments of His opponents
that His witness alone (without other witnesses) is not true.
But He goes on to remind them that *another*, His Father,
witnesses to the validity of His claims (vv. 32, 37). Other
witnesses cited are John the Baptist (v. 33), His miracles (v.
36), the Scriptures (v. 39), and Moses (v. 46). In 8:14 He
claims that His witness is true.

39 ¶ Search the scriptures; for in them ye think ye have eternal life: and they are they which testify of me.

40 And ye will not come to me, that ye might have life.

41 I receive not honour from men.

42 But I know you, that ye have not the love of God in you.

43 I am come in my Father's name, and ye receive me not: if another shall come in his own name, him ye will receive.

44 How can ye believe, which receive honour one of another, and seek not the honour that *cometh* from God only?

45 Do not think that I will accuse you to the Father: there is *one* that accuseth you, *even* Moses, in whom ye trust.

46 For had ye believed Moses, ye would have believed me: for he wrote of me.

47 But if ye believe not his writings, how shall ye believe my words?

B At Passover Time in Galilee, 6:1–71

1 *The miraculous sign,* 6:1–21

6 After these things Jesus went over the sea of Galilee, which is *the sea* of Tiberias.

2 And a great multitude followed him, because they saw his miracles which he did on them that were diseased.

3 And Jesus went up into a mountain, and there he sat with his disciples.

4 And the passover, a feast of the Jews, was nigh.

5 ¶ When Jesus then lifted up *his* eyes, and saw a great company come unto him, he saith unto Philip, Whence shall we buy bread, that these may eat?

6 And this he said to prove him: for he himself knew what he would do.

7 Philip answered him, Two hundred pennyworth of

5:39 *Search the scriptures.* This may be either a command or a statement of fact and is probably the latter.

5:43 *in my Father's name.* I.e., as His representative. Though you won't follow me, Christ says, you will, ironically, follow false Messiahs—which of course the Jews did periodically until finally crushed by Rome in A.D. 135.

6:1 *sea of Tiberias.* The first name for this lake was Gennesaret; later it was called Galilee, and finally Tiberias after the city built on its shore by Herod Antipas in honor of the Roman emperor Tiberius.

6:7 *two hundred pennyworth.* Better, 200 denarii, about $40. For the denarius, see note at Matt. 20:2.

bread is not sufficient for them, that every one of them may take a little.

8 One of his disciples, Andrew, Simon Peter's brother, saith unto him,

9 There is a lad here, which hath five barley loaves, and two small fishes: but what are they among so many?

10 And Jesus said, Make the men sit down. Now there was much grass in the place. So the men sat down, in number about five thousand.

11 And Jesus took the loaves; and when he had given thanks, he distributed to the disciples, and the disciples to them that were set down; and likewise of the fishes as much as they would.

12 When they were filled, he said unto his disciples, Gather up the fragments that remain, that nothing be lost.

13 Therefore they gathered *them* together, and filled twelve baskets with the fragments of the five barley loaves, which remained over and above unto them that had eaten.

14 Then those men, when they had seen the miracle that Jesus did, said, This is of a truth that prophet that should come into the world.

15 ¶When Jesus therefore perceived that they would come and take him by force, to make him a king, he departed again into a mountain himself alone.

16 And when even was *now* come, his disciples went down unto the sea,

17 And entered into a ship, and went over the sea toward Caper'naum. And it was now dark, and Jesus was not come to them.

18 And the sea arose by reason of a great wind that blew.

19 So when they had rowed about five and twenty or thirty furlongs, they see Jesus walking on the sea, and drawing nigh unto the ship: and they were afraid.

20 But he saith unto them, It is I; be not afraid.

21 Then they willingly received him into the ship: and immediately the ship was at the land whither they went.

6:9 *barley loaves*, the cheap food of the common people.
6:14 *that prophet*. See Deut. 18:15 and John 1:21.
6:15 *to make him a king*. Jesus had to escape from the enthusiasm of the crowd which would have forced Him to lead them in revolt against the Roman government. Jesus refused to become a political revolutionist.
6:19 *five and twenty or thirty furlongs*=3 or 4 miles.

2 *The discourse*, 6:22–40

22 ¶ The day following, when the people which stood on the other side of the sea saw that there was none other boat there, save that one whereinto his disciples were entered, and that Jesus went not with his disciples into the boat, but *that* his disciples were gone away alone;

23 (Howbeit there came other boats from Tiberias nigh unto the place where they did eat bread, after that the Lord had given thanks:)

24 When the people therefore saw that Jesus was not there, neither his disciples, they also took shipping, and came to Caper'naum, seeking for Jesus.

25 And when they had found him on the other side of the sea, they said unto him, Rabbi, when camest thou hither?

26 Jesus answered them and said, Verily, verily, I say unto you, Ye seek me, not because ye saw the miracles, but because ye did eat of the loaves, and were filled.

27 Labour not for the meat which perisheth, but for that meat which endureth unto everlasting life, which the Son of man shall give unto you: for him hath God the Father sealed.

28 Then said they unto him, What shall we do, that we might work the works of God?

29 Jesus answered and said unto them, This is the work of God, that ye believe on him whom he hath sent.

30 They said therefore unto him, What sign shewest thou then, that we may see, and believe thee? what dost thou work?

31 Our fathers did eat manna in the desert; as it is written, He gave them bread from heaven to eat.

32 Then Jesus said unto them, Verily, verily, I say unto you, Moses gave you not that bread from heaven; but my Father giveth you the true bread from heaven.

33 For the bread of God is he which cometh down from heaven, and giveth life unto the world.

34 Then said they unto him, Lord, evermore give us this bread.

35 And Jesus said unto them, I am the bread of life: he that cometh to me shall never hunger; and he that believeth on me shall never thirst.

36 But I said unto you, That ye also have seen me, and believe not.

6:27 The only work that a man can do that is acceptable to God is to believe in Christ (1 John 3:23).

6:31 *manna.* See Ex. 16:15; Num. 11:8; Neh. 9:15.

37 All that the Father giveth me shall come to me; and him that cometh to me I will in no wise cast out.

38 For I came down from heaven, not to do mine own will, but the will of him that sent me.

39 And this is the Father's will which hath sent me, that of all which he hath given me I should lose nothing, but should raise it up again at the last day.

40 And this is the will of him that sent me, that every one which seeth the Son, and believeth on him, may have everlasting life: and I will raise him up at the last day.

3 The reactions, 6:41–71

41 The Jews then murmured at him, because he said, I am the bread which came down from heaven.

42 And they said, Is not this Jesus, the son of Joseph, whose father and mother we know? how is it then that he saith, I came down from heaven?

43 Jesus therefore answered and said unto them, Murmur not among yourselves.

44 No man can come to me, except the Father which hath sent me draw him: and I will raise him up at the last day.

45 It is written in the prophets, And they shall be all taught of God. Every man therefore that hath heard, and hath learned of the Father, cometh unto me.

46 Not that any man hath seen the Father, save he which is of God, he hath seen the Father.

47 Verily, verily, I say unto you, He that believeth on me hath everlasting life.

48 I am that bread of life.

49 Your fathers did eat manna in the wilderness, and are dead.

50 This is the bread which cometh down from heaven, that a man may eat thereof, and not die.

51 I am the living bread which came down from heaven: if any man eat of this bread, he shall live for ever: and the bread that I will give is my flesh, which I will give for the life of the world.

52 The Jews therefore strove among themselves, saying, How can this man give us *his* flesh to eat?

6:39 It is the Father's will to preserve those who come to Christ.

6:43 *Murmur not*=Do not quibble.

6:45 See Isa. 54:13.

6:46 On seeing God, see note at 1:18.

6:51 *the bread that I will give is my flesh.* This is a reference to His sacrificial death on the cross.

53 Then Jesus said unto them, Verily, verily, I say unto you, Except ye eat the flesh of the Son of man, and drink his blood, ye have no life in you.

54 Whoso eateth my flesh, and drinketh my blood, hath eternal life; and I will raise him up at the last day.

55 For my flesh is meat indeed, and my blood is drink indeed.

56 He that eateth my flesh, and drinketh my blood, dwelleth in me, and I in him.

57 As the living Father hath sent me, and I live by the Father: so he that eateth me, even he shall live by me.

58 This is that bread which came down from heaven: not as your fathers did eat manna, and are dead: he that eateth of this bread shall live for ever.

59 These things said he in the synagogue, as he taught in Caper'naum.

60 Many therefore of his disciples, when they had heard *this*, said, This is an hard saying; who can hear it?

61 When Jesus knew in himself that his disciples murmured at it, he said unto them, Doth this offend you?

62 *What* and if ye shall see the Son of man ascend up where he was before?

63 It is the spirit that quickeneth; the flesh profiteth nothing: the words that I speak unto you, *they* are spirit, and *they* are life.

64 But there are some of you that believe not. For Jesus knew from the beginning who they were that believed not, and who should betray him.

65 And he said, Therefore said I unto you, that no man can come unto me, except it were given unto him of my Father.

66 ¶ From that *time* many of his disciples went back, and walked no more with him.

67 Then said Jesus unto the twelve, Will ye also go away?

68 Then Simon Peter answered him, Lord, to whom shall we go? thou hast the words of eternal life.

69 And we believe and are sure that thou art that Christ, the Son of the living God.

70 Jesus answered them, Have not I chosen you twelve, and one of you is a devil?

6:53-56 Just as one eats and drinks in order to have life, so it is necessary to appropriate Christ in order to have eternal life.
6:54 *hath eternal life*. I.e., already has it, and so can count on being raised.
6:60 *hear it*. I.e., accept it.
6:63 *quickeneth*=gives life. *profiteth nothing*=is of no account.

71 He spake of Judas Iscariot *the son* of Simon: for he it was that should betray him, being one of the twelve.

C At the Feast of Tabernacles in Jerusalem, 7:1–10:21

1 *Debate #1—the discourse*, 7:1–29

7 After these things Jesus walked in Galilee: for he would not walk in Jewry, because the Jews sought to kill him.

2 Now the Jews' feast of tabernacles was at hand.

3 His brethren therefore said unto him, Depart hence, and go into Judæa, that thy disciples also may see the works that thou doest.

4 For *there is* no man *that* doeth any thing in secret, and he himself seeketh to be known openly. If thou do these things, shew thyself to the world.

5 For neither did his brethren believe in him.

6 Then Jesus said unto them, My time is not yet come: but your time is always ready.

7 The world cannot hate you; but me it hateth, because I testify of it, that the works thereof are evil.

8 Go ye up unto this feast: I go not up yet unto this feast; for my time is not yet full come.

9 When he had said these words unto them, he abode *still* in Galilee.

10 ¶ But when his brethren were gone up, then went he also up unto the feast, not openly, but as it were in secret.

11 Then the Jews sought him at the feast, and said, Where is he?

12 And there was much murmuring among the people concerning him: for some said, He is a good man: others said, Nay; but he deceiveth the people.

13 Howbeit no man spake openly of him for fear of the Jews.

14 ¶ Now about the midst of the feast Jesus went up into the temple, and taught.

7:1 *Jewry*=Judea. For *Jews* here read Judeans.

7:2 *feast of tabernacles*. This was one of the three pilgrimage-festivals of the Jewish year, occurring in the autumn after the harvest. The Jews dwelt in booths made of the boughs of trees for the seven days of the festival (see Lev. 23:34–43).

7:6 *your time is always ready*. I.e., it doesn't make any difference when you go.

7:7 The world rejected Jesus because His words and acts were a witness against its evil deeds.

7:13 *the Jews*. Since *the people* (v. 12) were all of them Jews, here the Jewish authorities must be meant.

15 And the Jews marvelled, saying, How knoweth this man letters, having never learned?

16 Jesus answered them, and said, My doctrine is not mine, but his that sent me.

17 If any man will do his will, he shall know of the doctrine, whether it be of God, or *whether* I speak of myself.

18 He that speaketh of himself seeketh his own glory: but he that seeketh his glory that sent him, the same is true, and no unrighteousness is in him.

19 Did not Moses give you the law, and *yet* none of you keepeth the law? Why go ye about to kill me?

20 The people answered and said, Thou hast a devil: who goeth about to kill thee?

21 Jesus answered and said unto them, I have done one work, and ye all marvel.

22 Moses therefore gave unto you circumcision; (not because it is of Moses, but of the fathers;) and ye on the sabbath day circumcise a man.

23 If a man on the sabbath day receive circumcision, that the law of Moses should not be broken; are ye angry at me, because I have made a man every whit whole on the sabbath day?

24 Judge not according to the appearance, but judge righteous judgment.

25 Then said some of them of Jerusalem, Is not this he, whom they seek to kill?

26 But, lo, he speaketh boldly, and they say nothing unto him. Do the rulers know indeed that this is the very Christ?

27 Howbeit we know this man whence he is: but when Christ cometh, no man knoweth whence he is.

7:15 *having never learned*. Jesus was not trained in the rabbinical schools (Acts 4:13).

7:17 The thought is: Anyone who does God's will will be able to judge the authority of my teaching.

7:20 *a devil. Lit., a demon.* See Mark 3:22. The question of the last half of the verse overlooks 5:16, 18.

7:21 The *one work* which turned the authorities against Him was the healing of the man of 5:1–9 on the Sabbath day.

7:23 If circumcision be allowed on the Sabbath (Lev. 12:3), should not also a deed of mercy like the healing of an impotent man?

7:27 A popular idea associated with the coming of Messiah was that He would be a man of mystery coming out of the blue, so to speak. Jesus was known to have come from Nazareth and so did not fulfill the requirements.

28 Then cried Jesus in the temple as he taught, saying, Ye both know me, and ye know whence I am: and I am not come of myself, but he that sent me is true, whom ye know not.

29 But I know him: for I am from him, and he hath sent me.

2 The reactions, 7:30–36

30 Then they sought to take him: but no man laid hands on him, because his hour was not yet come.

31 And many of the people believed on him, and said, When Christ cometh, will he do more miracles than these which this *man* hath done?

32 ¶ The Pharisees heard that the people murmured such things concerning him; and the Pharisees and the chief priests sent officers to take him.

33 Then said Jesus unto them, Yet a little while am I with you, and *then* I go unto him that sent me.

34 Ye shall seek me, and shall not find *me:* and where I am, *thither* ye cannot come.

35 Then said the Jews among themselves, Whither will he go, that we shall not find him? will he go unto the dispersed among the Gentiles, and teach the Gentiles?

36 What *manner of* saying is this that he said, Ye shall seek me, and shall not find *me:* and where I am, *thither* ye cannot come?

3 Debate #2—the discourse, 7:37–39

37 In the last day, that great *day* of the feast, Jesus stood and cried, saying, If any man thirst, let him come unto me, and drink.

38 He that believeth on me, as the scripture hath said, out of his belly shall flow rivers of living water.

39 (But this spake he of the Spirit, which they that

7:28 Christ says, in effect, If you knew God you would recognize me.

7:34 The Jewish authorities will die in their sins (8:24) and so "cannot come" thither.

7:37–39 Though not mentioned in the O.T., the Jews had a ceremony of carrying water from the Pool of Siloam and pouring it into a silver basin by the altar of burnt offerings each day for the first seven days of the Feast of Tabernacles. On the eighth day this was not done, making Christ's offer of the water of eternal life from Himself even more startling.

7:38 *belly*=innermost being. The O.T. reference is probably to Isa. 55:1.

7:39 *was not yet given*. Though the Spirit had been active in the

believe on him should receive: for the Holy Ghost was not yet *given*; because that Jesus was not yet glorified.)

4 *The reactions,* 7:40–53

40 ¶ Many of the people therefore, when they heard this saying, said, Of a truth this is the Prophet.

41 Others said, This is the Christ. But some said, Shall Christ come out of Galilee?

42 Hath not the scripture said, That Christ cometh of the seed of David, and out of the town of Bethlehem, where David was?

43 So there was a division among the people because of him.

44 And some of them would have taken him; but no man laid hands on him.

45 ¶ Then came the officers to the chief priests and Pharisees; and they said unto them, Why have ye not brought him?

46 The officers answered, Never man spake like this man.

47 Then answered them the Pharisees, Are ye also deceived?

48 Have any of the rulers or of the Pharisees believed on him?

49 But this people who knoweth not the law are cursed.

50 Nicodemus saith unto them, (he that came to Jesus by night, being one of them,)

51 Doth our law judge *any* man, before it hear him, and know what he doeth?

52 They answered and said unto him, Art thou also of Galilee? Search, and look: for out of Galilee ariseth no prophet.

53 And every man went unto his own house.

world from the beginning (Gen. 1:2), the epoch of the Spirit, in which He would indwell God's people empowering and energizing them, would not begin until the day of Pentecost (see 14:26; 15:26; 16:7).

7:42 *seed of David.* See 2 Sam. 7:12.   *town of Bethlehem.* See Mic. 5:2.

7:43 *So there was a division.* John records three occasions of division over Christ in his Gospel: here concerning His person; in 9:16 concerning His power; and in 10:19 concerning His passion.

7:49 *this people.* I.e., the crowd, the *am ha-arez*, the people of the land, whom the Pharisees despised because they no longer observed the minutiae of the Jewish law.

7:53–8:11 This story, though probably authentic, is omitted in

5 Debate #3—the discourses, 8:1–58

8 Jesus went unto the mount of Olives.
2 And early in the morning he came again into the temple, and all the people came unto him; and he sat down, and taught them.

3 And the scribes and Pharisees brought unto him a woman taken in adultery; and when they had set her in the midst,

4 They say unto him, Master, this woman was taken in adultery, in the very act.

5 Now Moses in the law commanded us, that such should be stoned: but what sayest thou?

6 This they said, tempting him, that they might have to accuse him. But Jesus stooped down, and with *his* finger wrote on the ground, *as though he heard them not.*

7 So when they continued asking him, he lifted up himself, and said unto them, He that is without sin among you, let him first cast a stone at her.

8 And again he stooped down, and wrote on the ground.

9 And they which heard *it*, being convicted by *their own* conscience, went out one by one, beginning at the eldest, *even* unto the last: and Jesus was left alone, and the woman standing in the midst.

10 When Jesus had lifted up himself, and saw none but the woman, he said unto her, Woman, where are those thine accusers? hath no man condemned thee?

11 She said, No man, Lord. And Jesus said unto her, Neither do I condemn thee: go, and sin no more.

12 ¶ Then spake Jesus again unto them, saying, I am the light of the world: he that followeth me shall not walk in darkness, but shall have the light of life.

13 The Pharisees therefore said unto him, Thou bearest record of thyself; thy record is not true.

14 Jesus answered and said unto them, Though I bear record of myself, *yet* my record is true: for I know whence I came, and whither I go; but ye cannot tell whence I come, and whither I go.

many manuscripts and may not have been originally a part of this Gospel.

8:5 See Lev. 20:10; Deut. 22:22–24.

8:12 *I am the light of the world.* Our Lord here draws an analogy between the sun as the physical light of the world and Himself as the spiritual light of the world (see 9:4–5; 11:9–10). This theme permeates chapter 9 also.

8:14 *Though*=Even if. Even if, Christ says, I am testifying about myself, still my testimony is to be believed and trusted. Furthermore, my testimony is attested by the Father (v. 18).

15 Ye judge after the flesh; I judge no man.

16 And yet if I judge, my judgment is true: for I am not alone, but I and the Father that sent me.

17 It is also written in your law, that the testimony of two men is true.

18 I am one that bear witness of myself, and the Father that sent me beareth witness of me.

19 Then said they unto him, Where is thy Father? Jesus answered, Ye neither know me, nor my Father: if ye had known me, ye should have known my Father also.

20 These words spake Jesus in the treasury, as he taught in the temple: and no man laid hands on him; for his hour was not yet come.

21 Then said Jesus again unto them, I go my way, and ye shall seek me, and shall die in your sins: whither I go, ye cannot come.

22 Then said the Jews, Will he kill himself? because he saith, Whither I go, ye cannot come.

23 And he said unto them, Ye are from beneath; I am from above: ye are of this world; I am not of this world.

24 I said therefore unto you, that ye shall die in your sins: for if ye believe not that I am *he*, ye shall die in your sins.

25 Then said they unto him, Who art thou? And Jesus saith unto them, Even *the same* that I said unto you from the beginning.

26 I have many things to say and to judge of you: but he that sent me is true; and I speak to the world those things which I have heard of him.

27 They understood not that he spake to them of the Father.

28 Then said Jesus unto them, When ye have lifted up the Son of man, then shall ye know that I am *he*, and *that* I do nothing of myself; but as my Father hath taught me, I speak these things.

29 And he that sent me is with me: the Father hath not left me alone; for I do always those things that please him.

30 As he spake these words, many believed on him.

31 Then said Jesus to those Jews which believed on him, If ye continue in my word, *then* are ye my disciples indeed;

32 And ye shall know the truth, and the truth shall make you free.

8:24 This remark would have infuriated the Jewish authorities, for it ranked them among the sinners.

8:32 *the truth.* I.e., of the divine revelation, not some current Gnostic truth about the cosmos, the soul, its relation to the body, etc.

33 ¶ They answered him, We be Abraham's seed, and were never in bondage to any man: how sayest thou, Ye shall be made free?

34 Jesus answered them, Verily, verily, I say unto you, Whosoever committeth sin is the servant of sin.

35 And the servant abideth not in the house for ever: *but* the Son abideth ever.

36 If the Son therefore shall make you free, ye shall be free indeed.

37 I know that ye are Abraham's seed; but ye seek to kill me, because my word hath no place in you.

38 I speak that which I have seen with my Father: and ye do that which ye have seen with your father.

39 They answered and said unto him, Abraham is our father. Jesus saith unto them, If ye were Abraham's children, ye would do the works of Abraham.

40 But now ye seek to kill me, a man that hath told you the truth, which I have heard of God: this did not Abraham.

41 Ye do the deeds of your father. Then said they to him, We be not born of fornication; we have one Father, *even* God.

42 Jesus said unto them, If God were your Father, ye would love me: for I proceeded forth and came from God; neither came I of myself, but he sent me.

43 Why do ye not understand my speech? *even* because ye cannot hear my word.

44 Ye are of *your* father the devil, and the lusts of your father ye will do. He was a murderer from the beginning, and abode not in the truth, because there is no truth in him. When he speaketh a lie, he speaketh of his own: for he is a liar, and the father of it.

45 And because I tell *you* the truth, ye believe me not.

46 Which of you convinceth me of sin? And if I say the truth, why do ye not believe me?

8:39 *If we were Abraham's children.* The Jews were all the natural descendants of Abraham (vv. 33, 37), but not all were spiritual descendants because of their unbelief. Their father was the devil (v. 44; see also Eph. 2:2–3; 1 John 3:8–10).

8:40 *this did not Abraham*=this is not what Abraham did (see v. 56).

8:43 *my speech*=what I say. *cannot hear.* I.e., do not wish to, even cannot bear to, accept my teaching. It is not a matter of intellectual capacity but of inner response.

8:44 the true reason for their failure to receive Christ was their relationship to the devil. Notice a similar harsh condemnation in Matt. 23:15.

47 He that is of God heareth God's words: ye therefore hear *them* not, because ye are not of God.

48 Then answered the Jews, and said unto him, Say we not well that thou art a Samaritan, and hast a devil?

49 Jesus answered, I have not a devil; but I honour my Father, and ye do dishonour me.

50 And I seek not mine own glory: there is one that seeketh and judgeth.

51 Verily, verily, I say unto you, If a man keep my saying, he shall never see death.

52 Then said the Jews unto him, Now we know that thou hast a devil. Abraham is dead, and the prophets; and thou sayest, If a man keep my saying, he shall never taste of death.

53 Art thou greater than our father Abraham, which is dead? and the prophets are dead: whom makest thou thyself?

54 Jesus answered, If I honour myself, my honour is nothing: it is my Father that honoureth me; of whom ye say, that he is your God:

55 Yet ye have not known him; but I know him: and if I should say, I know him not, I shall be a liar like unto you: but I know him, and keep his saying.

56 Your father Abraham rejoiced to see my day: and he saw *it*, and was glad.

57 Then said the Jews unto him, Thou art not yet fifty years old, and hast thou seen Abraham?

58 Jesus said unto them, Verily, verily, I say unto you, Before Abraham was, I am.

6 *The reaction,* 8:59

59 Then took they up stones to cast at him: but Jesus hid himself, and went out of the temple, going through the midst of them, and so passed by.

8:51 *he shall never see death.* This means that the believer shall not see spiritual death (separation from God), because through faith he possesses spiritual life (5:24). It may also have the meaning that he shall not see death forever; that is, though the believer dies physically, that death is only temporary, being reversed eventually by the resurrection of the body.

8:53 *whom makest thou thyself?* I.e., who do you claim to be?

8:58 *Before Abraham was, I am.* The "I am" denotes absolute existence always, not simply existence prior to Abraham, and it is a claim to be Yahweh of the O.T. That the Jews understood the significance of this claim is clear from their reaction to this supposed blasphemy (v. 59).

7 *Debate #4—the miraculous sign*, 9:1–12

9 And as *Jesus* passed by, he saw a man which was blind
from *his* birth.

2 And his disciples asked him, saying, Master, who did
sin, this man, or his parents, that he was born blind?

3 Jesus answered, Neither hath this man sinned, nor
his parents: but that the works of God should be made
manifest in him.

4 I must work the works of him that sent me, while it
is day: the night cometh, when no man can work.

5 As long as I am in the world, I am the light of the
world.

6 When he had thus spoken, he spat on the ground, and
made clay of the spittle, and he anointed the eyes of the
blind man with the clay,

7 And said unto him, Go, wash in the pool of Siloam,
(which is by interpretation, Sent.) He went his way therefore, and washed, and came seeing.

8 ¶ The neighbours therefore, and they which before
had seen him that he was blind, said, Is not this he that
sat and begged?

9 Some said, This is he: others *said*, He is like him: *but*
he said, I am *he*.

10 Therefore said they unto him, How were thine eyes
opened?

11 He answered and said, A man that is called Jesus
made clay, and anointed mine eyes, and said unto me, Go
to the pool of Siloam, and wash: and I went and washed,
and I received sight.

12 Then said they unto him, Where is he? He said, I
know not.

8 *The reactions*, 9:13–41

13 ¶ They brought to the Pharisees him that aforetime
was blind.

14 And it was the sabbath day when Jesus made the
clay, and opened his eyes.

15 Then again the Pharisees also asked him how he had

9:2 Sickness and suffering were commonly held to be the consequences of sin. The religious problem became troublesome
when clearly the victim came into the world with a handicap
such as blindness. Jesus shifts the focus from the cause to the
purpose of such suffering. It provided an occasion for revealing God's glory.

9:7 *pool of Siloam*. This lay at the southern extremity of the
Tyropoeon Valley, at the southern end of Hezekiah's tunnel.

received his sight. He said unto them, He put clay upon mine eyes, and I washed, and do see.

16 Therefore said some of the Pharisees, This man is not of God, because he keepeth not the sabbath day. Others said, How can a man that is a sinner do such miracles? And there was a division among them.

17 They say unto the blind man again, What sayest thou of him, that he hath opened thine eyes? He said, He is a prophet.

18 But the Jews did not believe concerning him, that he had been blind, and received his sight, until they called the parents of him that had received his sight.

19 And they asked them, saying, Is this your son, who ye say was born blind? how then doth he now see?

20 His parents answered them and said, We know that this is our son, and that he was born blind:

21 But by what means he now seeth, we know not; or who hath opened his eyes, we know not: he is of age; ask him: he shall speak for himself.

22 These *words* spake his parents, because they feared the Jews: for the Jews had agreed already, that if any man did confess that he was Christ, he should be put out of the synagogue.

23 Therefore said his parents, He is of age; ask him.

24 Then again called they the man that was blind, and said unto him, Give God the praise: we know that this man is a sinner.

25 He answered and said, Whether he be a sinner *or no*, I know not: one thing I know, that, whereas I was blind, now I see.

26 Then said they to him again, What did he to thee? how opened he thine eyes?

27 He answered them, I have told you already, and ye did not hear: wherefore would ye hear *it* again? will ye also be his disciples?

28 Then they reviled him, and said, Thou art his disciple; but we are Moses' disciples.

9:16 *he keepeth not the sabbath day*. The Pharisees considered the making of clay (v. 14) a kind of work that violated the Sabbath (se 5:10).

9:17 *that*=since or because.

9:22 *be put out of the synagogue*. I.e., excommunicated from worship and fellowship.

9:27 *will ye*=do you wish also to be His disciples? The man is using sarcasm.

29 We know that God spake unto Moses: *as for* this *fellow*, we know not from whence he is.

30 The man answered and said unto them, Why herein is a marvellous thing, that ye know not from whence he is, and *yet* he hath opened mine eyes.

31 Now we know that God heareth not sinners: but if any man be a worshipper of God, and doeth his will, him he heareth.

32 Since the world began was it not heard that any man opened the eyes of one that was born blind.

33 If this man were not of God, he could do nothing.

34 They answered and said unto him, Thou wast altogether born in sins, and dost thou teach us? And they cast him out.

35 Jesus heard that they had cast him out; and when he had found him, he said unto him, Dost thou believe on the Son of God?

36 He answered and said, Who is he, Lord, that I might believe on him?

37 And Jesus said unto him, Thou hast both seen him, and it is he that talketh with thee.

38 And he said, Lord, I believe. And he worshipped him.

39 ¶ And Jesus said, For judgment I am come into this world, that they which see not might see; and that they which see might be made blind.

40 And *some* of the Pharisees which were with him heard these words, and said unto him, Are we blind also?

41 Jesus said unto them, If ye were blind, ye should have no sin: but now ye say, We see; therefore your sin remaineth.

9 Debate #5—
the discourse on the Good Shepherd, 10:1-18

10 Verily, verily, I say unto you, He that entereth not by the door into the sheepfold, but climbeth up some other way, the same is a thief and a robber.

9:29 A typical statement of Pharisaic orthodoxy. The man refused to be coerced away from the plain fact that he had been cured (vv. 25, 30).

9:34 Their hostility now borders on the fanatical.

9:39 *For judgment I am come into this world.* His coming was not for the purpose of judgment (3:17), but it inevitably resulted in judgment because some decided against Him. Compare Mark 4:12 and Isa. 6:9.

9:41 The Pharisees' insistence that they could see makes their sin willful.

2 But he that entereth in by the door is the shepherd of the sheep.

3 To him the porter openeth; and the sheep hear his voice: and he calleth his own sheep by name, and leadeth them out.

4 And when he putteth forth his own sheep, he goeth before them, and the sheep follow him: for they know his voice.

5 And a stranger will they not follow, but will flee from him: for they know not the voice of strangers.

6 This parable spake Jesus unto them: but they understood not what things they were which he spake unto them.

7 Then said Jesus unto them again, Verily, verily, I say unto you, I am the door of the sheep.

8 All that ever came before me are thieves and robbers: but the sheep did not hear them.

9 I am the door: by me if any man enter in, he shall be saved, and shall go in and out, and find pasture.

10 The thief cometh not, but for to steal, and to kill, and to destroy: I am come that they might have life, and that they might have *it* more abundantly.

11 I am the good shepherd: the good shepherd giveth his life for the sheep.

12 But he that is an hireling, and not the shepherd, whose own the sheep are not, seeth the wolf coming, and leaveth the sheep, and fleeth: and the wolf catcheth them, and scattereth the sheep.

13 The hireling fleeth, because he is an hireling, and careth not for the sheep.

14 I am the good shepherd, and know my *sheep*, and am known of mine.

15 As the Father knoweth me, even so know I the Father: and I lay down my life for the sheep.

16 And other sheep I have, which are not of this fold: them also I must bring, and they shall hear my voice; and there shall be one fold, *and* one shepherd.

10:8 *thieves and robbers.* I.e., false Messiahs, false teachers, of whom Palestine knew many in the first century A.D.

10:11 *I am the good shepherd.* As good shepherd Christ gave His life for the sheep and became the door to God's fold (v. 7); as great shepherd (Heb. 13:20–21) He rose from the dead to care for His sheep; as chief shepherd (1 Pet. 5:4) He will come again for His sheep.

10:16 *other sheep I have.* These are the Gentiles who would believe and who would, with the converted Jews, form one body (Eph. 2:16). *fold;* better, flock.

17 Therefore doth my Father love me, because I lay down my life, that I might take it again.

18 No man taketh it from me, but I lay it down of myself. I have power to lay it down, and I have power to take it again. This commandment have I received of my Father.

10 *The reactions,* 10:19–21

19 ¶ There was a division therefore again among the Jews for these sayings.

20 And many of them said, He hath a devil, and is mad; why hear ye him?

21 Others said, These are not the words of him that hath a devil. Can a devil open the eyes of the blind?

D At the Feast of Dedication in Jerusalem, 10:22–42

1 *The discourse,* 10:22–30

22 ¶ And it was at Jerusalem the feast of the dedication, and it was winter.

23 And Jesus walked in the temple in Solomon's porch.

24 Then came the Jews round about him, and said unto him, How long dost thou make us to doubt? If thou be the Christ, tell us plainly.

25 Jesus answered them, I told you, and ye believed not: the works that I do in my Father's name, they bear witness of me.

26 But ye believe not, because ye are not of my sheep, as I said unto you.

27 My sheep hear my voice, and I know them, and they follow me:

28 And I give unto them eternal life; and they shall never perish, neither shall any *man* pluck them out of my hand.

29 My Father, which gave *them* me, is greater than all; and no *man* is able to pluck *them* out of my Father's hand.

30 I and *my* Father are one.

10:22 *the feast of the dedication.* This was instituted in 165 B.C. by Judas Maccabeus in commemoration of the cleansing and reopening of the temple after its desecration by the Syrian ruler Antiochus Epiphanes in 168 B.C. (Dan. 11:31; 1 Macc. 4:52–59). It is also called the Feast of Lights or Hanukkah. The date falls near the winter solstice, Dec. 22.

10:30 *one.* The Father and Son are in perfect unity in their actions. The neuter rules out the meaning that they are one person.

2 *The rejection,* 10:31–42

31 Then the Jews took up stones again to stone him.

32 Jesus answered them, Many good works have I shewed you from my Father; for which of those works do ye stone me?

33 The Jews answered him, saying, For a good work we stone thee not; but for blasphemy; and because that thou, being a man, makest thyself God.

34 Jesus answered them, Is it not written in your law, I said, Ye are gods?

35 If he called them gods, unto whom the word of God came, and the scripture cannot be broken;

36 Say ye of him, whom the Father hath sanctified, and sent into the world, Thou blasphemest; because I said, I am the Son of God?

37 If I do not the works of my Father, believe me not.

38 But if I do, though ye believe not me, believe the works: that ye may know, and believe, that the Father *is* in me, and I in him.

39 Therefore they sought again to take him: but he escaped out of their hand,

40 And went away again beyond Jordan into the place where John at first baptized; and there he abode.

41 And many resorted unto him, and said, John did no miracle: but all things that John spake of this man were true.

42 And many believed on him there.

E At Bethany, 11:1–12:11

1 *The miraculous sign,* 11:1–44

11 Now a certain *man* was sick, *named* Lazarus, of Bethany, the town of Mary and her sister Martha.

10:33 *blasphemy.* See note at Mark 14:64.
10:34 *written in your law.* I.e., in Ps. 82.6. The term "law" was sometimes applied to the entire O.T. Christ's point is that if the O.T. uses the word "God" (Elohim) of men who were representative of God, then the Jews should not oppose Him for calling Himself the Son of God.
10:35 *the scripture cannot be broken.* I.e., loosed or deprived of its binding authority. Jesus here employs some rather technical exegesis of the O.T.
10:38 *believe the works.* Even if the leaders could not test Jesus' verbal claims, they could see His works, and those miracles should lead them to acknowledge the truth of His claims.
10:39 *he escaped.* Apparently He moved without walking, another supernatural phenomenon.

2 (It was *that* Mary which anointed the Lord with ointment, and wiped his feet with her hair, whose brother Lazarus was sick.)

3 Therefore his sisters sent unto him, saying, Lord, behold, he whom thou lovest is sick.

4 When Jesus heard *that*, he said, This sickness is not unto death, but for the glory of God, that the Son of God might be glorified thereby.

5 Now Jesus loved Martha, and her sister, and Lazarus.

6 When he had heard therefore that he was sick, he abode two days still in the same place where he was.

7 Then after that saith he to *his* disciples, Let us go into Judæa again.

8 *His* disciples say unto him, Master, the Jews of late sought to stone thee; and goest thou thither again?

9 Jesus answered, Are there not twelve hours in the day? If any man walk in the day, he stumbleth not, because he seeth the light of this world.

10 But if a man walk in the night, he stumbleth, because there is no light in him.

11 These things said he: and after that he saith unto them, Our friend Lazarus sleepeth; but I go, that I may awake him out of sleep.

12 Then said his disciples, Lord, if he sleep, he shall do well.

13 Howbeit Jesus spake of his death: but they thought that he had spoken of taking of rest in sleep.

14 Then said Jesus unto them plainly, Lazarus is dead.

15 And I am glad for your sakes that I was not there, to the intent ye may believe; nevertheless let us go unto him.

16 Then said Thomas, which is called Did'ymus, unto his fellowdisciples, Let us also go, that we may die with him.

11:2 *Mary*. See John 12:3; Matt. 26:7; Mark 14:3.
11:4 *for the glory of God*. The resurrection of Lazarus would demonstrate the glory of God even more than restoration from a sick bed.
11:8–10 Jesus states that He could safely go back to Judea, where an attempt had been made to stone Him (11:8), as long as He was walking in the light of His Father's will.
11:11 *sleepeth*. Though the disciples understood this to mean natural sleep (v. 12), Jesus used it as a metaphor to denote death (Mark 5:39; Acts 7:60; 1 Thess. 4:13).
11:16 *Didymus=twin*. Possibly Thomas was a twin of Matthew, with whose name his is coupled in Matt. 10:3, Mark 3:18, and Luke 6:15.

17 Then when Jesus came, he found that he had *lain* in the grave four days already.

18 Now Bethany was nigh unto Jerusalem, about fifteen furlongs off:

19 And many of the Jews came to Martha and Mary, to comfort them concerning their brother.

20 Then Martha, as soon as she heard that Jesus was coming, went and met him: but Mary sat *still* in the house.

21 Then said Martha unto Jesus, Lord, if thou hadst been here, my brother had not died.

22 But I know, that even now, whatsoever thou wilt ask of God, God will give *it* thee.

23 Jesus saith unto her, Thy brother shall rise again.

24 Martha saith unto him, I know that he shall rise again in the resurrection at the last day.

25 Jesus said unto her, I am the resurrection, and the life: he that believeth in me, though he were dead, yet shall he live:

26 And whosoever liveth and believeth in me shall never die. Believest thou this?

27 She saith unto him, Yea, Lord: I believe that thou art the Christ, the Son of God, which should come into the world.

28 And when she had so said, she went her way, and called Mary her sister secretly, saying, The Master is come, and calleth for thee.

29 As soon as she heard *that*, she arose quickly, and came unto him.

30 Now Jesus was not yet come into the town, but was in that place where Martha met him.

31 The Jews then which were with her in the house, and comforted her, when they saw Mary, that she rose up hastily and went out, followed her, saying, She goeth unto the grave to weep there.

32 Then when Mary was come where Jesus was, and saw him, she fell down at his feet, saying unto him, Lord, if thou hadst been here, my brother had not died.

33 When Jesus therefore saw her weeping, and the

11:17 *grave*=tomb.
11:18 *about fifteen furlongs*=about 2 miles.
11:25–26 *he that believeth in me*, even if he die physically he shall live spiritually and eternally. *And whosoever liveth* physically *and believeth in me shall never die* spiritually and eternally.
11:33 *he groaned in the spirit*. I.e., He was deeply moved within because of the sorrow sickness and death brought.

Jews also weeping which came with her, he groaned in the spirit, and was troubled,

34 And said, Where have ye laid him? They said unto him, Lord, come and see.

35 Jesus wept.

36 Then said the Jews, Behold how he loved him!

37 And some of them said, Could not this man, which opened the eyes of the blind, have caused that even this man should not have died?

38 Jesus therefore again groaning in himself cometh to the grave. It was a cave, and a stone lay upon it.

39 Jesus said, Take ye away the stone. Martha, the sister of him that was dead, saith unto him, Lord, by this time he stinketh: for he hath been *dead* four days.

40 Jesus saith unto her, Said I not unto thee, that, if thou wouldest believe, thou shouldest see the glory of God?

41 Then they took away the stone *from the place* where the dead was laid. And Jesus lifted up *his* eyes, and said, Father, I thank thee that thou hast heard me.

42 And I knew that thou hearest me always: but because of the people which stand by I said *it*, that they may believe that thou hast sent me.

43 And when he thus had spoken, he cried with a loud voice, Lazarus, come forth.

44 And he that was dead came forth, bound hand and foot with graveclothes: and his face was bound about with a napkin. Jesus saith unto them, Loose him, and let him go.

2 *The reactions*, 11:45–57

45 Then many of the Jews which came to Mary, and had seen the things which Jesus did, believed on him.

46 But some of them went their ways to the Pharisees, and told them what things Jesus had done.

47 ¶ Then gathered the chief priests and the Pharisees a council, and said, What do we? for this man doeth many miracles.

48 If we let him thus alone, all *men* will believe on him: and the Romans shall come and take away both our place and nation.

49 And one of them, *named* Ca'iaphas, being the high priest that same year, said unto them, Ye know nothing at all,

11:43 *Lazarus, come forth*. Only Jesus can call the dead to life 5:25); others could move the stone (v. 39) and grave clothes (v. 44).
11:48 *our place*. I.e., the holy place, the temple.

50 Nor consider that it is expedient for us, that one man should die for the people, and that the whole nation perish not.

51 And this spake he not of himself: but being high priest that year, he prophesied that Jesus should die for that nation;

52 And not for that nation only, but that also he should gather together in one the children of God that were scattered abroad.

53 Then from that day forth they took counsel together for to put him to death.

54 Jesus therefore walked no more openly among the Jews; but went thence unto a country near to the wilderness, into a city called Ē'phraim, and there continued with his disciples.

55 ¶And the Jews' passover was nigh at hand: and many went out of the country up to Jerusalem before the passover, to purify themselves.

56 Then sought they for Jesus, and spake among themselves, as they stood in the temple, What think ye, that he will not come to the feast?

57 Now both the chief priests and the Pharisees had given a commandment, that, if any man knew where he were, he should shew it, that they might take him.

3 The anointing by Mary, 12:1–8

12 Then Jesus six days before the passover came to Bethany, where Lazarus was which had been dead, whom he raised from the dead.

2 There they made him a supper; and Martha served: but Lazarus was one of them that sat at the table with him.

3 Then took Mary a pound of ointment of spikenard, very costly, and anointed the feet of Jesus, and wiped his feet with her hair: and the house was filled with the odour of the ointment.

4 Then saith one of his disciples, Judas Iscariot, Simon's son, which should betray him,

---

11:50 Caiaphas could hardly realize the full meaning of his words (18:14). He was simply expressing the thought of a political collaborator with Rome; and yet those words express the central doctrine of the Christian faith, the substitutionary atonement of Christ.

11:56 stood in the temple, after undergoing the purification rites (v. 55).

5 Why was not this ointment sold for three hundred pence, and given to the poor?

6 This he said, not that he cared for the poor; but because he was a thief, and had the bag, and bare what was put therein.

7 Then said Jesus, Let her alone: against the day of my burying hath she kept this.

8 For the poor always ye have with you; but me ye have not always.

4 *The reactions,* 12:9–11

9 Much people of the Jews therefore knew that he was there: and they came not for Jesus' sake only, but that they might see Lazarus also, whom he had raised from the dead.

10 ¶ But the chief priests consulted that they might put Lazarus also to death;

11 Because that by reason of him many of the Jews went away, and believed on Jesus.

F At Jerusalem, 12:12–50

1 *The triumphal entry,* 12:12–19

12 ¶ On the next day much people that were come to the feast, when they heard that Jesus was coming to Jerusalem,

13 Took branches of palm trees, and went forth to meet him, and cried, Hosanna: Blessed *is* the King of Israel that cometh in the name of the Lord.

14 And Jesus, when he had found a young ass, sat thereon; as it is written,

15 Fear not, daughter of Sion: behold, thy King cometh, sitting on an ass's colt.

16 These things understood not his disciples at the first: but when Jesus was glorified, then remembered they that these things were written of him, and *that* they had done these things unto him.

17 The people therefore that was with him when he

12:5 *three hundred pence*=300 denarii, approximately what a worker would earn in one year.

12:6 *had the bag.* Judas was evidently the treasurer of the group. Bag may mean small chest or money-box.

12:15 Quoting Zech. 9:9.

12:16 *that these things were written of him.* I.e., in the Hebrew Scriptures, which Christ's followers searched carefully after His death.

called Lazarus out of his grave, and raised him from the dead, bare record.

18 For this cause the people also met him, for that they heard that he had done this miracle.

19 The Pharisees therefore said among themselves, Perceive ye how ye prevail nothing? behold, the world is gone after him.

2 The teaching, 12:20–50

20 ¶ And there were certain Greeks among them that came up to worship at the feast:

21 The same came therefore to Philip, which was of Bethsā'ida of Galilee, and desired him, saying, Sir, we would see Jesus.

22 Philip cometh and telleth Andrew: and again Andrew and Philip tell Jesus.

23 ¶ And Jesus answered them, saying, The hour is come, that the Son of man should be glorified.

24 Verily, verily, I say unto you, Except a corn of wheat fall into the ground and die, it abideth alone: but if it die, it bringeth forth much fruit.

25 He that loveth his life shall lose it; and he that hateth his life in this world shall keep it unto life eternal.

26 If any man serve me, let him follow me; and where I am, there shall also my servant be: if any man serve me, him will *my* Father honour.

27 Now is my soul troubled; and what shall I say? Father, save me from this hour: but for this cause came I unto this hour.

28 Father, glorify thy name. Then came there a voice from heaven, *saying*, I have both glorified *it*, and will glorify *it* again.

29 The people therefore, that stood by, and heard *it*, said that it thundered: others said, An angel spake to him.

30 Jesus answered and said, This voice came not because of me, but for your sakes.

31 Now is the judgment of this world: now shall the prince of this world be cast out.

12:23 *The hour is come.* The time has come for which He has been working throughout His ministry; namely, the time of His death and resurrection. This is the beginning of the climax of His ministry.

12:31 *the judgment of this world.* The cross is the condemnation of, the judgment upon, those who reject it; it is also the basis for the ultimate victory over Satan.

32 And I, if I be lifted up from the earth, will draw all *men* unto me.

33 This he said, signifying what death he should die.

34 The people answered him, We have heard out of the law that Christ abideth for ever: and how sayest thou, The Son of man must be lifted up? who is this Son of man?

35 Then Jesus said unto them, Yet a little while is the light with you. Walk while ye have the light, lest darkness come upon you: for he that walketh in darkness knoweth not whither he goeth.

36 While ye have light, believe in the light, that ye may be the children of light. These things spake Jesus, and departed, and did hide himself from them.

37 ¶ But though he had done so many miracles before them, yet they believed not on him:

38 That the saying of Ēsā'ias the prophet might be fulfilled, which he spake, Lord, who hath believed our report? and to whom hath the arm of the Lord been revealed?

39 Therefore they could not believe, because that Ēsā'ias said again,

40 He hath blinded their eyes, and hardened their heart; that they should not see with *their* eyes, nor understand with *their* heart, and be converted, and I should heal them.

41 These things said Ēsā'ias, when he saw his glory, and spake of him.

42 ¶ Nevertheless among the chief rulers also many believed on him; but because of the Pharisees they did not confess *him*, lest they should be put out of the synagogue:

43 For they loved the praise of men more than the praise of God.

44 ¶ Jesus cried and said, He that believeth on me, believeth not on me, but on him that sent me.

45 And he that seeth me seeth him that sent me.

46 I am come a light into the world, that whosoever believeth on me should not abide in darkness.

12:32 *lifted up* on the cross. *will draw all men.* His saving grace will be available to Greeks (like those present, v. 20) as well as to Jews.

12:34 They could not conceive of the heavenly Son of man being lifted up to die.

12:37–50 These verses summarize the public ministry of Jesus Christ, and explain the rejections which are equated with the rejection of God.

12:38–41 See Isa. 6:10; 53:1.

12:41 *when.* Better, because.

47 And if any man hear my words, and believe not, I judge him not: for I came not to judge the world, but to save the world.

48 He that rejecteth me, and receiveth not my words, hath one that judgeth him: the word that I have spoken, the same shall judge him in the last day.

49 For I have not spoken of myself; but the Father which sent me, he gave me a commandment, what I should say, and what I should speak.

50 And I know that his commandment is life everlasting: whatsoever I speak therefore, even as the Father said unto me, so I speak.

IV INSTRUCTION BY THE SON OF GOD,
13:1–16:33

A Concerning Forgiveness, 13:1–20

13 Now before the feast of the passover, when Jesus knew that his hour was come that he should depart out of this world unto the Father, having loved his own which were in the world, he loved them unto the end.

2 And supper being ended, the devil having now put into the heart of Judas Iscariot, Simon's *son*, to betray him;

3 Jesus knowing that the Father had given all things into his hands, and that he was come from God, and went to God;

4 He riseth from supper, and laid aside his garments; and took a towel, and girded himself.

5 After that he poureth water into a bason, and began to wash the disciples' feet, and to wipe *them* with the towel wherewith he was girded.

6 Then cometh he to Simon Peter: and Peter saith unto him, Lord, dost thou wash my feet?

7 Jesus answered and said unto him, What I do thou knowest not now; but thou shalt know hereafter.

8 Peter saith unto him, Thou shalt never wash my feet. Jesus answered him, If I wash thee not, thou hast no part with me.

9 Simon Peter saith unto him, Lord, not my feet only, but also *my* hands and *my* head.

12:47 See note at 9:39.
13:1 *unto the end.* Lit., to the fullest extent.
13:3–11 This dramatic scene of the foot-washing is an acted parable, a lesson in humility, and a vivid dramatization of Christ's self-humiliation and exaltation.

10 Jesus saith to him, He that is washed needeth not save to wash *his* feet, but is clean every whit: and ye are clean, but not all.

11 For he knew who should betray him; therefore said he, Ye are not all clean.

12 So after he had washed their feet, and had taken his garments, and was set down again, he said unto them, Know ye what I have done to you?

13 Ye call me Master and Lord: and ye say well; for *so* I am.

14 If I then, *your* Lord and Master, have washed your feet; ye also ought to wash one another's feet.

15 For I have given you an example, that ye should do as I have done to you.

16 Verily, verily, I say unto you, The servant is not greater than his lord; neither he that is sent greater than he that sent him.

17 If ye know these things, happy are ye if ye do them.

18 ¶ I speak not of you all: I know whom I have chosen: but that the scripture may be fulfilled, He that eateth bread with me hath lifted up his heel against me.

19 Now I tell you before it come, that, when it is come to pass, ye may believe that I am *he.*

20 Verily, verily, I say unto you, He that receiveth whomsoever I send receiveth me; and he that receiveth me receiveth him that sent me.

B Concerning His Betrayal, 13:21–30

21 When Jesus had thus said, he was troubled in spirit, and testified, and said, Verily, verily, I say unto you, that one of you shall betray me.

13:10 *He that is washed needeth not save to wash his feet.* There are two different words here for "wash" so that the phrase literally reads, "He that has bathed needs not wash except his feet." Just as in the natural life a man who has bathed needs only to wash the dust off his sandaled feet when he returns home, so in the spiritual life a man who has been cleansed from sin need not think that all is lost when he sins in his walk through life. He needs only to confess those sins to be entirely clean again.

13:14 *ye also ought to wash one another's feet.* Since the illustration has to do with forgiveness, this phrase means that believers ought to forgive one another (Matt. 5:23–24; Eph. 4:32).

13:18 *scripture.* Ps. 41:9 is referred to.

13:19 *I am he.* I.e., the one to whom Ps. 41:9 refers.

13:20 Those who are sent are the apostles, as in v. 16.

22 Then the disciples looked one on another, doubting of whom he spake.

23 Now there was leaning on Jesus' bosom one of his disciples, whom Jesus loved.

24 Simon Peter therefore beckoned to him, that he should ask who it should be of whom he spake.

25 He then lying on Jesus' breast saith unto him, Lord, who is it?

26 Jesus answered, He it is, to whom I shall give a sop, when I have dipped *it*. And when he had dipped the sop, he gave *it* to Judas Iscariot, *the son* of Simon.

27 And after the sop Satan entered into him. Then said Jesus unto him, That thou doest, do quickly.

28 Now no man at the table knew for what intent he spake this unto him.

29 For some *of them* thought, because Judas had the bag, that Jesus had said unto him, Buy *those things* that we have need of against the feast; or, that he should give something to the poor.

30 He then having received the sop went immediately out: and it was night.

C Concerning His Departure, 13:31-38

31 ¶ Therefore, when he was gone out, Jesus said, Now is the Son of man glorified, and God is glorified in him.

32 If God be glorified in him, God shall also glorify him in himself, and shall straightway glorify him.

33 Little children, yet a little while I am with you. Ye shall seek me: and as I said unto the Jews, Whither I go, ye cannot come; so now I say to you.

34 A new commandment I give unto you, That ye love one another; as I have loved you, that ye also love one another.

13:23 *one of his disciples, whom Jesus loved.* I.e., John.

13:26 *the sop*=the morsel. At Eastern meals it was customary for the host to offer one of the guests a morsel of bread as a gesture of special friendship. By this Jesus was showing His love for the betrayer.

13:30 *and it was night.* The "hour" for which Christ, the light of the world, has been waiting, when the powers of darkness would engulf Him, begins in darkness.

13:31-32 In His death Christ and God will be glorified (v. 31). In the resurrection and exaltation God will glorify Christ and validate all His claims (v. 32).

35 By this shall all *men* know that ye are my disciples, if ye have love one to another.

36 ¶ Simon Peter said unto him, Lord, whither goest thou? Jesus answered him, Whither I go, thou canst not follow me now; but thou shalt follow me afterwards.

37 Peter said unto him, Lord, why cannot I follow thee now? I will lay down my life for thy sake.

38 Jesus answered him, Wilt thou lay down thy life for my sake? Verily, verily, I say unto thee, The cock shall not crow, till thou hast denied me thrice.

D Concerning Heaven, 14:1–14

14 Let not your heart be troubled: ye believe in God, believe also in me.

2 In my Father's house are many mansions: if *it were* not *so*, I would have told you. I go to prepare a place for you.

3 And if I go and prepare a place for you, I will come again, and receive you unto myself; that where I am, *there* ye may be also.

4 And whither I go ye know, and the way ye know.

5 Thomas saith unto him, Lord, we know not whither thou goest; and how can we know the way?

6 Jesus saith unto him, I am the way, the truth, and the life: no man cometh unto the Father, but by me.

7 If ye had known me, ye should have known my Father also: and from henceforth ye know him, and have seen him.

8 Philip saith unto him, Lord, shew us the Father, and it sufficeth us.

9 Jesus saith unto him, Have I been so long time with you, and yet hast thou not known me, Philip? he that hath

---

13:35 Your mutual love will be the strongest possible argument for the Christian faith.

14:1 In view of His departure from them, Christ gives the disciples in this chapter specific encouragements. They include the provision in the Father's house (v. 2), the promise to return (v. 3), the prospect of doing greater works (v. 12), the promise of answered prayer (v. 14), the coming of the Holy Spirit (v. 16), and the legacy of peace (v. 27). *ye believe . . . believe*. Both verbs are probably to be understood as imperatives: believe . . . believe.

14:2 *mansions*. The same word is used elsewhere in the N.T. only in v. 23, where it is translated "abode."

14:3 *I will come again*. See 1 Thess. 4:13–18. This is not the coming of the Spirit nor the believer's death, but Christ's personal return.

seen me hath seen the Father; and how sayest thou *then,*
Shew us the Father?

10 Believest thou not that I am in the Father, and the
Father in me? the words that I speak unto you I speak not
of myself: but the Father that dwelleth in me, he doeth
the works.

11 Believe me that I *am* in the Father, and the Father
in me: or else believe me for the very works' sake.

12 Verily, verily, I say unto you, He that believeth on
me, the works that I do shall he do also; and greater *works*
than these shall he do; because I go unto my Father.

13 And whatsoever ye shall ask in my name, that will
I do, that the Father may be glorified in the Son.

14 If ye shall ask any thing in my name, I will do *it.*

E Concerning the Holy Spirit, 14:15–26

15 ¶ If ye love me, keep my commandments.

16 And I will pray the Father, and he shall give you
another Comforter, that he may abide with you for ever;

17 *Even* the Spirit of truth; whom the world cannot
receive, because it seeth him not, neither knoweth him: but

14:9 *he that hath seen me hath seen the Father.* See note at
1:18.

14:12 *greater works than these shall he do.* Greater in extent
(through the world-wide preaching of the gospel) and effect
(the spiritual redemption and placing in the body of Christ
of multitudes of people since the day of Pentecost). These
will be done through prayer in His name (v. 13).

14:13 *in my name.* This is not a formula to be tacked on to the
end of prayers, but it means praying for the same things which
Christ would desire to see accomplished. It is like using a
power of attorney which a very dear loved one has given you.

14:16 *another Comforter.* The Holy Spirit is called the Comforter (Greek; *paraclete,* as also in 14:26; 15:26; 16:7). In
the root of this word are the ideas of advising, exhorting, comforting, strengthening, interceding, and encouraging. The only
other occurrence of the word outside this discourse in the
N.T. is in 1 John 2:1 applied to Christ and translated "Advocate." Here and in the other passages in John cited above,
Christ teaches that the Holy Spirit (1) will indwell Christians
(vv. 16–17); (2) will help the disciples recall the events of
His life (14:26); (3) will convince the world of sin, righteousness and judgment (16:7–11); (4) will teach believers the
truth (15:26; 16:13–15).

14:17 *he dwelleth with you, and shall be in you.* The Holy Spirit
was active in O.T. times, but His dwelling in the lives of
believers after Pentecost is different in that (1) it is permanent
and (2) it is true of every individual believer.

ye know him; for he dwelleth with you, and shall be in you.

18 I will not leave you comfortless: I will come to you.

19 Yet a little while, and the world seeth me no more; but ye see me: because I live, ye shall live also.

20 At that day ye shall know that I *am* in my Father, and ye in me, and I in you.

21 He that hath my commandments, and keepeth them, he it is that loveth me: and he that loveth me shall be loved of my Father, and I will love him, and will manifest myself to him.

22 Judas saith unto him, not Iscariot, Lord, how is it that thou wilt manifest thyself unto us, and not unto the world?

23 Jesus answered and said unto him, If a man love me, he will keep my words: and my Father will love him, and we will come unto him, and make our abode with him.

24 He that loveth me not keepeth not my sayings: and the word which ye hear is not mine, but the Father's which sent me.

25 These things have I spoken unto you, being *yet* present with you.

26 But the Comforter, *which is* the Holy Ghost, whom the Father will send in my name, he shall teach you all things, and bring all things to your remembrance, whatsoever I have said unto you.

F Concerning Peace, 14:27–31

27 Peace I leave with you, my peace I give unto you: not as the world giveth, give I unto you. Let not your heart be troubled, neither let it be afraid.

28 Ye have heard how I said unto you, I go away, and come *again* unto you. If ye loved me, ye would rejoice, because I said, I go unto the Father: for my Father is greater than I.

29 And now I have told you before it come to pass, that, when it is come to pass, ye might believe.

30 Hereafter I will not talk much with you: for the prince of this world cometh, and hath nothing in me.

14:21 The Christian faith works through love, and the measure of one's love is the extent to which he keeps Christ's commandments. These are, of course, found only in the N.T.

14:26 *Holy Ghost*=Holy Spirit.

14:30 *and hath nothing in me.* Satan (*the prince of this world*) possesses nothing in the person of Christ and has no power over Him whatsoever. This is another evidence of Christ's sinlessness.

31 But that the world may know that I love the Father; and as the Father gave me commandment, even so I do. Arise, let us go hence.

G Concerning Fruitfulness, 15:1–17

15 I am the true vine, and my Father is the husbandman.

2 Every branch in me that beareth not fruit he taketh away: and every *branch* that beareth fruit, he purgeth it, that it may bring forth more fruit.

3 Now ye are clean through the word which I have spoken unto you.

4 Abide in me, and I in you. As the branch cannot bear fruit of itself, except it abide in the vine; no more can ye, except ye abide in me.

5 I am the vine, ye *are* the branches: He that abideth in me, and I in him, the same bringeth forth much fruit: for without me ye can do nothing.

6 If a man abide not in me, he is cast forth as a branch, and is withered; and men gather them, and cast *them* into the fire, and they are burned.

7 If ye abide in me, and my words abide in you, ye shall ask what ye will, and it shall be done unto you.

8 Herein is my Father glorified, that ye bear much fruit; so shall ye be my disciples.

15:1 Chapters 15 and 16 contain the second Farewell Discourse. In 15 are the themes of fruit-bearing and the hatred of the world for Christ's disciples. The theme of persecution is continued in ch. 16 along with teaching concerning the ministry of the Holy Spirit.

15:2 *taketh away*. The word may mean this literally (as in 11:39) and would therefore be a reference to the physical death of fruitless Christians (1 Cor. 11:30); or it may mean lift up (as in 8:59) which would indicate that the *husbandman* (vinedresser) encourages and makes it easier for the fruitless believer, hoping he will respond and begin to bear fruit. *purgeth*=prunes. This is done through the Word of God which cleans the life (same root word as in v. 3).

15:4 *abide in me*. John explains what this means when he uses the same word ("dwelleth") in 1 John 3:24. Abiding depends on keeping His commandments.

15:6 *they are burned*. This refers to the works of the believer. The Christian who does not abide cannot do what pleases God; therefore, his works will be burned at the judgment seat of Christ though he himself will be saved (1 Cor. 3:11–15).

15:8 *Herein*. I.e., in answered prayer. Note the progression: the step from fruit to more fruit involves cleansing through the

9 As the Father hath loved me, so have I loved you: continue ye in my love.

10 If ye keep my commandments, ye shall abide in my love; even as I have kept my Father's commandments, and abide in his love.

11 These things have I spoken unto you, that my joy might remain in you, and *that* your joy might be full.

12 This is my commandment, That ye love one another, as I have loved you.

13 Greater love hath no man than this, that a man lay down his life for his friends.

14 Ye are my friends, if ye do whatsoever I command you.

15 Henceforth I call you not servants; for the servant knoweth not what his lord doeth: but I have called you friends; for all things that I have heard of my Father I have made known unto you.

16 Ye have not chosen me, but I have chosen you, and ordained you, that ye should go and bring forth fruit, and *that* your fruit should remain: that whatsover ye shall ask of the Father in my name, he may give it you.

17 These things I command you, that ye love one another.

H Concerning the World, 15:18–16:6

18 If the world hate you, ye know that it hated me before *it hated* you.

19 If ye were of the world, the world would love his own: but because ye are not of the world, but I have chosen you out of the world, therefore the world hateth you.

20 Remember the word that I said unto you, The servant is not greater than his lord. If they have persecuted me, they will also persecute you; if they have kept my saying, they will keep yours also.

21 But all these things will they do unto you for my name's sake, because they know not him that sent me.

22 If I had not come and spoken unto them, they had

Word of God (v. 2), and the step from more fruit to much fruit involves a life of answered prayer.

15:13 The highest expression of love is self-sacrifice which spares not life itself (see 1 John 3:16).

15:16 *ordained*=appointed.

15:21 *for my name's sake*. Better, on my account, i.e., because you are my followers.

15:22 *cloke*=excuse.

not had sin: but now they have no cloke for their sin.

23 He that hateth me hateth my Father also.

24 If I had not done among them the works which none other man did, they had not had sin: but now have they both seen and hated both me and my Father.

25 But *this cometh to pass*, that the word might be fulfilled that is written in their law, They hated me without a cause.

26 But when the Comforter is come, whom I will send unto you from the Father, *even* the Spirit of truth, which proceedeth from the Father, he shall testify of me:

27 And ye also shall bear witness, because ye have been with me from the beginning.

16 These things have I spoken unto you, that ye should not be offended.

2 They shall put you out of the synagogues: yea, the time cometh, that whosoever killeth you will think that he doeth God service.

3 And these things will they do unto you, because they have not known the Father, nor me.

4 But these things have I told you, that when the time shall come, ye may remember that I told you of them. And these things I said not unto you at the beginning, because I was with you.

5 But now I go my way to him that sent me; and none of you asketh me, Whither goest thou?

6 But because I have said these things unto you, sorrow hath filled your heart.

15:25 The reference here is to Ps. 35:19; 69:4. In this section Christ states: (1) the world hates me (v. 18); (2) Christians are aliens in the world (v. 19); (3) the world will persecute you because you are my followers (v. 20); (4) the persecutors do not know God (v. 21); (5) my words (v. 22) and my works (v. 24) rebuke them. These arguments are found in many early Christian writings addressed both to the faithful and polemically to pagans and Jews.

15:26 *Comforter*. See note at 14:16. *which proceedeth from the Father*. This refers to the mission of the Spirit which is from the Father; therefore, the Spirit's witness is that of the Father Himself. The creeds of the church have related this statement to the person of the Spirit proceeding eternally from the Father (and, in the Western church, from the Son).

16:1 *be offended*. Better, fall away.

16:2 *whosoever killeth you will think that he doeth God service*. The history of religious persecution is the fulfillment of this prophecy (Acts 7:57-60).

I Concerning the Holy Spirit, 16:7–15

7 Nevertheless I tell you the truth; It is expedient for you that I go away: for if I go not away, the Comforter will not come unto you; but if I depart, I will send him unto you.

8 And when he is come, he will reprove the world of sin, and of righteousness, and of judgment:

9 Of sin, because they believe not on me;

10 Of righteousness, because I go to my Father, and ye see me no more;

11 Of judgment, because the prince of this world is judged.

12 I have yet many things to say unto you, but ye cannot bear them now.

13 Howbeit when he, the Spirit of truth, is come, he will guide you into all truth: for he shall not speak of himself; but whatsoever he shall hear, *that* shall he speak: and he will shew you things to come.

14 He shall glorify me: for he shall receive of mine, and shall shew *it* unto you.

15 All things that the Father hath are mine: therefore

16:7 *it is expedient for you.* Better, it is to your advantage.

16:8–11 Christ teaches here that the Spirit through apostles, evangelists, and preachers will *reprove* the world. Reprove means to set the truth of the Gospel in such a clear light that men will either accept or reject it intelligently; i.e., to convince men of the truthfulness of the Gospel. The Spirit will help break down the indifference of the typical pagan who had no conviction of sin, who held a low regard for righteousness, and who paid no heed to warnings of the coming judgment.

16:9 *because they believe not on me.* The greatest sin is unbelief.

16:10 Jesus' return to the Father will vindicate His righteous life and the truthfulness of all He said.

16:11 *the prince of this world is judged.* At the cross Christ triumphed over Satan, serving notice on unbelievers of their judgment to come.

16:12 *many things . . . bear them now.* These things would become clear after the resurrection.

16:13 *of himself.* Lit., from himself, i.e., on his own authority. *he will show you things to come.* These things include the meaning of Christ's death and resurrection (which the disciples did not fully understand) as well as things yet in the future concerning the return of Christ. See Paul's statement in 1 Cor. 2:10.

16:14 *receive of mine*=take what is mine, i.e., my teachings and whatever relates to me. *shew*=declare it, also in v. 15.

16:15 The teaching ministry of the Holy Spirit has guided the

said I, that he shall take of mine, and shall shew *it* unto you.

J Concerning His Return, 16:16–33

16 A little while, and ye shall not see me: and again, a little while, and ye shall see me, because I go to the Father.

17 Then said *some* of his disciples among themselves, What is this that he saith unto us, A little while, and ye shall not see me: and again, a little while, and ye shall see me: and, Because I go to the Father?

18 They said therefore, What is this that he saith, A little while? we cannot tell what he saith.

19 Now Jesus knew that they were desirous to ask him, and said unto them, Do ye enquire among yourselves of that I said, A little while, and ye shall not see me: and again, a little while, and ye shall see me?

20 Verily, verily, I say unto you, That ye shall weep and lament, but the world shall rejoice: and ye shall be sorrowful, but your sorrow shall be turned into joy.

21 A woman when she is in travail hath sorrow, because her hour is come: but as soon as she is delivered of the child, she remembereth no more the anguish, for joy that a man is born into the world.

22 And ye now therefore have sorrow: but I will see you again, and your heart shall rejoice, and your joy no man taketh from you.

23 And in that day ye shall ask me nothing. Verily, verily, I say unto you, Whatsoever ye shall ask the Father in my name, he will give *it* you.

24 Hitherto have ye asked nothing in my name: ask, and ye shall receive, that your joy may be full.

25 These things have I spoken unto you in proverbs: but the time cometh, when I shall no more speak unto you in proverbs, but I shall shew you plainly of the Father.

26 At that day ye shall ask in my name: and I say not unto you, that I will pray the Father for you:

27 For the Father himself loveth you, because ye have loved me, and have believed that I came out from God.

church since the Spirit's coming. Doctrine, therefore, does not have to be traced back to the earthly ministry of Jesus to be authoritative, *for he* (the Spirit) *shall take of mine* (Christ's), *and shall shew it unto you.*

16:23 *in that day.* I.e., after His ascension.

16:25 *in proverbs.* Better, in parables or obscure sayings (see v. 29).

16:26 *ask in my name.* To address the Father through the Son has been the normal Christian practice ever since.

28 I came forth from the Father, and am come into the world: again, I leave the world, and go to the Father.

29 His disciples said unto him, Lo, now speakest thou plainly, and speakest no proverb.

30 Now are we sure that thou knowest all things, and needest not that any man should ask thee: by this we believe that thou camest forth from God.

31 Jesus answered them, Do ye now believe?

32 Behold, the hour cometh, yea, is now come, that ye shall be scattered, every man to his own, and shall leave me alone: and yet I am not alone, because the Father is with me.

33 These things I have spoken unto you, that in me ye might have peace. In the world ye shall have tribulation: but be of good cheer; I have overcome the world.

V INTERCESSION OF THE SON OF GOD, 17:1-26

17 These words spake Jesus, and lifted up his eyes to heaven, and said, Father, the hour is come; glorify thy Son, that thy Son also may glorify thee:

2 As thou hast given him power over all flesh, that he should give eternal life to as many as thou hast given him.

3 And this is life eternal, that they might know thee the only true God, and Jesus Christ, whom thou hast sent.

4 I have glorified thee on the earth: I have finished the work which thou gavest me to do.

5 And now, O Father, glorify thou me with thine own

16:33 *In the world ye shall have tribulation.* Better, ye have tribulation. There are three aspects of this: (1) general trials which come simply because we live in a sinful world (Rom. 8:36); (2) afflictions which God allows to come into our lives (2 Cor. 12:7); and (3) chastisement which comes more directly from God (Heb. 12:6). *I have overcome the world.* See Rom. 8:37; 1 John 5:4.

17:1 In this great so-called "high-priestly" prayer the Lord prays for: (1) His own glorification (vv. 2, 5); (2) believers' protection (v. 11); (3) believers' sanctification (v. 17); (4) the unity of believers (vv. 21-23); (5) the ultimate glorification of believers (v. 24). It is essentially an intercession for those who will form the church (vv. 6-26).

17:3 This is John's definition of salvation, especially if we add what is clearly understood: *sent* to be the Savior of the world (3:16; 4:42; 6:33; 1 John 4:14; 5:20).

17:5 *with thine own self.* I.e., in thy presence, "at the right hand of God."

self with the glory which I had with thee before the world was.

6 I have manifested thy name unto the men which thou gavest me out of the world: thine they were, and thou gavest them me; and they have kept thy word.

7 Now they have known that all things whatsoever thou hast given me are of thee.

8 For I have given unto them the words which thou gavest me; and they have received *them*, and have known surely that I came out from thee, and they have believed that thou didst send me.

9 I pray for them: I pray not for the world, but for them which thou hast given me; for they are thine.

10 And all mine are thine, and thine are mine; and I am glorified in them.

11 And now I am no more in the world, but these are in the world, and I come to thee. Holy Father, keep through thine own name those whom thou hast given me, that they may be one, as we *are*.

12 While I was with them in the world, I kept them in thy name: those that thou gavest me I have kept, and none of them is lost, but the son of perdition; that the scripture might be fulfilled.

13 And now come I to thee; and these things I speak in the world, that they might have my joy fulfilled in themselves.

14 I have given them thy word; and the world hath hated them, because they are not of the world, even as I am not of the world.

15 I pray not that thou shouldest take them out of the world, but that thou shouldest keep them from the evil.

16 They are not of the world, even as I am not of the world.

17 Sanctify them through thy truth: thy word is truth.

18 As thou hast sent me into the world, even so have I also sent them into the world.

17:6 *manifested thy name.* I.e., revealed your true nature. This divine revelation is the basis on which the church is established.
17:8 *the words.* I.e., the divine message.
17:12 *the son of perdition*=Judas. See Ps. 41:9.
17:15 *from the evil.* The word can be neuter (*from evil*) or masculine (*from the evil one, Satan*). It should be noted that Christ does not teach withdrawal from the world, but that Christians should be "in the world but not of it."
17:17 *Sanctify* means to set apart for God and holy purposes, so also v. 19.
17:18 A great text for the mission of the church.

19 And for their sakes I sanctify myself, that they also might be sanctified through the truth.

20 Neither pray I for these alone, but for them also which shall believe on me through their word;

21 That they all may be one; as thou, Father, *art* in me, and I in thee, that they also may be one in us: that the world may believe that thou hast sent me.

22 And the glory which thou gavest me I have given them; that they may be one, even as we are one:

23 I in them, and thou in me, that they may be made perfect in one; and that the world may know that thou hast sent me, and hast loved them, as thou hast loved me.

24 Father, I will that they also, whom thou hast given me, be with me where I am; that they may behold my glory, which thou hast given me: for thou lovedst me before the foundation of the world.

25 O righteous Father, the world hath not known thee: but I have known thee, and these have known that thou hast sent me.

26 And I have declared unto them thy name, and will declare *it*: that the love wherewith thou hast loved me may be in them, and I in them.

VI CRUCIFIXION OF THE SON OF GOD,
18:1–19:42

A The Arrest, 18:1–11

18 When Jesus had spoken these words, he went forth with his disciples over the brook Ce′dron, where was a garden, into the which he entered, and his disciples.

2 And Judas also, which betrayed him, knew the place: for Jesus ofttimes resorted thither with his disciples.

3 Judas then, having received a band *of men* and officers from the chief priests and Pharisees, cometh thither with lanterns and torches and weapons.

4 Jesus therefore, knowing all things that should come

17:21 *That they all may be one.* All believers do belong to the one body of Christ (1 Cor. 12:13) and to the same household of God (Eph. 2:19). That spiritual unity should have visible expression in the exercise of spiritual gifts (Eph. 4:3–16), prayer, and exhortation (2 Cor. 1:11; Heb. 10:25).

17:23 *perfect in one, and*=perfectly one, so that.

18:1 *brook Cedron.* Better, Kidron Valley, a ravine E. of Jerusalem, between the city and the Mount of Olives.

18:3 *band of men.* I.e., Roman soldiers.

upon him, went forth, and said unto them, Whom seek ye?

5 They answered him, Jesus of Nazareth. Jesus saith unto them, I am *he*. And Judas also, which betrayed him, stood with them.

6 As soon then as he had said unto them, I am *he*, they went backward, and fell to the ground.

7 Then asked he them again, Whom seek ye? And they said, Jesus of Nazareth.

8 Jesus answered, I have told you that I am *he*: if therefore ye seek me, let these go their way:

9 That the saying might be fulfilled, which he spake, Of them which thou gavest me have I lost none.

10 Then Simon Peter having a sword drew it, and smote the high priest's servant, and cut off his right ear. The servant's name was Mal'chus.

11 Then said Jesus unto Peter, Put up thy sword into the sheath: the cup which my Father hath given me, shall I not drink it?

B The Trials, 18:12–19:15

1 *Before Annas*, 18:12–23

12 Then the band and the captain and officers of the Jews took Jesus, and bound him,

13 And led him away to Annas first; for he was father in law to Ca'iaphas, which was the high priest that same year.

14 Now Ca'iaphas was he, which gave counsel to the Jews, that it was expedient that one man should die for the people.

15 ¶ And Simon Peter followed Jesus, and *so did* another disciple: that disciple was known unto the high priest, and went in with Jesus into the palace of the high priest.

16 But Peter stood at the door without. Then went out that other disciple, which was known unto the high priest, and spake unto her that kept the door, and brought in Peter.

17 Then saith the damsel that kept the door unto Peter,

18:10 *cut off his right ear*. For the sequel see Luke 22:51.
18:12 *officers of the Jews*. Better, servants of the Jewish authorities (high priests).
18:13 A small inner circle of high priests headed by Annas and Caiaphas ruled Jerusalem regardless of which was officially *the* high priest. See note at Luke 3:2.
18:15 *another disciple*=John.

Art not thou also *one* of this man's disciples? He saith, I
am not.

18 And the servants and officers stood there, who had
made a fire of coals; for it was cold: and they warmed themselves: and Peter stood with them, and warmed himself.

19 ¶ The high priest then asked Jesus of his disciples,
and of his doctrine.

20 Jesus answered him, I spake openly to the world; I
ever taught in the synagogue, and in the temple, whither
the Jews always resort; and in secret have I said nothing.

21 Why askest thou me? ask them which heard me,
what I have said unto them: behold, they know what I
said.

22 And when he had thus spoken, one of the officers
which stood by struck Jesus with the palm of his hand,
saying, Answerest thou the high priest so?

23 Jesus answered him, If I have spoken evil, bear witness of the evil: but if well, why smitest thou me?

2 *Before Caiaphas*, 18:24–27

24 Now Annas had sent him bound unto Cả'aphas the
high priest.

25 And Simon Peter stood and warmed himself. They
said therefore unto him, Art not thou also *one* of his disciples? He denied *it*, and said, I am not.

26 One of the servants of the high priest, being *his*
kinsman whose ear Peter cut off, saith, Did not I see thee
in the garden with him?

27 Peter then denied again: and immediately the cock
crew.

3 *Before Pilate*, 18:28–19:16

28 ¶ Then led they Jesus from Cả'aphas unto the hall
of judgment: and it was early; and they themselves went

18:23 *evil*. Better, wrongly.

18:24 No examination before *Caiaphas* is reported by John. See
    note at Matt. 26:57. Under Roman law, as with us today,
    a prisoner was assumed to be innocent until proved guilty.

18:28 *they themselves went not into the judgment hall*. This
    was the Roman praetorium or headquarters, the barracks (also
    in v. 33). As a dwelling place of Gentiles it was unclean. Thus
    the Jewish authorities would not enter lest they be defiled for
    the Passover. However, they were willing to see the murder of
    Jesus committed without fearing defilement! See note at
    Matt. 27:27.

not into the judgment hall, lest they should be defiled;
but that they might eat the passover.

29 Pilate then went out unto them, and said, What
accusation bring ye against this man?

30 They answered and said unto him, If he were not a
malefactor, we would not have delivered him up unto thee.

31 Then said Pilate unto them, Take ye him, and judge
him according to your law. The Jews therefore said unto
him, It is not lawful for us to put any man to death:

32 That the saying of Jesus might be fulfilled, which he
spake, signifying what death he should die.

33 Then Pilate entered into the judgment hall again,
and called Jesus, and said unto him, Art thou the King of
the Jews?

34 Jesus answered him, Sayest thou this thing of thyself, or did others tell it thee of me?

35 Pilate answered, Am I a Jew? Thine own nation and
the chief priests have delivered thee unto me: what hast
thou done?

36 Jesus answered, My kingdom is not of this world: if
my kingdom were of this world, then would my servants
fight, that I should not be delivered to the Jews: but now
is my kingdom not from hence.

37 Pilate therefore said unto him, Art thou a king then?
Jesus answered, Thou sayest that I am a king. To this end
was I born, and for this cause came I into the world, that
I should bear witness unto the truth. Every one that is of
the truth heareth my voice.

38 Pilate saith unto him, What is truth? And when he
had said this, he went out again unto the Jews, and saith
unto them, I find in him no fault *at all*.

18:31 *It is not lawful for us*. The Sanhedrin could condemn a
man to death, but the Roman government had to approve the
sentence and then execute it. See note at Luke 22:66.

18:34 Jesus asks whether Pilate's question arises from a Roman
viewpoint (*sayest thou this thing of thyself*) or from a Jewish
viewpoint (*or did others tell it thee of me?*).

18:36 Because Pilate's answer indicated that he was concerned
only about a possible rival kingdom to Rome (v. 35), our
Lord replied as He did in this verse indicating that His kingdom was not a political rival to Rome. Because Pilate was
satisfied that Jesus was not a political threat he wished to
release Him. *kingdom*; better, kingship; i.e., my authority is
not of human origin.

18:38 *What is truth?* Pilate is not being philosophical but expressing frustration and irritation at the avoidance of a direct
answer to what seemed to him to be a simple question. He
does not understand the charges (18:31, 35, 38; 19:4, 12).

39 But ye have a custom, that I should release unto you one at the passover: will ye therefore that I release unto you the King of the Jews?

40 Then cried they all again, saying, Not this man, but Barabbas. Now Barabbas was a robber.

16

Then Pilate therefore took Jesus, and scourged him.

2 And the soldiers platted a crown of thorns, and put *it* on his head, and they put on him a purple robe,

3 And said, Hail, King of the Jews! and they smote him with their hands.

4 Pilate therefore went forth again, and saith unto them, Behold, I bring him forth to you, that ye may know that I find no fault in him.

5 Then came Jesus forth, wearing the crown of thorns, and the purple robe. And *Pilate* saith unto them, Behold the man!

6 When the chief priests therefore and officers saw him, they cried out, saying, Crucify *him*, crucify *him*. Pilate saith unto them, Take ye him, and crucify *him*: for I find no fault in him.

7 The Jews answered him, We have a law, and by our law he ought to die, because he made himself the Son of God.

8 ¶ When Pilate therefore heard that saying, he was the more afraid;

9 And went again into the judgment hall, and saith unto Jesus, Whence art thou? But Jesus gave him no answer.

10 Then saith Pilate unto him, Speakest thou not unto me? knowest thou not that I have power to crucify thee, and have power to release thee?

19:1 *scourged*. See note at Matt. 27:26.

19:2 *plaited*=wove.

19:4 Perhaps Pilate is now seeking a compromise.

19:5 *Behold the man!* Pilate's remark is sarcastic: "Look at your so-called king now!"

19:7 *by our law he ought to die*. A reference to Jesus' alleged blasphemy because He claimed to be God (Lev. 24:16).

19:8 *afraid*. Perhaps of several things: of possible violence; of loss of favor at Rome for his inability to control the turbulent Jews (v. 15); of some sense of Jesus' true nature (this may be indicated by the question in v. 9).

19:9 *no answer*. See Isa. 53:7.

11 Jesus answered, Thou couldest have no power *at all* against me, except it were given thee from above: therefore he that delivered me unto thee hath the greater sin.

12 And from thenceforth Pilate sought to release him: but the Jews cried out, saying, If thou let this man go, thou art not Cæsar's friend: whosoever maketh himself a king speaketh against Cæsar.

13 ¶ When Pilate therefore heard that saying, he brought Jesus forth, and sat down in the judgment seat in a place that is called the Pavement, but in the Hebrew, Gab'batha.

14 And it was the preparation of the passover, and about the sixth hour: and he saith unto the Jews, Behold your King!

15 But they cried out, Away with *him*, away with *him*, crucify him. Pilate saith unto them, Shall I crucify your King? The chief priests answered, We have no king but Cæsar.

16 Then delivered he him therefore unto them to be crucified. And they took Jesus, and led *him* away.

C The Crucifixion, 19:17–37

17 And he bearing his cross went forth into a place called *the place* of a skull, which is called in the Hebrew Golgotha:

18 Where they crucified him, and two other with him, on either side one, and Jesus in the midst.

19:11 *he that delivered me.* Evidently a reference to Caiaphas (18:28).

19:12 The Jewish authorities revert to the political charge against Jesus. This posed a potent threat to a provincial governor who served at the whim of the emperor (Tiberius); and the Jews had already protested to Rome Pilate's actions in other matters where he was insensitive to their customs (see note on Pilate at Mark 15:1).

19:13 *Pavement.* Almost certainly the large paved area that was part of the Castle of Antonia at the northwest corner of the temple area beneath Ecce Homo Arch.

19:14 *preparation of the passover*=Friday of Passover week. In v. 31 *preparation* refers to Friday as the day of preparation for the Sabbath (see note at Luke 23:54).

19:14–15 Pilate's sarcasm is directed to the chief priests (whom he hates and mistrusts) and their clique. He draws from them the response "*We have no king but Cæsar,*" which is a blasphemous denial of the kingship of God over their nation.

19:16 *to be crucified.* See note at Matt. 27:31.

19:17 *Golgotha.* See note at Matt. 27:33.

19 ¶ And Pilate wrote a title, and put *it* on the cross. And the writing was, JESUS OF NAZARETH THE KING OF THE JEWS.

20 This title then read many of the Jews: for the place where Jesus was crucified was nigh to the city: and it was written in Hebrew, *and* Greek, *and* Latin.

21 Then said the chief priests of the Jews to Pilate, Write not, The King of the Jews: but that he said, I am King of the Jews.

22 Pilate answered, What I have written I have written.

23 ¶ Then the soldiers, when they had crucified Jesus, took his garments, and made four parts, to every soldier a part; and also *his* coat: now the coat was without seam, woven from the top throughout.

24 They said therefore among themselves, Let us not rend it, but cast lots for it, whose it shall be: that the scripture might be fulfilled, which saith, They parted my raiment among them, and for my vesture they did cast lots. These things therefore the soldiers did.

25 ¶ Now there stood by the cross of Jesus his mother, and his mother's sister, Mary the *wife* of Cle'ophas, and Mary Magdalene.

26 When Jesus therefore saw his mother, and the disciple standing by, whom he loved, he saith unto his mother, Woman, behold thy son!

27 Then saith he to the disciple, Behold thy mother! And from that hour that disciple took her unto his own *home*.

28 ¶ After this, Jesus knowing that all things were now accomplished, that the scripture might be fulfilled, saith, I thirst.

29 Now there was set a vessel full of vinegar: and they filled a spunge with vinegar, and put *it* upon hyssop, and put *it* to his mouth.

30 When Jesus therefore had received the vinegar, he said, It is finished: and he bowed his head, and gave up the ghost.

31 The Jews therefore, because it was the preparation,

19:24. Quoting Ps. 22:18. See note at Matt. 27:35.

19:25 *Mary.* On the Marys of the N.T. see note at Luke 8:2.

19:29 *vinegar . . . hyssop.* The vinegar was a sour, cheap wine. Hyssop was likely the caper plant, which has stems 2–3 feet long.

19:31 *for that sabbath day was an high day.* I.e., the first day of the Feast of Unleavened Bread fell that year on a Sabbath, making it a "high" festival (Ex. 12:16; Lev. 23:7). They were anxious that the body not remain on the cross because

that the bodies should not remain upon the cross on the
sabbath day, (for that sabbath day was an high day,) besought Pilate that their legs might be broken, and *that*
they might be taken away.

32 Then came the soldiers, and brake the legs of the
first, and of the other which was crucified with him.

33 But when they came to Jesus, and saw that he was
dead already, they brake not his legs:

34 But one of the soldiers with a spear pierced his side,
and forthwith came there out blood and water.

35 And he that saw *it* bare record, and his record is true:
and he knoweth that he saith true, that ye might believe.

36 For these things were done, that the scripture should
be fulfilled, A bone of him shall not be broken.

37 And again another scripture saith, They shall look
on him whom they pierced.

D The Burial, 19:38–42

38 ¶ And after this Joseph of Arimathǽ'a, being a disciple of Jesus, but secretly for fear of the Jews, besought
Pilate that he might take away the body of Jesus: and
Pilate gave *him* leave. He came therefore, and took the
body of Jesus.

39 And there came also Nicodḗ'mus, which at the first
came to Jesus by night, and brought a mixture of myrrh
and aloes, about an hundred pound *weight.*

40 Then took they the body of Jesus, and wound it in
linen clothes with the spices, as the manner of the Jews is
to bury.

41 Now in the place where he was crucified there was a
garden; and in the garden a new sepulchre, wherein was
never man yet laid.

42 There laid they Jesus therefore because of the Jews'
preparation *day*; for the sepulchre was nigh at hand.

of Deut. 21:22–23. *their legs might be broken.* This was done
to hasten death, since the victim could no longer raise himself
up on the nail through his feet in order to allow himself to
breathe.
19:36 See Ex. 12:46; Num. 9:12; Ps. 34:20.
19:37 See Zech. 12:10.
19:38 *Arimathea* was a town 20 miles NW. of Jerusalem.
19:39 *Nicodemus* apparently became a secret follower of Christ.
19:40 *linen clothes.* I.e., long strips of linen.
19:41 See Isa. 53:9.

VII RESURRECTION OF THE SON OF GOD,
20:1–21:25

A The Empty Tomb, 20:1–10

20 The first *day* of the week cometh Mary Magdalene early, when it was yet dark, unto the sepulchre, and seeth the stone taken away from the sepulchre.

2 Then she runneth, and cometh to Simon Peter, and to the other disciple, whom Jesus loved, and saith unto them, They have taken away the Lord out of the sepulchre, and we know not where they have laid him.

3 Peter therefore went forth, and that other disciple, and came to the sepulchre.

4 So they ran both together: and the other disciple did outrun Peter, and came first to the sepulchre.

5 And he stooping down, *and looking in,* saw the linen clothes lying; yet went he not in.

6 Then cometh Simon Peter following him, and went into the sepulchre, and seeth the linen clothes lie,

7 And the napkin, that was about his head, not lying with the linen clothes, but wrapped together in a place by itself.

8 Then went in also that other disciple, which came first to the sepulchre, and he saw, and believed.

9 For as yet they knew not the scripture, that he must rise again from the dead.

20:1 The order of Christ's appearances after His resurrection seems to be as follows: (1) To Mary Magdalene and the other woman (Matt. 28:8–10; John 20:11–18; Mark 16:9–10); (2) to Peter, probably in the afternoon (Luke 24:34; 1 Cor. 15:5); (3) to the disciples on the Emmaus road toward evening (Luke 24:13–32; Mark 16:12); (4) to the disciples, except Thomas, in the upper room (Luke 24:36–43; John 20:19–25; Mark 16:14); (5) to the disciples, including Thomas, on the next Sunday night (John 20:26–29); (6) to seven disciples beside the Sea of Galilee (John 21:1–24); (7) to the apostles and more than 500 brethren and James, the Lord's half-brother (1 Cor. 15:6–7); (8) to those who witnessed the ascension (Matt. 28:18–20; Mark 16:19; Luke 24:44–53; Acts 1:3–12).

20:6 *seeth the linen clothes lie.* If the body had been stolen, the thieves would not have taken time to unwrap it; but even if they had, then the wrappings would have been strewn around the tomb and not lying in perfect order as they were. See note at Luke 24:12.

10 Then the disciples went away again unto their own home.

B The Appearances of the Risen Lord, 20:11–21:25

1 To Mary Magdalene, 20:11–18

11 ¶ But Mary stood without at the sepulchre weeping: and as she wept, she stooped down, *and looked* into the sepulchre,

12 And seeth two angels in white sitting, the one at the head, and the other at the feet, where the body of Jesus had lain.

13 And they say unto her, Woman, why weepest thou? She saith unto them, Because they have taken away my Lord, and I know not where they have laid him.

14 And when she had thus said, she turned herself back, and saw Jesus standing, and knew not that it was Jesus.

15 Jesus saith unto her, Woman, why weepest thou? whom seekest thou? She, supposing him to be the gardener, saith unto him, Sir, if thou have borne him hence, tell me where thou hast laid him, and I will take him away.

16 Jesus saith unto her, Mary. She turned herself, and saith unto him, Rabbō'nī; which is to say, Master.

17 Jesus saith unto her, Touch me not; for I am not yet ascended to my Father: but go to my brethren, and say unto them, I ascend unto my Father, and your Father; and *to* my God, and your God.

18 Mary Magdalene came and told the disciples that she had seen the Lord, and *that* he had spoken these things unto her.

2 To the disciples, Thomas absent, 20:19–25

19 ¶ Then the same day at evening, being the first *day* of the week, when the doors were shut where the disciples were assembled for fear of the Jews, came Jesus and stood in the midst, and saith unto them, Peace *be* unto you.

20 And when he had so said, he shewed unto them *his* hands and his side. Then were the disciples glad, when they saw the Lord.

20:14 *she turned herself back*=she turned around.
20:17 *Touch me not.* More accurately the command was "Do not continue holding or clinging to me" (in order to restrain me). This was inappropriate because of His new relationship as resurrected Lord.
20:19 *the Jews.* I.e., the Jewish authorities.

21 Then said Jesus to them again, Peace *be* unto you: as *my* Father hath sent me, even so send I you.

22 And when he had said this, he breathed on *them*, and saith unto them, Receive ye the Holy Ghost:

23 Whose soever sins ye remit, they are remitted unto them; *and* whose soever *sins* ye retain, they are retained.

24 ¶ But Thomas, one of the twelve, called Did'ymus, was not with them when Jesus came.

25 The other disciples therefore said unto him, We have seen the Lord. But he said unto them, Except I shall see in his hands the print of the nails, and put my finger into the print of the nails, and thrust my hand into his side, I will not believe.

3 *To the disciples, Thomas present*, 20:26–31

26 ¶ And after eight days again his disciples were within, and Thomas with them: *then* came Jesus, the doors being shut, and stood in the midst, and said, Peace *be* unto you.

27 Then saith he to Thomas, Reach hither thy finger, and behold my hands; and reach hither thy hand, and thrust *it* into my side: and be not faithless, but believing.

28 And Thomas answered and said unto him, My Lord and my God.

29 Jesus saith unto him, Thomas, because thou hast seen me, thou hast believed: blessed *are* they that have not seen, and *yet* have believed.

20:21 Another great verse on the mission of the church (see also 17:18).

20:22 *Receive ye the Holy Ghost*. This was a filling with the Spirit for power until the regularized relationship of the Spirit begins at Pentecost.

20:23 *they are remitted . . . they are retained*. Since only God can forgive sins (Mark 2:7), the disciples and the church are here given the authority to declare what God does when a man either accepts or rejects His Son. See note at Matt. 16:19.

20:28 *My Lord and my God*. Thomas, the doubter, recognizes the full deity of Jesus Christ. This marks the climax of John's Gospel. The Lord had claimed deity throughout His ministry. Note: (1) the names of deity which He uses (Matt. 22:42–45; John 8:58); (2) the attributes of deity which He claimed to have (holiness, John 8:46; omnipotence and omnipresence, Matt. 28:20; omniscience, John 11:11–14); (3) the things He claimed to be able to do which only God does (forgive sins, Mark 2:5–7; raise the dead, John 5:28–30; 11:43; judge all men, John 5:22, 27).

30 ¶ And many other signs truly did Jesus in the presence of his disciples, which are not written in this book:

31 But these are written, that ye might believe that Jesus is the Christ, the Son of God; and that believing ye might have life through his name.

4 To *seven disciples*, 21:1–14

21 After these things Jesus shewed himself again to the disciples at the sea of Tiberias; and on this wise shewed he *himself*.

2 There were together Simon Peter, and Thomas called Did'ymus, and Nathanael of Cana in Galilee, and the *sons* of Zebedee, and two other of his disciples.

3 Simon Peter saith unto them, I go a fishing. They say unto him, We also go with thee. They went forth, and entered into a ship immediately; and that night they caught nothing.

4 But when the morning was now come, Jesus stood on the shore: but the disciples knew not that it was Jesus.

5 Then Jesus saith unto them, Children, have ye any meat? They answered him, No.

6 And he said unto them, Cast the net on the right side of the ship, and ye shall find. They cast therefore, and now they were not able to draw it for the multitude of fishes.

7 Therefore that disciple whom Jesus loved saith unto Peter, It is the Lord. Now when Simon Peter heard that it was the Lord, he girt *his* fisher's coat *unto him*, (for he was naked,) and did cast himself into the sea.

8 And the other disciples came in a little ship; (for they were not far from land, but as it were two hundred cubits,) dragging the net with fishes.

9 As soon then as they were come to land, they saw a fire of coals there, and fish laid thereon, and bread.

10 Jesus saith unto them, Bring of the fish which ye have now caught.

11 Simon Peter went up, and drew the net to land full of great fishes, an hundred and fifty and three: and for all there were so many, yet was not the net broken.

21:3 *ship*=boat. A Galilean fishing boat is about 15 feet long.
21:5 *children*=boys or lads. *meat*. I.e., fish.
21:7 *for he was naked*. I.e., stripped for work. He swam ashore. The others followed in the boat, dragging the net behind them as they rowed ashore.
21:8 *two hundred cubits*=about 100 yards.

12 Jesus saith unto them, Come *and* dine. And none of the disciples durst ask him, Who art thou? knowing that it was the Lord.

13 Jesus then cometh, and taketh bread, and giveth them, and fish likewise.

14 This is now the third time that Jesus shewed himself to his disciples, after that he was risen from the dead.

5 *To Peter and the beloved disciple,* 21:15–25

15 ¶ So when they had dined, Jesus saith to Simon Peter, Simon, *son* of Jonas, lovest thou me more than these? He saith unto him, Yea, Lord; thou knowest that I love thee. He saith unto him, Feed my lambs.

16 He saith to him again the second time, Simon, *son* of Jonas, lovest thou me? He saith unto him, Yea, Lord; thou knowest that I love thee. He saith unto him, Feed my sheep.

17 He saith unto him the third time, Simon, *son* of Jonas, lovest thou me? Peter was grieved because he said unto him the third time, Lovest thou me? And he said unto him, Lord, thou knowest all things; thou knowest that I love thee. Jesus saith unto him, Feed my sheep.

18 Verily, verily, I say unto thee, When thou wast young, thou girdedst thyself, and walkedst whither thou wouldest: but when thou shalt be old, thou shalt stretch forth thy hands, and another shall gird thee, and carry *thee* whither thou wouldest not.

19 This spake he, signifying by what death he should glorify God. And when he had spoken this, he saith unto him, Follow me.

20 Then Peter, turning about, seeth the disciple whom Jesus loved following; which also leaned on his breast at supper, and said, Lord, which is he that betrayeth thee?

21 Peter seeing him saith to Jesus, Lord, and what *shall* this man *do?*

21:12 *dine.* Lit., have breakfast.
21:14 *the third time.* See 20:19 and 20:26 for the other two.
21:15–17 Peter's three denials are offset here by three protestations of his love for Christ. John probably uses the two different words for love in these verses synonymously (compare 3:35, *agapao,* with 5:20, *phileo*) *more than these* (v. 15) means "more than the other disciples" (see Matt. 26:33; Mark 14:29). *Feed* (v. 16) is a different word than the one used in vv. 15 and 17 and means "tend" or "shepherd."
21:18–19 This is a prophecy of the martyrdom of Peter.

22 Jesus saith unto him, If I will that he tarry till I come, what *is that* to thee? follow thou me.

23 Then went this saying abroad among the brethren, that that disciple should not die: yet Jesus said not unto him, He shall not die; but, If I will that he tarry till I come, what *is that* to thee?

24 This is the disciple which testifieth of these things, and wrote these things: and we know that his testimony is true.

25 And there are also many other things which Jesus did, the which, if they should be written every one, I suppose that even the world itself could not contain the books that should be written. Amen.

21:22 The Lord rebukes Peter for being distracted over John's future. Peter's only responsibility was to *follow* Christ.

21:25 The Gospels were not intended to be complete accounts of the life of Christ.

INTRODUCTION TO

The Acts

OF THE APOSTLES

AUTHOR: Luke   DATE: 61

The Author   That the author of Acts was a companion of Paul is clear from the passages in the book in which "we" and "us" are used (16:10–17; 20:5–21:18; 27:1–28:16). These sections themselves eliminate known companions of Paul other than Luke, and Colossians 4:14 and Philemon 24 point affirmatively to Luke, who was a physician. The incidence of medical terms substantiates the conclusion (1:3; 3:7 ff.; 9:18, 33; 13:11; 28:1–10). Luke answered the Macedonian call along with Paul, was in charge of the work at Philippi for about six years, and later was with Paul in Rome during the period of Paul's house arrest. It was probably during this time that the book was written. If it were written later it would be very difficult to explain the absence of mention of such momentous events as the burning of Rome, the martyrdom of Paul, or the destruction of Jerusalem.

The Importance of the Book   (1) Acts gives us the record of the spread of Christianity from the coming of the Spirit on the day of Pentecost to Paul's arrival in Rome to preach the gospel in the world's capital. In this regard, then, it is the record of the continuation of those things which Jesus began to do while on earth and which He continued to do as the risen Head of the church and the one who sent the Holy Spirit (1:2; 2:33). The book is sometimes called The Acts of the Holy Spirit.

(2) The thirty years covered by the book were important years of transition. The gospel was preached first only to Jews, and the early church was composed of Jewish believers. Eventually Gentiles were included, and the church became distinct from Judaism.

(3) Doctrines which are later developed in the epistles

318

appear in seed form in Acts (the Spirit, 1:8; the kingdom, 3:21; 15:16; union with Christ, 9:4; elders, 11:30; Gentile salvation, 15:14). However, the book emphasizes the practice of doctrine more than the statement of doctrine.

(4) Acts furnishes principles for missionary work. (5) The book reveals the pattern for church life. (6) Archeological discoveries have confirmed in a remarkable way the historical accuracy of Luke's writing.

The Contents In the first twelve chapters of the book the important figures are Peter, Stephen, Philip, Barnabas, and James. From chapter 13 to the end the dominant person is Paul. The book may also be divided according to the geographical divisions mentioned in the Great Commission (1:8).

OUTLINE OF THE GOSPEL OF ACTS

I Christianity in Jerusalem, 1:1–8:3
  A The Risen Lord, 1:1–26
    1 The Lord confirming, 1:1–5
    2 The Lord commissioning, 1:6–11
    3 The Lord choosing, 1:12–26
  B Pentecost: Birthday of the Church, 2:1–47
    1 The power of Pentecost, 2:1–13
    2 The preaching of Pentecost, 2:14–36
    3 The results of Pentecost, 2:37–47
  C The Healing of a Lame Man, 3:1–26
    1 The miracle, 3:1–11
    2 The message, 3:12–26
  D The Beginning of Persecution, 4:1–37
    1 The persecution, 4:1–22
    2 The prayer, 4:23–31
    3 The provision, 4:32–37
  E Purging and Persecution, 5:1–42
    1 Purging from within, 5:1–11
    2 Purging from without, 5:12–42
  F Choosing Co-laborers, 6:1–7
  G Stephen, the First Martyr, 6:8–8:3
    1 The stirring of the people, 6:8–15
    2 The sermon of Stephen, 7:1–53
    3 The stoning of Stephen, 7:54–8:3
II Christianity in Palestine and Syria, 8:4–12:25
  A The Christians Scattered, 8:4–40
    1 The preaching in Samaria, 8:5–25
    2 The preaching on the Gaza road, 8:26–40
  B The Conversion of Paul, 9:1–31
    1 The account of Paul's conversion, 9:1–19
    2 The aftermath of Paul's conversion, 9:20–31

The Acts
OF THE APOSTLES

I CHRISTIANITY IN JERUSALEM, 1:1–8:3

A The Risen Lord, 1:1–26

1 *The Lord confirming*, 1:1–5

1 The former treatise have I made, O Thēoph'ilus, of all that Jesus began both to do and teach,

2 Until the day in which he was taken up, after that he through the Holy Ghost had given commandments unto the apostles whom he had chosen:

3 To whom also he shewed himself alive after his passion by many infallible proofs, being seen of them forty days, and speaking of the things pertaining to the kingdom of God:

4 And, being assembled together with *them*, commanded them that they should not depart from Jerusalem, but wait for the promise of the Father, which, *saith he*, ye have heard of me.

5 For John truly baptized with water; but ye shall be baptized with the Holy Ghost not many days hence.

2 *The Lord commissioning*, 1:6–11

6 When they therefore were come together, they asked of him, saying, Lord wilt thou at this time restore again the kingdom to Israel?

7 And he said unto them, It is not for you to know

1:1 *The former treatise*=the Gospel of Luke. *Theophilus* means "dear to God" or "friend of God." He was probably a Roman official, since the title "most excellent" given to him in Luke 1:3 indicates an official position in Acts 23:26; 24:3; 26:25.

1:3 *forty days*. This is the only reference to the length of Christ's ministry on earth between His resurrection and His ascension.

1:5 *baptized with the Holy Ghost*. This promise was first fulfilled on the day of Pentecost (see 11:15–16) and affects every believer by joining him to the body of Christ (1 Cor. 12:13). See notes at Matt. 3:11.

1:6 *the kingdom to Israel*=the Messianic, Davidic, millennial kingdom on earth. The time of its coming is unrevealed (Matt. 24:36, 42).

1:7 There is no rebuke in Christ's answer, for God is not through with Israel and the kingdom will come (Rom. 11:26). In the meantime, the gospel must be preached throughout the whole world (v. 8).

the times or the seasons, which the Father hath put in his own power.

8 But ye shall receive power, after that the Holy Ghost is come upon you: and ye shall be witnesses unto me both in Jerusalem, and in all Judæa, and in Samaria, and unto the uttermost part of the earth.

9 And when he had spoken these things, while they beheld, he was taken up; and a cloud received him out of their sight.

10 And while they looked stedfastly toward heaven as he went up, behold, two men stood by them in white apparel;

11 Which also said, Ye men of Galilee, why stand ye gazing up into heaven? this same Jesus, which is taken up from you into heaven, shall so come in like manner as ye have seen him go into heaven.

3 The Lord choosing, 1:12–26

12 Then returned they unto Jerusalem from the mount called Ol'ivet, which is from Jerusalem a sabbath day's journey.

13 And when they were come in, they went up into an upper room, where abode both Peter, and James, and John, and Andrew, Philip, and Thomas, Bartholomew, and Matthew, James the son of Alphæ'us, and Simon Zēlō'tēs, and Judas the brother of James.

14 These all continued with one accord in prayer and supplication, with the women, and Mary the mother of Jesus, and with his brethren.

15 ¶ And in those days Peter stood up in the midst of the disciples, and said, (the number of names together were about an hundred and twenty,)

16 Men and brethren, this scripture must needs have been fulfilled, which the Holy Ghost by the mouth of David spake before concerning Judas, which was guide to them that took Jesus.

1:11 in like manner. The second coming of Christ, like the ascension, will be personal and visible (Rev. 1:8; 19:11–16).
1:12 a sabbath day's journey. This was about 2000 cubits, or a little more than half a mile, and was the distance the rabbis allowed the people to journey on the Sabbath. This limitation was apparently arrived at on the basis of Ex. 16:29 interpreted by Num. 35:5.
1:13 Simon Zelotes. See note at Matt. 10:4.
1:15 Peter has made a full recovery of confidence and authority from the night of his denial, and is now fulfilling Matt. 16:19.
1:16 See Ps. 41:9.

17 For he was numbered with us, and had obtained part of this ministry.

18 Now this man purchased a field with the reward of iniquity; and falling headlong, he burst asunder in the midst, and all his bowels gushed out.

19 And it was known unto all the dwellers at Jerusalem; insomuch as that field is called in their proper tongue, Acel'dama, that is to say, The field of blood.

20 For it is written in the book of Psalms, Let his habitation be desolate, and let no man dwell therein: and his bishoprick let another take.

21 Wherefore of these men which have companied with us all the time that the Lord Jesus went in and out among us,

22 Beginning from the baptism of John, unto that same day that he was taken up from us, must one be ordained to be a witness with us of his resurrection.

23 And they appointed two, Joseph called Bar'sabas, who was surnamed Justus, and Matthias.

24 And they prayed, and said, Thou, Lord, which knowest the hearts of all *men*, shew whether of these two thou hast chosen,

25 That he may take part of this ministry and apostleship, from which Judas by transgression fell, that he might go to his own place.

26 And they gave forth their lots; and the lot fell upon Matthias; and he was numbered with the eleven apostles.

B Pentecost: Birthday of the Church, 2:1–47

1 *The power of Pentecost,* 2:1–13

2 And when the day of Pentecost was fully come, they were all with one accord in one place.

1:18 *burst asunder in the midst*=burst open in the middle. This was probably due to Judas' ineptness in trying to hang himself (Matt. 27:5).

1:20 See Ps. 69:25; 109:8. *bishoprick*=his office as overseer.

1:26 *gave forth their lots*. The two names written on stones having been placed in an urn, the one that fell out first was taken to be the Lord's choice (Prov. 16:33; Jon. 1:7). The occasion was unique, for the Lord was not there in person to appoint and the Spirit had not been given in the special way of Pentecost.

2:1 *the day of Pentecost*. The fourth of the annual feasts of the Jews (after Passover, Unleavened Bread, and Firstfruits), it came 50 days after Firstfruits (a type of the resurrection of Christ, 1 Cor. 15:23). Pentecost was the Greek name for the Jewish Feast of Weeks, so called because it fell seven (a week

2 And suddenly there came a sound from heaven as of a rushing mighty wind, and it filled all the house where they were sitting.

3 And there appeared unto them cloven tongues like as of fire, and it sat upon each of them.

4 And they were all filled with the Holy Ghost, and began to speak with other tongues, as the Spirit gave them utterance.

5 And there were dwelling at Jerusalem Jews, devout men, out of every nation under heaven.

6 Now when this was noised abroad, the multitude came together, and were confounded, because that every man heard them speak in his own language.

7 And they were all amazed and marvelled, saying one to another, Behold, are not all these which speak Galilæans?

8 And how hear we every man in our own tongue, wherein we were born?

9 Par'thians, and Medes, and Elamites, and the dwellers in Mesopotā'mia, and in Judæa, and Cappadō'cia, in Pontus, and Asia.

10 Phrygia, and Pamphyl'ia, in Egypt, and in the parts of Libya about Cȳrē'nē, and strangers of Rome, Jews and proselytes,

11 Cretes and Arabians, we do hear them speak in our tongues the wonderful works of God.

12 And they were all amazed, and were in doubt, saying one to another, What meaneth this?

13 Others mocking said, These men are full of new wine.

2 *The preaching of Pentecost,* 2:14–36

14 ¶ But Peter, standing up with the eleven, lifted up his voice, and said unto them, Ye men of Judæa, and all *ye*

---

of) weeks after Firstfruits. It celebrated the wheat harvest (Ex. 23:16). This day of Pentecost in Acts 2 marked the beginning of the church (Matt. 16:18).

2:2 The *sound from heaven* was like a wind; it was not wind.

2:3 The *tongues* were like fire in that, like a flame of fire, they divided and rested on each of the disciples. Probably at this point the group left the house and went to the temple.

2:4 *with other tongues.* These were actual languages unknown to the speakers but understood by the hearers (v. 8).

2:9–11 These countries form a circuit around the Mediterranean Sea.

2:10 *strangers of Rome.* I.e., Romans who were temporarily residing in Jerusalem.

2:14 Here begins Peter's great sermon with an explanation of the phenomena they were witnessing (vv. 14–21). Then he moves

that dwell at Jerusalem, be this known unto you, and hearken to my words:

15 For these are not drunken, as ye suppose, seeing it is *but* the third hour of the day.

16 But this is that which was spoken by the prophet Joel;

17 And it shall come to pass in the last days, saith God, I will pour out of my Spirit upon all flesh: and your sons and your daughters shall prophesy, and your young men shall see visions, and your old men shall dream dreams:

18 And on my servants and on my handmaidens I will pour out in those days of my Spirit; and they shall prophesy:

19 And I will shew wonders in heaven above, and signs in the earth beneath; blood, and fire, and vapour of smoke:

20 The sun shall be turned into darkness, and the moon into blood, before that great and notable day of the Lord come:

21 And it shall come to pass, *that* whosoever shall call on the name of the Lord shall be saved.

22 Ye men of Israel, hear these words; Jesus of Nazareth, a man approved of God among you by miracles and wonders and signs, which God did by him in the midst of you, as ye yourselves also know:

23 Him, being delivered by the determinate counsel and foreknowledge of God, ye have taken, and by wicked hands have crucified and slain:

24 Whom God hath raised up, having loosed the pains of death: because it was not possible that he should be holden of it.

on to proclaim the gospel (vv. 22–35) and apply the message (v. 36).

2:15 *the third hour*=9 a.m. Jews who were engaged in the exercises of the synagogue on feast days abstained from eating and drinking until 10 a.m. or noon; therefore, this could not be drunkenness.

2:16–17 See Joel 2:28–32. The fulfillment of this prophecy will be in the last days immediately preceding the return of Christ, when all the particulars of the prophecy will come to pass (e.g., v. 20 and see Rev. 6:12). Peter reminds his hearers that, knowing Joel's prophecy, they should have recognized what they were seeing then as a work of the Spirit, not a result of drunkenness.

2:22–36 In vv. 22–24 Peter reviews the life and death of Jesus of Nazareth. In vv. 25–31 he recites the prophecy of the resurrection, quoting Ps. 16:8–11. Since David was speaking of the Messiah (v. 31), and since Jesus was raised from the dead, Jesus must be the Messiah (v. 36).

25 For David speaketh concerning him, I foresaw the Lord always before my face, for he is on my right hand, that I should not be moved:

26 Therefore did my heart rejoice, and my tongue was glad; moreover also my flesh shall rest in hope:

27 Because thou wilt not leave my soul in hell, neither wilt thou suffer thine Holy One to see corruption.

28 Thou hast made known to me the ways of life; thou shalt make me full of joy with thy countenance.

29 Men *and* brethren, let me freely speak unto you of the patriarch David, that he is both dead and buried, and his sepulchre is with us unto this day.

30 Therefore being a prophet, and knowing that God had sworn with an oath to him, that of the fruit of his loins, according to the flesh, he would raise up Christ to sit on his throne;

31 He seeing this before spake of the resurrection of Christ, that his soul was not left in hell, neither his flesh did see corruption.

32 This Jesus hath God raised up, whereof we all are witnesses.

33 Therefore being by the right hand of God exalted, and having received of the Father the promise of the Holy Ghost, he hath shed forth this, which ye now see and hear.

34 For David is not ascended into the heavens: but he saith himself, The LORD said unto my Lord, Sit thou on my right hand,

35 Until I make thy foes thy footstool.

36 Therefore let all the house of Israel know assuredly, that God hath made that same Jesus, whom ye have crucified, both Lord and Christ.

3 The results of Pentecost, 2:37–47

37 ¶ Now when they heard *this*, they were pricked in their heart, and said unto Peter and to the rest of the apostles, Men *and* brethren, what shall we do?

2:27 *hell. Lit.*, hades. The unseen world, sometimes specifically a place of torment (see note at Luke 16:23) and sometimes merely the grave, as here. The meaning is that Christ's body and spirit would not be allowed to remain separated (v. 31).

2:33 Returning to the original point, Peter declares that it is the exalted Jesus who has sent the Holy Spirit.

2:34 Quoting Ps. 110:1.

2:37 *pricked in their heart*=cut to the heart.

38 Then Peter said unto them, Repent, and be baptized every one of you in the name of Jesus Christ for the remission of sins, and ye shall receive the gift of the Holy Ghost.

39 For the promise is unto you, and to your children, and to all that are afar off, *even* as many as the Lord our God shall call.

40 And with many other words did he testify and exhort, saying, Save yourselves from this untoward generation.

41 ¶ Then they that gladly received his word were baptized: and the same day there were added *unto them* about three thousand souls.

42 And they continued stedfastly in the apostles' doctrine and fellowship, and in breaking of bread, and in prayers.

43 And fear came upon every soul: and many wonders and signs were done by the apostles.

44 And all that believed were together, and had all things common;

45 And sold their possessions and goods, and parted them to all *men*, as every man had need.

46 And they, continuing daily with one accord in the temple, and breaking bread from house to house, did eat their meat with gladness and singleness of heart,

47 Praising God, and having favour with all the people. And the Lord added to the church daily such as should be saved.

2:38 *Repent.* This means to change one's mind, specifically, here, about Jesus of Nazareth, and to acknowledge Him as Lord (=God) and Christ (=Messiah). Such repentance brings salvation. There is also a repentance needed in the Christian life in relation to specific sins (2 Cor. 7:9; Rev. 2:5). *be baptized for the remission of sins.* On baptism see note at Matt. 3:11. Water baptism was the outward sign of repentance and remission of sins. The remission is through faith in Christ, not through baptism (*for* may mean "because of" here as in Matt. 12:41). *the gift of the Holy Ghost.* The Spirit is a gift to all who believe, not a reward to some.
2:40 *untoward*=crooked.
2:42 *breaking of bread*=celebrating the Lord's Supper.
2:44 *had all things common.* This community of goods seems to have been limited to the early years of the Jerusalem church only. It may have been necessitated by the many pilgrims who lingered in Jerusalem to learn more of their new Christian faith.

C The Healing of a Lame Man, 3:1–26

1 *The miracle*, 3:1–11

3 Now Peter and John went up together into the temple at the hour of prayer, *being* the ninth *hour*.

2 And a certain man lame from his mother's womb was carried, whom they laid daily at the gate of the temple which is called Beautiful, to ask alms of them that entered into the temple;

3 Who seeing Peter and John about to go into the temple asked an alms.

4 And Peter, fastening his eyes upon him with John, said, Look on us.

5 And he gave heed unto them, expecting to receive something of them.

6 Then Peter said, Silver and gold have I none; but such as I have give I thee: In the name of Jesus Christ of Nazareth rise up and walk.

7 And he took him by the right hand, and lifted *him* up: and immediately his feet and ankle bones received strength.

8 And he leaping up stood, and walked, and entered with them into the temple, walking, and leaping, and praising God.

9 And all the people saw him walking and praising God:

10 And they knew that it was he which sat for alms at the Beautiful gate of the temple: and they were filled with wonder and amazement at that which had happened unto him.

11 And as the lame man which was healed held Peter and John, all the people ran together unto them in the porch that is called Solomon's, greatly wondering.

2 *The message*, 3:12–26

12 ¶ And when Peter saw *it*, he answered unto the people, Ye men of Israel, why marvel ye at this? or why

3:1 *the ninth hour*=3 p.m., the hour of prayer associated with the evening sacrifice.
3:2 *the gate . . . Beautiful*. Probably the Nicanor Gate, the eastern gate of the temple buildings, leading from the Court of the Gentiles into the Women's Court.
3:6 *In the name of Jesus Christ*. His power and authority are invoked.
3:11 *the porch that is called Solomon's*. A colonnade running the length of the E. side of the outer court of the temple.

look ye so earnestly on us, as though by our own power or holiness we had made this man to walk?

13 The God of Abraham, and of Isaac, and of Jacob, the God of our fathers, hath glorified his Son Jesus; whom ye delivered up, and denied him in the presence of Pilate, when he was determined to let *him* go.

14 But ye denied the Holy One and the Just, and desired a murderer to be granted unto you;

15 And killed the Prince of life, whom God hath raised from the dead; whereof we are witnesses.

16 And his name through faith in his name hath made this man strong, whom ye see and know: yea, the faith which is by him hath given him this perfect soundness in the presence of you all.

17 And now, brethren, I wot that through ignorance ye did *it*, as *did* also your rulers.

18 But those things, which God before had shewed by the mouth of all his prophets, that Christ should suffer, he hath so fulfilled.

19 ¶ Repent ye therefore, and be converted, that your sins may be blotted out, when the times of refreshing shall come from the presence of the Lord;

20 And he shall send Jesus Christ, which before was preached unto you:

21 Whom the heaven must receive until the times of restitution of all things, which God hath spoken by the mouth of all his holy prophets since the world began.

22 For Moses truly said unto the fathers, A prophet shall the Lord your God raise up unto you of your brethren, like unto me; him shall ye hear in all things whatsoever he shall say unto you.

23 And it shall come to pass, *that* every soul, which will

3:13 *his Son*=his Servant; i.e., the "servant" of Isa. 42:1–9; 49:1–13; 52:13–53:12.

3:15 *Prince of life*. Lit., Author of life; i.e., originator.

3:16 *through faith*. I.e., through the apostles' faith or possibly the lame man's faith. *the faith which is by him*=the faith which is through Jesus.

3:19 *be converted*=turn around, i.e., turn from sin to God by reversing their verdict about Jesus and confessing Him as the Messiah. *the times of refreshing* and the *restitution of all things* (v. 21) refer to the millennial kingdom.

3:22 The Jews expected a *prophet* and the Messiah—two distinct persons (John 1:20–21; 7:40–41). The Christian view united them in the one person of Jesus Christ (Deut. 18:15).

3:23 See Lev. 23:29; Deut. 18:19.

not hear that prophet, shall be destroyed from among the people.

24 Yea, and all the prophets from Samuel and those that follow after, as many as have spoken, have likewise foretold of these days.

25 Ye are the children of the prophets, and of the covenant which God made with our fathers, saying unto Abraham, And in thy seed shall all the kindreds of the earth be blessed.

26 Unto you first God, having raised up his Son Jesus, sent him to bless you, in turning away every one of you from his iniquities.

D The Beginning of Persecution, 4:1-37

1 *The persecution,* 4:1-22

4 And as they spake unto the people, the priests, and the captain of the temple, and the Sadducees, came upon them,

2 Being grieved that they taught the people, and preached through Jesus the resurrection from the dead.

3 And they laid hands on them, and put *them* in hold unto the next day: for it was now eventide.

4 Howbeit many of them which heard the word believed; and the number of the men was about five thousand.

5 ¶ And it came to pass on the morrow, that their rulers, and elders, and scribes,

6 And Annas the high priest, and Ca'aphas, and John, and Alexander, and as many as were of the kindred of the high priest, were gathered together at Jerusalem.

7 And when they had set them in the midst, they asked, By what power, or by what name, have ye done this?

8 Then Peter, filled with the Holy Ghost, said unto them, Ye rulers of the people, and elders of Israel,

3:26 *his Son*=his Servant (see note at 3:13).
4:1 *the captain of the temple.* An official second only to the high priest. He was responsible for order in the temple. The *Sadducees* hated the idea of resurrection which the apostles were preaching (v. 2).
4:3 *in hold*=in custody.
4:6 *Annas . . . and Caiaphas. See note at Luke* 3:2. *We know* nothing about *John and Alexander.*
4:8-12 In his answer (reported in 92 words in the Greek text) Peter actually puts his hearers on trial. He calls attention to the fact that the miracle was a good deed, not a crime (v. 9), and that it took place by the power of Jesus whom they had

9 If we this day be examined of the good deed done to the impotent man, by what means he is made whole;

10 Be it known unto you all, and to all the people of Israel, that by the name of Jesus Christ of Nazareth, whom ye crucified, whom God raised from the dead, *even* by him doth this man stand here before you whole.

11 This is the stone which was set at nought of you builders, which is become the head of the corner.

12 Neither is there salvation in any other: for there is none other name under heaven given among men, whereby we must be saved.

13 ¶ Now when they saw the boldness of Peter and John, and perceived that they were unlearned and ignorant men, they marvelled; and they took knowledge of them, that they had been with Jesus.

14 And beholding the man which was healed standing with them, they could say nothing against it.

15 But when they had commanded them to go aside out of the council, they conferred among themselves,

16 Saying, What shall we do to these men? for that indeed a notable miracle hath been done by them *is* manifest to all them that dwell in Jerusalem; and we cannot deny *it*.

17 But that it spread no further among the people, let us straitly threaten them, that they speak henceforth to no man in this name.

18 And they called them, and commanded them not to speak at all nor teach in the name of Jesus.

19 But Peter and John answered and said unto them, Whether it be right in the sight of God to hearken unto you more than unto God, judge ye.

20 For we cannot but speak the things which we have seen and heard.

21 So when they had further threatened them, they let them go, finding nothing how they might punish them, because of the people: for all *men* glorified God for that which was done.

crucified (v. 10). His rejection was predicted in the O.T. (v. 11; Ps. 118:22), and salvation is only through Him (v. 12).

4:13 *unlearned and ignorant men.* This means that Peter and John were not formally trained in the rabbinic schools; they were not professional scholars or ordained teachers (see also John 7:15).

4:15-17 Though the Sanhedrin forbade further preaching, they did not try to disprove the resurrection of Jesus, which would have been the simplest way to stop the apostles.

22 For the man was above forty years old, on whom this miracle of healing was shewed.

2 The prayer, 4:23–31

23 ¶ And being let go, they went to their own company, and reported all that the chief priests and elders had said unto them.

24 And when they heard that, they lifted up their voice to God with one accord, and said, Lord, thou *art* God, which hast made heaven, and earth, and the sea, and all that in them is:

25 Who by the mouth of thy servant David hast said, Why did the heathen rage, and the people imagine vain things?

26 The kings of the earth stood up, and the rulers were gathered together against the Lord, and against his Christ.

27 For of a truth against thy holy child Jesus, whom thou hast anointed, both Herod, and Pontius Pilate, with the Gentiles, and the people of Israel, were gathered together,

28 For to do whatsoever thy hand and thy counsel determined before to be done.

29 And now, Lord, behold their threatenings: and grant unto thy servants, that with all boldness they may speak thy word,

30 By stretching forth thine hand to heal; and that signs and wonders may be done by the name of thy holy child Jesus.

31 ¶ And when they had prayed, the place was shaken where they were assembled together; and they were all filled with the Holy Ghost, and they spake the word of God with boldness.

4:24–31 This is a prayer of thanksgiving for the sovereign power of God, and not a prayer for deliverance from further opposition. The only petition in the prayer is for boldness (v. 31).

4:25–26 The quotation is from Ps. 2:1–2.

4:27 The responsibility for the death of Christ is laid upon both Jews and Gentiles.

4:31 *the Holy Ghost.* There are a number of references to the activity of the Holy Spirit in Acts: (1) He baptizes believers into the body of Christ, thus forming the church (1:5; 11:15–16). (2) His presence in the believer is evidence of the new birth (2:38; 5:32; 10:44; 15:8). (3) He fills believers for witnessing (4:8), for leadership (6:3), for strength (7:55), and for special discernment (13.9). (4) He leads (13:4; 16:7).

3 The provision, 4:32-37

32 And the multitude of them that believed were of one heart and of one soul: neither said any *of them* that ought of the things which he possessed was his own; but they had all things common.

33 And with great power gave the apostles witness of the resurrection of the Lord Jesus: and great grace was upon them all.

34 Neither was there any among them that lacked: for as many as were possessors of lands or houses sold them, and brought the prices of the things that were sold,

35 And laid *them* down at the apostles' feet: and distribution was made unto every man according as he had need.

36 And Joses, who by the apostles was surnamed Barnabas, (which is, being interpreted, The son of consolation,) a Levite, *and* of the country of Cyprus,

37 Having land, sold *it*, and brought the money, and laid *it* at the apostles' feet.

E Purging and Persecution, 5:1-42

1 Purging from within, 5:1-11

5 But a certain man named Anani'as, with Sapphira his wife, sold a possession,

2 And kept back *part* of the price, his wife also being privy *to it*, and brought a certain part, and laid *it* at the apostles' feet.

3 But Peter said, Anani'as, why hath Satan filled thine heart to lie to the Holy Ghost, and to keep back *part* of the price of the land?

4 Whiles it remained, was it not thine own? and after it was sold, was it not in thine own power? why hast thou conceived this thing in thine heart? thou hast not lied unto men, but unto God.

5 And Anani'as hearing these words fell down, and

4:32 *they had all things common.* This display of Christian charity did not abolish the right to possess personal property. Such community of goods was not compulsory but voluntary, as a way of eliminating need among them.

5:2 *being privy to it*=knowing about it.

5:3 *to lie.* The sin of Ananias and Sapphira was not in not selling all their property, or in keeping part of the proceeds of the sale, but in lying about how much they had received. Lying to the Spirit is lying to God, because the Holy Spirit is God (v. 4).

gave up the ghost: and great fear came on all them that heard these things.

6 And the young men arose, wound him up, and carried *him* out, and buried *him*.

7 And it was about the space of three hours after, when his wife, not knowing what was done, came in.

8 And Peter answered unto her, Tell me whether ye sold the land for so much? And she said, Yea, for so much.

9 Then Peter said unto her, How is it that ye have agreed together to tempt the Spirit of the Lord? behold, the feet of them which have buried thy husband *are* at the door, and shall carry thee out.

10 Then fell she down straightway at his feet, and yielded up the ghost: and the young men came in, and found her dead, and, carrying *her* forth, buried *her* by her husband.

11 And great fear came upon all the church, and upon as many as heard these things.

2 *Purging from without,* 5:12–42

12 ¶ And by the hands of the apostles were many signs and wonders wrought among the people; (and they were all with one accord in Solomon's porch.

13 And of the rest durst no man join himself to them: but the people magnified them.

14 And believers were the more added to the Lord, multitudes both of men and women.)

15 Insomuch that they brought forth the sick into the streets, and laid *them* on beds and couches, that at the least the shadow of Peter passing by might overshadow some of them.

16 There came also a multitude *out* of the cities round about unto Jerusalem, bringing sick folks, and them which were vexed with unclean spirits: and they were healed every one.

17 ¶ Then the high priest rose up, and all they that were with him, (which is the sect of the Sadducees,) and were filled with indignation,

---

5:6 *wound him up*=wrapped him (in his or their robes).

5:9 *to tempt.* I.e., to see how far you could go in presuming on God's goodness.

5:12 *Solomon's porch.* See note at 3:11.

5:17 Again the *Sadducees*, who did not believe in resurrection (23:8), were particularly riled at the disciples' preaching the resurrection of Christ (4:33).

18 And laid their hands on the apostles, and put them in the common prison.

19 But the angel of the Lord by night opened the prison doors, and brought them forth, and said,

20 Go, stand and speak in the temple to the people all the words of this life.

21 And when they heard *that*, they entered into the temple early in the morning, and taught. But the high priest came, and they that were with him, and called the council together, and all the senate of the children of Israel, and sent to the prison to have them brought.

22 But when the officers came, and found them not in the prison, they returned, and told,

23 Saying, The prison truly found we shut with all safety, and the keepers standing without before the doors: but when we had opened, we found no man within.

24 Now when the high priest and the captain of the temple and the chief priests heard these things, they doubted of them whereunto this would grow.

25 Then came one and told them, saying, Behold, the men whom ye put in prison are standing in the temple, and teaching the people.

26 Then went the captain with the officers, and brought them without violence: for they feared the people, lest they should have been stoned.

27 And when they had brought them, they set *them* before the council: and the high priest asked them,

28 Saying, Did not we straitly command you that ye should not teach in this name? and, behold, ye have filled Jerusalem with your doctrine, and intend to bring this man's blood upon us.

29 ¶ Then Peter and the *other* apostles answered and said, We ought to obey God rather than men.

30 The God of our fathers raised up Jesus, whom ye slew and hanged on a tree.

31 Him hath God exalted with his right hand *to be* a Prince and a Saviour, for to give repentance to Israel, and forgiveness of sins.

32 And we are his witnesses of these things; and *so is* also the Holy Ghost, whom God hath given to them that obey him.

5:21 *council . . . senate.* These are the same body, the Jewish Sanhedrin.
5:28 *straitly*=strictly.
5:31 *Prince*=Author (3:15; Heb. 12:2), or Leader.

33 ¶ When they heard *that*, they were cut *to the heart*, and took counsel to slay them.

34 Then stood there up one in the council, a Pharisee, named Gamā'liel, a doctor of the law, had in reputation among all the people, and commanded to put the apostles forth a little space;

35 And said unto them, Ye men of Israel, take heed to yourselves what ye intend to do as touching these men.

36 For before these days rose up Theu'das, boasting himself to be somebody; to whom a number of men, about four hundred, joined themselves: who was slain; and all, as many as obeyed him, were scattered, and brought to nought.

37 After this man rose up Judas of Galilee in the days of the taxing, and drew away much people after him: he also perished; and all, *even* as many as obeyed him, were dispersed.

38 And now I say unto you, Refrain from these men, and let them alone: for if this counsel or this work be of men, it will come to nought:

39 But if it be of God, ye cannot overthrow it; lest haply ye be found even to fight against God.

40 And to him they agreed: and when they had called the apostles, and beaten *them*, they commanded that they should not speak in the name of Jesus, and let them go.

41 ¶ And they departed from the presence of the council, rejoicing that they were counted worthy to suffer shame for his name.

42 And daily in the temple, and in every house, they ceased not to teach and preach Jesus Christ.

F Choosing Co-laborers, 6:1–7

6 And in those days, when the number of the disciples was multiplied, there arose a murmuring of the

---

5:34 *Gamaliel* was a respected rabbi who followed the liberal interpretations of Hillel, another rabbi who lived shortly before the time of Christ. His popularity demanded that the Sanhedrin listen to him. Paul was a student of Gamaliel (22:3).

5:36 *Theudas.* This is the only historical reference to him.

5:37 *Judas.* This revolt (in A.D. 6) is described by the historian Josephus. The followers of this Judas became the original "Zealots."

6:1 *Grecians . . . Hebrews.* The former were Greek-speaking Jewish Christians and the latter were Aramaic-speaking Jewish Christians.

Grecians against the Hebrews, because their widows were neglected in the daily ministration.

2 Then the twelve called the multitude of the disciples *unto them*, and said, It is not reason that we should leave the word of God, and serve tables.

3 Wherefore, brethren, look ye out among you seven men of honest report, full of the Holy Ghost and wisdom, whom we may appoint over this business.

4 But we will give ourselves continually to prayer, and to the ministry of the word.

5 ¶ And the saying pleased the whole multitude: and they chose Stephen, a man full of faith and of the Holy Ghost, and Philip, and Proch'orus, and Nīcā'nor, and Timon, and Par'menas, and Nicolas a proselyte of An'tioch:

6 Whom they set before the apostles: and when they had prayed, they laid *their* hands on them.

7 And the word of God increased; and the number of the disciples multiplied in Jerusalem greatly; and a great company of the priests were obedient to the faith.

G Stephen, the First Martyr, 6:8–8:3

1 *The stirring of the people*, 6:8–15

8 And Stephen, full of faith and power, did great wonders and miracles among the people.

9 ¶ Then there arose certain of the synagogue, which is called *the synagogue* of the Līber'tīnes, and Cȳrē'nians, and Alexandrians, and of them of Cīlic'ia and of Asia, disputing with Stephen.

6:2 *serve tables*. I.e., of food for the widows or of money (as "tables" in John 2:15). The word "serve" is the one we derive "deacon" from, but these men were "deacons" only in the sense of being servants. They were not yet deacons in the later sense of officers in the church (see note at 1 Tim. 3:8). All seven have Greek, not Jewish, names; two, Stephen and Philip, quickly achieve prominence for their vigorous evangelism.

6:6 *laid their hands on them*. The laying on of hands was a formal sign of their appointment to this service. The rite indicates a link or association between the parties involved. Sometimes it was related to healing (Mark 5:23), or to the impartation of the Spirit (Acts 6:17; 9:17; 19:6), or, as here, a sign of ordination for special service (13:3; 1 Tim. 4:14).

6:9 *Libertines*=Freedmen. These were Jewish freedmen or descendants of freedmen from the various places mentioned in the verse. They had their own synagogue in Jerusalem.

10 And they were not able to resist the wisdom and the spirit by which he spake.

11 Then they suborned men, which said, We have heard him speak blasphemous words against Moses, and *against* God.

12 And they stirred up the people, and the elders, and the scribes, and came upon *him*, and caught him, and brought *him* to the council,

13 And set up false witnesses, which said, This man ceaseth not to speak blasphemous words against this holy place, and the law:

14 For we have heard him say, that this Jesus of Nazareth shall destroy this place, and shall change the customs which Moses delivered us.

15 And all that sat in the council, looking stedfastly on him, saw his face as it had been the face of an angel.

2 *The sermon of Stephen,* 7:1–53

7 Then said the high priest, Are these things so?

2 And he said, Men, brethren, and fathers, hearken; The God of glory appeared unto our father Abraham, when he was in Mesopotā′mia, before he dwelt in Char′ran,

3 And said unto him, Get thee out of thy country, and from thy kindred, and come into the land which I shall shew thee.

4 Then came he out of the land of the Chaldæ′ans, and dwelt in Char′ran: and from thence, when his father was dead, he removed him into this land, wherein ye now dwell.

5 And he gave him none inheritance in it, no, not *so much as* to set his foot on: yet he promised that he would give it to him for a possession, and to his seed after him, when *as yet* he had no child.

6 And God spake on this wise, That his seed should sojourn in a strange land; and that they should bring them into bondage, and entreat *them* evil four hundred years.

6:11 *suborned*=secretly instigated.

6:12 *to the council,* the Sanhedrin. See note at Luke 22:66.

7:1 *the high priest*=Caiaphas.

7:2–53 Stephen's sermon is the longest recorded in Acts. The text is: "as your fathers did, so do ye" (v. 51). Stephen recites the privileges of the nation Israel and their rejection of God's messengers; then he lays the blame for the slaying of Jesus squarely on them (v. 52).

7:2 God's call to *Abraham* came first when he was in *Mesopotamia* (Gen. 15:7; Neh. 9:7). Then he went to Charran (Haran, Gen. 11:31–32) and later to Palestine.

7 And the nation to whom they shall be in bondage will I judge, said God: and after that shall they come forth, and serve me in this place.

8 And he gave him the covenant of circumcision: and so *Abraham* begat Isaac, and circumcised him the eighth day; and Isaac *begat* Jacob; and Jacob *begat* the twelve patriarchs.

9 And the patriarchs, moved with envy, sold Joseph into Egypt: but God was with him,

10 And delivered him out of all his afflictions, and gave him favour and wisdom in the sight of Phār′āōh king of Egypt; and he made him governor over Egypt and all his house.

11 Now there came a dearth over all the land of Egypt and Chā′naan, and great affliction: and our fathers found no sustenance.

12 But when Jacob heard that there was corn in Egypt, he sent out our fathers first.

13 And at the second *time* Joseph was made known to his brethren; and Joseph's kindred was made known unto Phār′āōh.

14 Then sent Joseph, and called his father Jacob to *him*, and all his kindred, threescore and fifteen souls.

15 So Jacob went down into Egypt, and died, he, and our fathers,

16 And were carried over into Sȳ′chem, and laid in the sepulchre that Abraham bought for a sum of money of the sons of Em′mor *the father* of Sychem.

17 But when the time of the promise drew nigh, which God had sworn to Abraham, the people grew and multiplied in Egypt,

18 Till another king arose, which knew not Joseph.

7:8 *circumcision*. See Gen. 17:9–14.

7:9 *Joseph*. See Gen. 37:11.

7:14 *threescore and fifteen souls*. This number follows the Septuagint (Greek translation of the O.T.), which arrives at 75 by including the son and grandson of Manasseh and two sons and a grandson of Ephraim. See Gen. 46:27, which reflects a different way of numbering Jacob's family, totaling 70. 7:15–16. Jacob was buried at Hebron in the Cave of Machpelah which Abraham bought from Ephron the Hittite (Gen. 23:16), and Joseph was buried at Shechem in a piece of ground Jacob bought from the sons of Hamor (Josh. 24:32). The two transactions are simply telescoped in these verses because of the pressure of Stephen's circumstances and need for brevity.

7:16 *Sychem*=Shechem. the *father of Sychem*; better, in Shechem.

19 The same dealt subtilly with our kindred, and evil entreated our fathers, so that they cast out their young children, to the end they might not live.

20 In which time Moses was born, and was exceeding fair, and nourished up in his father's house three months:

21 And when he was cast out, Phār'āōh's daughter took him up, and nourished him for her own son.

22 And Moses was learned in all the wisdom of the Egyptians, and was mighty in words and in deeds.

23 And when he was full forty years old, it came into his heart to visit his brethren the children of Israel.

24 And seeing one of them suffer wrong, he defended him, and avenged him that was oppressed, and smote the Egyptian:

25 For he supposed his brethren would have understood how that God by his hand would deliver them: but they understood not.

26 And the next day he shewed himself unto them as they strove, and would have set them at one again, saying, Sirs, ye are brethren; why do ye wrong one to another?

27 But he that did his neighbour wrong thrust him away, saying, Who made thee a ruler and a judge over us?

28 Wilt thou kill me, as thou diddest the Egyptian yesterday?

29 Then fled Moses at this saying, and was a stranger in the land of Madian, where he begat two sons.

30 And when forty years were expired, there appeared to him in the wilderness of mount Sina an angel of the Lord in a flame of fire in a bush.

31 When Moses saw it, he wondered at the sight: and as he drew near to behold it, the voice of the Lord came unto him,

32 Saying, I am the God of thy fathers, the God of Abraham, and the God of Isaac, and the God of Jacob. Then Moses trembled, and durst not behold.

33 Then said the Lord to him, Put off thy shoes from thy feet: for the place where thou standest is holy ground.

34 I have seen, I have seen the affliction of my people which is in Egypt, and I have heard their groaning, and am come down to deliver them. And now come, I will send thee into Egypt.

35 This Moses whom they refused, saying, Who made

7:19 The same dealt subtilly . . .=And he exploited our kindred and forced our fathers . . .
7:20 Moses. See Ex. 2 and Heb. 11:24–26.
7:30 in the bush. Ex. 3:2.

thee a ruler and a judge? the same did God send *to be* a ruler and a deliverer by the hand of the angel which appeared to him in the bush.

36 He brought them out, after that he had shewed wonders and signs in the land of Egypt, and in the Red sea, and in the wilderness forty years.

37 ¶ This is that Moses, which said unto the children of Israel, A prophet shall the Lord your God raise up unto you of your brethren, like unto me; him shall ye hear.

38 This is he, that was in the church in the wilderness with the angel which spake to him in the mount Sina, and *with* our fathers: who received the lively oracles to give unto us:

39 To whom our fathers would not obey, but thrust *him* from them, and in their hearts turned back again into Egypt,

40 Saying unto Aaron, Make us gods to go before us: for *as for* this Moses, which brought us out of the land of Egypt, we wot not what is become of him.

41 And they made a calf in those days, and offered sacrifice unto the idol, and rejoiced in the works of their own hands.

42 Then God turned, and gave them up to worship the host of heaven; as it is written in the book of the prophets, O ye house of Israel, have ye offered to me slain beasts and sacrifices *by the space of* forty years in the wilderness?

43 Yea, ye took up the tabernacle of Mō′loch, and the star of your god Remphan, figures which ye made to worship them: and I will carry you away beyond Babylon.

44 Our fathers had the tabernacle of witness in the wilderness, as he had appointed, speaking unto Moses, that

7:38 *the church in the wilderness.* Lit., the assembly in the wilderness; i.e., the gathering of the people to receive the law. The word "church" means an assembly or gathering and is used in the N.T. of four kinds of groups: (1) here, the children of Israel gathered as a nation; (2) in Acts 19:32, 39, 41, a group of townspeople assembled in a town meeting; (3) in a technical sense, all believers who are gathered together in the one body of Christ, the church universal (Col. 1:18); (4) most frequently, in reference to a local group of professing Christians; e.g., "the church at Antioch" (13:1).

7:43 *Moloch . . . Remphan.* See Amos 5:25–27. Moloch is a title for various Canaanite deities to whom human sacrifices were offered. Remphan (better, Rephan) is the name of a god connected with the planet Saturn.

7:44 *tabernacle of witness.* I.e., the tabernacle was a witness to the presence of God in their midst.

he should make it according to the fashion that he had seen.

45 Which also our fathers that came after brought in with Jesus into the possession of the Gentiles, whom God drave out before the face of our fathers, unto the days of David;

46 Who found favour before God, and desired to find a tabernacle for the God of Jacob.

47 But Solomon built him an house.

48 Howbeit the most High dwelleth not in temples made with hands; as saith the prophet,

49 Heaven *is* my throne, and earth *is* my footstool: what house will ye build me? saith the Lord: or what *is* the place of my rest?

50 Hath not my hand made all these things?

51 ¶ Ye stiffnecked and uncircumcised in heart and ears, ye do always resist the Holy Ghost: as your fathers *did*, so *do* ye.

52 Which of the prophets have not your fathers persecuted? and they have slain them which shewed before of the coming of the Just One; of whom ye have been now the betrayers and murderers:

53 Who have received the law by the disposition of angels, and have not kept *it*.

3 *The stoning of Stephen*, 7:54—8:3

54 ¶ When they heard these things, they were cut to the heart, and they gnashed on him with *their* teeth.

55 But he, being full of the Holy Ghost, looked up stedfastly into heaven, and saw the glory of God, and Jesus standing on the right hand of God,

56 And said, Behold, I see the heavens opened, and the Son of man standing on the right hand of God.

57 Then they cried out with a loud voice, and stopped their ears, and ran upon him with one accord,

58 And cast *him* out of the city, and stoned *him*: and

7:47 *Solomon*. See 2 Sam. 7:1–13; 1 Kings 8:20.

7:49–50 Quoting Isa. 66:1–2.

7:51–53 contain Stephen's indictment, amply illustrated in the previously cited history of Israel.

7:55 *Jesus standing on the right hand of God*. Jesus' priestly work of offering a sacrifice for sin was finished on the cross; therefore, He is sometimes pictured as seated at the right hand of God (Heb. 1:3). His priestly work of sustaining His people continues (as here with Stephen); therefore, He is seen as standing to minister (Rev. 2:1).

7:58 The mention of *witnesses* suggests that they went through

the witnesses laid down their clothes at a young man's feet, whose name was Saul.

59 And they stoned Stephen, calling upon God, and saying, Lord Jesus, receive my spirit.

60 And he kneeled down, and cried with a loud voice, Lord, lay not this sin to their charge. And when he had said this, he fell asleep.

8 And Saul was consenting unto his death. And at that time there was a great persecution against the church which was at Jerusalem; and they were all scattered abroad throughout the regions of Judæa and Samaria, except the apostles.

2 And devout men carried Stephen to his burial, and made great lamentation over him.

3 As for Saul, he made havock of the church, entering into every house, and haling men and women committed them to prison.

II CHRISTIANITY IN PALESTINE AND SYRIA, 8:4–12:25

A The Christians Scattered, 8:4–40

4 Therefore they that were scattered abroad went every where preaching the word.

1 The preaching in Samaria, 8:5–25

5 Then Philip went down to the city of Samaria, and preached Christ unto them.

6 And the people with one accord gave heed unto those things which Philip spake, hearing and seeing the miracles which he did.

7 For unclean spirits, crying with loud voice, came out of many that were possessed with them: and many taken with palsies, and that were lame, were healed.

8 And there was great joy in that city.

the motions of a legal execution (Lev. 24:14), though probably without securing the official approval of Pilate.

7:60 he fell asleep. This expression is used of the physical death of believers (John 11:11; 1 Thess. 4:13, 15).

8:4 went everywhere. See 11:19 for details.

8:5 Philip. See 6:5. the city of Samaria was then called Sebaste. Some texts read "a city of Samaria," which would mean some smaller city in Samaria. On the Samaritans see the note at Luke 10:33.

9 But there was a certain man, called Simon, which beforetime in the same city used sorcery, and bewitched the people of Samaria, giving out that himself was some great one:

10 To whom they all gave heed, from the least to the greatest, saying, This man is the great power of God.

11 And to him they had regard, because that of long time he had bewitched them with sorceries.

12 But when they believed Philip preaching the things concerning the kingdom of God, and the name of Jesus Christ, they were baptized, both men and women.

13 Then Simon himself believed also: and when he was baptized, he continued with Philip, and wondered, beholding the miracles and signs which were done.

14 Now when the apostles which were at Jerusalem heard that Samaria had received the word of God, they sent unto them Peter and John:

15 Who, when they were come down, prayed for them, that they might receive the Holy Ghost:

16 (For as yet he was fallen upon none of them: only they were baptized in the name of the Lord Jesus.)

17 Then laid they *their* hands on them, and they received the Holy Ghost.

18 And when Simon saw that through laying on of the apostles' hands the Holy Ghost was given, he offered them money,

19 Saying, Give me also this power, that on whomsoever I lay hands, he may receive the Holy Ghost.

8:9 *sorcery.* Simon was a practitioner of magic, quackery, and various kinds of sorcery which bewitched the people. He may have been making Messianic claims.

8:13 *Simon himself believed also.* Peter's denunciation in vv. 20–23 indicates that Simon's faith was not unto salvation (Jas. 2:14–20).

8:15–17 Though the Samaritans had been baptized in water (v. 12), the gift of the Holy Spirit was delayed until Peter and John came and laid their hands on them. Normally the Spirit is given at the moment of faith (10:44; 19:2; Eph. 1:13). In this instance, however, it was imperative that the Samaritans be identified with the apostles and the Jerusalem church so that there would be no rival Samaritan Christian church.

8:18–24 Simon thought he could buy the gift of God (v. 20). When Peter urges him to repent, Simon replies, in effect, "Pray for me that I may escape punishment" (v. 24). He was still thinking in terms of magical powers rather than repentance of heart.

20 But Peter said unto him, Thy money perish with thee, because thou hast thought that the gift of God may be purchased with money.

21 Thou hast neither part nor lot in this matter: for thy heart is not right in the sight of God.

22 Repent therefore of this thy wickedness, and pray God, if perhaps the thought of thine heart may be forgiven thee.

23 For I perceive that thou art in the gall of bitterness, and *in* the bond of iniquity.

24 Then answered Simon, and said, Pray ye to the Lord for me, that none of these things which ye have spoken come upon me.

25 And they, when they had testified and preached the word of the Lord, returned to Jerusalem, and preached the gospel in many villages of the Samaritans.

2 *The preaching on the Gaza road*, 8:26–40

26 And the angel of the Lord spake unto Philip, saying, Arise, and go toward the south unto the way that goeth down from Jerusalem unto Gaza, which is desert.

27 And he arose and went: and, behold, a man of Ethiopia, an eunuch of great authority under Can'dacē queen of the Ethiopians, who had the charge of all her treasure, and had come to Jerusalem for to worship,

28 Was returning, and sitting in his chariot read Ēsâ'as the prophet.

29 Then the Spirit said unto Philip, Go near, and join thyself to this chariot.

30 And Philip ran thither to *him*, and heard him read the prophet Ēsâ'as, and said, Understandest thou what thou readest?

31 And he said, How can I, except some man should guide me? And he desired Philip that he would come up and sit with him.

32 The place of the scripture which he read was this, He

8:26 *which is desert*. Probably a reference to Desert Gaza, the old city which was destroyed in 93 B.C. and which was inland from the Gaza of N.T. times. However, some understand the phrase to mean that it was a desert road.

8:27 *Ethiopia*. Not present-day Abyssinia but ancient Nubia, south of Aswan. The story shows how far the gospel was spreading. *Candace*. The hereditary title of Ethiopian queens.

8:32–33 He was reading Isa. 53:7–8.

was led as a sheep to the slaughter; and like a lamb dumb before his shearer, so opened he not his mouth:

33 In his humiliation his judgment was taken away: and who shall declare his generation? for his life is taken from the earth.

34 And the eunuch answered Philip, and said, I pray thee, of whom speaketh the prophet this? of himself, or of some other man?

35 Then Philip opened his mouth, and began at the same scripture, and preached unto him Jesus.

36 And as they went on *their* way, they came unto a certain water: and the eunuch said, See, *here is* water; what doth hinder me to be baptized?

37 And Philip said, If thou believest with all thine heart, thou mayest. And he answered and said, I believe that Jesus Christ is the Son of God.

38 And he commanded the chariot to stand still: and they went down both into the water, both Philip and the eunuch; and he baptized him.

39 And when they were come up out of the water, the Spirit of the Lord caught away Philip, that the eunuch saw him no more: and he went on his way rejoicing.

40 But Philip was found at Azō'tus: and passing through he preached in all the cities, till he came to Cæsarea.

B The Conversion of Paul, 9:1–31

1 *The account of Paul's conversion*, 9:1–19

9 And Saul, yet breathing out threatenings and slaughter against the disciples of the Lord, went unto the high priest,

---

8:32–35 *preached unto Him Jesus*. Before the coming of Jesus the Jews understood Isa. 53 as referring to the Messiah. This interpretation was abandoned as Christians applied the prophecy to Jesus of Nazareth, and Isa. 53 was then considered by the Jews to be referring either to Isaiah himself or to the people of Israel, who would be a light to the nations, etc.

8:37 Most manuscripts do not contain this verse.

8:40 *Azotus*=O.T. Ashdod, 20 miles N. of Gaza.

9:1–19 Luke here records Paul's conversion (22:4 ff. and 26:12 ff. also give accounts of it to the crowd in Jerusalem and to Herod Agrippa II). In his own writings Paul refers to it only a few times. He related it to the supernatural purposes of God (Gal. 1:15); he spoke of the suddenness of it (1 Cor. 15:8; Phil. 3:12); he called it an act of new creation by God (2 Cor. 4:6); he acknowledged the merciful character of it (1 Tim. 1:13); and he epitomized it as seeing the

2 And desired of him letters to Damascus to the synagogues, that if he found any of this way, whether they were men or women, he might bring them bound unto Jerusalem.

3 And as he journeyed, he came near Damascus: and suddenly there shined round about him a light from heaven:

4 And he fell to the earth, and heard a voice saying unto him, Saul, Saul, why persecutest thou me?

5 And he said, Who art thou, Lord? And the Lord said, I am Jesus whom thou persecutest: *it is* hard for thee to kick against the pricks.

6 And he trembling and astonished said, Lord, what wilt thou have me to do? And the Lord *said* unto him, Arise, and go into the city, and it shall be told thee what thou must do.

7 And the men which journeyed with him stood speechless, hearing a voice, but seeing no man.

8 And Saul arose from the earth; and when his eyes were opened, he saw no man: but they led him by the hand, and brought *him* into Damascus.

9 And he was three days without sight, and neither did eat nor drink.

10 ¶ And there was a certain disciple at Damascus, named Anani′as; and to him said the Lord in a vision, Ananias. And he said, Behold, I *am here*, Lord.

11 And the Lord *said* unto him, Arise, and go into the street which is called Straight, and enquire in the house of Judas for *one* called Saul, of Tarsus: for, behold, he prayeth,

12 And hath seen in a vision a man named Anani′as coming in, and putting *his* hand on him, that he might receive his sight.

Lord (1 Cor. 9:1). He was, therefore, just as qualified as the apostles, for his conversion experience was just as objective a reality as their meetings with the risen Christ before the ascension.

9:2 *of this way.* I.e., Christians, John 14:6.

9:5 *I am Jesus.* In this moment Paul identified the Lord Yahweh of the O.T. whom he so zealously served, with Jesus of Nazareth whom he so ferociously persecuted through His saints. *it is hard for thee to kick against the pricks.* Pricks or goads were sharp-pointed sticks used to make animals go. Paul was evidently under conviction and was trying to stifle the goading of his conscience by increasing the intensity of his persecution of the Christians.

9:10 *Ananias.* According to 22:12 Ananias was an unimpeachable witness to the reality of Paul's conversion.

13 Then Anani'as answered, Lord, I have heard by many of this man, how much evil he hath done to thy saints at Jerusalem:

14 And here he hath authority from the chief priests to bind all that call on thy name.

15 But the Lord said unto him, Go thy way: for he is a chosen vessel unto me, to bear my name before the Gentiles, and kings, and the children of Israel:

16 For I will shew him how great things he must suffer for my name's sake.

17 And Anani'as went his way, and entered into the house; and putting his hands on him said, Brother Saul, the Lord, *even* Jesus, that appeared unto thee in the way as thou camest, hath sent me, that thou mightest receive thy sight, and be filled with the Holy Ghost.

18 And immediately there fell from his eyes as it had been scales: and he received sight forthwith, and arose, and was baptized.

19 And when he had received meat, he was strengthened. Then was Saul certain days with the disciples which were at Damascus.

2 *The aftermath of Paul's conversion,* 9:20-31

20 And straightway he preached Christ in the synagogues, that he is the Son of God.

21 But all that heard *him* were amazed, and said; Is not this he that destroyed them which called on this name in Jerusalem, and came hither for that intent, that he might bring them bound unto the chief priests?

22 But Saul increased the more in strength, and confounded the Jews which dwelt at Damascus, proving that this is very Christ.

23 ¶ And after that many days were fulfilled, the Jews took counsel to kill him:

24 But their laying await was known of Saul. And they watched the gates day and night to kill him.

25 Then the disciples took him by night, and let *him* down by the wall in a basket.

26 And when Saul was come to Jerusalem, he assayed to join himself to the disciples: but they were all afraid of him, and believed not that he was a disciple.

9:17 Through Ananias' *putting his hands on him* Paul is identified with the people he had been persecuting.

9:23 *And after that many days were fulfilled.* During this time Paul went to Arabia (see note at Gal. 1:17), so that three years elapsed between his conversion and his going to Jerusalem (v. 26).

27 But Barnabas took him, and brought *him* to the apostles, and declared unto them how he had seen the Lord in the way, and that he had spoken to him, and how he had preached boldly at Damascus in the name of Jesus.

28 And he was with them coming in and going out at Jerusalem.

29 And he spake boldly in the name of the Lord Jesus, and disputed against the Grecians: but they went about to slay him.

30 *Which* when the brethren knew, they brought him down to Cæsarea, and sent him forth to Tarsus.

31 Then had the churches rest throughout all Judæa and Galilee and Samaria, and were edified; and walking in the fear of the Lord, and in the comfort of the Holy Ghost, were multiplied.

C The Conversion of Gentiles, 9:32—11:30

1 *The preparation of Peter*, 9:32—10:22

32 ¶ And it came to pass, as Peter passed throughout all *quarters*, he came down also to the saints which dwelt at Lydda.

33 And there he found a certain man named Æne͞'as, which had kept his bed eight years, and was sick of the palsy.

34 And Peter said unto him, Æne͞'as, Jesus Christ maketh thee whole: arise, and make thy bed. And he arose immediately.

35 And all that dwelt at Lydda and Saron saw him, and turned to the Lord.

36 ¶ Now there was at Joppa a certain disciple named Tabitha, which by interpretation is called Dorcas: this woman was full of good works and almsdeeds which she did.

37 And it came to pass in those days, that she was sick, and died: whom when they had washed, they laid *her* in an upper chamber.

38 And forasmuch as Lydda was nigh to Joppa, and the disciples had heard that Peter was there, they sent unto

9:27 *Barnabas*. See 4:36.
9:29 *Grecians*=Greek-speaking Jews.
9:32 *Lydda*. A town between Jerusalem and Joppa.
9:33 *sick of the palsy*=paralyzed.
9:35 *Saron*=Sharon. The plain along the Mediterranean Sea, not the name of a city.
9:36 *Tabitha* means "gazelle" (*Dorcas* is Greek for the same).

him two men, desiring *him* that he would not delay to come to them.

39 Then Peter arose and went with them. When he was come, they brought him into the upper chamber: and all the widows stood by him weeping, and shewing the coats and garments which Dorcas made, while she was with them.

40 But Peter put them all forth, and kneeled down, and prayed; and turning *him* to the body said, Tabitha, arise. And she opened her eyes: and when she saw Peter, she sat up.

41 And he gave her *his* hand, and lifted her up, and when he had called the saints and widows, presented her alive.

42 And it was known throughout all Joppa; and many believed in the Lord.

43 And it came to pass, that he tarried many days in Joppa with one Simon a tanner.

10 There was a certain man in Cæsarea called Cornelius, a centurion of the band called the Italian *band,*

2 A devout *man,* and one that feared God with all his house, which gave much alms to the people, and prayed to God alway.

3 He saw in a vision evidently about the ninth hour of the day an angel of God coming in to him, and saying unto him, Cornelius.

4 And when he looked on him, he was afraid, and said, What is it, Lord? And he said unto him, Thy prayers and thine alms are come up for a memorial before God.

5 And now send men to Joppa, and call for *one* Simon, whose surname is Peter:

6 He lodgeth with one Simon a tanner, whose house is by the sea side: he shall tell thee what thou oughtest to do.

7 And when the angel which spake unto Cornelius was departed, he called two of his household servants, and a devout soldier of them that waited on him continually;

8 And when he had declared all *these* things unto them, he sent them to Joppa.

9 ¶ On the morrow, as they went on their journey, and

10:1 *a centurion* was a non-commissioned officer who was in command of 100 men. Cornelius commanded the *Italian* cohort.
10:2 Cornelius was a semi-proselyte to Judaism, accepting Jewish beliefs and practices but stopping short of circumcision.

drew nigh unto the city, Peter went up upon the housetop to pray about the sixth hour:

10 And he became very hungry, and would have eaten: but while they made ready, he fell into a trance,

11 And saw heaven opened, and a certain vessel descending unto him, as it had been a great sheet knit at the four corners, and let down to the earth:

12 Wherein were all manner of fourfooted beasts of the earth, and wild beasts, and creeping things, and fowls of the air.

13 And there came a voice to him, Rise, Peter; kill, and eat.

14 But Peter said, Not so, Lord; for I have never eaten any thing that is common or unclean.

15 And the voice *spake* unto him again the second time, What God hath cleansed, *that* call not thou common.

16 This was done thrice: and the vessel was received up again into heaven.

17 Now while Peter doubted in himself what this vision which he had seen should mean, behold, the men which were sent from Cornelius had made enquiry for Simon's house, and stood before the gate,

18 And called, and asked whether Simon, which was surnamed Peter, were lodged there.

19 ¶ While Peter thought on the vision, the Spirit said unto him, Behold, three men seek thee.

20 Arise therefore, and get thee down, and go with them, doubting nothing: for I have sent them.

21 Then Peter went down to the men which were sent unto him from Cornelius; and said, Behold, I am he whom ye seek: what *is* the cause wherefore ye are come?

22 And they said, Cornelius the centurion, a just man, and one that feareth God, and of good report among all the nation of the Jews, was warned from God by an holy angel to send for thee into his house, and to hear words of thee.

2 *The preaching of Peter*, 10:23–48

23 Then called he them in, and lodged *them*. And on the morrow Peter went away with them, and certain brethren from Joppa accompanied him.

24 And the morrow after they entered into Cæsarea.

10:14 *common or unclean*. The Mosaic law prohibited the eating of certain unclean animals (Lev. 11). God was teaching Peter a lesson about people (see v. 28).

10:23 *certain brethren*. There were six of them (11:12).

And Cornelius waited for them, and had called together his kinsmen and near friends.

25 And as Peter was coming in, Cornelius met him, and fell down at his feet, and worshipped *him*.

26 But Peter took him up, saying, Stand up; I myself also am a man.

27 And as he talked with him, he went in, and found many that were come together.

28 And he said unto them, Ye know how that it is an unlawful thing for a man that is a Jew to keep company, or come unto one of another nation; but God hath shewed me that I should not call any man common or unclean.

29 Therefore came I *unto you* without gainsaying, as soon as I was sent for: I ask therefore for what intent ye have sent for me?

30 And Cornelius said, Four days ago I was fasting until this hour; and at the ninth hour I prayed in my house, and, behold, a man stood before me in bright clothing,

31 And said, Cornelius, thy prayer is heard, and thine alms are had in remembrance in the sight of God.

32 Send therefore to Joppa, and call hither Simon, whose surname is Peter; he is lodged in the house of *one* Simon a tanner by the sea side: who, when he cometh, shall speak unto thee.

33 Immediately therefore I sent to thee; and thou hast well done that thou art come. Now therefore are we all here present before God, to hear all things that are commanded thee of God.

34 ¶ Then Peter opened *his* mouth, and said, Of a truth I perceive that God is no respecter of persons:

35 But in every nation he that feareth him, and worketh righteousness, is accepted with him.

36 The word which God sent unto the children of Israel, preaching peace by Jesus Christ: (he is Lord of all:)

37 That word, *I say*, ye know, which was published throughout all Judæa, and began from Galilee, after the baptism which John preached;

38 How God anointed Jesus of Nazareth with the Holy Ghost and with power: who went about doing good, and

---

10:28 The case of Cornelius was the first of its kind and crucial to the spread of Christianity. Can the new faith (still so closely associated with Judaism) admit into fellowship an uncircumcised Gentile? The issue would not be completely resolved for some time.

10:34 God *is no respecter of persons*. This fact was taught in the O.T. (Deut. 10:17; 2 Sam. 14:14; 2 Chron. 19:7).

healing all that were oppressed of the devil; for God was with him.

39 And we are witnesses of all things which he did both in the land of the Jews, and in Jerusalem; whom they slew and hanged on a tree:

40 Him God raised up the third day, and shewed him openly;

41 Not to all the people, but unto witnesses chosen before of God, *even* to us, who did eat and drink with him after he rose from the dead.

42 And he commanded us to preach unto the people, and to testify that it is he which was ordained of God *to be* the Judge of quick and dead.

43 To him give all the prophets witness, that through his name whosoever believeth in him shall receive remission of sins.

44 ¶ While Peter yet spake these words, the Holy Ghost fell on all them which heard the word.

45 And they of the circumcision which believed were astonished, as many as came with Peter, because that on the Gentiles also was poured out the gift of the Holy Ghost.

46 For they heard them speak with tongues, and magnify God. Then answered Peter,

47 Can any man forbid water, that these should not be baptized, which have received the Holy Ghost as well as we?

48 And he commanded them to be baptized in the name of the Lord. Then prayed they him to tarry certain days.

3 *The plea of Peter,* 11:1–18

11 And the apostles and brethren that were in Judæa heard that the Gentiles had also received the word of God.

2 And when Peter was come up to Jerusalem, they that were of the circumcision contended with him,

---

10:44 *the Holy Ghost fell on all them.* In the case of these Gentile converts the gift of the Spirit came before they were baptized in water (v. 48). The authentication of the gift was the speaking in tongues (v. 46), entirely apart from the laying on of hands. All this demonstrated, especially to the Jewish brethren who accompanied Peter, that God had received these Gentiles into the church on an equal basis with Jewish believers because they had believed in Christ (v. 43).

11:2 *they that were of the circumcision*=Jewish Christians, the so-called "circumcision party," who were unhappy at the

3 Saying, Thou wentest in to men uncircumcised, and didst eat with them.

4 But Peter rehearsed *the matter* from the beginning, and expounded *it* by order unto them, saying,

5 I was in the city of Joppa praying: and in a trance I saw a vision, A certain vessel descend, as it had been a great sheet, let down from heaven by four corners; and it came even to me:

6 Upon the which when I had fastened mine eyes, I considered, and saw fourfooted beasts of the earth, and wild beasts, and creeping things, and fowls of the air.

7 And I heard a voice saying unto me, Arise, Peter; slay and eat.

8 But I said, Not so, Lord: for nothing common or unclean hath at any time entered into my mouth.

9 But the voice answered me again from heaven, What God hath cleansed, *that* call not thou common.

10 And this was done three times: and all were drawn up again into heaven.

11 And, behold, immediately there were three men already come unto the house where I was, sent from Cæsarea unto me.

12 And the Spirit bade me go with them, nothing doubting. Moreover these six brethren accompanied me, and we entered into the man's house:

13 And he shewed us how he had seen an angel in his house, which stood and said unto him, Send men to Joppa, and call for Simon, whose surname is Peter;

14 Who shall tell thee words, whereby thou and all thy house shall be saved.

15 And as I began to speak, the Holy Ghost fell on them, as on us at the beginning.

16 Then remembered I the word of the Lord, how that he said, John indeed baptized with water; but ye shall be baptized with the Holy Ghost.

17 Forasmuch then as God gave them the like gift as *he did* unto us, who believed on the Lord Jesus Christ; what was I, that I could withstand God?

report that Gentiles were being saved without ritual induction into Judaism. After Peter's review of what happened, they were satisfied that this was God's doing (v. 18).

11:12 *nothing doubting.* I.e., without hesitation.

11:15 *at the beginning.* I.e., on the day of Pentecost. Since God had done for the Gentiles in Cornelius' house the same as He had done for the Jews at Pentecost, to refuse to accept these Gentile converts would be to resist the work of God (v. 17).

18 When they heard these things, they held their peace, and glorified God, saying, Then hath God also to the Gentiles granted repentance unto life.

4 The church at Antioch, 11:19–30

19 ¶ Now they which were scattered abroad upon the persecution that arose about Stephen travelled as far as Phēni'cē, and Cyprus, and An'tioch, preaching the word to none but unto the Jews only.

20 And some of them were men of Cyprus and Cȳrē'nē, which, when they were come to An'tioch, spake unto the Grecians, preaching the Lord Jesus.

21 And the hand of the Lord was with them: and a great number believed, and turned unto the Lord.

22 ¶ Then tidings of these things came unto the ears of the church which was in Jerusalem: and they sent forth Barnabas, that he should go as far as An'tioch.

23 Who, when he came, and had seen the grace of God, was glad, and exhorted them all, that with purpose of heart they would cleave unto the Lord.

24 For he was a good man, and full of the Holy Ghost and of faith: and much people was added unto the Lord.

25 Then departed Barnabas to Tarsus, for to seek Saul:

26 And when he had found him, he brought him unto

11:19 *Phenice* =Phoenicia. *Antioch* on the Orontas River about 300 miles from Jerusalem was the capital of the Roman province of Syria. It was the third largest city in the empire, with a population of about 500,000. It was one of the cosmopolitan centers of the world of that day and a center of commerce, Seleucia (16 miles away) being its seaport (13:4). Replacing Jerusalem as the number one Christian city, it was the center of the early missionary activity of the church (6:5; 13:1; 14:26; 15:35; 18:22).

11:22 *Barnabas*, whose character is described by Luke as one who (=son of) consoles or exhorts (Acts 4:36), *a good man* who was *full of the Holy Ghost* (v. 24), played an important role in the early life of the church on four occasions: (1) he convinced the apostles of the genuineness of Paul's conversion (Acts 9:27); (2) he represented the apostles at Antioch and recognized that the movement there was the work of God (11:22–24); (3) he and Paul were sent by the Spirit on the first missionary journey (13:2); and (4) he defended the work among Gentiles at the Jerusalem council (15:12, 22, 25).

11:25 *to seek Saul.* Paul had been in Tarsus, his home city, and in Syria and Cilicia (Gal. 1:21) about 9 years since going there from Jerusalem (Acts 9:30).

11:26 *Christians.* The word appears only here, in 26:28, and

An'tioch. And it came to pass, that a whole year they assembled themselves with the church, and taught much people. And the disciples were called Christians first in Antioch.

27 ¶ And in these days came prophets from Jerusalem unto An'tioch.

28 And there stood up one of them named Ag'abus, and signified by the Spirit that there should be great dearth throughout all the world: which came to pass in the days of Claudius Cæsar.

29 Then the disciples, every man according to his ability, determined to send relief unto the brethren which dwelt in Judæa:

30 Which also they did, and sent it to the elders by the hands of Barnabas and Saul.

D The Christians Persecuted by Herod, 12:1–25

1 The death of James, 12:1–2

12 Now about that time Herod the king stretched forth his hands to vex certain of the church.

2 And he killed James the brother of John with the sword.

2 The deliverance of Peter, 12:3–19

3 And because he saw it pleased the Jews, he proceeded further to take Peter also. (Then were the days of unleavened bread.)

4 And when he had apprehended him, he put him in prison, and delivered him to four quaternions of soldiers to keep him; intending after Easter to bring him forth to the people.

5 Peter therefore was kept in prison: but prayer was made without ceasing of the church unto God for him.

in 1 Pet. 4:16. It means partisans or followers of Christ, "Christ's man."

11:28 *great dearth*=shortage or famine. Josephus reports that a famine occurred in about A.D. 46.

11:30 *elders*. See note at 1 Tim 3:1.

12:1 *Herod.* Herod Agrippa I, grandson of the Herod the Great who ruled at the birth of Jesus. Agrippa, at least on the surface, was a zealous practicer of Jewish rites and a religious patriot.

12:2 *James.* The first of the Twelve to be martyred.

12:4 *Easter*=Passover time. See note at Mark 14:1.

6 And when Herod would have brought him forth, the same night Peter was sleeping between two soldiers, bound with two chains: and the keepers before the door kept the prison.

7 And, behold, the angel of the Lord came upon *him*, and a light shined in the prison: and he smote Peter on the side, and raised him up, saying, Arise up quickly. And his chains fell off from *his* hands.

8 And the angel said unto him, Gird thyself, and bind on thy sandals. And so he did. And he saith unto him, Cast thy garment about thee, and follow me.

9 And he went out, and followed him; and wist not that it was true which was done by the angel; but thought he saw a vision.

10 When they were past the first and the second ward, they came unto the iron gate that leadeth unto the city; which opened to them of his own accord: and they went out, and passed on through one street; and forthwith the angel departed from him.

11 And when Peter was come to himself, he said, Now I know of a surety, that the Lord hath sent his angel, and hath delivered me out of the hand of Herod, and *from* all the expectation of the people of the Jews.

12 And when he had considered *the thing*, he came to the house of Mary the mother of John, whose surname was Mark; where many were gathered together praying.

13 And as Peter knocked at the door of the gate, a damsel came to hearken, named Rhoda.

14 And when she knew Peter's voice, she opened not the gate for gladness, but ran in, and told how Peter stood before the gate.

15 And they said unto her, Thou art mad. But she constantly affirmed that it was even so. Then said they, It is his angel.

16 But Peter continued knocking: and when they had opened *the door*, and saw him, they were astonished.

17 But he, beckoning unto them with the hand to hold

12:6 *Peter was sleeping*. He had Christ's promise that he would live to an old age (John 21:18).

12:10 *ward*=guard.

12:11 *hath delivered me*. God's ways are inscrutable—Peter was delivered, but James was killed (v. 2).

12:12 *the house of Mary*. Traditionally it was here that the Last Supper was held and here now was the nerve center of the church in Jerusalem.

12:15 *his angel*. For other guardian angels in scripture, see Gen. 48:16; Dan. 10:20–21; 12:1; Matt. 18:10; Heb. 1:14.

their peace, declared unto them how the Lord had brought him out of the prison. And he said, Go shew these things unto James, and to the brethren. And he departed, and went into another place.

18 Now as soon as it was day, there was no small stir among the soldiers, what was become of Peter.

19 And when Herod had sought for him, and found him not, he examined the keepers, and commanded that *they* should be put to death. And he went down from Judæa to Cæsarea, and *there* abode.

3 *The death of Herod,* 12:20–23

20 ¶ And Herod was highly displeased with them of Tyre and Sidon: but they came with one accord to him, and, having made Blastus the king's chamberlain their friend, desired peace; because their country was nourished by the king's *country.*

21 And upon a set day Herod, arrayed in royal apparel, sat upon his throne, and made an oration unto them.

22 And the people gave a shout, *saying, It is* the voice of a god, and not of a man.

23 And immediately the angel of the Lord smote him, because he gave not God the glory: and he was eaten of worms, and gave up the ghost.

4 *The dissemination of the Word,* 12:24–25

24 ¶ But the word of God grew and multiplied.

25 And Barnabas and Saul returned from Jerusalem, when they had fulfilled *their* ministry, and took with them John, whose surname was Mark.

III CHRISTIANITY TO THE UTTERMOST PART OF THE WORLD, 13:1–28:31

A The First Missionary Journey, 13:1–14:28

1 *Events in Antioch,* 13:1–3

13 Now there were in the church that was at An'tioch certain prophets and teachers; as Barnabas, and

---

12:20 *Tyre and Sidon* had to import grain; the fields of Galilee produced large supplies (1 Kings 5:9).

12:23 Josephus states that Herod was struck down while delivering his oration and after five days of suffering he died (A.D. 44).

13:1 Here begins what has been called "The Acts of Paul," be-

Simeon that was called Niger, and Lucius of Cȳrē′nē, and Man′āen, which had been brought up with Herod the tē′trarch, and Saul.

2 As they ministered to the Lord, and fasted, the Holy Ghost said, Separate me Barnabas and Saul for the work whereunto I have called them.

3 And when they had fasted and prayed, and laid *their* hands on them, they sent *them* away.

2 *Events in Cyprus,* 13:4–12

4 ¶ So they, being sent forth by the Holy Ghost, departed unto Selêu′cia; and from thence they sailed to Cyprus.

5 And when they were at Sal′amis, they preached the word of God in the synagogues of the Jews: and they had also John to *their* minister.

6 And when they had gone through the isle unto Pā′-phos, they found a certain sorcerer, a false prophet, a Jew, whose name *was* Bar-jesus:

7 Which was with the deputy of the country, Sergius Paulus, a prudent man; who called for Barnabas and Saul, and desired to hear the word of God.

8 But El′ymas the sorcerer (for so is his name by interpretation) withstood them, seeking to turn away the deputy from the faith.

9 Then Saul, (who also *is called* Paul,) filled with the Holy Ghost, set his eyes on him,

10 And said, O full of all subtilty and all mischief, *thou*

cause Paul becomes the dominant figure. *Simeon who was called Niger.* Niger was his Latin name and probably indicates that he was an African. *which had been brought up with.* Lit., foster brother, a designation given to boys of the same age as royal children with whom they were brought up. *Herod the tetrarch.* Herod Antipas, who ruled Galilee during the public ministry of Christ.

13:3 *laid their hands on them.* See note at 6:6.

13:5 *John to their minister.* Lit., John as their attendant. This was John Mark, son of Mary (12:12) and cousin to Barnabas (Col. 4:10). 13:13; 15:38–40; 2 Tim. 4:11.

13:7 *Which was with the deputy*=who was with the proconsul. Cyprus was a Roman senatorial province.

13:8 *Elymas* was the name given to Bar-Jesus by Greek-speaking acquaintances.

13:9 *Saul,* (*who also is called Paul*). Saul was his Jewish name and Paul his Roman or Gentile name. Both were given him at the time of his birth, but he now begins to use his Gentile name in this Gentile environment.

child of the devil, *thou* enemy of all righteousness, wilt thou not cease to pervert the right ways of the Lord?

11 And now, behold, the hand of the Lord *is* upon thee, and thou shalt be blind, not seeing the sun for a season. And immediately there fell on him a mist and a darkness; and he went about seeking some to lead him by the hand.

12 Then the deputy, when he saw what was done, believed, being astonished at the doctrine of the Lord.

3 *Events in Galatian cities*, 13:13–14:20

13 Now when Paul and his company loosed from Pā́phos, they came to Perga in Pamphylia: and John departing from them returned to Jerusalem.

14 ¶ But when they departed from Perga, they came to An'tioch in Pīsid'ia, and went into the synagogue on the sabbath day, and sat down.

15 And after the reading of the law and the prophets the rulers of the synagogue sent unto them, saying, *Ye* men *and* brethren, if ye have any word of exhortation for the people, say on.

16 Then Paul stood up, and beckoning with *his* hand said, Men of Israel, and ye that fear God, give audience.

17 The God of this people of Israel chose our fathers, and exalted the people when they dwelt as strangers in the land of Egypt, and with an high arm brought he them out of it.

18 And about the time of forty years suffered he their manners in the wilderness.

19 And when he had destroyed seven nations in the land of Chā́naan, he divided their land to them by lot.

20 And after that he gave *unto them* judges about the space of four hundred and fifty years, until Samuel the prophet.

21 And afterward they desired a king: and God gave unto them Saul the son of Cis, a man of the tribe of Benjamin, by the space of forty years.

22 And when he had removed him, he raised up unto them David to be their king; to whom also he gave testimony, and said, I have found David the *son* of Jesse, a man after mine own heart, which shall fulfil all my will.

13:14 *Antioch in Pisidia.* Actually it was in Phrygia, but near the border of Pisidia. This Antioch was so called to distinguish it from the larger Antioch in Syria.

13:20 The *four hundred and fifty years* extends from the Patriarchs to the Judges.

23 Of this man's seed hath God according to *his* promise raised unto Israel a Saviour, Jesus:

24 When John had first preached before his coming the baptism of repentance to all the people of Israel.

25 And as John fulfilled his course, he said, Whom think ye that I am? I am not *he*. But, behold, there cometh one after me, whose shoes of *his* feet I am not worthy to loose.

26 Men *and* brethren, children of the stock of Abraham, and whosoever among you feareth God, to you is the word of this salvation sent.

27 For they that dwell at Jerusalem, and their rulers, because they knew him not, nor yet the voices of the prophets which are read every sabbath day, they have fulfilled *them* in condemning *him*.

28 And though they found no cause of death *in him*, yet desired they Pilate that he should be slain.

29 And when they had fulfilled all that was written of him, they took *him* down from the tree, and laid *him* in a sepulchre.

30 But God raised him from the dead:

31 And he was seen many days of them which came up with him from Galilee to Jerusalem, who are his witnesses unto the people.

32 And we declare unto you glad tidings, how that the promise which was made unto the fathers,

33 God hath fulfilled the same unto us their children, in that he hath raised up Jesus again; as it is also written in the second psalm, Thou art my Son, this day have I begotten thee.

34 And as concerning that he raised him up from the dead, *now* no more to return to corruption, he said on this wise, I will give you the sure mercies of David.

35 Wherefore he saith also in another *psalm*, Thou shalt not suffer thine Holy One to see corruption.

36 For David, after he had served his own generation by the will of God, fell on sleep, and was laid unto his fathers, and saw corruption:

37 But he, whom God raised again, saw no corruption.

38 ¶ Be it known unto you therefore, men *and* brethren, that through this man is preached unto you the forgiveness of sins:

13:33 *Thou art my Son* . . . Quoting Ps. 2:7.
13:34 *the sure mercies of David*. Quoting from Isa. 55:3.
13:35 The Psalm referred to is 16:10.

39 And by him all that believe are justified from all things, from which ye could not be justified by the law of Moses.

40 Beware therefore, lest that come upon you, which is spoken of in the prophets;

41 Behold, ye despisers, and wonder, and perish: for I work a work in your days, a work which ye shall in no wise believe, though a man declare it unto you.

42 And when the Jews were gone out of the synagogue, the Gentiles besought that these words might be preached to them the next sabbath.

43 Now when the congregation was broken up, many of the Jews and religious proselytes followed Paul and Barnabas: who, speaking to them, persuaded them to continue in the grace of God.

44 ¶ And the next sabbath day came almost the whole city together to hear the word of God.

45 But when the Jews saw the multitudes, they were filled with envy, and spake against those things which were spoken by Paul, contradicting and blaspheming.

46 Then Paul and Barnabas waxed bold, and said, It was necessary that the word of God should first have been spoken to you: but seeing ye put it from you, and judge yourselves unworthy of everlasting life, lo, we turn to the Gentiles.

47 For so hath the Lord commanded us, *saying*, I have set thee to be a light of the Gentiles, that thou shouldest be for salvation unto the ends of the earth.

48 And when the Gentiles heard this, they were glad, and glorified the word of the Lord: and as many as were ordained to eternal life believed.

49 And the word of the Lord was published throughout all the region.

50 But the Jews stirred up the devout and honourable women, and the chief men of the city, and raised persecution against Paul and Barnabas, and expelled them out of their coasts.

51 But they shook off the dust of their feet against them, and came unto Īcō'nium.

13:40 *spoken of in the prophets*. See Hab. 1:5.

13:47 The quotation is from Isa. 49:6.

13:48 *they were glad*. The Gentiles' reception and the Jews' rejection (v. 50) of the gospel is a recurring theme in Acts now.

13:51 *they shook off the dust*. A good Jew took pains not to carry back into Palestine any dust from non-Jewish countries. To "shake off the dust" was a vivid gesture of complete break

52 And the disciples were filled with joy, and with the Holy Ghost.

14 And it came to pass in Īcō'nium, that they went both together into the synagogue of the Jews, and so spake, that a great multitude both of the Jews and also of the Greeks believed.

2 But the unbelieving Jews stirred up the Gentiles, and made their minds evil affected against the brethren.

3 Long time therefore abode they speaking boldly in the Lord, which gave testimony unto the word of his grace, and granted signs and wonders to be done by their hands.

4 But the multitude of the city was divided: and part held with the Jews, and part with the apostles.

5 And when there was an assault made both of the Gentiles, and also of the Jews with their rulers, to use *them* despitefully, and to stone them,

6 They were ware of *it*, and fled unto Lystra and Der'bē, cities of Lȳcāō'nia, and unto the region that lieth round about:

7 And there they preached the gospel.

8 ¶ And there sat a certain man at Lystra, impotent in his feet, being a cripple from his mother's womb, who never had walked:

9 The same heard Paul speak: who stedfastly beholding him, and perceiving that he had faith to be healed,

10 Said with a loud voice, Stand upright on thy feet. And he leaped and walked.

11 And when the people saw what Paul had done, they lifted up their voices, saying in the speech of Lȳcāō'nia, The gods are come down to us in the likeness of men.

12 And they called Barnabas, Jupiter; and Paul, Mercū'rius, because he was the chief speaker.

13 Then the priest of Jupiter, which was before their city, brought oxen and garlands unto the gates, and would have done sacrifice with the people.

14 *Which* when the apostles, Barnabas and Paul, heard *of*, they rent their clothes, and ran in among the people, crying out,

15 And saying, Sirs, why do ye these things? We also

of fellowship and renunciation of responsibility for the person or community gestured at. See Christ's command at Luke 9:5; 10:11; and note at Mark 6:11.

14:6 *Lystra.* About 20 miles from Iconium.

14:12 *Jupiter*= Zeus, the chief god of the Greek Pantheon. *Mercurius*=Hermes, the patron god of orators. In two Greek

are men of like passions with you, and preach unto you
that ye should turn from these vanities unto the living
God, which made heaven, and earth, and the sea, and all
things that are therein:

16 Who in times past suffered all nations to walk in
their own ways.

17 Nevertheless he left not himself without witness, in
that he did good, and gave us rain from heaven, and fruitful
seasons, filling our hearts with food and gladness.

18 And with these sayings scarce restrained they the
people, that they had not done sacrifice unto them.

19 ¶ And there came thither *certain* Jews from An'tioch
and Ico'nium, who persuaded the people, and, having
stoned Paul, drew *him* out of the city, supposing he had
been dead.

20 Howbeit, as the disciples stood round about him, he
rose up, and came into the city: and the next day he departed with Barnabas to Der'be.

4 Events on the return to Antioch, 14:21–28

21 And when they had preached the gospel to that city,
and had taught many, they returned again to Lystra, and
to Ico'nium, and An'tioch,

22 Confirming the souls of the disciples, *and* exhorting
them to continue in the faith, and that we must through
much tribulation enter into the kingdom of God.

23 And when they had ordained them elders in every
church, and had prayed with fasting, they commended
them to the Lord, on whom they believed.

24 And after they had passed throughout Pisid'ia, they
came to Pamphylia.

25 And when they had preached the word in Perga, they
went down into Ata'lia:

legends connected with Lystra (and familiar to Paul's listeners) Zeus and Hermes had come down "in the likeness of
men" (v. 11).

14:19 *having stoned Paul.* After suffering the crushing blows of
the stones, the victim was dragged outside the city and left
to the dogs and beasts. It was a miracle that Paul could get
up and leave the next day. Some think the vision mentioned
in 2 Cor. 12:1–5 occurred at this time, and it is also possible
that he received the marks spoken of in Gal. 6:17 during this
stoning.

14:23 *ordained them elders.* Better, appointed or designated
elders. See note at 1 Tim. 3:1.

26 And thence sailed to An'tioch, from whence they had been recommended to the grace of God for the work which they fulfilled.

27 And when they were come, and had gathered the church together, they rehearsed all that God had done with them, and how he had opened the door of faith unto the Gentiles.

28 And there they abode long time with the disciples.

B The Council at Jerusalem, 15:1–35

1 *The dissension,* 15:1–5

15 And certain men which came down from Judæa taught the brethren, *and said,* Except ye be circumcised after the manner of Moses, ye cannot be saved.

2 When therefore Paul and Barnabas had no small dissension and disputation with them, they determined that Paul and Barnabas, and certain other of them, should go up to Jerusalem unto the apostles and elders about this question.

3 And being brought on their way by the church, they passed through Phēnī'cē and Samaria, declaring the conversion of the Gentiles: and they caused great joy unto all the brethren.

4 And when they were come to Jerusalem, they were received of the church, and of the apostles and elders, and they declared all things that God had done with them.

5 But there rose up certain of the sect of the Pharisees which believed, saying, That it was needful to circumcise them, and to command *them* to keep the law of Moses.

15:1 *Except ye be circumcised . . . ye cannot be saved.* The problems raised by the presence of Gentiles in the church now come to a head. Peter had learned that no man should be called unclean—not even Gentiles (10:34), and the Jerusalem church had accepted the first Gentile converts on an equal basis with Jewish converts and without the necessity of being circumcised. However, the ultra-Judaistic party went on the offensive and insisted that Gentile converts be circumcised. A parallel question was also being raised; should there be unrestricted social intercourse between Jewish and Gentile Christians? The Judaistic party separated themselves from those who did not follow the dietary laws and would not partake of the common meals. Chapter 15 is concerned with these two questions: circumcision and foods (socializing). Had the division over these questions prevailed, the unity of the church would have been shattered from the start.

2 *The discussion,* 15:6–18

6 ¶ And the apostles and elders came together for to consider of this matter.

7 And when there had been much disputing, Peter rose up, and said unto them, Men *and* brethren, ye know how that a good while ago God made choice among us, that the Gentiles by my mouth should hear the word of the gospel, and believe.

8 And God, which knoweth the hearts, bare them witness, giving them the Holy Ghost, even as *he did* unto us;

9 And put no difference between us and them, purifying their hearts by faith.

10 Now therefore why tempt ye God, to put a yoke upon the neck of the disciples, which neither our fathers nor we were able to bear?

11 But we believe that through the grace of the Lord Jesus Christ we shall be saved, even as they.

12 ¶ Then all the multitude kept silence, and gave audience to Barnabas and Paul, declaring what miracles and wonders God had wrought among the Gentiles by them.

13 ¶ And after they had held their peace, James answered, saying, Men *and* brethren, hearken unto me:

14 Simeon hath declared how God at the first did visit the Gentiles, to take out of them a people for his name.

15 And to this agree the words of the prophets; as it is written,

16 After this I will return, and will build again the tabernacle of David, which is fallen down; and I will build again the ruins thereof, and I will set it up:

17 That the residue of men might seek after the Lord,

15:7 *the Gentiles by my mouth.* A reference to Peter's ministry in the house of Cornelius (10:44).

15:10 *a yoke.* I.e., that of the law, which in its complexities had become a burden, almost literally impossible to keep.

15:11 Peter means that both Jew and Gentile will be saved through grace without the yoke of the law.

15:13 *James.* See notes at Matt. 4:21 and the Introduction to James.

15:15–17 The quotation is from the Greek version of Amos 9:11–12. James specifies that the prophecy of Amos will be fulfilled "after this," i.e., after the present worldwide witness. Then, after the return of Christ, the tabernacle of David (the millennial kingdom) will be established, and Jew and Gentile will know the Lord in that day. James assures them that God's program for Israel has not been abandoned by the coming of Gentiles into the church.

and all the Gentiles, upon whom my name is called, saith the Lord, who doeth all these things.

18 Known unto God are all his works from the beginning of the world.

3 *The decision*, 15:19–29

19 Wherefore my sentence is, that we trouble not them, which from among the Gentiles are turned to God:

20 But that we write unto them, that they abstain from pollutions of idols, and *from* fornication, and *from* things strangled, and *from* blood.

21 For Moses of old time hath in every city them that preach him, being read in the synagogues every sabbath day.

22 Then pleased it the apostles and elders, with the whole church, to send chosen men of their own company to An'tioch with Paul and Barnabas; *namely*, Judas surnamed Barsabas, and Silas, chief men among the brethren:

23 And they wrote *letters* by them after this manner; The apostles and elders and brethren *send* greeting unto the brethren which are of the Gentiles in An'tioch and Syria and Cīlic'ia:

24 Forasmuch as we have heard, that certain which went out from us have troubled you with ʾords, subverting your souls, saying, Ye *must* be circumcised, and keep the law: to whom we gave no *such* commandment:

25 It seemed good unto us, being assembled with one accord, to send chosen men unto you with our beloved Barnabas and Paul,

26 Men that have hazarded their lives for the name of our Lord Jesus Christ.

27 We have sent therefore Judas and Silas, who shall also tell *you* the same things by mouth.

15:19 *we trouble not them*. The clear verdict of James, as president of the council, was that Gentile converts need not be circumcised.

15:20 In order to promote peace between Jewish and Gentile believers, the Gentiles were asked to abstain from any practice of things most abhorrent to Jewish Christians. Then the Jewish Christians would socialize with them. This is an illustration of 1 Cor. 8:13. *fornication*. It does not seem likely that the word means illicit sexual relations in this instance (though it does elsewhere), for this would be wrong for any Christian, Gentile, or Jew. It evidently has the special meaning here of marriage contracted between too-near relatives as forbidden in Lev. 18.

15:26 *hazarded their lives*. For some of the risks incurred see 13:50; 14:5, 19.

28 For it seemed good to the Holy Ghost, and to us, to lay upon you no greater burden than these necessary things;

29 That ye abstain from meats offered to idols, and from blood, and from things strangled, and from fornication: from which if ye keep yourselves, ye shall do well. Fare ye well.

4 *The letter delivered to Antioch,* 15:30–35

30 So when they were dismissed, they came to An'tioch: and when they had gathered the multitude together, they delivered the epistle:

31 *Which* when they had read, they rejoiced for the consolation.

32 And Judas and Silas, being prophets also themselves, exhorted the brethren with many words, and confirmed *them*.

33 And after they had tarried *there* a space, they were let go in peace from the brethren unto the apostles.

34 Notwithstanding it pleased Silas to abide there still.

35 Paul also and Barnabas continued in An'tioch, teaching and preaching the word of the Lord, with many others also.

C The Second Missionary Journey, 15:36–18:22

1 *The personnel chosen,* 15:36–40

36 ¶ And some days after Paul said unto Barnabas, Let us go again and visit our brethren in every city where we have preached the word of the Lord, *and see* how they do.

37 And Barnabas determined to take with them John, whose surname was Mark.

38 But Paul thought not good to take him with them, who departed from them from Pamphylia, and went not with them to the work.

39 And the contention was so sharp between them, that they departed asunder one from the other: and so Barnabas took Mark, and sailed unto Cyprus;

15:29 *do well.* I.e., act rightly.

15:38 *who departed from them.* See 13:13.

15:39 *they departed asunder one from the other.* Here is an example of separation on personality or practicality, not doctrine, and it seemed to be the only solution to the problem. God brought good out of it in that two missionary teams were sent out, and Barnabas' continued interest in John Mark rescued him from possible uselessness. (For separation on doctrinal grounds see Gal. 1:8; 2 Thess. 3:14; 2 Tim. 1 John 2:18; 2 John 10).

40 And Paul chose Silas, and departed, being recommended by the brethren unto the grace of God.

2 The churches revisited, 15:41–16:5

41 And he went through Syria and Cĭlic'ia, confirming the churches.

16 Then came he to Der'bē and Lystra: and, behold, a certain disciple was there, named Tīmoth'eus, the son of a certain woman, which was a Jewess, and believed; but his father was a Greek:

2 Which was well reported of by the brethren that were at Lystra and Ĭcō'nium.

3 Him would Paul have to go forth with him; and took and circumcised him because of the Jews which were in those quarters: for they knew all that his father was a Greek.

4 And as they went through the cities, they delivered them the decrees for to keep, that were ordained of the apostles and elders which were at Jerusalem.

5 And so were the churches established in the faith, and increased in number daily.

3 The call to Europe, 16:6–10

6 Now when they had gone throughout Phryg'ia and the region of Galatia, and were forbidden of the Holy Ghost to preach the word in Asia,

7 After they were come to Mysia, they assayed to go into Bīthyn'ia: but the Spirit suffered them not.

8 And they passing by Mysia came down to Trō'as.

9 And a vision appeared to Paul in the night; There stood a man of Macedonia, and prayed him, saying, Come over into Macedonia, and help us.

16:1 *Timotheus.* See Introduction to 1 Timothy.

16:3 *circumcised him.* The Jerusalem council had declared that circumcision was not necessary for acceptance into the Christian church and for salvation (15:19), but because of Timothy's part-Jewish background it seemed expedient in his case in order to enlarge his usefulness locally in witnessing. In the case of Gentile Titus, Paul insisted that he not be circumcised (Gal. 2:3).

16:4 *the decrees.* The decisions arrived at in Jerusalem, 15:23–29.

16:6 Paul traveled in a northwesterly direction around Asia, to Troas and onto Greece. On north and south *Galatia* see the Introduction to Galatians.

10 And after he had seen the vision, immediately we endeavoured to go into Macedonia, assuredly gathering that the Lord had called us for to preach the gospel unto them.

4 The work at Philippi, 16:11–40

11 Therefore loosing from Trō'as, we came with a straight course to Samōthrā'cia, and the next day to Nēā'polis;

12 And from thence to Phĭlip'pī, which is the chief city of that part of Macedonia, and a colony: and we were in that city abiding certain days.

13 And on the sabbath we went out of the city by a river side, where prayer was wont to be made; and we sat down, and spake unto the women which resorted thither.

14 ¶ And a certain woman named Lydia, a seller of purple, of the city of Thȳatī'ra, which worshipped God, heard us: whose heart the Lord opened, that she attended unto the things which were spoken of Paul.

15 And when she was baptized, and her household, she besought us, saying, If ye have judged me to be faithful to the Lord, come into my house, and abide there. And she constrained us.

16 ¶ And it came to pass, as we went to prayer, a certain damsel possessed with a spirit of divination met us, which brought her masters much gain by soothsaying:

17 The same followed Paul and us, and cried, saying, These men are the servants of the most high God, which shew unto us the way of salvation.

18 And this did she many days. But Paul, being grieved, turned and said to the spirit, I command thee in the name of Jesus Christ to come out of her. And he came out the same hour.

16:10 we. Luke joined Paul and his group at Troas and went with them to Philippi, where he remained when the others left (v. 40). Six or seven years later he rejoined Paul (20:5) and remained with him until the end of the narrative.

16:12 Philippi. See the Introduction to Philippians. a colony. A Roman colony was like a piece of Rome transplanted abroad, so that those who held citizenship enjoyed the same rights they would have if they lived in Italy. Other colonies mentioned in Acts are Antioch in Pisidia, Lystra, Troas, Ptolemais, and Corinth.

16:13 out of the city by a river side. Apparently there was no synagogue in Philippi; it required ten men to organize one.

16:14 seller of purple. Thyatira in Asia Minor was famous for its purple dye.

16:16 a spirit of divination. The girl was demon-possessed and was being exploited by her masters (v. 19).

19 ¶ And when her masters saw that the hope of their gains was gone, they caught Paul and Silas, and drew *them* into the marketplace unto the rulers,

20 And brought them to the magistrates, saying, These men, being Jews, do exceedingly trouble our city,

21 And teach customs, which are not lawful for us to receive, neither to observe, being Romans.

22 And the multitude rose up together against them: and the magistrates rent off their clothes, and commanded to beat *them*.

23 And when they had laid many stripes upon them, they cast *them* into prison, charging the jailor to keep them safely:

24 Who, having received such a charge, thrust them into the inner prison, and made their feet fast in the stocks.

25 ¶ And at midnight Paul and Silas prayed, and sang praises unto God: and the prisoners heard them.

26 And suddenly there was a great earthquake, so that the foundations of the prison were shaken: and immediately all the doors were opened, and every one's bands were loosed.

27 And the keeper of the prison awaking out of his sleep, and seeing the prison doors open, he drew out his sword, and would have killed himself, supposing that the prisoners had been fled.

28 But Paul cried with a loud voice, saying, Do thyself no harm: for we are all here.

29 Then he called for a light, and sprang in, and came trembling, and fell down before Paul and Silas,

30 And brought them out, and said, Sirs, what must I do to be saved?

31 And they said, Believe on the Lord Jesus Christ, and thou shalt be saved, and thy house.

32 And they spake unto him the word of the Lord, and to all that were in his house.

33 And he took them the same hour of the night, and washed *their* stripes; and was baptized, he and all his, straightway.

16:20 *being Jews, do exceedingly trouble.* Judaism was not a prescribed religion (the cult of the emperor being the official religion), but propagandizing for it was regarded as a menace. Paul and Silas were regarded in this instance as Jews.

16:31 *and thy house.* These words must be connected with "believe" as well as "be saved." Each member of the household must believe in order to be saved.

34 And when he had brought them into his house, he set meat before them, and rejoiced, believing in God with all his house.

35 And when it was day, the magistrates sent the serjeants, saying, Let those men go.

36 And the keeper of the prison told this saying to Paul, The magistrates have sent to let you go: now therefore depart, and go in peace.

37 But Paul said unto them, They have beaten us openly uncondemned, being Romans, and have cast us into prison; and now do they thrust us out privily? nay verily; but let them come themselves and fetch us out.

38 And the serjeants told these words unto the magistrates: and they feared, when they heard that they were Romans.

39 And they came and besought them, and brought them out, and desired them to depart out of the city.

40 And they went out of the prison, and entered into the house of Lydia: and when they had seen the brethren, they comforted them, and departed.

5 The work at Thessalonica, Berea, and Athens, 17:1–34

17 Now when they had passed through Amphip'olis and Apollō'nia, they came to Thessalōnī'ca, where was a synagogue of the Jews:

2 And Paul, as his manner was, went in unto them, and three sabbath days reasoned with them out of the scriptures,

3 Opening and alleging, that Christ must needs have suffered, and risen again from the dead; and that this Jesus, whom I preach unto you, is Christ.

4 And some of them believed, and consorted with Paul and Silas; and of the devout Greeks a great multitude, and of the chief women not a few.

5 ¶ But the Jews which believed not, moved with envy, took unto them certain lewd fellows of the baser sort, and gathered a company, and set all the city on an uproar, and

16:37 *being Romans.* Paul was born a Roman citizen (22:28), which gave him certain rights including a public hearing. The scourging of Roman citizens was prohibited by law: the rights of Paul and Silas had already been violated.

16:39 *and besought them*=and apologized to them.

17:1 *Thessalonica.* See the Introduction to 1 Thessalonians.

17:5 *lewd fellows of the baser sort*=wicked fellows of the rabble.

assaulted the house of Jason, and sought to bring them out to the people.

6 And when they found them not, they drew Jason and certain brethren unto the rulers of the city, crying, These that have turned the world upside down are come hither also;

7 Whom Jason hath received: and these all do contrary to the decrees of Cæsar, saying that there is another king, *one* Jesus.

8 And they troubled the people and the rulers of the city, when they heard these things.

9 And when they had taken security of Jason, and of the other, they let them go.

10 ¶ And the brethren immediately sent away Paul and Silas by night unto Berē'a: who coming *thither* went into the synagogue of the Jews.

11 These were more noble than those in Thessalōnī'ca, in that they received the word with all readiness of mind, and searched the scriptures daily, whether those things were so.

12 Therefore many of them believed; also of honourable women which were Greeks, and of men, not a few.

13 But when the Jews of Thessalōnī'ca had knowledge that the word of God was preached of Paul at Berē'a, they came thither also, and stirred up the people.

14 And then immediately the brethren sent away Paul to go as it were to the sea: but Silas and Tīmoth'eus abode there still.

15 And they that conducted Paul brought him unto Athens: and receiving a commandment unto Silas and Tīmoth'eus for to come to him with all speed, they departed.

16 ¶ Now while Paul waited for them at Athens, his spirit was stirred in him, when he saw the city wholly given to idolatry.

17 Therefore disputed he in the synagogue with the Jews, and with the devout persons, and in the market daily with them that met with him.

18 Then certain philosophers of the Epicūrē'ans, and of the Stō'icks, encountered him. And some said, What will this babbler say? other some, He seemeth to be a

---

17:9 *taken security of Jason.* I.e., made Jason put up a bond, forfeitable if there were further trouble.

17:14 *to go as it were to the sea.* Better, on his way to the sea.

17:18 *Epicureans.* Philosopher-followers of Epicurus (341–270 B.C.), who believed that happiness was the chief end of life.

setter forth of strange gods: because he preached unto them Jesus, and the resurrection.

19 And they took him, and brought him unto Areop'-agus, saying, May we know what this new doctrine, whereof thou speakest, *is?*

20 For thou bringest certain strange things to our ears: we would know therefore what these things mean.

21 (For all the Athenians and strangers which were there spent their time in nothing else, but either to tell, or to hear some new thing.)

22 ¶ Then Paul stood in the midst of Mars' hill, and said, Ye men of Athens, I perceive that in all things ye are too superstitious.

23 For as I passed by, and beheld your devotions, I found an altar with this inscription, TO THE UNKNOWN GOD. Whom therefore ye ignorantly worship, him declare I unto you.

24 God that made the world and all things therein, seeing that he is Lord of heaven and earth, dwelleth not in temples made with hands;

25 Neither is worshipped with men's hands, as though he needed any thing, seeing he giveth to all life, and breath, and all things;

26 And hath made of one blood all nations of men for to dwell on all the face of the earth, and hath determined the times before appointed, and the bounds of their habitation;

27 That they should seek the Lord, if haply they might feel after him, and find him, though he be not far from every one of us:

28 For in him we live, and move, and have our being; as certain also of your own poets have said, For we are also his offspring.

Stoicks. The Stoics, who regarded Zeno (340–265 B.C.) as their founder and whose name came from *Stoa Poikile* (Painted Porch) where he taught in Athens, emphasized the rational over the emotional. They were pantheistic. Their ethics were characterized by moral earnestness and a high sense of duty, advocating conduct "according to nature."

17:19 *Areopagus.* The venerable council that had charge of religious and educational matters in Athens. It met in early times on the Hill of Ares W. of the Acropolis, the hill also being known as the Areopagus.

17:22 *superstitious.* May also be translated "religious."

17:24–25 Notice this echo of Stephen's words which Paul heard years before (7:48–50).

29 Forasmuch then as we are the offspring of God, we ought not to think that the Godhead is like unto gold, or silver, or stone, graven by art and man's device.

30 And the times of this ignorance God winked at; but now commandeth all men every where to repent:

31 Because he hath appointed a day, in the which he will judge the world in righteousness by *that* man whom he hath ordained; *whereof* he hath given assurance unto all *men*, in that he hath raised him from the dead.

32 ¶ And when they heard of the resurrection of the dead, some mocked: and others said, We will hear thee again of this *matter*.

33 So Paul departed from among them.

34 Howbeit certain men clave unto him, and believed: among the which *was* Dīōnys'ius the Areop'agīte, and a woman named Dam'aris, and others with them.

6 *The ministry at Corinth*, 18:1–17

18 After these things Paul departed from Athens, and came to Corinth;

2 And found a certain Jew named Aquila, born in Pontus, lately come from Italy, with his wife Priscilla; (because that Claudius had commanded all Jews to depart from Rome:) and came unto them.

3 And because he was of the same craft, he abode with them, and wrought: for by their occupation they were tentmakers.

4 And he reasoned in the synagogue every sabbath, and persuaded the Jews and the Greeks.

5 And when Silas and Timoth'eus were come from Macedonia, Paul was pressed in the spirit, and testified to the Jews *that* Jesus *was* Christ.

17:29 *we are the offspring of God.* Because God is the Creator of all.

17:30 *winked at.* Lit., overlooked.

17:34 *Dionysius the Areopagite.* Membership in the Areopagus was a high distinction. There is no record of a church in Athens. Paul calls some Corinthians the first converts on mainland Greece (1 Cor. 16:15).

18:1 *Corinth.* See the Introduction to 1 Corinthians.

18:2 *Aquila . . . his wife Priscilla.* See Rom. 16:3; 1 Cor. 16:19; 2 Tim. 4:19, where Priscilla is called Prisca. *because Claudius had commanded all Jews to depart from Rome.* This imperial edict was issued in A.D. 49 or 50.

18:3 *tentmakers.* Jewish fathers were urged to teach their sons a trade, and Paul learned tentmaking, an important industry in Tarsus.

6 And when they opposed themselves, and blasphemed, he shook *his* raiment, and said unto them, Your blood *be* upon your own heads; I *am* clean: from henceforth I will go unto the Gentiles.

7 ¶ And he departed thence, and entered into a certain *man's* house, named Justus, *one* that worshipped God, whose house joined hard to the synagogue.

8 And Crispus, the chief ruler of the synagogue, believed on the Lord with all his house; and many of the Corinthians hearing believed, and were baptized.

9 Then spake the Lord to Paul in the night by a vision, Be not afraid, but speak, and hold not thy peace:

10 For I am with thee, and no man shall set on thee to hurt thee: for I have much people in this city.

11 And he continued *there* a year and six months, teaching the word of God among them.

12 ¶ And when Gal′liō was the deputy of Acha′ia, the Jews made insurrection with one accord against Paul, and brought him to the judgment seat,

13 Saying, This *fellow* persuadeth men to worship God contrary to the law.

14 And when Paul was now about to open *his* mouth, Gal′liō said unto the Jews, If it were a matter of wrong or wicked lewdness, O *ye* Jews, reason would that I should bear with you:

15 But if it be a question of words and names, and *of* your law, look ye *to it*; for I will be no judge of such *matters*.

16 And he drave them from the judgment seat.

17 Then all the Greeks took Sos′thenēs, the chief ruler of the synagogue, and beat *him* before the judgment seat. And Gal′liō cared for none of those things.

18:12 *deputy.* Gallio was proconsul of Achaia in 51. He was characterized by contemporaries as an amiable witty, and lovable person.

18:14–16 Judaism was a "licensed religion" under Roman law. Christianity could take advantage of this protection as long as it sheltered itself under the tent of Judaism. The Jews must have complained that these Christians were not a division or sect of Judaism, and Gallio refuses to see it their way. He says, in effect, "Settle your own religious squabbles yourselves." This ruling was probably important for the spread of the gospel.

18:17 *Sosthenes* became the victim of the Greeks' anti-Jewish feelings. Obviously he was the head of the pro-Pauline faction in the synagogue and a Jew. If this is the same Sosthenes as mentioned in 1 Cor. 1:1, the beating helped him to become a Christian!

7 *The journey completed*, 18:18–22

18 ¶ And Paul *after this* tarried *there* yet a good while, and then took his leave of the brethren, and sailed thence into Syria, and with him Priscilla and Aquila; having shorn *his* head in Cenchrē'a: for he had a vow.

19 And he came to Ephesus, and left them there: but he himself entered into the synagogue, and reasoned with the Jews.

20 When they desired *him* to tarry longer time with them, he consented not;

21 But bade them farewell, saying, I must by all means keep this feast that cometh in Jerusalem: but I will return again unto you, if God will. And he sailed from Ephesus.

22 And when he had landed at Cæsarea, and gone up, and saluted the church, he went down to An'tioch.

D The Third Missionary Journey, 18:23–21:26

1 *Ephesus: The power of the Word*, 18:23–19:41

23 And after he had spent some time *there*, he departed, and went over *all* the country of Galatia and Phryg'ia in order, strengthening all the disciples.

24 ¶ And a certain Jew named Apol'los, born at Alexandria, an eloquent man, *and* mighty in the scriptures, came to Ephesus.

25 This man was instructed in the way of the Lord; and being fervent in the spirit, he spake and taught diligently the things of the Lord, knowing only the baptism of John.

26 And he began to speak boldly in the synagogue: whom when Aquila and Priscilla had heard, they took him unto *them*, and expounded unto him the way of God more perfectly.

27 And when he was disposed to pass into Acha'ia, the brethren wrote, exhorting the disciples to receive him: who, when he was come, helped them much which had believed through grace:

18:18 *having shorn his head*. The sign of the conclusion of a Nazarite vow (Num. 6:18; Acts 21:24). Just why he took the vow is not known. *Cenchrea*. The eastern port of Corinth.

18:21 *this feast*. Probably Passover. The date was late winter, A.D. 52 or 53.

18:24 *Apollos*. See note at 1 Cor. 1:12.

18:26 *more perfectly*=more accurately, including the facts of the gospel.

28 For he mightily convinced the Jews, *and that* publickly, shewing by the scriptures that Jesus was Christ.

19 And it came to pass, that, while Apol′los was at Corinth, Paul having passed through the upper coasts came to Ephesus: and finding certain disciples,

2 He said unto them, Have ye received the Holy Ghost since ye believed? And they said unto him, We have not so much as heard whether there be any Holy Ghost.

3 And he said unto them, Unto what then were ye baptized? And they said, Unto John's baptism.

4 Then said Paul, John verily baptized with the baptism of repentance, saying unto the people, that they should believe on him which should come after him, that is, on Christ Jesus.

5 When they heard *this*, they were baptized in the name of the Lord Jesus.

6 And when Paul had laid *his* hands upon them, the Holy Ghost came on them; and they spake with tongues, and prophesied.

7 And all the men were about twelve.

8 And he went into the synagogue, and spake boldly for the space of three months, disputing and persuading the things concerning the kingdom of God.

9 But when divers were hardened, and believed not, but spake evil of that way before the multitude, he departed from them, and separated the disciples, disputing daily in the school of one Tyrannus.

10 And this continued by the space of two years; so that all they which dwelt in Asia heard the word of the Lord Jesus, both Jews and Greeks.

19:1 *Ephesus.* See the Introduction to Ephesians and note at Rev. 2:1.

19:2 *Have ye received the Holy Ghost since ye believed.* Lit., Did ye receive the Holy Spirit, having believed; i.e., when you believed? The gift of the Spirit is given at the time of believing (10:44).

19:5 *they were baptized in the name of the Lord Jesus.* Though these men had been baptized by John the Baptist, baptism in the name of Christ was in order as a testimony to their new faith in Christ.

19:8 *synagogue.* Again Paul uses the synagogue as his center of witness on arriving at the city.

19:9 *school.* I.e., lecture hall owned by Tyrannus, probably used by him to teach students of rhetoric, and made available by him to traveling philosophers or teachers.

11 And God wrought special miracles by the hands of Paul:

12 So that from his body were brought unto the sick handkerchiefs or aprons, and the diseases departed from them, and the evil spirits went out of them.

13 ¶ Then certain of the vagabond Jews, exorcists, took upon them to call over them which had evil spirits the name of the Lord Jesus, saying, We adjure you by Jesus whom Paul preacheth.

14 And there were seven sons of *one* Scē'va, a Jew, *and* chief of the priests, which did so.

15 And the evil spirit answered and said, Jesus I know, and Paul I know; but who are ye?

16 And the man in whom the evil spirit was leaped on them, and overcame them, and prevailed against them, so that they fled out of that house naked and wounded.

17 And this was known to all the Jews and Greeks also dwelling at Ephesus; and fear fell on them all, and the name of the Lord Jesus was magnified.

18 And many that believed came, and confessed, and shewed their deeds.

19 Many of them also which used curious arts brought their books together, and burned them before all *men*: and they counted the price of them, and found *it* fifty thousand *pieces* of silver.

20 So mightily grew the word of God and prevailed.

21 ¶ After these things were ended, Paul purposed in the spirit, when he had passed through Macedonia and Achä'a, to go to Jerusalem, saying, After I have been there, I must also see Rome.

22 So he sent into Macedonia two of them that ministered unto him, Tĭmoth'eus and Erastus; but he himself stayed in Asia for a season.

23 And the same time there arose no small stir about that way.

24 For a certain *man* named Dēmē'trius, a silversmith,

19:11 *special miracles.* On other occasions Paul did not have this power (2 Cor. 12:8; Phil. 2:27; 1 Tim. 5:23; 2 Tim. 4:20).

19:13 *exorcists.* Magicians who could cast out demons. The lesson of this story (vv. 13–17) is that to use the name of Jesus effectively in exorcism one must be totally devoted to Him. Contrary to theories of magic of the time, the name by itself could do nothing; in fact such misuse backfired (v. 16).

19:19 *curious arts.* Magical spells written on scrolls. *pieces of silver*: if the silver drachma is meant, the value would have been $10,000 plus.

19:24 *silver shrines.* Small shrines, representing Diana in a niche, for votaries to dedicate in the temple. None in silver have been

which made silver shrines for Diana, brought no small gain unto the craftsmen;

25 Whom he called together with the workmen of like occupation, and said, Sirs, ye know that by this craft we have our wealth.

26 Moreover ye see and hear, that not alone at Ephesus, but almost throughout all Asia, this Paul hath persuaded and turned away much people, saying that they be no gods, which are made with hands:

27 So that not only this our craft is in danger to be set at nought; but also that the temple of the great goddess Diana should be despised, and her magnificence should be destroyed, whom all Asia and the world worshippeth.

28 And when they heard *these sayings,* they were full of wrath, and cried out, saying, Great *is* Diana of the Ephesians.

29 And the whole city was filled with confusion: and having caught Ga´us and Aristar´chus, men of Macedonia, Paul's companions in travel, they rushed with one accord into the theatre.

30 And when Paul would have entered in unto the people, the disciples suffered him not.

31 And certain of the chief of Asia, which were his friends, sent unto him, desiring *him* that he would not adventure himself into the theatre.

32 Some therefore cried one thing, and some another: for the assembly was confused; and the more part knew not wherefore they were come together.

33 And they drew Alexander out of the multitude, the Jews putting him forward. And Alexander beckoned with the hand, and would have made his defence unto the people.

34 But when they knew that he was a Jew, all with one voice about the space of two hours cried out, Great *is* Diana of the Ephesians.

35 And when the townclerk had appeased the people,

found, though some in terra-cotta have. *brought no small gain.* Big profits are clearly implied.

19:27 The gospel was endangering the business of these idol-makers, but to stir up opposition against the Christians, the craftsmen appealed to the civic pride of the Ephesians. The temple of Diana was one of the Seven Wonders of the ancient world—a magnificent structure with 127 columns 60 feet high standing on an area 425 feet in length and 220 feet in width.

19:32 39, 41 *assembly.* The people of Ephesus had the right to meet in a legislative assembly, though this particular gathering was an unlawful one. See note at 7:38.

he said, Ye men of Ephesus, what man is there that knoweth not how that the city of the Ephesians is a worshipper of the great goddess Diana, and of the *image* which fell down from Jupiter?

36 Seeing then that these things cannot be spoken against, ye ought to be quiet, and to do nothing rashly.

37 For ye have brought hither these men, which are neither robbers of churches, nor yet blasphemers of your goddess.

38 Wherefore if Dēmē'trius, and the craftsmen which are with him, have a matter against any man, the law is open, and there are deputies: let them implead one another.

39 But if ye enquire any thing concerning other matters, it shall be determined in a lawful assembly.

40 For we are in danger to be called in question for this day's uproar, there being no cause whereby we may give an account of this concourse.

41 And when he had thus spoken, he dismissed the assembly.

2 Greece, 20:1–5

20 And after the uproar was ceased, Paul called unto him the disciples, and embraced *them*, and departed for to go into Macedonia.

2 And when he had gone over those parts, and had given them much exhortation, he came into Greece,

3 And *there* abode three months. And when the Jews laid wait for him, as he was about to sail into Syria, he purposed to return through Macedonia.

4 And there accompanied him into Asia Sō'pater of Berē'a; and of the Thessalō'nians, Aristar'chus and Secun'dus; and Gāi'us of Der'bē, and Tīmoth'eus; and of Asia, Tych'icus and Troph'imus.

5 These going before tarried for us at Trō'as.

3 Asia Minor: Troas and the elders of Ephesus, 20:6–38

6 And we sailed away from Phīlip'pī after the days of unleavened bread, and came unto them to Trō'as in five days; where we abode seven days.

7 And upon the first *day* of the week, when the disciples

20:1–4 Luke's brevity here, a mere mention of the missionary team and a journey through Macedonia revisiting established communities, suggests that Acts could have been a much longer book.

20:7 *upon the first day of the week.* This became the regular day

came together to break bread, Paul preached unto them, ready to depart on the morrow; and continued his speech until midnight.

8 And there were many lights in the upper chamber, where they were gathered together.

9 And there sat in a window a certain young man named Eû'tychus, being fallen into a deep sleep: and as Paul was long preaching, he sunk down with sleep, and fell down from the third loft, and was taken up dead.

10 And Paul went down, and fell on him, and embracing *him* said, Trouble not yourselves; for his life is in him.

11 When he therefore was come up again, and had broken bread, and eaten, and talked a long while, even till break of day, so he departed.

12 And they brought the young man alive, and were not a little comforted.

13 ¶ And we went before to ship, and sailed unto Assos, there intending to take in Paul: for so had he appointed, minding himself to go afoot.

14 And when he met with us at Assos, we took him in, and came to Mitylē'nē.

15 And we sailed thence, and came the next *day* over against Chī'os; and the next *day* we arrived at Samos, and tarried at Trōgyl'lium; and the next *day* we came to Mīlē'tus.

16 For Paul had determined to sail by Ephesus, because he would not spend the time in Asia: for he hasted, if it were possible for him, to be at Jerusalem the day of Pentecost.

17 ¶ And from Mīlē'tus he sent to Ephesus, and called the elders of the church.

18 And when they were come to him, he said unto them, Ye know, from the first day that I came into Asia, after what manner I have been with you at all seasons,

19 Serving the Lord with all humility of mind, and with many tears, and temptations, which befell me by the lying in wait of the Jews:

20 *And* how I kept back nothing that was profitable

---

of worship for the Christians in remembrance of Christ's resurrection on Sunday.

20:16 If Paul were to stop at Ephesus, friends would surely delay him. He *determined* to take a boat that had no plans to stop at Ephesus.

20:17 *elders.* These leaders of the group were recognized by all, since they knew whom to send when Paul *called the elders.* See note at 1 Tim. 3:1.

unto you, but have shewed you, and have taught you publickly, and from house to house,

21 Testifying both to the Jews, and also to the Greeks, repentance toward God, and faith toward our Lord Jesus Christ.

22 And now, behold, I go bound in the spirit unto Jerusalem, not knowing the things that shall befall me there:

23 Save that the Holy Ghost witnesseth in every city, saying that bonds and afflictions abide me.

24 But none of these things move me, neither count I my life dear unto myself, so that I might finish my course with joy, and the ministry, which I have received of the Lord Jesus, to testify the gospel of the grace of God.

25 And now, behold, I know that ye all, among whom I have gone preaching the kingdom of God, shall see my face no more.

26 Wherefore I take you to record this day, that I *am* pure from the blood of all *men*.

27 For I have not shunned to declare unto you all the counsel of God.

28 ¶ Take heed therefore unto yourselves, and to all the flock, over the which the Holy Ghost hath made you overseers, to feed the church of God, which he hath purchased with his own blood.

29 For I know this, that after my departing shall grievous wolves enter in among you, not sparing the flock.

30 Also of your own selves shall men arise, speaking perverse things, to draw away disciples after them.

31 Therefore watch, and remember, that by the space of three years I ceased not to warn every one night and day with tears.

32 And now, brethren, I commend you to God, and to the word of his grace, which is able to build you up, and to give you an inheritance among all them which are sanctified.

33 I have coveted no man's silver, or gold, or apparel.

34 Yea, ye yourselves know, that these hands have ministered unto my necessities, and to them that were with me.

35 I have shewed you all things, how that so labouring ye ought to support the weak, and to remember the words

20:24 Compare Paul's words in 2 Tim. 4:7.
20:28 *with his own blood*. Lit., with the blood of His own (Son).
20:28–30 For what happened at Ephesus later, see 1 Tim. 1:3–7.
20:35 *remember the words of the Lord Jesus*. This saying is not recorded in the Gospels.

of the Lord Jesus, how he said, It is more blessed to give than to receive.

36 ¶ And when he had thus spoken, he kneeled down, and prayed with them all.

37 And they all wept sore, and fell on Paul's neck, and kissed him,

38 Sorrowing most of all for the words which he spake, that they should see his face no more. And they accompanied him unto the ship.

4 From Miletus to Caesarea, 21:1-14

21 And it came to pass, that after we were gotten from them, and had launched, we came with a straight course unto Cō'os, and the *day* following unto Rhodes, and from thence unto Patara:

2 And finding a ship sailing over unto Phēnic'ia, we went aboard, and set forth.

3 Now when we had discovered Cyprus, we left it on the left hand, and sailed into Syria, and landed at Tyre: for there the ship was to unlade her burden.

4 And finding disciples, we tarried there seven days: who said to Paul through the Spirit, that he should not go up to Jerusalem.

5 And when we had accomplished those days, we departed and went our way; and they all brought us on our way, with wives and children, till *we were* out of the city: and we kneeled down on the shore, and prayed.

6 And when we had taken our leave one of another, we took ship; and they returned home again.

7 And when we had finished *our* course from Tyre, we came to Ptolemā'is, and saluted the brethren, and abode with them one day.

8 And the next *day* we that were of Paul's company departed, and came unto Cæsarea: and we entered into the house of Philip the evangelist, which was *one* of the seven; and abode with him.

9 And the same man had four daughters, virgins, which did prophesy.

10 And as we tarried *there* many days, there came down from Judæa a certain prophet, named Ag'abus.

21:1 Luke obviously enjoys describing a sea voyage. His masterpiece comes later (ch. 27).

21:8 *Philip the evangelist.* He was previously mentioned in 6:5 and 8:5.

21:10 *Agabus.* Presumably the same one who prophesied in 11:28.

11 And when he was come unto us, he took Paul's girdle, and bound his own hands and feet, and said, Thus saith the Holy Ghost, So shall the Jews at Jerusalem bind the man that owneth this girdle, and shall deliver *him* into the hands of the Gentiles.

12 And when we heard these things, both we, and they of that place, besought him not to go up to Jerusalem.

13 Then Paul answered, What mean ye to weep and to break mine heart? for I am ready not to be bound only, but also to die at Jerusalem for the name of the Lord Jesus.

14 And when he would not be persuaded, we ceased, saying, The will of the Lord be done.

5 *Paul with the Jerusalem church,* 21:15–26

15 And after those days we took up our carriages, and went up to Jerusalem.

16 There went with us also *certain* of the disciples of Cæsarea, and brought with them one Mnā'son of Cyprus, an old disciple, with whom we should lodge.

17 And when we were come to Jerusalem, the brethren received us gladly.

18 And the *day* following Paul went in with us unto James; and all the elders were present.

19 And when he had saluted them, he declared particularly what things God had wrought among the Gentiles by his ministry.

20 And when they heard *it*, they glorified the Lord, and said unto him, Thou seest, brother, how many thousands of Jews there are which believe; and they are all zealous of the law:

21 And they are informed of thee, that thou teachest all the Jews which are among the Gentiles to forsake Moses, saying that they ought not to circumcise *their* children, neither to walk after the customs.

22 What is it therefore? the multitude must needs come together: for they will hear that thou art come.

23 Do therefore this that we say to thee: We have four men which have a vow on them;

24 Them take, and purify thyself with them, and be at

21:15 *took up our carriages.* This probably means "packed our baggage" or "hired horses."

21:20 The old division reappears (see note at 15:1).

21:24 *be at charges with them.* Paul was being asked to pay the expenses involved in the offerings required at the completion of the Nazarite vow these four men had taken (Num. 6:13–21). He was being urged to take actions that would indicate that he was, after all, a middle-of-the-road Jewish-Christian.

charges with them, that they may shave *their* heads: and all may know that those things, whereof they were informed concerning thee, are nothing; but *that* thou thyself also walkest orderly, and keepest the law.

25 As touching the Gentiles which believe, we have written *and* concluded that they observe no such thing, save only that they keep themselves from *things* offered to idols, and from blood, and from strangled, and from fornication.

26 Then Paul took the men, and the next day purifying himself with them entered into the temple, to signify the accomplishment of the days of purification, until that an offering should be offered for every one of them.

E The Journey to Rome, 21:27–28:31

1 Paul's arrest and defense, 21:27–22:29

27 And when the seven days were almost ended, the Jews which were of Asia, when they saw him in the temple, stirred up all the people, and laid hands on him,

28 Crying out, Men of Israel, help: This is the man, that teacheth all *men* every where against the people, and the law, and this place: and further brought Greeks also into the temple, and hath polluted this holy place.

29 (For they had seen before with him in the city Troph'imus an Ephesian, whom they supposed that Paul had brought into the temple.)

30 And all the city was moved, and the people ran together: and they took Paul, and drew him out of the temple: and forthwith the doors were shut.

31 And as they went about to kill him, tidings came unto the chief captain of the band, that all Jerusalem was in an uproar.

32 Who immediately took soldiers and centurions, and ran down unto them: and when they saw the chief captain and the soldiers, they left beating of Paul.

33 Then the chief captain came near, and took him, and commanded *him* to be bound with two chains; and demanded who he was, and what he had done.

34 And some cried one thing, some another, among the multitude: and when he could not know the certainty

21:25 See note at 15:19.

21:28 *brought Greeks also into the temple.* Verse 29 explains that the crowd assumed (though it was untrue) that Paul had taken Trophimus, a Gentile, into the inner courts of the temple which were reserved for Jews only. This was an offense punishable by death.

for the tumult, he commanded him to be carried into the castle.

35 And when he came upon the stairs, so it was, that he was borne of the soldiers for the violence of the people.

36 For the multitude of the people followed after, crying, Away with him.

37 And as Paul was to be led into the castle, he said unto the chief captain, May I speak unto thee? Who said, Canst thou speak Greek?

38 Art not thou that Egyptian, which before these days madest an uproar, and leddest out into the wilderness four thousand men that were murderers?

39 But Paul said, I am a man *which am* a Jew of Tarsus, *a city* in Cĭlic′ia, a citizen of no mean city: and, I beseech thee, suffer me to speak unto the people.

40 And when he had given him licence, Paul stood on the stairs, and beckoned with the hand unto the people. And when there was made a great silence, he spake unto *them* in the Hebrew tongue, saying,

22 Men, brethren, and fathers, hear ye my defence *which I make* now unto you.

2 (And when they heard that he spake in the Hebrew tongue to them, they kept the more silence: and he saith,)

3 I am verily a man *which am* a Jew, born in Tarsus, *a city* in Cĭlic′ia, yet brought up in this city at the feet of Gămā′liel, *and* taught according to the perfect manner of the law of the fathers, and was zealous toward God, as ye all are this day.

4 And I persecuted this way unto the death, binding and delivering into prisons both men and women.

5 As also the high priest doth bear me witness, and all the estate of the elders: from whom also I received letters unto the brethren, and went to Damascus, to bring them which were there bound unto Jerusalem, for to be punished.

6 And it came to pass, that, as I made my journey, and was come nigh unto Damascus about noon, suddenly there shone from heaven a great light round about me.

7 And I fell unto the ground, and heard a voice saying unto me, Saul, Saul, why persecutest thou me?

8 And I answered, Who art thou, Lord? And he said unto me, I am Jesus of Nazareth, whom thou persecutest.

21:38 *that Egyptian.* Josephus the historian records such an event in A.D. 54. The leader disappeared. The tribune jumps to the conclusion that Paul is he.

9 And they that were with me saw indeed the light, and were afraid; but they heard not the voice of him that spake to me.

10 And I said, What shall I do, Lord? And the Lord said unto me, Arise, and go into Damascus; and there it shall be told thee of all things which are appointed for thee to do.

11 And when I could not see for the glory of that light, being led by the hand of them that were with me, I came into Damascus.

12 And one Anani′as, a devout man according to the law, having a good report of all the Jews which dwelt *there*,

13 Came unto me, and stood, and said unto me, Brother Saul, receive thy sight. And the same hour I looked up upon him.

14 And he said, The God of our fathers hath chosen thee, that thou shouldest know his will, and see that Just One, and shouldest hear the voice of his mouth.

15 For thou shalt be his witness unto all men of what thou hast seen and heard.

16 And now why tarriest thou? arise, and be baptized, and wash away thy sins, calling on the name of the Lord.

17 And it came to pass, that, when I was come again to Jerusalem, even while I prayed in the temple, I was in a trance;

18 And saw him saying unto me, Make haste, and get thee quickly out of Jerusalem: for they will not receive thy testimony concerning me.

19 And I said, Lord, they know that I imprisoned and beat in every synagogue them that believed on thee:

20 And when the blood of thy martyr Stephen was shed, I also was standing by, and consenting unto his death, and kept the raiment of them that slew him.

21 And he said unto me, Depart: for I will send thee far hence unto the Gentiles.

22 And they gave him audience unto this word, and *then* lifted up their voices, and said, Away with such a *fellow* from the earth: for it is not fit that he should live.

22:9 *heard not the voice*. I.e., heard not the *voice* (the verb is followed by an accusative), whereas 9:7 states that they did hear the *sound* (the verb there is followed by a genitive). There is no contradiction.

22:16 Translate literally thus: "having arisen, be baptized; and wash away your sins, having called on the name of the Lord."

22:21–23 The reference to the Gentiles, joined with Paul's claiming a divine commission, sets off the mob again.

23 And as they cried out, and cast off *their* clothes, and threw dust into the air,

24 The chief captain commanded him to be brought into the castle, and bade that he should be examined by scourging; that he might know wherefore they cried so against him.

25 And as they bound him with thongs, Paul said unto the centurion that stood by, Is it lawful for you to scourge a man that is a Roman, and uncondemned?

26 When the centurion heard *that,* he went and told the chief captain, saying, Take heed what thou doest: for this man is a Roman.

27 Then the chief captain came, and said unto him, Tell me, art thou a Roman? He said, Yea.

28 And the chief captain answered, With a great sum obtained I this freedom. And Paul said, But I was *free* born.

29 Then straightway they departed from him which should have examined him: and the chief captain also was afraid, after he knew that he was a Roman, and because he had bound him.

2 *Paul brought before the Sanhedrin,* 22:30–23:10

30 On the morrow, because he would have known the certainty wherefore he was accused of the Jews, he loosed him from *his* bands, and commanded the chief priests and all their council to appear, and brought Paul down, and set him before them.

23 And Paul, earnestly beholding the council, said, Men *and* brethren, I have lived in all good conscience before God until this day.

2 And the high priest Anani′as commanded them that stood by him to smite him on the mouth.

22:28 *With a great sum.* In the reign of Claudius, contemporaneous to these events, Roman citizenship could be purchased for what would be a princely sum for a soldier. Somehow Paul's parents had earned Roman citizenship before Paul's birth.

22:30 *their council*=the Sanhedrin. See note at Luke 22:66. Somehow the Sanhedrin had interposed itself so that Paul's case did not get directly and immediately referred to the Roman governor in Caesarea.

23:2 *commanded them . . . to smite him.* Ananias (high priest about A.D. 48–58) was reported to be an insolent and overbearing man. He was probably angered at Paul's bold claims and ordered him struck.

3 Then said Paul unto him, God shall smite thee, *thou whited wall:* for sittest thou to judge me after the law, and commandest me to be smitten contrary to the law?

4 And they that stood by said, Revilest thou God's high priest?

5 Then said Paul, I wist not, brethren, that he was the high priest: for it is written, Thou shalt not speak evil of the ruler of thy people.

6 But when Paul perceived that the one part were Sadducees, and the other Pharisees, he cried out in the council, Men *and* brethren, I am a Pharisee, the son of a Pharisee: of the hope and resurrection of the dead I am called in question.

7 And when he had so said, there arose a dissension between the Pharisees and the Sadducees: and the multitude was divided.

8 For the Sadducees say that there is no resurrection, neither angel, nor spirit: but the Pharisees confess both.

9 And there arose a great cry: and the scribes *that were* of the Pharisees' part arose, and strove, saying, We find no evil in this man: but if a spirit or an angel hath spoken to him, let us not fight against God.

10 And when there arose a great dissension, the chief captain, fearing lest Paul should have been pulled in pieces of them, commanded the soldiers to go down, and to take him by force from among them, and to bring *him* into the castle.

3 *Paul escorted to Caesarea,* 23:11-35

11 And the night following the Lord stood by him, and said, Be of good cheer, Paul: for as thou hast testified of me in Jerusalem, so must thou bear witness also at Rome.

12 And when it was day, certain of the Jews banded together, and bound themselves under a curse, saying that they would neither eat nor drink till they had killed Paul.

23:5 *I wist not, brethren, that he was the high priest.* Some think Paul's weak eyes caused him to fail to recognize the high priest; however, the remark may have been sarcasm—"I didn't think the high priest would ever speak like that!" Paul's quotation is from Ex. 22:28.

23:6 In effect Paul says: I, a Pharisee by inheritance and training, can hardly be regarded as a subversive teacher! Paul proceeds to split the Sanhedrin into its two factions.

23:11 Christ appeared to Paul four times: at his conversion (9:5), on his first visit to Jerusalem (22:17-18), in Corinth (18:9-10), and here during his last visit to Jerusalem.

13 And they were more than forty which had made this conspiracy.

14 And they came to the chief priests and elders, and said, We have bound ourselves under a great curse, that we will eat nothing until we have slain Paul.

15 Now therefore ye with the council signify to the chief captain that he bring him down unto you to morrow, as though ye would enquire something more perfectly concerning him: and we, or ever he come near, are ready to kill him.

16 And when Paul's sister's son heard of their lying in wait, he went and entered into the castle, and told Paul.

17 Then Paul called one of the centurions unto *him*, and said, Bring this young man unto the chief captain: for he hath a certain thing to tell him.

18 So he took him, and brought *him* to the chief captain, and said, Paul the prisoner called me unto *him*, and prayed me to bring this young man unto thee, who hath something to say unto thee.

19 Then the chief captain took him by the hand, and went *with him* aside privately, and asked *him*, What is that thou hast to tell me?

20 And he said, The Jews have agreed to desire thee that thou wouldest bring down Paul to morrow into the council, as though they would enquire somewhat of him more perfectly.

21 But do not thou yield unto them: for there lie in wait for him of them more than forty men, which have bound themselves with an oath, that they will neither eat nor drink till they have killed him: and now are they ready, looking for a promise from thee.

22 So the chief captain *then* let the young man depart, and charged *him*, See thou tell no man that thou hast shewed these things to me.

23 And he called unto *him* two centurions, saying, Make ready two hundred soldiers to go to Cæsarea, and horsemen threescore and ten, and spearmen two hundred, at the third hour of the night;

24 And provide *them* beasts, that they may set Paul on, and bring *him* safe unto Felix the governor.

25 And he wrote a letter after this manner:

23:16 *Paul's sister's son.* Only here is made any mention of Paul's immediate relatives.

23:24 *Felix the governor.* Roman procurator of Judea (A.D. 52 to probably 58) with headquarters in Caesarea.

26 Claudius Lys'ias unto the most excellent governor Felix *sendeth* greeting.

27 This man was taken of the Jews, and should have been killed of them: then came I with an army, and rescued him, having understood that he was a Roman.

28 And when I would have known the cause wherefore they accused him, I brought him forth into their council:

29 Whom I perceived to be accused of questions of their law, but to have nothing laid to his charge worthy of death or of bonds.

30 And when it was told me how that the Jews laid wait for the man, I sent straightway to thee, and gave commandment to his accusers also to say before thee what *they had* against him. Farewell.

31 Then the soldiers, as it was commanded them, took Paul, and brought *him* by night to Antip'atris.

32 On the morrow they left the horsemen to go with him, and returned to the castle:

33 Who, when they came to Cæsarea, and delivered the epistle to the governor, presented Paul also before him.

34 And when the governor had read *the letter*, he asked of what province he was. And when he understood that *he was* of Cilic'ia;

35 I will hear thee, said he, when thine accusers are also come. And he commanded him to be kept in Herod's judgment hall.

4 Paul's defense before Felix, 24:1–27

24 And after five days Anani'as the high priest descended with the elders, and *with* a certain orator *named* Tertul'lus, who informed the governor against Paul.

2 And when he was called forth, Tertul'lus began to accuse *him*, saying, Seeing that by thee we enjoy great

---

23:34 *of what province he was.* Roman law required that this question be asked at the opening of a hearing, for Paul had the right to be tried in his home province or in the province where the alleged crime was committed. Tarsus was in Cilicia. Felix was a deputy of the legate of Syria and Cilicia, and so claimed the right to conduct the hearing, whichever choice Paul made. Such a detail is strong proof that Luke was with Paul at the hearing.

24:1 *Ananias* heads the group that presents the complaint against Paul. Tertullus (Roman name) was probably a lawyer hired by the Jews in Caesarea to present their case.

quietness, and that very worthy deeds are done unto this nation by thy providence,

3 We accept *it* always, and in all places, most noble Felix, with all thankfulness.

4 Notwithstanding, that I be not further tedious unto thee, I pray thee that thou wouldest hear us of thy clemency a few words.

5 For we have found this man *a* pestilent *fellow*, and a mover of sedition among all the Jews throughout the world, and a ringleader of the sect of the Nazarenes:

6 Who also hath gone about to profane the temple: whom we took, and would have judged according to our law.

7 But the chief captain Lys′ias came *upon us*, and with great violence took *him* away out of our hands,

8 Commanding his accusers to come unto thee: by examining of whom thyself mayest take knowledge of all these things, whereof we accuse him.

9 And the Jews also assented, saying that these things were so.

10 Then Paul, after that the governor had beckoned unto him to speak, answered, Forasmuch as I know that thou hast been of many years a judge unto this nation, I do the more cheerfully answer for myself:

11 Because that thou mayest understand, that there are yet but twelve days since I went up to Jerusalem for to worship.

12 And they neither found me in the temple disputing with any man, neither raising up the people, neither in the synagogues, nor in the city:

13 Neither can they prove the things whereof they now accuse me.

14 But this I confess unto thee, that after the way which they call heresy, so worship I the God of my fathers, believing all things which are written in the law and in the prophets:

15 And have hope toward God, which they themselves also allow, that there shall be a resurrection of the dead, both of the just and unjust.

24:5 Tertullus broadens the charge, and makes it more serious in Roman eyes by, for the first time, accusing Paul of being an insurrectionist (*mover of sedition*).

24:8 Tertullus now argues that Lysias had exceeded his authority in removing Paul from trial by Jewish authorities on the charge of profaning the temple.

24:14 *after the way which they call heresy*. Better, according to the Way, which they call a sect.

16 And herein do I exercise myself, to have always a conscience void of offence toward God, and *toward* men.

17 Now after many years I came to bring alms to my nation, and offerings.

18 Whereupon certain Jews from Asia found me purified in the temple, neither with multitude, nor with tumult.

19 Who ought to have been here before thee, and object, if they had ought against me.

20 Or else let these same *here* say, if they have found any evil doing in me, while I stood before the council,

21 Except it be for this one voice, that I cried standing among them, Touching the resurrection of the dead I am called in question by you this day.

22 And when Felix heard these things, having more perfect knowledge of *that* way, he deferred them, and said, When Lys'ias the chief captain shall come down, I will know the uttermost of your matter.

23 And he commanded a centurion to keep Paul, and to let *him* have liberty, and that he should forbid none of his acquaintance to minister or come unto him.

24 And after certain days, when Felix came with his wife Drŭsil'la, which was a Jewess, he sent for Paul, and heard him concerning the faith in Christ.

25 And as he reasoned of righteousness, temperance, and judgment to come, Felix trembled, and answered, Go thy way for this time; when I have a convenient season, I will call for thee.

26 He hoped also that money should have been given him of Paul, that he might loose him: wherefore he sent for him the oftener, and communed with him.

27 But after two years Por'cius Festus came into Felix' room: and Felix, willing to shew the Jews a pleasure, left Paul bound.

24:19 *Who*=the Jews from Asia. They are not here, Paul points out, as witnesses.

24:22 *he deferred them* because Lysias wasn't there to be heard from.

24:23 *have liberty.* Paul was under a relatively loose military confinement.

24:25 *Felix trembled.* Felix had stolen Drusilla from her first husband. He also was corrupt as a governor (v. 26), and Paul may have challenged him concerning his morality.

24:27 *Porcius Festus* was Felix' successor. The change came about A.D. 58. A Roman magistrate could decide when a case could be called; often the delays were long, as here.

5 Paul's defense before Festus, 25:1–27

25 Now when Festus was come into the province, after three days he ascended from Cæsarea to Jerusalem.

2 Then the high priest and the chief of the Jews informed him against Paul, and besought him,

3 And desired favour against him, that he would send for him to Jerusalem, laying wait in the way to kill him.

4 But Festus answered, that Paul should be kept at Cæsarea, and that he himself would depart shortly *thither*.

5 Let them therefore, said he, which among you are able, go down with *me*, and accuse this man, if there be any wickedness in him.

6 And when he had tarried among them more than ten days, he went down unto Cæsarea; and the next day sitting on the judgment seat commanded Paul to be brought.

7 And when he was come, the Jews which came down from Jerusalem stood round about, and laid many and grievous complaints against Paul, which they could not prove.

8 While he answered for himself, Neither against the law of the Jews, neither against the temple, nor yet against Cæsar, have I offended any thing at all.

9 But Festus, willing to do the Jews a pleasure, answered Paul, and said, Wilt thou go up to Jerusalem, and there be judged of these things before me?

10 Then said Paul, I stand at Cæsar's judgment seat, where I ought to be judged: to the Jews have I done no wrong, as thou very well knowest.

11 For if I be an offender, or have committed anything worthy of death, I refuse not to die: but if there be none of these things whereof these accuse me, no man may deliver me unto them. I appeal unto Cæsar.

25:1 *to Jerusalem.* Since there was much unrest, Festus thought it prudent to make an early visit to the religious capital, Jerusalem. The Jews saw in this an opportunity to ask that Paul be returned there. If the request was granted they would try to kill him on the way (v. 3).

25:11 *I appeal unto Cæsar.* Festus' suggestion that Paul appear in Jerusalem for trial (v. 9) provoked this appeal to Caesar, for Paul realized that the trial would not be impartial if conducted by Festus, especially if the case were transferred to Jerusalem, and that he would be in great danger if he was returned to the jurisdiction of the Sanhedrin. The right of appeal was one of the most ancient and cherished rights of a Roman citizen. Nero was emperor at this time (A.D. 54–68).

12 Then Festus, when he had conferred with the council, answered, Hast thou appealed unto Cæsar? unto Cæsar shalt thou go.

13 And after certain days king Agrip'pa and Bernī'cē came unto Cæsarea to salute Festus.

14 And when they had been there many days, Festus declared Paul's cause unto the king, saying, There is a certain man left in bonds by Felix:

15 About whom, when I was at Jerusalem, the chief priests and the elders of the Jews informed *me*, desiring *to have* judgment against him.

16 To whom I answered, It is not the manner of the Romans to deliver any man to die, before that he which is accused have the accusers face to face, and have licence to answer for himself concerning the crime laid against him.

17 Therefore, when they were come hither, without any delay on the morrow I sat on the judgment seat, and commanded the man to be brought forth.

18 Against whom when the accusers stood up, they brought none accusation of such things as I supposed:

19 But had certain questions against him of their own superstition, and of one Jesus, which was dead, whom Paul affirmed to be alive.

20 And because I doubted of such manner of questions, I asked *him* whether he would go to Jerusalem, and there be judged of these matters.

21 But when Paul had appealed to be reserved unto the hearing of Augustus, I commanded him to be kept till I might send him to Cæsar.

22 Then Agrip'pa said unto Festus, I would also hear the man myself. To morrow, said he, thou shalt hear him.

23 And on the morrow, when Agrip'pa was come, and Bernī'cē, with great pomp, and was entered into the place of hearing, with the chief captains, and principal men of the city, at Festus' commandment Paul was brought forth.

24 And Festus said, King Agrip'pa, and all men which are here present with us, ye see this man, about whom all the multitude of the Jews have dealt with me, both at

25:13 *Agrippa*=Herod Agrippa II, son of Herod Agrippa I (12:1) and great-grandson of Herod the Great (Matt. 2:1), all of whose territories he ultimately ruled under Rome's jurisdiction. Bernice was his sister; they were living together incestuously. Paul was not required to defend himself before them, since he had already appealed to Caesar, but he took the opportunity to witness to the Jewish king.

25:19 *had certain questions . . . own superstition.* Better, had certain points of dispute with him about religious beliefs.

Jerusalem, and *also* here, crying that he ought not to live any longer.

25 But when I found that he had committed nothing worthy of death, and that he himself hath appealed to Augustus, I have determined to send him.

26 Of whom I have no certain thing to write unto my lord. Wherefore I have brought him forth before you, and specially before thee, O king Agrip'pa, that, after examination had, I might have somewhat to write.

27 For it seemeth to me unreasonable to send a prisoner, and not withal to signify the crimes *laid* against him.

6 Paul's defense before Agrippa, 26:1–32

26 Then Agrip'pa said unto Paul, Thou art permitted to speak for thyself. Then Paul stretched forth the hand, and answered for himself:

2 I think myself happy, king Agrip'pa, because I shall answer for myself this day before thee touching all the things whereof I am accused of the Jews:

3 Especially *because I know* thee to be expert in all customs and questions which are among the Jews: wherefore I beseech thee to hear me patiently.

4 My manner of life from my youth, which was at the first among mine own nation at Jerusalem, know all the Jews;

5 Which knew me from the beginning, if they would testify, that after the most straitest sect of our religion I lived a Pharisee.

6 And now I stand and am judged for the hope of the promise made of God unto our fathers:

7 Unto which *promise* our twelve tribes, instantly serving God day and night, hope to come. For which hope's sake, king Agrip'pa, I am accused of the Jews.

8 Why should it be thought a thing incredible with you, that God should raise the dead?

9 I verily thought with myself, that I ought to do many things contrary to the name of Jesus of Nazareth.

10 Which thing I also did in Jerusalem: and many of the saints did I shut up in prison, having received authority from the chief priests; and when they were put to death, I gave my voice against *them*.

11 And I punished them oft in every synagogue, and

26:6 *the promise.* I.e., of the Messiah (Gen. 22:18; 49:10).
26:8 That Paul preached the resurrection of Jesus Christ was the heart of the complaint of the Jewish authorities.
26:11 *compelled them to blaspheme.* I.e., was forcing them to

compelled *them* to blaspheme; and being exceedingly mad against them, I persecuted *them* even unto strange cities.

12 Whereupon as I went to Damascus with authority and commission from the chief priests,

13 At midday, O king, I saw in the way a light from heaven, above the brightness of the sun, shining round about me and them which journeyed with me.

14 And when we were all fallen to the earth, I heard a voice speaking unto me, and saying in the Hebrew tongue, Saul, Saul, why persecutest thou me? *it is* hard for thee to kick against the pricks.

15 And I said, Who art thou, Lord? And he said, I am Jesus whom thou persecutest.

16 But rise, and stand upon thy feet: for I have appeared unto thee for this purpose, to make thee a minister and a witness both of these things which thou hast seen, and of those things in the which I will appear unto thee:

17 Delivering thee from the people, and *from* the Gentiles, unto whom now I send thee,

18 To open their eyes, *and* to turn *them* from darkness to light, and *from* the power of Satan unto God, that they may receive forgiveness of sins, and inheritance among them which are sanctified by faith that is in me.

19 Whereupon, O king Agrip'pa, I was not disobedient unto the heavenly vision:

20 But shewed first unto them of Damascus, and at Jerusalem, and throughout all the coasts of Judæa, and *then* to the Gentiles, that they should repent and turn to God, and do works meet for repentance.

21 For these causes the Jews caught me in the temple, and went about to kill *me*.

22 Having therefore obtained help of God, I continue unto this day, witnessing both to small and great, saying none other things than those which the prophets and Moses did say should come:

23 That Christ should suffer, *and* that he should be the first that should rise from the dead, and should shew light unto the people, and to the Gentiles.

24 And as he thus spake for himself, Festus said with a loud voice, Paul, thou art beside thyself; much learning doth make thee mad.

---

blaspheme against Christ, which would not be blasphemy to the Jews.

26:24 *Paul, thou art . . . mad.* Festus, a Roman, simply cannot comprehend Paul's line of thought and language. Agrippa, a Jew, had no such semantic problems.

25 But he said, I am not mad, most noble Festus; but speak forth the words of truth and soberness.

26 For the king knoweth of these things, before whom also I speak freely: for I am persuaded that none of these things are hidden from him; for this thing was not done in a corner.

27 King Agrip′pa, believest thou the prophets? I know that thou believest.

28 Then Agrip′pa said unto Paul, Almost thou persuadest me to be a Christian.

29 And Paul said, I would to God, that not only thou, but also all that hear me this day, were both almost, and altogether such as I am, except these bonds.

30 And when he had thus spoken, the king rose up, and the governor, and Berni′cē, and they that sat with them:

31 And when they were gone aside, they talked between themselves, saying, This man doeth nothing worthy of death or of bonds.

32 Then said Agrip′pa unto Festus, This man might have been set at liberty, if he had not appealed unto Cæsar.

7 Paul's voyage and shipwreck, 27:1–44

27 And when it was determined that we should sail into Italy, they delivered Paul and certain other prisoners unto *one* named Julius, a centurion of Augustus' band.

2 And entering into a ship of Adramyt′tium, we launched, meaning to sail by the coasts of Asia; *one* Aristar′chus, a Macedonian of Thessalōni′ca, being with us.

3 And the next *day* we touched at Sidon. And Julius courteously entreated Paul, and gave *him* liberty to go unto his friends to refresh himself.

4 And when we had launched from thence, we sailed

26:25 *soberness* = good sense.

26:28 *Almost . . .*; Lit., in a little thou persuadest . . . This enigmatic statement may mean: "In such a short time are you trying to make a Christian of me?" or "With so few words you are persuading me to be a Christian."

26:29 *were both almost, and altogether*. Lit., were with little or much; i.e., in a short time or a long time, or with few or many words. This is Paul's response to Agrippa's "in a little thou persuadest . . ."

27:1 *centurion*. A commander of 100 soldiers.

27:2 *Adramyttium*. A port on the west coast of Asia Minor (modern Turkey), just south of Troas.

27:4 *under Cyprus* = under the ice of Cyprus. The prevailing

under Cyprus, because the winds were contrary.

5 And when we had sailed over the sea of Cĭlic′ia and Pamphylia, we came to Myra, *a city* of Lyc′ia.

6 And there the centurion found a ship of Alexandria sailing into Italy; and he put us therein.

7 And when we had sailed slowly many days, and scarce were come over against Cnĭ′dus, the wind not suffering us, we sailed under Crete, over against Salmō′nē;

8 And, hardly passing it, came unto a place which is called The fair havens; nigh whereunto was the city *of* Lasē′a.

9 Now when much time was spent, and when sailing was now dangerous, because the fast was now already past, Paul admonished *them*,

10 And said unto them, Sirs, I perceive that this voyage will be with hurt and much damage, not only of the lading and ship, but also of our lives.

11 Nevertheless the centurion believed the master and the owner of the ship, more than those things which were spoken by Paul.

12 And because the haven was not commodious to winter in, the more part advised to depart thence also, if by any means they might attain to Phēnĭ′cē, *and there* to winter; *which is* an haven of Crete, and lieth toward the south west and north west.

13 And when the south wind blew softly, supposing that they had obtained *their* purpose, loosing *thence*, they sailed close by Crete.

14 But not long after there arose against it a tempestuous wind, called Eûroc′lydon.

15 And when the ship was caught, and could not bear up into the wind, we let *her* drive.

early autumn winds came from the northwest, headwinds difficult for a coastal sailing vessel to handle in open ocean. So the ship sailed around the east end of Cyprus, the lee side, and headed north for the coast of Cilicia, where it would head west, close to shore for many miles.

27:9 *the fast was now already past.* Only one fast was prescribed by the law and that was on the Day of Atonement (Lev. 16:29–34). If this was the year 59, then the fast was on Oct. 5. This means Paul left Caesarea in August or September, and he did not arrive in Rome until the following March.

27:12 *the move part*=the majority.

27:14 *Euroclydon.* A hybrid word, half Greek, half Latin, meaning east-north and standing for a treacherous east-northeast wind.

16 And running under a certain island which is called Clauda, we had much work to come by the boat:

17 Which when they had taken up, they used helps, undergirding the ship; and, fearing lest they should fall into the quicksands, strake sail, and so were driven.

18 And we being exceedingly tossed with a tempest, the next *day* they lightened the ship;

19 And the third *day* we cast out with our own hands the tackling of the ship.

20 And when neither sun nor stars in many days appeared, and no small tempest lay on *us*, all hope that we should be saved was then taken away.

21 But after long abstinence Paul stood forth in the midst of them, and said, Sirs, ye should have hearkened unto me, and not have loosed from Crete, and to have gained this harm and loss.

22 And now I exhort you to be of good cheer: for there shall be no loss of *any man's* life among you, but of the ship.

23 For there stood by me this night the angel of God, whose I am, and whom I serve,

24 Saying, Fear not, Paul; thou must be brought before Cæsar: and, lo, God hath given thee all them that sail with thee.

25 Wherefore, sirs, be of good cheer: for I believe God, that it shall be even as it was told me.

26 Howbeit we must be cast upon a certain island.

27 But when the fourteenth night was come, as we were driven up and down in Adria, about midnight the shipmen deemed that they drew near to some country;

28 And sounded, and found *it* twenty fathoms: and when they had gone a little further, they sounded again, and found *it* fifteen fathoms.

29 Then fearing lest we should have fallen upon rocks, they cast four anchors out of the stern, and wished for the day.

30 And as the shipmen were about to flee out of the ship, when they had let down the boat into the sea, under

27:16 *to come by the boat.* Better, to secure the boat (i.e., the dinghy), probably being towed and starting to fill up.

27:17 *they used helps, undergirding the ship.* Some sort of rope truss to stiffen the timbers seems indicated.

27:27 *in Adria.* In this period Adria was applied to the Mediterranean E. of Sicily, and not merely to the present Adriatic Sea.

27:28 *fathoms.* A fathom is about 6 feet.

27:30 *under colour as though . . . foreship.* Read, under pretense of laying out anchors from the bow.

colour as though they would have cast anchors out of the
foreship,

31 Paul said to the centurion and to the soldiers, Except
these abide in the ship, ye cannot be saved.

32 Then the soldiers cut off the ropes of the boat, and
let her fall off.

33 And while the day was coming on, Paul besought
them all to take meat, saying, This day is the fourteenth
day that ye have tarried and continued fasting, having taken
nothing.

34 Wherefore I pray you to take *some* meat: for this
is for your health: for there shall not an hair fall from
the head of any of you.

35 And when he had thus spoken, he took bread, and
gave thanks to God in presence of them all: and when he
had broken *it*, he began to eat.

36 Then were they all of good cheer, and they also took
some meat.

37 And we were in all in the ship two hundred threescore
and sixteen souls.

38 And when they had eaten enough, they lightened the
ship, and cast out the wheat into the sea.

39 And when it was day, they knew not the land: but
they discovered a certain creek with a shore, into the
which they were minded, if it were possible, to thrust in
the ship.

40 And when they had taken up the anchors, they
committed *themselves* unto the sea, and loosed the rudder
bands, and hoised up the mainsail to the wind, and made
toward shore.

41 And falling into a place where two seas met, they
ran the ship aground; and the forepart stuck fast, and remained unmoveable, but the hinder part was broken with
the violence of the waves.

42 And the soldiers' counsel was to kill the prisoners,
lest any of them should swim out, and escape.

43 But the centurion, willing to save Paul, kept them

27:31–36 Paul the prisoner has risen to a place of commanding
    leadership.
27:38 The purpose of lightening the ship was to raise her in the
    water and let run as far up the beach as possible before
    grounding.
27:40 *taken up the anchors . . . sea.* Better, cast off the anchors
    and left them in the sea.
27:41 *a place where two seas meet.* They did not reach the shore
    but ran aground on a shoal extending offshore.

from *their* purpose; and commanded that they which could swim should cast *themselves* first *into the sea*, and get to land:

44 And the rest, some on boards, and some on *broken pieces* of the ship. And so it came to pass, that they escaped all safe to land.

8 *Paul in Malta and on to Rome*, 28:1-16

28 And when they were escaped, then they knew that the island was called Melita.

2 And the barbarous people shewed us no little kindness: for they kindled a fire, and received us every one, because of the present rain, and because of the cold.

3 And when Paul had gathered a bundle of sticks, and laid *them* on the fire, there came a viper out of the heat, and fastened on his hand.

4 And when the barbarians saw the *venomous* beast hang on his hand, they said among themselves, No doubt this man is a murderer, whom, though he hath escaped the sea, yet vengeance suffereth not to live.

5 And he shook off the beast into the fire, and felt no harm.

6 Howbeit they looked when he should have swollen, or fallen down dead suddenly: but after they had looked a great while, and saw no harm come to him, they changed their minds, and said that he was a god.

7 In the same quarters were possessions of the chief man of the island, whose name was Publius; who received us, and lodged us three days courteously.

8 And it came to pass, that the father of Publius lay sick of a fever and of a bloody flux: to whom Paul entered in, and prayed, and laid his hands on him, and healed him.

9 So when this was done, others also, which had diseases in the island, came, and were healed:

10 Who also honoured us with many honours; and when we departed, they laded *us* with such things as were necessary.

11 And after three months we departed in a ship of Alexandria, which had wintered in the isle, whose sign was Castor and Pollux.

28:1 *Melita*=Malta.
28:2 *barbarous people.* The primary meaning of the Greek word is "people who speak a foreign tongue."
28:4 *vengeance*=justice.
28:8 *bloody flux*=dysentery.
28:11 *after three months.* I.e., in the middle of February.

12 And landing at Sȳr′acûse, we tarried *there* three days.

13 And from thence we fetched a compass, and came to Rhē′gium: and after one day the south wind blew, and we came the next day to Pūtē′oli:

14 Where we found brethren, and were desired to tarry with them seven days: and so we went toward Rome.

15 And from thence, when the brethren heard of us, they came to meet us as far as Ap′pii forum, and The three taverns: whom when Paul saw, he thanked God, and took courage.

16 And when we came to Rome, the centurion delivered the prisoners to the captain of the guard: but Paul was suffered to dwell by himself with a soldier that kept him.

9 Paul in Rome, 28:17–31

17 And it came to pass, that after three days Paul called the chief of the Jews together: and when they were come together, he said unto them, Men *and* brethren, though I have committed nothing against the people, or customs of our fathers, yet was I delivered prisoner from Jerusalem into the hands of the Romans.

18 Who, when they had examined me, would have let *me* go, because there was no cause of death in me.

19 But when the Jews spake against *it*, I was constrained to appeal unto Cæsar; not that I had ought to accuse my nation of.

20 For this cause therefore have I called for you, to see *you*, and to speak with *you*: because that for the hope of Israel I am bound with this chain.

21 And they said unto him, We neither received letters out of Judæa concerning thee, neither any of the brethren that came shewed or spake any harm of thee.

22 But we desire to hear of thee what thou thinkest: for as concerning this sect, we know that every where it is spoken against.

23 And when they had appointed him a day, there came

28:13 *Rhegium.* A town on the "toe" of Italy, modern Reggio di Calabria. *Puteoli.* A port on the bay of Naples. Ostia, Rome's harbor, wasn't a deep enough harbor at this time to receive Alexandrian grain ships.

28:16 *kept.* Lit., guarded.

28:17 Paul wants to forfend any derogatory report from his Jewish enemies in Jerusalem.

28:20 *the hope of Israel.* This was the Messianic hope, incarnate in Jesus Christ and climaxed in His resurrection.

28:23 *persuading* the Jews meant to prove to them from scrip-

many to him into *his* lodging; to whom he expounded and testified the kingdom of God, persuading them concerning Jesus, both out of the law of Moses, and *out of* the prophets, from morning till evening.

24 And some believed the things which were spoken, and some believed not.

25 And when they agreed not among themselves, they departed, after that Paul had spoken one word, Well spake the Holy Ghost by Ēsā'as the prophet unto our fathers,

26 Saying, Go unto this people, and say, Hearing ye shall hear, and shall not understand; and seeing ye shall see, and not perceive:

27 For the heart of this people is waxed gross, and their ears are dull of hearing, and their eyes have they closed; lest they should see with *their* eyes, and hear with *their* ears, and understand with *their* heart, and should be converted, and I should heal them.

28 Be it known therefore unto you, that the salvation of God is sent unto the Gentiles, and *that* they will hear it.

29 And when he had said these words, the Jews departed, and had great reasoning among themselves.

30 And Paul dwelt two whole years in his own hired house, and received all that came in unto him,

31 Preaching the kingdom of God, and teaching those things which concern the Lord Jesus Christ, with all confidence, no man forbidding him.

ture and His resurrection that Jesus was the Messiah (see 13:30–39).

28:25–27 Paul's citation of this passage (Isa. 6:9–10) has been regarded as a parting shot on their obtuseness. He follows with a declaration that henceforth salvation will be preached to the Gentiles, the Jews having refused it.

28:30 *two whole years in his own hired house.* During this time of confinement Paul wrote Ephesians, Philippians, Colossians, and Philemon. See the Introduction to Ephesians. Knowing that they could not get a verdict of guilty, his accusers probably never showed up and Paul's case went by default. He would then have been released and engaged in the ministry that is reflected in the Pastoral Epistles before being rearrested and finally martyred. See the Introduction to Titus.

INTRODUCTION TO
THE LETTER OF PAUL TO THE
Romans

AUTHOR: Paul   DATE: 58

The Church at Rome   *Though both Paul and Peter were apparently martyred in Rome, it is unlikely that either was the founder of the church in that city. Possibly some who were converted on the day of Pentecost carried the gospel back to the imperial city (Acts 2:10); or it may be that converts of Paul or other apostles founded the church there. The membership was predominantly Gentile (1:13; 11:13; 15:5–6).*

The Occasion of the Letter   *Paul was anxious to minister in this church which was already widely known (1:8), so he wrote this letter to prepare the way for his visit (15:14–17). It was written from Corinth, where Paul was completing the collection for the poor in Palestine. From there he went to Jerusalem to deliver the money, intending to continue on to to Rome and Spain (15:24). These plans were, of course, changed by his arrest in Jerusalem, though Paul did eventually get to Rome as a prisoner. A first-century inscription discovered at Corinth mentions a city official named Erastus who is likely the same as the one mentioned in 16:23. Phoebe, who belonged to the church at Cenchrea near Corinth (16:1), probably carried the letter to Rome.*

The Question about Chapter 16   *The mention by name of 26 people in a church Paul had never visited (and particularly Priscilla and Aquila, who were most recently associated with Ephesus, Acts 18:18–19) has caused some scholars to consider chapter 16 part of an epistle sent to Ephesus. However, it would be natural for Paul to emphasize to a church to which he was a stranger his acquaintance with mutual friends. The only other long series of greetings is in Colossians—a letter sent also to a church he had not visited.*

The Contents More formal than Paul's other letters, Romans sets forth the doctrine of justification by faith (and its ramifications) in a systematic way. The theme is the righteousness of God (1:16–17). A number of basic Christian doctrines are discussed in the letter: natural revelation (1:19–20), universality of sin (3:9–20), justification (3:24), propitiation (3:25), faith (4), original sin (5:12), union with Christ (6), the election and rejection of Israel (9:11), spiritual gifts (12:3–8), and relation to government (13:1–7).

OUTLINE OF ROMANS

THE LETTER OF
PAUL THE APOSTLE TO THE
Romans

I SALUTATION AND STATEMENT OF THEME, 1:1–17

A Greeting, 1:1–7

1 Paul, a servant of Jesus Christ, called *to be* an apostle, separated unto the gospel of God,

1:1 *servants.* Lit., slave, from a word that means "to bind." The believer who voluntarily takes the position of slave to Christ has no rights or will of his own. He does always and only

2 (Which he had promised afore by his prophets in the holy scriptures,)

3 Concerning his Son Jesus Christ our Lord, which was made of the seed of David according to the flesh;

4 And declared *to be* the Son of God with power, according to the spirit of holiness, by the resurrection from the dead:

5 By whom we have received grace and apostleship, for obedience to the faith among all nations, for his name:

6 Among whom are ye also the called of Jesus Christ:

7 To all that be in Rome, beloved of God, called *to be* saints: Grace to you and peace from God our Father, and the Lord Jesus Christ.

B Paul's Interest, 1:8–15

8 First, I thank my God through Jesus Christ for you all, that your faith is spoken of throughout the whole world.

9 For God is my witness, whom I serve with my spirit in the gospel of his Son, that without ceasing I make mention of you always in my prayers;

10 Making request, if by any means now at length I

the will of his master. For His part, the Lord binds Himself to care for His servant (Deut. 15:12–18). *the gospel* is the good news that the death of Jesus Christ provided the full payment for the penalty of sin, and that anyone who trusts that living Christ is forgiven and has eternal life.

1:3 *made of the seed of David according to the flesh.* Jesus was descended from David. See notes at Matt. 1:1, 1:11; John 1:14.

1:4 *declared.* Better, designated, i.e., Jesus was designated or proved to be the Son of God by His own *resurrection from the dead.* Some understand *according to the spirit of holiness* to refer to the Holy Spirit, while others consider it a reference to Christ's own holy being. Thus the verse may be understood this way: the resurrection of Jesus is the mighty proof of His deity, and this is declared by the Holy Spirit.

1:5 *for his name.* Lit., on behalf of His name.

1:6 *the called.* I.e., those who have been summoned by God to salvation (8:30).

1:7 *saints.* The word means "holy ones" or "God's set-apart ones." The N.T. designates all believers as "saints" because they are by position holy and set apart to God (Phil. 4:21; Col. 1:2).

1:10 *Making request.* Arrest, trial, two years' languishing in prison (Acts 24:27), and shipwreck intervened before Paul's prayer was answered.

might have a prosperous journey by the will of God to come unto you.

11 For I long to see you, that I may impart unto you some spiritual gift, to the end ye may be established;

12 That is, that I may be comforted together with you by the mutual faith both of you and me.

13 Now I would not have you ignorant, brethren, that oftentimes I purposed to come unto you, (but was let hitherto,) that I might have some fruit among you also, even as among other Gentiles.

14 I am debtor both to the Greeks, and to the Barbarians; both to the wise, and to the unwise.

15 So, as much as in me is, I am ready to preach the gospel to you that are at Rome also.

C Theme, 1:16–17

16 For I am not ashamed of the gospel of Christ: for it is the power of God unto salvation to every one that believeth; to the Jew first, and also to the Greek.

17 For therein is the righteousness of God revealed from faith to faith: as it is written, The just shall live by faith.

1:11 *impart.* I.e., exercise his gifts for their benefit (as explained in v. 12).

1:13 *but was let hitherto*=but was hindered up to now.

1:14 *Greeks*=those who spoke Greek and who had adopted Hellenistic culture in contrast to *Barbarians* who had not. However, in v. 16 *Greek* means "Gentile." *wise*=educated.

1:16 *salvation* has three facets: past salvation from the penalties of sin (Luke 7:50); present salvation from the power of sin in the daily life (Rom. 5:10); and, in the future, salvation from the actual presence of sin in heaven (1 Cor. 3:15; 5:5). This salvation comes *to every one that believeth.* We receive and experience it through faith which is both assent to the truths of the gospel and confidence in the Savior Himself.

1:17 *the righteousness of God.* I.e., the restoration of right relations between man and God which proceeds from God's gift through His Son (see note at 3:21). *from faith to faith.* I.e., faith from start to finish. *The just shall live by faith.* Quoting Hab. 2:4, Paul is emphasizing that one can be just in God's sight only through faith; i.e., he who is just through faith shall live now and forever by faith. See notes at Gal. 3:11 and Heb. 10:38. In vv. 16–17 is the essence of Paul's theology, and it is: Believe in the Lord Jesus, and you will be saved.

II RIGHTEOUSNESS NEEDED; CONDEMNATION, SIN, 1:18–3:20

A The Condemnation of the Gentile, 1:18–32

1 *The cause of the condemnation: willful ignorance, 1:18–23*

18 For the wrath of God is revealed from heaven against all ungodliness and unrighteousness of men, who hold the truth in unrighteousness;

19 Because that which may be known of God is manifest in them; for God hath shewed *it* unto them.

20 For the invisible things of him from the creation of the world are clearly seen, being understood by the things that are made, *even* his eternal power and Godhead; so that they are without excuse:

21 Because that, when they knew God, they glorified *him* not as God, neither were thankful; but became vain in their imaginations, and their foolish heart was darkened.

22 Professing themselves to be wise, they became fools,

23 And changed the glory of the uncorruptible God into an image made like to corruptible man, and to birds, and four-footed beasts, and creeping things.

2 *The consequences of the condemnation: divine abandonment, 1:24–32*

24 Wherefore God also gave them up to uncleanness through the lusts of their own hearts, to dishonour their own bodies between themselves:

25 Who changed the truth of God into a lie, and wor-

1:18 From here to 3:20 is God's indictment of the world, showing why man needs the righteousness of God. *hold;* lit., hold down or suppress. Man is condemned because truth was given to him (vv. 19–20) and because he by his actions rejected it (vv. 21–32).

1:20 *they are without excuse.* The things that are made (creation) reveal to all men the *power and Godhead* (= divinity) of the true God, so that the rejection of this truth makes a man without excuse before God.

1:24 *God also gave them up.* Note the repetition of this phrase in vv. 26 and 28. Paul is attacking the frank idolatry of most of the Gentile world in which animals had become gods (v. 23), perversion was prevalent (vv. 26–27), and sin was rampant (vv. 29–32).

shipped and served the creature more than the Creator, who is blessed for ever. Amen.

26 For this cause God gave them up unto vile affections: for even their women did change the natural use into that which is against nature:

27 And likewise also the men, leaving the natural use of the woman, burned in their lust one toward another; men with men working that which is unseemly, and receiving in themselves that recompence of their error which was meet.

28 And even as they did not like to retain God in *their* knowledge, God gave them over to a reprobate mind, to do those things which are not convenient;

29 Being filled with all unrighteousness, fornication, wickedness, covetousness, maliciousness; full of envy, murder, debate, deceit, malignity; whisperers,

30 Backbiters, haters of God, despiteful, proud, boasters, inventors of evil things, disobedient to parents,

31 Without understanding, covenantbreakers, without natural affection, implacable, unmerciful:

32 Who knowing the judgment of God, that they which commit such things are worthy of death, not only do the same, but have pleasure in them that do them.

B The Condemnation of the Moralist, 2:1–16

2 Therefore thou art inexcusable, O man, whosoever thou art that judgest: for wherein thou judgest another, thou condemnest thyself; for thou that judgest doest the same things.

2 But we are sure that the judgment of God is according to truth against them which commit such things.

3 And thinkest thou this, O man, that judgest them which do such things, and doest the same, that thou shalt escape the judgment of God?

4 Or despisest thou the riches of his goodness and forbearance and longsuffering; not knowing that the goodness of God leadeth thee to repentance?

5 But after thy hardness and impenitent heart treasurest

1:28 *not convenient* = improper.
1:32 *have pleasure in them that do them.* Not only did the people sin themselves, but they received a vicarious satisfaction in the sins of others.
2:1 Paul now shows that the Jews are defenseless, first subtly (vv. 1–16), then openly.
2:4 *despisest* = entertain wrong ideas about. Grace rejected brings *wrath* (v. 5).

up unto thyself wrath against the day of wrath and revelation of the righteous judgment of God;

6 Who will render to every man according to his deeds:

7 To them who by patient continuance in well doing seek for glory and honour and immortality, eternal life:

8 But unto them that are contentious, and do not obey the truth, but obey unrighteousness, indignation and wrath,

9 Tribulation and anguish, upon every soul of man that doeth evil, of the Jew first, and also of the Gentile;

10 But glory, honour, and peace, to every man that worketh good, to the Jew first, and also to the Gentile:

11 For there is no respect of persons with God.

12 For as many as have sinned without law shall also perish without law: and as many as have sinned in the law shall be judged by the law;

13 (For not the hearers of the law *are* just before God, but the doers of the law shall be justified.

14 For when the Gentiles, which have not the law, do by nature the things contained in the law, these, having not the law, are a law unto themselves:

15 Which shew the work of the law written in their hearts, their conscience also bearing witness, and *their* thoughts the mean while accusing or else excusing one another;)

16 In the day when God shall judge the secrets of men by Jesus Christ according to my gospel.

C The Condemnation of the Jew, 2:17–3:8

1 *He did not keep the law of God*, 2:17–29

17 Behold, thou art called a Jew, and restest in the law, and makest thy boast of God,

2:7 *eternal life.* Good works do not save (Eph. 2:8–9) but are the proof of a changed life. Much of Romans is devoted to this thesis.

2:9–10 *the Jew first.* The Jews' priority of privilege was also one of responsibility, but the principles of God's judgment are the same for all (v. 11).

2:12 *without law.* I.e., Gentiles to whom the Mosaic law had not been given (9:4).

2:14 *by nature*=instinctively. The interaction of conscience and innate morality may result in a good life. To such persons God sends the gospel (Acts 4:12; 10:4).

2:17 *thou art called a Jew.* The failure of the Jew is culpable because of privileges he had in the law and the promises of God. He could have become a *guide* and *light* of those in darkness (v. 19).

18 And knowest *his* will, and approvest the things that are more excellent, being instructed out of the law;

19 And art confident that thou thyself art a guide of the blind, a light of them which are in darkness,

20 An instructor of the foolish, a teacher of babes, which hast the form of knowledge and of the truth in the law.

21 Thou therefore which teachest another, teachest thou not thyself? thou that preachest a man should not steal, dost thou steal?

22 Thou that sayest a man should not commit adultery, dost thou commit adultery? thou that abhorrest idols, dost thou commit sacrilege?

23 Thou that makest thy boast of the law, through breaking the law dishonourest thou God?

24 For the name of God is blasphemed among the Gentiles through you, as it is written.

25 For circumcision verily profiteth, if thou keep the law: but if thou be a breaker of the law, thy circumcision is made uncircumcision.

26 Therefore if the uncircumcision keep the righteousness of the law, shall not his uncircumcision be counted for circumcision?

27 And shall not uncircumcision which is by nature, if it fulfil the law, judge thee, who by the letter and circumcision dost transgress the law?

28 For he is not a Jew, which is one outwardly; neither *is that* circumcision, which is outward in the flesh:

29 But he *is* a Jew, which is one inwardly; and circumcision *is that* of the heart, in the spirit, *and* not in the letter; whose praise *is* not of men, but of God.

2 He did not believe the promises of God, 3:1–8

3 What advantage then hath the Jew? or what profit *is there* of circumcision?

2:24 See Isa. 52:5; Ezek. 36:21–23.

2:25 *thy circumcision is made uncircumcision.* I.e., a Jewish lawbreaker stands before God in the same place as a pagan, and Paul emphasizes that the Jewish law was impossible to keep.

2:29 *circumcision is that of the heart.* Circumcision is used in three senses in this passage: (1) it stands for the Jews (note that *uncircumcision* in v. 27 means Gentiles; see also Gen. 17:10); (2) it indicates the physical rite commanded in the law (v. 25a and Lev. 12:3); (3) it represents a life that is separated from the flesh and unto God (v. 27 and Deut. 10:16). See note at Acts 16:3.

3:1 *advantage.* The Jew did have the advantage of special revela-

2 Much every way: chiefly, because that unto them were committed the oracles of God.

3 For what if some did not believe? shall their unbelief make the faith of God without effect?

4 God forbid: yea, let God be true, but every man a liar; as it is written, That thou mightest be justified in thy sayings, and mightest overcome when thou art judged.

5 But if our unrighteousness commend the righteousness of God, what shall we say? Is God unrighteous who taketh vengeance? (I speak as a man)

6 God forbid: for then how shall God judge the world?

7 For if the truth of God hath more abounded through my lie unto his glory; why yet am I also judged as a sinner?

8 And not *rather*, (as we be slanderously reported, and as some affirm that we say,) Let us do evil, that good may come? whose damnation is just.

D The Condemnation of All Men, 3:9–20

9 What then? are we better *than they*? No, in no wise: for we have before proved both Jews and Gentiles, that they are all under sin;

10 As it is written, There is none righteous, no, not one:

11 There is none that understandeth, there is none that seeketh after God.

12 They are all gone out of the way, they are together become unprofitable; there is none that doeth good, no, not one.

13 Their throat *is* an open sepulchre; with their tongues they have used deceit; the poison of asps *is* under their lips:

14 Whose mouth *is* full of cursing and bitterness:

15 Their feet *are* swift to shed blood:

16 Destruction and misery *are* in their ways:

tion; yet this cannot save him, for he has not kept it. The law increases his responsibility, and deepens his despair.

3:2 *the oracles of God*=the promises of God to the Jews, found in the Scriptures.

3:3 *the faith of God*=the faithfulness of God.

3:4 *but every man a liar.* Believe that all men have broken their word rather than that God has broken His. See Ps. 51:4.

3:5 Does God use man's sin to glorify Himself? No, otherwise He would have to abandon all judgment.

3:9 *are we better than they?* Possibly this should be translated, "Are we Jews disadvantaged?" i.e., in a worse position than Gentiles.

3:10–18 In these verses Paul quotes and paraphrases Ps. 5:9; 10:7; 14:1–3; 36:1; 140:3; Isa. 59:7–8. This indictment of the Jews has the authority of scripture behind it.

17 And the way of peace have they not known:

18 There is no fear of God before their eyes.

19 Now we know that what things soever the law saith, it saith to them who are under the law: that every mouth may be stopped, and all the world may become guilty before God.

20 Therefore by the deeds of the law there shall no flesh be justified in his sight: for by the law *is* the knowledge of sin.

III RIGHTEOUSNESS IMPUTED: JUSTIFICATION, SALVATION, 3:21–5:21

A The Description of Righteousness, 3:21–31

21 But now the righteousness of God without the law is manifested, being witnessed by the law and the prophets:

22 Even the righteousness of God *which is* by faith of Jesus Christ unto all and upon all them that believe: for there is no difference:

23 For all have sinned, and come short of the glory of God;

24 Being justified freely by his grace through the redemption that is in Christ Jesus:

25 Whom God hath set forth *to be* a propitiation

3:20 The function of the law, Paul says, is to give knowledge of or about sin, but not to save one from sin (Acts 13:39; 1 Tim. 1:9–10).

3:21 *righteousness.* Used in various relationships in the Bible, righteousness refers: (1) to God's character (John 17:25); (2) to the gift which is given to every one who receives Christ (here and 5:17); and (3) to standards of right living (6:18; 2 Tim. 2:22).

3:23 *all have sinned.* Sin is defined in 1 John 3:4 as lawlessness, and here as lack of conformity to the *glory of God.* These are complementary ideas, since the law of God is an expression of His character.

3:24 *justified.* Justification is a legal term meaning to secure a favorable verdict, to acquit, to vindicate, to declare someone righteous (Deut. 25:1). It is an act of God (8:33), who takes the initiative and provides the means *through the redemption that is in Christ Jesus.* The sinner who believes in Christ receives God's gift of righteousness (5:17), which then enables God to pronounce him righteous, and that is justification. On *redemption* see the note at Eph. 1:7.

3:25 *propitiation.* Here this may mean the "place of propitiation"; i.e., the mercy seat (as in Heb. 9:5). Christ is pictured

through faith in his blood, to declare his righteousness for the remission of sins that are past, through the forbearance of God;

26 To declare, *I say*, at this time his righteousness: that he might be just, and the justifier of him which believeth in Jesus.

27 Where *is* boasting then? It is excluded. By what law? of works? Nay: but by the law of faith.

28 Therefore we conclude that a man is justified by faith without the deeds of the law.

29 *Is he* the God of the Jews only? *is he* not also of the Gentiles? Yes, of the Gentiles also:

30 Seeing *it is* one God, which shall justify the circumcision by faith, and uncircumcision through faith.

31 Do we then make void the law through faith? God forbid: yea, we establish the law.

B The Illustration of Righteousness, 4:1–25

1 *Abraham's faith was apart from works, 4:1–8*

4 What shall we say then that Abraham our father, as pertaining to the flesh, hath found?

2 For if Abraham were justified by works, he hath *whereof* to glory; but not before God.

3 For what saith the scripture? Abraham believed God, and it was counted unto him for righteousness.

4 Now to him that worketh is the reward not reckoned of grace, but of debt.

5 But to him that worketh not, but believeth on him that justifieth the ungodly, his faith is counted for righteousness.

as the mercy seat where God's holy demands were satisfied (Lev. 16:14). See note at Heb. 2:17. *sins that are past.* The death of Christ also paid for sins committed before He died.

3:26 *that he might be just, and the justifier of him which believeth in Jesus.* Because of the death of Christ, God can remain just when declaring righteous the one who believes in Jesus and who is thus forgiven of his sins.

3:31 *we establish the law.* The role of the law in making men conscious of sin (v. 20) is confirmed by everyone who acknowledges sin and turns to Christ in faith.

4:1 Paul's point in this chapter is that the faith-righteousness principle is not something new, and he uses Abraham as proof.

4:3 See Gen. 15:6. Abraham was justified by faith and not by works.

4:4 Wages have nothing to do with *grace* (unmerited favor) but with what is due.

6 Even as David also describeth the blessedness of the man, unto whom God imputeth righteousness without works,

7 *Saying,* Blessed *are* they whose iniquities are forgiven, and whose sins are covered.

8 Blessed *is* the man to whom the Lord will not impute sin.

2 *Abraham's faith was apart from circumcision,* 4:9–12

9 *Cometh* this blessedness then upon the circumcision *only,* or upon the uncircumcision also? for we say that faith was reckoned to Abraham for righteousness.

10 How was it then reckoned? when he was in circumcision, or in uncircumcision? Not in circumcision, but in uncircumcision.

11 And he received the sign of circumcision, a seal of the righteousness of the faith which *he had yet* being uncircumcised: that he might be the father of all them that believe, though they be not circumcised; that righteousness might be imputed unto them also:

12 And the father of circumcision to them who are not of the circumcision only, but who also walk in the steps of that faith of our father Abraham, which *he had* being *yet* uncircumcised.

3 *Abraham's faith was apart from the law,* 4:13–15

13 For the promise, that he should be the heir of the world, *was* not to Abraham, or to his seed, through the law, but through the righteousness of faith.

14 For if they which are of the law *be* heirs, faith is made void, and the promise made of none effect:

15 Because the law worketh wrath: for where no law is, *there is* no transgression.

4 *Abraham's faith was in God,* 4:16–25

16 Therefore *it is* of faith, that *it might be* by grace; to the end the promise might be sure to all the seed; not to

4:7 See Ps. 32:1–2.
4:9–25 The points Paul makes from the illustrations are these: (1) justification did not come to Abraham by faith plus circumcision (vv. 9–12); (2) justification was not by faith plus keeping the law (vv. 13–17); (3) justification was by faith alone (vv. 18–25).
4:10 Abraham's acceptance with God on the basis of faith preceded his circumcision (Gen. 15 is before Gen. 17).

that only which is of the law, but to that also which is of the faith of Abraham; who is the father of us all,

17 (As it is written, I have made thee a father of many nations,) before him whom he believed, *even* God, who quickeneth the dead, and calleth those things which be not as though they were.

18 Who against hope believed in hope, that he might become the father of many nations, according to that which was spoken, So shall thy seed be.

19 And being not weak in faith, he considered not his own body now dead, when he was about an hundred years old, neither yet the deadness of Sara's womb:

20 He staggered not at the promise of God through unbelief; but was strong in faith, giving glory to God;

21 And being fully persuaded that, what he had promised, he was able also to perform.

22 And therefore it was imputed to him for righteousness.

23 Now it was not written for his sake alone, that it was imputed to him;

24 But for us also, to whom it shall be imputed, if we believe on him that raised up Jesus our Lord from the dead;

25 Who was delivered for our offences, and was raised again for our justification.

C The Benefits of Righteousness, 5:1–11

5 Therefore being justified by faith, we have peace with God through our Lord Jesus Christ:

2 By whom also we have access by faith into this grace wherein we stand, and rejoice in hope of the glory of God.

3 And not only *so*, but we glory in tribulations also: knowing that tribulation worketh patience;

4:17 See Gen. 17:5.
4:18 See Gen. 15:5.
4:19 *not* is omitted by some manuscripts. Abraham fully faced the difficulty, yet he believed God.
4:24 Christian faith is faith in the Giver of miraculous life, demonstrated in the resurrection of Jesus.
4:25 *for our justification.* Christ's resurrection was because of our justification; i.e., as a proof of God's acceptance of His sacrifice.
5:1–11 For Paul justification is no sterile doctrine, but a source of blessing in one's life. *we have* (v. 1). Some manuscripts read "let us have."
5:2 *rejoice in hope of the glory of God.* Better, we boast in the hope of the glory which God will manifest.
5:3 *patience*=endurance.

4 And patience, experience; and experience, hope:

5 And hope maketh not ashamed; because the love of God is shed abroad in our hearts by the Holy Ghost which is given unto us.

6 For when we were yet without strength, in due time Christ died for the ungodly.

7 For scarcely for a righteous man will one die: yet peradventure for a good man some would even dare to die.

8 But God commendeth his love toward us, in that, while we were yet sinners, Christ died for us.

9 Much more then, being now justified by his blood, we shall be saved from wrath through him.

10 For if, when we were enemies, we were reconciled to God by the death of his Son, much more, being reconciled, we shall be saved by his life.

11 And not only so, but we also joy in God through our Lord Jesus Christ, by whom we have now received the atonement.

D The Applicability of Righteousness, 5:12-21

12 Wherefore, as by one man sin entered into the world, and death by sin; and so death passed upon all men, for that all have sinned:

5:5 *maketh not ashamed*=does not disappoint or deceive.

5:6-8 The extent of God's love is shown in the fact that Christ died for men in whom there was nothing that evoked that love.

5:6 *without strength*=weak (morally).

5:8 *commendeth.* I.e., shows or proves.

5:9 *Much more.* Note the repetition of this phrase in vv. 10, 15, 17, 20. Paul is teaching the vicariously sacrificial significance of Christ's death.

5:10 *we shall be saved by his life.* Christ's present resurrection ministry in heaven keeps us saved (Heb. 7:25).

5:11 *the atonement.* Lit., the reconciliation. The word "atonement" is exclusively an O.T. word, though theologically it has come to stand for the total significance of Christ's death. On reconciliation see note at 2 Cor. 5:18.

5:12-21 In the closely worded argument of this section Paul contrasts death in Adam with life in Christ. Just as Adam's sin brought certain results, so did the death of Christ. Yet this does not mean automatic salvation, for men must receive the *grace* God offers (v. 17).

5:12 *as by one man sin entered into the world.* After Adam sinned he could only beget sinners, so that all men are under the sentence of death, the penalty of sin. *all have sinned.* This is true because of the solidarity of the race (see Heb. 7:9-10).

13 (For until the law sin was in the world: but sin is not imputed when there is no law.

14 Nevertheless death reigned from Adam to Moses, even over them that had not sinned after the similitude of Adam's transgression, who is the figure of him that was to come.

15 But not as the offence, so also *is* the free gift. For if through the offence of one many be dead, much more the grace of God, and the gift by grace, *which is* by one man, Jesus Christ, hath abounded unto many.

16 And not as *it was* by one that sinned, *so is* the gift: for the judgment *was* by one to condemnation, but the free gift *is* of many offences unto justification.

17 For if by one man's offence death reigned by one; much more they which receive abundance of grace and of the gift of righteousness shall reign in life by one, Jesus Christ.)

18 Therefore as by the offence of one *judgment came* upon all men to condemnation; even so by the righteousness of one *the free gift came* upon all men unto justification of life.

19 For as by one man's disobedience many were made sinners, so by the obedience of one shall many be made righteous.

20 Moreover the law entered, that the offence might abound. But where sin abounded, grace did much more abound:

21 That as sin hath reigned unto death, even so might grace reign through righteousness unto eternal life by Jesus Christ our Lord.

5:13 *sin is not imputed.* I.e., sin is not charged as a specific violation of a particular command *when there is no law.* However, this does not mean that sin was not sin during the period from Adam to Moses, as proved by the fact of death during that period (v. 14).

5:18 Notice here and often in this passage the contrast between Adam and Christ, their deeds, and the results of those deeds. The contrast loses meaning if Adam were not an historical person.

IV RIGHTEOUSNESS IMPARTED;
SANCTIFICATION, SEPARATION, 6:1–8:39

A The Principles of
Sanctification; The Question of License, 6:1–23

1 *Shall we continue in sin?* 6:1–14

6 What shall we say then? Shall we continue in sin, that
grace may abound?

2 God forbid. How shall we, that are dead to sin, live
any longer therein?

3 Know ye not, that so many of us as were baptized
into Jesus Christ were baptized into his death?

4 Therefore we are buried with him by baptism into
death: that like as Christ was raised up from the dead by
the glory of the Father, even so we also should walk in
newness of life.

5 For if we have been planted together in the likeness
of his death, we shall be also *in the likeness* of *his* resurrection:

6 Knowing this, that our old man is crucified with *him*,
that the body of sin might be destroyed, that henceforth
we should not serve sin.

7 For he that is dead is freed from sin.

6:1 If grace abounds in the presence of sin (5:20), then shouldn't
we continue in sin, that grace may abound?

6:2 *God forbid*=by no means. Grace cannot be exploited for
evil ends! Because of our union with Christ we are *dead to
sin* and *alive unto God* (v. 11). The new moral life is based
on: (1) our union with Christ, 6:1–14); (2) our being slaves
to righteousness (6:15–23); and (3) the new marriage union
we have with Christ (7:1–6). *dead to sin.* Death is separation, not extinction. (1) Physical death is the separation of
body from spirit (Jas. 2:26). (2) Spiritual death is the separation of a person from God (Eph. 2:1). (3) The second death
is eternal separation from God (Rev. 20:14). (4) Death to
sin is separation from the ruling power of sin in one's life
(6:14).

6:3 *baptized into Jesus Christ.* Baptism with the Holy Spirit
joins the believer to Christ, separating him from the old life
and associating him with the new. He is no longer "in Adam"
but is "in Christ." Water baptism reminds us of this truth.

6:6 *old man.* I.e., our "old self"—all that a person is before
salvation which is made "old" by reason of the presence of
the new life in Christ. *destroyed;* i.e., made ineffective or
impotent (as in 2 Thess. 2:8).

8 Now if we be dead with Christ, we believe that we shall also live with him:

9 Knowing that Christ being raised from the dead dieth no more; death hath no more dominion over him.

10 For in that he died, he died unto sin once: but in that he liveth, he liveth unto God.

11 Likewise reckon ye also yourselves to be dead indeed unto sin, but alive unto God through Jesus Christ our Lord.

12 Let not sin therefore reign in your mortal body, that ye should obey it in the lusts thereof.

13 Neither yield ye your members *as* instruments of unrighteousness unto sin: but yield yourselves unto God, as those that are alive from the dead, and your members *as* instruments of righteousness unto God.

14 For sin shall not have dominion over you: for ye are not under the law, but under grace.

2 *Shall we continue to sin?* 6:15–23

15 What then? shall we sin, because we are not under the law, but under grace? God forbid.

16 Know ye not, that to whom ye yield yourselves servants to obey, his servants ye are to whom ye obey; whether of sin unto death, or of obedience unto righteousness?

17 But God be thanked, that ye were the servants of sin, but ye have obeyed from the heart that form of doctrine which was delivered you.

18 Being then made free from sin, ye became the servants of righteousness.

19 I speak after the manner of men because of the infirmity of your flesh: for as ye have yielded your members servants to uncleanness and to iniquity unto iniquity; even so now yield your members servants to righteousness unto holiness.

6:11 *reckon.* This means "calculate," i.e., by adding up the facts presented in vv. 1–10 and then acting accordingly.

6:12 We must either dethrone sin or obey its evil desires.

6:13 *Neither yield ye your members . . . but yield yourselves unto God.* The tenses may imply "stop yielding your members" . . . "but yield yourselves once for all unto God."

6:15–23 This passage is the ethical application of 5:12–21. When we were in Adam sin was the master, demanding shameful living and repaying with death. In Christ we may be slaves of righteousness.

6:17 *that form of doctrine*=Christian truth.

6:19 Paul uses the illustration of slaves and masters because of their dullness of understanding.

20 For when ye were the servants of sin, ye were free from righteousness.

21 What fruit had ye then in those things whereof ye are now ashamed? for the end of those things *is* death.

22 But now being made free from sin, and become servants to God, ye have your fruit unto holiness, and the end everlasting life.

23 For the wages of sin *is* death; but the gift of God *is* eternal life through Jesus Christ our Lord.

B The Practice of Sanctification; The Question of Law, 7:1–25

1 *Is the believer under law?* 7:1–6

7 Know ye not, brethren, (for I speak to them that know the law,) how that the law hath dominion over a man as long as he liveth?

2 For the woman which hath an husband is bound by the law to *her* husband so long as he liveth; but if the husband be dead, she is loosed from the law of *her* husband.

3 So then if, while *her* husband liveth, she be married to another man, she shall be called an adulteress: but if her husband be dead, she is free from that law; so that she is no adulteress, though she be married to another man.

4 Wherefore, my brethren, ye also are become dead to the law by the body of Christ; that ye should be married to another, *even* to him who is raised from the dead, that we should bring forth fruit unto God.

5 For when we were in the flesh, the motions of sins, which were by the law, did work in our members to bring forth fruit unto death.

6 But now we are delivered from the law, that being

6:21 *then*. I.e., when you were slaves to sin what fruit did you have?

6:23 *the gift of God*. Sanctification of life does not earn one eternal life; it is still God's gift.

7:1–6 Paul here introduces a new metaphor, that of a fruitful marriage. The Christian because of his death with Christ is free from the law and brought into a new marriage with Christ. This new union demands good living as its progeny.

7:1 *know the law*. Legal principles, not the Mosaic law here.

7:4 The believer who has died with Christ is released from the bondage of the law and hence to sin, and is free to experience the abundant life of Christ.

7:5 *when we were in the flesh*. I.e., before we were saved.

dead wherein we were held; that we should serve in newness of spirit, and not *in* the oldness of the letter.

2 *Is the law an evil thing?* 7:7–12

7 What shall we say then? *Is* the law sin? God forbid. Nay, I had not known sin, but by the law: for I had not known lust, except the law had said, Thou shalt not covet.

8 But sin, taking occasion by the commandment, wrought in me all manner of concupiscence. For without the law sin *was* dead.

9 For I was alive without the law once: but when the commandment came, sin revived, and I died.

10 And the commandment, which *was ordained* to life, I found *to be* unto death.

11 For sin, taking occasion by the commandment, deceived me, and by it slew *me*.

12 Wherefore the law *is* holy, and the commandment holy, and just, and good.

3 *Is the law a cause of death?* 7:13–14

13 Was then that which is good made death unto me? God forbid. But sin, that it might appear sin, working death in me by that which is good; that sin by the commandment might become exceeding sinful.

14 For we know that the law is spiritual: but I am carnal, sold under sin.

4 *How can I resolve the struggle within my being?* 7:15–25

15 For that which I do, I allow not: for what I would, that do I not; but what I hate, that do I.

16 If then I do that which I would not, I consent unto the law that *it is* good.

17 Now then it is no more I that do it, but sin that dwelleth in me.

7:8 *concupiscence*=lust (same word as in v. 7).

7:9 When Paul understood the true meaning of the law, he realized that he was a sinner and worthy of death.

7:12 The law is fundamentally good, but the result of the law is to bring into the open the power of sin. It is sin that deceives and kills (v. 11).

7:15–25 The intensely personal character of these verses seems to indicate that this was probably Paul's own experience as a believer. This is his diagnosis of what happens when one tries to be sanctified by keeping the law.

7:17 *sin that dwelleth in me*. Though Paul has written of acts

18 For I know that in me (that is, in my flesh,) dwelleth no good thing: for to will is present with me; but *how* to perform that which is good I find not.

19 For the good that I would I do not: but the evil which I would not, that I do.

20 Now if I do that I would not, it is no more I that do it, but sin that dwelleth in me.

21 I find then a law, that, when I would do good, evil is present with me.

22 For I delight in the law of God after the inward man:

23 But I see another law in my members, warring against the law of my mind, and bringing me into captivity to the law of sin which is in my members.

24 O wretched man that I am! who shall deliver me from the body of this death?

25 I thank God through Jesus Christ our Lord. So then with the mind I myself serve the law of God; but with the flesh the law of sin.

C The Power of Sanctification; The Question of Living, 8:1–39

1 *Emancipated living,* 8:1–11

8 *There is* therefore now no condemnation to them which are in Christ Jesus, who walk not after the flesh, but after the Spirit.

2 For the law of the Spirit of life in Christ Jesus hath made me free from the law of sin and death.

3 For what the law could not do, in that it was weak

of sin in 1:21–32, here he speaks of sin as something deep in a man's life which produces those acts.

7:18 *flesh*. Paul uses flesh in several ways. (1) It denotes the personality of man controlled by sin and directed to selfish pursuits rather than the service of God (here; v. 25; 8:5–7; Gal. 5:17). (2) It sometimes refers simply to physical descent (1:3; 9:3). (3) It also stands for the physical existence of a person; i.e., being in the body, and there is no blame attached to this significance of the word (Eph. 2:15; Philem. 16).

7:24 The *body* dominated by sin endures a living *death*.

8:1 *who walk not after the flesh, but after the Spirit*. This phrase is not in the best manuscripts.

8:2 *the law of the Spirit of life*. The working of the Holy Spirit in the life of a believer is regular (like a *law*) but not mechanical (for it is *life*).

8:3 *in the likeness of sinful flesh*. The word "likeness" is crucial, for it indicates that Jesus was a true man but not a sinful man. *flesh*=body.

through the flesh, God sending his own Son in the likeness of sinful flesh, and for sin, condemned sin in the flesh:

4 That the righteousness of the law might be fulfilled in us, who walk not after the flesh, but after the Spirit.

5 For they that are after the flesh do mind the things of the flesh; but they that are after the Spirit the things of the Spirit.

6 For to be carnally minded *is* death; but to be spiritually minded *is* life and peace.

7 Because the carnal mind *is* enmity against God: for it is not subject to the law of God, neither indeed can be.

8 So then they that are in the flesh cannot please God.

9 But ye are not in the flesh, but in the Spirit, if so be that the Spirit of God dwell in you. Now if any man have not the Spirit of Christ, he is none of his.

10 And if Christ *be* in you, the body *is* dead because of sin; but the Spirit *is* life because of righteousness.

11 But if the Spirit of him that raised up Jesus from the dead dwell in you, he that raised up Christ from the dead shall also quicken your mortal bodies by his Spirit that dwelleth in you.

2 *Exalted living,* 8:12–17

12 Therefore, brethren, we are debtors, not to the flesh, to live after the flesh.

13 For if ye live after the flesh, ye shall die: but if ye through the Spirit do mortify the deeds of the body, ye shall live.

14 For as many as are led by the Spirit of God, they are the sons of God.

15 For ye have not received the spirit of bondage again to fear; but ye have received the Spirit of adoption, whereby we cry, Abba, Father.

8:4–8 The contrast here is between a life dominated by the flesh (=sinful nature within) and one controlled by the Holy Spirit.

8:9 *if so be*=since. There is no doubt in the statement; those who belong to Christ have the Holy Spirit.

8:13 *mortify*=put to death; i.e., separate from the deeds of the body (see Col. 3:5).

8:15 *adoption.* The act of God which places the believer in His family as an adult son (v. 23; 9:4; Gal. 4:5; Eph. 1:5). At the same time he is born into the family of God as a child who needs to grow and develop. His position is one of full privilege; his practice involves growth in grace. *Abba.* Aramaic for father.

16 The Spirit itself beareth witness with our spirit, that we are the children of God:

17 And if children, then heirs; heirs of God, and joint-heirs with Christ; if so be that we suffer with *him*, that we may be also glorified together.

3 *Expectant living*, 8:18–30

18 For I reckon that the sufferings of this present time *are* not worthy *to be compared* with the glory which shall be revealed in us.

19 For the earnest expectation of the creature waiteth for the manifestation of the sons of God.

20 For the creature was made subject to vanity, not willingly, but by reason of him who hath subjected *the same* in hope.

21 Because the creature itself also shall be delivered from the bondage of corruption into the glorious liberty of the children of God.

22 For we know that the whole creation groaneth and travaileth in pain together until now.

23 And not only *they*, but ourselves also, which have the firstfruits of the Spirit, even we ourselves groan within ourselves, waiting for the adoption, *to wit*, the redemption of our body.

24 For we are saved by hope: but hope that is seen is not hope: for what a man seeth, why doth he yet hope for?

25 But if we hope for that we see not, *then* do we with patience wait for *it*.

26 Likewise the Spirit also helpeth our infirmities: for

8:18–25 Here is a statement of the Christian hope as it affects the individual (v. 18) and the entire creation (vv. 19–25). Compare 2 Cor. 4:17.

8:19 *the creatures*=the whole creation, also in vv. 20–21.

8:20 *was made subject to vanity.* After Adam sinned, God was obliged to subject the creation to futility so that man in his sinful state might retain some measure of dominion over creation. Nature was involved for evil in man's fall; she will be emancipated when man receives the adoption as sons (v. 23).

8:23 The culmination of our position as adopted sons is the resurrection state.

8:24 *by hope.* I.e., in the just-expressed hope (vv. 21–23) of the future redemption of the body.

8:26 The Holy Spirit helps our *infirmities* (our inability to pray intelligently about situations) by praying with unutterable *groanings* (=sighs). Such intercession is in accord with God's will (v. 27).

we know not what we should pray for as we ought: but the Spirit itself maketh intercession for us with groanings which cannot be uttered.

27 And he that searcheth the hearts knoweth what *is* the mind of the Spirit, because he maketh intercession for the saints according to *the will of* God.

28 And we know that all things work together for good to them that love God, to them who are the called according to *his* purpose.

29 For whom he did foreknow, he also did predestinate *to be* conformed to the image of his Son, that he might be the firstborn among many brethren.

30 Moreover whom he did predestinate, them he also called: and whom he called, them he also justified: and whom he justified, them he also glorified.

4 *Exultant living*, 8:31–39

31 What shall we then say to these things? If God *be* for us, who *can be* against us?

32 He that spared not his own Son, but delivered him up for us all, how shall he not with him also freely give us all things?

33 Who shall lay any thing to the charge of God's elect? *It is* God that justifieth.

34 Who *is* he that condemneth? *It is* Christ that died, yea rather, that is risen again, who is even at the right hand of God, who also maketh intercession for us.

35 Who shall separate us from the love of Christ? *shall* tribulation, or distress, or persecution, or famine, or nakedness, or peril, or sword?

36 As it is written, For thy sake we are killed all the day long; we are accounted as sheep for the slaughter.

37 Nay, in all these things we are more than conquerors through him that loved us.

8:28 This promise is only for those *that love God.*
8:29 *predestinate.* See note at Eph. 1:5. The destiny of the elect is to be conformed to Christ.
8:30 *called.* See note at 1:6. *justified.* See note at 3:24. *glorified.* The tense of this word shows that our future glorification is so certain that it can be said to be done. Those who were foreknown will all be glorified without loss of a single one.
8:33–34 God has declared us righteous, so He will not condemn us, and Christ died, rose, and lives for us, so He will not either.
8:36 See Ps. 44:22. Difficulties are not necessarily obstacles for God's children, but His appointed way.

38 For I am persuaded, that neither death, nor life, nor angels, nor principalities, nor powers, nor things present, nor things to come,

39 Nor height, nor depth, nor any other creature, shall be able to separate us from the love of God, which is in Christ Jesus our Lord.

V RIGHTEOUSNESS VINDICATED; DISPENSATION, SOVEREIGNTY, 9:1–11:36

A Israel's Past; Election, 9:1–29

1 *Paul's sorrow*, 9:1–5

9 I say the truth in Christ, I lie not, my conscience also bearing me witness in the Holy Ghost,

2 That I have great heaviness and continual sorrow in my heart.

3 For I could wish that myself were accursed from Christ for my brethren, my kinsmen according to the flesh:

4 Who are Israelites; to whom *pertaineth* the adoption, and the glory, and the covenants, and the giving of the law, and the service *of God*, and the promises;

5 Whose *are* the fathers, and of whom as concerning the flesh Christ *came*, who is over all, God blessed for ever. Amen.

2 *God's sovereignty*, 9:6–29

6 Not as though the word of God hath taken none effect. For they *are* not all Israel, which are of Israel:

8:39 *nor any other creature.* Nothing in the universe is not under God's control; therefore, nothing can separate us from His love.

9:1 Here begins Paul's discussion of perplexing questions about the Jewish people. Why were they refusing the gospel? How does this new scheme of righteousness apart from the law relate to the privileged position of the Jews? Have the promises contained in their covenants failed?

9:4–5 The privileges of the Jewish people included adoption as a nation (Ex. 4:22), glory (Ex. 16:10), covenants (Eph. 2:12), the Mosaic law, service in the tabernacle and temple, thousands of promises, the patriarchs, and Christ.

9:5 *who is over all . . . Amen.* Some regard these words as comprising a grammatically separate sentence, a doxology. Although early manuscripts were not punctuated, the punctuation in the text seems correct. Paul's anguish over the Jew's rejection of Christ drives him to avow his own recognition of Him as God. A doxology does not fit the train of thought here.

7 Neither, because they are the seed of Abraham, *are they* all children: but, In Isaac shall thy seed be called.

8 That is, They which are the children of the flesh, these *are* not the children of God: but the children of the promise are counted for the seed.

9 For this *is* the word of promise, At this time will I come, and Sara shall have a son.

10 And not only *this*; but when Rebecca also had conceived by one, *even* by our father Isaac;

11 (For *the children* being not yet born, neither having done any good or evil, that the purpose of God according to election might stand, not of works, but of him that calleth;)

12 It was said unto her, The elder shall serve the younger.

13 As it is written, Jacob have I loved, but Esau have I hated.

14 What shall we say then? *Is there* unrighteousness with God? God forbid.

15 For he saith to Moses, I will have mercy on whom I will have mercy, and I will have compassion on whom I will have compassion.

16 So then *it is* not of him that willeth, nor of him that runneth, but of God that sheweth mercy.

17 For the scripture saith unto Phār′aōh, Even for this same purpose have I raised thee up, that I might shew my power in thee, and that my name might be declared throughout all the earth.

18 Therefore hath he mercy on whom he will *have mercy*, and whom he will be hardeneth.

19 Thou wilt say then unto me, Why doth he yet find fault? For who hath resisted his will?

20 Nay but, O man, who art thou that repliest against God? Shall the thing formed say to him that formed *it*, Why hast thou made me thus?

9:9 See Gen. 18:10.
9:12 See Gen. 25:23.
9:13 See Mal. 1:2–3.
9:15 See Ex. 33:19. If God were not free to show His mercy, no one would be blessed, for no one deserves His grace, and it cannot be earned.
9:17 See Ex. 9:16.
9:19 An opponent might say that Paul's conclusion of v. 18 leads to fatalism. Paul does not give an analytical answer but rebukes the questioner for such a preposterous conclusion. If a potter can do what he wishes with his vessels, certainly God can with His.

21 Hath not the potter power over the clay, of the same lump to make one vessel unto honour, and another unto dishonour?

22 What if God, willing to shew *his* wrath, and to make his power known, endured with much longsuffering the vessels of wrath fitted to destruction:

23 And that he might make known the riches of his glory on the vessels of mercy, which he had afore prepared unto glory,

24 Even us, whom he hath called, not of the Jews only, but also of the Gentiles?

25 As he saith also in Ō'sĕe, I will call them my people, which were not my people; and her beloved, which was not beloved.

26 And it shall come to pass, *that* in the place where it was said unto them, Ye *are* not my people; there shall they be called the children of the living God.

27 Ēsāi'as also crieth concerning Israel, Though the number of the children of Israel be as the sand of the sea, a remnant shall be saved:

28 For he will finish the work, and cut *it* short in righteousness: because a short work will the Lord make upon the earth.

29 And as Ēsāi'as said before, Except the Lord of Sabā'ōth had left us a seed, we had been as Sod'oma, and been made like unto Gōmor'rha.

B Israel's Present; Rejection, 9:30–10:21

30 What shall we say then? That the Gentiles, which followed not after righteousness, have attained to righteousness, even the righteousness which is of faith.

31 But Israel, which followed after the law of righteousness, hath not attained to the law of righteousness.

32 Wherefore? Because *they sought it* not by faith, but as it were by the works of the law. For they stumbled at that stumblingstone;

33 As it is written, Behold, I lay in Sion a stumblingstone and rock of offence: and whosoever believeth on him shall not be ashamed.

9:25 See Hos. 1:9–10.
9:27 See Isa. 10:22–23.
9:29 See Isa. 1:9.
9:33 See Isa. 28:16. The stumbling-stone was Christ (1 Pet. 2:8).

10 Brethren, my heart's desire and prayer to God for Israel is, that they might be saved.

2 For I bear them record that they have a zeal of God, but not according to knowledge.

3 For they being ignorant of God's righteousness, and going about to establish their own righteousness, have not submitted themselves unto the righteousness of God.

4 For Christ *is* the end of the law for righteousness to every one that believeth.

5 For Moses describeth the righteousness which is of the law, That the man which doeth those things shall live by them.

6 But the righteousness which is of faith speaketh on this wise, Say not in thine heart, Who shall ascend into heaven? (that is, to bring Christ down *from above*:)

7 Or, Who shall descend into the deep? (that is, to bring up Christ again from the dead.)

8 But what saith it? The word is nigh thee, *even* in thy mouth, and in thy heart: that is, the word of faith, which we preach;

9 That if thou shalt confess with thy mouth the Lord Jesus, and shalt believe in thine heart that God hath raised him from the dead, thou shalt be saved.

10 For with the heart man believeth unto righteousness; and with the mouth confession is made unto salvation.

11 For the scripture saith, Whosoever believeth on him shall not be ashamed.

12 For there is no difference between the Jew and the Greek: for the same Lord over all is rich unto all that call upon him.

10:1–21 Paul expresses his deep longing for the salvation of Israel (v. 1), who tried to substitute law-righteousness for faith-righteousness (vv. 2–4), though the latter was universally available (vv. 5–13). God gave the Jews every opportunity to receive the gospel but they have not responded in faith (vv. 14–21).

10:4 Christ is the termination of the law. It could not provide righteousness earned on merit, but Christ can through God's grace in response to faith (3:20; Acts 13:39).

10:6–8 Quoting Deut. 30:12–14, which emphasize the initiative of divine grace and humble reception of God's word. Paul applies this to the gospel which is *nigh* (near) ready for a man to take on his lips and into his heart (v. 9).

10:9 *the Lord Jesus.* Lord or Yahweh is the O.T. name for God; thus he who confesses that Jesus is Lord affirms His deity.

10:11 See Isa. 28:16; 49:23.

13 For whosoever shall call upon the name of the Lord shall be saved.

14 How then shall they call on him in whom they have not believed? and how shall they believe in him of whom they have not heard? and how shall they hear without a preacher?

15 And how shall they preach, except they be sent? as it is written, How beautiful are the feet of them that preach the gospel of peace, and bring glad tidings of good things!

16 But they have not all obeyed the gospel. For Ēsa'̄as saith, Lord, who hath believed our report?

17 So then faith *cometh* by hearing, and hearing by the word of God.

18 But I say, Have they not heard? Yes verily, their sound went into all the earth, and their words unto the ends of the world.

19 But I say, Did not Israel know? First Moses saith, I will provoke you to jealousy by *them that are* no people, *and* by a foolish nation I will anger you.

20 But Ēsa'̄as is very bold, and saith, I was found of them that sought me not; I was made manifest unto them that asked not after me.

21 But to Israel he saith, All day long I have stretched forth my hands unto a disobedient and gainsaying people.

C Israel's Future; Salvation, 11:1–36

1 *The extent of Israel's rejection (partial)*, 11:1–10

11 I say then, Hath God cast away his people? God forbid. For I also am an Israelite, of the seed of Abraham, of the tribe of Benjamin.

10:13 See Joel 2:32.
10:14–15 Though God's election of His people is of His own free choice and not based on human merit (9:11, 23), the elect are not saved without believing the message which is preached by those who are sent (Isa. 52:7).
10:16 See Isa. 53:1.
10:17 *by the word of God.* This is the word for the spoken word rather than the written Bible. Of course, our oral testimony (our preaching of Christ) is based on the Bible.
10:18 See Ps. 19:4.
10:19 See Deut. 32:21.
10:20 *gainsaying*=obstinate.
11:1–36 In this chapter Paul assures us that God has not forgotten His people, the Jews, and His promises to them. After the full number of Gentiles have been incorporated into the

2 God hath not cast away his people which he foreknew. Wot ye not what the scripture saith of Ēlī'as? how he maketh intercession to God against Israel, saying,

3 Lord, they have killed thy prophets, and digged down thine altars; and I am left alone, and they seek my life.

4 But what saith the answer of God unto him? I have reserved to myself seven thousand men, who have not bowed the knee to *the image of* Bā'al.

5 Even so then at this present time also there is a remnant according to the election of grace.

6 And if by grace, then *is it* no more of works: otherwise grace is no more grace. But if *it be* of works, then is it no more grace: otherwise work is no more work.

7 What then? Israel hath not obtained that which he seeketh for; but the election hath obtained it, and the rest were blinded

8 (According as it is writtten, God hath given them the spirit of slumber, eyes that they should not see, and ears that they should not hear;) unto this day.

9 And David saith, Let their table be made a snare, and a trap, and a stumblingblock, and a recompence unto them:

10 Let their eyes be darkened, that they may not see, and bow down their back alway.

2 *The purpose of Israel's rejection,* 11:11–24

11 I say then, Have they stumbled that they should fall? God forbid: but *rather* through their fall salvation *is come* unto the Gentiles, for to provoke them to jealousy.

12 Now if the fall of them *be* the riches of the world, and the diminishing of them the riches of the Gentiles; how much more their fulness?

13 For I speak to you Gentiles, inasmuch as I am the apostle of the Gentiles, I magnify mine office:

14 If by any means I may provoke to emulation *them which are* my flesh, and might save some of them.

15 For if the casting away of them *be* the reconciling of

church, all the Jews will turn to the Lord, not the mere handful as now. Paul does not assert that the O.T. promises to Israel have been transferred to the largely Gentile church.

11:1 *God forbid*=by no means.

11:3 See 1 Kings 19:10–18.

11:7 *the election.* I.e., the elect minority of Jews who are being saved today.

11:8 See Isa. 29:10.

11:9 See Ps. 69:22–23.

11:15 When Israel rejected Jesus Christ, the nation lost her

the world, what *shall* the receiving *of them be*, but life from the dead?

16 For if the firstfruit *be* holy, the lump *is* also *holy*: and if the root *be* holy, so *are* the branches.

17 And if some of the branches be broken off, and thou, being a wild olive tree, wert graffed in among them, and with them partakest of the root and fatness of the olive tree;

18 Boast not against the branches. But if thou boast, thou bearest not the root, but the root thee.

19 Thou wilt say then, The branches were broken off, that I might be graffed in.

20 Well; because of unbelief they were broken off, and thou standest by faith. Be not highminded, but fear:

21 For if God spared not the natural branches, *take heed* lest he also spare not thee.

22 Behold therefore the goodness and severity of God: on them which fell, severity; but toward thee, goodness, if thou continue in *his* goodness: otherwise thou also shalt be cut off.

23 And they also, if they abide not still in unbelief, shall be graffed in: for God is able to graff them in again.

24 For if thou wert cut out of the olive tree which is wild by nature, and wert graffed contrary to nature into a good olive tree: how much more shall these, which be the natural *branches*, be graffed into their own olive tree?

3 The duration of
Israel's rejection (temporary), 11:25–32

25 For I would not, brethren, that ye should be ignorant of this mystery, lest ye should be wise in your own conceits; that blindness in part is happened to Israel, until the fulness of the Gentiles be come in.

favored position before God, and the gospel was preached to Gentiles, so that hopefully the Jews would become jealous and be saved (v. 11). But the casting off is only temporary. When the Lord returns, the Jewish people will be regathered, judged, restored to favor, and redeemed (v. 26).

11:17–24 The olive tree is the place of privilege which was first occupied by the natural branches (the Jews). The wild branches are Gentiles who because of the unbelief of Israel now occupy the place of privilege. The root of the tree is the Abrahamic covenant which promised blessing to both Jew and Gentile through Christ.

11:25 *the fulness of the Gentiles.* I.e., the full number of Gentiles who will be saved (Acts 15:14). After this, God will

26 And so all Israel shall be saved: as it is written, There shall come out of Sion the Deliverer, and shall turn away ungodliness from Jacob:

27 For this *is* my covenant unto them, when I shall take away their sins.

28 As concerning the gospel, *they are* enemies for your sakes: but as touching the election, *they are* beloved for the fathers' sakes.

29 For the gifts and calling of God *are* without repentance.

30 For as ye in times past have not believed God, yet have now obtained mercy through their unbelief:

31 Even so have these also now not believed, that through your mercy they also may obtain mercy.

32 For God hath concluded them all in unbelief, that he might have mercy upon all.

4 Peroration on God's wisdom, 11:33–36

33 O the depth of the riches both of the wisdom and knowledge of God! how unsearchable *are* his judgments, and his ways past finding out!

34 For who hath known the mind of the Lord? or who hath been his counsellor?

35 Or who hath first given to him, and it shall be recompensed unto him again?

36 For of him, and through him, and to him, *are* all things: to whom *be* glory for ever. Amen.

VI RIGHTEOUSNESS PRACTICED; APPLICATION, SERVICE, 12:1–15:13

A In Relation to Ourselves, 12:1–2

12 I beseech you therefore, brethren, by the mercies of God, that ye present your bodies a living sacrifice, holy, acceptable unto God, *which is* your reasonable service.

---

turn again to the Jews and will save all those who are alive at the Lord's return (v. 26).

11:26 See Isa. 59:20–21.

11:32 *all . . . all*=Jews and Gentiles alike.

11:36 God is the source (*of him*), sustainer (*through him*), and goal (*to him*) of all things.

12:1 *by the mercies of God* which have been described in the preceding chapters. *reasonable service.* I.e., a service involving all of one's rational powers.

2 And be not conformed to this world: but be ye transformed by the renewing of your mind, that ye may prove what *is* that good, and acceptable, and perfect, will of God.

B In Relation to the Church, 12:3–8

3 For I say, through the grace given unto me, to every man that is among you, not to think *of himself* more highly than he ought to think; but to think soberly, according as God hath dealt to every man the measure of faith.

4 For as we have many members in one body, and all members have not the same office:

5 So we, *being* many, are one body in Christ, and every one members one of another.

6 Having then gifts differing according to the grace that is given to us, whether prophecy, *let us prophesy* according to the proportion of faith;

7 Or ministry, *let us wait* on *our* ministering: or he that teacheth, on teaching;

8 Or he that exhorteth, on exhortation: he that giveth, *let him do it* with simplicity; he that ruleth, with diligence; he that sheweth mercy, with cheerfulness.

C In Relation to Society, 12:9–21

9 *Let* love be without dissimulation. Abhor that which is evil; cleave to that which is good.

10 *Be* kindly affectioned one to another with brotherly love; in honour preferring one another;

12:2 *be not conformed.* I.e., do not live according to the style or manner of this present age, but live as if the new age had already arrived. The only other occurrence of this Greek word in the N.T. is in 1 Pet. 1:14.

12:3 In introducing the subject of the use of spiritual gifts, Paul warns against high-mindedness and exhorts sober-mindedness based on the *measure of faith* to work for God which has been given each one.

12:4 *one body.* For this concept see the note at 1 Cor. 12:12–31.

12:6 *gifts.* On spiritual gifts see note at 1 Cor. 1:7.   *according to the proportion of faith;* i.e., the revelations that come through the prophet must be in agreement with the already revealed body of truth.

12:7 *ministry*=service in a general sense.

12:8 *simplicity.* Better, generosity.

12:9 *dissimulation*=hypocrisy; or, let love be genuine.

11 Not slothful in business; fervent in spirit; serving the Lord;

12 Rejoicing in hope; patient in tribulation; continuing instant in prayer;

13 Distributing to the necessity of saints; given to hospitality.

14 Bless them which persecute you: bless, and curse not.

15 Rejoice with them that do rejoice, and weep with them that weep.

16 *Be* of the same mind one toward another. Mind not high things, but condescend to men of low estate. Be not wise in your own conceits.

17 Recompense to no man evil for evil. Provide things honest in the sight of all men.

18 If it be possible, as much as lieth in you, live peaceably with all men.

19 Dearly beloved, avenge not yourselves, but *rather* give place unto wrath: for it is written, Vengeance *is* mine; I will repay, saith the Lord.

20 Therefore if thine enemy hunger, feed him; if he thirst, give him drink: for in so doing thou shalt heap coals of fire on his head.

21 Be not overcome of evil, but overcome evil with good.

D In Relation to Government, 13:1–14

13 Let every soul be subject unto the higher powers. For there is no power but of God: the powers that be are ordained of God.

2 Whosoever therefore resisteth the power, resisteth the ordinance of God: and they that resist shall receive to themselves damnation.

3 For rulers are not a terror to good works, but to the evil. Wilt thou then not be afraid of the power? do that which is good, and thou shalt have praise of the same:

12:11 *Not slothful in business*=Do not let your zeal slacken. *fervent in*=boiling with.

12:12 *continuing instant*=continuing steadfastly.

12:19 See Deut. 32:35.

13:1 *be subject*. This is the same verb that is used later by Paul in Tit. 3:1 and by Peter in 1 Pet. 2:13, where essentially the same view of the individual's proper attitude to the state is set forth. *the powers that be are ordained of God*. This does not say that only certain forms of government are ordained of God. God established and upholds the principle of government even though some governments do not fulfill His desires.

4 For he is the minister of God to thee for good. But if thou do that which is evil, be afraid; for he beareth not the sword in vain: for he is the minister of God, a revenger to *execute* wrath upon him that doeth evil.

5 Wherefore *ye* must needs be subject, not only for wrath, but also for conscience sake.

6 For this cause pay ye tribute also: for they are God's ministers, attending continually upon this very thing.

7 Render therefore to all their dues: tribute to whom tribute *is due*; custom to whom custom; fear to whom fear; honour to whom honour.

8 Owe no man any thing, but to love one another: for he that loveth another hath fulfilled the law.

9 For this, Thou shalt not commit adultery, Thou shalt not kill, Thou shalt not steal, Thou shalt not bear false witness, Thou shalt not covet; and if *there be* any other commandment, it is briefly comprehended in this saying, namely, Thou shalt love thy neighbour as thyself.

10 Love worketh no ill to his neighbour: therefore love *is* the fulfilling of the law.

11 And that, knowing the time, that now *it is* high time to awake out of sleep: for now *is* our salvation nearer than when we believed.

12 The night is far spent, the day is at hand: let us therefore cast off the works of darkness, and let us put on the armour of light.

13 Let us walk honestly, as in the day; not in rioting and drunkenness, not in chambering and wantoness, not in strife and envying.

14 But put ye on the Lord Jesus Christ, and make not provision for the flesh, to *fulfil* the lusts *thereof.*

13:4 *for he beareth not the sword in vain.* God has given the state the power of life and death over its subjects in order to maintain order. Therefore, one should hold government in healthy respect.

13:6 *tribute*=taxes.

13:8 Love is a debt one can never fully discharge.

13:9 See Ex. 20:13–17; Lev. 19:18.

13:11 *out of sleep.* I.e., out of insensitivity to sin.   *our salvation.* The future culmination of our salvation at the return of the Lord is nearer every day.

13:13 *chambering.* Lit., beds, i.e., illicit sex. *wantonness*= sexual excesses.

13:14 An illustration of obedience to this command is in Acts 19:19.

E In Relation to Other Believers, 14:1–15:13

1 *Do not judge one another*, 14:1–12

14 Him that is weak in the faith receive ye, *but* not to doubtful disputations.

2 For one believeth that he may eat all things: another, who is weak, eateth herbs.

3 Let not him that eateth despise him that eateth not; and let not him which eateth not judge him that eateth: for God hath received him.

4 Who art thou that judgest another man's servant? to his own master he standeth or falleth. Yea, he shall be holden up: for God is able to make him stand.

5 One man esteemeth one day above another: another esteemeth every day *alike*. Let every man be fully persuaded in his own mind.

6 He that regardeth the day, regardeth *it* unto the Lord; and he that regardeth not the day, to the Lord he doth not regard *it*. He that eateth, eateth to the Lord, for he giveth God thanks; and he that eateth not, to the Lord he eateth not, and giveth God thanks.

7 For none of us liveth to himself, and no man dieth to himself.

8 For whether we live, we live unto the Lord; and whether we die, we die unto the Lord: whether we live therefore, or die, we are the Lord's.

9 For to this end Christ both died, and rose, and revived, that he might be Lord both of the dead and living.

10 But why dost thou judge thy brother? or why dost thou set at nought thy brother? for we shall all stand before the judgment seat of Christ.

11 For it is written, *As* I live, saith the Lord, every knee shall bow to me, and every tongue shall confess to God.

12 So then every one of us shall give account of himself to God.

14:1–12 Here Paul discusses the proper attitude Christians should have toward each other in debatable areas of conduct (not things which are clearly stated to be wrong). He says that we are not to judge one another, because God has received both the weaker and stronger believer (vv. 1–3); because we can differ in good conscience (vv. 4–6); because we all shall be judged by the Lord (vv. 7–12).

14:1 *weak in the faith*. I.e., one who does not yet have full knowledge of how to live as a Christian. In this case it is one who eats only *herbs* (=vegetables), v. 2, and not meat.

14:10 *the judgment seat of Christ*. See 1 Cor. 3:10–15; 2 Cor. 5:10.

14:11 See Isa. 45:23.

2 Do not hinder one another, 14:13–23

13 Let us not therefore judge one another any more: but judge this rather, that no man put a stumblingblock or an occasion to fall in *his* brother's way.

14 I know, and am persuaded by the Lord Jesus, that *there is* nothing unclean of itself: but to him that esteemeth any thing to be unclean, to him *it is* unclean.

15 But if thy brother be grieved with *thy* meat, now walkest thou not charitably. Destroy not him with thy meat, for whom Christ died.

16 Let not then your good be evil spoken of:

17 For the kingdom of God is not meat and drink; but righteousness, and peace, and joy in the Holy Ghost.

18 For he that in these things serveth Christ *is* acceptable to God, and approved of men.

19 Let us therefore follow after the things which make for peace, and things wherewith one may edify another.

20 For meat destroy not the work of God. All things indeed *are* pure; but *it is* evil for that man who eateth with offence.

21 *It is* good neither to eat flesh, nor to drink wine, nor *any thing* whereby thy brother stumbleth, or is offended, or is made weak.

22 Hast thou faith? have *it* to thyself before God. Happy *is* he that condemneth not himself in that thing which he alloweth.

23 And he that doubteth is damned if he eat, because *he eateth* not of faith: for whatsoever *is* not of faith is sin.

3 Do imitate Christ, 15:1–13

15 We then that are strong ought to bear the infirmities of the weak, and not to please ourselves.

2 Let every one of us please *his* neighbour for *his* good to edification.

14:13 *occasion to fall*=temptation to sin.

14:14 *unclean*. This refers to meats not permitted by the law (Lev. 11). Though these restrictions no longer applied (v. 20), some immature believers still applied them to their own lives. The mature brother is exhorted to abstain from those meats and also from wine so as not to be a hindrance to his brother (v. 21). Abstention, even though one may personally think it unnecessary, is better than placing temptation in a brother's way.

14:22 *faith*. I.e., conviction or a standard in regard to these matters. Every believer should have standards and see that they are used to help others, never to hinder them (15:2).

3 For even Christ pleased not himself; but, as it is written, The reproaches of them that reproached thee fell on me.

4 For whatsoever things were written aforetime were written for our learning, that we through patience and comfort of the scriptures might have hope.

5 Now the God of patience and consolation grant you to be likeminded one toward another according to Christ Jesus:

6 That ye may with one mind *and* one mouth glorify God, even the Father of our Lord Jesus Christ.

7 Wherefore receive ye one another, as Christ also received us to the glory of God.

8 Now I say that Jesus Christ was a minister of the circumcision for the truth of God, to confirm the promises *made* unto the fathers:

9 And that the Gentiles might glorify God for *his* mercy; as it is written, For this cause I will confess to thee among the Gentiles, and sing unto thy name.

10 And again he saith, Rejoice, ye Gentiles, with his people.

11 And again, Praise the Lord, all ye Gentiles; and laud him, all ye people.

12 And again, Esaías saith, There shall be a root of Jesse, and he that shall rise to reign over the Gentiles; in him shall the Gentiles trust.

13 Now the God of hope fill you with all joy and peace in believing, that ye may abound in hope, through the power of the Holy Ghost.

VII PERSONAL MESSAGES AND BENEDICTION, 15:14–16:27

A Paul's Plans, 15:14–33

14 And I myself also am persuaded of you, my brethren, that ye also are full of goodness, filled with all knowledge, able also to admonish one another.

15 Nevertheless, brethren, I have written the more

15:3 Here Paul answers the question, Why should I restrict myself, by pointing to the example of Christ (Ps. 69:9).

15:8 *a minister of the circumcision.* Jesus ministered to his fellow-Jews.

15:9–12 Quoting Ps. 18:49; Deut. 32:43; Ps. 117:1; Isa. 11:10, all from the Greek version of the O.T.

boldly unto you in some sort, as putting you in mind, because of the grace that is given to me of God,

16 That I should be the minister of Jesus Christ to the Gentiles, ministering the gospel of God, that the offering up of the Gentiles might be acceptable, being sanctified by the Holy Ghost.

17 I have therefore whereof I may glory through Jesus Christ in those things which pertain to God.

18 For I will not dare to speak of any of those things which Christ hath not wrought by me, to make the Gentiles obedient, by word and deed,

19 Through mighty signs and wonders, by the power of the Spirit of God; so that from Jerusalem, and round about unto Illyr'icum, I have fully preached the gospel of Christ.

20 Yea, so have I strived to preach the gospel, not where Christ was named, lest I should build upon another man's foundation:

21 But as it is written, To whom he was not spoken of, they shall see: and they that have not heard shall understand.

22 For which cause also I have been much hindered from coming to you.

23 But now having no more place in these parts, and having a great desire these many years to come unto you;

24 Whensoever I take my journey into Spain, I will come to you: for I trust to see you in my journey, and to be brought on my way thitherward by you, if first I be somewhat filled with your *company*.

25 But now I go unto Jerusalem to minister unto the saints.

26 For it hath pleased them of Macedonia and Acha'a to make a certain contribution for the poor saints which are at Jerusalem.

27 It hath pleased them verily; and their debtors they are. For if the Gentiles have been made partakers of their spiritual things, their duty is also to minister unto them in carnal things.

28 When therefore I have performed this, and have sealed to them this fruit, I will come by you into Spain.

29 And I am sure that, when I come unto you, I shall

15:16 *to the Gentiles*. See Gal. 2:9.
15:19 *Illyricum*. The eastern shore of the Adriatic (present-day Yugoslavia).
15:20 *not where Christ was named*. I.e., where Christ was unknown.
15:21 See Isa. 52:15.

come in the fulness of the blessing of the gospel of Christ.

30 Now I beseech you, brethren, for the Lord Jesus Christ's sake, and for the love of the Spirit, that ye strive together with me in *your* prayers to God for me;

31 That I may be delivered from them that do not believe in Judæa; and that my service which *I have* for Jerusalem may be accepted of the saints;

32 That I may come unto you with joy by the will of God, and may with you be refreshed.

33 Now the God of peace *be* with you all. Amen.

B Paul's Personal Greetings, 16:1–16

16 I commend unto you Phē′bē our sister, which is a servant of the church which is at Cenchrē′a:

2 That ye receive her in the Lord, as becometh saints, and that ye assist her in whatsoever business she hath need of you: for she hath been a succourer of many, and of myself also.

3 Greet Priṣcilla and Aquila my helpers in Christ Jesus:

4 Who have for my life laid down their own necks: unto whom not only I give thanks, but also all the churches of the Gentiles.

5 Likewise *greet* the church that is in their house. Salute my wellbeloved Epæ′netus, who is the firstfruits of Achā′a unto Christ.

6 Greet Mary, who bestowed much labour on us.

15:23 *no more place.* I.e., no more opportunity to preach Christ where He was unknown. Therefore, Paul proposed to go to Spain, stopping off in Rome on his way (v. 24).

15:25 *to minister.* I.e., to take the money that had been collected in Greece (see 2 Cor. 8–9).

15:27 *in carnal things.* I.e., in things that pertain to material needs.

15:28 *this fruit.* I.e., the money he was collecting.

16:1 *Phebe . . . a servant of the church.* The word "servant" is also the word for "deacon," which leads some to believe that Phebe was a deaconess. However, the word is more likely used here in an unofficial sense of helper. *Cenchrea.* The eastern port of Corinth.

16:2 *succourer*=helper.

16:3 *Priscilla and Aquila.* See Acts 18:2, 26 1 Cor. 16:19 2 Tim 4:19. Just how they risked their lives for Paul (v. 4), he does not say.

16:5 *the church that is in their house.* The early congregations met in homes (1 Cor. 16:19 Col. 4:15 Philem. 2). The several house churches in one city would constitute the church in that city (1 Cor. 1:2). *Achaia.* Lit., Asia.

7 Salute Andrōnī′cus and Jū′nia, my kinsmen, and my fellowprisoners, who are of note among the apostles, who also were in Christ before me.

8 Greet Am′plias my beloved in the Lord.

9 Salute Urbane, our helper in Christ, and Stach′ys my beloved.

10 Salute Apel′lēs approved in Christ. Salute them which are of Aristōbū′lus' *household*.

11 Salute Hērō′dion my kinsman. Greet them that be of the *household* of Narcissus, which are in the Lord.

12 Salute Tryphena and Tryphosa, who labour in the Lord. Salute the beloved Persis, which laboured much in the Lord.

13 Salute Rufus chosen in the Lord, and his mother and mine.

14 Salute Asyn′critus, Phlegon, Hermas, Pat′rōbas, Hermes, and the brethren which are with them.

15 Salute Philol′ogus, and Julia, Nē′rēus, and his sister, and Olympas, and all the saints which are with them.

16 Salute one another with an holy kiss. The churches of Christ salute you.

C Paul's Concluding
Admonition and Benediction, 16:17–27

17 Now I beseech you, brethren, mark them which cause divisions and offences contrary to the doctrine which ye have learned; and avoid them.

18 For they that are such serve not our Lord Jesus Christ, but their own belly; and by good words and fair speeches deceive the hearts of the simple.

19 For your obedience is come abroad unto all *men*. I am glad therefore on your behalf: but yet I would have you wise unto that which is good, and simple concerning evil.

20 And the God of peace shall bruise Satan under your feet shortly. The grace of our Lord Jesus Christ *be* with you. Amen.

16:7 *of note among the apostles.* Better, well known to the apostles.

16:18 *their own belly.* I.e., their own appetites.

16:19 *simple concerning evil.* I.e., guileless. The believer should not mix with evil rather, he should be knowledgeable about good things (see Matt. 10:16 and Phil. 2:15 for the only other occurrences of the word "simple," in them translated "harmless").

16:20 *bruise*=crush.

21 Tímoth'eus my workfellow, and Lucius, and Jason, and Sōsip'ater, my kinsmen, salute you.

22 I Tertius, who wrote *this* epistle, salute you in the Lord.

23 Ga͡i'us mine host, and of the whole church, saluteth you. Erastus the chamberlain of the city saluteth you, and Quartus a brother.

24 The grace of our Lord Jesus Christ *be* with you all. Amen.

25 Now to him that is of power to stablish you according to my gospel, and the preaching of Jesus Christ, according to the revelation of the mystery, which was kept secret since the world began,

26 But now is made manifest, and by the scriptures of the prophets, according to the commandment of the everlasting God, made known to all nations for the obedience of faith:

27 To God only wise, *be* glory through Jesus Christ for ever. Amen.

16:21 *my kinsmen*, not relatives, but fellow-countrymen (also v. 7).

16:22 *Tertius*. Paul's stenographer.

16:23 *Gaius*. Presumably the Gaius of 1 Cor. 1:14, whom Paul had baptized. *the chamberlain*=the treasurer. Erastus' name has been found on a pavement which he donated to Corinth.

16:25 *the mystery*. Here is a definition of a scriptural mystery: something unknown in times past but revealed in the N.T. See note at Eph. 3:3.

INTRODUCTION TO
THE FIRST LETTER OF PAUL TO THE
Corinthians

AUTHOR: Paul   DATE: 56

The City of Corinth   Located on the narrow isthmus between the Aegean and Adriatic Seas, Corinth was a port city and wealthy commercial center. Ships wanting to avoid the dangerous trip around the southern tip of Greece were dragged across that isthmus. The city boasted an outdoor theater that accommodated 20,000 people, athletic games second only to the Olympics, a Greek, Roman, and Oriental population, and the great temple of Aphrodite with its 1,000 prostitutes. The immoral condition of Corinth is vividly seen in the fact that Korinthiazomai (literally, to act the Corinthian) came to mean "to practice fornication." Taverns lined the south side of the marketplace, and many drinking vessels have been dug up from those liquor lockers. Corinth was noted for everything sinful.

The Church in Corinth   The gospel was first preached in Corinth by Paul on his second missionary journey (A.D. 50). While living and working with Aquila and Priscilla he preached in the synagogue until opposition forced him to move next door, to the house of Titus Justus. The Jews accused him before the Roman governor Gallio but the charge was dismissed, and Paul remained 18 months in the city (Acts 18:1–17; 1 Cor. 2:3). After leaving, Paul wrote the church a letter which has been lost (5:9), but disturbing news about the believers and questions they asked Paul in a letter they sent to him (7:1) prompted the writing of 1 Corinthians. Problems included divisions in the church (1:11) and immorality (5; 6:9–20), and the questions concerned marriage, meats, worship, and the resurrection. Aberrant beliefs and practices of an astonishing variety characterized this church.

The Place of Writing   *This letter was written from Ephesus (16:8).*

The Contents   *The letter is largely practical in its emphasis, dealing with the problems and questions brought to Paul. It is a case book of pastoral theology! Important passages include: the judgment seat of Christ (3:11–15), the temple of the Holy Spirit (6:19–20), the principle of the glory of God (10:31), the Lord's Supper (11:23–34), the great chapter on love (13), and the doctrine of the resurrection (15).*

OUTLINE OF 1 CORINTHIANS

THE FIRST LETTER OF
PAUL THE APOSTLE TO THE
Corinthians

I INTRODUCTION, 1:1–9

A The Salutation, 1:1–3

1 Paul, called *to be* an apostle of Jesus Christ through the will of God, and Sos'thenēs *our* brother,

2 Unto the church of God which is at Corinth, to them that are sanctified in Christ Jesus, called *to be* saints, with all that in every place call upon the name of Jesus Christ our Lord, both theirs and ours:

3 Grace *be* unto you, and peace, from God our Father, and *from* the Lord Jesus Christ.

B The Expression of Thanks, 1:4–9

4 I thank my God always on your behalf, for the grace of God which is given you by Jesus Christ;

1:1 *Sosthenes.* Possibly this is the ruler of the synagogue mentioned in Acts 18:17.

1:2 *sanctified.* I.e., set apart for God's possession and use. See note at 6:11. This was true of the Corinthians because of their position in Christ (1 Cor. 12:13) in spite of their blatant imperfections.

5 That in every thing ye are enriched by him, in all utterance, and *in* all knowledge;

6 Even as the testimony of Christ was confirmed in you:

7 So that ye come behind in no gift; waiting for the coming of our Lord Jesus Christ:

8 Who shall also confirm you unto the end, *that ye may be* blameless in the day of our Lord Jesus Christ.

9 God *is* faithful, by whom ye were called unto the fellowship of his Son Jesus Christ our Lord.

II DIVISIONS IN THE CHURCH, 1:10–4:21

A The Fact of Divisions, 1:10–17

10 Now I beseech you, brethren, by the name of our Lord Jesus Christ, that ye all speak the same thing, and *that* there be no divisions among you; but *that* ye be perfectly joined together in the same mind and in the same judgment.

11 For it hath been declared unto me of you, my brethren, by them *which are of the house* of Chlō′ē, that there are contentions among you.

12 Now this I say, that every one of you saith, I am

1:7 *gift.* Lit., spiritual gift (12:4–11). Spiritual gifts are abilities which God gives believers that they may serve Him. Every Christian has at least one gift (1 Pet. 4:10); at Corinth all the gifts were found within the group. Spiritual gifts are discussed in Rom. 12:3–8; 1 Cor. 12–14; and Ep. 4:7–16.

1:8 *confirm*=guarantee. The Corinthians had God's guarantee that they would be in Christ's presence when He returns, and they would be *blameless* then. The reason for this assurance is based on the fact that God is faithful (v.9).

1:10 *divisions.* This letter was written to a divided church. Here the word literally means "schisms" or "parties," divisions over personalities (v. 12). These are severely condemned, though factions ("heresies," 11:19) may have to exist in order that the approved ones may be recognized. Issues that also divided the church included libertinism (6:13), a kind of new freedom or emancipation (11:2–16), food laws (8:10; 10:25), speaking in tongues (14), and a denial of the resurrection of the dead (15). *perfectly joined together.* Paul appeals for adjustments to be made in these personality divisions so that there might be unity in the church.

1:11 *contentions*=strife, which, according to Gal. 5:20, is a work of the flesh or old nature.

1:12 The party of *Apollos* apparently preferred a polished style

of Paul; and I of Apol'los; and I of Cē'phas; and I of Christ.

13 Is Christ divided? was Paul crucified for you? or were ye baptized in the name of Paul?

14 I thank God that I baptized none of you, but Crispus and Gā'us;

15 Lest any should say that I had baptized in mine own name.

16 And I baptized also the household of Steph'anas: besides, I know not whether I baptized any other.

17 For Christ sent me not to baptize, but to preach the gospel: not with wisdom of words, lest the cross of Christ should be made of none effect.

B The Causes of Divisions, 1:18–2:16

1 The misunderstanding of God's message of the cross, 1:18–2:5

18 For the preaching of the cross is to them that perish foolishness; but unto us which are saved it is the power of God.

19 For it is written, I will destroy the wisdom of the wise, and will bring to nothing the understanding of the prudent.

20 Where is the wise? where is the scribe? where is the disputer of this world? hath not God made foolish the wisdom of this world?

21 For after that in the wisdom of God the world by wisdom knew not God, it pleased God by the foolishness of preaching to save them that believe.

in preaching (Acts 18:24). The party of *Cephas* (Peter) appealed to the traditionalists who wanted a link with the man who walked with Christ. The party of *Christ* included those who disdained attachment to any group and flaunted their liberty in Christ (6:12).

1:13 The impossibility of these things being true demonstrates the fallacy of factions.

1:17 *For Christ sent me not to baptize, but to preach the gospel.* Though Paul did baptize some (vv. 14, 16), it is clear from this statement that he did not consider baptism necessary for salvation.

1:18–25 In these verses Paul shows that worldly wisdom, which the Corinthians prized so highly, is the very antithesis of the wisdom of God.

1:19 See Isa. 29:14.

1:21 *preaching* refers to the content of the message, not the method of its delivery.

22 For the Jews require a sign, and the Greeks seek after wisdom:

23 But we preach Christ crucified, unto the Jews a stumblingblock, and unto the Greeks foolishness;

24 But unto them which are called, both Jews and Greeks, Christ the power of God, and the wisdom of God.

25 Because the foolishness of God is wiser than men; and the weakness of God is stronger than men.

26 For ye see your calling, brethren, how that not many wise men after the flesh, not many mighty, not many noble, *are called*:

27 But God hath chosen the foolish things of the world to confound the wise; and God hath chosen the weak things of the world to confound the things which are mighty;

28 And base things of the world, and things which are despised, hath God chosen, *yea*, and things which are not, to bring to nought things that are:

29 That no flesh should glory in his presence.

30 But of him are ye in Christ Jesus, who of God is made unto us wisdom, and righteousness, and sanctification, and redemption:

31 That, according as it is written, He that glorieth, let him glory in the Lord.

2 And I, brethren, when I came to you, came not with excellency of speech or of wisdom, declaring unto you the testimony of God.

2 For I determined not to know any thing among you, save Jesus Christ, and him crucified.

3 And I was with you in weakness, and in fear, and in much trembling.

4 And my speech and my preaching *was* not with enticing words of man's wisdom, but in demonstration of the Spirit and of power:

1:26–31 Not only is the message of the cross folly, but God uses those who would commonly be considered foolish, weak, and of no consequence to convey that message. They could see that by looking at their own church group, which did not include many *wise, mighty,* or *noble* (v. 26). God's purpose is to exclude all boasting in self (v. 29).

1:31 See Jer. 9:24.

2:3 Paul arrived in Corinth after a discouraging experience in Athens and anxious about the believers he had just left in Thessalonica (Acts 17). The overwhelming wickedness of Corinth undoubtedly added to his anxiety.

5 That your faith should not stand in the wisdom of men, but in the power of God.

2 The misunderstanding of the Spirit's ministry of revealing, 2:6–16

6 Howbeit we speak wisdom among them that are perfect: yet not the wisdom of this world, nor of the princes of this world, that come to nought:

7 But we speak the wisdom of God in a mystery, *even* the hidden *wisdom*, which God ordained before the world unto our glory:

8 Which none of the princes of this world knew: for had they known *it*, they would not have crucified the Lord of glory.

9 But as it is written, Eye hath not seen, nor ear heard, neither have entered into the heart of man, the things which God hath prepared for them that love him.

10 But God hath revealed *them* unto us by his Spirit: for the Spirit searcheth all things, yea, the deep things of God.

11 For what man knoweth the things of a man, save the spirit of man which is in him? even so the things of God knoweth no man, but the Spirit of God.

12 Now we have received, not the spirit of the world, but the spirit which is of God; that we might know the things that are freely given to us of God.

13 Which things also we speak, not in the words which man's wisdom teacheth, but which the Holy Ghost teacheth; comparing spiritual things with spiritual.

14 But the natural man receiveth not the things of the Spirit of God: for they are foolishness unto him: neither can he know *them*, because they are spiritually discerned.

2:5 *wisdom of men.* Paul did not want their faith to be placed in a clever argument but *in the power of God.*

2:6 *perfect*=mature.

2:8 *the princes of this world.* I.e., those who crucified Christ.

2:9 A free quotation of Isa. 64:4. The revelation of these things is not in heaven, but now by the Spirit (v. 10).

2:13 *comparing spiritual things with spiritual.* This difficult phrase may mean (1) interpreting spiritual truths to spiritual minds; or (2) combining spiritual truths with spiritual language.

2:14 *the natural man.* The unsaved man. See Jude 19, where the same word is used (translated "sensual") and explained as indicating a person who does not have the Spirit (see also Rom. 8:9).

15 But he that is spiritual judgeth all things, yet he himself is judged of no man.

16 For who hath known the mind of the Lord, that he may instruct him? But we have the mind of Christ.

C The Consequences of Divisions, 3:1—4:5

1 *Spiritual growth is stunted*, 3:1–9

3 And I, brethren, could not speak unto you as unto spiritual, but as unto carnal, *even* as unto babes in Christ.

2 I have fed you with milk, and not with meat: for hitherto ye were not able *to bear it*, neither yet now are ye able.

3 For ye are yet carnal: for whereas *there is* among you envying, and strife, and divisions, are ye not carnal, and walk as men?

4 For while one saith, I am of Paul; and another, I *am* of Apol'los; are ye not carnal?

5 Who then is Paul, and who *is* Apol'los, but ministers by whom ye believed, even as the Lord gave to every man?

6 I have planted, Apol'los watered; but God gave the increase.

7 So then neither is he that planteth any thing, neither he that watereth; but God that giveth the increase.

8 Now he that planteth and he that watereth are one: and every man shall receive his own reward according to his own labour.

9 For we are labourers together with God: ye are God's husbandry, *ye are* God's building.

2:15 *he that is spiritual*. The mature Christian who is led and taught by the Spirit *judgeth all things*, i.e., he can scrutinize and sift all things; but unbelievers and even carnally-minded Christians cannot judge (understand) him.

3:1 *carnal*. The Greek word *sarkinos* means "fleshly" or "of the flesh," with the idea of weakness; in v. 3 *carnal* has the overtone of willfulness. A carnal Christian (*brethren*) is a babe in Christ (i.e., undeveloped) who cannot understand the deeper truths of the Word of God (v. 2) and who is characterized by strife (v. 3).

3:3 *yet*=even yet, still. Their condition was inexcusable, for they had been saved long enough to be expected to have grown up. *walk as men*. The carnal Christian is scarcely distinguishable from the natural or unsaved man.

3:8 *are one*. I.e., in harmony, not competition.

3:9 *husbandry*=field.

2 Rewards will be lost, 3:10–4:5

10 According to the grace of God which is given unto me, as a wise masterbuilder, I have laid the foundation, and another buildeth thereon. But let every man take heed how he buildeth thereupon.

11 For other foundation can no man lay than that is laid, which is Jesus Christ.

12 Now if any man build upon this foundation gold, silver, precious stones, wood, hay, stubble;

13 Every man's work shall be made manifest: for the day shall declare it, because it shall be revealed by fire; and the fire shall try every man's work of what sort it is.

14 If any man's work abide which he hath built thereupon, he shall receive a reward.

15 If any man's work shall be burned, he shall suffer loss: but he himself shall be saved; yet so as by fire.

16 Know ye not that ye are the temple of God, and that the Spirit of God dwelleth in you?

17 If any man defile the temple of God, him shall God destroy; for the temple of God is holy, which temple ye are.

18 Let no man deceive himself. If any man among you seemeth to be wise in this world, let him become a fool, that he may be wise.

19 For the wisdom of this world is foolishness with God. For it is written, He taketh the wise in their own craftiness.

20 And again, The Lord knoweth the thoughts of the wise, that they are vain.

21 Therefore let no man glory in men. For all things are yours;

22 Whether Paul, or Apol'los, or Ce'phas, or the world,

3:10–15 This passage describes the "judgment seat of Christ" (2 Cor. 5:10). Rewards (or loss of them) for service, not salvation, is the theme.

3:12 gold. Those works which are valuable and enduring; wood. Those which are ultimately worthless.

3:14 reward. Salvation is a free gift, but rewards for those who are saved are earned. The quality of our service (of what sort it is, v. 13) is the criterion, and rewards are often spoken of as crowns (see 9:25; 1 Thess. 2:19; 2 Tim. 4:8; Jas. 1:12; 1 Pet. 5:4; Rev. 2:10; 3:11; 4:4, 10).

3:15 suffer loss. I.e., of reward, not salvation, as is made clear in the latter part of the verse.

3:16 the temple of God. Here the local church is viewed as the temple of God inhabited by the Spirit; in 6:19 the individual is the temple of God.

3:18 seemeth. Better, thinks. let him become a fool by accepting God's wisdom which the world regards as folly.

or life, or death, or things present, or things to come; all are yours;

23 And ye are Christ's; and Christ *is* God's.

4 Let a man so account of us, as of the ministers of Christ, and stewards of the mysteries of God.

2 Moreover it is required in stewards, that a man be found faithful.

3 But with me it is a very small thing that I should be judged of you, or of man's judgment: yea, I judge not mine own self.

4 For I know nothing by myself; yet am I not hereby justified: but he that judgeth me is the Lord.

5 Therefore judge nothing before the time, until the Lord come, who both will bring to light the hidden things of darkness, and will make manifest the counsels of the hearts: and then shall every man have praise of God.

D The Example of Paul, 4:6–21

6 And these things, brethren, I have in a figure transferred to myself and *to* Apol'los for your sakes; that ye might learn in us not to think *of men* above that which is written, that no one of you be puffed up for one against another.

7 For who maketh thee to differ *from another?* and what hast thou that thou didst not receive? now if thou didst receive *it*, why dost thou glory, as if thou hadst not received *it?*

8 Now ye are full, now ye are rich, ye have reigned as kings without us: and I would to God ye did reign, that we also might reign with you.

9 For I think that God hath set forth us the apostles

4:1 *ministers.* The word denotes subordination (originally an under-rower in a trireme) and is different from the one used in 3:5. *mysteries.* See note at Eph. 3:3.

4:2 *faithful.* Reliability is the one necessary virtue for stewards, who were managers or administrators of large estates.

4:4 *by myself.* Lit., against myself. Paul is saying, I have a clear conscience, but my final judgment rests with God.

4:6 *I have in a figure transferred.* I.e., though Paul had been speaking of himself and Apollos in 3:5–4:5, others, whom he did not name, were the real culprits. *that ye might learn in us not to think of men above that which is written*=that ye might learn by us to live according to the Scriptures.

4:8–13 With biting irony, Paul contrasts the imagined exaltation of the Corinthians with the degradation and distress which were the apostles' daily lot.

last, as it were appointed to death: for we are made a spectacle unto the world, and to angels, and to men.

10 We *are* fools for Christ's sake, but ye *are* wise in Christ; we *are* weak, but ye *are* strong; ye *are* honourable, but we *are* despised.

11 Even unto this present hour we both hunger, and thirst, and are naked, and are buffeted, and have no certain dwellingplace;

12 And labour, working with our own hands: being reviled, we bless; being persecuted, we suffer it:

13 Being defamed, we intreat: we are made as the filth of the world, *and are* the offscouring of all things unto this day.

14 I write not these things to shame you, but as my beloved sons I warn *you*.

15 For though ye have ten thousand instructors in Christ, yet *have ye* not many fathers: for in Christ Jesus I have begotten you through the gospel.

16 Wherefore I beseech you, be ye followers of me.

17 For this cause have I sent unto you Timoth'eus, who is my beloved son, and faithful in the Lord, who shall bring you into remembrance of my ways which be in Christ, as I teach every where in every church.

18 Now some are puffed up, as though I would not come to you.

19 But I will come to you shortly, if the Lord will, and will know, not the speech of them which are puffed up, but the power.

20 For the kingdom of God *is* not in word, but in power.

21 What will ye? shall I come unto you with a rod, or in love, and *in* the spirit of meekness?

III MORAL DISORDERS IN THE CHURCH, 5:1–6:20

A The Case of Incest, 5:1–13

1 *The problem stated*, 5:1–2

5 It is reported commonly *that there is* fornication among you, and such fornication as is not so much as named among the Gentiles, that one should have his father's wife.

4:15 *instructors*. The same word is used in Gal. 3:24 (see the note there) The Corinthians had many instructors but only one spiritual father, Paul.

5:1 *commonly*. Better, actually. *fornication;* i.e., incest, forbid-

2 And ye are puffed up, and have not rather mourned, that he that hath done this deed might be taken away from among you.

2 The punishment prescribed, 5:3–13

3 For I verily, as absent in body, but present in spirit, have judged already, as though I were present, *concerning* him that hath so done this deed,

4 In the name of our Lord Jesus Christ, when ye are gathered together, and my spirit, with the power of our Lord Jesus Christ,

5 To deliver such an one unto Satan for the destruction of the flesh, that the spirit may be saved in the day of the Lord Jesus.

6 Your glorying *is* not good. Know ye not that a little leaven leaveneth the whole lump?

7 Purge out therefore the old leaven, that ye may be a new lump, as ye are unleavened. For even Christ our passover is sacrificed for us:

8 Therefore let us keep the feast, not with old leaven, neither with the leaven of malice and wickedness; but with the unleavened *bread* of sincerity and truth.

9 I wrote unto you in an epistle not to company with fornicators:

den by the law (Lev. 18:8; Deut. 22:22). *should have.* Lit., has, suggesting some sort of permanent relationship. *his father's wife,* not the offender's mother, but a stepmother, possibly divorced from his father.

5:2 *be taken away* refers to church discipline and excommunication.

5:5 *To deliver such an one unto Satan for the destruction of the flesh.* This evidently means that the church was to discipline this sinning brother by committing him to Satan's domain, the world (1 John 5:19), and to Satan's chastisement, the destruction or ruin of his body (*flesh* means "body" here) through sickness or even physical death. *destruction* does not mean annihilation, but ruin. Persistent sin often leads to physical punishment (1 Cor. 11:30; 1 John 5:16–17).

5:7 *leaven.* A symbol of impurity (see note at Matt. 13:33). By position they were *unleavened;* Paul urges that their practice conform. *passover.* See Ex. 12:1–28. Christ was already sacrificed, and as Passover was followed by the Feast of Unleavened Bread, so should the Corinthians who were cleansed now walk in holiness.

5:8 *the feast.* I.e., of Unleavened Bread, Ex. 12:15–20; 13:1–10.

5:9 *to company*=to associate closely, have familiar fellowship. It is impossible not to have some contact with the evil people of the world in the daily pursuits of life (v. 10), but Paul says it

10 Yet not altogether with the fornicators of this world, or with the covetous, or extortioners, or with idolaters; for then must ye needs go out of the world.

11 But now I have written unto you not to keep company, if any man that is called a brother be a fornicator, or covetous, or an idolater, or a railer, or a drunkard, or an extortioner; with such an one no not to eat.

12 For what have I to do to judge them also that are without? do not ye judge them that are within?

13 But them that are without God judgeth. Therefore put away from among yourselves that wicked person.

B The Problem of Litigation in Heathen Courts, 6:1-8

6 Dare any of you, having a matter against another, go to law before the unjust, and not before the saints?

2 Do ye not know that the saints shall judge the world? and if the world shall be judged by you, are ye unworthy to judge the smallest matters?

3 Know ye not that we shall judge angels? how much more things that pertain to this life?

4 If then ye have judgments of things pertaining to this life, set them to judge who are least esteemed in the church.

5 I speak to your shame. Is it so, that there is not a wise man among you? no, not one that shall be able to judge between his brethren?

6 But brother goeth to law with brother, and that before the unbelievers.

7 Now therefore there is utterly a fault among you, because ye go to law one with another. Why do ye not rather take wrong? why do ye not rather *suffer yourselves to* be defrauded?

8 Nay, ye do wrong, and defraud, and that *your* brethren.

it is improper to have fellowship with a Christian who is under discipline (v. 11).

5:12-13 Leave the judgment of unbelievers to God; the church must set its own house in order.

6:1 *a matter.* I.e., a cause for trial, a case.

6:2 *the saints shall judge the world.* Because of our union with Christ we shall be associated with Him in this judgment (during the millennium, see Matt. 19:28). We shall also *judge angels* (v. 3). See 2 Pet. 2:4, 9; Jude 6.

6:4 *set them* ... Better, are you setting them ... ?

6:7 *a fault.* Better, a defeat. Going to court against a brother brings defeat before the case is even heard. It is better to be wronged and take a loss.

C The Warning against Moral Laxity, 6:9–20

9 Know ye not that the unrighteous shall not inherit the kingdom of God? Be not deceived: neither fornicators, nor idolaters, nor adulterers, nor effeminate, nor abusers of themselves with mankind,

10 Nor thieves, nor covetous, nor drunkards, nor revilers, nor extortioners, shall inherit the kingdom of God.

11 And such were some of you: but ye are washed, but ye are sanctified, but ye are justified in the name of the Lord Jesus, and by the Spirit of our God.

12 All things are lawful unto me, but all things are not expedient: all things are lawful for me, but I will not be brought under the power of any.

13 Meats for the belly, and the belly for meats: but God shall destroy both it and them. Now the body *is* not for fornication, but for the Lord; and the Lord for the body.

14 And God hath both raised up the Lord, and will also raise up us by his own power.

15 Know ye not that your bodies are the members of Christ? shall I then take the members of Christ, and make *them* the members of an harlot? God forbid.

6:9 *effeminate, nor abusers of themselves with mankind.* Both expressions refer to homosexuals, the first to those who allow themselves to be used in this manner, and the second to active homosexuals. Paul's warning is given against the background of incest, homosexuality, pederasty, and unnatural vice which were prevalent among the Greeks and Romans. Paul did not want Christianity confused with sects that permitted such things.

6:11 *washed.* I.e., regenerated (Tit. 3:5). *sanctified*=set apart for God's use. There are three aspects to sanctification: (1) positional sanctification, which is true of every believer from the moment of his conversion. It is his perfect standing in holiness (Acts 20:32; 1 Cor. 1:2); (2) progressive sanctification, which is the daily growth in grace, becoming in practice more and more set apart for God's use (John 17:17; Eph. 5:26); (3) ultimate sanctification, when we shall be fully and completely set apart to God in heaven (1 Thess. 5:23). *justified.* See note at Rom. 3:24.

6:12 *are lawful.* Apparently some of the Corinthians were using this to justify their sins. Christian liberty is limited here by two considerations: Is the practice expedient (helpful) and will it enslave?

6:13 Some were saying that just as *meats* (better, food) and the belly necessarily go together, so the body and sexual indulgence go together. Not so, says Paul. Rather, the body should glorify the Lord.

16 What? know ye not that he which is joined to an harlot is one body? for two, saith he, shall be one flesh.

17 But he that is joined unto the Lord is one spirit.

18 Flee fornication. Every sin that a man doeth is without the body; but he that committeth fornication sinneth against his own body.

19 What? know ye not that your body is the temple of the Holy Ghost *which is* in you, which ye have of God, and ye are not your own?

20 For ye are bought with a price: therefore glorify God in your body, and in your spirit, which are God's.

IV DISCUSSION CONCERNING MARRIAGE, 7:1–40

A Marriage and Celibacy, 7:1–9

7 Now concerning the things whereof ye wrote unto me: *It is* good for a man not to touch a woman.

2 Nevertheless, *to avoid* fornication, let every man have his own wife, and let every woman have her own husband.

3 Let the husband render unto the wife due benevolence: and likewise also the wife unto the husband.

4 The wife hath not power of her own body, but the husband: and likewise also the husband hath not power of his own body, but the wife.

5 Defraud ye not one the other, except *it be* with consent for a time, that ye may give yourselves to fasting

6:18 *Flee fornication.* Lit., make it your habit to flee fornication. For an illustration of this, see Joseph's experience in Gen. 39:12.

6:19 *your body is the temple.* A sharp contrast to the temple of Aphrodite in Corinth where the priestesses were prostitutes.

6:20 *and in your spirit, which are God's.* Some manuscripts omit this phrase.

7:1 *ye wrote unto me.* In this chapter Paul is not writing a treatise on marriage but answering questions which had been sent to him. We are only reading one side of the correspondence. It is clear that Paul favored celibacy (vv. 1, 7, 8, 9, 27, 38), though he countenances marriage (vv. 2, 27). For the complete N.T. teaching concerning marriage, see John 2:1–11; Eph. 5:21–33; 1 Tim. 5:14; Heb. 13:4; 1 Pet. 3:1–7. *It is good* . . . Probably a position taken by some at Corinth. Paul grants its validity but states that marriage is better for those who might be overcome by the practices of the evil society in which they live.

7:2–5 In the mutuality of marriage each partner has rights of his or her own and debts to the other (*benevolence*=debt).

and prayer; and come together again, that Satan tempt you not for your incontinency.

6 But I speak this by permission, *and* not of commandment.

7 For I would that all men were even as I myself. But every man hath his proper gift of God, one after this manner, and another after that.

8 I say therefore to the unmarried and widows, It is good for them if they abide even as I.

9 But if they cannot contain, let them marry: for it is better to marry than to burn.

B Marriage and Divorce, 7:10–24

10 And unto the married I command, *yet* not I, but the Lord, Let not the wife depart from *her* husband:

11 But and if she depart, let her remain unmarried, or be reconciled to *her* husband: and let not the husband put away *his* wife.

12 But to the rest speak I, not the Lord: If any brother hath a wife that believeth not, and she be pleased to dwell with him, let him not put her away.

13 And the woman which hath an husband that believeth not, and if he be pleased to dwell with her, let her not leave him.

14 For the unbelieving husband is sanctified by the wife, and the unbelieving wife is sanctified by the husband: else were your children unclean; but now are they holy.

7:7 *one after this manner* (celibate), *and another after that* (married).

7:8 *even as I.* Paul was obviously unmarried when he wrote these words. He might have been a widower. However, it is difficult to substantiate that he was married on the basis that he was a member of the Sanhedrin (Acts 26:10) because it is uncertain that he was a member and it is not clear that members had to be married in the period before A.D. 70.

7:9 *contain*=exercise self-control. *burn.* I.e., with passion.

7:10–11 Believers should not divorce, according to Paul's and Christ's teachings (Mark 10:1–12). If a separation does occur, then the wife must either remain unmarried permanently or be reconciled permanently.

7:12–13 These verses deal with marriages in which one partner becomes a believer after the marriage occurs. Again the rule is, no separation. *speak I, not the Lord* means that Christ did not give any teaching concerning these spiritually mixed marriages, but Paul does, and his teaching is not any less authoritative.

7:14 sanctified. The presence of a believer in the home sets the home apart and gives it a Christian influence it would not

15 But if the unbelieving depart, let him depart. A brother or a sister is not under bondage in such *cases*: but God hath called us to peace.

16 For what knowest thou, O wife, whether thou shalt save *thy* husband? or how knowest thou, O man, whether thou shalt save *thy* wife?

17 But as God hath distributed to every man, as the Lord hath called every one, so let him walk. And so ordain I in all churches.

18 Is any man called being circumcised? let him not become uncircumcised. Is any called in uncircumcision? let him not be circumcised.

19 Circumcision is nothing, and uncircumcision is nothing, but the keeping of the commandments of God.

20 Let every man abide in the same calling wherein he was called.

21 Art thou called *being* a servant? care not for it: but if thou mayest be made free, use *it* rather.

22 For he that is called in the Lord, *being* a servant, is the Lord's freeman: likewise also he that is called, *being* free, is Christ's servant.

23 Ye are bought with a price; be not ye the servants of men.

24 Brethren, let every man, wherein he is called, therein abide with God.

C Marriage and Christian Service, 7:25–38

25 Now concerning virgins I have no commandment of the Lord: yet I give my judgment, as one that hath obtained mercy of the Lord to be faithful.

26 I suppose therefore that this is good for the present distress, *I say*, that *it is* good for a man so to be.

otherwise have. That is why the believing partner should stay with the unbeliever. However, this does not mean that children born into such a home are automatically Christians. They are *holy* in the same sense of being set apart by the presence of one believing parent.

7:15 *depart*. If the unbelieving partner does choose to separate, the believer must accept it, though everything should be done to prevent the separation. Nothing is said about a second marriage for the believer.

7:17–24 The principle of abiding in one's marital relationship is part of a more general principle: in everything the Christian is to remain in his calling, unless it be immoral (v. 24).

7:25–35 Celibacy is presented as a desirable though not necessary state.

7:26 *the present distress*. Probably some particularly difficult

27 Art thou bound unto a wife? seek not to be loosed. Art thou loosed from a wife? seek not a wife.

28 But and if thou marry, thou hast not sinned; and if a virgin marry, she hath not sinned. Nevertheless such shall have trouble in the flesh: but I spare you.

29 But this I say, brethren, the time *is* short: it remaineth, that both they that have wives be as though they had none;

30 And they that weep, as though they wept not; and they that rejoice, as though they rejoiced not; and they that buy, as though they possessed not;

31 And they that use this world, as not abusing *it*: for the fashion of this world passeth away.

32 But I would have you without carefulness. He that is unmarried careth for the things that belong to the Lord, how he may please the Lord:

33 But he that is married careth for the things that are of the world, how he may please *his* wife.

34 There is difference *also* between a wife and a virgin. The unmarried woman careth for the things of the Lord, that she may be holy both in body and in spirit: but she that is married careth for the things of the world, how she may please *her* husband.

35 And this I speak for your own profit; not that I may cast a snare upon you, but for that which is comely, and that ye may attend upon the Lord without distraction.

36 But if any man think that he behaveth himself uncomely toward his virgin, if she pass the flower of *her* age, and need so require, let him do what he will, he sinneth not: let them marry.

37 Nevertheless he that standeth stedfast in his heart, having no necessity, but hath power over his own will, and hath so decreed in his heart that he will keep his virgin, doeth well.

38 So then he that giveth *her* in marriage doeth well; but he that giveth *her* not in marriage doeth better.

D Marriage and Remarriage, 7:39-40

39 The wife is bound by the law as long as her husband liveth; but if her husband be dead, she is at liberty to be married to whom she will; only in the Lord.

circumstances through which the Corinthian Christians were passing.

7:36 *if she pass the flower of her age.* I.e., if a virgin daughter is getting beyond marriageable age, then her father may arrange a marriage if her *need so require.*

7:39 *only in the Lord.* I.e., only to another Christian.

40 But she is happier if she so abide, after my judgment: and I think also that I have the Spirit of God.

V DIFFICULTIES CAUSED BY FOOD OFFERED TO IDOLS, 8:1–11:1

A The Enquiry: May a Christian Eat Food Consecrated to a Pagan God? 8:1–13

8 Now as touching things offered unto idols, we know that we all have knowledge. Knowledge puffeth up, but charity edifieth.

2 And if any man think that he knoweth any thing, he knoweth nothing yet as he ought to know.

3 But if any man love God, the same is known of him.

4 As concerning therefore the eating of those things that are offered in sacrifice unto idols, we know that an idol *is* nothing in the world, and that *there is* none other God but one.

5 For though there be that are called gods, whether in heaven or in earth, (as there be gods many, and lords many,)

6 But to us *there is but* one God, the Father, of whom *are* all things, and we in him; and one Lord Jesus Christ, by whom *are* all things, and we by him.

7 Howbeit *there is* not in every man that knowledge: for some with conscience of the idol unto this hour eat *it* as a thing offered unto an idol; and their conscience being weak is defiled.

8 But meat commendeth us not to God: for neither, if we eat, are we the better; neither, if we eat not, are we the worse.

9 But take heed lest by any means this liberty of yours become a stumblingblock to them that are weak.

10 For if any man see thee which hast knowledge sit

8:1 *things offered unto idols.* These were the remainders of animals which had been sacrificed to heathen idols. If the offering was private, the remainders were claimed by the offerer; if public, they were sold in the market. What should a Christian do about buying such meat or eating it when served to him at a banquet?

8:4 *an idol is nothing in the world.* Better, there is no idol in the world. Yet, Paul admits (v. 5), there are those that *are called gods.*

8:7 *with conscience of the idol.* Better, because of being long accustomed to idols.

8:10 *in the idol's temple.* Probably refers to some official function or festival.

at meat in the idol's temple, shall not the conscience of him which is weak be emboldened to eat those things which are offered to idols;

11 And through thy knowledge shall the weak brother perish, for whom Christ died?

12 But when ye sin so against the brethren, and wound their weak conscience, ye sin against Christ.

13 Wherefore, if meat make my brother to offend, I will eat no flesh while the world standeth, lest I make my brother to offend.

B The Example of Paul, 9:1–27

1 Paul's rights, 9:1–14

9 Am I not an apostle? am I not free? have I not seen Jesus Christ our Lord? are not ye my work in the Lord?

2 If I be not an apostle unto others, yet doubtless I am to you: for the seal of mine apostleship are ye in the Lord.

3 Mine answer to them that do examine me is this,

4 Have we not power to eat and to drink?

5 Have we not power to lead about a sister, a wife, as well as other apostles, and as the brethren of the Lord, and Cĕ′phas?

6 Or I only and Barnabas, have not we power to forbear working?

7 Who goeth a warfare any time at his own charges? who planteth a vineyard, and eateth not of the fruit thereof? or who feedeth a flock, and eateth not of the milk of the flock?

8 Say I these things as a man? or saith not the law the same also?

8:11 *perish*, not eternally, but be ruined in his spiritual life.
8:13 Here is the great principle that regulates conduct in morally indifferent matters. It is the principle of love regulating liberty voluntarily (Gal. 5:13). *offend*=stumble.
9:1 This chapter is an illustration of the principle of 8:13 from Paul's own life, for he did not use the privileges he had a right to use as an apostle.
9:4 *power*=right.
9:5 *to lead about a sister, a wife*. I.e., to be married. Peter was married (Matt. 8:14), as were *other apostles* and Christ's brothers.
9:6 *to forbear working*. I.e., Is it only Barnabas and I who must not refrain from working for a living? Paul had the right to expect to be supported by those to whom he ministered, but he did not always insist on this right (1 Thess. 2:9).
9:7 Others derive their living from their occupation.

9 For it is written in the law of Moses, Thou shalt not muzzle the mouth of the ox that treadeth out the corn. Doth God take care for oxen?

10 Or saith he *it* altogether for our sakes? For our sakes, no doubt, *this* is written: that he that ploweth should plow in hope; and that he that thresheth in hope should be partaker of his hope.

11 If we have sown unto you spiritual things, *is it* a great thing if we shall reap your carnal things?

12 If others be partakers of *this* power over you, *are* not we rather? Nevertheless we have not used this power; but suffer all things, lest we should hinder the gospel of Christ.

13 Do ye not know that they which minister about holy things live *of the things* of the temple? and they which wait at the altar are partakers with the altar?

14 Even so hath the Lord ordained that they which preach the gospel should live of the gospel.

2 *Paul's restrictions*, 9:15–27

15 But I have used none of these things: neither have I written these things, that it should be so done unto me: for *it were* better for me to die, than that any man should make my glorying void.

16 For though I preach the gospel, I have nothing to glory of: for necessity is laid upon me; yea, woe is unto me, if I preach not the gospel!

17 For if I do this thing willingly, I have a reward: but if against my will, a dispensation *of the gospel* is committed unto me.

18 What is my reward then? V*erily* that, when I preach the gospel, I may make the gospel of Christ without charge, that I abuse not my power in the gospel.

19 For though I be free from all *men*, yet have I made myself servant unto all, that I might gain the more.

20 And unto the Jews I became as a Jew, that I might

9:9 The law (Deut. 25:4) also vindicates Paul's claim.
9:11 *your carnal things.* I.e., your material support.
9:13 The priests were supported by the people (Num. 18:8–24).
9:14 See Matt. 10:10; Luke 10:7.
9:17 Willingly or unwillingly, Paul could not escape his responsibility to preach the gospel because a *dispensation* (=stewardship responsibility), had been committed to him and he was under orders to preach even though he was never paid (Luke 17:10).
9:20 *as under the law.* I.e., I became as one under the law. After these words many manuscripts add parenthetically: "not being

gain the Jews; to them that are under the law, as under the law, that I might gain them that are under the law;

21 To them that are without law, as without law, (being not without law to God, but under the law to Christ,) that I might gain them that are without law.

22 To the weak became I as weak, that I might gain the weak: I am made all things to all *men*, that I might by all means save some.

23 And this I do for the gospel's sake, that I might be partaker thereof with *you*.

24 Know ye not that they which run in a race run all, but one receiveth the prize? So run, that ye may obtain.

25 And every man that striveth for the mastery is temperate in all things. Now they *do it* to obtain a corruptible crown; but we an incorruptible.

26 I therefore so run, not as uncertainly; so fight I, not as one that beateth the air:

27 But I keep under my body, and bring *it* into subjection: lest that by any means, when I have preached to others, I myself should be a castaway.

C The Exhortations, 10:1–11:1

1 *Avoid self-indulgence*, 10:1–13

10 Moreover, brethren, I would not that ye should be ignorant, how that all our fathers were under the cloud, and all passed through the sea;

---

myself under the law." Though Paul had broken with the law of Moses, he adds (v. 21) that he was not lawless, *but under the law to Christ*.

9:24 *race*. Paul draws on his readers' knowledge of the Isthmian games which were held every two years near Corinth.

9:25 *is temperate*=practices self-discipline. To be a winner one must train diligently. *a corruptible crown*. In the Isthmian games it was a wreath of pine.

9:26 *not as uncertainly*=not aimlessly. *not as one that beateth the air*. This does not refer to shadowboxing but to wild misses during an actual boxing match.

9:27 *But I keep under my body*. Better, I treat severely or buffet my body. Paul changes the metaphor: his opponent is now his own body. By self-discipline he gives it knockout blows. *a castaway*. *Lit*., disapproved. This is a reference to the possible loss of reward (see note at 3:14; 2 John 8).

10:1 *our fathers*. The nation Israel is now used as an illustration of some who were disapproved (9:27). *under the cloud* that guided them (Ex. 13:21–22; 14:19). *through the sea*. See Ex. 14:15–22.

2 And were all baptized unto Moses in the cloud and in the sea;

3 And did all eat the same spiritual meat;

4 And did all drink the same spiritual drink: for they drank of that spiritual Rock that followed them: and that Rock was Christ.

5 But with many of them God was not well pleased: for they were overthrown in the wilderness.

6 Now these things were our examples, to the intent we should not lust after evil things, as they also lusted.

7 Neither be ye idolaters, as *were* some of them; as it is written, The people sat down to eat and drink, and rose up to play.

8 Neither let us commit fornication, as some of them committed, and fell in one day three and twenty thousand.

9 Neither let us tempt Christ, as some of them also tempted, and were destroyed of serpents.

10 Neither murmur ye, as some of them also murmured, and were destroyed of the destroyer.

11 Now all these things happened unto them for ensamples: and they are written for our admonition, upon whom the ends of the world are come.

12 Wherefore let him that thinketh he standeth take heed lest he fall.

13 There hath no temptation taken you but such as is common to man: but God *is* faithful, who will not suffer you to be tempted above that ye are able; but will with the temptation also make a way to escape, that ye may be able to bear *it*.

10:2 *baptized unto Moses.* I.e., united to Moses as their leader.

10:3 *spiritual meat.* Lit., spiritual food; i.e., the manna (Ex. 16:1–36; Ps. 78:25).

10:4 *that spiritual Rock* which provided water (Ex. 17:1–9; Num. 20:1–13). The rock appeared twice in different settings, giving rise to a rabbinic legend that a material rock actually followed them. Paul, however, says that it was Christ who was with Israel all the way.

10:6 *lusted.* I.e., desired, when they preferred the food of Egypt to God's manna (Num. 11:4).

10:7 *idolaters.* See Ex. 32:1–14 for the making of the golden calf.

10:8 *three and twenty thousand* was the number killed *in one day.* Num. 25:9 indicates that there were additional deaths afterwards.

10:9 *tempt Christ . . . destroyed of serpents.* See Num. 21:6.

10:10 *murmured* after the judgment on the rebellion led by Korah (Num. 16:41–50).

10:13 *a way to escape.* Lit., a way out. This is not necessarily relief, but power to be able to bear the testing.

2 *Do not participate in idol feasts*, 10:14–22

14 Wherefore, my dearly beloved, flee from idolatry.

15 I speak as to wise men; judge ye what I say.

16 The cup of blessing which we bless, is it not the communion of the blood of Christ? The bread which we break, is it not the communion of the body of Christ?

17 For we *being* many are one bread, *and* one body: for we are all partakers of that one bread.

18 Behold Israel after the flesh: are not they which eat of the sacrifices partakers of the altar?

19 What say I then? that the idol is any thing, or that which is offered in sacrifice to idols is any thing?

20 But *I say*, that the things which the Gentiles sacrifice, they sacrifice to devils, and not to God: and I would not that ye should have fellowship with devils.

21 Ye cannot drink the cup of the Lord, and the cup of devils: ye cannot be partakers of the Lord's table, and of the table of devils.

22 Do we provoke the Lord to jealousy? are we stronger than he?

3 *Glorify God by seeking the welfare of your brother*, 10:23–11:1

23 All things are lawful for me, but all things are not expedient: all things are lawful for me, but all things edify not.

24 Let no man seek his own, but every man another's *wealth*.

25 Whatsoever is sold in the shambles, *that* eat, asking no question for conscience sake:

26 For the earth *is* the Lord's, and the fulness thereof.

27 If any of them that believe not bid you *to a feast*, and ye be disposed to go; whatsoever is set before you, eat, asking no question for conscience sake.

10:14–22 Paul's point here is that partaking in a religious feast means fellowshipping with the one worshiped at that feast. This is true of the Lord's Supper (vv. 16–17), it was true of Israel in O.T. times (v. 18), and it is true of a pagan feast (vv. 19–22). Therefore, believers must not fellowship at pagan feasts since they may open themselves up to demonic attacks (v. 20).

10:24 *wealth*=welfare.

10:25 *the shambles*. A seventeenth-century word meaning the meat market. The subject now changes from meat sacrificed to idols and served at pagan feasts to meat sacrificed to idols that is bought in the market and served at private dinner parties (v. 27). Again, liberty should be restricted.

28 But if any man say unto you, This is offered in sacrifice unto idols, eat not for his sake that shewed it, and for conscience sake: for the earth is the Lord's, and the fulness thereof:

29 Conscience, I say, not thine own, but of the other: for why is my liberty judged of another man's conscience?

30 For if I by grace be a partaker, why am I evil spoken of for that for which I give thanks?

31 Whether therefore ye eat, or drink, or whatsoever ye do, do all to the glory of God.

32 Give none offence, neither to the Jews, nor to the Gentiles, nor to the church of God:

33 Even as I please all men in all things, not seeking mine own profit, but the profit of many, that they may be saved.

11 Be ye followers of me, even as I also am of Christ.

VI DISORDERS IN PUBLIC WORSHIP, 11:2–14:40

A The Veiling of Women, 11:2–16

2 Now I praise you, brethren, that ye remember me in all things, and keep the ordinances, as I delivered them to you.

3 But I would have you know, that the head of every man is Christ; and the head of the woman is the man; and the head of Christ is God.

4 Every man praying or prophesying, having his head covered, dishonoureth his head.

10:31 *do all to the glory of God.* This is the all-inclusive principle concluding the discussion that began in 8:1. It is: Test all conduct by whether or not it manifests the characteristics of God. Other principles for guiding the believer's conduct in this book are: (1) is it beneficial (*expedient*, 6:12)? (2) is it enslaving (6:12)? (3) will it hinder the spiritual growth of a brother (8:13)? (4) does it edify (build up, 10:23)?

11:1 This passage belongs in thought with chapter 10. The Corinthians are urged to imitate the self-sacrificing example of Paul and Christ.

11:2 *ordinances.* I.e., oral teaching.

11:3 *the head of the woman is the man.* This is based on Gen. 3:16, and Paul makes it the basis for the wearing of a covering.

5 But every woman that prayeth or prophesieth with *her* head uncovered dishonoureth her head: for that is even all one as if she were shaven.

6 For if the woman be not covered, let her also be shorn: but if it be a shame for a woman to be shorn or shaven, let her be covered.

7 For a man indeed ought not to cover *his* head, forasmuch as he is the image and glory of God: but the woman is the glory of the man.

8 For the man is not of the woman; but the woman of the man.

9 Neither was the man created for the woman; but the woman for the man.

10 For this cause ought the woman to have power on *her* head because of the angels.

11 Nevertheless neither is the man without the woman, neither the woman without the man, in the Lord.

12 For as the woman *is* of the man, even so *is* the man also by the woman; but all things of God.

13 Judge in yourselves: is it comely that a woman pray unto God uncovered?

14 Doth not even nature itself teach you, that, if a man have long hair, it is a shame unto him?

15 But if a woman have long hair, it is a glory to her: for *her* hair is given her for a covering.

16 But if any man seem to be contentious, we have no such custom, neither the churches of God.

11:5 *prayeth or prophesieth.* In the light of what he says in 14:34–35 it is doubtful that Paul approved of those activities on the part of the women at Corinth. He is simply acknowledging what was going on unauthorized. *with her head uncovered.* Women should be veiled or covered in the meeting of the church, and men should not. Paul's reasons are based on theology (headship, v. 5), the order in creation (vv. 7–9), and the presence of angels in the meeting (v. 10). Actually none of these reasons is based on contemporary social custom.

11:10 *power.* I.e., the covering is the sign of man's authority over the woman. *because of the angels.* The insubordination of an uncovered woman (signifying her refusal to recognize the authority of her husband) would offend the angels who observe the conduct of believers in their church gathering (1 Pet. 1:12).

11:15 *her hair is given her for a covering.* This is not the same word as that used in vv. 5–6. The point here is that as the hair represents the proper covering in the natural realm, so the veil is the proper covering in the supernatural.

11:16 *no such custom.* I.e., no custom of women worshiping without a covering.

B The Lord's Supper, 11:17–34

17 Now in this that I declare *unto you* I praise *you* not, that ye come together not for the better, but for the worse.

18 For first of all, when ye come together in the church, I hear that there be divisions among you; and I partly believe it.

19 For there must be also heresies among you, that they which are approved may be made manifest among you.

20 When ye come together therefore into one place, *this* is not to eat the Lord's supper.

21 For in eating every one taketh before *other* his own supper: and one is hungry, and another is drunken.

22 What? have ye not houses to eat and to drink in? or despise ye the church of God, and shame them that have not? What shall I say to you? shall I praise you in this? I praise *you* not.

23 For I have received of the Lord that which also I delivered unto you, That the Lord Jesus the *same* night in which he was betrayed took bread:

24 And when he had given thanks, he brake *it*, and said, Take, eat: this is my body, which is broken for you: this do in remembrance of me.

25 After the same manner also *he took* the cup, when he had supped, saying, This cup is the new testament in my blood: this do ye, as oft as ye drink *it*, in remembrance of me.

26 For as often as ye eat this bread, and drink this cup, ye do shew the Lord's death till he come.

27 Wherefore whosover shall eat this bread, and drink *this* cup of the Lord, unworthily, shall be guilty of the body and blood of the Lord.

11:20 *when ye come together*. The early Christians held a love-feast in connection with the Lord's Supper during which they gathered for a fellowship meal, sent and received communications from other churches, and collected money for widows and orphans. Apparently some of the wealthier members were not sharing their food but greedily consumed it before the poor showed up (v. 21). If the purposes of the love-feast are not being realized, then it is better to eat at home (v. 22).

11:24 *this is my body*. The bread represents Christ's body and the *cup* (v. 25) His blood. See note at Luke 22:19.

11:25 *the new testament*. See note at Matt. 26:28.

11:26 *ye do shew the Lord's death till he come*. The Lord's Supper is an acted sermon (*shew*), looking back on Christ's life and death, and looking forward to His second coming.

28 But let a man examine himself, and so let him eat of *that* bread, and drink of *that* cup.

29 For he that eateth and drinketh unworthily, eateth and drinketh damnation to himself, not discerning the Lord's body.

30 For this cause many *are* weak and sickly among you, and many sleep.

31 For if we would judge ourselves, we should not be judged.

32 But when we are judged, we are chastened of the Lord, that we should not be condemned with the world.

33 Wherefore, my brethren, when ye come together to eat, tarry one for another.

34 And if any man hunger, let him eat at home; that ye come not together unto condemnation. And the rest will I set in order when I come.

C The Use of Spiritual Gifts, 12:1–14:40

1 *The varieties of gifts,* 12:1–11

12 Now concerning spiritual *gifts,* brethren, I would not have you ignorant.

2 Ye know that ye were Gentiles, carried away unto these dumb idols, even as ye were led.

3 Wherefore I give you to understand, that no man speaking by the Spirit of God calleth Jesus accursed: and *that* no man can say that Jesus is the Lord, but by the Holy Ghost.

4 Now there are diversities of gifts, but the same Spirit.

5 And there are differences of administrations, but the same Lord.

6 And there are diversities of operations, but it is the same God which worketh all in all.

7 But the manifestation of the Spirit is given to every man to profit withal.

11:29 *unworthily.* I.e., with unconfessed sin (so also in v. 27). This may result in judgment, even sickness or physical death v. 30). Therefore, each one is to examine himself before partaking (v. 31).

12:1 In chapters 12–14 Paul deals with the subject of *spiritual gifts* against the background of divisions and moral laxity in a church that lacked no gift (1:7, see note). Chapter 12 deals with the unity and diversity of the gifts, ch. 13 with the power of love, and ch. 14 with the specific gifts of prophecy and tongues.

12:5 *administrations.* Lit., ministries.

12:6 *operations.* I.e., energizing of the gifts. Each person of the Godhead is related to the gifts.

8 For to one is given by the Spirit the word of wisdom; to another the word of knowledge by the same Spirit;

9 To another faith by the same Spirit; to another the gifts of healing by the same Spirit;

10 To another the working of miracles; to another prophecy; to another discerning of spirits; to another *divers* kinds of tongues; to another the interpretation of tongues:

11 But all these worketh that one and the selfsame Spirit, dividing to every man severally as he will.

2 *The purpose of gifts: unity in diversity*, 12:12–31

12 For as the body is one, and hath many members, and all the members of that one body, being many, are one body: so also *is* Christ.

13 For by one Spirit are we all baptized into one body, whether *we be* Jews or Gentiles, whether *we be* bond or free; and have been all made to drink into one Spirit.

14 For the body is not one member, but many.

15 If the foot shall say, Because I am not the hand, I am not of the body; is it therefore not of the body?

16 And if the ear shall say, Because I am not the eye, I am not of the body; is it therefore not of the body?

17 If the whole body *were* an eye, where *were* the hearing? If the whole *were* hearing, where *were* the smelling?

18 But now hath God set the members every one of them in the body, as it hath pleased him.

12:8–10 *the word of wisdom* (v. 8) = the communication of spiritual wisdom. *the word of knowledge* (v. 8) = the communication of practical truth. *faith* (v. 9) = unusual reliance on God. *gifts of healing* (v. 9) included restoration of life (Acts 9:40; 20:9). *prophecy* (v. 10) = the ability to tell new revelation from God. *tongues* and *interpretation of tongues* (v. 10) = the ability to speak and interpret languages unknown to the speaker or interpreter. These gifts were obviously necessary before the Word of God was written.

12:12–31 Here Paul describes the relationship of gifted believers to each other, using the illustration of the human body. The Spirit has formed an organic unity of the many dissimilar members of the body of Christ (vv. 12–13). The constitutions of the human body and the body of Christ demand that all members (even those which seem unimportant) function in harmony (vv. 14–20). Finally, he emphasizes the need for mutual dependence, respect, and care for each other (vv. 21–31).

12:13 *are we all baptized*. The Spirit joins all believers to the body of Christ. The tense of the verb indicates a past action, and it is something all believers (even carnal ones) have experienced.

19 And if they were all one member, where *were* the body?

20 But now *are they* many members, yet but one body.

21 And the eye cannot say unto the hand, I have no need of thee: nor again the head to the feet, I have no need of you.

22 Nay, much more those members of the body, which seem to be more feeble, are necessary:

23 And those *members* of the body, which we think to be less honourable, upon these we bestow more abundant honour; and our uncomely *parts* have more abundant comeliness.

24 For our comely *parts* have no need: but God hath tempered the body together, having given more abundant honour to that *part* which lacked:

25 That there should be no schism in the *body*; but *that* the members should have the same care one for another.

26 And whether one member suffer, all the members suffer with it; or one member be honoured, all the members rejoice with it.

27 Now ye are the body of Christ, and members in particular.

28 And God hath set some in the church, first apostles, secondarily prophets, thirdly teachers, after that miracles, then gifts of healings, helps, governments, diversities of tongues.

29 *Are* all apostles? *are* all prophets? *are* all teachers? *are* all workers of miracles?

30 Have all the gifts of healing? do all speak with tongues? do all interpret?

31 But covet earnestly the best gifts: and yet shew I unto you a more excellent way.

3 *The supremacy of love over gifts*, 13:1–13

13 Though I speak with the tongues of men and of angels, and have not charity, I am become *as* sounding brass, or a tinkling cymbal.

12:23 *we bestow more abundant honour* by way of clothing.

12:24 *tempered*=blended.

12:25 *schism*=dissension, division.

12:28 *first . . .* The gifts are ranked in order of honor.

12:29–30 The answer expected to all of these questions is "No."

12:31 *the best gifts.* Lit., the greater gifts (as ranked in v. 28).

13:1 *charity*=love, and throughout this chapter. The Greek word used is *agape*. The Greek word used for love of an adorable

2 And though I have *the gift of* prophecy, and understand all mysteries, and all knowledge; and though I have all faith, so that I could remove mountains, and have not charity, I am nothing.

3 And though I bestow all my goods to feed *the poor*, and though I give my body to be burned, and have not charity, it profiteth me nothing.

4 Charity suffereth long, *and* is kind; charity envieth not; charity vaunteth not itself, is not puffed up,

5 Doth not behave itself unseemly, seeketh not her own, is not easily provoked, thinketh no evil;

6 Rejoiceth not in iniquity, but rejoiceth in the truth;

7 Beareth all things, believeth all things, hopeth all things, endureth all things.

8 Charity never faileth: but whether *there be* prophecies, they shall fail; whether *there be* tongues, they shall cease; whether *there be* knowledge, it shall vanish away.

9 For we know in part, and we prophesy in part.

10 But when that which is perfect is come, then that which is in part shall be done away.

11 When I was a child, I spake as a child, I understood as a child, I thought as a child: but when I became a man, I put away childish things.

12 For now we see through a glass, darkly; but then face

object, especially for love between man and woman, was *eros*. Another Greek word, *phileo*, means to have the kind of love that is found in friendship. *Charity* is from the Latin *caritas*, and means basically benevolence or alms-giving. *Agape* is what God is (1 John 4:8) and what He manifested in the gift of His Son (John 3:16). It is more than "mutuality"; it expresses an unselfish esteem of the object loved. Christ's love for us is undeserved and without thought of return. The love which His followers show, Paul now says, should be the same. *sounding brass*=noisy gong, which along with the *cymbal* was associated with pagan worship.

13:4 *envieth not*=is not jealous. *vaunteth not itself*=does not play the braggart.

13:5 *unseemly*=unbecomingly (see 7:36; 11:5-6, 21). *seeketh not her own.* See 6:7.

13:10 . . . *that which is perfect.* A reference to Christ's second coming.

13:11 There are stages of growth within this imperfect time before Christ's return. After the church began there was a period of immaturity during which spectacular gifts were needed for growth and authentication (Heb. 2:3-4). With the completion of the N.T. and the growing maturity of the church, the need for such gifts disappeared.

to face: now I know in part; but then shall I know even as also I am known.

13 And now abideth faith, hope, charity, these three; but the greatest of these *is* charity.

4 *The superiority of prophecy over tongues,* 14:1–25

14 Follow after charity, and desire spiritual *gifts,* but rather that ye may prophesy.

2 For he that speaketh in an *unknown* tongue speaketh not unto men, but unto God: for no man understandeth *him;* howbeit in the spirit he speaketh mysteries.

3 But he that prophesieth speaketh unto men *to* edification, and exhortation, and comfort.

4 He that speaketh in an *unknown* tongue edifieth himself; but he that prophesieth edifieth the church.

5 I would that ye all spake with tongues, but rather that ye prophesied: for greater *is* he that prophesieth than he that speaketh with tongues, except he interpret, that the church may receive edifying.

6 Now, brethren, if I come unto you speaking with tongues, what shall I profit you, except I shall speak to you either by revelation, or by knowledge, or by prophesying, or by doctrine?

7 And even things without life giving sound, whether pipe or harp, except they give a distinction in the sounds, how shall it be known what is piped or harped?

8 For if the trumpet give an uncertain sound, who shall prepare himself to the battle?

9 So likewise ye, except ye utter by the tongue words easy to be understood, how shall it be known what is spoken? for ye shall speak into the air.

10 There are, it may be, so many kinds of voices in the world, and none of them *is* without signification.

11 Therefore if I know not the meaning of the voice,

13:13 *abideth.* Since these three virtues abide even after all the gifts have ceased, they should be cultivated. Love is the *greatest* since it expressed God and Calvary.

14:1 *rather that ye may prophesy.* Prophecy is preferred over tongues because it is clear (v. 2) and it edifies the whole church (v. 4).

14:2 *an unknown tongue.* The word "unknown" is not in the original text and has been supplied throughout this chapter. Though many understand these tongues to be ecstatic speech, it may well be that they were languages, as in Acts 2:4, 6, 8, 11.

14:6–15 *tongues* are really useless without interpretation.

I shall be unto him that speaketh a barbarian, and he that speaketh *shall be* a barbarian unto me.

12 Even so ye, forasmuch as ye are zealous of spiritual *gifts,* seek that ye may excel to the edifying of the church.

13 Wherefore let him that speaketh in an *unknown* tongue pray that he may interpret.

14 For if I pray in an *unknown* tongue, my spirit prayeth, but my understanding is unfruitful.

15 What is it then? I will pray with the spirit, and I will pray with the understanding also: I will sing with the spirit, and I will sing with the understanding also.

16 Else when thou shalt bless with the spirit, how shall he that occupieth the room of the unlearned say Amen at thy giving of thanks, seeing he understandeth not what thou sayest?

17 For thou verily givest thanks well, but the other is not edified.

18 I thank my God, I speak with tongues more than ye all:

19 Yet in the church I had rather speak five words with my understanding, that *by my voice* I might teach others also, than ten thousand words in an *unknown* tongue.

20 Brethren, be not children in understanding: howbeit in malice be ye children, but in understanding be men.

21 In the law it is written, With *men of* other tongues and other lips will I speak unto this people; and yet for all that will they not hear me, saith the Lord.

22 Wherefore tongues are for a sign, not to them that believe, but to them that believe not: but prophesying *serveth* not for them that believe not, but for them which believe.

23 If therefore the whole church be come together into one place, and all speak with tongues, and there come in *those that are* unlearned, or unbelievers, will they not say that ye are mad?

24 But if all prophesy, and there come in one that believeth not, or *one* unlearned, he is convinced of all, he is judged of all:

25 And thus are the secrets of his heart made manifest;

14:16 *the room of the unlearned.* Better, the place of the un-instructed; i.e., the untaught believer, or perhaps the outsider.

14:20–25 Prophecy is not only more profitable for those within the church, but also for outsiders.

14:21 See Isa. 28:11–12. Tongues were given as a sign to pro-voke the Jews to a consideration of the truth of the Christian message.

and so falling down on *his* face he will worship God, and report that God is in you of a truth.

5 *The regulations for the use of gifts*, 14:26–40

26 How is it then, brethren? when ye come together, every one of you hath a psalm, hath a doctrine, hath a tongue, hath a revelation, hath an interpretation. Let all things be done unto edifying.

27 If any man speak in an *unknown* tongue, *let it be* by two, or at the most *by* three, and *that* by course; and let one interpret.

28 But if there be no interpreter, let him keep silence in the church; and let him speak to himself, and to God.

29 Let the prophets speak two or three, and let the other judge.

30 If *any thing* be revealed to another that sitteth by, let the first hold his peace.

31 For ye may all prophesy one by one, that all may learn, and all may be comforted.

32 And the spirits of the prophets are subject to the prophets.

33 For God is not *the author* of confusion, but of peace, as in all churches of the saints.

34 Let your women keep silence in the churches: for it is not permitted unto them to speak; but *they are commanded* to be under obedience, as also saith the law.

35 And if they will learn any thing, let them ask their husbands at home: for it is a shame for women to speak in the church.

36 What? came the word of God out from you? or came it unto you only?

14:26 Free participation in the service is indicated by this verse, but not to the point of disorder.
14:27 *by course*=in turn. Only *two* or *three* should speak in tongues in a service, never at the same time, but in turn, and not at all if no interpreter is present (v. 28).
14:29 *two* or *three* prophets can be heard profitably in a meeting.
14:32 This means that the spiritual activities of the prophets are under the full control of the prophets. No true prophet can claim a hearing on the ground that he is under a power over which he has no control.
14:34 *Let your women keep silence in the churches*. Whatever this restriction means, it must include tongues and prophecy (see vv. 27, 29 where the same verb *speak* is used). See also 1 Tim. 2:12.
14:36 Is Corinth the sole repository of truth?!

37 If any man think himself to be a prophet, or spiritual, let him acknowledge that the things that I write unto you are the commandments of the Lord.

38 But if any man be ignorant, let him be ignorant.

39 Wherefore, brethren, covet to prophesy, and forbid not to speak with tongues.

40 Let all things be done decently and in order.

VII THE DOCTRINE OF THE RESURRECTION, 15:1–58

A The Importance of the Resurrection, 15:1–11

15 Moreover, brethren, I declare unto you the gospel which I preached unto you, which also ye have received, and wherein ye stand;

2 By which also ye are saved, if ye keep in memory what I preached unto you, unless ye have believed in vain.

3 For I delivered unto you first of all that which I also received, how that Christ died for our sins according to the scriptures;

4 And that he was buried, and that he rose again the third day according to the scriptures:

5 And that he was seen of Cĕ′phas, then of the twelve:

6 After that, he was seen of above five hundred brethren at once; of whom the greater part remain unto this present, but some are fallen asleep.

7 After that, he was seen of James; then of all the apostles.

14:38 *let him be ignorant.* I.e., the one ignorant of Paul's words is to be left in that condition. However, a variant reading may be translated "he is ignored" (by God).

15:2 *unless ye have believed in vain.* That would be the case if the resurrection of Christ were not true.

15:4 *And that he was buried.* This is certain proof that Christ actually died. *and that he rose again.* The perfect tense indicates that He is still alive.

15:6 *five hundred brethren.* The citation of these and other witnesses to Christ's resurrection is of great apologetic value, especially in view of the fact that since most of them were alive when Paul wrote, this means that the resurrection was still attested to by living witnesses 25 years after the event.

15:7 *he was seen of James.* This is our Lord's half-brother, the author of the letter of James (see John 7:5; Acts 1:14). This appearance is nowhere else recorded in the N.T.

8 And last of all he was seen of me also, as of one born out of due time.

9 For I am the least of the apostles, that am not meet to be called an apostle, because I persecuted the church of God.

10 But by the grace of God I am what I am: and his grace which *was bestowed* upon me was not in vain; but I laboured more abundantly than they all: yet not I, but the grace of God which was with me.

11 Therefore whether *it were* I or they, so we preach, and so ye believed.

B The Consequences of
Denying the Resurrection, 15:12–19

12 Now if Christ be preached that he rose from the dead, how say some among you that there is no resurrection of the dead?

13 But if there be no resurrection of the dead, then is Christ not risen:

14 And if Christ be not risen, then *is* our preaching vain, and your faith *is* also vain.

15 Yea, and we are found false witnesses of God; because we have testified of God that he raised up Christ: whom he raised not up, if so be that the dead rise not.

16 For if the dead rise not, then is not Christ raised:

17 And if Christ be not raised, your faith *is* vain; ye are yet in yours sins.

15:8 *one born out of due time.* Paul may be referring to his own conversion as premature when viewed in relation to Israel's future conversion (Rom. 11:26); or he is likely regarding himself as a miscarried infant when compared to the other apostles; that is, one thrust suddenly into apostleship without the nurture of Christ's friendship and direct teaching.

15:12 *no resurrection of the dead.* Nothing in the Greek background of the Gentile converts at Corinth led them to believe in the resurrection of the dead. In general, they believed in the immortality of the soul, but not the resurrection of the body. To them, the body was the source of man's weakness and sin; death, therefore, was the welcome means by which the soul was liberated from the body. Resurrection, then, would enslave the soul again.

15:13–19 If the bodily resurrection of Christ is untrue, then we preach a lie (v. 15), our faith is without content (v. 17), and we are hopeless concerning the future (vv. 18–19).

18 Then they also which are fallen asleep in Christ are perished.

19 If in this life only we have hope in Christ, we are of all men most miserable.

C The Christian Hope, 15:20–34

20 But now is Christ risen from the dead, *and* become the firstfruits of them that slept.

21 For since by man *came* death, by man *came* also the resurrection of the dead.

22 For as in Adam all die, even so in Christ shall all be made alive.

23 But every man in his own order: Christ the firstfruits; afterward they that are Christ's at his coming.

24 Then *cometh* the end, when he shall have delivered up the kingdom to God, even the Father; when he shall have put down all rule and all authority and power.

25 For he must reign, till he hath put all enemies under his feet.

26 The last enemy *that* shall be destroyed *is* death.

27 For he hath put all things under his feet. But when he saith all things are put under *him, it is* manifest that he is excepted, which did put all things under him.

28 And when all things shall be subdued unto him, then shall the Son also himself be subject unto him that put all things under him, that God may be all in all.

29 Else what shall they do which are baptized for the dead, if the dead rise not at all? why are they then baptized for the dead?

30 And why stand we in jeopardy every hour?

15:20 *the firstfruits.* Christ's resurrection is an earnest or sample of resurrections to come (see Lev. 23:9–14).

15:22 *in Christ shall all be made alive.* This refers to the resurrection of believers only (those *in Christ*).

15:23–24 The order of resurrections is as follows: first, Christ; then believers at His coming (1 Thess. 4:13–18); finally, at the end of the millennial kingdom.

15:29 *baptized for the dead.* Various interpretations have been given for this difficult expression. (1) This sanctions being baptized vicariously for another in order to assure him a place in heaven—a view which is heretical. (2) This refers to those who were baptized because of the testimony of those who had died. (3) Most likely it means being baptized in the place of those who had died; i.e., new converts taking the place of older ones who died. Paul's point is: unless one believes in the resurrection of the dead (rather than the Greek idea of "immortality") what's the point of such behavior?

31 I protest by your rejoicing which I have in Christ Jesus our Lord, I die daily.

32 If after the manner of men I have fought with beasts at Ephesus, what advantageth it me, if the dead rise not? let us eat and drink; for to morrow we die.

33 Be not deceived: evil communications corrupt good manners.

34 Awake to righteousness, and sin not; for some have not the knowledge of God: I speak *this* to your shame.

D The Resurrection Body, 15:35–50

35 But some *man* will say, How are the dead raised up? and with what body do they come?

36 *Thou* fool, that which thou sowest is not quickened, except it die:

37 And that which thou sowest, thou sowest not that body that shall be, but bare grain, it may chance of wheat, or of some other *grain:*

38 But God giveth it a body as it hath pleased him, and to every seed his own body.

39 All flesh *is* not the same flesh: but *there is* one *kind of* flesh of men, another flesh of beasts, another of fishes, *and* another of birds.

40 *There are* also celestial bodies, and bodies terrestrial: but the glory of the celestial *is* one, and the *glory* of the terrestrial *is* another.

41 *There is* one glory of the sun, and another glory of the moon, and another glory of the stars: for *one* star differeth from *another* star in glory.

42 So also *is* the resurrection of the dead. It is sown in corruption; it is raised in incorruption:

15:31 *I die daily.* Paul was exposed to so many physical dangers and violent attacks on himself and his teachings, that "daily" cannot be an exaggeration.

15:33 *Be not deceived.* The same Greek phrase occurs in 6:9; Gal. 6:7; Jas. 1:16. The verse is a Greek proverb, first appearing in a play by Menander. It may be translated: "Bad company ruins good morals."

15:34 *Awake to righteousness.* Better, come to your right mind.

15:35–50 Here Paul deals with two common errors in regard to the nature of the resurrection body: (1) that it is the same body that was laid in the grave, simply reformed; and (2) that the new body is unrelated to the original one. It is the body God has chosen (v. 38), related to the former (v. 36), yet different (vv. 39–41).

15:42 *raised in incorruption* with no possibility of decay.

43 It is sown in dishonour; it is raised in glory: it is sown in weakness; it is raised in power:

44 It is sown a natural body: it is raised a spiritual body. There is a natural body, and there is a spiritual body.

45 And so it is written, The first man Adam was made a living soul; the last Adam *was made* a quickening spirit.

46 Howbeit that *was* not first which is spiritual, but that which is natural; and afterward that which is spiritual.

47 The first man *is* of the earth, earthy: the second man *is* the Lord from heaven.

48 As *is* the earthy, such *are* they also that are earthy: and as *is* the heavenly, such *are* they also that are heavenly.

49 And as we have borne the image of the earthy, we shall also bear the image of the heavenly.

50 Now this I say, brethren, that flesh and blood cannot inherit the kingdom of God; neither doth corruption inherit incorruption.

E The Christian's Victory through Christ, 15:51–58

51 Behold, I shew you a mystery; We shall not all sleep, but we shall all be changed,

52 In a moment, in the twinkling of an eye, at the last trump: for the trumpet shall sound, and the dead shall be raised incorruptible, and we shall be changed.

53 For this corruptible must put on incorruption, and this mortal *must* put on immortality.

54 So when this corruptible shall have put on incorruption, and this mortal shall have put on immortality, then shall be brought to pass the saying that is written, Death is swallowed up in victory.

55 O death, where *is* thy sting? O grave, where *is* thy victory?

56 The sting of death *is* sin; and the strength of sin *is* the law.

15:45 See Gen. 2:7.

15:49 *the image of the heavenly*. I.e., the resurrection body will be like Christ's.

15:51–58 Here Paul answers the question, What happens to those who do not die?

15:51 *We shall not all sleep*. I.e., not all die (1 Thess. 4:15). Some will be alive when the Lord returns, but all will *be changed*.

15:53 *corruptible*=those who have died. *mortal*=those who are living.

15:54 The reference is to Isa. 25:8.

15:55 *grave*. Lit., death.

15:56 *The sting of death is sin* because it is by sin that death

57 But thanks *be* to God, which giveth us the victory through our Lord Jesus Christ.

58 Therefore, my beloved brethren, be ye stedfast, unmoveable, always abounding in the work of the Lord, forasmuch as ye know that your labour is not in vain in the Lord.

VIII PRACTICAL AND PERSONAL MATTERS, 16:1–24

A The Collection for the Saints in Jerusalem, 16:1–4

16 Now concerning the collection for the saints, as I have given order to the churches of Galatia, even so do ye.

2 Upon the first *day* of the week let every one of you lay by him in store, as God hath prospered him, that there be no gatherings when I come.

3 And when I come, whomsoever ye shall approve by *your* letters, them will I send to bring your liberality unto Jerusalem.

4 And if it be meet that I go also, they shall go with me.

B The Planned Visit of Paul, 16:5–9

5 Now I will come unto you, when I shall pass through Macedonia: for I do pass through Macedonia.

6 And it may be that I will abide, yea, and winter with you, that ye may bring me on my journey whithersoever I go.

7 For I will not see you now by the way; but I trust to tarry a while with you, if the Lord permit.

8 But I will tarry at Ephesus until Pentecost.

9 For a great door and effectual is opened unto me, and *there are* many adversaries.

gains authority over man, *and the strength of sin is the law* because the law stirs up sin (Rom. 5:12: 7:8–11).

15:58 A firm belief in the resurrection and a solid hope for the future will give incentive for service in the present.

16:1 *the saints* in Jerusalem.

16:2 The Christian's giving is to be done (1) regularly on Sunday; (2) into a private store ("by him") at home from which store he makes distributions; and (3) in proportion to God's prospering.

16:3 Paul would let others handle the money.

16:9 *door* of opportunity.

C Exhortations, Greetings, and Benediction, 16:10–24

10 Now if Timoth'eus come, see that he may be with you without fear: for he worketh the work of the Lord, as I also *do.*

11 Let no man therefore despise him: but conduct him forth in peace, that he may come unto me: for I look for him with the brethren.

12 As touching *our* brother Apol'los, I greatly desired him to come unto you with the brethren: but his will was not at all to come at this time; but he will come when he shall have convenient time.

13 Watch ye, stand fast in the faith, quit you like men, be strong.

14 Let all your things be done with charity.

15 I beseech you, brethren, (ye know the house of Steph'anas, that it is the firstfruits of Achā'a, and *that* they have addicted themselves to the ministry of the saints,)

16 That ye submit yourselves unto such, and to every one that helpeth with *us,* and laboureth.

17 I am glad of the coming of Steph'anas and Fortūnā'-tus and Achā'icus: for that which was lacking on your part they have supplied.

18 For they have refreshed my spirit and yours: therefore acknowledge ye them that are such.

19 The churches of Asia salute you. Aquila and Priscilla salute you much in the Lord, with the church that is in their house.

20 All the brethren greet you. Greet ye one another with an holy kiss.

21 The salutation of *me* Paul with mine own hand.

22 If any man love not the Lord Jesus Christ, let him be Anath'ema Maran-a'tha.

23 The grace of our Lord Jesus Christ *be* with you.

24 My love *be* with you all in Christ Jesus. Amen.

16:12 *his will.* I.e., Apollos'.

16:13 *quit you like men*=be a man!

16:15 *firstfruits.* I.e., first converts. *addicted.* Better, appointed.

16:17 *Stephanas and Fortunatus and Achaicus* probably brought Paul the letter from the Corinthians mentioned in 7:1.

16:20 *an holy kiss.* See note at 1 Pet. 5:14.

16:22 *Anathema.* Lit., a thing devoted to destruction; i.e., accursed (12:3; Rom. 9:3; Gal. 1:8–9). *Maranatha*=our Lord, come! See also Rev. 22:20.

INTRODUCTION TO
THE SECOND LETTER OF PAUL TO THE
Corinthians

AUTHOR: Paul   DATE: 57

The Occasion   After writing 1 Corinthians Paul found it necessary to make a hurried, painful visit to Corinth, since the problems that occasioned the first letter had not been resolved (2 Cor. 2:1; 12:14; 13:1–2). Following this visit he wrote the church a severe and sorrowful letter, to which he refers in 2:4 but which has been lost to us. Titus carried that letter. Paul, unable to wait to meet Titus on his return to Troas, hurried on to Macedonia where Titus related the good news that the church had repented of their rebelliousness against Paul. From Macedonia Paul wrote 2 Corinthians and followed it up with his final recorded visit to the church (Acts 20:1–4).

A popular theory claims that chapters 10–13 are part of that lost "sorrowful letter." Although some features of those chapters correspond to what must have been the contents of that lost letter, the principal subject of that letter, the offender of 2 Corinthians 2–5, is nowhere mentioned in those chapters. Further, there is no manuscript evidence for partitioning 2 Corinthians.

The Purposes   The purposes of this letter were: (1) to express joy at the favorable response of the church to Paul's ministry (1–7); (2) to remind the believers of their commitment to give to the collection for the Christians in Judea (8–9); and (3) to defend his own apostolic authority (10–13).

The Contents   The letter contains many personal and autobiographical glimpses into Paul's life (4:8–18; 11:22–33). The longest discussion of giving in the N.T. is in chapters 8 and 9. Important verses include 5:10, 20–21; 6:14; 8:9; 10:5; 11:14; 12:9; and 13:14.

OUTLINE OF 2 CORINTHIANS

THE SECOND LETTER OF
PAUL THE APOSTLE TO THE
Corinthians

I INTRODUCTION, 1:1–11

A Salutation, 1:1–2

1 Paul, an apostle of Jesus Christ by the will of God, and Timothy *our* brother, unto the church of God which is at Corinth, with all the saints which are in all Achа́'a:

2 Grace *be* to you and peace from God our Father, and *from* the Lord Jesus Christ.

E Paul's Gratitude for God's Goodness, 1:3–11

3 Blessed *be* God, even the Father of our Lord Jesus Christ, the Father of mercies, and the God of all comfort;

4 Who comforteth us in all our tribulation, that we may be able to comfort them which are in any trouble, by the comfort wherewith we ourselves are comforted of God.

5 For as the sufferings of Christ abound in us, so our consolation also aboundeth by Christ.

1:1 *Achaia.* The Roman province comprising all of Greece south of Macedonia, including Athens and Cenchrea (Rom. 16:1).
1:2 God *our Father.* Paul says a number of things about God the Father in this epistle: (1) He is the living God (3:3; 6:16); (2) He is the God of grace, mercy, and comfort (1:2–3); (3) He is faithful (1:18, *true*=faithful); (4) His power is available to His people (4:7; 6:7; 13:4); (5) He is the Father of Christ (1:3) and of His people (6:18). Concerning *the Lord Jesus Christ* Paul says: (1) He is the Son of God (1:19); (2) He is the image of God (4:44); (3) He is sinless (5:21). But he seems to be more interested in what Christ does: (1) Victory is in Him (2:14); (2) He is the judge (5:10); (3) He reconciles (5:19; 8:9); (4) He appoints and motivates His ambassadors (5:20); (5) He makes men new creatures (5:17).
1:5 *the sufferings of Christ abound in us.* Paul's own sufferings are identified as Christ's sufferings (see 4:10; Phil. 3:10; Col. 1:24). What Paul suffered was intended to encourage others (v. 6).

6 And whether we be afflicted, *it is* for your consolation and salvation, which is effectual in the enduring of the same sufferings which we also suffer: or whether we be comforted, *it is* for your consolation and salvation.

7 And our hope of you *is* stedfast, knowing, that as ye are partakers of the sufferings, so *shall ye be* also of the consolation.

8 For we would not, brethren, have you ignorant of our trouble which came to us in Asia, that we were pressed out of measure, above strength, insomuch that we despaired even of life:

9 But we had the sentence of death in ourselves, that we should not trust in ourselves, but in God which raiseth the dead:

10 Who delivered us from so great a death, and doth deliver: in whom we trust that he will yet deliver *us*;

11 Ye also helping together by prayer for us, that for the gift *bestowed* upon us by the means of many persons thanks may be given by many on our behalf.

II THE APOSTLE'S CONCILIATION WITH RESPECT TO THE PROBLEM AT CORINTH, 1:12–2:13

A The Change in Paul's Plans, 1:12–2:4

12 For our rejoicing is this, the testimony of our conscience, that in simplicity and godly sincerity, not with fleshly wisdom, but by the grace of God, we have had our conversation in the world, and more abundantly to youward.

13 For we write none other things unto you, than what ye read or acknowledge; and I trust ye shall acknowledge even to the end;

14 As also ye have acknowledged us in part, that we

1:8 *our trouble which came to us in Asia.* Since Paul offers no details, probably the Corinthians knew what the trouble was. It may have been one of the dangers described in 11:23–26, or the mob violence of Acts 19:23–41, or some serious illness (*we despaired even of life*).

1:11 *by prayer.* The good report of the church brought by Titus encourages Paul to exhort the Corinthians to prayer. Paul's great confidence in intercessory prayer is seen also in Rom. 15:30–31; Phil. 1:9; Col. 4:12.

1:12 *simplicity.* Better, holiness. *we have had our conversation=* we behaved ourselves.

are your rejoicing, even as ye also *are* ours in the day of the Lord Jesus.

15 And in this confidence I was minded to come unto you before, that ye might have a second benefit;

16 And to pass by you into Macedonia, and to come again out of Macedonia unto you, and of you to be brought on my way toward Judæa.

17 When I therefore was thus minded, did I use lightness? or the things that I purpose, do I purpose according to the flesh, that with me there should be yea yea, and nay nay?

18 But *as* God *is* true, our word toward you was not yea and nay.

19 For the Son of God, Jesus Christ, who was preached among you by us, *even* by me and Silvā′nus and Tīmoth′-eus, was not yea and nay, but in him was yea.

20 For all the promises of God in him *are* yea, and in him Amen, unto the glory of God by us.

21 Now he which stablisheth us with you in Christ, and hath anointed us, *is* God;

22 Who hath also sealed us, and given the earnest of the Spirit in our hearts.

23 Moreover I call God for a record upon my soul, that to spare you I came not as yet unto Corinth.

24 Not for that we have dominion over your faith, but are helpers of your joy: for by faith ye stand.

1:16 Paul intended to visit them twice, going to and returning from Macedonia, but he changed his plans. This was dubbed vacillation and unspirituality (*according to the flesh*, v. 17) by his opponents, charges he denies.

1:17 *did I use lightness*=was I vacillating? The verse may be paraphrased like this: Did my change of plans indicate that I couldn't make up my mind? Am I like a worldly man who says "Yes" and "No" at the same time? In 1 Cor. 16:5 Paul had promised to go to Corinth. In the second lost letter (between 1 and 2 Cor.) he may have said something different which seemed to make him say yes and no at the same time. The itinerary of his present plan was Ephesus to Troas to Macedonia to Corinth.

1:20 *in him are yea*. I.e., the promises of God find their certain fulfillment, their Yes, in Christ. *and in him Amen*. I.e., we give our concurrence through saying Amen.

1:22 The seal indicates security, and the *earnest* is a guarantee that God will fulfill His promises. See notes at Eph. 1:13 and 1:14.

1:24 *Not for that we have dominion over your faith*. Apostolic authority did not give Paul the right to lord it over their faith

2 But I determined this with myself, that I would not come again to you in heaviness.

2 For if I make you sorry, who is he then that maketh me glad, but the same which is made sorry by me?

3 And I wrote this same unto you, lest, when I came, I should have sorrow from them of whom I ought to rejoice; having confidence in you all, that my joy is *the joy* of you all.

4 For out of much affliction and anguish of heart I wrote unto you with many tears; not that ye should be grieved, but that ye might know the love which I have more abundantly unto you.

B The Change in the Offender's Punishment, 2:5-11

5 But if any have caused grief, he hath not grieved me, but in part: that I may not overcharge you all.

6 Sufficient to such a man *is* this punishment, which *was inflicted* of many.

7 So that contrariwise ye *ought* rather to forgive *him,* and comfort *him,* lest perhaps such a one should be swallowed up with overmuch sorrow.

8 Wherefore I beseech you that ye would confirm *your* love toward him.

9 For to this end also did I write, that I might know the proof of you, whether ye be obedient in all things.

10 To whom ye forgive any thing, I *forgive* also: for if I forgave any thing, to whom I forgave *it,* for your sakes *forgave I it* in the person of Christ;

11 Lest Satan should get an advantage of us: for we are not ignorant of his devices.

(see 1 Pet. 5:1-3). They stand *by* faith, i.e., their own faith, not by Paul's *dominion* or control.

2:2 The meaning is this: If I hurt you, who will be left to make me glad but sad people? That won't be any comfort!

2:4 *I wrote . . . unto you.* See the Introduction to 2 Corinthians for a discussion of this "sorrowful letter."

2:6 *of many.* Lit., by the majority. The rebel had been punished sufficiently and had repented. Apparently some wanted a severer penalty (vv. 6-8).

2:9 *whether ye be obedient.* Though they had accepted Paul's authority in the case of the rebel, they had yet to prove that they accepted it *in all things* (compare 10:6).

2:11 *Lest Satan should get an advantage of us.* The forgiven brother needed to be restored to fellowship lest Satan put him under the pressure of continued self-accusation and introspec-

C The Meeting with Titus, 2:12–13

12 Furthermore, when I came to Trō'as to *preach* Christ's gospel, and a door was opened unto me of the Lord,

13 I had no rest in my spirit, because I found not Titus my brother: but taking my leave of them, I went from thence into Macedonia.

III THE APOSTOLIC MINISTRY, 2:14–6:10

A The Confidence of the Ministry: Victory, 2:14–17

14 Now thanks *be* unto God, which always causeth us to triumph in Christ, and maketh manifest the savour of his knowledge by us in every place.

15 For we are unto God a sweet savour of Christ, in them that are saved, and in them that perish:

16 To the one *we are* the savour of death unto death; and to the other the savour of life unto life. And who *is* sufficient for these things?

17 For we are not as many, which corrupt the word of God: but as of sincerity, but as of God, in the sight of God speak we in Christ.

**B The Commendation of the Ministry:
Changed Lives, 3:1–3**

3 Do we begin again to commend ourselves? or need we, as some *others*, epistles of commendation to you, or *letters* of commendation from you?

2 Ye are our epistle written in our hearts, known and read of all men:

3 *Forasmuch as ye are* manifestly declared to be the

tion. Also as long as the matter was not settled, Satan kept Paul and the church estranged.

2:13 *I had no rest* wondering how his severe letter had been received.

2:14 *which always causeth us to triumph in Christ.* Better, who leads us in triumph in Christ. The picture is of a Roman conqueror leading his captives in triumph. Paul gladly considers himself one of Christ's captives being led in triumph to the glory of Christ. For *savour* read fragrance; for *by us*, through us.

2:15–16 The same gospel brings life to the believer and death to the rejector.

2:17 *corrupt.* Lit., hawking or peddling.

3:1–3 The work of the Spirit in the lives of the Corinthians was sufficient recommendation of Paul's ministry.

epistle of Christ ministered by us, written not with ink, but with the Spirit of the living God; not in tables of stone, but in fleshy tables of the heart.

C The Covenant for the Ministry:
The New Covenant, 3:4–18

4 And such trust have we through Christ to God-ward:

5 Not that we are sufficient of ourselves to think any thing as of ourselves; but our sufficiency *is* of God;

6 Who also hath made us able ministers of the new testament; not of the letter, but of the spirit: for the letter killeth, but the spirit giveth life.

7 But if the ministration of death, written *and* engraven in stones, was glorious, so that the children of Israel could not stedfastly behold the face of Moses for the glory of his countenance; which *glory* was to be done away:

8 How shall not the ministration of the spirit be rather glorious?

9 For if the ministration of condemnation *be* glory, much more doth the ministration of righteousness exceed in glory.

10 For even that which was made glorious had no glory in this respect, by reason of the glory that excelleth.

11 For if that which is done away *was* glorious, much more that which remaineth *is* glorious.

12 Seeing then that we have such hope, we use great plainness of speech:

3:5 *our sufficiency is of God.* This answers the question raised in 2:16.

3:6 *able*=sufficient or competent. *the new testament.* Lit., a new covenant, the message of the grace of Christ (Matt. 26:28). *the letter killeth, but the spirit giveth life.* The *letter* stands for the whole Mosaic law. It kills because of itself it could not give life (Acts 13:39). The work of the law was to make men conscious of sin (Gal. 3:21–25; 1 Tim. 1:9). The Spirit, by contrast, gives life to believers.

3:7 *the ministration of death.* This refers to the law and particularly to the Ten Commandments which were *written and engraven in stones* (Deut. 9:10). Since the law showed man his sinfulness and gave him no power to break out of it, it ministered death. Note that the law is done away (v. 11). Moses stood before God with unveiled face, see Ex. 34:29–35.

3:8 *rather glorious.* I.e., more glorious than the old order.

3:11 There is no question that the law was glorious for its time and purpose, but its temporariness and limited purpose cause that glory to fade in the blazing light of the grace of Christ which has as its eternal purpose the bringing of many sons into glory (John 1:17; Heb. 2:10).

13 And not as Moses, *which* put a vail over his face, that the children of Israel could not stedfastly look to the end of that which is abolished:

14 But their minds were blinded: for until this day remaineth the same vail untaken away in the reading of the old testament; which *vail* is done away in Christ.

15 But even unto this day, when Moses is read, the vail is upon their heart.

16 Nevertheless when it shall turn to the Lord, the vail shall be taken away.

17 Now the Lord is that Spirit: and where the Spirit of the Lord *is*, there *is* liberty.

18 But we all, with open face beholding as in a glass the glory of the Lord, are changed into the same image from glory to glory, *even* as by the Spirit of the Lord.

D The Character of the Ministry: Supernatural, 4:1–7

4 Therefore seeing we have this ministry, as we have received mercy, we faint not;

2 But have renounced the hidden things of dishonesty, not walking in craftiness, nor handling the word of God deceitfully; but by manifestation of the truth commending ourselves to every man's conscience in the sight of God.

3 But if our gospel be hid, it is hid to them that are lost:

4 In whom the god of this world hath blinded the

3:13 Paul means here that Moses veiled his face that the Israelites might not see the fading away of that transitory glory.

3:15 *the vail is upon their heart* as long as they find permanence in the law and do not turn to Christ who takes away the veil (v. 14).

3:16 *it*; i.e., the heart.

3:17 *Now the Lord is that Spirit.* Lit., the Lord is the Spirit—a strong statement that Christ and the Holy Spirit are one in essence, though Paul also recognized the distinction between them (13:14).

3:18 *with open face beholding.* Paul is building on the experience of Moses in Ex. 34:29–35. We Christians, he says, behold constantly Christ's divine glory; and this beholding changes or transforms us *from glory to glory*; i.e., from one degree of glory to another.

4:1 *we faint not.* Not a physical fainting but a losing of courage. Note the other occurrences of the Greek word in Luke 18:1; 2 Cor. 4:16; Gal. 6:9; Eph. 3:13; 2 Thess. 3:13. His effectiveness Paul credits to the *mercy of God.*

4:2 *dishonesty*=shame; i.e., shameful, hidden things. *handling the word of God deceitfully*=adulterating the Word of God.

4:4 *the god of this world*=Satan.

minds of them which believe not, lest the light of the glorious gospel of Christ, who is the image of God, should shine unto them.

5 For we preach not ourselves, but Christ Jesus the Lord; and ourselves your servants for Jesus' sake.

6 For God, who commanded the light to shine out of darkness, hath shined in our hearts, to *give* the light of the knowledge of the glory of God in the face of Jesus Christ.

7 But we have this treasure in earthen vessels, that the excellency of the power may be of God, and not of us.

E The Circumstances of the Ministry, 4:8–18

8 *We are* troubled on every side, yet not distressed; *we are* perplexed, but not in despair;

9 Persecuted, but not forsaken; cast down, but not destroyed;

10 Always bearing about in the body the dying of the Lord Jesus, that the life also of Jesus might be made manifest in our body.

11 For we which live are alway delivered unto death for Jesus' sake, that the life also of Jesus might be made manifest in our mortal flesh.

12 So then death worketh in us, but life in you.

13 We having the same spirit of faith, according as it is written, I believed, and therefore have I spoken; we also believe, and therefore speak;

14 Knowing that he which raised up the Lord Jesus shall raise up us also by Jesus, and shall present *us* with you.

15 For all things *are* for your sakes, that the abundant grace might through the thanksgiving of many redound to the glory of God.

4:7 *this treasure*=the glorious gospel of Jesus Christ. *in earthen vessels*. I.e., in our frail human bodies. *the excellency of the power*. Paul makes clear that this power belongs to God, not to some leader within the church (see 1 Cor. 1:12).

4:10–11 Paul here compares his own constant persecution and suffering with that of Jesus, thus causing him to share in His dying and in His resurrection life (Gal. 2:20; Col. 1:24).

4:12 Paul's physical sufferings (*death worketh in us*) are the means by which spiritual *life* comes to the Corinthians.

4:13 See Ps. 116:10.

4:13–18 Though oppressed, Paul's prospect is one of hope (v. 14). Therefore, he does not lose heart (v. 16) though his *outward man perish*, for this *affliction* is *light* and temporary. *worketh for us*=prepares for us (v. 17).

16 For which cause we faint not; but though our outward man perish, yet the inward *man* is renewed day by day.

17 For our light affliction, which is but for a moment, worketh for us a far more exceeding *and* eternal weight of glory;

18 While we look not at the things which are seen, but at the things which are not seen: for the things which are seen *are* temporal; but the things which are not seen *are* eternal.

F The Compulsions of the Ministry, 5:1-21

1 *The assurance of resurrection, 5:1-9*

5 For we know that if our earthly house of *this* tabernacle were dissolved, we have a building of God, an house not made with hands, eternal in the heavens.

2 For in this we groan, earnestly desiring to be clothed upon with our house which is from heaven:

3 If so be that being clothed we shall not be found naked.

4 For we that are in *this* tabernacle do groan, being burdened: not for that we would be unclothed, but clothed upon, that mortality might be swallowed up of life.

5 Now he that hath wrought us for the selfsame thing *is* God, who also hath given unto us the earnest of the Spirit.

6 Therefore *we are* always confident, knowing that, whilst we are at home in the body, we are absent from the Lord:

7 (For we walk by faith, not by sight:)

8 We are confident, *I say*, and willing rather to be absent from the body, and to be present with the Lord.

9 Wherefore we labour, that, whether present or absent, we may be accepted of him.

5:1 *our earthly house . . . an house not made with hands.* The present earthly body contrasted with the resurrection body.

5:2 *in this* earthly body we *groan* because of the burdens of life (Rom. 8:23). *house which is from heaven.* Lit., dwelling place which is from heaven.

5:3 *we shall not be found naked.* We shall not be bodiless at death.

5:4 While in this body we are burdened; so we long not to be disembodied but to have a resurrection body which God will give us (v. 5).

5:6 *confident.* Lit., of good cheer.

5:9 *we labour.* Lit., we are ambitious. The Greek word is found

2 *The judgment seat of Christ,* 5:10–13

10 For we must all appear before the judgment seat of Christ; that every one may receive the things *done* in *his* body, according to that he hath done, whether *it be* good or bad.

11 Knowing therefore the terror of the Lord, we persuade men; but we are made manifest unto God; and I trust also are made manifest in your consciences.

12 For we commend not ourselves again unto you, but give you occasion to glory on our behalf, that ye may have somewhat to *answer* them which glory in appearance, and not in heart.

13 For whether we be beside ourselves, *it is* to God: or whether we be sober, *it is* for your cause.

3 *The love of Christ,* 5:14–21

14 For the love of Christ constraineth us; because we thus judge, that if one died for all, then were all dead:

15 And *that* he died for all, that they which live should not henceforth live unto themselves, but unto him which died for them, and rose again.

16 Wherefore henceforth know we no man after the flesh: yea, though we have known Christ after the flesh, yet now henceforth know we *him* no more.

17 Therefore if any man *be* in Christ, *he is* a new

elsewhere only in Rom. 15:20 and 1 Thess. 4:11. *we may be accepted to him.* Better, we may be well-pleasing to Him.

5:10 *the judgment seat of Christ.* The *bema* (judgment seat) was well known to the Corinthians (see Acts 18:21). Believers will be judged in a review of their works for the purpose of rewards (see note at 1 Cor. 3:14). *bad*=worthless.

5:11 *terror*=fear or awe of the Lord (Christ) in view of His judging us.

5:13 *beside ourselves.* Lit., we went mad, probably referring to some specific occasion when Paul's critics charged him with madness (for a similar charge against Jesus see Mark 3:21; see also Acts 26:24).

5:14 *For the love of Christ constraineth us.* Christ's love for us (and possibly it may also mean our love for Christ) controls us; i.e., keeps us within bounds, not unwillingly, but because *we thus judge* (=are convinced). *then were all dead.* Believers are regarded by God as having died in Christ so that they may live to please Him (Rom. 6:8).

5:15 Christ's death was for the purpose of bringing His followers into the experience of unselfish living for others.

5:16 Before his conversion, Paul regarded Christ as merely another man.

5:17 *a new creature.* Lit., a new creation. Old things are passed

creature: old things are passed away; behold, all things are become new.

18 And all things *are* of God, who hath reconciled us to himself by Jesus Christ, and hath given to us the ministry of reconciliation;

19 To wit, that God was in Christ, reconciling the world unto himself, not imputing their trespasses unto them; and hath committed unto us the word of reconciliation.

20 Now then we are ambassadors for Christ, as though God did beseech *you* by us: we pray *you* in Christ's stead, be ye reconciled to God.

21 For he hath made him *to be* sin for us, who knew no sin; that we might be made the righteousness of God in him.

G The Conduct of the Ministry, 6:1–10

6 We then, *as* workers together *with him*, beseech *you* also that ye receive not the grace of God in vain.

2 (For he saith, I have heard thee in a time accepted, and in the day of salvation have I succoured thee: behold, now *is* the accepted time; behold, now *is* the day of salvation.)

3 Giving no offence in any thing, that the ministry be not blamed:

4 But in all *things* approving ourselves as the ministers of God, in much patience, in afflictions, in necessities, in distresses,

---

away (aorist tense indicating the decisive change salvation brings); *behold all things are become new.* Lit., the new has come (perfect tense indicating abiding results of the new life in Christ). The grace of God not only justifies but also makes "a new creation" which results in a changed style of life (v. 15).

5:18 *reconciliation* involves a changed relationship because our trespasses have been imputed to Christ (v. 19). We are now to announce to others this message of God's grace.

5:19 *To wit.* Paul here restates v. 18.

5:20 *in Christ's stead.* I.e., on His behalf and in His place.

5:21 Here is the heart of the gospel: the sinless Savior taking our sins that we might have God's righteousness.

6:2 The quotation is from Isa. 49:8, Greek version. Paul's emphasis is on the *now.*

6:3–10 The theme of the apostolic ministry which was first introduced in 2:14 is here recapitulated.

6:4 *approving.* Lit., commending. *patience.* Lit., endurance.

5 In stripes, in imprisonments, in tumults, in labours, in watchings, in fastings;

6 By pureness, by knowledge, by longsuffering, by kindness, by the Holy Ghost, by love unfeigned,

7 By the word of truth, by the power of God, by the armour of righteousness on the right hand and on the left,

8 By honour and dishonour, by evil report and good report: as deceivers, and *yet* true;

9 As unknown, and *yet* well known; as dying, and, behold, we live; as chastened, and not killed;

10 As sorrowful, yet alway rejoicing; as poor, yet making many rich; as having nothing, and *yet* possessing all things.

IV THE APOSTLE'S EXHORTATIONS TO THE CORINTHIANS, 6:11–7:16

A Be Open toward Him, 6:11–13

11 O *ye* Corinthians, our mouth is open unto you, our heart is enlarged.

12 Ye are not straitened in us, but ye are straitened in your own bowels.

13 Now for a recompence in the same, (I speak as unto *my* children,) be ye also enlarged.

B Be Separated from Evil, 6:14–7:1

14 Be ye not unequally yoked together with unbelievers: for what fellowship hath righteousness with unrighteousness? and what communion hath light with darkness?

15 And what concord hath Christ with Bē′lial? or what part hath he that believeth with an infidel?

6:5 See 11:23–24.
6:6 *by pureness*=in purity. God-given qualities of character are proof of Paul's integrity.
6:8 *as deceivers*. Paul was hardly a deceiver, but was apparently called one by his enemies (see Matt. 27:63). Paul says he fights his way through the slanders and faithfully carries on for Christ.
6:9 *as unknown*. His opponents said Paul was an insignificant teacher, a "nobody."
6:11 This means: our speech is frank and our heart is ready to take you in.
6:12 *straitened*=restricted.   *bowels*=affection.
6:14 *be ye not unequally yoked together with unbelievers*. This injunction applies to marriage, business, and ecclesiastical and intimate personal relationships.
6:15 *Belial*=Satan.

16 And what agreement hath the temple of God with idols? for ye are the temple of the living God; as God hath said, I will dwell in them, and walk in *them*; and I will be their God, and they shall be my people.

17 Wherefore come out from among them, and be ye separate, saith the Lord, and touch not the unclean *thing*; and I will receive you,

18 And will be a Father unto you, and ye shall be my sons and daughters, saith the Lord Almighty.

7 Having therefore these promises, dearly beloved, let us cleanse ourselves from all filthiness of the flesh and spirit, perfecting holiness in the fear of God.

C Be Assured of His Joy over Their Repentance, 7:2–16

2 Receive us; we have wronged no man, we have corrupted no man, we have defrauded no man.

3 I speak not *this* to condemn *you*: for I have said before, that ye are in our hearts to die and live with *you*.

4 Great *is* my boldness of speech toward you, great *is* my glorying of you: I am filled with comfort, I am exceeding joyful in all our tribulation.

5 For, when we were come into Macedonia, our flesh had no rest, but we were troubled on every side; without *were* fightings, within *were* fears.

6 Nevertheless God, that comforteth those that are cast down, comforted us by the coming of Titus;

7 And not by his coming only, but by the consolation wherewith he was comforted in you, when he told us your earnest desire, your mourning, your fervent mind toward me; so that I rejoiced the more.

6:17 *be ye separate*. The quotation found in vv. 16b–18 is basically Isa. 52:11. Personal separation involves not being unequally yoked (v. 14); not loving the world (1 John 2:15–17) though using it (1 Cor. 7:31); not having fellowship with sinning brethren (1 Cor. 5:11); and on the positive side, exhibiting Christlikeness. See note at Acts 15:39.

7:2 *Receive us*. Lit., make room (in your heart) for us.

7:5–13a resumes the discussion of his journey to Macedonia introduced in 2:13. Paul describes his relief because of the good news Titus brought (vv. 5–7), and his reflections on the severe letter he had written and its consequences.

7:6 *the coming of Titus* from Corinth with the news that the church had accepted the severe letter.

8 For though I made you sorry with a letter, I do not repent, though I did repent: for I perceive that the same epistle hath made you sorry, though *it were* but for a season.

9 Now I rejoice, not that ye were made sorry, but that ye sorrowed to repentance: for ye were made sorry after a godly manner, that ye might receive damage by us in nothing.

10 For godly sorrow worketh repentance to salvation not to be repented of: but the sorrow of the world worketh death.

11 For behold this selfsame thing, that ye sorrowed after a godly sort, what carefulness it wrought in you, yea, *what* clearing of yourselves, yea, *what* indignation, yea, *what* fear, yea, *what* vehement desire, yea, *what* zeal, yea, *what* revenge! In all *things* ye have approved yourselves to be clear in this matter.

12 Wherefore, though I wrote unto you, *I did it* not for his cause that had done the wrong, nor for his cause that suffered wrong, but that our care for you in the sight of God might appear unto you.

13 Therefore we were comforted in your comfort: yea, and exceedingly the more joyed we for the joy of Titus, because his spirit was refreshed by you all.

14 For if I have boasted any thing to him of you, I am not ashamed; but as we spake all things to you in truth, even so our boasting, which *I made* before Titus, is found a truth.

15 And his inward affection is more abundant toward you, whilst he remembereth the obedience of you all, how with fear and trembling ye received him.

16 I rejoice therefore that I have confidence in you in all *things*.

7:8 *repent*. The word can also mean regret, as it does here.

7:9 *repentance*. A different word, meaning repentance, a change of mind.

7:10 *repentance to salvation not to be repented of*. Lit., repentance, a change of mind. (same word as in v. 9) . . . not to be regretted (same word as in v. 8).

7:11 *carefulness*=earnestness. *clearing of yourselves* of Paul's accusations by change of behavior. Their sorrow had worked the right kind of repentance.

7:12 *that had done the wrong*. I.e., the offended (2:6). *that suffered wrong*. I.e., Paul.

V THE APOSTLE'S SOLICITATION (OR COLLECTION) FOR THE JUDEAN SAINTS, 8:1–9:15

A Principles for Giving, 8:1–6

8 Moreover, brethren, we do you to wit of the grace of God bestowed on the churches of Macedonia;

2 How that in a great trial of affliction the abundance of their joy and their deep poverty abounded unto the riches of their liberality.

3 For to *their* power, I bear record, yea, and beyond *their* power *they were* willing of themselves;

4 Praying us with much intreaty that we would receive the gift, and *take upon us* the fellowship of the ministering to the saints.

5 And *this they did*, not as we hoped, but first gave their own selves to the Lord, and unto us by the will of God.

6 Insomuch that we desired Titus, that as he had begun, so he would also finish in you the same grace also.

B Purposes for Giving, 8:7–15

7 Therefore, as ye abound in every *thing*, *in* faith, and utterance, and knowledge, and *in* all diligence, and *in* your love to us, *see* that ye abound in this grace also.

8 I speak not by commandment, but by occasion of the forwardness of others, and to prove the sincerity of your love.

9 For ye know the grace of our Lord Jesus Christ, that, though he was rich, yet for your sakes he became poor, that ye through his poverty might be rich.

10 And herein I give *my* advice: for this is expedient for you, who have begun before, not only to do, but also to be forward a year ago.

8:1–6 Some principles of N.T. giving are: (1) it is a grace (vv. 1, 6); (2) it can be experienced even in poverty (v. 2); (3) it is a form of fellowship (v. 4); (4) it should be preceded by the dedication of self (v. 5). Apparently the church at Corinth had never, up to now at least, supported Paul (see 11:8–9; 12:13; 1 Cor. 9:11–12).

8:7–15 Some purposes in giving are: (1) to abound in all aspects of Christian experience (v. 7); (2) to prove the reality of one's love (v. 8); (3) to imitate Christ (v. 9); and (4) to help meet the needs of others (v. 14).

11 Now therefore perform the doing of it; that as there was a readiness to will, so there may be a performance also out of that which ye have.

12 For if there be first a willing mind, it is accepted according to that a man hath, and not according to that he hath not.

13 For I mean not that other men be eased, and ye burdened:

14 But by an equality, that now at this time your abundance may be a supply for their want, that their abundance also may be a supply for your want: that there may be equality:

15 As it is written, He that had gathered much had nothing over; and he that had gathered little had no lack.

C Policies in Giving, 8:16–9:5

16 But thanks be to God, which put the same earnest care into the heart of Titus for you.

17 For indeed he accepted the exhortation; but being more forward, of his own accord he went unto you.

18 And we have sent with him the brother, whose praise is in the gospel throughout all the churches;

19 And not that only, but who was also chosen of the churches to travel with us with this grace, which is administered by us to the glory of the same Lord, and declaration of your ready mind:

20 Avoiding this, that no man should blame us in this abundance which is administered by us:

21 Providing for honest things, not only in the sight of the Lord, but also in the sight of men.

22 And we have sent with them our brother, whom we have oftentimes proved diligent in many things, but now much more diligent, upon the great confidence which I have in you.

23 Whether any do enquire of Titus, he is my partner and fellowhelper concerning you: or our brethren be enquired of, they are the messengers of the churches, and the glory of Christ.

8:15 Paul quotes Ex. 16:18 and urges the believers to share their resources.

8:17 being more forward=more diligent.

8:18 the brother. I.e., fellow-Christian. He was obviously well known for his preaching of the gospel, although we do not know who he was (perhaps Luke or Trophimus). Titus, this brother, and a third brother (v. 22) acted as trustees of the money to insure complete propriety in the handling of it (v. 21).

24 Wherefore shew ye to them, and before the churches, the proof of your love, and of our boasting on your behalf.

9 For as touching the ministering to the saints, it is superfluous for me to write to you:

2 For I know the forwardness of your mind, for which I boast of you to them of Macedonia, that Achái'a was ready a year ago; and your zeal hath provoked very many.

3 Yet have I sent the brethren, lest our boasting of you should be in vain in this behalf; that, as I said, ye may be ready:

4 Lest haply if they of Macedonia come with me, and find you unprepared, we (that we say not, ye) should be ashamed in this same confident boasting.

5 Therefore I thought it necessary to exhort the brethren, that they would go before unto you, and make up beforehand your bounty, whereof ye had notice before, that the same might be ready, as *a matter of* bounty, and not as *of* covetousness.

D Promises in Giving, 9:6–15

6 But this I *say*, He which soweth sparingly shall reap also sparingly; and he which soweth bountifully shall reap also bountifully.

7 Every man according as he purposeth in his heart, *so let him give*; not grudgingly, or of necessity: for God loveth a cheerful giver.

8 And God *is* able to make all grace abound toward you; that ye, always having all sufficiency in all *things*, may abound to every good work:

9 (As it is written, He hath dispersed abroad; he hath given to the poor: his righteousness remaineth for ever.

10 Now he that ministereth seed to the sower both minister bread for *your* food, and multiply your seed sown, and increase the fruits of your righteousness;)

9:2 *forwardness*=eagerness (8:10). The Corinthians' *zeal* had been an example and incentive to *many* to give also; now if they did not fulfill their promise it would be a disgrace to them and to Paul (v. 4).

9:6 See Prov. 11:24; 19:17; Luke 6:38.

9:7b Quoting Prov. 22:9, Greek version.

9:8 God will supply the generous giver with enough to meet his own needs and enough to give to *every good work*.

9:9 Quoting Ps. 112:9. This is the same thought as in v. 8.

9:10 The generous giver will be given increasing means to give (*multiply your seed sown*) and increasing fruit. See Hos. 10:12.

11 Being enriched in every thing to all bountifulness, which causeth through us thanksgiving to God.

12 For the administration of this service not only supplieth the want of the saints, but is abundant also by many thanksgivings unto God;

13 Whiles by the experiment of this ministration they glorify God for your professed subjection unto the gospel of Christ, and for *your* liberal distribution unto them, and unto all *men;*

14 And by their prayer for you, which long after you for the exceeding grace of God in you.

15 Thanks *be* unto God for his unspeakable gift.

VI THE APOSTLE'S VINDICATION OF HIMSELF,
10:1–12:18

A The Authority of His Apostleship, 10:1–18

10 Now I Paul myself beseech you by the meekness and gentleness of Christ, who in presence *am* base among you, but being absent am bold toward you:

2 But I beseech *you,* that I may not be bold when I am present with that confidence, wherewith I think to be bold against some, which think of us as if we walked according to the flesh.

3 For though we walk in the flesh, we do not war after the flesh:

4 (For the weapons of our warfare *are* not carnal, but mighty through God to the pulling down of strong holds;)

5 Casting down imaginations, and every high thing that exalteth itself against the knowledge of God, and bringing into captivity every thought to the obedience of Christ;

9:12–14 The gift of money will (1) supply a need (v. 12); (2) be a cause for thanksgiving (v. 12); (3) prove their obedience (v. 13); (4) draw the Jerusalem Christians to them (v. 14, *which long after you*).

9:15 *unspeakable*=indescribable.

10:1 In spite of Paul's general satisfaction with the church, there were still some who challenged his apostolic authority and followed certain leaders whom Paul calls "false apostles" (11:13). These leaders were apparently Jewish Christians (11:22) who claimed higher authority than Paul's (10:7) and who spoiled the church (11:20). base=lowly.

10:3 *in the flesh.* I.e., in a human body (with its limitations). *after the flesh.* I.e., after the impulses of the sinful nature.

10:5 *imaginations*=reasoning.

6 And having in a readiness to revenge all disobedience, when your obedience is fulfilled.

7 Do ye look on things after the outward appearance? If any man trust to himself that he is Christ's, let him of himself think this again, that, as he *is* Christ's, even so *are* we Christ's.

8 For though I should boast somewhat more of our authority, which the Lord hath given us for edification, and not for your destruction, I should not be ashamed:

9 That I may not seem as if I would terrify you by letters.

10 For *his* letters, say they, *are* weighty and powerful; but *his* bodily presence *is* weak, and *his* speech contemptible.

11 Let such an one think this, that, such as we are in word by letters when we are absent, such *will we be* also in deed when we are present.

12 For we dare not make ourselves of the number, or compare ourselves with some that commend themselves: but they measuring themselves by themselves, and comparing themselves among themselves, are not wise.

13 But we will not boast of things without *our* measure, but according to the measure of the rule which God hath distributed to us, a measure to reach even unto you.

14 For we stretch not ourselves beyond *our measure*, as though we reached not unto you: for we are come as far as to you also in *preaching* the gospel of Christ:

15 Not boasting of things without *our* measure, *that is*, of other men's labours; but having hope, when your faith is increased, that we shall be enlarged by you according to our rule abundantly,

16 To preach the gospel in the *regions* beyond you, *and* not to boast in another man's line of things made ready to our hand.

10:6 Being ready to punish every disobedience when your obedience is complete.

10:7–9 You look, Paul says, only at what lies before your eyes. I belong to Christ as much as they do (v. 7). As a matter of fact, I could claim higher authority (v. 8), but that might frighten you (v. 9)!

10:10 *contemptible*=of no account.

10:13 *without our measure*. I.e., beyond our limit or assigned region, the territory God had assigned to Paul. In that territory, which included Corinth, he would boast, but not in areas in which others had labored.

10:15–16 When their *faith is increased* and his presence is no longer necessary, Paul can turn to other fields.

17 But he that glorieth, let him glory in the Lord.
18 For not he that commendeth himself is approved, but whom the Lord commendeth.

B The Marks of His Apostleship, 11:1–12:18

1 *Paul's conduct*, 11:1–15

11 Would to God ye could bear with me a little in *my* folly: and indeed bear with me.

2 For I am jealous over you with godly jealousy: for I have espoused you to one husband, that I may present *you as* a chaste virgin to Christ.

3 But I fear, lest by any means, as the serpent beguiled Eve through his subtilty, so your minds should be corrupted from the simplicity that is in Christ.

4 For if he that cometh preacheth another Jesus, whom we have not preached, or *if* ye receive another spirit, which ye have not received, or another gospel, which ye have not accepted, ye might well bear with *him*.

5 For I suppose I was not a whit behind the very chiefest apostles.

6 But though I *be* rude in speech, yet not in knowledge; but we have been throughly made manifest among you in all things.

7 Have I committed an offence in abasing myself that ye might be exalted, because I have preached to you the gospel of God freely?

8 I robbed other churches, taking wages *of them*, to do you service.

9 And when I was present with you, and wanted, I was chargeable to no man: for that which was lacking to me the brethren which came from Macedonia supplied: and in all *things* I have kept myself from being burdensome unto you, and *so* will I keep *myself*.

11:1 *my folly*. I.e., the boasting of vv. 21–33, but Paul knows he must do it to make the false apostles appear in their true colors.

11:3 Some texts read "from the simplicity and purity which is in Christ."

11:4 Paul here and in v. 5 is speaking sarcastically. Of course he did not want them to submit to false teachers, nor did he regard these smooth talkers as "apostles" in any sense, let alone among the *chiefest apostles*.

11:6 *rude in speech*. I.e., unskilled, not an orator.

11:8 *robbed* in the sense of accepting gifts which other churches could ill afford to give in order not to be a financial burden to the Corinthians.

10 As the truth of Christ is in me, no man shall stop me of this boasting in the regions of Achaï'a.

11 Wherefore? because I love you not? God knoweth.

12 But what I do, that I will do, that I may cut off occasion from them which desire occasion; that wherein they glory, they may be found even as we.

13 For such *are* false apostles, deceitful workers, transforming themselves into the apostles of Christ.

14 And no marvel; for Satan himself is transformed into an angel of light.

15 Therefore *it is* no great thing if his ministers also be transformed as the ministers of righteousness; whose end shall be according to their works.

2 *Paul's sufferings*, 11:16–33

16 I say again, Let no man think me a fool; if otherwise, yet as a fool receive me, that I may boast myself a little.

17 That which I speak, I speak *it* not after the Lord, but as it were foolishly, in this confidence of boasting.

18 Seeing that many glory after the flesh, I will glory also.

19 For ye suffer fools gladly, seeing ye *yourselves* are wise.

20 For ye suffer, if a man bring you into bondage, if a man devour *you*, if a man take *of you*, if a man exalt himself, if a man smite you on the face.

21 I speak as concerning reproach, as though we had been weak. Howbeit whereinsoever any is bold, (I speak foolishly,) I am bold also.

22 Are they Hebrews? so *am* I. Are they Israelites? so *am* I. Are they the seed of Abraham? so *am* I.

23 Are they ministers of Christ? (I speak as a fool) I *am* more; in labours more abundant, in stripes above measure, in prisons more frequent, in deaths oft.

24 Of the Jews five times received I forty *stripes* save one.

11:12 By not accepting support Paul cuts off his opponents' *occasion* or opening for attacking him.

11:14–15 Satan's masterful deception is to appear in the guise of an angel of light, so these teachers, Satan's servants, appear as preachers of righteousness.

11:17 *not after the Lord.* Paul means that his forced boasting finds no example in the life of Christ. He has had to indulge in it, he says, against his natural instincts, so that he can call some significant facts to their attention.

11:20 *devour* by exacting money (as in Mark 12:40).

11:24 *forty stripes save one.* This refers to beatings administered

25 Thrice was I beaten with rods, once was I stoned, thrice I suffered shipwreck, a night and a day I have been in the deep;

26 *In* journeyings often, *in* perils of waters, *in* perils of robbers, *in* perils by *mine own* countrymen, *in* perils by the heathen, *in* perils in the city, *in* perils in the wilderness, *in* perils in the sea, *in* perils among false brethren;

27 In weariness and painfulness, in watchings often, in hunger and thirst, in fastings often, in cold and nakedness.

28 Beside those things that are without, that which cometh upon me daily, the care of all the churches.

29 Who is weak, and I am not weak? who is offended, and I burn not?

30 If I must needs glory, I will glory of the things which concern mine infirmities.

31 The God and Father of our Lord Jesus Christ, which is blessed for evermore, knoweth that I lie not.

32 In Damascus the governor under Ar'etas the king kept the city of the Dam'ascēnes with a garrison, desirous to apprehend me:

33 And through a window in a basket was I let down by the wall, and escaped his hands.

3 *Paul's vision,* 12:1–10

12 It is not expedient for me doubtless to glory. I will come to visions and revelations of the Lord.

2 I knew a man in Christ above fourteen years ago, (whether in the body, I cannot tell; or whether out of the body, I cannot tell: God knoweth;) such an one caught up to the third heaven.

3 And I knew such a man, (whether in the body, or out of the body, I cannot tell: God knoweth;)

4 How that he was caught up into paradise, and heard unspeakable words, which it is not lawful for a man to utter.

in the synagogue. The law prescribed forty lashes (Deut. 25:1–3) but only 39 were given in order to be certain of not exceeding the limit.

11:25 *beaten with rods.* This was a Roman punishment. We know that it was done to Paul at Philippi (Acts 16:23). *stoned* at Lystra (Acts 14:11–19). Being *shipwrecked* is not mentioned by Luke although Paul later experienced one (Acts 27).

11:32 The record of the events in *Damascus* is in Acts 9:24–25.

12:2–4 Paul here speaks of a personal and actual experience when he was caught up into heaven and given revelations he could not speak about. Some think this occurred when he was stoned (Acts 14:19).

5 Of such an one will I glory: yet of myself I will not glory, but in mine infirmities.

6 For though I would desire to glory, I shall not be a fool; for I will say the truth: but *now* I forbear, lest any man should think of me above that which he seeth me *to be*, or *that* he heareth of me.

7 And lest I should be exalted above measure through the abundance of the revelations, there was given to me a thorn in the flesh, the messenger of Satan to buffet me, lest I should be exalted above measure.

8 For this thing I besought the Lord thrice, that it might depart from me.

9 And he said unto me, My grace is sufficient for thee: for my strength is made perfect in weakness. Most gladly therefore will I rather glory in my infirmities, that the power of Christ may rest upon me.

10 Therefore I take pleasure in infirmities, in reproaches, in necessities, in persecutions, in distresses for Christ's sake: for when I am weak, then am I strong.

4 Paul's unselfishness, 12:11–18

11 I am become a fool in glorying; ye have compelled me: for I ought to have been commended of you: for in nothing am I behind the very chiefest apostles, though I be nothing.

12 Truly the signs of an apostle were wrought among you in all patience, in signs, and wonders, and mighty deeds.

13 For what is it wherein ye were inferior to other churches, except *it be* that I myself was not burdensome to you? forgive me this wrong.

14 Behold, the third time I am ready to come to you; and I will not be burdensome to you: for I seek not yours, but you: for the children ought not to lay up for the parents, but the parents for the children.

12:6 Paul wants to be judged only on the evidence before their eyes.

12:7 *a thorn in the flesh.* This seems to have been some recurrent physical affliction. Migraine headaches, eye trouble (ophthalmia?), malaria, and epilepsy have all been seriously suggested (but see note at Gal. 4:12–15). Paul views it as the work of Satan, permitted by God for a good purpose (keeping him humble). It could not be relieved through prayer (v. 8).

12:9 *the power of Christ* upon him was more important than freedom from pain.

12:13 Do you think I made you *inferior to other churches* because I didn't sponge off you?

15 And I will very gladly spend and be spent for you: though the more abundantly I love you, the less I be loved.

16 But be it so, I did not burden you: nevertheless, being crafty, I caught you with guile.

17 Did I make a gain of you by any of them whom I sent unto you?

18 I desired Titus, and with *him* I sent a brother. Did Titus make a gain of you? walked we not in the same spirit? *walked we* not in the same steps?

VII CONCLUDING REMARKS, 12:19—13:14

A An Appeal for Repentance, 12:19—21

19 Again, think ye that we excuse ourselves unto you? we speak before God in Christ: but *we do* all things, dearly beloved, for your edifying.

20 For I fear, lest, when I come, I shall not find you such as I would, and *that* I shall be found unto you such as ye would not: lest *there be* debates, envyings, wraths, strifes, backbitings, whisperings, swellings, tumults:

21 *And* lest, when I come again, my God will humble me among you, and *that* I shall bewail many which have sinned already, and have not repented of the uncleanness and fornication and lasciviousness which they have committed.

B Statement of Plans, 13:1—10

13 This *is* the third *time* I am coming to you. In the mouth of two or three witnesses shall every word be established.

12:15 *for you.* I.e., for your spiritual good. The last half of the verse is often translated as a question: If I love you more abundantly, am I to be loved the less?

12:16 After *nevertheless* add, "they say." Sure, they say, he didn't take any money while he was here, but what about that collection for the saints? Who knows in whose pockets that will go?

12:21 *God will humble among you* if when He comes He finds them still acting like pagans (v. 20).

13:1 *the third time I am coming to you.* Acts 18:1 records the first visit; the second was likely the "painful visit" (2:1); and the third is the one he is about to undertake. *in the mouth of two or three witnesses.* Paul warns that trials are going to be held if necessary when he comes in which Jewish rules of evidence-giving will be applied (Deut. 19:15).

2 I told you before, and foretell you, as if I were present, the second time; and being absent now I write to them which heretofore have sinned, and to all other, that, if I come again, I will not spare:

3 Since ye seek a proof of Christ speaking in me, which to you-ward is not weak, but is mighty in you.

4 For though he was crucified through weakness, yet he liveth by the power of God. For we also are weak in him, but we shall live with him by the power of God toward you.

5 Examine yourselves, whether ye be in the faith; prove your own selves. Know ye not your own selves, how that Jesus Christ is in you, except ye be reprobates?

6 But I trust that ye shall know that we are not reprobates.

7 Now I pray to God that ye do no evil; not that we should appear approved, but that ye should do that which is honest, though we be as reprobates.

8 For we can do nothing against the truth, but for the truth.

9 For we are glad, when we are weak, and ye are strong: and this also we wish, *even* your perfection.

10 Therefore I write these things being absent, lest being present I should use sharpness, according to the power which the Lord hath given me to edification, and not to destruction.

C Greetings and Benediction, 13:11–14

11 Finally, brethren, farewell. Be perfect, be of good comfort, be of one mind, live in peace; and the God of love and peace shall be with you.

12 Greet one another with an holy kiss.

13 All the saints salute you.

14 The grace of the Lord Jesus Christ, and the love of God, and the communion of the Holy Ghost, *be* with you all. Amen.

¶ The second *letter* to the Corinthians was written from Phĭlip'pĭ, *a city* of Macedonia, by Titus and Lucas.

13:5 *yourselves* is emphatic; i.e., it's yourselves, not I whom you should examine. *reprobates*=disapproved; i.e., they fail to pass the test and are not members of the household of faith (also v. 6).

13:9 *your perfection*=your full restoration to spiritual health also v. 11).

13:12 *an holy kiss*. See note at 1 Pet. 5:14.

13:14 Here is an early witness to belief in the Trinity.

INTRODUCTION TO
THE LETTER OF PAUL TO THE
Galatians

AUTHOR: Paul   DATE: 49 OR 55

The Galatians   *At the time of the writing of this letter the term "Galatia" denoted two areas: (1) north central Asia Minor, north of the cities of Pisidian Antioch, Iconium, Lystra, and Derbe; and (2) the Roman province (organized in 25 B.C.) which included southern districts and those cities mentioned. If the letter was written to Christians in North Galatia, the churches were founded on the second missionary journey and the epistle was written on the third missionary journey, either early from Ephesus (about 53) or later (about 55) from Macedonia. In favor of this is the fact that Luke seems to use "Galatia" only to describe North Galatia (Acts 16:6; 18:23).*

If the letter was written to Christians in South Galatia, the churches were founded on the first missionary journey, the letter was written after the end of the journey, probably from Antioch (about 49, making it the earliest of Paul's epistles), and the Jerusalem council (Acts 15) convened shortly after the writing of Galatians. In favor of this is the fact that Paul does not mention in Galatians the decision of the Jerusalem council which bore directly on his argument, indicating that the council had not yet taken place.

The Problem   *How can men (by nature sinful) come to God (by nature holy)? Paul's answer is: There is only one way—accept the grace of God which Christ makes available through His death. Forget about merit-salvation through obedience to the law of Moses. Man is too weak by nature to accomplish anything by way of self-salvation or self-sanctification. Certain Jewish Christians (the Judaizers) were teaching that works are necessary and that Paul's gospel was not a true one, for he was not a genuine apostle. Paul's answer is to proclaim the doctrine of justification by faith plus nothing, and sanctification by the Holy Spirit, not the Mosaic law. This answer was backed by full* apostolic authority received from Christ. All theologies that teach salvation by faith plus human effort are negated by this great letter.

The Contents The theme, justification by faith, is defended, explained, and applied in these chapters. Significant passages include the mention of Paul's three years in Arabia (1:17), Paul's correcting Peter (2:11), the law as a schoolmaster (3:24), and the fruit of the Spirit (5:22–23).

OUTLINE OF GALATIANS

THE LETTER OF
PAUL THE APOSTLE TO THE
Galatians

I INTRODUCTION: THE RIGHTNESS OF PAUL'S GOSPEL ASSERTED, 1:1–10

1 Paul, an apostle, (not of men, neither by man, but by Jesus Christ, and God the Father, who raised him from the dead;)

1:1 Paul's apostleship was *not of men* (i.e., it did not originate from any man, but God), *neither by man* (i.e., it was not

2 And all the brethren which are with me, unto the churches of Galatia:

3 Grace *be* to you and peace from God the Father, and *from* our Lord Jesus Christ,

4 Who gave himself for our sins, that he might deliver us from this present evil world, according to the will of God and our Father:

5 To whom *be* glory for ever and ever. Amen.

6 I marvel that ye are so soon removed from him that called you into the grace of Christ unto another gospel:

7 Which is not another; but there be some that trouble you, and would pervert the gospel of Christ.

8 But though we, or an angel from heaven, preach any other gospel unto you than that which we have preached unto you, let him be accursed.

9 As we said before, so say I now again, If any *man* preach any other gospel unto you than that ye have received, let him be accursed.

10 For do I now persuade men, or God? or do I seek to please men? for if I yet pleased men, I should not be the servant of Christ.

II JUSTIFICATION BY FAITH DEFENDED: PAUL'S AUTHORITY, 1:11–2:21

A His Authority Acquired through Revelation, 1:11–24

11 But I certify you, brethren, that the gospel which was preached of me is not after man.

mediated through any man, but came directly from *Jesus Christ*).

1:3–5 Here in his greeting Paul neatly summarizes his whole preaching message.

1:6 *ye are so soon removed.* Lit., you are so soon removing yourselves. *from him that called you*=God the Father. They were deserting "grace" to retreat into "law," and they bore the responsibility for their defection.

1:7 *the gospel of Christ*=the good news of God's grace in Christ who gave Himself for our sins (v. 4). Those teaching an easier way threatened the true gospel.

1:8 *accursed.* Lit., anathema or devoted to destruction. Ecclesiastically, it was accompanied by excommunication.

1:10 *do I now persuade men* (by toning down my message), or do I seek God's favor? Paul is being accused of preaching a cheap form of admission to God's kingdom. He counters by saying that he is a *servant of Christ* (lit., slave). How can this cross-centered way be viewed as seeking *to please men*?

1:11–17 In these verses Paul defends his authority as an apostle.

12 For I neither received it of man, neither was I taught *it*, but by the revelation of Jesus Christ.

13 For ye have heard of my conversation in time past in the Jews' religion, how that beyond measure I persecuted the church of God, and wasted it:

14 And profited in the Jews' religion above many my equals in mine own nation, being more exceedingly zealous of the traditions of my fathers.

15 But when it pleased God, who separated me from my mother's womb, and called *me* by his grace,

16 To reveal his Son in me, that I might preach him among the heathen; immediately I conferred not with flesh and blood:

17 Neither went I up to Jerusalem to them which were apostles before me; but I went into Arabia, and returned again unto Damascus.

18 Then after three years I went up to Jerusalem to see Peter, and abode with him fifteen days.

19 But other of the apostles saw I none, save James the Lord's brother.

20 Now the things which I write unto you, behold, before God, I lie not.

On the one hand he shows that his teaching was not derived from any human agency; on the other, that it was acknowledged by the apostles as truly from God.

1:13 *my conversation*=my manner of life, conduct. *wasted* is translated "destroyed" in Acts 9:21 in describing Paul's activities.

1:14 *profited*. Better, progressed.

1:15 Paul was set apart from birth for his work (as was Jeremiah, 1:5).

1:16 *with flesh and blood*. I.e., with other people.

1:17 *Arabia*. This may mean anywhere in the kingdom of the Nabataeans, from near Damascus down to the Sinaitic peninsula. Paul's point is not to pinpoint the location but to emphasize that it was a place, in contrast to Jerusalem, where there was no apostle to instruct him. In Arabia he was alone with God, thinking through the implications of his encounter with the risen Christ on the Damascus road. Though not mentioned in Acts, this period in Paul's life probably came between Acts 9:21 and 9:22.

1:18—2:21 This is Paul's account of his relations with the Jerusalem apostles. Though independent of men, Paul makes it clear that he is within the stream of apostolic tradition represented by James, Peter, and John.

1:18 *see*=visit. The purpose of Paul's visit to Peter was to become acquainted with him rather than to confer with him. He also saw James, the Lord's half-brother (v. 19), but did not visit the Judean churches (v. 22).

21 Afterwards I came into the regions of Syria and Cilic'ia;

22 And was unknown by face unto the churches of Judæa which were in Christ:

23 But they had heard only, That he which persecuted us in times past now preacheth the faith which once he destroyed.

24 And they glorified God in me.

B His Authority
Approved by the Church in Jerusalem, 2:1-10

2 Then fourteen years after I went up again to Jerusalem with Barnabas, and took Titus with *me* also.

2 And I went up by revelation, and communicated unto them that gospel which I preach among the Gentiles, but privately to them which were of reputation, lest by any means I should run, or had run, in vain.

3 But neither Titus, who was with me, being a Greek, was compelled to be circumcised:

4 And that because of false brethren unawares brought in, who came in privily to spy out our liberty which we have in Christ Jesus, that they might bring us into bondage:

5 To whom we gave place by subjection, no, not for an hour; that the truth of the gospel might continue with you.

6 But of these who seemed to be somewhat, (whatsoever they were, it maketh no matter to me: God accepteth no man's person:) for they who seemed *to be somewhat* in conference added nothing to me:

7 But contrariwise, when they saw that the gospel of the uncircumcision was committed unto me, as *the gospel* of the circumcision *was* unto Peter;

8 (For he that wrought effectually in Peter to the apos-

2:1-10 is Paul's account of the events recorded in Acts 11 (if the letter was written to the churches in South Galatia) or Acts 15 (if written to North Galatia).

2:3 *Titus* was a test case: if he was compelled to be circumcised, then other Gentile believers could be too. If not, then freedom from the law was confirmed.

2:5 *the truth of the gospel* is that grace is everything, and for everyone. To compromise this is unthinkable.

2:7 *the gospel of the uncircumcision.* I.e., the gospel for the uncircumcision, the Gentiles. Paul was especially responsible for spreading the gospel to Gentiles (Rom. 1:5) and Peter to the *circumcision*, the Jews.

tleship of the circumcision, the same was mighty in me toward the Gentiles:)

9 And when James, Cē'phas, and John, who seemed to be pillars, perceived the grace that was given unto me, they gave to me and Barnabas the right hands of fellowship; that we *should go* unto the heathen, and they unto the circumcision.

10 Only *they would* that we should remember the poor; the same which I also was forward to do.

C His Authority
Acknowledged in the Rebuke of Peter, 2:11–21

11 But when Peter was come to An'tioch, I withstood him to the face, because he was to be blamed.

12 For before that certain came from James, he did eat with the Gentiles: but when they were come, he withdrew and separated himself, fearing them which were of the circumcision.

13 And the other Jews dissembled likewise with him; insomuch that Barnabas also was carried away with their dissimulation.

14 But when I saw that they walked not uprightly according to the truth of the gospel, I said unto Peter before *them* all, If thou, being a Jew, livest after the manner of Gentiles, and not as do the Jews, why compellest thou the Gentiles to live as do the Jews?

15 We *who are* Jews by nature, and not sinners of the Gentiles,

16 Knowing that a man is not justified by the works of the law, but by the faith of Jesus Christ, even we have believed in Jesus Christ, that we might be justified by the faith of Christ, and not by the works of the law: for by the works of the law shall no flesh be justified.

17 But if, while we seek to be justified by Christ, we ourselves also are found sinners, *is* therefore Christ the minister of sin? God forbid.

2:10 *the poor.* The saints in Jerusalem were notoriously poor (Rom. 15:26; see also 1 Cor. 16:1–4).

2:11–13 Peter was not preaching heresy but was not practicing consistently the gospel of grace. When pressured to do so by Hebrew Christians, he withdrew from eating with uncircumcised Gentile believers.

2:13 *dissimulation*=hypocrisy or pretense.

2:16 *justified.* I.e., to be declared righteous in God's sight and to be vindicated of any charge of sin in connection with failure to keep God's law.

18 For if I build again the things which I destroyed, I make myself a transgressor.

19 For I through the law am dead to the law, that I might live unto God.

20 I am crucified with Christ: nevertheless I live; yet not I, but Christ liveth in me: and the life which I now live in the flesh I live by the faith of the Son of God, who loved me, and gave himself for me.

21 I do not frustrate the grace of God: for if righteousness *come* by the law, then Christ is dead in vain.

III JUSTIFICATION BY FAITH EXPLAINED: PAUL'S GOSPEL, 3:1–4:31

A The Argument from Experience, 3·1–5

3 O foolish Galatians, who hath bewitched you, that ye should not obey the truth, before whose eyes Jesus Christ hath been evidently set forth, crucified among you?

2 This only would I learn of you, Received ye the Spirit by the works of the law, or by the hearing of faith?

3 Are ye so foolish? having begun in the Spirit, are ye now made perfect by the flesh?

4 Have ye suffered so many things in vain? if *it be* yet in vain.

5 He therefore that ministereth to you the Spirit, and worketh miracles among you, *doeth he it* by the works of the law, or by the hearing of faith?

2:19 *dead to the law*, because Christ paid the penalty for sin that the law demanded. Paul could cease giving further thought to legal obedience as a means of winning God's acceptance.

2:20 *I am crucified with Christ*. Crucifixion with Christ means death to or separation from the reigning power of the old sinful life and freedom to experience the power of the resurrection life of Christ by faith (see Rom. 6:6). *nevertheless I live; yet not I*. Better, and it is no longer I but Christ . . . Christ has taken up His abode in Paul, yet without submerging Paul's own personality.

2:21 *frustrate*=set aside. It is the Galatians, not Paul, who are nullifying the grace of God by wanting to retain law. If God wanted obedience through law, then why send His Son to suffering and death on a cross?

3:3 Paul brought the gospel and the *Spirit* worked in them. Now they are reverting to flesh-works in the hope that a combination of faith (Spirit) and works (flesh) will work more easily or better.

B The Argument from Abraham, 3:6–9

6 Even as Abraham believed God, and it was accounted to him for righteousness.

7 Know ye therefore that they which are of faith, the same are the children of Abraham.

8 And the scripture, foreseeing that God would justify the heathen through faith, preached before the gospel unto Abraham, *saying*, In thee shall all nations be blessed.

9 So then they which be of faith are blessed with faithful Abraham.

C The Argument from the Law, 3:10–4:11

10 For as many as are of the works of the law are under the curse: for it is written, Cursed *is* every one that continueth not in all things which are written in the book of the law to do them.

11 But that no man is justified by the law in the sight of God, *it is* evident: for, The just shall live by faith.

12 And the law is not of faith: but, The man that doeth them shall live in them.

13 Christ hath redeemed us from the curse of the law, being made a curse for us: for it is written, Cursed *is* every one that hangeth on a tree:

14 That the blessing of Abraham might come on the

3:6 Paul now appeals to Scripture (Gen. 15:6) to show that the patriarch Abraham depended on faith *for righteousness*.

3:7 *children of Abraham.* Abraham's physical descendants through Isaac and Jacob are the Jewish people, but his spiritual descendants are those who believe in God for salvation, men of faith, as contrasted with men of works or men of circumcision.

3:8 Quoting Gen. 12:3.

3:10 Having shattered the Jews' confidence in their physical relation to Abraham, Paul now shows that the law brings a curse. Paul quotes Deut. 27:26 (from the Greek O.T.) and argues that man cannot possibly keep all the laws, hence his bondage (Jas. 2:10).

3:11 *The just shall live by faith.* Paul's use of this quotation from Hab. 2:4 is to stress that one can become just in God's sight only by faith; i.e., he who is righteous by faith (rather than works) shall live. See note at Heb. 10:38.

3:12 See Lev. 18:5.

3:13 The law brings a curse. The believer is delivered from that curse through Christ who was *made a curse for us*. The crucifixion brought Him under the curse of the law as explained in the last half of the verse quoted from Deut. 21:23.

Gentiles through Jesus Christ; that we might receive the promise of the Spirit through faith.

15 Brethren, I speak after the manner of men; Though *it be* but a man's covenant, yet *if it be* confirmed, no man disannulleth, or addeth thereto.

16 Now to Abraham and his seed were the promises made. He saith not, And to seeds, as of many; but as of one, And to thy seed, which is Christ.

17 And this I say, *that* the covenant, that was confirmed before of God in Christ, the law, which was four hundred and thirty years after, cannot disannul, that it should make the promise of none effect.

18 For if the inheritance *be* of the law, *it is* no more of promise: but God gave *it* to Abraham by promise.

19 Wherefore then *serveth* the law? It was added because of transgressions, till the seed should come to whom the promise was made; *and it was* ordained by angels in the hand of a mediator.

20 Now a mediator is not *a mediator* of one, but God is one.

21 *Is* the law then against the promises of God? God forbid: for if there had been a law given which could have given life, verily righteousness should have been by the law.

22 But the scripture hath concluded all under sin, that the promise by faith of Jesus Christ might be given to them that believe.

23 But before faith came, we were kept under the law, shut up unto the faith which should afterwards be revealed.

24 Wherefore the law was our schoolmaster *to bring us* unto Christ, that we might be justified by faith.

25 But after that faith is come, we are no longer under a schoolmaster.

3:16 *seed.* Gen. 22:13. Since Paul's argument here is based on the singular rather than the plural, he must have believed in the accuracy of the very words of scripture.

3:17 The Mosaic law did not set aside the promises made to Abraham, and during those hundreds of years before the law, God justified men by faith.

3:19-20 The law was mediated through angels and Moses, whereas the covenant with Abraham was given by God sovereignly (Gen. 15:18). The presence of a *mediator* assumes two parties, and the need of a mediator shows the inferiority of the law. God dealt with Abraham directly.

3:24 *schoolmaster.* The Greek word here means not a "teacher" but an attendant, a custodian, usually a slave whose job it was to insure the safe arrival of the child at school. Christ is the true teacher.

26 For ye are all the children of God by faith in Christ Jesus.

27 For as many of you as have been baptized into Christ have put on Christ.

28 There is neither Jew nor Greek, there is neither bond nor free, there is neither male nor female: for ye are all one in Christ Jesus.

29 And if ye *be* Christ's, then are ye Abraham's seed, and heirs according to the promise.

4 Now I say, *That* the heir, as long as he is a child, differeth nothing from a servant, though he be lord of all;

2 But is under tutors and governors until the time appointed of the father.

3 Even so we, when we were children, were in bondage under the elements of the world:

4 But when the fulness of the time was come, God sent forth his Son, made of a woman, made under the law,

5 To redeem them that were under the law, that we might receive the adoption of sons.

6 And because ye are sons, God hath sent forth the Spirit of his Son into your hearts, crying, Abba, Father.

7 Wherefore thou art no more a servant, but a son; and if a son, then an heir of God through Christ.

8 Howbeit then, when ye knew not God, ye did service unto them which by nature are no gods.

9 But now, after that ye have known God, or rather are known of God, how turn ye again to the weak and beggarly elements, whereunto ye desire again to be in bondage?

10 Ye observe days, and months, and times, and years.

3:26 *children of God.* Lit., sons of God. *by faith.* Better, through faith.

3:27 *baptized into Christ.* Not water baptism but Spirit baptism which brings believers into a living union with Christ (1 Cor. 12:13). *have put in Christ.* I.e., clothing oneself with Christ, a responsible act of appropriating all that Christ is.

4:3 *the elements of the world.* I.e., the bondage of a legalistic practice of Judaism, also v. 9.

4:4 *made under the law.* Christ was reared in conformity to the Mosaic law.

4:5 *the adoption of sons.* See note on Rom. 8:15.

4:6 The Holy *Spirit* in the heart of the believer of his acceptance with God as a son and heir (v. 7). *Abba* is the Aramaic word for father.

4:8–11 Here Paul tells the Galatians they are not acting like heirs of God!

11 I am afraid of you, lest I have bestowed upon you labour in vain.

D The Argument from Personal Testimony, 4:12–20

12 Brethren, I beseech you, be as I *am*; for I *am* as ye *are*: ye have not injured me at all.

13 Ye know how through infirmity of the flesh I preached the gospel unto you at the first.

14 And my temptation which was in my flesh ye despised not, nor rejected; but received me as an angel of God, *even* as Christ Jesus.

15 Where is then the blessedness ye spake of? for I bear you record, that, if *it had been* possible, ye would have plucked out your own eyes, and have given them to me.

16 Am I therefore become your enemy, because I tell you the truth?

17 They zealously affect you, *but* not well; yea, they would exclude you, that ye might affect them.

18 But *it is* good to be zealously affected always in *a* good *thing*, and not only when I am present with you.

19 My little children, of whom I travail in birth again until Christ be formed in you,

20 I desire to be present with you now, and to change my voice; for I stand in doubt of you.

E The Argument from an Allegory, 4:21–31

21 Tell me, ye that desire to be under the law, do ye not hear the law?

22 For it is written, that Abraham had two sons, the one by a bondmaid, the other by a freewoman.

23 But he *who was* of the bondwoman was born after the flesh; but he of the freewoman *was* by promise.

4:12–15 Paul is saying that he has had a good relationship with the Galatians: you have in the past been ready to "pluck out your eyes for me," a common expression of the time for giving up everything for another (and not an indication of eye trouble). Though ill on my former visit, you did not scorn me, but treated me as Christ had treated them. Now, then, he wants them to hold firm to the truth he had taught them.

4:17 The Judaizers were apparently using flattery and threats on the Galatians.

4:18 *not only when I am present with you.* I.e., Paul was not averse to having others minister to them as long as they spoke the truth.

4:20 *for I stand in doubt of you.* Better, for I am perplexed about you.

24 Which things are an allegory: for these are the two covenants; the one from the mount Sinai, which gendereth to bondage, which is Agar.

25 For this Agar is mount Sinai in Arabia, and answereth to Jerusalem which now is, and is in bondage with her children.

26 But Jerusalem which is above is free, which is the mother of us all.

27 For it is written, Rejoice, *thou* barren that bearest not; break forth and cry, thou that travailest not: for the desolate hath many more children than she which hath an husband.

28 Now we, brethren, as Isaac was, are the children of promise.

29 But as then he that was born after the flesh persecuted him *that was born* after the Spirit, even so *it is* now.

30 Nevertheless what saith the scripture? Cast out the bondwoman and her son: for the son of the bondwoman shall not be heir with the son of the freewoman.

31 So then, brethren, we are not children of the bondwoman, but of the free.

IV JUSTIFICATION BY FAITH APPLIED: PAUL'S ETHICS, 5:1–6:10

A In Relation to Christian Liberty, 5:1–12

5 Stand fast therefore in the liberty wherewith Christ hath made us free, and be not entangled again with the yoke of bondage.

2 Behold, I Paul say unto you, that if ye be circumcised, Christ shall profit you nothing.

3 For I testify again to every man that is circumcised, that he is a debtor to do the whole law.

4 Christ is become of no effect unto you, whosoever of you are justified by the law; ye are fallen from grace.

4:24 *are an allegory*. Lit., are allegorized. The allegory Paul offers here—of Ishmael and Isaac (Gen. 16:15; 21:3, 9)—expresses something in addition to the simple facts of the case—in this instance that the Judaizers (related to Hagar, Sinai, and the law) did not have the authority or blessing of God.

5:1 *Stand fast . . .* More accurately, For freedom Christ has freed us; stand fast, therefore, and be not entangled again . . .

5:2 Law (circumcision) and grace (Christ) simply do not mix, Paul says.

5:4 *fallen from grace.* To use the impossible ground of justifica-

5 For we through the Spirit wait for the hope of righteousness by faith.

6 For in Jesus Christ neither circumcision availeth anything, nor uncircumcision; but faith which worketh by love.

7 Ye did run well; who did hinder you that ye should not obey the truth?

8 This persuasion *cometh* not of him that calleth you.

9 A little leaven leaveneth the whole lump.

10 I have confidence in you through the Lord, that ye will be none otherwise minded: but he that troubleth you shall bear his judgment, whosoever he be.

11 And I, brethren, if I yet preach circumcision, why do I yet suffer persecution? then is the offence of the cross ceased.

12 I would they were even cut off which trouble you.

B In Relation to License and Love, 5:13-15

13 For, brethren, ye have been called unto liberty; only *use* not liberty for an occasion to the flesh, but by love serve one another.

14 For all the law is fulfilled in one word, *even* in this; Thou shalt love thy neighbour as thyself.

15 But if ye bite and devour one another, take heed that ye be not consumed one of another.

C In Relation to the Flesh and the Spirit, 5:16-26

16 *This* I say then, Walk in the Spirit, and ye shall not fulfil the lust of the flesh.

17 For the flesh lusteth against the Spirit, and the Spirit against the flesh: and these are contrary the one to the other: so that ye cannot do the things that ye would.

18 But if ye be led of the Spirit, ye are not under the law.

19 Now the works of the flesh are manifest, which are *these*; Adultery, fornication, uncleanness, lasciviousness,

---

tion by law is to leave, abandon, fall from, the way of grace as the only basis for justification.

5:11 *the offense of the cross.* I.e., that man can be saved only by faith alone. This is an offense to his pride.

5:14 Compare Rom. 13:8-10.

5:16 *in the Spirit.* Better, by the Spirit which will give victory over the flesh and its works.

5:19 *manifest*=plain, or open, with overtones of unashamed and blatant. *lasciviousness*=lewdness.

20 Idolatry, witchcraft, hatred, variance, emulations, wrath, strife, seditions, heresies,

21 Envyings, murders, drunkenness, revellings, and such like: of the which I tell you before, as I have also told *you* in time past, that they which do such things shall not inherit the kingdom of God.

22 But the fruit of the Spirit is love, joy, peace, long-suffering, gentleness, goodness, faith,

23 Meekness, temperance: against such there is no law.

24 And they that are Christ's have crucified the flesh with the affections and lusts.

25 If we live in the Spirit, let us also walk in the Spirit.

26 Let us not be desirous of vain glory, provoking one another, envying one another.

D In Relation to a Sinning Brother, 6:1–5

6 Brethren, if a man be overtaken in a fault, ye which are spiritual, restore such an one in the spirit of meekness; considering thyself, lest thou also be tempted.

2 Bear ye one another's burdens, and so fulfil the law of Christ.

3 For if a man think himself to be something, when he is nothing, he deceiveth himself.

4 But let every man prove his own work, and then shall he have rejoicing in himself alone, and not in another.

5 For every man shall bear his own burden.

E In Relation to Giving, 6:6–10

6 Let him that is taught in the word communicate unto him that teacheth in all good things.

5:20 *witchcraft.* Lit., pharmacy, the use of drugs and magical potions (see also Rev. 9:21; 18:23; 21:8; 22:15). *variance*= strife. *emulations*=jealousy. *strife*=rivalries.

5:22 *gentleness.* Better, kindness. *faith*=faithful in word and deed.

5:23 *temperance* here means "self-control."

5:24 *crucified.* See 2:20.

6:1 *be overtaken*=be apprehended, taken by surprise, caught red-handed.

6:2 *burdens*=the excess burdens which we need to share with one another, in contrast to the different Greek word in v. 5 which means the normal load each must carry for himself. *the law of Chirst.* I.e., the commands of Christ, especially the new commandment to love one another (John 13:34). Living under grace is not license; it is a life of love and service (5:6, 13).

6:6 *communicate unto.* I.e., share material things.

7 Be not deceived; God is not mocked: for whatsoever a man soweth, that shall he also reap.

8 For he that soweth to his flesh shall of the flesh reap corruption; but he that soweth to the Spirit shall of the Spirit reap life everlasting.

9 And let us not be weary in well doing: for in due season we shall reap, if we faint not.

10 As we have therefore opportunity, let us do good unto all *men*, especially unto them who are of the household of faith.

V CONCLUSION: THE
SUBSTANCE OF PAUL'S INSTRUCTION, 6:11-18

11 Ye see how large a letter I have written unto you with mine own hand.

12 As many as desire to make a fair shew in the flesh, they constrain you to be circumcised; only lest they should suffer persecution for the cross of Christ.

13 For neither they themselves who are circumcised keep the law; but desire to have you circumcised, that they may glory in your flesh.

14 But God forbid that I should glory, save in the cross of our Lord Jesus Christ, by whom the world is crucified unto me, and I unto the world.

15 For in Christ Jesus neither circumcision availeth any thing, nor uncircumcision, but a new creature.

16 And as many as walk according to this rule, peace *be* on them, and mercy, and upon the Israel of God.

17 From henceforth let no man trouble me: for I bear in my body the marks of the Lord Jesus.

18 Brethren, the grace of our Lord Jesus Christ *be* with your spirit. Amen.

6:10 *the household of faith*=believers. Concern for this group is especially the obligation of the children of God.

6:11 *how large a letter*. Lit., with what large letters. Paul took the pen from his scribe to write this closing section in large letters for emphasis (though some think this indicates that his illness was in his eyes, 4:15).

6:16 *the Israel of God*=Christian Jews, those who are both the physical and spiritual seed of Abraham.

6:17 *marks*. I.e., scars suffered in persecution, which spoke more eloquently than the mark of circumcision which the Judaizers sought to impose.

INTRODUCTION TO
THE LETTER OF PAUL TO THE
Ephesians

AUTHOR: Paul DATE: 61

The Prison Letters Ephesians, Philippians, Colossians, and Philemon are sometimes referred to as the "Prison Letters," since they were all written during Paul's Roman imprisonment (Eph. 3:1; Phil. 1:6; Col. 4:10; Philem. 9). Whether he was imprisoned once or twice in Rome is debated, though two imprisonments seem to fit the facts better. During the first, Paul was kept in or near the barracks of the Praetorian Guard or in rented quarters at his own expense (Acts 28:30) for two years, during which these "Prison Letters" were written. He anticipated being released (Philem. 22) and following his release he made several trips, wrote 1 Timothy and Titus, was rearrested, wrote 2 Timothy, and was martyred (see the Introduction to Titus). Strictly speaking, these are the first Roman imprisonment letters, while 2 Timothy is the second Roman imprisonment letter.

An Encyclical Several things indicate that Ephesians was a circular letter—a doctrinal treatise in the form of a letter —to the churches in Asia Minor. Some good Greek manuscripts omit the words "at Ephesus" in 1:1. There is an absence of controversy in this letter, and it does not deal with problems of particular churches. Since Paul had worked at Ephesus for about three years, and since Paul normally mentions many friends at his churches, the absence of any mention of personal names strongly supports the encyclical character of the letter. It was likely sent to Ephesus first by Tychicus (Eph. 6:21–22; Col. 4:7–8), and it is probably the same letter that is called the "letter to the Laodiceans" in Colossians 4:16.

Ephesus Christianity probably came first to Ephesus with

Aquila and Priscilla when Paul made a brief stop there on his second missionary journey (Acts 18:18–19). On his third journey he stayed in the city for about three years and the gospel spread throughout all of Asia Minor (Acts 19:10). The city was a commercial and religious center, the great temple of Diana being there. It was also a major trading center ranking with Alexandria and Antioch. After Paul, Timothy had charge of the church in Ephesus for a time (1 Tim. 1:3), and later the apostle John made the city his headquarters.

The Contents   The great theme of this letter is God's eternal purpose to establish and complete the church of Christ, His body. In developing this theme Paul discusses predestination (1:3–14); Christ's headship over the body (1:22–23; 4:15–16), the church as the building and temple of God (2:21–22), the mystery (3:1–21), spiritual gifts to the body (4:7–16), and the church as the bride of Christ.

OUTLINE OF EPHESIANS

THE LETTER OF
PAUL THE APOSTLE TO THE
Ephesians

I GREETINGS, 1:1–2

1 Paul, an apostle of Jesus Christ by the will of God, to the saints which are at Ephesus, and to the faithful in Christ Jesus:

2 Grace *be* to you, and peace, from God our Father, and *from* the Lord Jesus Christ.

II THE POSITION OF BELIEVERS, 1:3–3:21

A Chosen and Sealed, 1:3–23

3 Blessed *be* the God and Father of our Lord Jesus Christ, who hath blessed us with all spiritual blessings in heavenly *places* in Christ:

4 According as he hath chosen us in him before the foundation of the world, that we should be holy and without blame before him in love:

5 Having predestinated us unto the adoption of children by Jesus Christ to himself, according to the good pleasure of his will,

6 To the praise of the glory of his grace, wherein he hath made us accepted in the beloved.

1:3 *in heavenly places.* Lit., in the heavenlies, i.e., in the realm of heavenly possessions and experiences into which the Christian has been brought because of his association with the risen Christ. The word also occurs in 1:20; 2:6; 3:10; 6:12; John 3:12.

1:4 It is possible that the words *in love* begin v. 5: "In love having predestinated us."

1:5 *predestinated.* This means that God determined beforehand the destiny of those who believe in Christ to be adopted into His family and conformed to His Son (Rom. 8:29). It involves a choice on His part (v. 4); it is done in love (v. 4); it is based on the good pleasure of His perfect will (vv. 5, 19, 11); its purpose is to glorify God (v. 14); but it does not relieve man of his responsibility to believe the gospel in order to bring to pass personally God's predestination (v. 13). *adoption of children.* Lit., adoption of sons. See note at Rom. 8:15.

1:6 *in the beloved.* I.e., in Christ.

7 In whom we have redemption through his blood, the forgiveness of sins, according to the riches of his grace;

8 Wherein he hath abounded toward us in all wisdom and prudence;

9 Having made known unto us the mystery of his will, according to his good pleasure which he hath purposed in himself:

10 That in the dispensation of the fulness of times he might gather together in one all things in Christ, both which are in heaven, and which are on earth; *even* in him:

11 In whom also we have obtained an inheritance, being predestinated according to the purpose of him who worketh all things after the counsel of his own will:

12 That we should be to the praise of his glory, who first trusted in Christ.

13 In whom ye also *trusted*, after that ye heard the word of truth, the gospel of your salvation: in whom also after that ye believed, ye were sealed with that holy Spirit of promise,

14 Which is the earnest of our inheritance until the redemption of the purchased possession, unto the praise of his glory.

15 Wherefore I also, after I heard of your faith in the Lord Jesus, and love unto all the saints,

16 Cease not to give thanks for you, making mention of you in my prayers;

1:7 *redemption.* Three ideas are involved in the doctrine of redemption: (1) paying the ransom with the blood of Christ (1 Cor. 6:20; Rev. 5:9); (2) removal from the curse of the law (Gal. 3:13; 4:5); (3) release from the bondage of sin into the freedom of grace (1 Pet. 1:18). It is always *through his blood*; i.e., through the death of Christ (Col. 1:14).

1:9 *mystery.* See note at 3:3.

1:10 *the dispensation of the fulness of times* refers to the plan, the arrangement, of the millennial kingdom. *gather together in one all things in Christ.* I.e., that God might head up everything in Christ and bring everything into harmony (Col. 1:16).

1:11 *we have obtained an inheritance* may be translated "we were made His inheritance." Both ideas are true: we are Christ's inheritance as He is ours.

1:12 *trusted in Christ.* Lit., hoped in the Christ, the Messiah.

1:13 *after that ye believed.* Better, when you believed. The time of sealing is coincident with the time of believing. *sealed with that holy Spirit.* A seal indicates possession and security. The presence of the Holy Spirit, the seal, is the believer's guarantee of the security of his salvation.

1:14 *earnest*=deposit, down payment. The presence of the Spirit is God's pledge that our salvation will be consummated.

17 That the God of our Lord Jesus Christ, the Father of glory, may give unto you the spirit of wisdom and revelation in the knowledge of him:

18 The eyes of your understanding being enlightened; that ye may know what is the hope of his calling, and what the riches of the glory of his inheritance in the saints,

19 And what *is* the exceeding greatness of his power to us-ward who believe, according to the working of his mighty power,

20 Which he wrought in Christ, when he raised him from the dead, and set *him* at his own right hand in the heavenly *places*,

21 Far above all principality, and power, and might, and dominion, and every name that is named, not only in this world, but also in that which is to come:

22 And hath put all *things* under his feet, and gave him *to be* the head over all *things* to the church,

23 Which is his body, the fulness of him that filleth all in all.

B Saved by Grace, 2:1–10

2 And you *hath he quickened*, who were dead in trespasses and sins;

2 Wherein in time past ye walked according to the course of this world, according to the prince of the

---

1:18 *of your understanding*. Lit., of your heart. "Heart" in scripture is considered the very center and core of life.

1:20 *at his own right hand*. See Ps. 110:1. The right hand is a figure for the place of honor and sovereign power.

1:21 *principality, and power, and might, and dominion*. These are names that were in rabbinic thought of the time with regard to different orders of angels (see Rom. 8:38; Eph. 3:10; 6:12; Col. 1:16; 2:10, 15; Tit. 3:1).

1:22–23 *the church, which is his body*=the universal church to which every true believer belongs regardless of local church affiliation. It is a spiritual organism entered by means of the baptism of the Spirit (1 Cor. 12:13). Christ is the risen head of the church and its members are subject to Him (Eph. 5:24). Local churches should be miniatures of the body of Christ, though it is possible to have unbelieving members of local churches who are not, therefore, members of the body of Christ.

2:1 *dead*. I.e., separated from God because of sins. This is spiritual death. If a man continues in this state by continuing to reject Christ, spiritual death becomes the second death, eternal separation from God (Rev. 20:14).

2:2 *prince . . . spirit* both refer to Satan. *children of disobedience* is a Hebraism for "disobedient people."

power of the air, the spirit that now worketh in the children of disobedience:

3 Among whom also we all had our conversation in times past in the lusts of our flesh, fulfilling the desires of the flesh and of the mind; and were by nature the children of wrath, even as others.

4 But God, who is rich in mercy, for his great love wherewith he loved us,

5 Even when we were dead in sins, hath quickened us together with Christ, (by grace ye are saved;)

6 And hath raised *us* up together, and made *us* sit together in heavenly *places* in Christ Jesus:

7 That in the ages to come he might shew the exceeding riches of his grace in *his* kindness toward us through Christ Jesus.

8 For by grace are ye saved through faith; and that not of yourselves: *it is* the gift of God:

9 Not of works, lest any man should boast.

10 For we are his workmanship, created in Christ Jesus unto good works, which God hath before ordained that we should walk in them.

C United in One Body, 2:11–22

11 Wherefore remember, that ye *being* in time past Gentiles in the flesh, who are called Uncircumcision by that which is called the Circumcision in the flesh made by hands;

12 That at that time ye were without Christ, being aliens from the commonwealth of Israel, and strangers from the covenants of promise, having no hope, and without God in the world:

13 But now in Christ Jesus ye who sometimes were far off are made nigh by the blood of Christ.

14 For he is our peace, who hath made both one, and hath broken down the middle wall of partition *between us;*

2:3 *conversation*=manner of life, social intercourse. Man's *nature* has been affected by sin. *children of wrath*. A Hebraism, difficult to translate, but meaning "deserving of wrath."

2:5 *quickened*=made alive. *grace*. See note at John 1:17.

2:7 Believers will be an eternal display of the grace of God.

2:8 Salvation is *by grace through faith*. Faith involves knowledge of the gospel (Rom. 10:14), acknowledgment of the truth of its message, and personal reception of the Savior (John 1:12). Works cannot save (v. 9), but good works always accompany salvation (v. 10; Jas. 2:17).

2:11–22 Paul now expands the concept he put forward in 1:23.

2:13 *nigh*=near (to God).

2:14 *the middle wall of partition*. An allusion to the wall which

15 Having abolished in his flesh the enmity, *even* the law of commandments *contained* in ordinances; for to make in himself of twain one new man, so making peace;

16 And that he might reconcile both unto God in one body by the cross, having slain the enmity thereby:

17 And came and preached peace to you which were afar off, and to them that were nigh.

18 For through him we both have access by one Spirit unto the Father.

19 Now therefore ye are no more strangers and foreigners, but fellow citizens with the saints, and of the household of God;

20 And are built upon the foundation of the apostles and prophets, Jesus Christ himself being the chief corner *stone*;

21 In whom all the building fitly framed together groweth unto an holy temple in the Lord:

22 In whom ye also are builded together for an habitation of God through the Spirit.

D Equal in the Body (the Mystery), 3:1-21

3 For this cause I Paul, the prisoner of Jesus Christ for you Gentiles,

2 If ye have heard of the dispensation of the grace of God which is given me to you-ward:

3 How that by revelation he made known unto me the mystery; (as I wrote afore in few words,

separated the Court of the Gentiles from the Court of the Jews in the temple. An inscription warned Gentiles of the death penalty for going beyond it.

2:15 *in his flesh.* For an explanation of Paul's understanding of this shorthand phrase in this context, see Gal. 4:4 and Heb. 2:14. *the law*=the whole Jewish legal system. *of twain.* I.e., of Jew and Gentile.

2:20-21 In the figure of the church as a temple, Christ is the *corner stone*, the *apostles and N.T. prophets* are the *foundation*, and each Christian is a stone in the building (1 Pet. 2:4-8). In 1 Cor. 3:11 Paul says that Christ is the sole foundation.

3:2 *dispensation*=stewardship. Paul was entrusted with the message of the grace of God as the apostle to the Gentiles (v. 1; Gal. 2:7).

3:3 *the mystery.* A mystery was not something mysterious but something unknown until revealed to the initiated (Rom. 16:25). The mystery spoken of here is not that Gentiles would be blessed (for that was predicted in the O.T.), but that Jews and Gentiles would be equal heirs in the one body of Christ (v. 6). This was unknown in O.T. prophecy but was revealed by the N.T. apostles and prophets (v. 5). Other mysteries in

4 Whereby, when ye read, ye may understand my knowledge in the mystery of Christ)

5 Which in other ages was not made known unto the sons of men, as it is now revealed unto his holy apostles and prophets by the Spirit;

6 That the Gentiles should be fellowheirs, and of the same body, and partakers of his promise in Christ by the gospel:

7 Whereof I was made a minister, according to the gift of the grace of God given unto me by the effectual working of his power.

8 Unto me, who am less than the least of all saints, is this grace given, that I should preach among the Gentiles the unsearchable riches of Christ;

9 And to make all *men* see what *is* the fellowship of the mystery, which from the beginning of the world hath been hid in God, who created all things by Jesus Christ:

10 To the intent that now unto the principalities and powers in heavenly *places* might be known by the church the manifold wisdom of God,

11 According to the eternal purpose which he purposed in Christ Jesus our Lord:

12 In whom we have boldness and access with confidence by the faith of him.

13 Wherefore I desire that ye faint not at my tribulations for you, which is your glory.

14 For this cause I bow my knees unto the Father of our Lord Jesus Christ,

15 Of whom the whole family in heaven and earth is named,

16 That he would grant you, according to the riches of his glory, to be strengthened with might by his Spirit in the inner man;

the N.T. are found in Matt. 13:11; Rom. 11:25; 1 Cor. 15:51–52; Eph. 5:32; 6:19; Col. 1:27; 2:2, 9; 2 Thess. 2:7; 1 Tim. 3:16; Rev. 1:20; 17:5, 7.

3:7–10 Paul here gives his concept of his own mission. Note that this was God's doing (v. 7); that he was to make available to all mankind Israel's hope for a Messiah (v. 8); that he was to be a theologian-teacher as well as a missionary (v. 9); that even angelic beings might see the wisdom of God in His plan for the church (v. 10). On *principalities and powers* see note at 1:21.

3:13 *faint*=be disheartened.

3:14 *For this cause*. Here Paul resumes the thought begun in 3:1.

17 That Christ may dwell in your hearts by faith; that ye, being rooted and grounded in love,

18 May be able to comprehend with all saints what *is* the breadth, and length, and depth, and height;

19 And to know the love of Christ, which passeth knowledge, that ye might be filled with all the fulness of God.

20 Now unto him that is able to do exceeding abundantly above all that we ask or think, according to the power that worketh in us,

21 Unto him *be* glory in the church by Christ Jesus throughout all ages, world without end. Amen.

III THE PRACTICE OF BELIEVERS, 4:1–6:9

A In Relation to Other Believers, 4:1–6

4 I therefore, the prisoner of the Lord, beseech you that ye walk worthy of the vocation wherewith ye are called,

2 With all lowliness and meekness, with longsuffering, forbearing one another in love;

3 Endeavouring to keep the unity of the Spirit in the bond of peace.

4 *There is* one body, and one Spirit, even as ye are called in one hope of your calling;

5 One Lord, one faith, one baptism,

6 One God and Father of all, who *is* above all, and through all, and in you all.

B In Relation to Spiritual Gifts, 4:7–16

7 But unto every one of us is given grace according to the measure of the gift of Christ.

3:17 *dwell*=be completely at home.

3:20 *the power that worketh in us*=the Holy Spirit.

4:1 Here begins Paul's exhortation to his readers to promote the unity of the church through godly living (vv. 1–6) and through the contribution of the common welfare of persons with a diversity of gifts (vv. 7–16). *vocation*=calling; i.e., our heavenly calling.

4:2 *lowliness*=humility. *meekness*=gentleness.

4:5 *one baptism*. I.e., the baptism of the Spirit which brings us into the unity of the body.

4:6 God is *Father* in four relationships: (1) here of all men by virtue of being the Creator; (2) of the Lord Jesus Christ (Matt. 3:17); (3) of Israel (Ex. 4:22); and (4) of believers in the Lord Jesus Christ (Gal. 3:26).

4:7 In 1 Cor. 12:7–11 Paul attributes the giving of spiritual gifts to the Spirit; here to the ascended Christ.

8 Wherefore he saith, When he ascended up on high, he led captivity captive, and gave gifts unto men.

9 (Now that he ascended, what is it but that he also descended first into the lower parts of the earth?

10 He that descended is the same also that ascended up far above all heavens, that he might fill all things.)

11 And he gave some, apostles; and some, prophets; and some, evangelists; and some, pastors and teachers;

12 For the perfecting of the saints, for the work of the ministry, for the edifying of the body of Christ:

13 Till we all come in the unity of the faith, and of the knowledge of the Son of God, unto a perfect man, unto the measure of the stature of the fulness of Christ:

14 That we *henceforth* be no more children, tossed to and fro, and carried about with every wind of doctrine, by the sleight of men, *and* cunning craftiness, whereby they lie in wait to deceive;

15 But speaking the truth in love, may grow up into him in all things, which is the head, *even* Christ:

16 From whom the whole body fitly joined together and compacted by that which every joint supplieth, according to the effectual working in the measure of every part, maketh increase of the body unto the edifying of itself in love.

4:8 *he led captivity captive*. Paul uses an illustration from Ps. 68:18 in which the triumphant warrior is elevated when he returns with hosts of prisoners, receiving gifts from the conquered people, and issuing gifts to his followers. Christ conquered Satan and all that had conquered us.

4:9–10 These verses are a parenthetical aside to comment on *he ascended* in v. 8 and to prove that only Christ fits the description.

4:9 *lower parts of the earth* may mean that Christ descended into Hades between His death and resurrection; or "of the earth" may be an appositional phrase meaning that He descended (at His incarnation) into the lower parts (of the universe), namely, the earth.

4:11 *apostles*. See note at Matt. 10.2. *prophets*. Strictly speaking, those who were given by God direct revelation to communicate to men. *evangelists*=preachers of the gospel. *pastors and teachers*. The two are linked together here, though separated elsewhere (Rom. 12:7; 1 Pet. 5:2).

4:12 Delete the commas as the clauses follow in sequence.

4:14 *sleight*=cunning.

C In Relation to the Former Life, 4:17–32

17 This I say therefore, and testify in the Lord, that ye henceforth walk not as other Gentiles walk, in the vanity of their mind,

18 Having the understanding darkened, being alienated from the life of God through the ignorance that is in them, because of the blindness of their heart:

19 Who being past feeling have given themselves over unto lasciviousness, to work all uncleanness with greediness.

20 But ye have not so learned Christ;

21 If so be that ye have heard him, and have been taught by him, as the truth is in Jesus:

22 That ye put off concerning the former conversation the old man, which is corrupt according to the deceitful lusts;

23 And be renewed in the spirit of your mind;

24 And that ye put on the new man, which after God is created in righteousness and true holiness.

25 Wherefore putting away lying, speak every man truth with his neighbour: for we are members one of another.

26 Be ye angry, and sin not: let not the sun go down upon your wrath:

27 Neither give place to the devil.

28 Let him that stole steal no more: but rather let him labour, working with *his* hands the thing which is good, that he may have to give to him that needeth.

29 Let no corrupt communication proceed out of your mouth, but that which is good to the use of edifying, that it may minister grace unto the hearers.

30 And grieve not the holy Spirit of God, whereby ye are sealed unto the day of redemption.

31 Let all bitterness, and wrath, and anger, and clamour, and evil speaking, be put away from you, with all malice:

4:17 Here begins a long passage (ending at 6:9) in which Paul draws the logical conclusions that follow from membership in Christ's body in terms of life and morals.

4:19 *being past feeling*=become callous.

4:22–24 *the old man . . . the new man*. The *old* is what we were before we were saved, and the *new* is the new life we have in Christ. See 2 Cor. 5:17; Gal. 2:20.

4:26 There is an anger which is not sinful, but even this must not be allowed to stay and fester and give the devil an opportunity.

4:30 The Holy *Spirit* is grieved or pained by sin, especially the sins of the tongue (vv. 29, 31). *sealed.* See note on 1:13.

4:31 *evil speaking*. Lit., blasphemy or slander.

32 And be ye kind one to another, tenderhearted, forgiving one another, even as God for Christ's sake hath forgiven you.

D In Relation to Evil, 5:1–17

5 Be ye therefore followers of God, as dear children;
2 And walk in love, as Christ also hath loved us, and hath given himself for us an offering and a sacrifice to God for a sweetsmelling savour.

3 But fornication, and all uncleanness, or covetousness, let it not be once named among you, as becometh saints;

4 Neither filthiness, nor foolish talking, nor jesting, which are not convenient: but rather giving of thanks.

5 For this ye know, that no whoremonger, nor unclean person, nor covetous man, who is an idolater, hath any inheritance in the kingdom of Christ and of God.

6 Let no man deceive you with vain words: for because of these things cometh the wrath of God upon the children of disobedience.

7 Be not ye therefore partakers with them.

8 For ye were sometimes darkness, but now *are ye* light in the Lord: walk as children of light:

9 (For the fruit of the Spirit *is* in all goodness and righteousness and truth;)

10 Proving what is acceptable unto the Lord.

11 And have no fellowship with the unfruitful works of darkness, but rather reprove *them*.

12 For it is a shame even to speak of those things which are done of them in secret.

13 But all things that are reproved are made manifest by the light: for whatsoever doth make manifest is light.

14 Wherefore he saith, Awake thou that sleepest, and arise from the dead, and Christ shall give thee light.

15 See then that ye walk circumspectly, not as fools, but as wise,

16 Redeeming the time, because the days are evil.

17 Wherefore be ye not unwise, but understanding what the will of the Lord *is*.

5:1 *followers.* Lit., imitators, especially in love.
5:2 *a sweetsmelling savour.* The sweet savour offerings of Lev. 1–3 prefigure the voluntary character of Christ's sacrifice.
5:4 *foolish talking, nor jesting.* I.e., unclean speech often veiled in innuendo or double meaning.
5:15 *circumspectly*=diligently, carefully.
5:16 *Redeeming the time*=making the most of time.

E In Relation to the Holy Spirit, 5:18-21

18 And be not drunk with wine, wherein is excess; but be filled with the Spirit;

19 Speaking to yourselves in psalms and hymns and spiritual songs, singing and making melody in your heart to the Lord;

20 Giving thanks always for all things unto God and the Father in the name of our Lord Jesus Christ;

21 Submitting yourselves one to another in the fear of God.

F In Relation to Home Life, 5:22-6:4

22 Wives, submit yourselves unto your own husbands, as unto the Lord.

23 For the husband is the head of the wife, even as Christ is the head of the church: and he is the saviour of the body.

24 Therefore as the church is subject unto Christ, so *let* the wives *be* to their own husbands in every thing.

25 Husbands, love your wives, even as Christ also loved the church, and gave himself for it;

26 That he might sanctify and cleanse it with the washing of water by the word,

27 That he might present it to himself a glorious church, not having spot, or wrinkle, or any such thing; but that it should be holy and without blemish.

5:18 *be filled with the Spirit*. Paul has taught in this epistle that all believers are sealed with the Spirit when they believe (1:13-14; 4:30), but not all are filled since this depends on yieldedness to God's will (v. 17). "Filling" describes an experience that can be repeated (Acts 2:4; 4:31), and here, as in Acts, it is connected with joy, courage, spirituality, and Christian character.

5:19 *to yourselves*. Better, to one another. Making music in one's heart is mentioned at the end of this verse.

5:21 *Submitting*. This is the key thought for understanding Paul's view of proper personal relationships in a Christian household; the subjection is to be mutual and based on reverence for God.

5:22 *Wives* are to submit to the leadership of their husbands in the home (vv. 22, 24); they are to reverence their husbands (v. 33); they are to love their husbands (Tit. 2:4), and live with them until death (Rom. 7:2-3).

5:25 *Husbands* are to love their wives, lead them (v. 23), nurture them in the things of Christ (v. 29), and live with them faithfully for life (Matt. 19:3-9).

28 So ought men to love their wives as their own bodies. He that loveth his wife loveth himself.

29 For no man ever yet hated his own flesh; but nourisheth and cherisheth it, even as the Lord the church:

30 For we are members of his body, of his flesh, and of his bones.

31 For this cause shall a man leave his father and mother, and shall be joined unto his wife, and they two shall be one flesh.

32 This is a great mystery: but I speak concerning Christ and the church.

33 Nevertheless let every one of you in particular so love his wife even as himself; and the wife *see* that she reverence *her* husband.

6 Children, obey your parents in the Lord: for this is right.

2 Honour thy father and mother; (which is the first commandment with promise;)

3 That it may be well with thee, and thou mayest live long on the earth.

4 And, ye fathers, provoke not your children to wrath: but bring them up in the nurture and admonition of the Lord.

G In Relation to Slaves and Masters, 6:5-9

5 Servants, be obedient to them that are *your* masters according to the flesh, with fear and trembling, in singleness of your heart, as unto Christ;

6 Not with eyeservice, as menpleasers; but as the servants of Christ, doing the will of God from the heart;

5:31 See Gen. 2:24.

5:32 The relationship between believing husbands and wives is illustrative of that which exists between Christ (the bridegroom) and the church (His bride). See also Matt. 25:1–13; Rev. 19:7–8; 21:2.

6:1 *in the Lord.* I.e., obedience to parents is part of a child's obligation to Christ. See the example of Christ in Luke 2:51 and Heb. 5:8.

6:2 Quoting Ex. 20:12. When a child marries, his relationship to his parents changes (5:31), but not his responsibility to provide for them (1 Tim. 5:4).

6:4 *provoke not.* I.e., do not nag or arbitrarily assert authority for its own sake.

6:5 *Servants.* Lit., slaves, *in singleness of your heart;* i.e., in reality and sincerity, not hypocrisy.

7 With good will doing service, as to the Lord, and not to men:

8 Knowing that whatsoever good thing any man doeth, the same shall he receive of the Lord, whether *he be* bond or free.

9 And, ye masters, do the same things unto them, forbearing threatening: knowing that your Master also is in heaven; neither is there respect of persons with him.

IV THE PROTECTION FOR BELIEVERS, 6:10–20

10 Finally, my brethren, be strong in the Lord, and in the power of his might.

A Against Whom? 6:11–12

11 Put on the whole armour of God, that ye may be able to stand against the wiles of the devil.

12 For we wrestle not against flesh and blood, but against principalities, against powers, against the rulers of the darkness of this world, against spiritual wickedness in high *places*.

B With What? 6:13–20

13 Wherefore take unto you the whole armour of God, that ye may be able to withstand in the evil day, and having done all, to stand.

14 Stand therefore, having your loins girt about with truth, and having on the breastplate of righteousness;

15 And your feet shod with the preparation of the gospel of peace;

16 Above all, taking the shield of faith, wherewith ye shall be able to quench all the fiery darts of the wicked.

17 And take the helmet of salvation, and the sword of the Spirit, which is the word of God:

18 Praying always with all prayer and supplication in the Spirit, and watching thereunto with all perserverance and supplication for all saints;

6:11 *wiles*=craftiness.
6:12 The believer's enemies are the demonic hosts of Satan, drawn up for mortal combat.
6:17 *take*. Lit., receive, a different word from that in v. 16. Salvation is a gift. *sword*, the only offensive weapon mentioned.

19 And for me, that utterance may be given unto me, that I may open my mouth boldly, to make known the mystery of the gospel,

20 For which I am an ambassador in bonds: that therein I may speak boldly, as I ought to speak.

V CONCLUDING WORDS, 6:21-24

21 But that ye also may know my affairs, *and* how I do, Tych'icus, a beloved brother and faithful minister in the Lord, shall make known to you all things:

22 Whom I have sent unto you for the same purpose, that ye might know our affairs, and *that* he might comfort your hearts.

23 Peace *be* to the brethren, and love with faith, from God the Father and the Lord Jesus Christ.

24 Grace *be* with all them that love our Lord Jesus Christ in sincerity. Amen.

6:19 Even in prison Paul was not thinking of his own personal welfare but of his testimony for Christ.

INTRODUCTION TO
THE LETTER OF PAUL TO THE
Philippians

AUTHOR: Paul DATE: 61

The Church at Philippi Founded by Paul on the second
missionary journey, this was the first church to be established by him in Europe (Acts 16). Philippi was but a small
city, founded by King Philip of Macedonia, father of
Alexander the Great. Its greatest fame came from the battle
fought nearby, in A.D. 42, between forces of Brutus and
Cassius and those of Anthony and Octavian (later Caesar
Augustus). It became a Roman "colony," a military out-
post city with special privileges.

Paul's relationship with the church at Philippi was always
close and cordial. Having helped him financially at least
two times before this letter was written (4:16), and having
heard of his confinement in Rome, the church sent
Epaphroditus with another gift. Philippians is a thank-you
letter for that gift, and it is the most personal of any letter
Paul wrote to a church. Epaphroditus had become nearly
fatally ill while with Paul (2:27), and on his recovery Paul
sent him back with this letter. Though somewhat obscured
by Paul's gentleness in this letter, some of the problems
in the church are seen beneath the surface. These included
rivalries and personal ambition (2:3–4; 4:2), the teaching of
Judaizers (3:1–3), perfectionism (3:12–14), and the influence of antinomian libertines (3:18–19).

The Place of Writing Paul was imprisoned when this
letter was written, but there is not agreement as to where.
Some think he was in Caesarea, others Ephesus, but he was
undoubtedly in Rome. In 1:13 (see note there) he mentions
the praetorium, a Roman body of troops assigned to the
emperor in Rome (see also 4:22). It is also quite clear that
in the trial facing Paul his life was at stake, indicating that
the trial was before Caesar in Rome (1:20). Although Paul
was confined in Caesarea two years, no final decision of his
case was even in prospect there (Acts 24). Ephesus has been

suggested as the place of writing on the basis of 1 Corinthians 15:32, but there is really no clear reference to an imprisonment in that verse.

The Contents One of the most important doctrinal passages in the New Testament is Philippians 2:5–8, the doctrine of the kenosis of self-humiliating, or self-emptying, of Christ. Important verses on prayer are 4:6–7, and other favorite verses include 1:21, 23b; 3:10, 20; 4:8, 13. An important autobiographical sketch appears in 3:4–14.

OUTLINE OF PHILIPPIANS

THE LETTER OF
PAUL THE APOSTLE TO THE
Philippians

I GREETINGS AND
EXPRESSIONS OF GRATITUDE, 1:1–11

1 Paul and Timoth'eus, the servants of Jesus Christ, to all the saints in Christ Jesus which are at Phi-lip'pi, with the bishops and deacons:

1:1 *Timotheus* (Timothy) had helped Paul found this church. *saints.* See note at Rom. 1:7. *bishops.* Lit., overseers. See note at 1 Tim. 3:1. *deacons.* See note at 1 Tim. 3:8. Both bishops

2 Grace *be* unto you, and peace, from God our Father, and *from* the Lord Jesus Christ.

3 I thank my God upon every remembrance of you,

4 Always in every prayer of mine for you all making request with joy,

5 For your fellowship in the gospel from the first day until now;

6 Being confident of this very thing, that he which hath begun a good work in you will perform *it* until the day of Jesus Christ:

7 Even as it is meet for me to think this of you all, because I have you in my heart; inasmuch as both in my bonds, and in the defence and confirmation of the gospel, ye all are partakers of my grace.

8 For God is my record, how greatly I long after you all in the bowels of Jesus Christ.

9 And this I pray, that your love may abound yet more and more in knowledge and *in* all judgment;

10 That ye may approve things that are excellent; that ye may be sincere and without offence till the day of Christ;

11 Being filled with the fruits of righteousness, which are by Jesus Christ, unto the glory and praise of God.

II PAUL'S PERSONAL CIRCUMSTANCES: THE PREACHING OF CHRIST, 1:12–30

12 But I would ye should understand, brethren, that the things *which happened* unto me have fallen out rather unto the furtherance of the gospel;

and deacons were recognizable groups within the church at this time.

1:5 Paul is here complimenting them on their cooperation from the beginning (see Acts 16:40; Phil. 4:16).

1:6 *he which hath begun*=He (God) who began. God will continue His good work of grace in them until the consummation at *the day of Jesus Christ* (the day when Christ returns).

1:7 *meet*=right. The Greek words underlying *bonds, defense,* and *confirmation* are courtroom terms. Paul is saying that they shared with him in his courageous witness in the court of law. Whether Paul had already appeared at trial or whether he is still anticipating it is unclear.

1:8 *bowels*=tenderness, compassion.

1:9 *judgment*=discernment.

1:10 *approve things that are excellent.* The idea is to differentiate between highest matters and side issues. *sincere and without offense.* Better, pure and blameless.

1:12–30 This passage tells us about all we know of Paul's im-

13 So that my bonds in Christ are manifest in all the palace, and in all other *places*;

14 And many of the brethren in the Lord, waxing confident by my bonds, are much more bold to speak the word without fear.

15 Some indeed preach Christ even of envy and strife; and some also of good will:

16 The one preach Christ of contention, not sincerely, supposing to add affliction to my bonds:

17 But the other of love, knowing that I am set for the defence of the gospel.

18 What then? notwithstanding, every way, whether in pretence, or in truth, Christ is preached; and I therein do rejoice, yea, and will rejoice.

19 For I know that this shall turn to my salvation through your prayer, and the supply of the Spirit of Jesus Christ,

20 According to my earnest expectation and *my* hope, that in nothing I shall be ashamed, but *that* with all boldness, as always, *so* now also Christ shall be magnified in my body, whether *it be* by life, or by death.

21 For to me to live *is* Christ, and to die *is* gain.

22 But if I live in the flesh, this *is* the fruit of my labour: yet what I shall choose I wot not.

23 For I am in a strait betwixt two, having a desire to depart, and to be with Christ; which is far better:

prisonment. He knows he is facing his great ordeal, but he takes great pains not to alarm his friends. His all-consuming concern is for the advancement of the gospel. People are beginning to talk about his bonds and his Christ, the church in Rome is becoming more confident, and he intends to follow his course. He exists only to help forward the cause of Christ (v. 21).

1:13 *palace.* Lit., praetorium. This group of imperial guards, distinct from the army or Roman police, about 9000 in Rome, had heard the gospel through their various members who had been assigned the duty of guarding Paul. Guard and prisoner were chained together, a captive audience for the gospel (see Eph. 6:20).

1:18 Regardless of the motive, if Christ is preached, Paul rejoiced. Wrong motives are seen in vv. 15–16.

1:19 *my salvation.* Paul's trial had probably begun. He was confident that either release or death would advance the cause of Christ (v. 20).

1:21 *to me to live is Christ.* I.e., life finds all its meaning in Christ. *to die is gain* because then there will be union with Christ without the limitations of this life.

1:22 *I wot not* = I perceive not.

24 Nevertheless to abide in the flesh *is* more needful for you.

25 And having this confidence, I know that I shall abide and continue with you all for your furtherance and joy of faith;

26 That your rejoicing may be more abundant in Jesus Christ for me by my coming to you again.

27 Only let your conversation be as it becometh the gospel of Christ: that whether I come and see you, or else be absent, I may hear of your affairs, that ye stand fast in one spirit, with one mind striving together for the faith of the gospel;

28 And in nothing terrified by your adversaries: which is to them an evident token of perdition, but to you of salvation, and that of God.

29 For unto you it is given in the behalf of Christ, not only to believe on him, but also to suffer for his sake;

30 Having the same conflict which ye saw in me, and now hear *to be* in me.

III THE PATTERN OF THE CHRISTIAN LIFE: THE HUMILITY OF CHRIST, 2:1-30

A The Exhortation to Humility, 2:1-4

2 If *there be* therefore any consolation in Christ, if any comfort of love, if any fellowship of the Spirit, if any bowels and mercies,

2 Fulfil ye my joy, that ye be likeminded, having the same love, *being* of one accord, of one mind.

3 *Let* nothing *be done* through strife or vainglory; but in lowliness of mind let each esteem other better than themselves.

1:25 Here Paul seems certain that he will be acquitted, but the only reason one can see for his momentary confidence is that he is still needed on earth.

1:26 *for me*. Better, So that, your pride in me may . . .

1:30 Paul is saying that the Philippians are in the same game (*conflict*) he is in.

2:1 *consolation*=support. *bowels and mercies*=affection and sympathy. Paul is saying that since (=if) men can count on Christ they can do the things described in the following verses.

2:2 *Fulfill ye my joy*. I.e., you would cap off my pleasure if you would work together harmoniously and clear up your petty quarrels. Paul has in mind particularly the division caused by two women, Euodia (=Euodias) and Syntyche (4:2).

4 Look not every man on his own things, but every man also on the things of others.

B The Epitome of Humility, 2:5–11

5 Let this mind be in you, which was also in Christ Jesus:

6 Who, being in the form of God, thought it not robbery to be equal with God:

7 But made himself of no reputation, and took upon him the form of a servant, and was made in the likeness of men:

8 And being found in fashion as a man, he humbled himself, and became obedient unto death, even the death of the cross.

9 Wherefore God also hath highly exalted him, and given him a name which is above every name:

10 That at the name of Jesus every knee should bow, of *things* in heaven, and *things* in earth, and *things* under the earth;

11 And *that* every tongue should confess that Jesus Christ *is* Lord, to the glory of God the Father.

2:4 The church was apparently evidencing petty jealousies among members over honors and rewards. Paul commends humility and that new disposition that comes from Christ (v. 5).

2:5–11 This passage on the humility of Christ is the high mark of the epistle. Unlike the informal, conversational style of the rest of the letter, vv. 5–11 are highly polished. It is also noteworthy in that it conveys in a few verses Paul's conception of the uniqueness of the person and work of Christ. Paul's point is that the disposition, the temper, of church members ought always to be that of Christ.

2:6 *the form of God* means that Christ is of the same nature and essence as God. *not robbery*. The verse may be paraphrased thus: Who, though of the same nature as God, did not think this something to be exploited to His own advantage.

2:7 *made himself of no reputation*. Lit., emptied himself. The *kenosis* (emptying) of Christ during His incarnation does not mean that He surrendered any attributes of deity, but that He took on the limitations of humanity. This mean a veiling of His preincarnate glory (John 17:5) and the voluntary nonuse of some of His divine prerogatives during the time He was on earth (Matt. 24:36).

2:9 Through self-denial and obedience Christ won sovereignty over all peoples and things (v. 10).

C The Exercise of Humility, 2:12–18

12 Wherefore, my beloved, as ye have always obeyed, not as in my presence only, but now much more in my absence, work out your own salvation with fear and trembling.

13 For it is God which worketh in you both to will and to do of *his* good pleasure.

14 Do all things without murmurings and disputings:

15 That ye may be blameless and harmless, the sons of God, without rebuke, in the midst of a crooked and perverse nation, among whom ye shine as lights in the world;

16 Holding forth the word or life; that I may rejoice in the day of Christ, that I have not run in vain, neither laboured in vain.

17 Yea, and if I be offered upon the sacrifice and service of your faith, I joy, and rejoice with you all.

18 For the same cause also do ye joy, and rejoice with me.

D The Examples of Timothy and Epaphroditus, 2:19–30

19 But I trust in the Lord Jesus to send Timoth'eus shortly unto you, that I also may be of good comfort, when I know your state.

20 For I have no man likeminded, who will naturally care for your state.

21 For all seek their own, not the things which are Jesus Christ's.

22 But ye know the proof of him, that, as a son with the father, he hath served with me in the gospel.

2:12–18 Paul now turns to the obligations that the example of Christ lays on Christians. You must learn to stand on your own feet, with a sense of human frailty, knowing that God is behind you (v. 13). So live in this corrupt human society of ours that you may reflect the light that comes from a heavenly source (vv. 14–15), constantly proclaiming the gospel of the new life (v. 16a). Thus at Christ's coming Paul will receive his reward (v. 16b). In vv. 17–18 Paul employs the language of the Jewish offerings and compares his death to a drink-offering which accompanies the Philippians' presentation of themselves as a burnt-offering (Num. 15:10; 28:7).

2:19–30 The letter now returns to personal matters. Paul is going to send Timothy later and is sending Epaphroditus now; and he wants them to be accepted as his representative with his authority. Nobody else with him at the moment except Timothy has the interest of Christ at heart (v. 21). Epaphroditus was a leader in the Philippian church; Paul is sending him home with this letter (v. 25).

23 Him therefore I hope to send presently, so soon as I shall see how it will go with me.

24 But I trust in the Lord that I also myself shall come shortly.

25 Yet I supposed it necessary to send to you Epaphrōdī'tus, my brother, and companion in labour, and fellowsoldier, but your messenger, and he that ministered to my wants.

26 For he longed after you all, and was full of heaviness, because that ye had heard that he had been sick.

27 For indeed he was sick nigh unto death: but God had mercy on him; and not on him only, but on me also, lest I should have sorrow upon sorrow.

28 I sent him therefore the more carefully, that, when ye see him again, ye may rejoice, and that I may be the less sorrowful.

29 Receive him therefore in the Lord with all gladness; and hold such in reputation:

30 Because for the work of Christ he was nigh unto death, not regarding his life, to supply your lack of service toward me.

IV THE PRIZE OF THE CHRISTIAN LIFE: THE KNOWLEDGE OF CHRIST, 3:1-21

A The Warning against Judaizers, 3:1-3

3 Finally, my brethren, rejoice in the Lord. To write the same things to you, to me indeed *is* not grievous, but for you *it is* safe.

2 Beware of dogs, beware of evil workers, beware of the concision.

2:30 *nigh unto death.* Some causes for sickness are: (1) violation of natural limitations illustrated here by Epaphroditus' being sick from overwork; (2) unconfessed sin in the life (1 Cor. 11:30); (3) to promote Christian character and growth (2 Cor. 12:7-9); (4) to display the power of God (John 9:3).

3:1 *the same things.* I.e., the content of vv. 2-3, a basic lesson which Paul as their teacher had undoubtedly gone over with them many times while with them: Do not let Christianity be debased into some form of the Jewish ritualistic religion. Obviously this was a danger in Philippi.

3:2 Paul here becomes polemical. He labels the Judaizers (who taught that circumcision was necessary for salvation) *dogs* (a term they used to describe Gentiles), *evil workers*, and *concision* which means mutilators. All three epithets are directed at the same people.

3 For we are the circumcision, which worship God in the spirit, and rejoice in Christ Jesus, and have no confidence in the flesh.

B The Example of Paul, 3:4–14

4 Though I might also have confidence in the flesh. If any other man thinketh that he hath whereof he might trust in the flesh, I more:

5 Circumcised the eighth day, of the stock of Israel, *of* the tribe of Benjamin, an Hebrew of the Hebrews; as touching the law, a Pharisee;

6 Concerning zeal, persecuting the church; touching the righteousness which is in the law, blameless.

7 But what things were gain to me, those I counted loss for Christ.

8 Yea doubtless, and I count all things *but* loss for the excellency of the knowledge of Christ Jesus my Lord: for whom I have suffered the loss of all things, and do count them *but* dung, that I may win Christ,

9 And be found in him, not having mine own righteousness, which is of the law, but that which is through the faith of Christ, the righteousness which is of God by faith:

10 That I may know him, and the power of his resurrection, and the fellowship of his sufferings, being made conformable unto his death;

11 If by any means I might attain unto the resurrection of the dead.

12 Not as though I had already attained, either were already perfect: but I follow after, if that I may apprehend that for which also I am apprehended of Christ Jesus.

13 Brethren, I count not myself to have apprehended: but *this* one thing I *do*, forgetting those things which are behind, and reaching forth unto those things which are before,

---

3:4–14 Paul reflects on the whole course of his life, which gives him the right to criticize Judaism.

3:8 *dung*=rubbish, refuse.

3:9 Here Paul contrasts works-righteousness, which is based on the law, with faith-righteousness, which is from God through faith in Christ. Rom. 3:21–5:21 is a commentary on this verse.

3:10 *being made conformable to his death* means becoming like Him in His death—passing through death into a new life, dying and rising with Christ (Rom. 6).

3:12 Paul makes it clear that he had not "arrived" but was still very much in the race of life.

14 I press toward the mark for the prize of the high calling of God in Christ Jesus.

C The Exhortation to Others, 3:15–21

15 Let us therefore, as many as be perfect, be thus minded: and if in any thing ye be otherwise minded, God shall reveal even this unto you.

16 Nevertheless, whereto we have already attained, let us walk by the same rule, let us mind the same thing.

17 Brethren, be followers together of me, and mark them which walk so as ye have us for an ensample.

18 (For many walk, of whom I have told you often, and now tell you even weeping, *that they are* the enemies of the cross of Christ:

19 Whose end *is* destruction, whose God *is their* belly, and *whose* glory *is* in their shame, who mind earthly things.)

20 For our conversation is in heaven; from whence also we look for the Saviour, the Lord Jesus Christ:

21 Who shall change our vile body, that it may be fashioned like unto his glorious body, according to the working whereby he is able even to subdue all things unto himself.

V THE PEACE OF THE CHRISTIAN LIFE: THE PRESENCE OF CHRIST, 4:1–23

A Peace with Others, 4:1–4

4 Therefore, my brethren dearly beloved and longed for, my joy and crown, so stand fast in the Lord, *my* dearly beloved.

2 I beseech Eû-ō′dias, and beseech Syn′tychē, that they be of the same mind in the Lord.

3:15 *perfect*=mature. In the last half of the verse Paul says, "If you don't agree, God will give you light on the subject."

3:18 *enemies of the cross of Christ*. Evil living (the libertines) is in view here. Their principal concern was their *belly* (v. 19); i.e., all sensual indulgences.

3:20 *conversation*. Lit., citizenship. This would have been particularly appreciated by the Philippians in view of their city's status as a Roman colony.

3:21 *vile body*. Lit., body of humiliation. Our present state of mortality is a lowly one.

4:1 Here begins Paul's closing section, consisting first of practical advice followed by personal messages.

4:2 *Euodias*. Lit., Euodia. *be of the same mind*=agree.

3 And I intreat thee also, true yokefellow, help those women which laboured with me in the gospel, with Clement also, and *with* other my fellowlabourers, whose names *are* in the book of life.

4 Rejoice in the Lord alway: *and* again I say, Rejoice.

B Peace with Self, 4:5-9

5 Let your moderation be known unto all men. The Lord *is* at hand.

6 Be careful for nothing; but in every thing by prayer and supplication with thanksgiving let your requests be made known unto God.

7 And the peace of God, which passeth all understanding, shall keep your hearts and minds through Christ Jesus.

8 Finally, brethren, whatsoever things are true, whatsoever things *are* honest, whatsoever things *are* just, whatsoever things *are* pure, whatsoever things *are* lovely, whatsoever things *are* of good report; if *there be* any virtue, and if *there be* any praise, think on these things.

9 Those things, which ye have both learned, and received, and heard, and seen in me, do: and the God of peace shall be with you.

C Peace with Circumstances, 4:10-23

10 But I rejoiced in the Lord greatly, that now at the last your care of me hath flourished again; wherein ye were also careful, but ye lacked opportunity.

11 Not that I speak in respect of want: for I have learned, in whatsoever state I am, *therewith* to be content.

12 I know both how to be abased, and I know how to abound: every where and in all things I am instructed both to be full and to be hungry, both to abound and to suffer need.

13 I can do all things through Christ which strengtheneth me.

14 Notwithstanding ye have well done, that ye did communicate with my affliction.

4:3 The identity of the *true yokefellow* is not revealed.
4:5 *moderation*=forbearance, gentleness.
4:6 *Be careful for nothing.* Lit., be anxious about nothing.
4:8 *honest*=worthy of respect. *lovely*=winsome.
4:11 *content.* Lit., self-sufficient, independent of external circumstances. The secret of such contentment is found in v. 13.
4:14 *communicate.* Lit., make common cause with. Paul refers to the sending of monetary gifts (vv. 10, 16).

15 Now ye Philippians know also, that in the beginning of the gospel, when I departed from Macedonia, no church communicated with me as concerning giving and receiving, but ye only.

16 For even in Thessalōnī'ca ye sent once and again unto my necessity.

17 Not because I desire a gift: but I desire fruit that may abound to your account.

18 But I have all, and abound: I am full, having received of Epaphrōdī'tus the things *which were sent* from you, an odour of a sweet smell, a sacrifice acceptable, wellpleasing to God.

19 But my God shall supply all your need according to his riches in glory by Christ Jesus.

20 Now unto God and our Father *be* glory for ever and ever. Amen.

21 Salute every saint in Christ Jesus. The brethren which are with me greet you.

22 All the saints salute you, chiefly they that are of Cæsar's household.

23 The grace of our Lord Jesus Christ *be* with you all. Amen.

4:19 The church that gives to missionaries will have its own needs supplied.

4:22 *Caesar's household.* Probably employees in the emperor's palace. There is no evidence of the conversion of a member of the imperial family until a generation later.

INTRODUCTION TO
THE LETTER OF PAUL TO THE
Colossians

AUTHOR: Paul   DATE: 61

The Church at Colosse   About 100 miles east of Ephesus
and near Laodicea and Hierapolis (4:13), Colosse was an
ancient but declining commercial center. The gospel may
have gone there during Paul's ministry at Ephesus (Acts
19:10), though it was Epaphras who played the major role
in the evangelism and growth of the Colossians. Paul was
personally unacquainted with the believers there (2:1), but
Epaphras either visited Paul in prison or was imprisoned
with him (Philem. 23) and reported on conditions in the
church.

The Place of Writing   Like Ephesians, Philippians, and
Philemon, Colossians was written during Paul's first imprisonment in Rome (see the Introduction to Titus and the
Introduction to Philippians for other suggestions as to the
place of writing). The many common personal references
between Colossians and Philemon and the many similarities
of ideas between Colossians and Ephesians link these letters
together. Tychicus was apparently the bearer of the letter
(Eph. 6:21; Col. 4:7).

The Colossian Heresy   From Paul's counter-emphases in
the epistle, we can discern some of the features of the false
teaching at Colosse. It was a syncretistic doctrine fusing
Jewish legalism, Greek philosophic speculation, and Oriental mysticism. Specifics included dietary and Sabbath
observances and circumcision rites (2:11, 16), the worship
of angels (2:18), and the practice of asceticism, which
stemmed from the belief that the body was evil (2:21–23).
In combating this heresy Paul emphasizes the cosmic significance of Christ as Lord of creation and Head of the
church. Any teaching or practice and all intermediaries that

detract from the uniqueness and centrality of Christ are attacks on the faith.

The Contents The theme is the all-sufficiency and supremacy of Christ. Important subjects include the major section on Christ (1:15–23), Paul's direct attack on the heresy (2:8–23), and the teaching on the believers' union with Christ (3:1–4).

OUTLINE OF COLOSSIANS

THE LETTER OF
PAUL THE APOSTLE TO THE
Colossians

I INTRODUCTION, 1:1–14

A Greetings, 1:1–2

1 Paul, an apostle of Jesus Christ by the will of God, and Timoth'eus *our* brother.

2 To the saints and faithful brethren in Christ which are at Colos'sē: Grace *be* unto you, and peace, from God our Father and the Lord Jesus Christ.

B Gratitude for the Colossians' Faith, 1:3–8

3 We give thanks to God and the Father of our Lord Jesus Christ, praying always for you,

4 Since we heard of your faith in Christ Jesus, and of the love *which ye have* to all the saints,

5 For the hope which is laid up for you in heaven, whereof ye heard before in the word of the truth of the gospel;

6 Which is come unto you, as *it is* in all the world; and bringeth forth fruit, as *it doth* also in you, since the day ye heard *of it*, and knew the grace of God in truth:

7 As ye also learned of Ep'aphras our dear fellowservant, who is for you a faithful minister of Christ;

8 Who also declared unto us your love in the Spirit.

C Prayer for the Colossians' Growth, 1:9–14

9 For this cause we also, since the day we heard *it*, do not cease to pray for you, and to desire that ye might be filled with the knowledge of his will in all wisdom and spiritual understanding;

10 That ye might walk worthy of the Lord unto all pleasing, being fruitful in every good work, and increasing in the knowledge of God;

11 Strengthened with all might, according to his glorious power, unto all patience and longsuffering with joyfulness;

12 Giving thanks unto the Father, which hath made us meet to be partakers of the inheritance of the saints in light:

1:4–5 Notice the mention of the triad of Christian graces: *faith*, *love*, and *hope* (1 Cor. 13:13).

1:6 The verse should read thus: Which is come unto you; as also in all the world it is bringing forth fruit and growing as it is among you . . .

1:7 *Epaphras* (see 4:12; Philem. 23). He was apparently the man who evangelized the cities of the Lycus Valley and founded the churches of Colossae, Hierapolis, and Laodicea. It was his report, brought to Paul in Rome, of the condition of these churches that prompted the writing of this letter. Epaphroditus of Phil. 2:25 and 4:18 is evidently a different individual.

1:10 *walk worthy of the Lord*=live a life worthy of the Lord.

1:11 *with joyfulness*. This is what distinguishes the Christian's *patience* and *longsuffering* from the Stoic's.

1:12 *made us meet*=made us fit, qualified us.

13 Who hath delivered us from the power of darkness, and hath translated *us* into the kingdom of his dear Son:

14 In whom we have redemption through his blood, *even* the forgiveness of sins:

II THE EXALTED CHRIST, 1:15–29

A Christ's Character, 1:15–23

15 Who is the image of the invisible God, the firstborn of every creature:

16 For by him were all things created, that are in heaven, and that are in earth, visible and invisible, whether *they be* thrones, or dominions, or principalities, or powers: all things were created by him, and for him:

17 And he is before all things, and by him all things consist.

18 And he is the head of the body, the church: who is the beginning, the firstborn from the dead; that in all *things* he might have the preeminence.

19 For it pleased *the Father* that in him should all fulness dwell;

20 And, having made peace through the blood of his cross, by him to reconcile all things unto himself; by him, I *say*, whether *they be* things in earth, or things in heaven.

21 And you, that were sometime alienated and enemies in *your* mind by wicked works, yet now hath he reconciled

22 In the body of his flesh through death, to present you holy and unblameable and unreproveable in his sight:

1:13 *the kingdom of his dear Son*. Lit., the kingdom of the Son of His love. Christians are already within the sphere of the new age.

1:14 *redemption*. See note at Eph. 1:7.

1:15 *the firstborn of every creature*. Lit., the firstborn of all creation; i.e., the Son has all the rights belonging to the first-born because of His preeminent position as supreme over all creation (v. 16).

1:16 *principalities, or powers*. See note at Eph. 1:21.

1:17 *consist*=hold together in unity.

1:18 *the church*. See note at Eph. 1:22–23. *the firstborn from the dead*. I.e., the first one to rise from the dead with a resurrection body (Rev. 1:5).

1:19 *all fulness*. The full essence (powers and attributes) of deity dwell in Christ (see 2:9).

1:20 *to reconcile all things unto himself*. Christ is the remedy for the alienation from God, and eventually all things will be changed and brought into a unity in Him, even though this will involve judgment (Heb. 9:23; 1 Cor. 15:24–28).

23 If ye continue in the faith grounded and settled, and *be* not moved away from the hope of the gospel, which ye have heard, *and* which was preached to every creature which is under heaven; whereof I Paul am made a minister;

B Christ's Commission to Paul, 1:24–29

24 Who now rejoice in my sufferings for you, and fill up that which is behind of the afflictions of Christ in my flesh for his body's sake, which is the church:

25 Whereof I am made a minister, according to the dispensation of God which is given to me for you, to fulfil the word of God;

26 *Even* the mystery which hath been hid from ages and from generations, but now is made manifest to his saints:

27 To whom God would make known what *is* the riches of the glory of this mystery among the Gentiles; which is Christ in you, the hope of glory:

28 Whom we preach, warning every man, and teaching every man in all wisdom; that we may present every man perfect in Christ Jesus:

29 Whereunto I also labour, striving according to his working, which worketh in me mightily.

III THE EXALTED CHRISTIANITY, 2:1–23

A Exalted Over Philosophy, 2:1–10

2 For I would that ye knew what great conflict I have for you, and *for* them at Lāodicē′a, and *for* as many as have not seen my face in the flesh;

2 That their hearts might be comforted, being knit together in love, and unto all riches of the full assurance of understanding, to the acknowledgement of the mystery of God, and of the Father, and of Christ;

3 In whom are hid all the treasures of wisdom and knowledge.

1:23 *to every creature which is under heaven.* Lit., in all creation under heaven.

1:24 Because of the union of believers with Christ, what Paul suffered for the sake of the church can be called Christ's sufferings as well.

1:25 *the dispensation*=the stewardship, assignment, office (1 Cor. 4:1).

1:26 *the mystery.* The secret known only by Divine revelation of the indwelling of Christ (see note at Eph. 3:3).

4 And this I say, lest any man should beguile you with enticing words.

5 For though I be absent in the flesh, yet am I with you in the spirit, joying and beholding your order, and the stedfastness of your faith in Christ.

6 As ye have therefore received Christ Jesus the Lord, so walk ye in him:

7 Rooted and built up in him, and stablished in the faith, as ye have been taught, abounding therein with thanksgiving.

8 Beware lest any man spoil you through philosophy and vain deceit, after the tradition of men, after the rudiments of the world, and not after Christ.

9 For in him dwelleth all the fulness of the Godhead bodily.

10 And ye are complete in him, which is the head of all principality and power:

B Exalted Over Legalism, 2:11–17

11 In whom also ye are circumcised with the circumcision made without hands, in putting off the body of the sins of the flesh by the circumcision of Christ:

12 Buried with him in baptism, wherein also ye are risen with *him* through the faith of the operation of God, who hath raised him from the dead.

2:4 *enticing words*=persuasive speech.

2:6 As . . . so. As Christ is received by faith, the believer is to walk (live) by faith, acknowledging the Lordship of Christ over his life (2 Cor. 5:7).

2:8 *vain deceit*. This is Paul's belittlement of the Colossian "philosophy." *after the rudiments of the world*=after the elemental spirits of the universe; i.e., the cosmic spirits of Hellenistic syncretism. Apparently their philosophy involved regulating their religious life by observing the movements of the stars which they associated with the powers of the angels who were worshiped by some (v. 18). In this passage Paul uses the vocabulary of the heretics, giving the words their proper meaning and defeating them using their own terms (e.g., *perfect*, 1:28; *mystery*, 2:2; *wisdom and knowledge*, 2:3; *rudiments of the world*, 2:8; *head*, 2:10).

2:9 In Jesus Christ deity (the divine attributes and nature) dwelt in His earthly body. This is a strong statement of the deity and humanity of the God-man.

2:11–12 *Putting off the body of the sins of the flesh* (the old nature which is corrupt in its unregenerate state of rebellion against God) is illustrated in the rite of circumcision and the ordinance of baptism, but is accomplished by a spiritual circumcision and Spirit baptism.

13 And you, being dead in your sins and the uncircumcision of your flesh, hath he quickened together with him, having forgiven you all trespasses;

14 Blotting out the handwriting of ordinances that was against us, which was contrary to us, and took it out of the way, nailing it to his cross;

15 *And* having spoiled principalities and powers, he made a shew of them openly, triumphing over them in it.

16 Let no man therefore judge you in meat, or in drink, or in respect of an holyday, or of the new moon, or of the sabbath *days*:

17 Which are a shadow of things to come; but the body *is* of Christ.

C Exalted Over Mystical Teaching, 2:18–19

18 Let no man beguile you of your reward in a voluntary humility and worshipping of angels, intruding into those things which he hath not seen, vainly puffed up by his fleshly mind,

19 And not holding the Head, from which all the body by joints and bands having nourishment ministered, and knit together, increaseth with the increase of God.

D Exalted Over Asceticism, 2:20–23

20 Wherefore if ye be dead with Christ from the rudiments of the world, why, as though living in the world, are ye subject to ordinances,

2:14 *handwriting of ordinances*=a certificate or acknowledgment of debt in the handwriting of the debtor. The Mosaic law (which Paul's phrase symbolizes) put us in debt to God with sin; this debt He has canceled by nailing it to the cross of Christ. Christ has made full payment.

2:15 *spoiled*. Lit., stripped (as was done to enemies).

2:16 False teachers were evidently imposing abstinence from certain foods and observance of certain days. These, Paul says, are in the shadows which have been dispersed by the coming of Christ (v. 17).

2:17 *body*. I.e., the reality.

2:18 Some were also teaching a false humility and the worship of angels as the proper form of it, claiming special mystic insights by way of visions (*intruding into those things which he hath not seen*). The basic problem is their egoistic or *fleshly mind*.

2:20–23 Christ has freed you from the taboos of asceticism. It can only give a pretense of wisdom, promote a self-imposed worship, deal severely with the body, yet without any success in combating the desires of the flesh.

21 (Touch not; taste not; handle not;

22 Which all are to perish with the using;) after the commandments and doctrines of men?

23 Which things have indeed a shew of wisdom in will worship, and humility, and neglecting of the body; not in any honour to the satisfying of the flesh.

IV THE EXALTED CALLING, 3:1–4:6

A The Certainties of Our Calling, 3:1–4

3 If ye then be risen with Christ, seek those things which are above, where Christ sitteth on the right hand of God.

2 Set your affection on things above, not on things on the earth.

3 For ye are dead, and your life is hid with Christ in God.

4 When Christ, *who is* our life, shall appear, then shall ye also appear with him in glory.

B The Characteristics of Our Calling, 3:5–4:6

1 *In every-day life,* 3:5–17

5 Mortify therefore your members which are upon the earth; fornication, uncleanness, inordinate affection, evil concupiscence, and covetousness, which is idolatry:

6 For which things' sake the wrath of God cometh on the children of disobedience:

7 In the which ye also walked some time, when ye lived in them.

8 But now ye also put off all these; anger, wrath, malice, blasphemy, filthy communication out of your mouth.

9 Lie not one to another, seeing that ye have put off the old man with his deeds;

10 And have put on the new *man*, which is renewed in knowledge after the image of him that created him:

3:1 Here begins the ethical section of the letter. Paul's appeal is simple: Become in experience what you already are by God's grace. The Christian is risen with Christ; let him exhibit that new life.

3:5 *Mortify*=put to death. *concupiscence*=desire.

3:9 *the old man*=that old nature or capacity to leave God out of one's life and actions which characterized the unregenerate state.

3:10 *the new man*=that new nature or capacity received when one is saved, with which he may serve God and righteousness

11 Where there is neither Greek nor Jew, circumcision nor uncircumcision, Barbarian, Scythian, bond *nor* free: but Christ *is* all, and in all.

12 Put on therefore, as the elect of God, holy and beloved, bowels of mercies, kindness, humbleness of mind, meekness, longsuffering;

13 Forbearing one another, and forgiving one another, if any man have a quarrel against any: even as Christ forgave you, so also *do* ye.

14 And above all these things *put on* charity, which is the bond of perfectness.

15 And let the peace of God rule in your hearts, to the which also ye are called in one body; and be ye thankful.

16 Let the word of Christ dwell in you richly in all wisdom; teaching and admonishing one another in psalms and hymns and spiritual songs, singing with grace in your hearts to the Lord.

17 And whatsoever ye do in word or deed, *do* all in the name of the Lord Jesus, giving thanks to God and the Father by him.

2 *In the home,* 3:18–21

18 Wives, submit yourselves unto your own husbands, as it is fit in the Lord.

19 Husbands, love *your* wives, and be not bitter against them.

20 Children, obey *your* parents in all things: for this is well pleasing unto the Lord.

21 Fathers, provoke not your children *to anger,* lest they be discouraged.

3 *In servant-master relationships,* 3:22–4:1

22 Servants, obey in all things *your* masters according to the flesh; not with eyeservice, as menpleasers; but in singleness of heart, fearing God:

(Rom. 6:18). Continual renewing is necessary, however, in order that the new life may have full dominion over their moral conduct.

3:11 *Barbarian.* At this time the word was applied to those who did not speak Greek. *Scythian* represents the lowest type of uncouth barbarian nomads of southern Russia. In Christ distinctions of race, class, and culture are transcended.

3:14 *charity*=love. *perfectness*=completeness.

3:16 The *psalms and hymns and spiritual songs* must be those which teach and admonish.

3:19 *Husbands.* See note at Eph. 5:25.

3:22 *in singleness of heart.* I.e., in sincerity, honesty.

23 And whatsoever ye do, do *it* heartily, as to the Lord, and not unto men;

24 Knowing that of the Lord ye shall receive the reward of the inheritance: for ye serve the Lord Christ.

25 But he that doeth wrong shall receive for the wrong which he hath done: and there is no respect of persons.

4 Masters, give unto *your* servants that which is just and equal; knowing that ye also have a Master in heaven.

4 *In prayer,* 4:2–4

2 Continue in prayer, and watch in the same with thanksgiving;

3 Withal praying also for us, that God would open unto us a door of utterance, to speak the mystery of Christ, for which I am also in bonds:

4 That I may make it manifest, as I ought to speak.

5 *In witness and speech,* 4:5–6

5 Walk in wisdom toward them that are without, redeeming the time.

6 Let your speech *be* alway with grace, seasoned with salt, that ye may know how ye ought to answer every man.

V CONCLUDING PERSONAL REMARKS, 4:7–18

7 All my state shall Tych′icus declare unto you, *who is* a beloved brother, and a faithful minister and fellowservant in the Lord:

8 Whom I have sent unto you for the same purpose, that he might know your estate, and comfort your hearts;

9 With Ones′imus, a faithful and beloved brother, who

3:25 *no respect of persons.* God will show no favoritism either for the unfaithful slave or the unjust master (4:1).

4:2 *watch in the same*=being watchful in it.

4:3 *a door of utterance.* Lit., a door of the word; i.e., an opportunity to *speak the mystery.*

4:5 *them that are without.* I.e., those who are not Christians, but pagans. The division between them was sharp: the church was the community and all others were shut-out unbelievers.

4:6 *seasoned with salt.* Since salt is a preservative that retards corruption, our speech should never be insipid, corrupt, or obscene. *every man.* I.e., them that are without.

4:7 *Tychicus.* One of the bearers of this letter (Acts 20:4).

4:9 *Onesimus.* See the Introduction to Philemon.

is *one* of you. They shall make known unto you all things which *are done* here.

10 Aristar'chus my fellowprisoner saluteth you, and Marcus, sister's son to Barnabas, (touching whom ye received commandments: if he come unto you, receive him;)

11 And Jesus, which is called Justus, who are of the circumcision. These only *are my* fellowworkers unto the kingdom of God, which have been a comfort unto me.

12 Ep'aphras, who is *one* of you, a servant of Christ, saluteth you, always labouring fervently for you in prayers, that ye may stand perfect and complete in all the will of God.

13 For I bear him record, that he hath a great zeal for you, and them *that are* in Lāodicē'a, and them in Hīerā'-polis.

14 Luke, the beloved physician, and Demas, greet you.

15 Salute the brethren which are in Lāodicē'a, and Nymphas, and the church which is in his house.

16 And when this epistle is read among you, cause that it be read also in the church of the Lāodicē'ans; and that ye likewise read the *epistle* from Lāodicē'a.

17 And say to Archip'pus, Take heed to the ministry which thou hast received in the Lord, that thou fulfil it.

18 The salutation by the hand of me Paul. Remember my bonds. Grace *be* with you. Amen.

4:10 *Aristarchus.* See Acts 19:29; 20:4; 27:2. *Marcus*=Mark, the author of the second Gospel. He has been restored to Paul's favor after his lapse on the first missionary journey (Acts 15:36–39).

4:11 *Jesus, which is called Justus.* Nothing else is known of him.

4:14 *Luke.* The author of the third Gospel. *Demas* later defected (2 Tim. 4:10).

4:15 *the church which is in his house.* See note at Rom. 16:5.

4:16 *the epistle from Laodicea.* Some think this is the circular letter to the Ephesians.

4:17 *Archippus.* See Philem. 2.

INTRODUCTION TO
THE FIRST LETTER OF PAUL TO THE
Thessalonians

Author: Paul Date: 51

The Work at Thessalonica Paul, Silas, and Timothy first went to the Macedonian port city of Thessalonica on the second missionary journey (Acts 17:1–14). This was the second place the gospel was preached in Europe, Philippi being the first. Because the preaching of the gospel depleted the ranks of the synagogue, the Jews charged Paul's host, Jason, with harboring traitors to Caesar. The rulers of the city took security of Jason (like a peace bond) and let the missionaries leave the city. When they arrived in Athens, Paul sent Timothy back to Thessalonica (3:1–2, 5) to encourage the believers and to report back to him on the condition of the church there. Timothy rejoined Paul in Corinth (3:6), where the two Thessalonian letters were written.

Some feel that Paul was in Thessalonica less than a month (only three Sabbaths are mentioned in Acts 17:2). In any case, he was anxious about leaving the church under pressure and without experienced leadership. Timothy's report gave Paul cause only for praise for the healthy state of the church. This is a letter from a relieved and grateful pastor to his growing flock.

The Purposes of the Letter In addition (1) to expressing his thankfulness, Paul (2) defended himself against a campaign to slander his ministry which asserted that it was done only for profit (2:9–10); (3) encouraged the new converts to stand not only against persecution but also against the pressure to revert to their former pagan standards (3:2–3; 4:1–12); (4) answered the question about what happens to Christians who die before the return of the Lord (4:13–18). (5) Finally, some problems in their church life needed to be dealt with (5:12–13, 19–20).

The Contents *The key passages in this letter are eschato-logical; that is, related to future events of the last days, like the rapture of the church (4:13–18) and the day of the Lord (5:1–11).*

OUTLINE OF 1 THESSALONIANS

I Personal and Historical, 1:1–3:13
  A Paul's Greeting, 1:1
  B Paul's Commendation of the Thessalonians, 1:2–10
  C Paul's Conduct among the Thessalonians, 2:1–12
    1 His uprightness, 2:1–4
    2 His industry, 2:5–9
    3 His blameless behavior, 2:10–12
  D Paul's Concern for the Thessalonians, 2:13–3:13
    1 For their sufferings, 2:13–20
    2 For their testings (Timothy's visit), 3:1–8
    3 For their continued growth, 3:9–13
II Practical and Hortatory, 4:1–5:28
  A Teaching Concerning Development, 4:1–12
    1 In sexual relations, 4:1–8
    2 In brotherly love, 4:9–10
    3 In orderly living, 4:11–12
  B Teaching Concerning the Dead, 4:13–18
  C Teaching Concerning the Day of the Lord, 5:1–11
  D Teaching Concerning Various Duties, 5:12–28

THE FIRST LETTER OF
PAUL THE APOSTLE TO THE
Thessalonians

I PERSONAL AND HISTORICAL, 1:1–3:13

A Paul's Greeting, 1:1

1 Paul, and Silvā'nus, and Tīmoth'eus, unto the church of the Thessalonians *which is* in God the Father and *in* the Lord Jesus Christ: Grace *be* unto you, and peace, from God our Father, and the Lord Jesus Christ.

B Paul's Commendation of the Thessalonians, 1:2–10

2 We give thanks to God always for you all, making mention of you in our prayers;

1:1 *Silvanus*=Silas, who replaced Barnabas on the second missionary journey (Acts 15:22–18:5).

3 Remembering without ceasing your work of faith, and labour of love, and patience of hope in our Lord Jesus Christ, in the sight of God and our Father;

4 Knowing, brethren beloved, your election of God.

5 For our gospel came not unto you in word only, but also in power, and in the Holy Ghost, and in much assurance; as ye know what manner of men we were among you for your sake.

6 And ye became followers of us, and of the Lord, having received the word in much affliction, with joy of the Holy Ghost:

7 So that ye were ensamples to all that believe in Macedonia and Achaľa.

8 For from you sounded out the word of the Lord not only in Macedonia and Achaľa, but also in every place your faith to God-ward is spread abroad; so that we need not to speak any thing.

9 For they themselves shew of us what manner of entering in we had unto you, and how ye turned to God from idols to serve the living and true God;

10 And to wait for his Son from heaven, whom he raised from the dead, *even* Jesus, which delivered us from the wrath to come.

1:4 The order of the words should be: "Knowing, brethren beloved of God, your election." *election* is choosing. In relation to believers, God's choosing is sovereign (Rom. 9:11), it is pre-temporal (Eph. 1:4), it is unto salvation (2 Thess. 2:13), and it is proved by the fruits which accompany salvation (v. 5; Col. 3:12).

1:5 *what manner of men.* Paul elaborates on this in 2:3–12.

1:6 *followers.* Lit., imitators (see 1 Cor. 4:16; 11:1). They imitated the Lord and the apostles because they responded to the gospel in spite of affliction.

1:7 *ensamples*=pattern or model. *Macedonia* was the northern province of Greece, *Achaia* the southern.

1:9 *they themselves.* I.e., people everywhere gave testimony to the conversion of the Thessalonians. *turned to God from idols.* This informs us that this church was comprised largely of converts from pagan religions and not from Judaism (see also 2:14, 16). The last part of this verse and v. 10 summarize the message Paul, Silvanus, and Timothy preached. *to serve* as slaves. *the living* (in contrast to lifeless idols) *and true* (not false gods) *God.*

1:10 *to wait.* The Christian's hope of the return of Christ is rooted in the fact that He was *raised from the dead.* *which delivered*=the Deliverer. *the wrath to come*=the judgments to come (5:9; Rev. 6:16).

C Paul's Conduct among the Thessalonians, 2:1–12

1 *His uprightness*, 2:1–4

2 For yourselves, brethren, know our entrance in unto you, that it was not in vain:

2 But even after that we had suffered before, and were shamefully entreated, as ye know, at Phĭlip′pī, we were bold in our God to speak unto you the gospel of God with much contention.

3 For our exhortation *was* not of deceit, nor of uncleanness, nor in guile:

4 But as we were allowed of God to be put in trust with the gospel, even so we speak; not as pleasing men, but God, which trieth our hearts.

2 *His industry*, 2:5–9

5 For neither at any time used we flattering words, as ye know, nor a cloke of covetousness; God *is* witness:

6 Nor of men sought we glory, neither of you, nor *yet* of others, when we might have been burdensome, as the apostles of Christ.

7 But we were gentle among you, even as a nurse cherisheth her children:

8 So being affectionately desirous of you, we were willing to have imparted unto you, not the gospel of God only, but also our own souls, because ye were dear unto us.

9 For ye remember, brethren, our labour and travail: for labouring night and day, because we would not be chargeable unto any of you, we preached unto you the gospel of God.

2:1 This verse builds on 1:5: *not in vain*=not without results. He returns to this subject in v. 13, after reviewing his ministry in vv. 1–12.

2:2 *at Philippi*. The account is in Acts 16:12–40.

2:3 Here Paul attacks what must have been charges against him, of *deceit* (i.e., that the gospel was based on error), of *uncleanness* (that Christianity encouraged sexual immorality), and of *guile* (that his methods were underhanded).

2:4 *allowed*=approved.

2:5 *flattering words*=cajolery, i.e., an attempt to persuade by use of insincere speech. *covetousness*=greed.

2:6 *been burdensome*. Better, made demands (on you), i.e., for support. Paul makes clear his right as an apostle to financial support, but says he behaved as selflessly as a nurse.

2:8 *affectionately desirous*. An unusual word word indicating the yearning love of a mother for her children. Paul's pastoral heart is laid bare in these verses.

3 *His blameless behavior*, 2:10–12

10 Ye *are* witnesses, and God *also*, how holily and justly and unblameably we behaved ourselves among you that believe:

11 As ye know how we exhorted and comforted and charged every one of you, as a father *doth* his children,

12 That ye would walk worthy of God, who hath called you unto his kingdom and glory.

D Paul's Concern for the Thessalonians, 2:13–3:13

1 *For their sufferings*, 2:13–20

13 For this cause also thank we God without ceasing, because, when ye received the word of God which ye heard of us, ye received *it* not *as* the word of men, but as it is in truth, the word of God, which effectually worketh also in you that believe.

14 For ye, brethren, became followers of the churches of God which in Judæa are in Christ Jesus: for ye also have suffered like things of your own countrymen, even as they *have* of the Jews:

15 Who both killed the Lord Jesus, and their own prophets, and have persecuted us; and they please not God, and are contrary to all men:

16 Forbidding us to speak to the Gentiles that they might be saved, to fill up their sins alway: for the wrath is come upon them to the uttermost.

17 But we, brethren, being taken from you for a short time in presence, not in heart, endeavoured the more abundantly to see your face with great desire.

18 Wherefore we would have come unto you, even I Paul, once and again; but Satan hindered us.

19 For what *is* our hope, or joy, or crown of rejoicing?

2:12 *walk*=live.

2:14 *followers*. Better, imitators. Paul compares the problems of the Christians at Thessalonica among their fellow-Greeks with those of the Christians in Judea, persecuted by Jews.

2:16 *to fill up their sins alway*. I.e., God allows His people to be persecuted in order to show the evil nature of men and the rightness of His judgment when it falls (Gen. 15:16). These persecutors were heaping sin upon sin.

2:17–18 Paul now expresses his desire to return to Thessalonica. *Satan hindered us* likely refers to the security taken of Jason (Acts 17:9) which probably included a guarantee that Paul would not return to the city.

2:19 may be paraphrased like this: "What is our hope, or joy, or

Are not even ye in the presence of our Lord Jesus Christ
at his coming?

20 For ye are our glory and joy.

2 For their testings (Timothy's visit), 3:1-8

3 Wherefore when we could no longer forbear, we
thought it good to be left at Athens alone:

2 And sent Timoth'eus, our brother, and minister of
God, and our fellowlabourer in the gospel of Christ, to
establish you, and to comfort you concerning your faith:

3 That no man should be moved my these afflictions: for
yourselves know that we are appointed thereunto.

4 For verily, when we were with you, we told you before
that we should suffer tribulation; even as it came to pass,
and ye know.

5 For this cause, when I could no longer forbear, I sent
to know your faith, lest by some means the tempter have
tempted you, and our labour be in vain.

6 But now when Timoth'eus came from you unto us,
and brought us good tidings of your faith and charity, and
that ye have good remembrance of us always, desiring
greatly to see us, as we also to see you:

7 Therefore, brethren, we were comforted over you in
all our affliction and distress by your faith:

8 For now we live, if ye stand fast in the Lord.

3 For their continued growth, 3:9-13

9 For what thanks can we render to God again for you,
for all the joy wherewith we joy for your sakes before our
God;

10 Night and day praying exceedingly that we might

crown of rejoicing? Nothing, if you are not such in the presence of our Lord Jesus Christ at His coming."

3:3 *moved*=beguiled, i.e., that they be not seduced away from
the faith by the heathen who were urging them to reject their
faith.

3:4 *suffer tribulation* means to endure the normal afflictions that
come to a believer in this life. Paul had told them these would
come (v. 3).

3:5 *to know*=to find out about. *the tempter.* Again (as in 2:18)
Paul traces events to Satan's working.

3:7 *over you*=about you.

3:8 The good news of their spiritual well-being was a breath of
life to Paul.

3:10 *perfect*=to make complete as one might repair fishing nets
(Matt. 4:21) or restore saints (Gal. 6:1; Eph. 4:12).

see your face, and might perfect that which is lacking in your faith?

11 Now God himself and our Father, and our Lord Jesus Christ, direct our way unto you.

12 And the Lord make you to increase and abound in love one toward another, and toward all *men*, even as we *do* toward you:

13 To the end he may stablish your hearts unblameable in holiness before God, even our Father, at the coming of our Lord Jesus Christ with all his saints.

II PRACTICAL AND HORTATORY, 4:1–5:28

A Teaching Concerning Development, 4:1–12

1 *In sexual relations*, 4:1–8

4 Furthermore then we beseech you, brethren, and exhort *you* by the Lord Jesus, that as ye have received of us how ye ought to walk and to please God, so ye would abound more and more.

2 For ye know what commandments we gave you by the Lord Jesus.

3 For this is the will of God, *even* your sanctification, that ye should abstain from fornication:

4 That every one of you should know how to possess his vessel in sanctification and honour;

5 Not in the lust of concupiscence, even as the Gentiles which know not God:

3:12 *the Lord.* Here=Christ.
3:13 *saints.* Lit., holy ones, probably referring here to angels who will accompany the return of Christ (Mark 8:38), or possibly also "holy men" (4:14). Here ends the "thanksgiving" portion of the letter, in a three-verse prayer.
4:3 *will of God.* I.e., His desire or purpose. *sanctification* (holiness) is viewed in three aspects in the N.T.: (1) There is a position of being set apart to God which every believer has at the moment of his salvation (1 Cor. 6:13). (2) There is a progressive holiness of life that ought to be true of every believer (4:3). (3) Finally, in heaven we shall be "unblameable in holiness" (3:13). *fornication.* The Greek word is more general, meaning all kinds of illicit or unnatural sexual indulgence. Greek cities like Thessalonica were wide open to all kinds of sexual looseness, even in religious rites.
4:4 *possess his vessel.* This means either mastery over one's body, keeping it pure (1 Cor. 9:24–27), or it refers to an honorable marriage (*vessel*=wife as 1 Pet. 3:7).
4:5 *lust of concupiscence*=passion of lust.

6 That no *man* go beyond and defraud his brother in *any* matter: because that the Lord *is* the avenger of all such, as we also have forewarned you and testified.

7 For God hath not called us unto uncleanness, but unto holiness.

8 He therefore that despiseth, despiseth not man, but God, who hath also given unto us his holy Spirit.

2 *In brotherly love,* 4:9–10

9 But as touching brotherly love ye need not that I write unto you: for ye yourselves are taught of God to love one another.

10 And indeed ye do it toward all the brethren which are in all Macedonia: but we beseech you, brethren, that ye increase more and more;

3 *In orderly living,* 4:11–12

11 And that ye study to be quiet, and to do your own business, and to work with your own hands, as we commanded you;

12 That ye may walk honestly toward them that are without, and *that* ye may have lack of nothing.

B Teaching Concerning the Dead, 4:13–18

13 But I would not have you to be ignorant, brethren, concerning them which are asleep, that ye sorrow not, even as others which have no hope.

4:6 *go beyond*=transgress. Sexual conduct is the subject of 4:3–8.

4:7 *holiness*. This same word is translated "sanctification" in v. 3.

4:8 *despiseth*. I. e., rejects or treats lightly these commands to sexual purity.

4:10 *increase more and more*. Better, do it (i.e., practice brotherly love with your fellow Macedonian Christians) more and more.

4:11 *study*. I.e., be ambitious, aspire. It is used only here, Rom. 15:20, and 2 Cor. 5:9. The problems mentioned in 2 Thess. 3:11–12 are the reason for these exhortations.

4:12 *honestly*=becomingly, fittingly. *them that are without.* I.e., non-Christians.

4:13–18 The question behind this paragraph is this: Does the death of a believer before the Lord comes cause him to lose all hope of sharing in the glorious reign of Christ? Paul's answer is the reassuring affirmation that the dead will be raised and will share in the kingdom.

4:13 *are asleep*. The body of the believer who dies is said to sleep during the time between death and resurrection.

14 For if we believe that Jesus died and rose again, even so them also which sleep in Jesus will God bring with him.

15 For this we say unto you by the word of the Lord, that we which are alive *and* remain unto the coming of the Lord shall not prevent them which are asleep.

16 For the Lord himself shall descend from heaven with a shout, with the voice of the archangel, and with the trump of God: and the dead in Christ shall rise first:

17 Then we which are alive *and* remain shall be caught up together with them in the clouds, to meet the Lord in the air: and so shall we ever be with the Lord.

18 Wherefore comfort one another with these words.

C Teaching Concerning the Day of the Lord, 5:1-11

5 But of the times and the seasons, brethren, ye have no need that I write unto you.

2 For yourselves know perfectly that the day of the Lord so cometh as a thief in the night.

3 For when they shall say, Peace and safety; then sudden destruction cometh upon them, as travail upon a woman with child; and they shall not escape.

4 But ye, brethren, are not in darkness, that that day should overtake you as a thief.

4:14 *if we believe.* Better, since we do believe. The certainty of the Christian's resurrection is based on the fact of Christ's resurrection.

4:15 *prevent*=precede.

4:16 *the trump* of God. See 1 Cor. 15:52.

4:17 When the Lord comes for His people *the dead in Christ shall rise first* (v. 16). Then living believers will be *caught up*. From the Latin for "caught up" comes the term "rapture." The rapture or catching up of believers described here involves both those who have died and those who are living when the Lord comes. His coming here is in the air, not to the earth, just prior to the beginning of the tribulation period (see Rev. 3:10). That period will end with His coming to the earth (Matt. 24:29-30; Rev. 19:11-16).

4:18 The *comfort* of the Christian's hope in resurrection is in sharp contrast to the hopelessness of the heathen in the face of death.

5:2 *the day of the Lord.* The phrase means an extended period of time, beginning with the tribulation period and including the events of the second coming of Christ and the millennial kingdom on earth. It will begin (*cometh*) unexpectedly (*as a thief in the night*).

5:3 *travail*=birth-pang.

5:4 *darkness.* A figure of the unbeliever's moral state and separation from God.

5 Ye are all the children of light, and the children of the day: we are not of the night, nor of darkness.

6 Therefore let us not sleep, as *do* others; but let us watch and be sober.

7 For they that sleep sleep in the night; and they that be drunken are drunken in the night.

8 But let us, who are of the day, be sober, putting on the breastplate of faith and love; and for an helmet, the hope of salvation.

9 For God hath not appointed us to wrath, but to obtain salvation by our Lord Jesus Christ,

10 Who died for us, that, whether we wake or sleep, we should live together with him.

11 Wherefore comfort yourselves together, and edify one another, even as also ye do.

D Teaching Concerning Various Duties, 5:12-28

12 And we beseech you, brethren, to know them which labour among you, and are over you in the Lord, and admonish you;

13 And to esteem them very highly in love for their work's sake. *And* be at peace among yourselves.

14 Now we exhort you, brethren, warn them that are unruly, comfort the feebleminded, support the weak, be patient toward all *men*.

15 See that none render evil for evil unto any *man*; but ever follow that which is good, both among yourselves, and to all *men*.

16 Rejoice evermore.

17 Pray without ceasing.

18 In every thing give thanks: for this is the will of God in Christ Jesus concerning you.

19 Quench not the Spirit.

5:6 *sleep,* not physically but morally (as in Mark 13:36; Eph. 5:14).

5:9 *wrath.* I.e., the anguish and tribulation associated with the beginning of the day of the Lord (v. 3). The believer is to be delivered from this (1:10).

5:12 *to know.* I.e., to know the value of, to appreciate.

5:14 *warn them that are unruly.* Better, admonish the idle. *feebleminded*=faint-hearted.

5:16 Compare Phil. 4:4. Vv. 16–18 are closely related; vv. 19–22 form another paragraph.

5:17 *without ceasing.* Paul prayed thus for the Thessalonians (1:3; 2:13).

5:19 *Quench. the Spirit* is often likened to fire (Matt. 3:11;

20 Despise not prophesyings.

21 Prove all things; hold fast that which is good.

22 Abstain from all appearance of evil.

23 And the very God of peace sanctify you wholly; and *I pray God* your whole spirit and soul and body be preserved blameless unto the coming of our Lord Jesus Christ.

24 Faithful *is* he that calleth you, who also will do *it*.

25 Brethren, pray for us.

26 Greet all the brethren with an holy kiss.

27 I charge you by the Lord that this epistle be read unto all the holy brethren.

28 The grace of our Lord Jesus Christ *be* with you. Amen.

Luke 3:16; Acts 2:3). The Spirit is quenched whenever his ministry is stifled in an individual or in the church.

5:21 *Prove*=test.

5:23 Here begins a two-verse prayer that closes the section of instruction and exhortation begun at 4:1. *spirit and soul and body* should not be understood as defining the parts of man, but the whole of man.

5:26 *an holy kiss*. For the kiss as a symbol of welcome in Jewish life see Luke 7:45; 22:48. As a symbol of Christian fellowship see note at 1 Pet. 5:14. Paul uses the phrase in Rom. 16:16; 1 Cor. 16:20; 2 Cor. 13:12.

INTRODUCTION TO
THE SECOND LETTER OF PAUL TO THE
Thessalonians

AUTHOR: Paul   DATE: 51

The Purpose   This is a letter of correction of doctrine and practice sent by Paul to the church at Thessalonica, not long after I Thessalonians, to meet a new situation. Word had reached Paul somehow that there had been misunderstanding, if not misrepresentation (2:2), of his teaching concerning the coming of the day of the Lord (I Thess. 5:1–11). Some thought that its judgments had already begun; yet they understood Paul to have taught that they would be exempt from those judgments. The practical ramification of this doctrinal confusion was that some, thinking the end of the world was at hand, had stopped working and were creating an embarrassing situation (3:6, 11). Paul corrects the teaching and reprimands the idlers.

The Contents   The major section in 2:1–12 on the man of sin should be compared with other passages which tell of this Antichrist (Dan. 9:27; Matt. 24:15, Rev. 11:7; 13:1–10).

OUTLINE OF 2 THESSALONIANS

I Salutation, 1:1–2
II Thanksgiving and Encouragement in Persecution, 1:3–12
III Correction concerning the Day of the Lord, 2:1–17
    A Its Relation to the Present, 2:1–2
    B Its Relation to the Apostasy, 2:3a
    C Its Relation to the Man of Sin, 2:3b–5
    D Its Relation to the Restrainer, 2:6–9
    E Its Relation to Unbelievers, 2:10–12
    F Its Relation to Believers, 2:13–17
IV Exhortations to Prayer and Discipline, 3:1–15
    A Paul's Confidence, 3:1–5
    B Paul's Commands, 3:6–15
V Concluding Benediction and Autograph Greeting, 3:16–18

THE SECOND LETTER OF
PAUL THE APOSTLE TO THE
Thessalonians

I SALUTATION, 1:1–2

1 Paul, and Silvā'nus, and Tīmoth'eus, unto the church
of the Thessalonians in God our Father and the Lord
Jesus Christ:

2 Grace unto you, and peace, from God our Father and
the Lord Jesus Christ.

II THANKSGIVING AND
ENCOURAGEMENT IN PERSECUTION, 1:3–12

3 We are bound to thank God always for you, brethren,
as it is meet, because that your faith groweth exceedingly,
and the charity of every one of you all toward each other
aboundeth;

4 So that we ourselves glory in you in the churches of
God for your patience and faith in all your persecutions
and tribulations that ye endure:

5 *Which is* a manifest token of the righteous judgment
of God, that ye may be counted worthy of the kingdom of
God, for which ye also suffer:

6 Seeing *it is* a righteous thing with God to recompense
tribulation to them that trouble you;

7 And to you who are troubled rest with us, when the
Lord Jesus shall be revealed from heaven with his mighty
angels,

8 In flaming fire taking vengeance on them that know

1:3–4 *your faith groweth exceedingly*. Paul's earlier fears about
their faith (1 Thess. 3:5, 10) have disappeared in the light
of their exceptional growth. *charity*=love (see 1 Thess. 3:12).

1:7 *rest with us*. I.e., with Paul, Silvanus, and Timothy who
knew what it was to be under persecution and pressure for
their faith (1 Thess. 1:6; 2:14–18). Rest is promised at the
return of Christ, who will then judge those who afflicted them
(v. 6).

not God, and that obey not the gospel of our Lord Jesus Christ:

9 Who shall be punished with everlasting destruction from the presence of the Lord, and from the glory of his power;

10 When he shall come to be glorified in his saints, and to be admired in all them that believe (because our testimony among you was believed) in that day.

11 Wherefore also we pray always for you, that our God would count you worthy of *this* calling, and fulfil all the good pleasure of *his* goodness, and the work of faith with power:

12 That the name of our Lord Jesus Christ may be glorified in you, and ye in him, according to the grace of our God and the Lord Jesus Christ.

III CORRECTION
CONCERNING THE DAY OF THE LORD, 2:1–17

A Its Relation to the Present, 2:1–2

2 Now we beseech you, brethren, by the coming of our Lord Jesus Christ, and *by* our gathering together unto him,

2 That ye be not soon shaken in mind, or be troubled, neither by spirit, nor by word, nor by letter as from us, as that the day of Christ is at hand.

1:9 *everlasting destruction*. Not annihilation, but ruin by reason of separation from the presence of the Lord. In 1 Thess. 5:3 the destruction is said to be sudden; here, eternal.

1:10 *in that day*. I.e., the day when the Lord Jesus shall be revealed (v. 7) on His return.

2:1 *by the coming of our Lord Jesus*. Better, concerning, or in the interest of the truth concerning, the Lord's coming. Paul denies the teaching, ascribed to him, that the day of the Lord had already begun. *our gathering together* is a reference to the rapture of the church referred to in 1 Thess. 4:13–18.

2:2 *shaken in mind*=excited, violently disturbed. The Thessalonians were being greatly disturbed by false teaching concerning future events, and Paul seeks to bring them back to true doctrine (2:1–12) and proper living (3:6–16). The sources of the false teaching were *by spirit* (some prophetic utterance), *by word* (some spoken teaching) and *by letter as from us* (some written communication purporting to be from Paul). The source of these is not given. *day of Christ*. Better manuscripts read "day of the Lord" (see note at 1 Thess. 5:2). *is at hand*=is already present.

B Its Relation to the Apostasy, 2:3a

3 Let no man deceive you by any means: for *that day shall not come*, except there come a falling away first, and that man of sin be revealed, the son of perdition;

C Its Relation to the Man of Sin, 2:3b–5

4 Who opposeth and exalteth himself above all that is called God, or that is worshipped; so that he as God sitteth in the temple of God, shewing himself that he is God.

5 Remember ye not, that, when I was yet with you, I told you these things?

D Its Relation to the Restrainer, 2:6–9

6 And now ye know what withholdeth that he might be revealed in his time.

7 For the mystery of iniquity doth already work: only he who now letteth *will let*, until he be taken out of the way.

8 And then shall that Wicked be revealed, whom the Lord shall consume with the spirit of his mouth, and shall destroy with the brightness of his coming:

2:3 *falling away*. Lit., the apostasy—an aggressive and climactic revolt against God which will prepare the way for the appearance of the man of sin (see 1 Tim. 4:1–5; 2 Tim. 3:1–5). *man of sin*. Lit., man of lawlessness. While it is true that the forces of lawlessness were at work in Paul's time (as well as today) (note v. 7, *the mystery of iniquity doth already work*), the man of lawlessness (also called *that Wicked*, v. 8; lit., the lawless one) is an individual of the future who will come to power during the tribulation days. John also recognized the presence of many antichrists in his time (1 John 2:18) as well as the coming of one great Antichrist in the future (Rev. 11:7; 13:1–10).

2:4 *sitteth in the temple of God*. At the mid-point of the tribulation period the Antichrist will desecrate the Jewish temple in Jerusalem by placing himself there to be worshipped (see note at Matt. 24:15). This will be the climax of the sin of self-deification of man in open defiance of God.

2:7 *he who now letteth will let*=he who now restrains will restrain. Antichrist is now being held back by a restrainer. Some understand this to be God indwelling His church by the Holy Spirit, while others see government as the restraint. In the former view the removal would be in the rapture of the church (1 Thess. 4:13–18); in the latter, the overthrow of government by Antichrist.

2:8 *then shall that Wicked be revealed*. Paul's argument is this: The day of the Lord will not begin until the Antichrist is revealed (v. 3); the Antichrist cannot begin to act until the

9 *Even him*, whose coming is after the working of Satan with all power and signs and lying wonders,

E Its Relation to Unbelievers, 2:10–12

10 And with all deceivableness of unrighteousness in them that perish; because they received not the love of the truth, that they might be saved.

11 And for this cause God shall send them strong delusion, that they should believe a lie:

12 That they all might be damned who believed not the truth, but had pleasure in unrighteousness.

F Its Relation to Believers, 2:13–17

13 But we are bound to give thanks alway to God for you, brethren beloved of the Lord, because God hath from the beginning chosen you to salvation through sanctification of the Spirit and belief of the truth:

14 Whereunto he called you by our gospel, to the obtaining of the glory of our Lord Jesus Christ.

15 Therefore, brethren, stand fast, and hold the traditions which ye have been taught, whether by word, or our epistle.

16 Now our Lord Jesus Christ himself, and God, even our Father, which hath loved us, and hath given *us* everlasting consolation and good hope through grace,

restrainer is removed (v. 7); since the restrainer has not yet been removed, the Thessalonians could be certain that the day of the Lord had not yet begun, regardless of what the false teachers were saying.

2:11–12 The *strong delusion* comes from God; it is both a punishment and a moral result of their rejection of the truth (vv. 10, 12). These verses reflect the O.T. concept that God is sovereign even in the activities of the powers of evil (Ex. 4:21; Josh. 11:20; 1 Kings 22:19–23; 1 Chron. 21:1; cf. 2 Sam. 24:1). The result will be that men will believe *a lie* (lit., the lie) of Satan working through Antichrist.

2:13 *through sanctification of the Spirit and belief of the truth*. God's activity (the Holy Spirit's work of regeneration) and man's responsibility (faith) are equally necessary in salvation.

2:15 *the traditions*. I.e., the whole corpus of the teachings Paul had shared with the Thessalonians.

2:16–17 Paul's prayer for steadfastness on the part of the Thessalonians closes this crucial section. Notice the other prayers in this letter: 1:11–12—that their lives may be such as can be commended by the Lord; 3:5—for love and patience; 3:16—for peace.

17 Comfort your hearts, and stablish you in every good word and work.

IV EXHORTATIONS TO PRAYER AND DISCIPLINE, 3:1-15

A Paul's Confidence, 3:1-5

3 Finally, brethren, pray for us, that the word of the Lord may have *free* course, and be glorified, even as *it is* with you:

2 And that we may be delivered from unreasonable and wicked men: for all *men* have not faith.

3 But the Lord is faithful, who shall stablish you, and keep *you* from evil.

4 And we have confidence in the Lord touching you, that ye both do and will do the things which we command you.

5 And the Lord direct your hearts into the love of God, and into the patient waiting for Christ.

B Paul's Commands, 3:6-15

6 Now we command you, brethren, in the name of our Lord Jesus Christ, that ye withdraw yourselves from every brother that walketh disorderly, and not after the tradition which he received of us.

7 For yourselves know how ye ought to follow us: for we behaved not ourselves disorderly among you;

8 Neither did we eat any man's bread for nought; but wrought with labour and travail night and day, that we might not be chargeable to any of you:

9 Not because we have not power, but to make ourselves an ensample unto you to follow us.

10 For even when we were with you, this we com-

3:2 *unreasonable and wicked men*. Lit., perverse and evil men: those "who disbelieve the truth" (2:10–12), Jews and Gentiles, whom Paul encountered in virtually every city he visited. His experiences at Thessalonica are recorded in Acts 17:5–10 and at Corinth (where he wrote this letter) in Acts 18:6–17.

3:3 *But*. I.e., in contrast to this wickedness of men.

3:5 *patient waiting for Christ*. This may refer to our expectation of Christ's coming or it may mean that the endurance or steadfastness of Christ during His life on earth should be our example.

3:6 *that walketh disorderly*. I.e., who is an idler. Paul had instructed them on this point earlier (1 Thess. 4:1; 5:14).

manded you, that if any would not work, neither should he eat.

11 For we hear that there are some which walk among you disorderly, working not at all, but are busybodies.

12 Now them that are such we command and exhort by our Lord Jesus Christ, that with quietness they work, and eat their own bread.

13 But ye, brethren, be not weary in well doing.

14 And if any man obey not our word by this epistle, note that man, and have no company with him, that he may be ashamed.

15 Yet count *him* not as an enemy, but admonish *him* as a brother.

V CONCLUDING BENEDICTION AND AUTOGRAPH GREETING, 3:16–18

16 Now the Lord of peace himself give you peace always by all means. The Lord *be* with you all.

17 The salutation of Paul with mine own hand, which is the token in every epistle: so I write.

18 The grace of our Lord Jesus Christ *be* with you all. Amen.

3:14 *have no company with him*. Idlers were to be ostracized from the company of believers in order to shame them into changing their ways. This is not formal excommunication but group disapproval and social ostracism, a serious thing for a believer in a heathen society.

3:15 *admonish him*. The aim of the discipline is reformation and restoration of the offender.

INTRODUCTION TO
THE FIRST LETTER OF PAUL TO
Timothy

AUTHOR: Paul   DATE: 63

The Pastorals The two letters to Timothy and the one to Titus are called the "Pastoral Epistles" because they contain principles for the pastoral care of churches and qualifications for ministers.

The Author Some have questioned whether Paul himself wrote these letters on the grounds that: (1) Paul's travels described in the Pastorals do not fit anywhere into the historical account of the book of Acts; (2) the church organization described is that of the second century; (3) the vocabulary and style of the Pastorals are significantly different from that of the other Pauline letters. Those who hold to the Pauline authorship reply that: (1) it is an assumption that Acts contains the complete history of the life of Paul. Since his death is not recorded in Acts, he was apparently released from house arrest in Rome, traveled over the empire for several years (perhaps even as far as Spain), was rearrested, imprisoned a second time in Rome, and martyred under Nero. (2) Nothing in the church organization of the Pastorals requires a later date (see Acts 14:23; Phil. 1:1). (3) The question of authorship cannot be decided solely on the basis of the numerical data involved in the vocabulary used without considering the considerable effect on such data of the different subject matter. Vocabulary used to describe church organization would be expected to be different from that used to teach the doctrine of the Holy Spirit, for instance. Actually there is no argument against the Pauline authorship that does not have a reasonable answer, and, of course, the letters themselves claim to have been written by Paul.

The Background of 1 Timothy Timothy, the son of a Greek Gentile father and a devout Jewish mother named

Eunice, was intimately associated with Paul from the
second missionary journey on (2 Tim. 1:5; Acts 16:1–3).
When Paul wrote 1 Timothy, probably from Macedonia
(1:3), he was on his way to Nicopolis (Tit. 3:12), but
Timothy had been left in charge of the work in Ephesus
and Asia Minor. Though Paul expressed his desire to visit
Timothy (3:14; 4:13), this letter, in the meantime, would
guide Timothy in the conduct of his pastoral responsibilities.

The Contents In relation to Timothy personally the
theme is "Warring a Good Warfare" (1:18). In relation to
the church corporately the theme is "Behaving in the
House of God" (3:15). Important subjects discussed in the
epistle include the law (1:7–11), prayer (2:1–8), appearance
and activity of women (2:9–15) qualifications for bishops
or elders and for deacons (3:1–13), the last days (4:1–3),
care of widows (5:3–16), and use of money (6:6–19).

OUTLINE OF 1 TIMOTHY

THE FIRST LETTER OF
PAUL THE APOSTLE TO
Timothy

I OPENING GREETINGS, 1:1–2

1 Paul, an apostle of Jesus Christ by the commandment of God our Saviour, and Lord Jesus Christ, *which is* our hope;

2 Unto Timothy, *my* own son in the faith: Grace, mercy, *and* peace, from God our Father and Jesus Christ our Lord.

II INSTRUCTION CONCERNING DOCTRINE, 1:3–20

A Paul's Warning against False Doctrines, 1:3–11

3 As I besought thee to abide still at Ephesus, when I went into Macedonia, that thou mightest charge some that they teach no other doctrine,

4 Neither give heed to fables and endless genealogies, which minister questions, rather than godly edifying which is in faith: *so do.*

5 Now the end of the commandment is charity out of a pure heart, and *of* a good conscience, and *of* faith unfeigned:

1:1 *apostle.* This is Paul's title of authority; it indicates his status, above elders and deacons. An apostle has the right to expect obedience from the churches. *God our Saviour.* 1 Timothy (here; 2:3; 4:10) and Titus (1:3; 2:10; 3:4) especially among N.T. books continue the O.T. title "Savior" applied to God, so frequent in the Psalms (106:21) and in Isaiah (45:21). The epithet also came to be ascribed to Christ (Phil. 3:20; Tit. 1:4).

1:3 *I went into Macedonia.* This journey evidently occurred after the close of Acts (see the Introduction to Titus). *no other doctrine.* I.e., any doctrine different from what Paul taught.

1:4 *fables and endless genealogies.* These were mythical legends added to O.T. history which may have led to Gnostic teachings concerning emanations extending from God to the creation (see discussion of Gnosticism in the Introduction to 1 John).

6 From which some having swerved have turned aside unto vain jangling;

7 Desiring to be teachers of the law; understanding neither what they say, nor whereof they affirm.

8 But we know that the law *is* good, if a man use it lawfully;

9 Knowing this, that the law is not made for a righteous man, but for the lawless and disobedient, for the ungodly and for sinners, for unholy and profane, for murderers of fathers and murderers of mothers, for manslayers,

10 For whoremongers, for them that defile themselves with mankind, for menstealers, for liars, for perjured persons, and if there be any other thing that is contrary to sound doctrine;

11 According to the glorious gospel of the blessed God, which was committed to my trust.

B Paul's Testimony concerning the Grace of God, 1:12–17

12 And I thank Christ Jesus our Lord, who hath enabled me, for that he counted me faithful, putting me into the ministry;

13 Who was before a blasphemer, and a persecutor, and injurious: but I obtained mercy, because I did *it* ignorantly in unbelief.

14 And the grace of our Lord was exceeding abundant with faith and love which is in Christ Jesus.

15 This *is* a faithful saying, and worthy of all acceptation, that Christ Jesus came into the world to save sinners; of whom I am chief.

16 Howbeit for this cause I obtained mercy, that in me first Jesus Christ might shew forth all longsuffering, for a pattern to them which should hereafter believe on him to life everlasting.

17 Now unto the King eternal, immortal, invisible, the only wise God, *be* honour and glory for ever and ever. Amen.

1:8 *the law is good*, if used lawfully, because it restrains evil people.

1:10 *sound doctrine*. Lit., healthy or wholesome in contrast to false doctrine, which is diseased. The words are used also in 6:3; 2 Tim. 1:13; 4:3; Tit. 1:9, 13; 2:1, 2.

1:13 *injurious*=insolent, violent.

1:15 *This is a faithful saying*. This formula, which introduces an axiomatic truth, appears only in the Pastorals (here; 3:1; 4:9; 2 Tim. 2:11; Tit. 3:8). *I am chief*. Paul considered himself the foremost of sinners even at the end of his illustrious life because of his previous opposition to Christ and His church.

C Paul's Charge to Timothy, 1:18–20

18 This charge I commit unto thee, son Timothy, according to the prophecies which went before on thee, that thou by them mightest war a good warfare;

19 Holding faith, and a good conscience; which some having put away concerning faith have made shipwreck:

20 Of whom is Hȳmenæ'us and Alexander; whom I have delivered unto Satan, that they may learn not to blaspheme.

III INSTRUCTION CONCERNING WORSHIP, 2:1–15

A Prayer in the Church, 2:1–8

2 I exhort therefore, that, first of all, supplications, prayers, intercessions, *and* giving of thanks, be made for all men;

2 For kings, and *for* all that are in authority; that we may lead a quiet and peaceable life in all godliness and honesty.

3 For this *is* good and acceptable in the sight of God our Saviour;

4 Who will have all men to be saved, and to come unto the knowledge of the truth.

5 For *there is* one God, and one mediator between God and men, the man Christ Jesus;

6 Who gave himself a ransom for all, to be testified in due time.

7 Whereunto I am ordained a preacher, and an apostle, (I speak the truth in Christ, *and* lie not;) a teacher of the Gentiles in faith and verity.

8 I will therefore that men pray every where, lifting up holy hands, without wrath and doubting.

1:20 *Hymenaeus and Alexander.* How they made shipwreck of their faith (v. 19) is not stated, though the false teaching of Hymenaeus is described in 2 Tim. 2:17–18. *I have delivered unto Satan.* As in 1 Cor. 5:5, this is remedial discipline by excluding such persons from the help and fellowship of the church, a kind of last-resort punishment.

2:2 *honesty*=seriousness, gravity, dignity.

2:4 *Who will have.* Better, who wishes. This is an expression of God's desire, not His decree.

2:5 *one mediator.* This statement rules out all other mediators in bringing God and man together; Jesus does this through His death on the cross (Heb. 9:15; 12:24).

2:8 *men*=males who are to lead in public prayer. *lifting up*

B Women in the Church, 2:9–15

9 In like manner also, that women adorn themselves in modest apparel, with shamefacedness and sobriety; not with broided hair, or gold, or pearls, or costly array;

10 But (which becometh women professing godliness) with good works.

11 Let the woman learn in silence with all subjection.

12 But I suffer not a woman to teach, nor to usurp authority over the man, but to be in silence.

13 For Adam was first formed, then Eve.

14 And Adam was not deceived, but the woman being deceived was in the transgression.

15 Notwithstanding she shall be saved in childbearing, if they continue in faith and charity and holiness with sobriety.

IV INSTRUCTION CONCERNING LEADERS, 3:1–16

A The Bishop, 3:1–7

3 This *is* a true saying, If a man desire the office of a bishop, he desireth a good work.

holy hands. A common posture for prayer and representative of the purity of life which is necessary for proper fellowship in prayer. *without wrath and doubting.* When these are present, prayer is impossible.

2:9 *modest apparel.* Respectable and honorable apparel reflects the godly woman's inner life. Elaborate interweaving of the hair with gold and pearls is discouraged, and orderliness, not ostentation, is the standard (*shamefacedness*=modesty). *good works* (v. 10) will be their ornament.

2:12 *I suffer not a woman to teach.* Women are not to assume the office of teacher in the church (see 1 Cor. 14:34). Women may teach as long as they do not usurp the place of leadership and authority of men in the church. The injunction is based on the relationship of man and woman in the original creation (Gen. 2:18; 3:6).

2:15 *saved in childbearing.* This may mean: (1) brought safely through childbirth; (2) saved through the birth of a Child, Jesus the Savior; or (3) that a woman's greatest achievement is found in her devotion to her divinely ordained role: to help her husband, to bear children, and to follow a faithful, chaste way of life.

3:1 *bishop.* Lit., overseer. The same person is also referred to as an elder in the N.T. (see Tit. 1:5, 7 where the terms are used interchangeably). The elder, the principal official in a local church, was called by the Holy Spirit (Acts 20:28), recog-

2 A bishop then must be blameless, the husband of one wife, vigilant, sober, of good behaviour, given to hospitality, apt to teach;

3 Not given to wine, no striker, not greedy of filthy lucre; but patient, not a brawler, not covetous;

4 One that ruleth well his own house, having his children in subjection with all gravity;

5 (For if a man know not how to rule his own house, how shall he take care of the church of God?)

6 Not a novice, lest being lifted up with pride he fall into the condemnation of the devil.

7 Moreover he must have a good report of them which are without; lest he fall into reproach and the snare of the devil.

B The Deacons, 3:8–16

8 Likewise *must* the deacons *be* grave, not double-tongued, not given to much wine, not greedy of filthy lucre;

9 Holding the mystery of the faith in a pure conscience.

10 And let these also first be proved; then let them use the office of a deacon, being *found* blameless.

---

nized by other elders (1 Tim. 4:14), and qualified according to the standards listed in this passage. His duties included ruling (5:17), pastoring or shepherding the flock (Acts 20:28; 1 Pet. 5:2), guarding the truth (Tit. 1:9), and general oversight of the work, including its finances (Acts 11:30).

3:2 *blameless*=without reproach. *the husband of one wife*= married only once (see note on Tit. 1:6). *vigilant*=temperate.

3:3 *no striker*=not pugnacious or a bully. *filthy lucre*=money. *not a brawler*=not contentious.

3:4–5 The elder's home provides him with a training-ground for the exercise of his leadership duties in the church. *gravity* =dignity, seriousness, i.e., disciplining or controlling them.

3:6 *Not a novice*=not a new convert, lest his rapid advancement into a place of leadership cause him to become proud.

3:8 *deacons*. The word means "minister" or "servant," and deacons were originally the helpers of the elders. Thus their qualifications were practically the same as those for the elders. The office had its beginnings in Acts 6:1–6. However, the word deacon is used in an unofficial sense throughout the N.T. of anyone who serves (Eph. 6:21), as well as in an official sense designating those who occupy the office of deacon (Phil. 1:1).

3:9 *the mystery of the faith*=the body of revealed doctrine. Truth must be united to a life lived with *a pure conscience*.

11 Even so *must their* wives *be* grave, not slanderers, sober, faithful in all things.

12 Let the deacons be the husbands of one wife, ruling their children and their own houses well.

13 For they that have used the office of a deacon well purchase to themselves a good degree, and great boldness in the faith which is in Christ Jesus.

14 These things write I unto thee, hoping to come unto thee shortly:

15 But if I tarry long, that thou mayest know how thou oughtest to behave thyself in the house of God, which is the church of the living God, the pillar and ground of the truth.

16 And without controversy great is the mystery of godliness: God was manifest in the flesh, justified in the Spirit, seen of angels, preached unto the Gentiles, believed on in the world, received up into glory.

V INSTRUCTION CONCERNING DANGERS, 4:1–16

A Description of the Dangers, 4:1–5

4 Now the Spirit speaketh expressly, that in the latter times some shall depart from the faith, giving heed to seducing spirits, and doctrines of devils;

2 Speaking lies in hypocrisy; having their conscience seared with a hot iron;

3:11 *their wives.* This most likely refers to the wives of the deacons rather than to a separate office of deaconesses, since the qualifications for deacons are continued in v. 12. If a new group was intended, it would seem more natural for Paul to finish the qualifications for deacons before introducing the office of deaconess.

3:13 *purchase to themselves a good degree*=acquire a good standing for themselves.

3:15 *the truth*=the Christian faith.

3:16 This seems to be a summary of the truth contained in what was likely a part of an early Christian hymn. *God was manifest in the flesh* refers to the incarnation of Christ (2 Tim. 1:10; Tit. 2:11). *justified in the Spirit* refers to the vindication of Christ by the Spirit in His resurrection. *received up into glory* refers to His ascension into heaven.

4:1–5 Paul returns to his attack on heresy. False teaching is inspired by demons and promulgated by men *speaking lies in hypocrisy* ("speaking" is masculine, referring to men). The ethics of heresy are not necessarily immoral (v. 3). Paul's position is found in vv. 4–5. The Christian should live affirma-

3 Forbidding to marry, *and commanding* to abstain from meats, which God hath created to be received with thanksgiving of them which believe and know the truth.

4 For every creature of God *is* good, and nothing to be refused, if it be received with thanksgiving:

5 For it is sanctified by the word of God and prayer.

B Defenses against the Dangers, 4:6–16

6 If thou put the brethren in remembrance of these things, thou shalt be a good minister of Jesus Christ, nourished up in the words of faith and of good doctrine, whereunto thou hast attained.

7 But refuse profane and old wives' fables, and exercise thyself *rather* unto godliness.

8 For bodily exercise profiteth little: but godliness is profitable unto all things, having promise of the life that now is, and of that which is to come.

9 This *is* a faithful saying and worthy of all acceptation.

10 For therefore we both labour and suffer reproach, because we trust in the living God, who is the Saviour of all men, specially of those that believe.

11 These things command and teach.

12 Let no man despise thy youth; but be thou an example of the believers, in word, in conversation, in charity, in spirit, in faith, in purity.

13 Till I come, give attendance to reading, to exhortation, to doctrine.

14 Neglect not the gift that is in thee, which was given thee by prophecy, with the laying on of the hands of the presbytery.

15 Meditate upon these things; give thyself wholly to them; that thy profiting may appear to all.

16 Take heed unto thyself, and unto the doctrine; continue in them: for in doing this thou shalt both save thyself, and them that hear thee.

tively, neither renouncing the world for a life of self-denial nor plunging into indulgence.

4:7 *old wives' fables.* See note at 1:4.

4:8 *little.* The benefits of bodily training are limited and transient when contrasted with the extensive and permanent benefits of godliness.

4:12 *conversation*=conduct.

4:13 *reading.* This refers to the public reading of the Scriptures, and should be accompanied by *exhortation* (preaching) and *doctrine* (teaching).

4:14 *the presbytery*=the body of elders.

VI INSTRUCTION
CONCERNING VARIOUS DUTIES, 5:1–6:21

A Toward those Older and Younger, 5:1–2

5 Rebuke not an elder, but intreat *him* as a father; *and* the younger men as brethren;

2 The elder women as mothers; the younger as sisters, with all purity.

B Toward Widows, 5:3–16

3 Honour widows that are widows indeed.

4 But if any widow have children or nephews, let them learn first to shew piety at home, and to requite their parents: for that is good and acceptable before God.

5 Now she that is a widow indeed, and desolate, trusteth in God, and continueth in supplications and prayers night and day.

6 But she that livest in pleasure is dead while she liveth.

7 And these things give in charge, that they may be blameless.

8 But if any provide not for his own, and specially for those of his own house, he hath denied the faith, and is worse than an infidel.

9 Let not a widow be taken into the number under threescore years old, having been the wife of one man,

10 Well reported of for good works; if she have brought up children, if she have lodged strangers, if she have washed the saints' feet, if she have relieved the afflicted, if she have diligently followed every good work.

11 But the younger widows refuse: for when they have begun to wax wanton against Christ, they will marry;

5:1 *intreat*=exhort.

5:3–16 Widows, who ordinarily would have no financial means of support, were to be cared for by their families first (v. 4); then, if support were not available from that source, the church should care for them (these are called *widows indeed*, v. 3). Younger widows are encouraged to remarry (v. 14), but those over 60 and destitute could be placed on the official relief roll of the church (v. 9). These "enrolled widows" constituted a kind of "order of widows" who were expected to devote themselves to prayer and good works (vv. 5, 10).

5:4 *nephews*. Lit., grandchildren.

5:7 The meaning is: See that these regulations are followed so that both widows and their families will be above criticism in their conduct.

12 Having damnation, because they have cast off their first faith.

13 And withal they learn *to be* idle, wandering about from house to house; and not only idle, but tattlers also and busybodies, speaking things which they ought not.

14 I will therefore that the younger women marry, bear children, guide the house, give none occasion to the adversary to speak reproachfully.

15 For some are already turned aside after Satan.

16 If any man or woman that believeth have widows, let them relieve them, and let not the church be charged; that it may relieve them that are widows indeed.

C Toward Elders, 5:17–25

17 Let the elders that rule well be counted worthy of double honour, especially they who labour in the word and doctrine.

18 For the scripture saith, Thou shalt not muzzle the ox that treadeth out the corn. And, The labourer *is* worthy of his reward.

19 Against an elder receive not an accusation, but before two or three witnesses.

20 Them that sin rebuke before all, that others also may fear.

21 I charge *thee* before God, and the Lord Jesus Christ, and the elect angels, that thou observe these things without preferring one before another, doing nothing by partiality.

22 Lay hands suddenly on no man, neither be partaker of other men's sins: keep thyself pure.

23 Drink no longer water, but use a little wine for thy stomach's sake and thine often infirmities.

24 Some men's sins are open beforehand, going before to judgment; and some *men* they follow after.

5:16 Relatives should assume the support of widows in their family (cf. vv. 4, 8).

5:17 *double honour*. This has two meanings: respect and remuneration. Both are intended here. The church was beginning to face the problem of financial support of its workers.

5:20 *Them that sin*. I.e., elders who do sin.

5:22 *Lay hands suddenly on no man*. This is often understood as forbidding hasty ordination, but it may well refer to overhasty receiving of a penitent backslider back into full fellowship.

5:23 *use a little wine*. The words imply that Timothy was a total abstainer and that the advice is given in relation to a medical problem.

25 Likewise also the good works *of some* are manifest beforehand; and they that are otherwise cannot be hid.

D Toward Masters and Slaves, 6:1–2

6 Let as many servants as are under the yoke count their own masters worthy of all honour, that the name of God and *his* doctrine be not blasphemed.

2 And they that have believing masters, let them not despise *them*, because they are brethren; but rather do *them* service, because they are faithful and beloved, partakers of the benefit. These things teach and exhort.

E Toward False Teachers, 6:3–5

3 If any man teach otherwise, and consent not to wholesome words, *even* the words of our Lord Jesus Christ, and to the doctrine which is according to godliness;

4 He is proud, knowing nothing, but doting about questions and strifes of words, whereof cometh envy, strife, railings, evil surmisings,

5 Perverse disputings of men of corrupt minds, and destitute of the truth, supposing that gain is godliness: from such withdraw thyself.

F Toward Money and Godliness, 6:6–19

6 But godliness with contentment is great gain.

7 For we brought nothing into *this* world, *and it is* certain we can carry nothing out.

8 And having food and raiment let us be therewith content.

9 But they that will be rich fall into temptation and a snare, and *into* many foolish and hurtful lusts, which drown men in destruction and perdition.

6:1–2 The problems of the master-slave relationship are discussed in 1 Cor. 7:21; Eph. 6:5–9; 3:22–4:1; Tit. 2:9–10 and Philem. 10–17. The N.T. writers do not question the institution of slavery but try to mitigate it via improved attitudes of both masters and slaves. In the church both met on equal terms as members of the fellowship, though there may have been instances when slaves were elders and thus in the church over masters whom they served all week.

6:4–5 Again heretical teachers are excoriated. Perhaps they charged fees (v. 5).

6:6 In contrast to the material gain of the heretics (v. 5), the Christian finds his gain of a non-financial sort, *godliness with contentment* or self-sufficiency which results from an inner satisfaction with the situation that God has ordained for him.

10 For the love of money is the root of all evil: which while some coveted after, they have erred from the faith, and pierced themselves through with many sorrows.

11 But thou, O man of God, flee these things; and follow after righteousness, godliness, faith, love, patience, meekness.

12 Fight the good fight of faith, lay hold on eternal life, whereunto thou art also called, and hast professed a good profession before many witnesses.

13 I give thee charge in the sight of God, who quickeneth all things, and *before* Christ Jesus, who before Pontius Pilate witnessed a good confession;

14 That thou keep *this* commandment without spot, unrebukeable, until the appearing of our Lord Jesus Christ:

15 Which in his times he shall shew, *who is* the blessed and only Potentate, the King of kings, and Lord of lords;

16 Who only hath immortality, dwelling in the light which no man can approach unto; whom no man hath seen, nor can see: to whom *be* honour and power everlasting. Amen.

17 Charge them that are rich in this world, that they be not highminded, nor trust in uncertain riches, but in the living God, who giveth us richly all things to enjoy;

18 That they do good, that they be rich in good works, ready to distribute, willing to communicate;

19 Laying up in store for themselves a good foundation against the time to come, that they may lay hold on eternal life.

G Toward One's Trust, 6:20–21

20 O Timothy, keep that which is committed to thy trust, avoiding profane *and* vain babblings, and oppositions of science falsely so called:

21 Which some professing have erred concerning the faith. Grace *be* with thee. Amen.

6:12 *hast professed a good profession.* This refers to Timothy's public confession of Christ at his baptism.

6:15 Better, This will be manifest at the proper time by the blessed and only Sovereign. In other words, the return of Christ (v. 14) will occur at the time ordered and appointed by God.

6:18 *willing to communicate*=to be generous.

INTRODUCTION TO
THE SECOND LETTER OF PAUL TO
Timothy

AUTHOR: Paul   DATE: 66

The Author   *See Introduction to 1 Timothy.*

The Background   See The Probable Order of Events under the Introduction to Titus. Paul, imprisoned in Rome as the result of persecution under Nero, realized that his death was near when he wrote this letter (1:8, 16; 4:6–8). Alone (4:10–11) and cold (4:13) in his dungeon, the veteran missionary wrote his young son in the faith this intensely personal and pastoral letter. Soon after, he was, according to tradition, beheaded on the Ostian Way, west of Rome.

The Contents   The theme may be taken from 2:3, "A Good Soldier of Jesus Christ." Important subjects mentioned include: the apostasy of the last days (3:1–9, see 1 Tim. 4:1–3), the inspiration of the Scriptures (3:16), and the crown of righteousness (4:8).

OUTLINE OF 2 TIMOTHY

THE SECOND LETTER OF
PAUL THE APOSTLE TO
Timothy

I THE SALUTATION, 1:1–2

1 Paul, an apostle of Jesus Christ by the will of God, according to the promise of life which is in Christ Jesus,

2 To Timothy, *my* dearly beloved son: Grace, mercy, *and* peace, from God the Father and Christ Jesus our Lord.

II THE EXPRESSION OF THANKS FOR TIMOTHY, 1:3–7

3 I thank God, whom I serve from *my* forefathers with pure conscience, that without ceasing I have remembrance of thee in my prayers night and day;

4 Greatly desiring to see thee, being mindful of thy tears, that I may be filled with joy;

5 When I call to remembrance the unfeigned faith that is in thee, which dwelt first in thy grandmother Lō'is, and thy mother Eûnĭ'cē; and I am persuaded that in thee also.

1:1 *life which is in Christ Jesus.* I.e., which is in union with Christ Jesus.

1:4 *thy tears.* Possibly those shed at some parting, such as Acts 20:37; or perhaps a reference to tears Paul knows Timothy has shed in the course of his service for Christ.

1:5 *Lois* is mentioned nowhere else. *thy mother Eunice.* See Acts 16:1. Apparently both had been converted under Paul's ministry.

6 Wherefore I put thee in remembrance that thou stir up the gift of God, which is in thee by the putting on of my hands.

7 For God hath not given us the spirit of fear; but of power, and of love, and of a sound mind.

III THE CALL OF A SOLDIER OF CHRIST, 1:8–18

A A Call to Courage, 1:8–12

8 Be not thou therefore ashamed of the testimony of our Lord, nor of me his prisoner: but be thou partaker of the afflictions of the gospel according to the power of God;

9 Who hath saved us, and called *us* with an holy calling, not according to our works, but according to his own purpose and grace, which was given us in Christ Jesus before the world began,

10 But is now made manifest by the appearing of our Saviour Jesus Christ, who hath abolished death, and hath brought life and immortality to light through the gospel:

11 Whereunto I am appointed a preacher, and an apostle, and a teacher of the Gentiles.

12 For the which cause I also suffer these things: nevertheless I am not ashamed: for I know whom I have believed, and am persuaded that he is able to keep that which I have committed unto him against that day.

B A Call to Faithfulness, 1:13–18

13 Hold fast the form of sound words, which thou hast heard of me, in faith and love which is in Christ Jesus.

14 That good thing which was committed unto thee keep by the Holy Ghost which dwelleth in us.

1:7 *fear.* Lit., cowardice, as in John 14:27 and Rev. 21:8. The believer is to have fear in the sense of awe (1 Pet. 1:17; 2:17) but not cowardice. *sound mind*=self-control or good sense.
1:8 *the testimony of our Lord.* I.e., testifying, including suffering, to our Lord.
1:10 *immortality*=incorruption, imperishability.
1:12 *whom I have believed.* I.e., on whose trustworthiness I have staked my faith. *that which I have committed.* Lit., the deposit. Paul's trust is well founded, for God will preserve this deposit of faith in Christ until the day of judgment when all dangers will be past. Some understand this to refer to God's deposit of gifts in Paul's life (as in v. 14 and 1 Tim. 6:20).
1:14 *That good thing.* Lit., the good deposit, i.e., the gospel.

15 This thou knowest, that all they which are in Asia be turned away from me; of whom are Phỹġel'lus and Hermoġ'enēs.

16 The Lord give mercy unto the house of Ōnesiph'orus, for he oft refreshed me, and was not ashamed of my chain:

17 But, when he was in Rome, he sought me out very diligently, and found *me*.

18 The Lord grant unto him that he may find mercy of the Lord in that day: and in how many things he ministered unto me at Ephesus, thou knowest very well.

IV THE CHARACTER OF A SOLDIER OF CHRIST, 2:1–26

A He Is Strong, 2:1–2

2 Thou therefore, my son, be strong in the grace that is in Christ Jesus.

2 And the things that thou hast heard of me among many witnesses, the same commit thou to faithful men, who shall be able to teach others also.

B He Is Single-minded, 2:3–4

3 Thou therefore endure hardness, as a good soldier of Jesus Christ.

4 No man that warreth entangleth himself with the affairs of *this* life; that he may please him who hath chosen him to be a soldier.

1:15 *all they which are in Asia.* I.e., all who are now in Asia who had formerly been with Paul in Rome. Asia is the Roman province, embracing the western part of what is now called Asia Minor (Turkey). *Phygellus and Hermogenes* were a special disappointment to Paul and were known to Timothy.

1:16–18 *Onesiphorus,* who had ministered to Paul in Ephesus, sought him out in the dungeon where Paul was confined in Rome and ministered to him.

2:1 This verse seems to sum up the teaching of chapter 1: Timothy, you have the gift of power from God through Christ (1:7); now find your strength in this gift of grace.

2:2 *heard of me.* The content of Paul's teaching is not stated but was clearly understood by Timothy. *among many witnesses.* Perhaps the elders at Timothy's ordination or likely the many who had at different times heard Paul's preaching.

2:4 *entangleth.* The minister must put priority on his calling and be completely dedicated to his task and his Commander.

C He Is Strict, 2:5–10

5 And if a man also strive for masteries, *yet* is he not crowned, except he strive lawfully.

6 The husbandman that laboureth must be first partaker of the fruits.

7 Consider what I say; and the Lord give thee understanding in all things.

8 Remember that Jesus Christ of the seed of David was raised from the dead according to my gospel:

9 Wherein I suffer trouble, as an evil doer, *even* unto bonds; but the word of God is not bound.

10 Therefore I endure all things for the elect's sakes, that they may also obtain the salvation which is in Christ Jesus with eternal glory.

D He Is Secure, 2:11–13

11 *It is* a faithful saying: For if we be dead with *him*, we shall also live with *him*:

12 If we suffer, we shall also reign with *him*: if we deny *him*, he also will deny us:

13 If we believe not, *yet* he abideth faithful: he cannot deny himself.

E He Is Sound of Faith, 2:14–19

14 Of these things put *them* in remembrance, charging *them* before the Lord that they strive not about words to no profit, *but* to the subverting of the hearers.

2:5 *strive for masteries*=contend in the games. The picture in this verse is of an athlete who must play according to the rules (*lawfully*). The minister must adhere to the requirements of his calling, making the Word and will of God his standard in all things.

2:6 *The husbandman that laboureth*=the hard-working farmer.

2:7 *Consider.* If you will reflect on my teachings (in the previous verses) Christ will open up for you the depths of their meanings.

2:9 *evil doer*=criminal. *even unto bonds.* I.e., even to the point of wearing fetters, like a brigand.

2:10 *Therefore.* I.e., because the Word of God remains unimprisoned (v. 9).

2:11 *a faithful saying*=a sure saying. *be dead.* Perhaps this refers to the crucifixion of the sin nature, as Gal. 2:20, but more likely a reference to physical death; i.e., if we die physically, we shall be raised physically.

2:13 *believe not. . . .* Lit., if we are unfaithful. He abides faithful. This is a statement of the consistency of God's character which is a strong promise to the believer of the security of his salvation even though he may lose all rewards (see 1 Cor. 3:15).

2:14 *strive not about words.* I.e., indulge in word-battles, wordy

15 Study to shew thyself approved unto God, a work-man that needeth not to be ashamed, rightly dividing the word of truth.

16 But shun profane *and* vain babblings: for they will increase unto more ungodliness.

17 And their word will eat as doth a canker: of whom is Hȳmenǽ'us and Phīlē'tus;

18 Who concerning the truth have erred, saying that the resurrection is past already; and overthrow the faith of some.

19 Nevertheless the foundation of God standeth sure, having this seal, The Lord knoweth them that are his. And, Let every one that nameth the name of Christ depart from iniquity.

F He Is Sanctified, 2:20–23

20 But in a great house there are not only vessels of gold and of silver, but also of wood and of earth; and some to honour, and some to dishonour.

21 If a man therefore purge himself from these, he shall be a vessel unto honour, sanctified, and meet for the master's use, *and* prepared unto every good work.

22 Flee also youthful lusts: but follow righteousness, faith, charity, peace, with them that call on the Lord out of a pure heart.

23 But foolish and unlearned questions avoid, knowing that they do gender strifes.

controversies, and quibbling about words. These are not only profitless but ruining to those who hear them.

2:15 *Study*=be diligent. *rightly dividing*=correct handling in analysis and presentation of the Word of God in contrast to the inane interpretations of false teachers.

2:17 *canker*=gangrene. *Hymenaeus and Philetus*. These trouble-makers (Hymenaeus is also mentioned in 1 Tim. 1:20) were probably teaching that the doctrine of resurrection had only an allegorical or spiritual meaning. Gnostic teaching conceived of resurrection allegorically as referring to acquaintance with truth and occurring at baptism.

2:19 *seal*. A mark of authentication and ownership.

2:20–21 The reality is, Paul says, there are going to be some wicked persons (of wood and earthenware) in every church, but (v. 21) no one need remain wicked.

2:22 *lusts* are not only things immoral but also things foolish. Temptation is avoided by fleeing what would hinder and by following what helps in the company of spiritual people.

2:23 *gender*=engender, breed.

G He Is a Servant, 2:24–26

24 And the servant of the Lord must not strive; but be gentle unto all *men*, apt to teach, patient,

25 In meekness instructing those that oppose themselves; if God peradventure will give them repentance to the acknowledging of the truth;

26 And *that* they may recover themselves out of the snare of the devil, who are taken captive by him at his will.

V THE CAUTION FOR A SOLDIER OF CHRIST, 3:1–17

A The Peril of Apostasy, 3:1–9

3 This know also, that in the last days perilous times shall come.

2 For men shall be lovers of their own selves, covetous, boasters, proud, blasphemers, disobedient to parents, unthankful, unholy,

3 Without natural affection, trucebreakers, false accusers, incontinent, fierce, despisers of those that are good,

4 Traitors, heady, highminded, lovers of pleasures more than lovers of God;

5 Having a form of godliness, but denying the power therof: from such turn away.

6 For of this sort are they which creep into houses, and lead captive silly women laden with sins, led away with divers lusts,

7 Ever learning, and never able to come to the knowledge of the truth.

8 Now as Jan'nēs and Jam'brēs withstood Moses, so do these also resist the truth: men of corrupt minds, reprobate concerning the faith.

2:24 *strive*=engage in strife, be quarrelsome.
2:26 *taken captive.* I.e., by Satan at Satan's will (see Eph. 2:3).
3:1 *in the last days.* This includes the whole period between the writing of this letter and the Lord's return. As His return draws near, these characteristics will intensify (see 1 Tim. 4:1–5). The description that follows in vv. 2–9 is of mass corruption, of a breakdown of law and tradition.
3:4 *heady*=headstrong, reckless.
3:5 *Having a form of godliness*=holding the form of religion, the outer semblence of it without its spiritual dynamic.
3:6 *silly women.* Women are here viewed as changeable of mind, prone to accept new ideas and swayed by impulses.
3:8 *Jannes and Jambres.* Though these names do not appear in

9 But they shall proceed no further: for their folly shall be manifest unto all *men*, as theirs also was.

B The Protection from Apostasy, 3:10–17

10 But thou hast fully known my doctrine, manner of life, purpose, faith, longsuffering, charity, patience,

11 Persecutions, afflictions, which came unto me at An'tioch, at Īcō'nium, at Lystra; what persecutions I endured: but out of *them* all the Lord delivered me.

12 Yea, and all that will live godly in Christ Jesus shall suffer persecution.

13 But evil men and seducers shall wax worse and worse, deceiving, and being deceived.

14 But continue thou in the things which thou hast learned and hast been assured of, knowing of whom thou hast learned *them;*

15 And that from a child thou hast known the holy scriptures, which are able to make thee wise unto salvation through faith which is in Christ Jesus.

16 All scripture *is* given by inspiration of God, and *is* profitable for doctrine, for reproof, for correction, for instruction in righteousness:

17 That the man of God may be perfect, throughly furnished unto all good works.

the O.T., in late Jewish, pagan, and certain early Christian writings they are given to the Egyptian magicians who did counterfeit miracles in opposition to Moses (Ex. 7:11, 22). They are symbols of the folly of opposing the truth.

3:11 *Persecutions.* See Acts 13–14.

3:12 To *live godly* will apparently involve an aggressive witness such as that Paul gave at the places listed in v. 11.

3:16 *All scripture is given by inspiration.* Lit., God-breathed; i.e., the Bible came from God through the men who wrote it (see 2 Pet. 1:21). God superintended these human authors so that, using their individual personalities, they composed and recorded without error God's Word to man. Christ attested to the fact that inspiration extends to the very words (Matt. 5:18; John 10:35). Paul quoted Deuteromony and Luke in the same verse as scripture (1 Tim. 5:18), and Peter declared Paul's epistles to be scripture (2 Pet. 3:16). Inspiration is not mechanical dictation, but it is the accurate recording of God's words. Inspiration does not extend beyond the original manuscripts, though the texts we possess today have been transmitted with high accuracy.

3:17 *throughly*=thoroughly.

VI THE CHARGE TO A SOLDIER OF CHRIST,
4:1-5

4 I charge *thee* therefore before God, and the Lord Jesus Christ, who shall judge the quick and the dead at his appearing and his kingdom;

2 Preach the word; be instant in season, out of season; reprove, rebuke, exhort with all longsuffering and doctrine.

3 For the time will come when they will not endure sound doctrine; but after their own lusts shall they heap to themselves teachers, having itching ears;

4 And they shall turn away *their* ears from the truth, and shall be turned unto fables.

5 But watch thou in all things, endure afflictions, do the work of an evangelist, make full proof of thy ministry.

VII THE COMFORT OF A SOLDIER OF CHRIST,
4:6-18

A A Good Finish to Life, 4:6-7

6 For I am now ready to be offered, and the time of my departure is at hand.

7 I have fought a good fight, I have finished *my* course, I have kept the faith:

B A Good Future after Life, 4:8

8 Henceforth there is laid up for me a crown of righteousness, which the Lord, the righteous judge, shall give me at that day: and not to me only, but unto all them also that love his appearing.

4:1 *quick*=living. *at his appearing and his kingdom*. When Christ appears He will inaugurate the judgment and His faithful will be gathered into His kingdom.

4:2 *be instant in season*. I.e., always be ready whether the time is opportune for preaching the gospel or not.

4:3-4 The description is of people who no longer are content to hear the sound teaching of Paul, but who are impelled to turn to teacher after teacher of novelty and untruth.

4:6 *departure*=release, i.e., his death.

4:7 *the faith*. I.e., the recognized body of Christian doctrine (also Jude 3). Paul *kept* it in two senses: he was obedient to it, and he passed it on as he received it.

4:8 *Henceforth*=from now on. *laid up*. I.e., safely kept. *crown of righteousness* is one of the rewards (prizes) offered Chris-

C Good Friends in Life, 4:9–18

9 Do thy diligence to come shortly unto me:

10 For Demas hath forsaken me, having loved this present world, and is departed unto Thessalōnī′ca; Cres′cens to Galatia, Titus unto Dalmatia.

11 Only Luke is with me. Take Mark, and bring him with thee: for he is profitable to me for the ministry.

12 And Tych′icus have I sent to Ephesus.

13 The cloke that I left at Trō′as with Carpus, when thou comest, bring *with thee,* and the books, *but* especially the parchments.

14 Alexander the coppersmith did me much evil: the Lord reward him according to his works:

15 Of whom be thou ware also; for he hath greatly withstood our words.

16 At my first answer no man stood with me, but all *men* forsook me: *I pray God* that it may not be laid to their charge.

17 Notwithstanding the Lord stood with me, and strengthened me; that by me the preaching might be fully known, and *that* all the Gentiles might hear: and I was delivered out of the mouth of the lion.

18 And the Lord shall deliver me from every evil work, and will preserve *me* unto his heavenly kingdom: to whom *be* glory for ever and ever. Amen.

tians, in this case for loving the coming of Christ. See note at 1 Cor. 3:14.

4:9–22 After this climactic testimony (vv. 6–8) Paul returns to treat worrisome, immediate personal affairs.

4:10 Why *Demas* deserted Paul is not known.

4:11 *Mark* and Paul had overcome their differences that caused their earlier separation (Acts 15:36–41). See Col. 4:10; Philem. 24.

4:13 *the books.* Papyrus rolls, but *the parchments* were skins of vellum which were used for more precious documents, in this case probably Paul's personal copies of portions of the O.T. This missionary-prisoner still wants to study!

4:14 *Alexander.* Probably not the same as the one mentioned in 1 Tim. 1:20, since he is further identified as the coppersmith or metalworker. We may infer from v. 15 that he may have caused the arrest of Paul in some city; that he was still active; and that he was hostile to Paul's teachings.

4:16 *my first answer.* I.e., the preliminary hearing with which Paul's final trial opened (though some refer this to Paul's first trial in Rome three years before).

4:17 *delivered out of the mouth of the lion.* Paul was not immediately condemned but was spared from execution.

VIII CONCLUDING GREETINGS, 4:19–22

19 Salute Prisca and Aquila, and the household of Ōnesiph′orus.

20 Erastus abode at Corinth: but Troph′imus have I left at Mīlē′tum sick.

21 Do thy diligence to come before winter. Eûbū′lus greeteth thee, and Pudens, and Linus, and Claudia, and all the brethren.

22 The Lord Jesus Christ *be* with thy spirit. Grace *be* with you. Amen.

4:19 *Prisca and Aquila.* They were devoted friends (Rom. 16:3; 1 Cor. 16:19; Acts 18:2, 26). *Onesiphorus.* See Note at 1:16–18.

4:20 *Trophimus.* This happening cannot be fitted into Acts and thus indicates two imprisonments in Rome for Paul. Trophimus was an Ephesian (Acts 20:4; 21:29).

4:21 The four persons named here, at least, had not deserted Paul (v. 16). Nothing more is known of them.

INTRODUCTION TO
THE LETTER OF PAUL TO
Titus

AUTHOR: Paul   DATE: 65

The Author See the Introduction to 1 Timothy for arguments that Paul was the author.

The Probable Order of Events (1) Paul was released from his confinement in Rome (where he is left at the end of Acts) under house arrest, probably because his accusers did not choose to press their charges against him before Caesar (Acts 24:1; 28:30). Therefore, their case was lost by default and Paul was freed. (2) Paul visited Ephesus, left Timothy there to supervise the churches, and went on to Macedonia (northern Greece). (3) From there he wrote 1 Timothy (1 Tim. 1:3). (4) He visited Crete, left Titus there to supervise those churches, and went to Nicopolis in Achaia (southern Greece) (Tit. 3:12). (5) Either from Macedonia or Nicopolis he wrote this letter to encourage Titus. (6) He visited Troas (2 Tim. 4:13), where he was suddenly arrested, taken to Rome, imprisoned, and finally beheaded. (7) From Rome during this second imprisonment he wrote 2 Timothy.

Titus A Gentile by birth (Gal. 2:3), Titus was converted through the ministry of Paul (Tit. 1:4). He accompanied Paul to Jerusalem at the time of the apostolic council (Acts 15:2; Gal. 2:1–3). He was Paul's emissary to the church at Corinth during the third missionary journey (2 Cor. 7:6–7; 8:6, 16). Titus and two others took the letter we call 2 Corinthians to Corinth and urged the Corinthians to make good their promise to give to the poor in Jerusalem. Paul left Titus in Crete to use his administrative gifts to consolidate the work there. Artemas or Tychicus probably relieved him in Crete so he could join Paul in Nicopolis (Tit. 3:12), from which place Paul sent him to Dalmatia

(Yugoslavia) (2 Tim. 4:10). Tradition says he returned to Crete and died there.

The Contents *Important topics discussed in the letter include: qualifications for elders (1:5–9), instructions to various age groups (2:1–8), relationship to government (3:1–2), and the relation of regeneration to human works and to the Spirit (3:5).*

OUTLINE OF TITUS

THE LETTER OF PAUL TO

Titus

I OPENING GREETINGS, 1:1–4

1 Paul, a servant of God, and an apostle of Jesus Christ, according to the faith of God's elect, and the acknowledging of the truth which is after godliness;

2 In hope of eternal life, which God, that cannot lie, promised before the world began;

3 But hath in due times manifested his word through preaching, which is committed unto me according to the commandment of God our Saviour;

4 To Titus, *mine* own son after the common faith: Grace, mercy, *and* peace, from God the Father and the Lord Jesus Christ our Saviour.

1:1 *according to . . . after godliness.* The meaning is this: Paul was commissioned to further the faith of God's elect so that they might acquire full knowledge of Christian truth.

1:4 *Titus.* Though not mentioned in Acts, other N.T. references

II OFFICERS IN THE CHURCH, 1:5–9

A The Desirability of Elders, 1:5

5 For this cause left I thee in Crete, that thou shouldest set in order the things that are wanting, and ordain elders in every city, as I had appointed thee:

B The Qualifications for Elders, 1:6–9

6 If any be blameless, the husband of one wife, having faithful children not accused of riot or unruly.

7 For a bishop must be blameless, as the steward of God; not selfwilled, not soon angry, not given to wine, no striker, not given to filthy lucre;

8 But a lover of hospitality, a lover of good men, sober, just, holy, temperate;

9 Holding fast the faithful word as he hath been taught, that he may be able by sound doctrine both to exhort and to convince the gainsayers.

III OFFENDERS IN THE CHURCH, 1:10–16

10 For there are many unruly and vain talkers and deceivers, specially they of the circumcision:

11 Whose mouths must be stopped, who subvert whole houses, teaching things which they ought not, for filthy lucre's sake.

12 One of themselves, *even* a prophet of their own, said, The Cretians *are* alway liars, evil beasts, slow bellies.

to Titus' activities are found in 2 Cor. 2:13; 7:5–7, 13–14; 8:6, 16–17, 23; 12:18; Gal. 2:1, 3; 2 Tim. 4:10. *son*. Lit., child, a term of affection used also by Paul of Timothy and Onesimus.

1:5 *the things that are wanting*. A church is defective unless it has constituted leaders. In Crete these were appointed (=ordained) by Titus. See note on the elders at 1 Tim. 3:1.

1:6 *husband of one wife*. Wherever mentioned in the N.T., elders are seen as being married and as having children. This phrase may mean having only one husband at a time or it may mean being married only once (see 1 Tim. 5:9, where the similar phrase can only mean the latter). See also 1 Cor. 7:39 and 1 Tim. 5:14, where remarriage of a widow is permitted.

1:7 In Greek cities of the first century A.D. these vices and bad qualities were common among men.

1:9 *gainsayers*=those who contradict (sound doctrine).

1:12 Quoted from the Cretan poet Epimenides, who exaggerates for effect. To Cretanize was to lie. *slow bellies*=idle gluttons.

13 This witness is true. Wherefore rebuke them sharply, that they may be sound in the faith;

14 Not giving heed to Jewish fables, and commandments of men, that turn from the truth.

15 Unto the pure all things *are* pure: but unto them that are defiled and unbelieving *is* nothing pure; but even their mind and conscience is defiled.

16 They profess that they know God; but in works they deny *him*, being abominable, and disobedient, and unto every good work reprobate.

IV ORDERLINESS IN THE CHURCH, 2:1–3:11

A The Duties of the Minister, 2:1–10

2 But speak thou the things which become sound doctrine:

2 That the aged men be sober, grave, temperate, sound in faith, in charity, in patience.

3 The aged women likewise, that *they be* in behaviour as becometh holiness, not false accusers, not given to much wine, teachers of good things;

4 That they may teach the young women to be sober, to love their husbands, to love their children,

5 *To be* discreet, chaste, keepers at home, good, obedient to their own husbands, that the word of God be not blasphemed.

6 Young men likewise exhort to be sober minded.

7 In all things shewing thyself a pattern of good works: in doctrine *shewing* uncorruptness, gravity, sincerity,

8 Sound speech, that cannot be condemned; that he

1:14 *Jewish fables*. Better, myths; what is meant is speculations based on O.T. scripture of a Gnostic sort. For Gnosticism see the Introduction to 1 John.

1:15 Purity is an interior matter, of the mind and conscience, not external, not an attribute of things. See Luke 11:41.

2:1 *But*. I.e., in contrast to false teachers. *sound doctrine*. Lit., healthy teaching (as in 1:9, 13; 2:2) is that which causes behavior to be in accord with belief.

2:3 *false accusers*. Lit., slanderers. Apparently some of the older women were given to gossiping and drinking.

2:5 *that the word of God be not blasphemed*. Failure to observe the matters mentioned in this verse would expose the Word of God to contempt by the world.

2:8 *Sound speech*. Lit., healthy speech (the adjectival form of the word in vv. 1–2).

that is of the contrary part may be ashamed, having no evil thing to say of you.

9 *Exhort* servants to be obedient unto their own masters, *and* to please *them* well in all *things*; not answering again;

10 Not purloining, but shewing all good fidelity; that they may adorn the doctrine of God our Saviour in all things.

B The Doctrine of the Grace of God, 2:11–15

11 For the grace of God that bringeth salvation hath appeared to all men,

12 Teaching us that, denying ungodliness and worldly lusts, we should live soberly, righteously, and godly, in this present world;

13 Looking for that blessed hope, and the glorious appearing of the great God and our Saviour Jesus Christ;

14 Who gave himself for us, that he might redeem us from all iniquity, and purify unto himself a peculiar people, zealous of good works.

15 These things speak, and exhort, and rebuke with all authority. Let no man despise thee.

C The Demonstration of Good Works, 3:1–11

1 *In relation to governments*, 3:1

3 Put them in mind to be subject to principalities and powers, to obey magistrates, to be ready to every good work,

---

2:10 *purloining* = petty stealing.

2:11 *appeared*. The tense of the verb indicates that this is a reference to the incarnation, Christ's first appearing.

2:12 *ungodliness*=irreverence. *worldly lusts*=passions, overpowering attractions for the secular world. *soberly*=sensibly, seriously.

2:14 *redeem*. I.e., release us from the bondage of sin. See note on redemption at Eph. 1:7. *peculiar people*=a people of His very own possession.

3:1 *be subject*=to submit or subject oneself it is the same word used in Rom. 13:1 and 1 Pet. 2:13. *principalities and powers* usually refer to angels (good angels in Eph. 3:10 or evil angels in Eph. 6:12), but here the reference is to human governmental rulers. Though Christians are a "special" people elected by God, redeemed from the world and no longer dependent upon it, they are not above the necessity of getting along with the civil rulers who govern them.

2 In relation to all people, 3:2–7

2 To speak evil of no man, to be no brawlers, *but* gentle, shewing all meekness unto all men.

3 For we ourselves also were sometimes foolish, disobedient, deceived, serving divers lusts and pleasures, living in malice and envy, hateful, *and* hating one another.

4 But after that the kindness and love of God our Saviour toward man appeared,

5 Not by works of righteousness which we have done, but according to his mercy he saved us, by the washing of regeneration, and renewing of the Holy Ghost;

6 Which he shed on us abundantly through Jesus Christ our Saviour;

7 That being justified by his grace, we should be made heirs according to the hope of eternal life.

3 In relation to false teachers, 3:8–11

8 *This is* a faithful saying, and these things I will that thou affirm constantly, that they which have believed in God might be careful to maintain good works. These things are good and profitable unto men.

9 But avoid foolish questions, and genealogies, and contentions, and strivings about the law; for they are unprofitable and vain.

10 A man that is an heretick after the first and second admonition reject;

3:2 *brawlers.* Better, quarrelers. Quarreling only arouses the hostility of non-Christians. Christian virtues are of an opposite sort.

3:3 *divers*=various.

3:5 *Not by works of righteousness . . . by the washing of regeneration.* Personal salvation is not achieved through good works but through the cleansing of the new birth. *renewing of the Holy Ghost* means either the initial act of conversion or, more probably, the continual renewing of the Spirit throughout the life of the believer. In any case salvation is God's doing and not a reward for man's meritorious acts.

3:8 *these things.* I.e., the counsels of vv. 1–7. *maintain good works* probably has the general meaning of "supply themselves to good deeds," though the phrase may have the technical meaning of "enter honorable occupations."

3:10 The Greek word here translated *heretick* means factious— one who willfully chooses for himself and sets up a faction (see 1 Cor. 11:19 Gal. 5:20). Our responsibility is to reprimand him twice, then avoid him.

11 Knowing that he that is such is subverted, and sinneth, being condemned of himself.

V PERSONAL MESSAGES AND GREETINGS, 3:12–15

12 When I shall send Ar'temas unto thee, or Tych'icus, be diligent to come unto me to Nicop'olis: for I have determined there to winter.

13 Bring Zenas the lawyer and Apol'los on their journey diligently, that nothing be wanting unto them.

14 And let ours also learn to maintain good works for necessary uses, that they be not unfruitful.

15 All that are with me salute thee. Greet them that love us in the faith. Grace *be* with you all. Amen.

3:11 *subverted.* I.e., perverted, turned aside, and hence self-condemned.

3:12 *Artemas.* Nothing more is known of him. *Tychicus.* See Acts 20:4; Eph. 6:21; Col. 4:7; 2 Tim. 4:12.

3:13 *Zenas.* Nothing more is known of him. *Apollos.* The well-known associate of Paul.

INTRODUCTION TO
THE LETTER OF PAUL TO
Philemon

AUTHOR: Paul   DATE: 61

The Background of the Letter *Like Ephesians, Philippians, and Colossians, Philemon is one of the "Prison Epistles" written during Paul's first confinement in Rome. Onesimus, one of the millions of slaves in the Roman Empire, had stolen from his master, Philemon, and had run away. Eventually, he made his way to Rome, where he crossed the path of the apostle Paul, who led him to faith in Christ (v. 10). Now Onesimus was faced with doing his Christian duty toward his master by returning to him. Death would normally have been his punishment, so Paul wrote this wonderful letter of intercession on Onesimus' behalf.*

Philemon was not the only slaveholder in the Colossian church (see Col. 4:1), so this letter gave guidelines for other Christian masters in their relationships to their slave-brothers. Paul did not deny the rights of Philemon over his slave (the law punished those who interfered with those rights), but he asked Philemon to relate the principle of Christian brotherhood to the situation with Onesimus (v. 16). At the same time Paul offered to pay personally whatever Onesimus owed. This letter is not an attack against slavery as such, but a suggestion as to how Christian masters and slaves could live their faith within that evil system. It is possible that Philemon did free Onesimus and send him back to Paul (v. 14). It has also been suggested that Onesimus became a minister and later bishop of the church at Ephesus (Ignatius, To the Ephesians, 1).

This is the most personal of all of Paul's letters.

OUTLINE OF PHILEMON

THE LETTER OF PAUL TO
Philemon

I GREETINGS, 1–3

Paul, a prisoner of Jesus Christ, and Timothy *our* brother, unto Phile′mon our dearly beloved, and fellowlabourer,

2 And to *our* beloved Apphia, and Archip′pus our fellowsoldier, and to the church in thy house:

3 Grace to you, and peace, from God our Father and the Lord Jesus Christ.

II PRAISE OF PHILEMON, 4–7

4 I thank my God, making mention of thee always in my prayers,

5 Hearing of thy love and faith, which thou hast toward the Lord Jesus, and toward all saints;

6 That the communication of thy faith may become effectual by the acknowledging of every good thing which is in you in Christ Jesus.

7 For we have great joy and consolation in thy love, because the bowels of the saints are refreshed by thee, brother.

III PLEA TO PHILEMON, 8–17

8 Wherefore, though I might be much bold in Christ to enjoin thee that which is convenient,

---

1 *a prisoner of Jesus Christ.* Better, for Jesus Christ, i.e., for His sake, in His service.
2 *Apphia* was likely Philemon's wife and *Archippus* his son.
6 *communication* = sharing.
7 *bowels* = innermost feelings or hearts.
8–9 *that which is convenient.* Better, what is proper or required. Paul could use his authority as an apostle to order Philemon.

9 Yet for love's sake I rather beseech *thee*, being such an one as Paul the aged, and now also a prisoner of Jesus Christ.

10 I beseech thee for my son Ōnes'imus, whom I have begotten in my bonds:

11 Which in time past was to thee unprofitable, but now profitable to thee and to me:

12 Whom I have sent again: thou therefore receive him, that is, mine own bowels:

13 Whom I would have retained with me, that in thy stead he might have ministered unto me in the bonds of the gospel:

14 But without thy mind would I do nothing; that thy benefit should not be as it were of necessity, but willingly.

15 For perhaps he therefore departed for a season, that thou shouldest receive him for ever;

16 Not now as a servant, but above a servant, a brother beloved, specially to me, but how much more unto thee, both in the flesh, and in the Lord?

17 If thou count me therefore a partner, receive him as myself.

IV PLEDGE TO PHILEMON, 18–21

18 If he hath wronged thee, or oweth *thee* ought, put that on mine account;

19 I Paul have written *it* with mine own hand, I will re-

Instead Paul pleads love, age, and his imprisoned state, and (in v. 10) he simply "asks."

10 The name Onesimus means useful, beneficial.

12 *mine own bowels*=my very heart. So also in v. 20.

14 *thy benefit*=your goodness (if Philemon decided to send Onesimus back to serve Paul).

15 *perhaps*. A suggestion of a deeper purpose of God's providence in Onesimus' running away.

16 *a brother beloved*. Not legal emancipation for Onesimus but an emancipation because of Philemon's changed attitude toward his slave, who was now also his brother in Christ.

18 *put that on mine account*. This seems to indicate that Onesimus' offense included some monetary loss to Philemon as well as running away. This phrase is translated "impute" in Rom. 5:13. Paul asks Philemon to impute or reckon Onesimus' debt to Paul's account and to *receive him as myself* (v. 17), a beautiful illustration of our sin imputed to Christ so that God receives us in the merit of His Son (2 Cor. 5:21).

19 *thou owest unto me even thine own self*. Philemon was apparently converted under Paul's ministry.

pay *it*: albeit I do not say to thee how thou owest unto me even thine own self besides.

20 Yea, brother, let me have joy of thee in the Lord: refresh my bowels in the Lord.

21 Having confidence in thy obedience I wrote unto thee, knowing that thou wilt also do more than I say.

V PERSONAL MATTERS, 22–25

22 But withal prepare me also a lodging: for I trust that through your prayers I shall be given unto you.

23 There salute thee Ep'aphras, my fellowprisoner in Christ Jesus;

24 Marcus, Aristar'chus, Demas, Lucas, my fellow-labourers.

25 The grace of our Lord Jesus Christ *be* with your spirit. Amen.

22 *I shall be given unto you.* Paul expected to be released from imprisonment soon (see Phil. 1:25–26).

INTRODUCTION TO
THE LETTER TO THE
Hebrews

AUTHOR: Unknown   DATE: 64–68

The Readers   *Three questions are involved in determining the readership of this letter. (1) What was the racial background of these readers?* Although some have held that they were Gentiles, all evidence points to their Jewish background—the title of the book, "to the Hebrews," the references to the prophets and angels ministering to Israel, and the citations concerning the Levitical worship. *(2) Where did they live?* Palestine or Italy have been the answers most often given. The preference seems to be Italy, for these readers were not poor (and the saints in Palestine were, 6:10; 10:34; Rom. 15:26); the Septuagint is used exclusively for quotations from the O.T. (one would not expect this if the readers were Palestinian); and "they of Italy salute you" (13:24) sounds as though Italians outside of Italy are sending greetings back home. *(3) What was their spiritual condition?* Most were believers (3:1), though, as in every church group, there were doubtless some who merely professed Christianity. The author calls this letter a "word of exhortation" (13:22) necessitated by the fact that some were in danger of abandoning their faith in Christ and reverting to Judaism. The readers were being persecuted, though not to the point of being martyrs (10:32–34; 12:4), and in the face of this some were running the risk of apostasizing. The letter is a stirring apologetic for the superiority of Christ and Christianity over Judaism in terms of the priesthood and sacrifice of Christ.

The Author   *Many suggestions have been made for the author of this anonymous book*—Paul, Barnabas, Apollos, Silas, Aquila and Priscilla, and Clement of Rome. There are both resemblances and dissimilarities to the theology and style of Paul, but Paul constantly appeals to his own apostolic authority in his letters, while this writer appeals to others who were eyewitnesses of Jesus' ministry (2:3). It is safest to say, as Origen did, that only God now knows who wrote Hebrews.

The Date Various dates have been suggested for the writing of Hebrews, from the 60's to the 90's. However, its use in 1 Clement, which was written in 95, requires a date some time before that. What strongly indicates a date before 70 is the lack in the book of any reference to the destruction of the temple in Jerusalem as the divine proof that the O.T. sacrificial system was finished. In addition, the mention of Timothy's recent release, if it was in connection with his ministry to Paul in Rome, requires a date in the late 60's.

The Style The author displays outstanding literary and rhetorical skill. The style of Hebrews is a model of perfect Hellenistic prose. Both the author and his readers are very familiar with the O.T. in the Greek translation (the Septuagint). There are 29 direct quotations from the O.T. plus 53 clear allusions to various O.T. passages. These are used to demonstrate both the finality of the Christian revelation and its superiority to the old covenant.

The Contents The theme of the book is the superiority of Christ and thus of Christianity. The words "better," "perfection," "heavenly" appear frequently. The outline shows how the theme is developed by proving that Christ is superior both in His person and His priesthood. Favorite passages include 2:3 (so great salvation), 4:12 (the living Word of God), 4:16 (the throne of grace), 7:25 (the intercession of Christ), 11:1 (the description of faith) 11:4–40 (the heroes of faith), 12:1–2 (the Christian race) and 13:20–21 (a great benediction).

OUTLINE OF HEBREWS

THE LETTER OF
PAUL THE APOSTLE TO THE
Hebrews

I THE SUPERIORITY OF
THE PERSON OF CHRIST, 1:1–4:16

A Christ Is Superior to the Prophets, 1:1–4

1 God, who at sundry times and in divers manners spake in time past unto the fathers by the prophets,

1:1-4 These verses comprise one majestic sentence in the Greek text and read like the opening of a formal Greek oration rather than the customary "greetings" of a letter.

2 Hath in these last days spoken unto us by *his* Son, whom he hath appointed heir of all things, by whom also he made the worlds;

3 Who being the brightness of *his* glory, and the express image of his person, and upholding all things by the word of his power, when he had by himself purged our sins, sat down on the right hand of the Majesty on high;

4 Being made so much better than the angels, as he hath by inheritance obtained a more excellent name than they.

B Christ Is Superior to the Angels, 1:5–2:18

1 *In His divine person,* 1:5–14

5 For unto which of the angels said he at any time, Thou art my Son, this day have I begotten thee? And again, I will be to him a Father, and he shall be to me a Son?

1:1 *at sundry times and in divers manners.* I.e., in many parts (of Israel's history) and in various ways (through laws, institutions, ceremonies, kings, judges, prophets). *fathers.* I.e., forefathers.

1:2 *in these last days.* The *last days* here means the entire gospel dispensation extending from the first to the second advent of Christ. *the worlds.* Lit., the ages, including time, space, and the material world.

1:3 *brightness*=effulgence or flood of resplendent light or radiance. The word means an "outshining," not a reflection. *the express image of his person.* Lit., the exact representation of God's essence or nature. These expressions in v. 3 are strong assertions of the deity of Christ. *sat down on* (=at) *the right hand of the Majesty on high.* The picture of Christ being seated indicates the finished character of His sacrifice once-for-all for sin (10:10, 12), and the right hand indicates the place of honor which He occupies.

1:5 *the angels.* The word "angel" means messenger. It usually refers to an order of spirit beings, though rarely it is used of human beings (Luke 7:24 Jas. 2:25). Apparently all angels were originally created in a holy state, but some followed Satan in his revolt against God and became the demons. Some demons are loose and some are confined (see notes at Matt. 7:22; 2 Pet. 2:4; Jude 6). Angels are created beings who must ultimately answer to their Creator (Col. 1:16). Since they are spirit beings they are not bound by some of the things that limit human beings (Heb. 1:14; Acts 12:5–10). They are organized and ranked (Isa. 6:1–3; Dan. 10:1; Eph. 3:10; Jude 9). Angels ministered to Christ often during His first advent and will accompany Him at His return (Matt. 2:13; 4:11; 26:53; 28:2, 5; Luke 22:43; 2 Thess. 1:7–8). They serve believers (Heb. 1:14) and observe them (1 Cor. 4:9; 11:10). Michael is the only one designated an archangel (Dan. 10:13,

6 And again, when he bringeth in the firstbegotten into the world, he saith, And let all the angels of God worship him.

7 And of the angels he saith, Who maketh his angels spirits, and his ministers a flame of fire.

8 But unto the Son *he saith*, Thy throne, O God, *is* for ever and ever: a sceptre of righteousness *is* the sceptre of thy kingdom.

9 Thou hast loved righteousness, and hated iniquity; therefore God, *even* thy God, hath anointed thee with the oil of gladness above thy fellows.

10 And, Thou, Lord, in the beginning hast laid the foundation of the earth; and the heavens are the works of thine hands:

11 They shall perish; but thou remainest; and they all shall wax old as doth a garment;

12 And as a vesture shalt thou fold them up, and they shall be changed: but thou art the same, and thy years shall not fail.

13 But to which of the angels said he at any time, Sit on my right hand, until I make thine enemies thy footstool?

14 Are they not all ministering spirits, sent forth to minister for them who shall be heirs of salvation?

21; Jude 9), though Gabriel also has an important position (Luke 1:19, 26). *said he.* Quoting 2 Sam. 7:14 and Ps. 2:7. Never to any angel did God say that He was a Son, only to and of Christ. Both O.T. passages are interpreted in a Christological sense (Ps. 2:7 may have been sung to a monarch on the day of his coronation, and 2 Sam. 7:14 was addressed to Solomon), since Christ is the ultimate fulfillment of these words.

1:6 A combination of Ps. 97:7 with Deut. 32:43 (Septuagint version, the Greek translation of the O.T.).

1:7 *spirits.* Better, winds, quoting Ps. 104:4. Angels are servants (as wind and *fire* are) and therefore subordinate to the Son.

1:8–9 Quoting Ps. 45:6–7. Historically the psalm was probably sung at a Hebrew monarch's wedding. What was true of the ancient king by virtue of his office, the writer to the Hebrews sees to be wholly true of Christ by virtue of His nature. *above thy fellows*=beyond thy comrades, i.e., beyond all others.

1:10–12 Quoting Ps. 102:25–27. Christ is the Creator of all things and the One who in the midst of change is unchanging.

1:13 Quoting Ps. 110:1.

1:14 *ministering spirits.* The ministry of angels on behalf of believers continues today. The mention of *salvation* leads the writer into a discussion of this topic (2:1–18).

2 In His saving proclamation, 2:1-4

2 Therefore we ought to give the more earnest heed to the things which we have heard, lest at any time we should let *them* slip.

2 For if the word spoken by angels was stedfast, and every transgression and disobedience received a just recompence of reward;

3 How shall we escape, if we neglect so great salvation; which at the first began to be spoken by the Lord, and was confirmed unto us by them that heard *him*;

4 God also bearing *them* witness, both with signs and wonders, and with divers miracles, and gifts of the Holy Ghost, according to his own will?

3 In His delivering purpose, 2:5-18

5 For unto the angels hath he not put in subjection the world to come, whereof we speak.

6 But one in a certain place testified, saying, What is man, that thou art mindful of him? or the son of man, that thou visitest him?

7 Thou madest him a little lower than the angels; thou crownedst him with glory and honour, and didst set him over the works of thy hands:

8 Thou hast put all things in subjection under his feet. For in that he put all in subjection under him, he left nothing *that is* not put under him. But now we see not yet all things put under him.

9 But we see Jesus, who was made a little lower than the angels for the suffering of death, crowned with glory

2:1 *slip*=drift away.

2:2 *the word spoken by angels* refers to the Mosaic law (Ps. 68:17; Acts 7:53). In later Judaism it was held that angels had delivered the law.

2:5 *the world to come*. Lit., the coming inhabited earth (as in Luke 2:1). This is a reference to the millennial kingdom on earth which will not be ruled by angels but by Christ and the redeemed.

2:6 Quoting Ps. 8:4-6.

2:7 *a little lower*. This may mean (1) for a little time, or more likely (2) a little lower as to station. In the order of creation, man is lower than angels, and in the incarnation Christ took this lower place also.

2:8 *his feet . . . him . . . him*. This refers to man (not Christ) who was given dominion over the creation (Gen. 1:23) but who lost it when he sinned (Rom. 8:20) and who will regain it in the future millennial kingdom because of Christ's death for sin (v. 10).

and honour; that he by the grace of God should taste death for every man.

10 For it became him, for whom *are* all things, and by whom *are* all things, in bringing many sons unto glory, to make the captain of their salvation perfect through sufferings.

11 For both he that sanctifieth and they who are sanctified *are* all of one: for which cause he is not ashamed to call them brethren,

12 Saying, I will declare thy name unto my brethren, in the midst of the church will I sing praise unto thee.

13 And again, I will put my trust in him. And again, Behold I and the children which God hath given me.

14 Forasmuch then as the children are partakers of flesh and blood, he also himself likewise took part of the same; that through death he might destroy him that had the power of death, that is, the devil;

15 And deliver them who through fear of death were all their lifetime subject to bondage.

16 For verily he took not on *him the nature of* angels; but he took on *him* the seed of Abraham.

17 Wherefore in all things it behoved him to be made like unto *his* brethren, that he might be a merciful and faithful high priest in things *pertaining* to God, to make reconciliation for the sins of the people.

18 For in that he himself hath suffered being tempted, he is able to succour them that are tempted.

2:10 *captain*=leader, author, pioneer. *to make . . . perfect.* I.e., the sufferings of Jesus made Him qualified to be the leader of man's salvation.
2:11 *all of one* (source). I.e., we have the same Father.
2:12 Quoting Ps. 22:22.
2:13 See Isa. 8:17–18.
2:14 *took part of the same*=partook of the same human nature. Flesh and blood is an O.T. figure for human nature. *destroy.* Lit., bring to nought or make inoperative or useless, but not annihilate, for the devil will live in torment in the lake of fire forever (Rev. 20:10). This verse states the overriding purpose of Christ's accepting "a lower state."
2:16 Better, He was not concerned with angels but with the descendants of Abraham; i.e., Christ did not come to save fallen angels, but to save fallen men.
2:17 *to make reconciliation.* Lit., to propitiate or expiate. Propitiation means that God's wrath is satisfied by the death of Christ (Rom. 3:25; 1 John 2:2). Expiation emphasizes the removal of sin by the sacrifice which satisfied God. Sin interrupts normal relations with God; expiation removes sins and restores the relationship.

C Christ Is Superior to Moses, 3:1–6

3 Wherefore, holy brethren, partakers of the heavenly calling, consider the Apostle and High Priest of our profession, Christ Jesus;

2 Who was faithful to him that appointed him, as also Moses *was faithful* in all his house.

3 For this *man* was counted worthy of more glory than Moses, inasmuch as he who hath builded the house hath more honour than the house.

4 For every house is builded by some *man*; but he that built all things *is* God.

5 And Moses verily *was* faithful in all his house, as a servant, for a testimony of those things which were to be spoken after;

6 But Christ as a son over his own house; whose house are we, if we hold fast the confidence and the rejoicing of the hope firm unto the end.

D Christ Is the Supreme Object of Faith, 3:7–4:16

1 *The catastrophe of unbelief*, 3:7–19

7 Wherefore (as the Holy Ghost saith, To day if ye will hear his voice,

8 Harden not your hearts, as in the provocation, in the day of temptation in the wilderness:

9 When your fathers tempted me, proved me, and saw my works forty years.

10 Wherefore I was grieved with that generation, and said, They do alway err in *their* heart; and they have not known my ways.

11 So I sware in my wrath, They shall not enter into my rest.

12 Take heed, brethren, lest there be in any of you an evil heart of unbelief, in departing from the living God.

13 But exhort one another daily, while it is called To day; lest any of you be hardened through the deceitfulness of sin.

14 For we are made partakers of Christ, if we hold the beginning of our confidence stedfast unto the end;

3:1 *profession.* Better, confession.
3:3 Christ is better than Moses because Christ is the builder of God's house while Moses was a servant in the house.
3:7–11 See Ps. 95:7–11. The children of Israel challenged God's authority over them by their rebellion in the wilderness (Num. 14–21). Because of this, they failed to enter into the rest of dwelling in Canaan and they perished in the wilderness.

15 While it is said, To day if ye will hear his voice, harden not your hearts, as in the provocation.

16 For some, when they had heard, did provoke: howbeit not all that came out of Egypt by Moses.

17 But with whom was he grieved forty years? *was it* not with them that had sinned, whose carcases fell in the wilderness?

18 And to whom sware he that they should not enter into his rest, but to them that believed not?

19 So we see that they could not enter in because of unbelief.

2 *The consequences of unbelief*, 4:1–10

4 Let us therefore fear, lest, a promise being left *us* of entering into his rest, any of you should seem to come short of it.

2 For unto us was the gospel preached, as well as unto them: but the word preached did not profit them, not being mixed with faith in them that heard *it*.

3 For we which have believed do enter into rest, as he said, As I have sworn in my wrath, if they shall enter into my rest: although the works were finished from the foundation of the world.

4 For he spake in a certain place of the seventh *day* on this wise, And God did rest the seventh day from all his works.

5 And in this *place* again, If they shall enter into my rest.

6 Seeing therefore it remaineth that some must enter therein, and they to whom it was first preached entered not in because of unbelief:

3:16 Better, But who, when they had heard, did provoke? Was it not all who came out of Egypt by Moses?

3:19 *because of unbelief*. See Num. 14; 1 Cor. 10:10–11.

4:1 Although God has promised believers today that they may enter His rest, some may fail to experience it because of unbelief.

4:4 See Gen. 2:2. After the work of creation was finished God rested; i.e., He enjoyed the sense of satisfaction and repose that comes with the completion of a task. It is in this sense that *rest* is used in vv. 1 and 3.

4:5–9 The divine promise still holds good: the believer may enter into God's rest through faith. This is true both of salvation and sanctification. Rest in the Christian life comes through complete reliance on God's promises and full surrender to His will (2 Cor. 5:7; Col. 2:6).

7 Again, he limiteth a certain day, saying in David, To day, after so long a time; as it is said, To day if ye will hear his voice, harden not your hearts.

8 For if Jesus had given them rest, then would he not afterward have spoken of another day.

9 There remaineth therefore a rest to the people of God.

10 For he that is entered into his rest, he also hath ceased from his own works, as God *did* from his.

3 *The cure for unbelief*, 4:11-16

11 Let us labour therefore to enter into that rest, lest any man fall after the same example of unbelief.

12 For the word of God *is* quick, and powerful, and sharper than any twoedged sword, piercing even to the dividing asunder of soul and spirit, and of the joints and marrow, and *is* a discerner of the thoughts and intents of the heart.

13 Neither is there any creature that is not manifest in his sight: but all things *are* naked and opened unto the eyes of him with whom we have to do.

14 Seeing then that we have a great high priest, that is passed into the heavens, Jesus the Son of God, let us hold fast *our* profession.

15 For we have not an high priest which cannot be touched with the feeling of our infirmities; but was in all points tempted like as *we are, yet* without sin.

4:8 *Jesus.* Not Jesus Christ, but Joshua (Jesus is the Greek form of the Hebrew Joshua). Joshua (Moses' successor) could not lead all the people into the rest of dwelling in their promised land because of their unbelief. Likewise the believer today cannot enjoy a fully satisfying Christian life unless he believes all the promises of God.

4:11 *Let us labor.* Lit., let us make every effort. The same Greek word is used in Eph. 4:3; 2 Tim. 2:15; 2 Pet. 1:10; 3:14.

4:12 *the word of God.* Here meaning His inspired word, the Scriptures. *quick, and powerful.* Lit., living and operative. It has the power to reach to the inmost parts of one's personality and discerns (lit., judges) the innermost thoughts.

4:13 *with whom we have to do.* Better, to whom we must give an account—lit., to whom is our word, a play on the word "word"; i.e., if our lives conform to the *word of God* (v. 12) then our word (account) in the day of judgment will be acceptable to God.

4:15 *but was in all points tempted like as we are, yet without sin.* This does not mean that Christ experienced every temptation man does, but rather that He was tempted in all areas in which

16 Let us therefore come boldly unto the throne of grace, that we may obtain mercy, and find grace to help in time of need.

II THE SUPERIORITY OF
THE PRIESTHOOD OF CHRIST, 5:1–10:39

A Christ Is Superior in His Qualifications, 5:1–10

5 For every high priest taken from among men is ordained for men in things *pertaining* to God, that he may offer both gifts and sacrifices for sins:

2 Who can have compassion on the ignorant, and on them that are out of the way; for that he himself also is compassed with infirmity.

3 And by reason hereof he ought, as for the people, so also for himself, to offer for sins.

4 And no man taketh this honour unto himself, but he that is called of God, as *was* Aaron.

5 So also Christ glorified not himself to be made an high priest; but he that said unto him, Thou art my Son, to day have I begotten thee.

6 As he saith also in another *place*, Thou *art* a priest for ever after the order of Melchis'edec.

7 Who in the days of his flesh, when he had offered up prayers and supplications with strong crying and tears unto him that was able to save him from death, and was heard in that he feared;

man is tempted (the lust of the flesh, the lust of the eyes, and the pride of life, 1 John 2:16), but with particular temptations specially suited to Him. This testing was possible only because He took the likeness of sinful flesh (Rom. 8:3), for had there not been an incarnation there would have been no temptation (Jas. 1:13). Yet our Lord was distinct from all other men in that He was "apart from sin"; i.e., He possessed no sin nature as we do. Because He endured and successfully passed His tests, He can now offer us mercy and grace to help in time of need, for He knows what we are going through.

5:1–10 The qualifications for high priest are stated in these verses, Aaron serving as the model.

5:4 See Ex. 28:1.

5:5 Quoting Ps. 2:7.

5:6 Quoting Ps. 110:4.

5:7 *Who.* I.e., Christ, referring back to v. 5. *Offered up prayers and supplications with strong crying and tears*: referring to occasions like John 12:27 and the experience in Gethsemane (Matt. 26:39–44).

8 Though he were a Son, yet learned he obedience by the things which he suffered;

9 And being made perfect, he became the author of eternal salvation unto all them that obey him;

10 Called of God an high priest after the order of Melchis'edec.

B Parenthetical Warning:
Don't Degenerate from Christ, 5:11–6:20

11 Of whom we have many things to say, and hard to be uttered, seeing ye are dull of hearing.

12 For when for the time ye ought to be teachers, ye have need that one teach you again which *be* the first principles of the oracles of God; and are become such as have need of milk, and not of strong meat.

13 For every one that useth milk *is* unskilful in the word of righteousness: for he is a babe.

14 But strong meat belongeth to them that are of full age, *even* those who by reason of use have their senses exercised to discern both good and evil.

6 Therefore leaving the principles of the doctrine of Christ, let us go on unto perfection; not laying again the foundation of repentance from dead works, and of faith toward God,

5:8 *Though he were*=Even though He was.

5:9 *author*=cause or source (not the same word that is translated "captain" in 2:10).

5:10 *after the order of Melchisedec.* Our Lord could never have been a Levitical priest because He was born of the tribe of Judah (7:14) and not the tribe of Levi. Thus He must be associated with another order of priests, that of Melchisedec. Both Christ and Melchisedec were men (Heb. 7:4; 1 Tim. 2:5); both were king-priests (Gen. 14:18; Zech. 6:12–13); both were appointed by God (Heb. 7:21); both were called King of righteousness and King of peace (Isa. 11:5–9; Heb. 7:1).

5:12 *when for the time.* Better, although by now, i.e., in consideration of the time they had been believers. *milk*=elementary truth (see 1 Cor. 3:1–3).

5:13 *unskilful.* Lit., without experience.

5:14 *them that are of full age.* Lit., mature. Christian maturity involves (1) time (v. 12); (2) growth in the knowledge of the Word of God (v. 13); (3) experience in the use of the Word in discerning between good and evil (vv. 13–14). *senses exercised.* I.e., perceptions trained.

6:1 *principles of the doctrine of Christ.* I.e., the basic teachings

2 Of the doctrine of baptisms, and of laying on of hands, and of resurrection of the dead, and of eternal judgment.

3 And this will we do, if God permit.

4 For *it is* impossible for those who were once enlightened, and have tasted of the heavenly gift, and were made partakers of the Holy Ghost,

5 And have tasted the good word of God, and the powers of the world to come,

6 If they shall fall away, to renew them again unto repentance; seeing they crucify to themselves the Son of God afresh, and put *him* to an open shame.

7 For the earth which drinketh in the rain that cometh oft upon it, and bringeth forth herbs meet for them by whom it is dressed, receiveth blessing from God:

8 But that which beareth thorns and briers *is* rejected, and *is* nigh unto cursing: whose end *is* to be burned.

about Christ and the Christian religion. *perfection.* Lit., maturity, The exhortation to these people is to go on to Christian maturity and to stop wasting time and opportunities. They know the first principles or basics of Christianity and are being exhorted to go on from there. *dead works.* I.e., sins.

6:2 *the doctrine of baptisms.* The distinction between various baptisms is a necessary part of basic Christian doctrine (e.g., the baptism of Jewish proselytes, John the Baptist's baptism, Christian baptism).

6:4–6 This much-debated passage has been understood in several ways. (1) Armenians hold that the people described in these verses are redeemed people who actually lose their salvation. If this be so, notice that the passage also teaches that it is impossible to be saved a second time. (2) Some hold that the passage refers not to genuine believers but to those who only profess to be believers. Thus the phrases in vv. 4–5 are understood to refer to experiences short of salvation. The "falling away" is from the knowledge of the truth, not the personal possession of it. (3) Others understand the passage to be a warning to genuine believers to urge them on in Christian growth and maturity. *If they shall fall away* is impossible (since according to this view true believers are eternally secure), but it is placed in the sentence to strengthen the warning. It is similar to saying something like this to a class of students: "It is impossible for a student once enrolled in this course, if he turns the clock back, to start the course over. Therefore, let all students go on to deeper knowledge." In this view the phrases in vv. 4–5 are understood to refer to the conversion experience. Notice how the words are used elsewhere in Hebrews: "illuminated" (enlightened) in 10:32, "tasted" in 2:9, and "partakers" in 12:8.

9 But, beloved, we are persuaded better things of you, and things that accompany salvation, though we thus speak.

10 For God *is* not unrighteous to forget your work and labour of love, which ye have shewed toward his name, in that ye have ministered to the saints, and do minister.

11 And we desire that every one of you do shew the same diligence to the full assurance of hope unto the end:

12 That ye be not slothful, but followers of them who through faith and patience inherit the promises.

13 For when God made promise to Abraham, because he could swear by no greater, he sware by himself,

14 Saying, Surely blessing I will bless thee, and multiplying I will multiply thee.

15 And so, after he had patiently endured, he obtained the promise.

16 For men verily swear by the greater: and an oath for confirmation *is* to them an end of all strife.

17 Wherein God, willing more abundantly to shew unto the heirs of promise the immutability of his counsel, confirmed *it* by an oath:

18 That by two immutable things, in which *it was* impossible for God to lie, we might have a strong consolation, who have fled for refuge to lay hold upon the hope set before us:

19 Which *hope* we have as an anchor of the soul, both sure and stedfast, and which entereth into that within the veil;

20 Whither the forerunner is for us entered, *even* Jesus, made an high priest for ever after the order of Melchis'edec.

6:9 This verse is an expression of confidence, though the writer speaks severely. *things that accompany salvation*=fruit in the Christian life.

6:12 *slothful*=dull.

6:14 See Gen. 22:16–17.

6:16 *and an oath for confirmation is to them an end of all strife.* Better, in all their disputes, an oath is final for confirmation.

6:17 *counsel*=purpose.

6:18 *two immutable things*=the promise made to Abraham and the oath which rests on the very being of God.

6:19 *within the veil.* I.e., in the presence of God. Believers have as strong encouragement as Abraham had in his time because Jesus has already entered into the presence of God and assures us of our entrance into heaven as well.

6:20 *forerunner.* A word used of a scout reconnoitering or of a herald announcing the coming of a king; both concepts imply that others are to follow.

**C Christ Is Superior
in the Order of His Priesthood, 7:1–8:13**

1 *The portrait of Melchisedec*, 7:1–3

7 For this Melchis'edec, king of Salem, priest of the
most high God, who met Abraham returning from the
slaughter of the kings, and blessed him;

2 To whom also Abraham gave a tenth part of all; first
being by interpretation King of righteousness, and after
that also King of Salem, which is, King of peace;

3 Without father, without mother, without descent,
having neither beginning of days, nor end of life; but
made like unto the Son of God; abideth a priest continually.

**2 *The preeminence
of the Melchisedec priesthood*, 7:4–8:13**

4 Now consider how great this man *was*, unto whom
even the patriarch Abraham gave the tenth of the spoils.

5 And verily they that are of the sons of Levi, who
receive the office of the priesthood, have a commandment
to take tithes of the people according to the law, that is,
of their brethren, though they come out of the loins of
Abraham:

6 But he whose descent is not counted from them
received tithes of Abraham, and blessed him that had the
promises.

7 And without all contradiction the less is blessed of
the better.

7:1 *Melchisedec* is clearly a type of Christ. Everything known
about him from the O.T. is found in Gen. 14:17–20 and Ps.
110:4. He was a great king-priest, and it is to his order of
priesthood that Christ belongs. *slaughter of the kings.* See
Gen. 14:1–16.

7:3 *Without father* . . . This does not mean that Melchisedec
had no parents or that he was not born or did not die, but
only that the Scriptures contain no record of these events so
that he might be more perfectly likened to Christ.

7:4 *gave the tenth.* By taking the role of the one who tithed and
the one who received the blessing (v. 1), Abraham, to whom
God gave the promises, doubly acknowledged his inferiority to
Melchisedec.

7:6 The proof that the Melchisedec priesthood (and Christ's)
is superior to the Aaronic or Levitical priesthood is that Levi's
great-grandfather Abraham paid tithes to Melchisedec, and
Levi, though unborn, was involved (v. 9).

8 And here men that die receive tithes; but there he *receiveth them*, of whom it is witnessed that he liveth.

9 And as I may so say, Levi also, who receiveth tithes, payed tithes in Abraham.

10 For he was yet in the loins of his father, when Melchis'edec met him.

11 If therefore perfection were by the Levitical priesthood, (for under it the people received the law,) what further need *was there* that another priest should rise after the order of Melchis'edec, and not be called after the order of Aaron?

12 For the priesthood being changed, there is made of necessity a change also of the law.

13 For he of whom these things are spoken pertaineth to another tribe, of which no man gave attendance at the altar.

14 For *it is* evident that our Lord sprang out of Juda; of which tribe Moses spake nothing concerning priesthood.

15 And it is yet far more evident: for that after the similitude of Melchis'edec there ariseth another priest,

16 Who is made, not after the law of a carnal commandment, but after the power of an endless life.

17 For he testifieth, Thou *art* a priest for ever after the order of Melchis'edec.

18 For there is verily a disannulling of the commandment going before for the weakness and unprofitableness thereof.

19 For the law made nothing perfect, but the bringing in of a better hope *did*; by the which we draw nigh unto God.

20 And inasmuch as not without an oath *he was made priest*:

21 (For those priests were made without an oath; but this with an oath by him that said unto him, The Lord sware and will not repent, Thou *art* a priest for ever after the order of Melchis'edec:)

7:8 *here men that die* refers to the Levitical priests, *there* refers to Melchisedec and his priesthood.

7:11 Another proof that Christ is superior to the law and its priesthood is that the law could not give the people *perfection*, i.e., complete communion with God. The sacrificial, Levitical system never achieved its aim.

7:12 For Paul's different argument on the abrogation of the Mosaic law, see Rom. 7:1–6; 2 Cor. 3:7–11; Gal. 3:19–25.

7:18 *disannulling*=abrogation or annulment. A *better hope* (v. 19) for effecting full and final removal of sin has been introduced, along with a new way of access to God.

22 By so much was Jesus made a surety of a better testament.

23 And they truly were many priests, because they were not suffered to continue by reason of death:

24 But this *man*, because he continueth ever, hath an unchangeable priesthood.

25 Wherefore he is able also to save them to the uttermost that come unto God by him, seeing he ever liveth to make intercession for them.

26 For such an high priest became us, *who is* holy, harmless, undefiled, separate from sinners, and made higher than the heavens;

27 Who needeth not daily, as those high priests, to offer up sacrifice, first for his own sins, and then for the people's: for this he did once, when he offered up himself.

28 For the law maketh men high priests which have infirmity; but the word of the oath, which was since the law, *maketh* the Son, who is consecrated for evermore.

8 Now of the things which we have spoken *this is* the sum: We have such an high priest, who is set on the right hand of the throne of the Majesty in the heavens;

2 A minister of the sanctuary, and of the true tabernacle, which the Lord pitched, and not man.

3 For every high priest is ordained to offer gifts and sacrifices: wherefore *it is* of necessity that this man have somewhat also to offer.

4 For if he were on earth, he should not be a priest, seeing that there are priests that offer gifts according to the law:

5 Who serve unto the example and shadow of heavenly things, as Moses was admonished of God when he was about to make the tabernacle: for, See, saith he, *that* thou make all things according to the pattern shewed to thee in the mount.

6 But now hath he obtained a more excellent ministry,

7:25 *to the uttermost*=completely and eternally. Christ's priesthood has authority (vv. 20–22) and permanence.
8:1 *the sum*=the chief point (of what follows). A priest must have something to offer (v. 3) and a sanctuary in which to do it. Christ was disqualified from using the earthly sanctuary because of His descent from the tribe of Judah; therefore, His sphere of service must be heaven (v. 2).
8:5 *the pattern*. See Ex. 25:40.
8:6 The covenant Christ mediates is a better covenant since it is enacted on better promises. In vv. 6–13 the new covenant is

by how much also he is the mediator of a better covenant, which was established upon better promises.

7 For if that first *covenant* had been faultless, then should no place have been sought for the second.

8 For finding fault with them, he saith, Behold, the days come, saith the Lord, when I will make a new covenant with the house of Israel and with the house of Judah:

9 Not according to the covenant that I made with their fathers in the day when I took them by the hand to lead them out of the land of Egypt; because they continued not in my covenant, and I regarded them not, saith the Lord.

10 For this *is* the covenant that I will make with the house of Israel after those days, saith the Lord; I will put my laws into their mind, and write them in their hearts: and I will be to them a God, and they shall be to me a people:

11 And they shall not teach every man his neighbour, and every man his brother, saying, Know the Lord: for all shall know me, from the least to the greatest.

12 For I will be merciful to their unrighteousness, and their sins and their iniquities will I remember no more.

13 In that he saith, A new *covenant*, he hath made the first old. Now that which decayeth and waxeth old *is* ready to vanish away.

D Christ Is Superior in His Priestly Ministry, 9:1–10:18

    1 *The earthly priesthood*, 9:1–10

9 Then verily the first *covenant* had also ordinances of divine service, and a worldly sanctuary.

2 For there was a tabernacle made; the first, wherein *was* the candlestick, and the table, and the shewbread; which is called the sanctuary.

3 And after the second veil, the tabernacle which is called the Holiest of all;

contrasted with "that first covenant" (v. 7); i.e., the Mosaic law (Ex. 19:5). Christ's blood is the basis of the new covenant (Matt. 26:28); Christians are ministers of it (2 Cor. 3:6); and it will yet have an aspect of its fulfillment in relation to Israel and Judah in the millennium (as predicted in Jer. 31:31–34).

8:8–11 Quoting Jer. 31:31–34.
8:10 *to me a*=my.
9:1 *worldly*=earthly.

4 Which had the golden censer, and the ark of the covenant overlaid round about with gold, wherein *was* the golden pot that had manna, and Aaron's rod that budded, and the tables of the covenant;

5 And over it the cher'ūbims of glory shadowing the mercyseat; of which we cannot now speak particularly.

6 Now when these things were thus ordained, the priests went always into the first tabernacle, accomplishing the service of God.

7 But into the second *went* the high priest alone once every year, not without blood, which he offered for himself, and *for* the errors of the people:

8 The Holy Ghost this signifying, that the way into the holiest of all was not yet made manifest, while as the first tabernacle was yet standing:

9 Which *was* a figure for the time then present, in which were offered both gifts and sacrifices, that could not make him that did the service perfect, as pertaining to the conscience;

10 Which *stood* only in meats and drinks, and divers washings, and carnal ordinances, imposed *on them* until the time of reformation.

2 Christ's priesthood, 9:11–14

11 But Christ being come an high priest of good things to come, by a greater and more perfect tabernacle, not made with hands, that is to say, not of this building;

12 Neither by the blood of goats and calves, but by his own blood he entered in once into the holy place, having obtained eternal redemption *for us*.

13 For if the blood of bulls and of goats, and the ashes of an heifer sprinkling the unclean, sanctifieth to the purifying of the flesh:

9:4 *the golden censer*. Better, the golden altar. Though the altar stood before the veil in the Holy Place, its ritual use was connected with the *Holiest of all* (lit., Holy of Holies (v. 3), especially on the Day of Atonement which is being described in these verses (see Lev. 16:12–13).

9:5 *particularly*=in detail.

9:7–10 The fact that the high priest only could go into the Holy of Holies and that he had to go each year signified that no final offering for sin was made in O.T. times and that the offerings that were made could not cleanse the conscience. *carnal ordinances*=regulations concerning the body. *reformation*. I.e., the change brought about by the completed sacrifice of Christ and His entering into heaven (vv. 11–12).

9:12 *by . . . by*. Better, through . . . through.

14 How much more shall the blood of Christ, who through the eternal Spirit offered himself without spot to God, purge your conscience from dead works to serve the living God?

3 Christ's fulfillment of the promise, 9:15–10:18

15 And for this cause he is the mediator of the new testament, that by means of death, for the redemption of the transgressions *that were* under the first testament, they which are called might receive the promise of eternal inheritance.

16 For where a testament *is*, there must also of necessity be the death of the testator.

17 For a testament *is* of force after men are dead: otherwise it is of no strength at all while the testator liveth.

18 Whereupon neither the first *testament* was dedicated without blood.

19 For when Moses had spoken every precept to all the people according to the law, he took the blood of calves and of goats, with water, and scarlet wool, and hyssop, and sprinkled both the book, and all the people,

20 Saying, This *is* the blood of the testament which God hath enjoined unto you.

21 Moreover he sprinkled with blood both the tabernacle, and all the vessels of the ministry.

22 And almost all things are by the law purged with blood; and without shedding of blood is no remission.

23 *It was* therefore necessary that the patterns of things in the heavens should be purified with these; but the heavenly things themselves with better sacrifices than these.

24 For Christ is not entered into the holy places made with hands, *which are* the figures of the true; but into heaven itself, now to appear in the presence of God for us:

9:15–16 *testament*. Better, covenant, as in O.T. usage.
9:16 *testator*. The one who made the covenant or will. This is strong proof that it is the death of Christ, not His life, which put into effect the new covenant with all its blessings. His sinless life qualified Him to be the suitable sacrifice for sin, but it was His death that made the payment for sin.
9:21 *he sprinkled*. See Ex. 29:12, 36.
9:22 *almost*. For exceptions to the requirement of blood for cleansing permitted by the law see Lev. 5:11–13; Num. 16:46; 31:50. *purged*=purified.

25 Nor yet that he should offer himself often, as the high priest entereth into the holy place every year with blood of others;

26 For then must he often have suffered since the foundation of the world: but now once in the end of the world hath he appeared to put away sin by the sacrifice of himself.

27 And as it is appointed unto men once to die, but after this the judgment:

28 So Christ was once offered to bear the sins of many; and unto them that look for him shall he appear the second time without sin unto salvation.

10 For the law having a shadow of good things to come, *and* not the very image of the things, can never with those sacrifices which they offered year by year continually make the comers thereunto perfect.

2 For then would they not have ceased to be offered? because that the worshippers once purged should have had no more conscience of sins.

3 But in those *sacrifices there is* a remembrance again *made* of sins every year.

4 For *it is* not possible that the blood of bulls and of goats should take away sins.

5 Wherefore when he cometh into the world, he saith, Sacrifice and offering thou wouldest not, but a body hast thou prepared me:

6 In burnt offerings and *sacrifices* for sin thou hast had no pleasure.

7 Then said I, Lo, I come (in the volume of the book it is written of me,) to do thy will, O God.

9:26 *once*=once for all. *the end of the world.* Lit., the end of the ages (1 Pet. 1:20). The first advent of Christ was a consummation of the ages.

9:28 *to bear the sins of many.* Quoted from Isa. 53:12, a significant source of early Christian interpretation of Christ. *without sin.* I.e., apart from the sin question. In His first coming Christ dealt with sin once for all; in His second coming He will take redeemed sinners to Himself in the consummation of their salvation.

10:1–39 In this chapter the author emphasizes the finality of Christ's sacrifice by contrasting it with the lack of finality of the O.T. system of law and sacrifices. Christ's redemption needs no repetition and no supplementation. Therefore, rejection of His sacrifice is final and unforgivable.

10:5–7 Quoting Ps. 40:6–8. *he cometh* (v. 5). I.e., Christ.

8 Above when he said, Sacrifice and offering and burnt offerings and *offering* for sin thou wouldest not, neither hadst pleasure *therein;* which are offered by the law;

9 Then said he, Lo, I come to do thy will, O God. He taketh away the first, that he may establish the second.

10 By the which will we are sanctified through the offering of the body of Jesus Christ once *for all.*

11 And every priest standeth daily ministering and offering oftentimes the same sacrifices, which can never take away sins:

12 But this man, after he had offered one sacrifice for sins for ever, sat down on the right hand of God;

13 From henceforth expecting till his enemies be made his footstool.

14 For by one offering he hath perfected for ever them that are sanctified.

15 *Whereof* the Holy Ghost also is a witness to us: for after that he had said before,

16 This *is* the covenant that I will make with them after those days, saith the Lord, I will put my laws into their hearts, and in their minds will I write them;

17 And their sins and iniquities will I remember no more.

18 Now where remission of these *is, there is* no more offering for sin.

E Parenthetical Warning: Don't Despise Christ, 10:19-39

19 Having therefore, brethren, boldness to enter into the holiest by the blood of Jesus,

20 By a new and living way, which he hath consecrated for us, through the veil, that is to say, his flesh;

21 And *having* an high priest over the house of God;

22 Let us draw near with a true heart in full assurance of faith, having our hearts sprinkled from an evil conscience, and our bodies washed with pure water.

23 Let us hold fast the profession of *our* faith without wavering; (for he *is* faithful that promised;)

24 And let us consider one another to provoke unto love and to good works:

10:10 *By the which will.* I.e., by Christ's doing the will of God in becoming the sacrifice for sin.

10:16-17 See Jer. 31:33-34, quoted earlier in Heb. 8:10-12.

10:20 *a new and living way.* Christ is that way (compare John 14:6; Heb. 4:14; 6:20; 7:24-25).

10:23 *the profession of our faith.* Lit., the confession of our hope.

10:24 *to provoke.* I.e., to stir up to an incitement or paroxysm

25 Not forsaking the assembling of ourselves together, as the manner of some *is*; but exhorting *one another*: and so much the more, as ye see the day approaching.

26 For if we sin wilfully after that we have received the knowledge of the truth, there remaineth no more sacrifice for sins,

27 But a certain fearful looking for of judgment and fiery indignation, which shall devour the adversaries.

28 He that despised Moses' law died without mercy under two or three witnesses:

29 Of how much sorer punishment, suppose ye, shall he be thought worthy, who hath trodden under foot the Son of God, and hath counted the blood of the covenant, wherewith he was sanctified, an unholy thing, and hath done despite unto the Spirit of grace?

30 For we know him that hath said, Vengeance *belongeth* unto me, I will recompense, saith the Lord. And again, The Lord shall judge his people.

31 *It is* a fearful thing to fall into the hands of the living God.

32 But call to remembrance the former days, in which, after ye were illuminated, ye endured a great fight of afflictions;

33 Partly, whilst ye were made a gazingstock both by reproaches and afflictions; and partly, whilst ye became companions of them that were so used.

34 For ye had compassion of me in my bonds, and took joyfully the spoiling of your goods, knowing in yourselves that ye have in heaven a better and an enduring substance.

---

of love and good works. To understand how strong this word is, see its use in Acts 15:39; 17:16; 1 Cor. 13:5; Eph. 6:4.

10:25 *the assembling of ourselves together*. The gathering of Christians for worship and edification. *the day*. I.e., of Christ's coming (also v. 37; 1 Cor. 3:13; Phil. 1:10).

10:26 *there remaineth no more sacrifice for sins*. The meaning is this: If a person rejects the truth of Christ's death for sin, there is no other sacrifice for sin and no other way to come to God. Only judgment remains for such a person (v. 27).

10:27 *looking for*=prospect. *fiery indignation*=a furious fire.

10:29 *done despite unto*=insulted, outraged. The three indictments specified in this verse describe the enormity of his treacherous behavior.

10:30 Quoting from Deut. 32:35–36 and Ps. 135:14.

10:32 *fights of afflications*=struggle with sufferings.

10:33 *a gazingstock*=being publicly exposed to.

10:34 *of me in my bonds*. The better reading is "on the prisoners." Some apparently had been imprisoned for their faith

35 Cast not away therefore your confidence, which hath great recompence of reward.

36 For ye have need of patience, that, after ye have done the will of God, ye might receive the promise.

37 For yet a little while, and he that shall come will come, and will not tarry.

38 Now the just shall live by faith: but if *any man* draw back, my soul shall have no pleasure in him.

39 But we are not of them who draw back unto perdition; but of them that believe to the saving of the soul.

III THE SUPERIORITY OF
THE POWER OF CHRIST, 11:1–13:19

A The Power of Faith in Christ, 11:1–40

1 *The description of faith*, 11:1

11 Now faith is the substance of things hoped for, the evidence of things not seen.

2 *The examples of faith*, 11:2–40

2 For by it the elders obtained a good report.

3 Through faith we understand that the worlds were framed by the word of God, so that things which are seen were not made of things which do appear.

4 By faith Abel offered unto God a more excellent

---

while others had experienced the *spoiling* (=seizure) of their possessions.

10:36 *endurance*=patience.

10:37 See Hab. 2:3.

10:38 This is a quotation from Hab. 2:4 and is used here to mean that the person who has been made righteous by God ("the just") lives (and survives the coming ordeal) by faith. The believer trusts God in everything. Hab. 2:4 is also quoted in Rom. 1:17 and Gal. 3:11 where Paul takes it to mean "He who is righteous by faith (rather than by works) shall live." Paul's emphasis is on salvation by faith; this writer's is on living by faith.

11:1 Faith is described in this great verse as the *substance* (assurance or reality, the same word is translated "person" in 1:3) *of things hoped for, and the evidence* (proof, as in John 16:8) *of things not seen.* Faith gives reality and proof of things unseen, treating them as if they were already objects of sight rather than of hope.

11:2 *elders*=men of old, i.e., the O.T. patriarchs and heroes. *obtained a good report*=received divine approval.

sacrifice than Cain, by which he obtained witness that he was righteous, God testifying of his gifts: and by it he being dead yet speaketh.

5 By faith Enoch was translated that he should not see death; and was not found, because God had translated him: for before his translation he had this testimony, that he pleased God.

6 But without faith *it is* impossible to please *him*: for he that cometh to God must believe that he is, and *that* he is a rewarder of them that diligently seek him.

7 By faith Noah, being warned of God of things not seen as yet, moved with fear, prepared an ark to the saving of his house; by the which he condemned the world, and became heir of the righteousness which is by faith.

8 By faith Abraham, when he was called to go out into a place which he should after receive for an inheritance, obeyed; and he went out, not knowing whither he went.

9 By faith he sojourned in the land of promise, as *in* a strange country, dwelling in tabernacles with Isaac and Jacob, the heirs with him of the same promise:

10 For he looked for a city which hath foundations, whose builder and maker *is* God.

11 Through faith also Sara herself received strength to conceive seed, and was delivered of a child when she was past age, because she judged him faithful who had promised.

12 Therefore sprang there even of one, and him as good as dead, *so many* as the stars of the sky in multitude, and as the sand which is by the sea shore innumerable.

13 These all died in faith, not having received the promises, but having seen them afar off, and were persuaded of *them*, and embraced *them*, and confessed that they were strangers and pilgrims on the earth.

11:3 *the worlds were framed.* Lit., the ages have been prepared (as in 1:3). This means the preparation of all that the successive periods of time contain.

11:4 *Abel.* See Gen. 4:3–5. Actually nothing is said here or in Gen. as to why Abel's sacrifice was more acceptable, though the fact that it involved blood sacrifice is significant (see Heb. 12:24).

11:5 *Enoch.* See Gen. 5:22–24. Enoch was saved from death by being carried aloft (*translated*).

11:7 *Noah.* See Gen. 6:13–22. His *fear* was fear of God=piety.

11:8 *Abraham.* See Gen. 12:1–4.

11:9 *strange country.* Better, foreign country.

11:11 *Sara.* See Gen. 21:1–5.

14 For they that say such things declare plainly that they seek a country.

15 And truly, if they had been mindful of that *country* from whence they came out, they might have had opportunity to have returned.

16 But now they desire a better *country*, that is, an heavenly: wherefore God is not ashamed to be called their God: for he hath prepared for them a city.

17 By faith Abraham, when he was tried, offered up Isaac: and he that had received the promises offered up his only begotten *son*,

18 Of whom it was said, That in Isaac shall thy seed be called:

19 Accounting that God *was* able to raise *him* up, even from the dead; from whence also he received him in a figure.

20 By faith Isaac blessed Jacob and Esau concerning things to come.

21 By faith Jacob, when he was a dying, blessed both the sons of Joseph; and worshipped, *leaning* upon the top of his staff.

22 By faith Joseph, when he died, made mention of the departing of the children of Israel; and gave commandment concerning his bones.

23 By faith Moses, when he was born, was hid three months of his parents, because they saw *he was* a proper child; and they were not afraid of the king's commandment.

24 By faith Moses, when he was come to years, refused to be called the son of Phār′aōh's daughter;

25 Choosing rather to suffer affliction with the people of God, than to enjoy the pleasures of sin for a season;

26 Esteeming the reproach of Christ greater riches than the treasures in Egypt: for he had respect unto the recompence of the reward.

11:17 *when he was tried* (=tested), *offered up Isaac*. See Gen. 22:1; Jas. 2:21. This was a severe test, for only through Isaac could Abraham have enjoyed the promises of the Lord.

11:18 Quoting the last part of Gen. 21:12.

11:20 *Isaac blessed Jacob and Esau*. See Gen. 27:26–40.

11:21 *Jacob . . . blessed both the sons of Joseph*. See Gen. 48:1–22.

11:22 *Joseph*. See Gen. 50:24–25. *departing*=the Exodus (from Egypt). Joseph showed his faith in God's promise to Abraham by requesting that his bones be buried in the Land of Promise.

11:23 *Moses*. See Ex. 2:1–15. *proper child*=beautiful child.

27 By faith he forsook Egypt, not fearing the wrath of the king: for he endured, as seeing him who is invisible.

28 Through faith he kept the passover, and the sprinkling of blood, lest he that destroyed the firstborn should touch them.

29 By faith they passed through the Red sea as by dry land: which the Egyptians assaying to do were drowned.

30 By faith the walls of Jericho fell down, after they were compassed about seven days.

31 By faith the harlot Rahab perished not with them that believed not, when she had received the spies with peace.

32 And what shall I more say? for the time would fail me to tell of Gedeon, and of Barak, and of Samson, and of Jeph'thæ; of David also, and Samuel, and of the prophets:

33 Who through faith subdued kingdoms, wrought righteousness, obtained promises, stopped the mouths of lions,

34 Quenched the violence of fire, escaped the edge of the sword, out of weakness were made strong, waxed valiant in fight, turned to flight the armies of the aliens.

35 Women received their dead raised to life again: and others were tortured, not accepting deliverance; that they might obtain a better resurrection:

36 And others had trial of *cruel* mockings and scourgings, yea, moreover of bonds and imprisonment:

37 They were stoned, they were sawn asunder, were tempted, were slain with the sword: they wandered about in sheepskins and goatskins; being destitute, afflicted, tormented;

38 (Of whom the world was not worthy:) they wan-

11:28 *the passover.* See Ex. 12:1-28.
11:29 *they passed through the Red Sea.* See Ex. 14:13-31.
11:30 *the walls of Jericho fell down.* See Josh. 6.
11:31 *Rahab.* See Josh. 2:1-21; 6:22-25; Jas. 2:25.
11:32 *Gideon* (Judg. 6:11; 8:32); *Barak* (Judg. 4:6-5:31); *Samson* (Judg. 13:24-16:31); *Jephthah* (Judg. 11:1-12:7); *David* (1 Sam. 16-17); *Samuel* (1 Sam. 7-10).
11:33 *stopped the mouths of lions.* See Dan. 6 (Daniel); Judg. 14:5 (Samson); 1 Sam. 17:34 (David).
11:34 *quenched the violence of fire.* See Dan. 3:23-28.
11:35 *Women received their dead raised to life again.* See 1 Kings 17:22-23 (the widow of Zarephath's son); 2 Kings 4:35-36 (the Shunammite's son).
11:35-38 The background for much of what is in these verses is likely from 2 Macc. 6:18-7:42.

dered in deserts, and *in* mountains, and *in* dens and caves of the earth.

39 And these all, having obtained a good report through faith, received not the promise:

40 God having provided some better thing for us, that they without us should not be made perfect.

B The Power of Hope in Christ, 12:1–29

1 *The debatable things of life,* 12:1–2

12 Wherefore seeing we also are compassed about with so great a cloud of witnesses, let us lay aside every weight, and the sin which doth so easily beset *us*, and let us run with patience the race that is set before us,

2 Looking unto Jesus the author and finisher of *our* faith; who for the joy that was set before him endured the cross, despising the shame, and is set down at the right hand of the throne of God.

2 *The disciplines of life,* 12:3–11

3 For consider him that endured such contradiction of sinners against himself, lest ye be wearied and faint in your minds.

4 Ye have not yet resisted unto blood, striving against sin.

5 And ye have forgotten the exhortation which speaketh unto you as unto children, My son, despise not thou the chastening of the Lord, nor faint when thou art rebuked of him:

11:39 *the promise.* I.e., all that was included in the actual coming of the Messiah.

12:1 *a cloud of witnesses*=the heroes of faith mentioned in chapter 11 and others. *every weight*=the encumbrances which hinder the believer from being a winner. *the sin which does so easily beset us*=unbelief.

12:3 *him*=Jesus. *contradiction*=opposition.

12:4 *Ye have not yet resisted unto blood.* None of the readers of this book had yet been martyred at the hand of sinful persecutors.

12:5–11 In these verses the writer discusses why Christians are chastened (better, disciplined). (1) It is part of the educational process by which a believer is fitted to share God's holiness (v. 10). (2) It is proof of a genuine love-relationship between the heavenly Father and His children (vv. 6, 8). (3) It helps train us to be obedient (v. 9). (4) It produces the fruit of righteousness in the life (v. 11). Other teaching on this subject is found in the book of Job; Rom. 8:18; 2 Cor. 1:3–4; 4:16–17; 12:7–9; Phil. 1:29; 2 Tim. 3:12.

6 For whom the Lord loveth he chasteneth, and scourgeth every son whom he receiveth.

7 If ye endure chastening, God dealeth with you as with sons; for what son is he whom the father chasteneth not?

8 But if ye be without chastisement, whereof all are partakers, then are ye bastards, and not sons.

9 Furthermore we have had fathers of our flesh which corrected *us*, and we gave *them* reverence: shall we not much rather be in subjection unto the Father of spirits, and live?

10 For they verily for a few days chastened *us* after their own pleasure; but he for *our* profit, that *we* might be partakers of his holiness.

11 Now no chastening for the present seemeth to be joyous, but grievous: nevertheless afterward it yieldeth the peaceable fruit of righteousness unto them which are exercised thereby.

3 *The direction of life,* 12:12–17

12 Wherefore lift up the hands which hang down, and the feeble knees;

13 And make straight paths for your feet, lest that which is lame be turned out of the way; but let it rather be healed.

14 Follow peace with all *men*, and holiness, without which no man shall see the Lord:

15 Looking diligently lest any man fail of the grace of God; lest any root of bitterness springing up trouble *you*, and thereby many be defiled;

16 Lest there *be* any fornicator, or profane person, as Esau, who for one morsel of meat sold his birthright.

17 For ye know how that afterward, when he would have inherited the blessing, he was rejected: for he found no place of repentance, though he sought it carefully with tears.

4 *The drive of life,* 12:18–24

18 For ye are not come unto the mount that might be touched, and that burned with fire, nor unto blackness, and darkness, and tempest,

12:10 *after their own pleasure.* Better, as it seemed good to them.
12:16 *Esau.* See Gen. 25:33. Though he was not a fornicator in the physical sense, he was immoral in the religious sense, being a worldly, materialistically-minded person.
12:18–24 The old covenant (the law) and the new covenant

19 And the sound of a trumpet, and the voice of words; which *voice* they that heard intreated that the word should not be spoken to them any more:

20 (For they could not endure that which was commanded, And if so much as a beast touch the mountain, it shall be stoned, or thrust through with a dart:

21 And so terrible was the sight, *that* Moses said, I exceedingly fear and quake:)

22 But ye are come unto mount Sion, and unto the city of the living God, the heavenly Jerusalem, and to an innumerable company of angels,

23 To the general assembly and church of the firstborn, which are written in heaven, and to God the Judge of all, and to the spirits of just men made perfect,

24 And to Jesus the mediator of the new covenant, and to the blood of sprinkling, that speaketh better things than *that of* Abel.

5 The duty of life, 12:25–29

25 See that ye refuse not him that speaketh. For if they escaped not who refused him that spake on earth, much more *shall not* we *escape*, if we turn away from him that *speaketh* from heaven:

26 Whose voice then shook the earth: but now he hath promised, saying, Yet once more I shake not the earth only, but also heaven.

27 And this *word*, Yet once more, signifieth the removing of those things that are shaken, as of things that are made, that those things which cannot be shaken may remain.

28 Wherefore we receiving a kingdom which cannot be moved, let us have grace, whereby we may serve God acceptably with reverence and godly fear:

29 For our God *is* a consuming fire.

are contrasted by comparing Mt. Sinai, where the law was given, with Mt. Zion, the spiritual city, eternal in the heavens.

12:23 *church of the firstborn.* Lit., church of firstborn ones. This refers to N.T. believers who belong to the church, the body of Christ. *spirits of just men made perfect.* These are believers of O.T. times.

12:26 Quoting Hag. 2:6.

12:27 *those things which cannot be shaken.* I.e., the eternal kingdom to which Christians belong (v. 28).

C The Power of the Love of Christ, 13:1–19

1 *In relation to social duties*, 13:1–6

13 Let brotherly love continue.
2 Be not forgetful to entertain strangers: for thereby some have entertained angels unawares.

3 Remember them that are in bonds, as bound with them; *and* them which suffer adversity, as being yourselves also in the body.

4 Marriage *is* honourable in all, and the bed undefiled: but whoremongers and adulterers God will judge.

5 *Let your* conversation *be* without covetousness; *and be* content with such things as ye have: for he hath said, I will never leave thee, nor forsake thee.

6 So that we may boldly say, The Lord *is* my helper, and I will not fear what man shall do unto me.

2 *In relation to spiritual duties*, 13:7–19

7 Remember them which have the rule over you, who have spoken unto you the word of God: whose faith follow, considering the end of *their* conversation.

8 Jesus Christ the same yesterday, and to day, and for ever.

9 Be not carried about with divers and strange doctrines. For *it is* a good thing that the heart be established with grace; not with meats, which have not profited them that have been occupied therein.

10 We have an altar, whereof they have no right to eat which serve the tabernacle.

11 For the bodies of those beasts, whose blood is brought into the sanctuary by the high priest for sin, are burned without the camp.

12 Wherefore Jesus also, that he might sanctify the people with his own blood, suffered without the gate.

13 Let us go forth therefore unto him without the camp, bearing his reproach.

13:2 *some have entertained angels unawares* (=unconsciously). The word "angel" may refer to superhuman beings (see Gen. 18:1–8 for an example of such entertaining) or it may refer to a human being who is a messenger from God (see Jas. 2:25 for an example of such entertaining).
13:4 *Marriage is honourable*=Let marriage be honorable.
13:5 *conversation*=way of life. *he hath said.* See Deut. 31:6. The idea is: Christians need not be anxious (Matt. 6:24–34).
13:11 *without the camp.* See Lev. 4:21; 16:27.
13:12 *Jesus . . . suffered without the gate.* See John 19:17–20.
13:16 *communicate.* I.e., share what you have (Phil. 4:18).

14 For here have we no continuing city, but we seek one to come.

15 By him therefore let us offer the sacrifice of praise to God continually, that is, the fruit of *our* lips giving thanks to his name.

16 But to do good and to communicate forget not: for with such sacrifices God is well pleased.

17 Obey them that have the rule over you, and submit yourselves: for they watch for your souls, as they that must give account, that they may do it with joy, and not with grief: for that *is* unprofitable for you.

18 Pray for us: for we trust we have a good conscience, in all things willing to live honestly.

19 But I beseech *you* the rather to do this, that I may be restored to you the sooner.

IV CONCLUDING BENEDICTIONS, 13:20–25

20 Now the God of peace, that brought again from the dead our Lord Jesus, that great shepherd of the sheep, through the blood of the everlasting covenant,

21 Make you perfect in every good work to do his will, working in you that which is wellpleasing in his sight, through Jesus Christ; to whom *be* glory for ever and ever. Amen.

22 And I beseech you, brethren, suffer the word of exhortation: for I have written a letter unto you in few words.

23 Know ye that *our* brother Timothy is set at liberty; with whom, if he come shortly, I will see you.

24 Salute all them that have the rule over you, and all the saints. They of Italy salute you.

25 Grace *be* with you all. Amen.

13:17 *have the rule over you.* Lit., lead you. This refers to church leaders as also in v. 7. *unprofitable to you*=not to your advantage.

13:21 *make you perfect*=equip, fully provide, adjust, make ready. Some other occurrences are in Matt. 4:21; Gal. 6:1; 1 Thess. 3:10.

13:22 *suffer*=be patient with. *in few words*=briefly, and perhaps also outspokenly.

13:23 *Timothy.* See Acts 16:1; Rom. 16:21. Apparently he had been imprisoned.

13:24 *all them that have the rule over you.* I.e., all your leaders. *saints*=believers.

INTRODUCTION TO
THE LETTER OF
James

AUTHOR: James   DATE: 45–50

The General Epistles   *James, 1 and 2 Peter, 1, 2, and 3 John, and Jude* were called by the early church the "General," "Universal," or "Catholic Epistles" because their addressees (with the exceptions of 2 and 3 John) were not limited to a single locality. James, for example, is addressed "to the twelve tribes which are scattered abroad" (1:1)—a designation for believers everywhere (likely all Jewish Christians at that early date).

The Author   *Of the four men bearing the name James in the New Testament, only two have been proposed as the author of this letter, James the son of Zebedee (and brother of John) and James the half-brother of Jesus. It is unlikely that the son of Zebedee was the author, for he was martyred in A.D. 44 (Acts 12:2). The authoritative tone of the letter not only rules out the two lesser known Jameses of the New Testament ("James the less" and the James of Luke 6:16) but points to the half-brother of Jesus who became the recognized leader of the Jerusalem church (Acts 12:17; 15:13; 21:18). This conclusion is supported by the resemblances in the Greek between this epistle and the speech of James at the Council of Jerusalem (1:1 and Acts 15:23; 1:27 and Acts 15:14; 2:5 and Acts 15:13; 2:7 and Acts 15:17). Furthermore, in the 108 verses of the epistle there are references or allusions from 22 books of the Old Testament and at least 15 allusions to the teachings of Christ which became embodied in the Sermon on the Mount.*

The Date   *Some, denying the authorship by James because of the excellent Greek, place the writing of the book at the very end of the first century. However, Galileans knew and used Greek well along with Aramaic and Hebrew. Further,* an early date is indicated by the lack of reference to the Jerusalem council (A.D. 49), by the use of the word "synagogue" for the church in 2:2, and by the strong expectation of the Lord's return (5:7–9).

Canonicity The canonical status of this letter was questioned until the church realized that its author was almost surely James the half-brother of Jesus. Luther did not question the genuineness of James, only its usefulness in comparison with Paul's epistles, because it says little about justification by faith, while elevating works.

The Contents The book is concerned with the practical aspects of Christian conduct; it tells how faith works in everyday life. James's purpose was to provide concrete ethical instruction. Compared to Paul, James shows much less interest in formal theology, though the letter is not without its theological statements (1:12; 2:1, 10–12, 19; 3:9; 5:7–9, 12, 14). Many subjects are discussed in this book, making it like a series of brief sayings arranged in the form of a letter. While there is little formal structure to the book, its many instructions explain how to be doers of the Word (1:22). Among the subjects discussed. are faith and works (2:14–26) the use of the tongue (3:1–12), and prayer for the sick (5:13–16).

OUTLINE OF JAMES

THE LETTER OF

James

I GREETING, 1:1

1 James, a servant of God and of the Lord Jesus Christ, to the twelve tribes which are scattered abroad, greeting.

II ON TRIALS, 1:2–18

A The Purpose of Trials, 1:2–12

2 My brethren, count it all joy when ye fall into divers temptations;

3 Knowing *this*, that the trying of your faith worketh patience.

4 But let patience have *her* perfect work, that ye may be perfect and entire, wanting nothing.

5 If any of you lack wisdom, let him ask of God, that giveth to all *men* liberally, and upbraideth not; and it shall be given him.

6 But let him ask in faith, nothing wavering. For he that wavereth is like a wave of the sea driven with the wind and tossed.

7 For let not that man think that he shall receive any thing of the Lord.

8 A double minded man *is* unstable in all his ways.

1:1 *to the twelve tribes which are scattered abroad.* The letter is addressed to Jews scattered throughout the world, though the author, realizing that the letter would be read chiefly by Christians, addresses most of his sayings to them.

1:2 *divers*=various.

1:3 *patience*=steadfastness, endurance.

1:5 *upbraideth not*=without reproaching.

1:6 *wavering* means to go back and forth between belief and unbelief (Rom. 4:20).

1:8 A *double minded man*=a man of divided allegiance.

9 Let the brother of low degree rejoice in that he is exalted:

10 But the rich, in that he is made low: because as the flower of the grass he shall pass away.

11 For the sun is no sooner risen with a burning heat, but it withereth the grass, and the flower thereof falleth, and the grace of the fashion of it perisheth: so also shall the rich man fade away in his ways.

12 Blessed *is* the man that endureth temptation: for when he is tried, he shall receive the crown of life, which the Lord hath promised to them that love him.

B The Pedigree of Trials, 1:13–16

13 Let no man say when he is tempted, I am tempted of God: for God cannot be tempted with evil, neither tempteth he any man:

14 But every man is tempted, when he is drawn away of his own lust, and enticed.

15 Then when lust hath conceived, it bringeth forth sin: and sin, when it is finished, bringeth forth death.

16 Do not err, my beloved brethren.

C The Purpose of God, 1:17–18

17 Every good gift and every perfect gift is from above, and cometh down from the Father of lights, with whom is no variableness, neither shadow of turning.

1:10 *made low*. Either by losing his money or by being brought through some circumstance to realize that money means little and is at best transitory.

1:12 *temptation*. Better, trial. *when he is tried*. Better, when he has stood the test. *crown of life*. One of the rewards or prizes for the Christian, kingly glory and life. See note at 1 Cor. 3:14.

1:13 *tempted*. To tempt is to test, try, prove, or solicit to evil. In vv. 2 and 12 the word is used to mean trials which are designed to prove the quality of one's character. In this verse the same word means "a solicitation to evil," and this, James says, is not from God but from man's own inner lust. The man seeks a self-excuse based on ignorance of both God and the nature of temptation.

1:14 *drawn away . . . enticed*. The picture behind these words is that of the hunter or fisherman luring his prey from its safe retreat.

1:16 *Do not err*. Lit., be not deceived, used also in 1 Cor. 6:9; 15:33; Gal. 6:7.

1:17 *Every good gift*. The word means both the gift and the act of giving. The point is that these good things come from above. This statement may have come from an early Christian hymn.

18 Of his own will begat he us with the word of truth, that we should be a kind of firstfruits of his creatures.

III ON THE WORD, 1:19-27

19 Wherefore, my beloved brethren, let every man be swift to hear, slow to speak, slow to wrath:

20 For the wrath of man worketh not the righteousness of God.

21 Wherefore lay apart all filthiness and superfluity of naughtiness, and receive with meekness the engrafted word, which is able to save your souls.

22 But be ye doers of the word, and not hearers only, deceiving your own selves.

23 For if any be a hearer of the word, and not a doer, he is like unto a man beholding his natural face in a glass:

24 For he beholdeth himself, and goeth his way, and straightway forgetteth what manner of man he was.

25 But whoso looketh into the perfect law of liberty, and continueth *therein*, he being not a forgetful hearer, but a doer of the work, this man shall be blessed in his deed.

Father of lights. God is the source of all light in the physical, intellectual, moral, and spiritual realms, and He does not change.

1:18 *Of his own will.* God's own will or purpose is the cause of our regeneration (*begat he us*) by means of the gospel message. *firstfruits.* These first believers, largely Jewish in background, were the guarantee of a fuller harvest of believers to come.

1:21 *superfluity of naughtiness*=remainder of wickedness. *engrafted word*=implanted word, i.e., the gospel received as in v. 18, the word of truth.

1:23 *his natural face.* Lit., the face of his birth, his physical features. The contrast in vv. 23-25 is a simple one: the careless man looks in a mirror and forgets what he saw. The earnest man looks into the Word of God and acts upon what he sees there. *unto a man.* The word for man is "male" and indicates that men, in contrast to women who are more sensitive by nature, need this exhortation to careful observance of what they see in the Word.

1:25 *the perfect law of liberty* is the Bible itself, though at the time this letter was written it was only the O.T. and the teachings of Christ. The Word of God is the means of regeneration (1:18), a mirror reflecting man's defects (1:23), the ethical guide for Christian living (1:25; 2:8), and the standard for judgment (2:12).

26 If any man among you seem to be religious, and bridleth not his tongue, but deceiveth his own heart, this man's religion *is* vain.

27 Pure religion and undefiled before God and the Father is this, To visit the fatherless and widows in their affliction, *and* to keep himself unspotted from the world.

IV ON PARTIALITY, 2:1–13

A The Command, 2:1

2 My brethren, have not the faith of our Lord Jesus Christ, *the Lord* of glory, with respect of persons.

B The Conduct, 2:2–3

2 For if there come unto your assembly a man with a gold ring, in goodly apparel, and there come in also a poor man in vile raiment;

3 And ye have respect to him that weareth the gay clothing, and say unto him, Sit thou here in a good place; and say to the poor, Stand thou there, or sit here under my footstool:

C The Consequences, 2:4–13

4 Are ye not then partial in yourselves, and are become judges of evil thoughts?

5 Hearken, my beloved brethren, Hath not God chosen the poor of this world rich in faith, and heirs of the kingdom which he hath promised to them that love him?

6 But ye have despised the poor. Do not rich men oppress you, and draw you before the judgment seats?

7 Do not they blaspheme that worthy name by the which ye are called?

2:1 *respect of persons*=partiality; i.e., show no partiality especially in regard to people of position or wealth in the assembly.

2:2 *gold ring.* It was not uncommon for several to be worn as a mark of wealth and social distinction (Luke 15:22). *vile raiment*=shabby clothing.

2:3 *gay.* Gorgeous in color and ornamentation. *under my footstool.* I.e., in a lowly place, on the floor.

2:4 *judges of evil thoughts.* Better, with or full of evil thoughts. It is wrong to show favoritism to the rich because it shows one's own value system to be false (v. 3); it fails to honor the poor whom God honors (v. 5); it favors those who oppress you (v. 6); and it is sin (v. 9).

8 If ye fulfil the royal law according to the scripture,
Thou shalt love thy neighbour as thyself, ye do well:

9 But if ye have respect to persons, ye commit sin, and
are convinced of the law as transgressors.

10 For whosoever shall keep the whole law, and yet
offend in one *point*, he is guilty of all.

11 For he that said, Do not commit adultery, said also,
Do not kill. Now if thou commit no adultery, yet if thou
kill, thou art become a transgressor of the law.

12 So speak ye, and so do, as they that shall be judged
by the law of liberty.

13 For he shall have judgment without mercy, that hath
shewed no mercy; and mercy rejoiceth against judgment.

V ON FAITH AND WORKS, 2:14–26

A The Inquiry, 2:14

14 What *doth it* profit, my brethren, though a man say
he hath faith, and have not works? can faith save him?

B The Illustration, 2:15–17

15 If a brother or sister be naked, and destitute of daily
food,

16 And one of you say unto them, Depart in peace, be
ye warmed and filled; notwithstanding ye give them not
those things which are needful to the body; what *doth it*
profit?

17 Even so faith, if it hath not works, is dead, being
alone.

C The Indoctrination, 2:18–26

18 Yea, a man may say, Thou hast faith, and I have
works: shew me thy faith without thy works, and I will
shew thee my faith by my works.

2:10 *he is guilty of all.* One sin, small or great, makes a man a
sinner and brings him under condemnation.

2:14 *can faith save him?* Lit., can that (i.e., a non-working, dead,
spurious) faith save him? James is not saying that we are saved
by works, but that a faith that does not produce good works
is a dead faith. James was refuting not the Pauline doctrine
of justification by faith but a perversion of it which did not
define faith, as both Paul and James did, as a living, productive
trust in Christ. Genuine faith cannot be "dead" to morality
or barren to works. An illustration of spurious faith is given
in vv. 15–16.

2:15 *naked.* I.e., ill-clad.

19 Thou believest that there is one God; thou doest well: the devils also believe, and tremble.

20 But wilt thou know, O vain man, that faith without works is dead?

21 Was not Abraham our father justified by works, when he had offered Isaac his son upon the altar?

22 Seest thou how faith wrought with his works, and by works was faith made perfect?

23 And the scripture was fulfilled which saith, Abraham believed God, and it was imputed unto him for righteousness: and he was called the Friend of God.

24 Ye see then how that by works a man is justified, and not by faith only.

25 Likewise also was not Rahab the harlot justified by works, when she had received the messengers, and had sent *them* out another way?

26 For as the body without the spirit is dead, so faith without works is dead also.

VI ON SINS OF THE TONGUE, 3:1-12

A Its Bridling, 3:1-4

3 My brethren, be not many masters, knowing that we shall receive the greater condemnation.

2:19 *one God*. Lit., God is one. The unity of God was a fundamental belief in Judaism, but if that belief does not produce good deeds it is no better than the monotheism of the demons. *devils*=demons. *tremble*=shudder.

2:21 *justified by works*. In Paul "justification" means to declare a sinner righteous in the sight of God; here in James it means "to vindicate" or "show to be righteous" before God and men. Abraham's justification (in Paul's sense) is recorded in Gen. 15:6; Abraham's justification (in James's sense) took place 30 or more years later in this crowning act of obedience in offering Isaac (Gen. 22). By this act he proved the reality of his Gen. 15 faith.

2:23 *Friend of God*. This title comes from 2 Chron. 20:7 and Isa. 41:8.

2:24 This verse is the reply to the question of v. 14. Unproductive faith cannot save, because it is not genuine faith. Faith and works are like a two-coupon ticket to heaven. The coupon of works is not good for passage, and the coupon of faith is not good if detached from works.

2:25 *Rahab*. Her story is told in Josh. 2:1-21.

3:1 *masters*. Lit. teachers. Since teachers use their tongues more, they will be judged more strictly.

2 For in many things we offend all. If any man offend not in word, the same *is* a perfect man, *and* able also to bridle the whole body.

3 Behold, we put bits in the horses' mouths, that they may obey us; and we turn about their whole body.

4 Behold also the ships, which though *they be* so great, and *are* driven of fierce winds, yet are they turned about with a very small helm, whithersoever the governor listeth.

B Its Boasting, 3:5–12

5 Even so the tongue is a little member, and boasteth great things. Behold, how great a matter a little fire kindleth!

6 And the tongue *is* a fire, a world of iniquity: so is the tongue among our members, that it defileth the whole body, and setteth on fire the course of nature; and it is set on fire of hell.

7 For every kind of beasts, and of birds, and of serpents, and of things in the sea, is tamed, and hath been tamed of mankind:

8 But the tongue can no man tame; *it is* an unruly evil, full of deadly poison.

9 Therewith bless we God, even the Father; and therewith curse we men, which are made after the similitude of God.

10 Out of the same mouth proceedeth blessing and cursing. My brethren, these things ought not so to be.

11 Doth a fountain send forth at the same place sweet *water* and bitter?

12 Can the fig tree, my brethren, bear olive berries? either a vine, figs? so *can* no fountain both yield salt water and fresh.

3:2 *we offend all.* Lit., we all stumble. The theme of vv. 1–12 is found in the second clause, *if any man . . . a perfect man.* *perfect*=mature, of full moral growth.

3:4 *whithersoever the governor listeth*=wherever the pilot directs.

3:6 *the course of nature*=the whole course of human existence. This tremendous power for the tongue comes from *hell* (lit., Gehenna; see note at Matt. 5:22).

3:9 *after the similitude of God.* The divine image has been marred by sin, but not totally obliterated. Here, the fact that man was made in the image of God is the basis for not cursing our fellow man.

VII ON TRUE WISDOM, 3:13–18

13 Who *is* a wise man and endued with knowledge among you? let him shew out of a good conversation his works with meekness of wisdom.

14 But if ye have bitter envying and strife in your hearts, glory not, and lie not against the truth.

15 This wisdom descendeth not from above, but *is* earthly, sensual, devilish.

16 For where envying and strife *is*, there *is* confusion and every evil work.

17 But the wisdom that is from above is first pure, then peaceable, gentle, *and* easy to be intreated, full of mercy and good fruits, without partiality, and without hypocrisy.

18 And the fruit of righteousness is sown in peace of them that make peace.

VIII ON WORLDLINESS, 4:1–17

A Its Cause, 4:1–2

4 From whence *come* wars and fightings among you? *come they* not hence, *even* of your lusts that war in your members?

2 Ye lust, and have not: ye kill, and desire to have, and cannot obtain: ye fight and war, yet ye have not, because ye ask not.

B Its Consequences, 4:3–6

3 Ye ask, and receive not, because ye ask amiss, that ye may consume *it* upon your lusts.

4 Ye adulterers and adulteresses, know ye not that the friendship of the world is enmity with God? whosoever therefore will be a friend of the world is the enemy of God.

3:13 The question sets the theme for vv. 13–18. The answer is: The person who remembers his moral responsibilities.

3:17 *easy to be intreated*=compliant, open to reason.

3:18 *the fruit of righteousness.* I.e., the fruit which is righteousness. This is in contrast to 1:20.

4:2 *kill.* The logical, but not necessarily usual, outcome of lust. See Matt. 5:21–22.

4:4 *adulterers* is not in the best text, and *adulteresses* is symbolic language for "unfaithful creatures," as often in the O.T.

5 Do ye think that the scripture saith in vain, The spirit that dwelleth in us lusteth to envy?

6 But he giveth more grace. Wherefore he saith, God resisteth the proud, but giveth grace unto the humble.

C Its Cure, 4:7–10

7 Submit yourselves therefore to God. Resist the devil, and he will flee from you.

8 Draw nigh to God, and he will draw nigh to you. Cleanse *your* hands, *ye* sinners; and purify *your* hearts, *ye* double minded.

9 Be afflicted, and mourn, and weep: let your laughter be turned to mourning, and *your* joy to heaviness.

10 Humble yourselves in the sight of the Lord, and he shall lift you up.

D Its Characteristics, 4:11–17

11 Speak not evil one of another, brethren. He that speaketh evil of *his* brother, and judgeth his brother, speaketh evil of the law, and judgeth the law: but if thou judge the law, thou art not a doer of the law, but a judge.

12 There is one lawgiver, who is able to save and to destroy: who art thou that judgest another?

13 Go to now, ye that say, To day or to morrow we will go into such a city, and continue there a year, and buy and sell, and get gain:

14 Whereas ye know not what *shall be* on the morrow. For what *is* your life? It is even a vapour, that appeareth for a little time, and then vanisheth away.

15 For that ye *ought* to say, If the Lord will, we shall live, and do this, or that.

4:5 The thought is this: Do you imagine there is no meaning to the scripture that says, "The Spirit that dwells in us longs jealously over us?"

4:7–10 There are 10 verbs, all commands, in these verses in a tense which indicates the need for a decisive and urgent break with the old life.

4:8 *double minded.* See 1:8. Worldliness is basically divided allegiance.

4:9 *laughter.* Laughter is sometimes desirable (Ps. 126:2), but not when it reflects the frivolity of the world.

4:11–12 The person who judges his brother disobeys the law, thus putting himself above it and treating it with contempt.

4:13–17 The folly of forgetting God in business, as illustrated in these verses, is another illustration of worldliness. The itinerant merchants addressed here were Jews who carried on a lucrative trade throughout the world.

16 But now ye rejoice in your boastings: all such rejoicing is evil.

17 Therefore to him that knoweth to do good, and doeth *it* not, to him it is sin.

IX ON RICHES, PATIENCE, AND SWEARING, 5:1–12

5 Go to now, *ye* rich men, weep and howl for your miseries that shall come upon *you.*

2 Your riches are corrupted, and your garments are motheaten.

3 Your gold and silver is cankered; and the rust of them shall be a witness against you, and shall eat your flesh as it were fire. Ye have heaped treasure together for the last days.

4 Behold, the hire of the labourers who have reaped down your fields, which is of you kept back by fraud, crieth: and the cries of them which have reaped are entered into the ears of the Lord of sabaoth.

5 Ye have lived in pleasure on the earth, and been wanton; ye have nourished your hearts, as in a day of slaughter.

6 Ye have condemned *and* killed the just; *and* he doth not resist you.

7 Be patient therefore, brethren, unto the coming of the Lord. Behold, the husbandman waiteth for the precious fruit of the earth, and hath long patience for it, until he receive the early and latter rain.

8 Be ye also patient; stablish your hearts: for the coming of the Lord draweth nigh.

9 Grudge not one against another, brethren, lest ye be condemned: behold, the judge standeth before the door.

10 Take, my brethren, the prophets, who have spoken in the name of the Lord, for an example of suffering affliction, and of patience.

5:3 *is cankered*=is rusted. The rich did not realize that *the last days* were already present (2 Tim. 3:1).

5:4 *hire*=wages. *Lord of sabaoth*=Lord of Hosts (a familiar O.T. title), or the Lord Almighty, the omnipotent sovereign who is not oblivious to injustice.

5:6 *killed the just.* This probably refers to the practice of the rich in taking the poor ("the just") to court to take away what little he might have, thus "murdering" him.

5:7 *the early* (Oct.–Nov.) *and latter* (Apr.–May) *rain.* Palestine has two rainy seasons annually.

5:9 *Grudge*=murmur or grumble.

11 Behold, we count them happy which endure. Ye have heard of the patience of Job, and have seen the end of the Lord; that the Lord is very pitiful, and of tender mercy.

12 But above all things, my brethren, swear not, neither by heaven, neither by the earth, neither by any other oath: but let your yea be yea; and *your* nay, nay; lest ye fall into condemnation.

X ON PRAYERS, 5:13–18

13 Is any among you afflicted? let him pray. Is any merry? let him sing psalms.

14 Is any sick among you? let him call for the elders of the church; and let them pray over him, anointing him with oil in the name of the Lord:

15 And the prayer of faith shall save the sick, and the Lord shall raise him up; and if he have committed sins, they shall be forgiven him.

16 Confess *your* faults one to another, and pray one for another, that ye may be healed. The effectual fervent prayer of a righteous man availeth much.

5:11 *the patience of Job.* Job was steadfast in his moral integrity. See Job. 1:21; 2:10; 13:15; 16:19; 19:25.   *pitiful*=very compassionate.

5:12 *swear not.* Not all oaths are forbidden by this verse, only flippant, profane, or blasphemous ones. Oaths in the sense of solemn affirmations were enjoined in the Law (Ex. 22:11) and were practiced by Christ (Matt. 26:63–64) and Paul (Rom. 1:9).

5:14–15 God may heal directly, through medicine or in answer to prayer, as here. The oil is a symbol of the presence of God (Ps. 23:5); it may also have been considered medicinal in James's day (Luke 10:34), though hardly for all diseases. Prayers of faith are answered not simply because they are prayed in faith but only if they are prayed in the will of God (1 John 5:14). God does not always think it best to heal (2 Cor. 12:8), and here the healing is dependent on confession of sin. Historically, extreme unction developed out of this rite, but the significance is entirely changed, for the Roman Catholic rite has death in view, not recovery.

5:14 *the elders of the church.* Elders are first mentioned in Acts 11:30 as recognized leaders of the churches. Their mention here and in Acts 14:23 relates to about the same time. They were the first leaders, before deacons and long before bishops arose in the churches.

17 Ēlī′as was a man subject to like passions as we are, and he prayed earnestly that it might not rain: and it rained not on the earth by the space of three years and six months.

18 And he prayed again, and the heaven gave rain, and the earth brought forth her fruit.

XI ON THE CONVERSION OF THE ERRING,
5:19–20

19 Brethren, if any of you do err from the truth, and one convert him;

20 Let him know, that he which converteth the sinner from the error of his way shall save a soul from death, and shall hide a multitude of sins.

5:19–20 *any of you*. The reference is evidently to Christians, and the *death* is physical death which sin may cause (1 Cor. 11:30).

INTRODUCTION TO
THE FIRST LETTER OF
Peter

AUTHOR: Peter   DATE: 63

The Readers   This letter is addressed to the "strangers scattered" or, literally, the "sojourners of the dispersion" (1:1). These were Christians who, like Israel of old, were scattered throughout the world, though the readers of this epistle were predominantly of Gentile background rather than Jewish (1:14; 2:9–10; 4:3–4). Their situation was one of suffering and trial (4:12), but not because of any empire-wide ban on Christianity, since that came later (3:13). The sufferings referred to are those which often come to Christians as they live Christianity in a pagan and hostile society. The persecution took the forms of slander, riots, local police action, and social ostracism. The readers are encouraged to rejoice and live above reproach.

The Circumstances of Writing   That the apostle Peter was the writer (as stated in 1:1) is confirmed by the many similarities between this letter and Peter's sermons recorded in Acts (1:20 and Acts 2:23; 4:5 and Acts 10:42). The same Silas (also called Silvanus) who accompanied Paul on the second missionary journey was his amanuensis (5:12; Acts 15:40).

The place of writing was "Babylon" (5:13), a symbolic name for Rome much used by writers who wished to avoid trouble with the Roman authorities. In Revelation 17:5 and 9 idolatrous Babylon is linked with Rome. Peter was in Rome during the last decade of his life and wrote this epistle about A.D. 63, just before the outbreak of Nero's persecution in 64. Peter was martyred about 67.

The Contents   Peter himself states the theme of his letter in 5:12 as an explanation of what "the true grace of God" means in the life of a believer.

OUTLINE OF 1 PETER

THE FIRST LETTER OF
Peter

I SALUTATION, 1:1–2

1 Peter, an apostle of Jesus Christ, to the strangers scattered throughout Pontus, Galatia, Cappadō'cia, Asia, and Bithyn'ia,

1:1 ~~strangers~~=sojourners, exiles, foreign residents. The word is
applied to those who settled in a town or region without
making it their permanent place of residence. The readers,
whose citizenship was in heaven, are viewed as temporary
residents of the provinces of Asia Minor named in this verse.
1:2 The idea expressed in this verse is that God in His wisdom
has chosen us to salvation through the work of the Holy
Spirit applying the worth of the death of Christ so that we
might be obedient to Him. *foreknowledge.* God's prior knowledge of all things based on His causative relation to them is
the basis of our election. Foreknowledge involves active consciousness of God's part of all that comes to pass (see 1:20;
Rom. 8:29; 11:2 for the same word and concept; and see note

2 Elect according to the foreknowledge of God the Father, through sanctification of the Spirit, unto obedience and sprinkling of the blood of Jesus Christ: Grace unto you, and peace, be multiplied.

II GRACE MEANS SECURITY, 1:3–12

A Doxology, 1:3–9

3 Blessed *be* the God and Father of our Lord Jesus Christ, which according to his abundant mercy hath begotten us again unto a lively hope by the resurrection of Jesus Christ from the dead,

4 To an inheritance incorruptible, and undefiled, and that fadeth not away, reserved in heaven for you,

5 Who are kept by the power of God through faith unto salvation ready to be revealed in the last time.

6 Wherein ye greatly rejoice, though now for a season, if need be, ye are in heaviness through manifold temptations:

7 That the trial of your faith, being much more precious than of gold that perisheth, though it be tried with fire, might be found unto praise and honour and glory at the appearing of Jesus Christ:

8 Whom having not seen, ye love; in whom, though now ye see *him* not, yet believing, ye rejoice with joy unspeakable and full of glory:

9 Receiving the end of your faith, *even* the salvation of *your* souls.

B The Prophets and the Gospel, 1:10–12

10 Of which salvation the prophets have enquired and searched diligently, who prophesied of the grace *that should come* unto you:

at Eph. 1:5). *Father . . . Spirit . . . Christ.* Here is an early formulation of the doctrine of the Trinity. *sprinkling of the blood* signifies the personal application of the sacrifice of Christ.
1:3 Here begins Peter's recital of the blessings of God's redeemed children, concluding at 2:10. *begotten us*=regenerated us. *lively*=living.
1:4 *incorruptible*=indestructible. *undefiled*=unstained by evil. *that fadeth not away*=unimpaired by time.
1:6 *manifold temptations*=various trials.
1:9 *end*=outcome.
1:10–12 Though the O.T. prophets spoke of grace being given to Gentiles, they did not understand all that was involved in

11 Searching what, or what manner of time the Spirit of Christ which was in them did signify, when it testified beforehand the sufferings of Christ, and the glory that should follow.

12 Unto whom it was revealed, that not unto themselves, but unto us they did minister the things, which are now reported unto you by them that have preached the gospel unto you with the Holy Ghost sent down from heaven; which things the angels desire to look into.

III GRACE MEANS SOBRIETY, 1:13–2:10

A In Holiness, 1:13–16

13 Wherefore gird up the loins of your mind, be sober, and hope to the end for the grace that is to be brought unto you at the revelation of Jesus Christ;

14 As obedient children, not fashioning yourselves according to the former lusts in your ignorance:

15 But as he which hath called you is holy, so be ye holy in all manner of conversation;

16 Because it is written, Be ye holy; for I am holy.

B In Fear, 1:17–21

17 And if ye call on the Father, who without respect of persons judgeth according to every man's work, pass the time of your sojourning *here* in fear:

18 Forasmuch as ye know that ye were not redeemed with corruptible things, *as* silver and gold, from your vain conversation *received* by tradition from your fathers;

God's saving Gentiles through a suffering Messiah (see Col. 1:26–27). The O.T. prophets did predict both the suffering (Isa. 53) and glory (Isa. 11) of the Messiah without distinguishing that the former would be fulfilled at His first coming and the latter at His second advent.

1:12 *angels.* See Eph. 3:10.

1:13 *gird up the loins of your mind*=be disciplined in your thinking, a figure of speech based on the gathering and fastening up of the long Eastern garments so that they would not interfere with the individual's activity.

1:14 *not fashioning yourselves.* This word is translated "be not conformed" in Rom. 12:2, the only other occurrence of it.

1:15 *conversation*=conduct or behavior.

1:16 *Be ye holy.* See Lev. 11:44–45.

1:17 *in fear*=reverently.

1:18 *from your vain . . .* Better, from your foolish way of life inherited from your fathers.

19 But with the precious blood of Christ, as of a lamb without blemish and without spot:

20 Who verily was foreordained before the foundation of the world, but was manifest in these last times for you,

21 Who by him do believe in God, that raised him up from the dead, and gave him glory; that your faith and hope might be in God.

C In Love, 1:22–25

22 Seeing ye have purified your souls in obeying the truth through the Spirit unto unfeigned love of the brethren, *see that ye* love one another with a pure heart fervently:

23 Being born again, not of corruptible seed, but of incorruptible, by the word of God, which liveth and abideth for ever.

24 For all flesh *is* as grass, and all the glory of man as the flower of grass. The grass withereth, and the flower thereof falleth away:

25 But the word of the Lord endureth for ever. And this is the word which by the gospel is preached unto you.

D In Growth, 2:1–10

2 Wherefore laying aside all malice, and all guile, and hypocrisies, and envies, and all evil speakings,

2 As newborn babes, desire the sincere milk of the word, that ye may grow thereby:

3 If so be ye have tasted that the Lord *is* gracious.

4 To whom coming, *as unto* a living stone, disallowed indeed of men, but chosen of God, *and* precious,

5 Ye also, as lively stones, are built up a spiritual house, an holy priesthood, to offer up spiritual sacrifices, acceptable to God by Jesus Christ.

6 Wherefore also it is contained in the scripture, Behold, I lay in Sion a chief corner stone, elect, precious: and he that believeth on him shall not be confounded.

7 Unto you therefore which believe *he is* precious: but unto them which be disobedient, the stone which the

1:19 *without blemish and without spot.* This refers to the sinlessness of Christ (see Lev. 22:19–25).

1:22 *fervently*=earnestly.

1:24–25 See Isa. 40:6–8.

2:2 *sincere milk of the word.* Lit., pure, spiritual unadulterated milk.

2:4–8 Christ is the living stone (v. 4), the cornerstone (v. 6), the head stone (v. 7), and the stumbling-stone (v. 8).

builders disallowed, the same is made the head of the corner,

8 And a stone of stumbling, and a rock of offence, *even to them* which stumble at the word, being disobedient: whereunto also they were appointed.

9 But ye *are* a chosen generation, a royal priesthood, an holy nation, a peculiar people; that ye should shew forth the praises of him who hath called you out of darkness into his marvellous light:

10 Which in time past *were* not a people, but *are* now the people of God: which had not obtained mercy, but now have obtained mercy.

IV GRACE MEANS SUBMISSION, 2:11–3:12

11 Dearly beloved, I beseech *you* as strangers and pilgrims, abstain from fleshly lusts, which war against the soul;

12 Having your conversation honest among the Gentiles: that, whereas they speak against you as evildoers, they may by *your* good works, which they shall behold, glorify God in the day of visitation.

A To Governments, 2:13–17

13 Submit yourselves to every ordinance of man for the Lord's sake: whether it be to the king, as supreme;

14 Or unto governors, as unto them that are sent by him for the punishment of evildoers, and for the praise of them that do well.

15 For so is the will of God, that with well doing ye may put to silence the ignorance of foolish men:

16 As free, and not using *your* liberty for a cloke of maliciousness, but as the servants of God.

17 Honour all *men*. Love the brotherhood. Fear God. Honour the king.

2:8 *appointed*. The same divine purpose which chose some ordains those who are disobedient to the only alternative.

2:9 *peculiar people*. I.e., people possessed by God, God's own people.

2:11 In this section beginning here, and ending at 4:11, Peter sets forth the duties of Christians in the world.

2:13–17 Christians are to be law-abiding citizens. If the law of country violates the revealed will of God, then, of course, the believer must obey God, though he may suffer the penalties of that country's laws. See Rom. 13:1–7 and Tit. 3:1–2.

2:15 *foolish men*. I.e., the slanderers of v. 12.

2:16 *a cloke of maliciousness*=a pretext for evil.

B To Masters, 2:18–25

18 Servants, *be* subject to *your* masters with all fear; not only to the good and gentle, but also to the froward.

19 For this *is* thankworthy, if a man for conscience toward God endure grief, suffering wrongfully.

20 For what glory *is it*, if, when ye be buffeted for your faults, ye shall take it patiently? but if, when ye do well, and suffer *for it*, ye take it patiently, this *is* acceptable with God.

21 For even hereunto were ye called: because Christ also suffered for us, leaving us an example, that ye should follow his steps:

22 Who did no sin, neither was guile found in his mouth:

23 Who, when he was reviled, reviled not again; when he suffered, he threatened not; but committed *himself* to him that judgeth righteously:

24 Who his own self bare our sins in his own body on the tree, that we, being dead to sins, should live unto righteousness: by whose stripes ye were healed.

25 For ye were as sheep going astray; but are now returned unto the Shepherd and Bishop of your souls.

C To Husbands, 3:1–7

3 Likewise, ye wives, *be* in subjection to your own husband; that, if any obey not the word, they also may without the word be won by the conversation of the wives;

2 While they behold your chaste conversation *coupled* with fear.

3 Whose adorning let it not be that outward *adorning*

2:20 *buffeted* = beaten.

2:22–24 *Who did no sin . . . who bore our sins.* The sinless Jesus was the perfect substitute for the sins of mankind in His death.

2:24 *on the tree.* This was the instrument of death for slaves also. *stripes* = wounds.

2:25 *Bishop* = Guardian or Caretaker.

3:1 *without the words.* Lit., without *a* word; i.e., an unsaved husband can better be won to Christianity by seeing it work in his wife's godly life than by always hearing about it from her lips.

3:3 *plaiting.* I.e., elaborate braiding. This verse does not prohibit all jewelry; if it did, it would also prohibit all clothing! It condemns outward ostentation and enjoins modesty and meekness.

of plaiting the hair, and of wearing of gold, or of putting on of apparel;

4 But *let it be* the hidden man of the heart, in that which is not corruptible, *even the ornament* of a meek and quiet spirit, which is in the sight of God of great price.

5 For after this manner in the old time the holy women also, who trusted in God, adorned themselves, being in subjection unto their own husbands:

6 Even as Sara obeyed Abraham, calling him lord: whose daughters ye are, as long as ye do well, and are not afraid with any amazement.

7 Likewise, ye husbands, dwell with *them* according to knowledge, giving honour unto the wife, as unto the weaker vessel, and as being heirs together of the grace of life; that your prayers be not hindered.

D Recapitulation, 3:8–12

8 Finally, *be ye* all of one mind, having compassion one of another, love as brethren, *be* pitiful, *be* courteous:

9 Not rendering evil for evil, or railing for railing: but contrariwise blessing; knowing that ye are thereunto called, that ye should inherit a blessing.

10 For he that will love life, and see good days, let him refrain his tongue from evil, and his lips that they speak no guile:

11 Let him eschew evil, and do good; let him seek peace, and ensue it.

12 For the eyes of the Lord *are* over the righteous, and his ears *are open* unto their prayers: but the face of the Lord *is* against them that do evil.

V GRACE MEANS SUFFERING, 3:13–4:19

A Reasons for Suffering, 3:13–4:6

13 And who *is* he that will harm you, if ye be followers of that which is good?

3:4 *hidden man*=hidden *person* (see Eph. 3:16).

3:6 *Sara.* See Gen. 18:12.

3:7 *according to knowledge.* I.e., considerately. *that your prayers be not hindered.* The man who fails to give his wife due consideration can hardly pray with her.

3:8 *having compassion*=sympathetic. *pitiful*=compassionate.

3:9 *railing*=abuse. This is an echo of Christ's words (Luke 6:27–28).

3:11 *eschew*=turn aside from. *ensue*=pursue.

14 But and if ye suffer for righteousness' sake, happy *are ye*: and be not afraid of their terror, neither be troubled;

15 But sanctify the Lord God in your hearts: and *be* ready always to *give* an answer to every man that asketh you a reason of the hope that is in you with meekness and fear:

16 Having a good conscience; that, whereas they speak evil of you, as of evildoers, they may be ashamed that falsely accuse your good conversation in Christ.

17 For *it is* better, if the will of God be so, that ye suffer for well doing, than for evil doing.

18 For Christ also hath once suffered for sins, the just for the unjust, that he might bring us to God, being put to death in the flesh, but quickened by the Spirit:

19 By which also he went and preached unto the spirits in prison;

20 Which sometime were disobedient, when once the longsuffering of God waited in the days of Noah, while the ark was a preparing, wherein few, that is, eight souls were saved by water.

21 The like figure whereunto *even* baptism doth also now save us (not the putting away of the filth of the flesh, but the answer of a good conscience toward God,) by the resurrection of Jesus Christ:

22 Who is gone into heaven, and is on the right hand of God; angels and authorities and powers being made subject unto him.

4 Forasmuch then as Christ hath suffered for us in the flesh, arm yourselves likewise with the same mind: for he that hath suffered in the flesh hath ceased from sin;

3:15 *sanctify the Lord*=reverence the Lord.

3:18 *suffered*. Some texts read "died."

3:19 *preached unto the spirits in prison*. Some understand this to mean that Christ between His death and resurrection descended into Hades and offered to the antediluvians a second chance for salvation. Others say that it was simply an announcement of His victory over sin to those in Hades without offering a second chance. Still others understand this as a reference to the preincarnate Christ preaching through Noah to those who, because they rejected that message, are now spirits in prison.

3:21 *baptism*. Though water itself cannot save, baptism with water is the vivid symbol of the changed life of one who has a conscience at peace with God through faith in Christ.

4:1 The thought is: Christ suffered in the flesh. He is your

2 That he no longer should live the rest of *his* time in the flesh to the lusts of men, but to the will of God.

3 For the time past of *our* life may suffice us to have wrought the will of the Gentiles, when we walked in lasciviousness, lusts, excess of wine, revellings, banquetings, and abominable idolatries:

4 Wherein they think it strange that ye run not with *them* to the same excess of riot, speaking evil of *you*:

5 Who shall give account to him that is ready to judge the quick and the dead.

6 For for this cause was the gospel preached also to them that are dead, that they might be judged according to men in the flesh, but live according to God in the spirit.

B Reactions in Suffering, 4:7–19

7 But the end of all things is at hand: be ye therefore sober, and watch unto prayer.

8 And above all things have fervent charity among yourselves: for charity shall cover the multitude of sins.

9 Use hospitality one to another without grudging.

10 As every man hath received the gift, *even so* minister the same one to another, as good stewards of the manifold grace of God.

11 If any man speak, *let him speak* as the oracles of God; if any man minister, *let him do it* as of the ability which God giveth: that God in all things may be glorified through Jesus Christ, to whom be praise and dominion for ever and ever. Amen.

12 Beloved, think it not strange concerning the fiery

example. So, arm yourselves by taking the same view of suffering as Christ took, which is to do the will of God. Thereby is the dominion of sin broken in practical experience.

4:3 *banquetings*=drinking bouts.

4:5 *the quick and the dead*=the living and the dead, i.e., all generations.

4:6 *them that are dead.* I.e., deceased Christians. The gospel was preached to those martyrs now dead. They were judged in the flesh and condemned to martyrdom according to human standards, but they are alive in the spirit after death. Another interpretation refers this to the preaching of 3:19.

4:9 *grudging*=murmuring.

4:10 *the gift*=the spiritual gift. See note at 1 Cor. 1:7. This is the only occurrence of the word in the N.T. outside of the writings of Paul.

4:11 *oracles*=sayings; i.e., one who speaks should preach God's words.

4:12 *think it not strange*=do not be surprised. Peter now turns to the trials of Christians in the world, concluding at 5:11.

trial which is to try you, as though some strange thing happened unto you:

13 But rejoice, inasmuch as ye are partakers of Christ's sufferings; that, when his glory shall be revealed, ye may be glad also with exceeding joy.

14 If ye be reproached for the name of Christ, happy *are ye*; for the spirit of glory and of God resteth upon you: on their part he is evil spoken of, but on your part he is glorified.

15 But let none of you suffer as a murderer, or. *as* a thief, or *as* an evildoer, or as a busybody in other men's matters.

16 Yet if *any man suffer* as a Christian, let him not be ashamed; but let him glorify God on this behalf.

17 For the time *is come* that judgment must begin at the house of God: and if *it* first *begin* at us, what shall the end *be* of them that obey not the gospel of God?

18 And if the righteous scarcely be saved, where shall the ungodly and the sinner appear?

19 Wherefore let them that suffer according to the will of God commit the keeping of their souls *to him* in well doing, as unto a faithful Creator.

VI GRACE MEANS SERVICE, 5:1–11

5 The elders which are among you I exhort, who am also an elder, and a witness of the sufferings of Christ, and also a partaker of the glory that shall be revealed:

2 Feed the flock of God which is among you, taking the oversight *thereof*, not by constraint, but willingly; not for filthy lucre, but of a ready mind;

3 Neither as being lords over God's heritage, but being ensamples to the flock.

4 And when the chief Shepherd shall appear, ye shall receive a crown of glory that fadeth not away.

4:16 *Christian*. See note at Acts 11:26. *on this behalf*. Lit., by this name (Christian).

4:17 The idea is this: If even Christians must be judged (for purging), what fate must await unbelievers who will be punished for their sins?

5:1 *elders*. See note at 1 Tim. 3:1. Elders are to feed, lead (but not lord over), and be an example to their people.

5:2 *constraint*=compulsion. *not for filthy lucre*. Lit., not in fondness for dishonest gain.

5:4 *crown of glory*. Faithful church leaders, who are often dishonored on earth, will receive glory in heaven from Christ the

5 Likewise, ye younger, submit yourselves unto the elder. Yea, all *of you* be subject one to another, and be clothed with humility: for God resisteth the proud, and giveth grace to the humble.

6 Humble yourselves therefore under the mighty hand of God, that he may exalt you in due time:

7 Casting all your care upon him; for he careth for you.

8 Be sober, be vigilant; because your adversary the devil, as a roaring lion, walketh about, seeking whom he may devour:

9 Whom resist stedfast in the faith, knowing that the same afflictions are accomplished in your brethren that are in the world.

10 But the God of all grace, who hath called us unto his eternal glory by Christ Jesus, after that ye have suffered a while, make you perfect, stablish, strengthen, settle *you.*

11 To him *be* glory and dominion for ever and ever. Amen.

VII CONCLUDING REMARKS, 5:12–14

12 By Silvā'nus, a faithful brother unto you, as I suppose, I have written briefly, exhorting, and testifying that this is the true grace of God wherein ye stand.

13 The *church that is* at Babylon, elected together with *you,* saluteth you; and *so doth* Marcus my son.

14 Greet ye one another with a kiss of charity. Peace *be* with you all that are in Christ Jesus. Amen.

chief Shepherd. Athletes were awarded floral crowns for victory; theirs faded away. See note at 1 Cor. 3:14.

5:5 *humility.* Christianity made humility a major virtue. It is an attitude of mind that realizes that one is without any reason for distinction in God's sight.

5:7 *he careth for you.* Lit., it matters to Him concerning you.

5:8 *be vigilant*=be watchful.

5:13 *Marcus my son.* This is John Mark the writer of the Gospel, who was not Peter's natural son but his son in the faith.

5:14 *kiss of charity.* The "holy kiss" (Paul's term, Rom. 16:16) was an expression of Christian love and was apparently restricted to one's own sex.

INTRODUCTION TO
THE SECOND LETTER OF
Peter

AUTHOR: Peter   DATE: 66

The Author Many have suggested that someone other than Peter wrote this letter after A.D. 80 because of (1) differences in style, (2) its supposed dependence on Jude, and (3) the mention of Paul's letters having been collected (3:16). However, (1) using a different scribe or no scribe would result in stylistic changes; (2) there is no reason why Peter should not have borrowed from Jude, though it is more likely that Jude was written later than 2 Peter; and (3) 3:16 does not need to imply all of Paul's letters but only those written up to that time. Furthermore, similarities between 1 and 2 Peter point to the same author, and its acceptance in the canon demands apostolic authority behind it. Assuming Petrine authorship, the letter was written just before his martyrdom in 67 and most likely from Rome.

The Contents The letter is a reminder (1:12; 3:1) of the truth of Christianity as opposed to the heresies of false teachers. Important passages include the reference to the transfiguration (1:16–18), the inspiration of scripture (1:21), and the certainty of the second coming of Christ (3:4–10).

OUTLINE OF 2 PETER

THE SECOND LETTER OF
Peter

I GREETINGS, 1:1–2

1 Simon Peter, a servant and an apostle of Jesus Christ, to them that have obtained like precious faith with us through the righteousness of God and our Saviour Jesus Christ:

2 Grace and peace be multiplied unto you through the knowledge of God, and of Jesus our Lord,

II THE DEVELOPMENT OF FAITH, 1:3–21

A The Growth of Faith, 1:3–11

3 According as his divine power hath given unto us all things that *pertain* unto life and godliness, through the knowledge of him that hath called us to glory and virtue:

4 Whereby are given unto us exceeding great and precious promises: that by these ye might be partakers of the divine nature, having escaped the corruption that is in the world through lust.

5 And beside this, giving all diligence, add to your faith virtue; and to virtue knowledge;

1:1 *to them that have obtained like precious faith with us*. The thought is this: I write to those who have obtained a faith of equal standing with ours (i.e., the apostles') by reason of the impartiality of Christ's blessings.

1:2 *knowledge*. Lit., full of true knowledge (also in v. 3).

1:4 *Whereby*=through which; i.e., through the glory and virtue (v. 3). *partakers of the divine nature*. The believer shares in the life of God by means of Christ and the Spirit living in him (Rom. 8:9; Gal. 2:20).

1:5 *virtue*=moral uprightness.

6 And to knowledge temperance; and to temperance patience; and to patience godliness;

7 And to godliness brotherly kindness; and to brotherly kindness charity.

8 For if these things be in you, and abound, they make *you that ye shall* neither *be* barren nor unfruitful in the knowledge of our Lord Jesus Christ.

9 But he that lacketh these things is blind, and cannot see afar off, and hath forgotten that he was purged from his old sins.

10 Wherefore the rather, brethren, give diligence to make your calling and election sure: for if ye do these things, ye shall never fall:

11 For so an entrance shall be ministered unto you abundantly into the everlasting kingdom of our Lord and Saviour Jesus Christ.

B The Ground of Faith, 1:12–21

12 Wherefore I will not be negligent to put you always in remembrance of these things, though ye know *them*, and be established in the present truth.

13 Yea, I think it meet, as long as I am in this tabernacle, to stir you up by putting *you* in remembrance;

14 Knowing that shortly I must put off *this* my tabernacle, even as our Lord Jesus Christ hath shewed me.

15 Moreover I will endeavour that ye may be able after my decease to have these things always in remembrance.

16 For we have not followed cunningly devised fables, when we made known unto you the power and coming of our Lord Jesus Christ, but were eyewitnesses of his majesty.

1:6 *temperance*=self-control (as in Gal. 5:23). *godliness*. The attitude and conduct of a person who is God-fearing.

1:7 *charity*=love.

1:9 *old sins*. Sins committed prior to conversion.

1:10 *make your calling and election sure*. I.e., confirm by godly living your profession of faith.

1:11 *abundantly*. A Christian life that can be rewarded will provide that abundant entrance into heaven.

1:13 *I think it meet*=I think it right. *this tabernacle*. I.e., Peter's human body.

1:14 *I must put off this my tabernacle*. Peter knew because of Christ's prediction (John 21:18) that he would soon die.

1:16 *eyewitnesses of his majesty*. Peter is referring here to witnessing the transfiguration of Christ (Matt. 17:1–8). This event confirmed the truth of the O.T. prophecies and made them even more sure from a human viewpoint (v. 19).

17 For he received from God the Father honour and glory, when there came such a voice to him from the excellent glory, This is my beloved Son, in whom I am well pleased.

18 And this voice which came from heaven we heard, when we were with him in the holy mount.

19 We have also a more sure word of prophecy; whereunto ye do well that ye take heed, as unto a light that shineth in a dark place, until the day dawn, and the day star arise in your hearts:

20 Knowing this first, that no prophecy of the scripture is of any private interpretation.

21 For the prophecy came not in old time by the will of man: but holy men of God spake *as they were* moved by the Holy Ghost.

III THE DENOUNCING OF FALSE TEACHERS, 2:1-22

A Their Conduct, 2:1-3

2 But there were false prophets also among the people, even as there shall be false teachers among you, who privily shall bring in damnable heresies, even denying the Lord that bought them, and bring upon themselves swift destruction.

2 And many shall follow their pernicious ways; by reason of whom the way of truth shall be evil spoken of.

3 And through covetousness shall they with feigned

1:19 *until the day dawn.* Possibly a reference to the second coming of Christ.

1:20 *private interpretation.* Several interpretations are suggested: (1) Prophecies must be interpreted in the light of other Scriptures; (2) prophecies are often capable of several fulfillments; (3) prophecies must be interpreted only with God's help since they were given only as the prophets were moved by God, and not by any impulse of man.

1:21 *moved.* Lit., borne along. This shows the dual authorship of God's Word—the Holy Spirit guiding and guarding the men involved in the actual writing. See note at 2 Tim. 3:16.

2:1 *privily*=secretly. *denying the Lord that bought them.* The price for the sins of all men (including these false teachers) was paid by the death of Christ, though no man can know forgiveness of his sins except through faith in the Savior. See 1 Cor. 6:20; 1 Pet. 1:18-19.

2:2 *pernicious ways.* Lit., licentiousness.

2:3 *feigned words.* Lit., false words. *make merchandise of you*= exploit you for their own ends.

words make merchandise of you: whose judgment now of a long time lingereth not, and their damnation slumbereth not.

B Their Condemnation, 2:4–9

4 For if God spared not the angels that sinned, but cast *them* down to hell, and delivered *them* into chains of darkness, to be reserved unto judgment;

5 And spared not the old world, but saved Noah the eighth *person*, a preacher of righteousness, bringing in the flood upon the world of the ungodly;

6 And turning the cities of Sodom and Gōmor'rha into ashes condemned *them* with an overthrow, making *them* an ensample unto those that after should live ungodly;

7 And delivered just Lot, vexed with the filthy conversation of the wicked:

8 (For that righteous man dwelling among them, in seeing and hearing, vexed *his* righteous soul from day to day with *their* unlawful deeds;)

9 The Lord knoweth how to deliver the godly out of temptations, and to reserve the unjust unto the day of judgment to be punished:

C Their Characteristics, 2:10–22

10 But chiefly them that walk after the flesh in the lust of uncleanness, and despise government. Presumptuous *are they*, selfwilled, they are not afraid to speak evil of dignities.

11 Whereas angels, which are greater in power and

2:4 *angels that sinned.* These are the fallen angels who sinned grievously by cohabiting with women, as described in Gen. 6:1–4. See Jude 6. The logic is that if this happened to angels, surely God will not spare these false teachers.

2:5 *the eighth person.* Noah was the eighth along with the seven other members of his family (his wife and his three sons and their wives).

2:6 *Sodom and Gomorrha.* See Gen. 19:15–29.

2:7 *just Lot.* Lit., righteous Lot. He was a righteous man in that he believed God and he was vexed at the licentiousness of the wicked people about him, though his life was lived for himself.

2:10 *despise government.* I.e., authority, especially God's. The last part of the verse may be translated: Daring, self-willed, they tremble not at blaspheming the glorious ones (i.e., angels). False teachers speak rashly in disbelief of the power and authority of angels.

2:11 *against them.* Probably a reference to the false teachers. In other words, even though the false teachers speak evil of angels, angels do not denounce them but leave all judgment to God.

might, bring not railing accusation against them before the Lord.

12 But these, as natural brute beasts, made to be taken and destroyed, speak evil of the things that they understand not; and shall utterly perish in their own corruption;

13 And shall receive the reward of unrighteousness, *as* they that count it pleasure to riot in the day time. Spots *they are* and blemishes, sporting themselves with their own deceivings while they feast with you;

14 Having eyes full of adultery, and that cannot cease from sin; beguiling unstable souls: an heart they have exercised with covetous practices; cursed children:

15 Which have forsaken the right way, and are gone astray, following the way of Bā'lāam *the son* of Bosor, who loved the wages of unrighteousness;

16 But was rebuked for his iniquity: the dumb ass speaking with man's voice forbad the madness of the prophet.

17 These are wells without water, clouds that are carried with a tempest; to whom the mist of darkness is reserved for ever.

18 For when they speak great swelling *words* of vanity, they allure through the lusts of the flesh, *through much* wantonness, those that were clean escaped from them who live in error.

19 While they promise them liberty, they themselves are the servants of corruption: for of whom a man is overcome, of the same is he brought in bondage.

20 For if after they have escaped the pollutions of the

2:13 *And shall receive the reward of unrighteousness.* Lit., suffering wrong for their wrongdoing.

2:13 *sporting themselves with their own deceivings.* Lit., reveling in their dissipation. The false teachers turn Christian fellowship meals into riotous drinking-parties.

2:14 *cursed children.* A phrase which simply means that they are accursed.

2:15 *the way of Balaam.* This is the covetousness of one who hires himself for personal gain (see Num. 22:28–30 and note at Jude 11). This "way" is contrasted with "the right way" (v. 15).

2:17 *wells without water.* The barrenness of the false teachers mocks the thirsty soul. *clouds that are carried with a tempest.* Lit., mists driven by a storm. These mists, like the false teachers, seem to promise refreshment, but in reality do no good. *mist of darkness.* Lit., gloom of darkness=eternal torment (Matt. 8:12).

2:18 *wantonness*=sexual excesses.

2:20 *escaped the pollutions of the world.* These false teachers had

world through the knowledge of the Lord and Saviour Jesus Christ, they are again entangled therein, and overcome, the latter end is worse with them than the beginning.

21 For it had been better for them not to have known the way of righteousness, than, after they have known *it*, to turn from the holy commandment delivered unto them.

22 But it is happened unto them according to the true proverb, The dog *is* turned to his own vomit again; and the sow that was washed to her wallowing in the mire.

IV THE DESIGN OF THE FUTURE, 3:1–18

A Derision, 3:1–7

3 This second epistle, beloved, I now write unto you; in *both* which I stir up your pure minds by way of remembrance:

2 That ye may be mindful of the words which were spoken before by the holy prophets, and of the commandment of us the apostles of the Lord and Saviour:

3 Knowing this first, that there shall come in the last days scoffers, walking after their own lusts,

4 And saying, Where is the promise of his coming? for since the fathers fell asleep, all things continue as *they were* from the beginning of the creation.

5 For this they willingly are ignorant of, that by the word of God the heavens were of old, and the earth standing out of the water and in the water:

6 Whereby the world that then was, being overflowed with water, perished:

7 But the heavens and the earth, which are now, by the same word are kept in store, reserved unto fire against the day of judgment and perdition of ungodly men.

apparently made some sort of profession of the truth without possessing the new life of Christ. They then rejected what they professed, becoming slaves of corruption (v. 19) and showing their true natural condition (v. 22).

3:1 *pure*=sincere.

3:5 *willingly ignorant of*. Lit., this escapes their notice willingly. Peter begins his attack on those who doubt the truth of Christ's return by referring to the dependability of God's word as demonstrated in Creation.

3:6 *overflowed with water*. The judgment of the flood in the days of Noah also demonstrates the truthfulness of God's word.

3:7 *perdition*=destruction.

B Delay, 3:8–9

8 But, beloved, be not ignorant of this one thing, that one day *is* with the Lord as a thousand years, and a thousand years as one day.

9 The Lord is not slack concerning his promise, as some men count slackness; but is longsuffering to us-ward, not willing that any should perish, but that all should come to repentance.

C Dissolution, 3:10–13

10 But the day of the Lord will come as a thief in the night; in the which the heavens shall pass away with a great noise, and the elements shall melt with fervent heat, the earth also and the works that are therein shall be burned up.

11 *Seeing* then *that* all these things shall be dissolved, what manner *of persons* ought ye to be in *all* holy conversation and godliness,

12 Looking for and hasting unto the coming of the day of God, wherein the heavens being on fire shall be dissolved, and the elements shall melt with fervent heat?

13 Nevertheless we, according to his promise, look for new heavens and a new earth, wherein dwelleth righteousness.

D Diligence, 3:14–18

14 Wherefore, beloved, seeing that ye look for such things, be diligent that ye may be found of him in peace, without spot, and blameless.

15 And account *that* the longsuffering of our Lord *is* salvation; even as our beloved brother Paul also according to the wisdom given unto him hath written unto you;

16 As also in all *his* epistles, speaking in them of these

3:8–9 To believers, Peter now says that the seeming delay of Christ's return is for the purpose of allowing more people to repent.

3:10 *the day of the Lord*. See note at 1 Thess. 5:2.

3:12 *hasting*=hastening. *wherein*. Lit., on account of which, i.e., after the dissolution of the present heavens the ray of God will come. This is eternity (Rev. 21:1). The certainty of this dissolution makes doubly urgent a life of godliness now.

3:15 *account that . . . is salvation*. I.e., understand that the delay of the return of the Lord is intended as an opportunity for men to be saved (see v. 9).

3:16 Paul's epistles are here put on a par with *other scriptures*.

things; in which are some things hard to be understood, which they that are unlearned and unstable wrest, as *they do* also the other scriptures, unto their own destruction.

17 Ye therefore, beloved, seeing ye know *these things* before, beware lest ye also, being led away with the error of the wicked, fall from your own stedfastness.

18 But grow in grace, and *in* the knowledge of our Lord and Saviour Jesus Christ. To him *be* glory both now and for ever. Amen.

INTRODUCTION TO
THE FIRST LETTER OF
John

AUTHOR: John   DATE: 90

The Author   *Though it is generally agreed that the same person wrote the Gospel of John and these three epistles, some feel that they were not written by John the apostle, the son of Zebedee (as traditionally held), but by another John, the elder or presbyter (2 John 1; 3 John 1). It is argued that (1) an unlettered man could not have written something so profound as the Gospel (Acts 4:13); (2) a fisherman's son would not have known the high priest as John the apostle did; and (3) an apostle would not call himself an elder. But (1) "unlettered" does not mean "illiterate," but without formal training in the rabbinic schools; (2) some fishermen were well-to-do people; and (3) Peter the apostle called himself an elder (1 Pet. 5:1). Further, if John the elder is the beloved disciple and the author of the Gospel, why did he not mention John the son of Zebedee, an important figure in the life of Christ, in that Gospel? Every evidence points to John the elder being the same as John the apostle and the author of this letter.*

Date and Place of Writing   *Strong tradition says that John spent his old age in Ephesus. Lack of personal references in this letter indicates that it was written in sermonic style to Christians all over Asia Minor (much like Ephesians). It was probably written after the Gospel was published and before the persecution under Domitian in 95, which places its writing in the late 80's or early 90's.*

Gnosticism   *The heresy of Gnosticism had begun to make inroads among churches in John's day. Among its teachings were: (1) knowledge is superior to virtue; (2) the nonliteral sense of scripture is correct and can be understood only*

690

by a select few; (3) evil in the world precludes God's being
the Creator; (4) the incarnation is incredible because deity
cannot unite itself with anything material such as a body
(Docetism); and (5) there is no resurrection of the flesh.
The ethical standards of many Gnostics were low, so John
emphasized the reality of the incarnation and the high
ethical standard of the earthly life of Christ.

The Contents   The letter shows John's obvious affection
and concern for the spiritual welfare of his "little children."
The book is filled with contrasts—light and darkness (1:6–
7; 2:8–11); love of world and love of God (2:15–17);
children of God and children of the devil (3:4–10); Spirit
of God and spirit of Antichrist (4:1–3); love and hate
(4:7–12, 16–21).

OUTLINE OF 1 JOHN

THE FIRST LETTER OF
John

I INTRODUCTION:
THE PURPOSE OF THE LETTER, 1:1–4

1 That which was from the beginning, which we have heard, which we have seen with our eyes, which we have looked upon, and our hands have handled, of the Word of life;

2 (For the life was manifested, and we have seen *it*, and bear witness, and shew unto you that eternal life, which was with the Father, and was manifested unto us;)

3 That which we have seen and heard declare we unto you, that ye also may have fellowship with us: and truly our fellowship *is* with the Father, and with his Son Jesus Christ.

4 And these things write we unto you, that your joy may be full.

II CONDITIONS FOR FELLOWSHIP, 1:5–2:2

A Conformity to a Standard, 1:5–7

5 This then is the message which we have heard of him, and declare unto you, that God is light, and in him is no darkness at all.

6 If we say that we have fellowship with him, and walk in darkness, we lie, and do not the truth:

7 But if we walk in the light, as he is in the light, we have fellowship one with another, and the blood of Jesus Christ his Son cleanseth us from all sin.

1:1 *was*. The verb means "was in existence" prior to Creation, not "came into existence." *handled*. The same word is used by Christ in one of His post-resurrection appearances (Luke 24:39).

1:5 *of him*. I.e., of Christ. *God is light* means that God is holy and pure. This symbol was much used by John (John 1:4, 3:19–21; 8:12). Notice also the other "God is . . ." phrases in John 4:24 and 1 John 4:8.

1:7 *But if we walk in the light*. To walk in the light is to live in obedience to God's commandments. The contrast of light and darkness characterizes the section 1:5–2:17.

B Confession of Sin, 1:8–2:2

8 If we say that we have no sin, we deceive ourselves, and the truth is not in us.

9 If we confess our sins, he is faithful and just to forgive us *our* sins, and to cleanse us from all unrighteousness.

10 If we say that we have not sinned, we make him a liar, and his word is not in us.

2 My little children, these things write I unto you, that ye sin not. And if any man sin, we have an advocate with the Father, Jesus Christ the righteous:

2 And he is the propitiation for our sins: and not for ours only, but also for *the sins of* the whole world.

III CONDUCT IN FELLOWSHIP, 2:3–27

A The Character of our Conduct—Imitation, 2:3–11

3 And hereby we do know that we know him, if we keep his commandments.

4 He that saith, I know him, and keepeth not his commandments, is a liar, and the truth is not in him.

5 But whoso keepeth his word, in him verily is the love of God perfected: hereby know we that we are in him.

6 He that saith he abideth in him ought himself also so to walk, even as he walked.

7 Brethren, I write no new commandment unto you, but an old commandment which ye had from the beginning. The old commandment is the word which ye have heard from the beginning.

8 Again, a new commandment I write unto you, which

1:8 *have no sin.* A reference to the indwelling principle of sin rather than the act of sin.

1:9 *confess* means to say the same thing about sin that God does.

1:10 *we have not sinned.* I.e., have not committed sin. Even believers sin, but if we deny past sin and present guilt, we are kidding ourselves, mocking God, and not walking in the light.

2:1 *advocate.* Lit., one summoned alongside, a helper or patron in a lawsuit. Used only by John in the N.T. and translated "Comforter" in John 14:16, 26; 15:26; 16:7.

2:2 *propitiation*=satisfaction. Christ is the offering that satisfied God concerning sin (Rom. 3:25).

2:3–5 Obedience to Christ's commandments is the down-to-earth test of our faith.

2:4 *truth.* Not merely correct knowledge, but the demonstration of the reality of God's love.

2:5 *perfected.* I.e., realized in practice.

2:8 *the true light*=the revelation of God in Christ.

thing is true in him and in you: because the darkness is past, and the true light now shineth.

9 He that saith he is in the light, and hateth his brother, is in darkness even until now.

10 He that loveth his brother abideth in the light, and there is none occasion of stumbling in him.

11 But he that hateth his brother is in darkness, and walketh in darkness, and knoweth not whither he goeth, because that darkness hath blinded his eyes.

B The Commandment for our Conduct—Separation, 2:12–17

12 I write unto you, little children, because your sins are forgiven you for his name's sake.

13 I write unto you, fathers, because ye have known him *that is* from the beginning. I write unto you, young men, because ye have overcome the wicked one. I write unto you, little children, because ye have known the Father.

14 I have written unto you, fathers, because ye have known him *that is* from the beginning. I have written unto you, young men, because ye are strong, and the word of God abideth in you, and ye have overcome the wicked one.

15 Love not the world, neither the things *that are* in the world. If any man love the world, the love of the Father is not in him.

16 For all that *is* in the world, the lust of the flesh, and the lust of the eyes, and the pride of life, is not of the Father, but is of the world.

17 And the world passeth away, and the lust thereof: but he that doeth the will of God abideth for ever.

C The Creed for our Conduct—Affirmation, 2:18–27

18 Little children, it is the last time: and as ye have

2:10 *there is none occasion of stumbling in him.* I.e., there is nothing in him that would cause others to stumble.

2:13 *the wicked one*=the devil.

2:15 *the world.* The world (Greek: *cosmos*) is that organized system headed by Satan which leaves God out and acts as a rival to Him. Though God loves the world of men (John 3:16), believers are not to love at all that which organizes them against God. See 1 John 5:19; John 3:19; Jas. 1:27; 4:4.

2:16 *pride of life.* This means vainglory, display, or boasting about one's possessions.

2:18–27 The author's contrast now becomes that between truth and falsehood.

heard that an'tichrīst shall come, even now are there many antichrists; whereby we know that it is the last time.

19 They went out from us, but they were not of us; for if they had been of us, they would *no doubt* have continued with us: but *they went out,* that they might be made manifest that they were not all of us.

20 But ye have an unction from the Holy One, and ye know all things.

21 I have not written unto you because ye know not the truth, but because ye know it, and that no lie is of the truth.

22 Who is a liar but he that denieth that Jesus is the Christ? He is an'tichrīst, that denieth the Father and the Son.

23 Whosoever denieth the Son, the same hath not the Father: [*but*] *he that acknowledgeth the Son hath the Father also.*

24 Let that therefore abide in you, which ye have heard from the beginning. If that which ye have heard from the beginning shall remain in you, ye also shall continue in the Son, and in the Father.

25 And this is the promise that he hath promised us, *even* eternal life.

26 These *things* have I written unto you concerning them that seduce you.

27 But the anointing which ye have received of him abideth in you, and ye need not that any man teach you: but as the same anointing teacheth you of all things, and is truth, and is no lie, and even as it hath taught you, ye shall abide in him.

2:18 *antichrist.* John speaks about (1) the spirit of Antichrist (4:3) which refers to demonic forces behind Antichristian teaching and activity; (2) the great coming Antichrist (Rev. 13:1–10); and (3) many antichrists present and active in his time and throughout church history. They belonged to the visible church but were not believers (v. 19). They denied the reality of the incarnation of Christ and His relationship to the Father (vv. 21–23; 2 John 7).

2:20 *ye have an unction from*=you have been anointed by the Holy Spirit (and thus can discern between truth and error).

2:22 *a liar.* Lit., the liar. The supreme liar is the one who denies that Jesus Christ came in the flesh; i.e., that He was both man and God. The separation of the human and the divine was an early (Docetic) heresy.

2:26 *seduce*=lead astray.

2:27 *ye need not that any man teach you.* The Spirit whom they had received would teach them how to distinguish truth from error.

IV CHARACTERISTICS OF FELLOWSHIP,
2:28–3:24

A In Relation to our Prospect: Purity, 2:28–3:3

28 And now, little children, abide in him; that, when he shall appear, we may have confidence, and not be ashamed before him at his coming.

29 If ye know that he is righteous, ye know that every one that doeth righteousness is born of him.

3 Behold, what manner of love the Father hath bestowed upon us, that we should be called the sons of God: therefore the world knoweth us not, because it knew him not.

2 Beloved, now are we the sons of God, and it doth not yet appear what we shall be: but we know that, when he shall appear, we shall be like him; for we shall see him as he is.

3 And every man that hath this hope in him purifieth himself, even as he is pure.

B In Relation to our Position:
Righteousness and Brotherly Love, 3:4–18

4 Whosoever committeth sin transgresseth also the law: for sin is the transgression of the law.

5 And ye know that he was manifested to take away our sins; and in him is no sin.

6 Whosoever abideth in him sinneth not: whosoever sinneth hath not seen him, neither known him.

7 Little children, let no man deceive you: he that doeth righteousness is righteous, even as he is righteous.

8 He that committeth sin is of the devil; for the devil sinneth from the beginning. For this purpose the Son of God was manifested, that he might destroy the works of the devil.

2:28–3:24 John's third great contrast is between life and death.

3:1 After *sons of God* should be inserted the words "and we are." *sons*=children, born ones as in John 1:12. We can know Him now as a child knows its father; the future relationship no words can describe.

3:4 *sin is the transgression of the law*. Lit., sin is lawlessness. Lawlessness is used here in its broadest sense of defection from God's standards.

3:8 *committeth*=continually practicing sin as a habit of life, not merely a single act.

9 Whosoever is born of God doth not commit sin; for his seed remaineth in him: and he cannot sin, because he is born of God.

10 In this the children of God are manifest, and the children of the devil: whosoever doeth not righteousness is not of God, neither he that loveth not his brother.

11 For this is the message that ye heard from the beginning, that we should love one another.

12 Not as Cain, *who* was of that wicked one, and slew his brother. And wherefore slew he him? Because his own works were evil, and his brother's righteous.

13 Marvel not, my brethren, if the world hate you.

14 We know that we have passed from death unto life, because we love the brethren. He that loveth not *his* brother abideth in death.

15 Whosoever hateth his brother is a murderer: and ye know that no murderer hath eternal life abiding in him.

16 Hereby perceive we the love *of God*, because he laid down his life for us: and we ought to lay down *our* lives for the brethren.

17 But whoso hath this world's good, and seeth his brother have need, and shutteth up his bowels *of compassion* from him, how dwelleth the love of God in him?

18 My little children, let us not love in word, neither in tongue; but in deed and in truth.

C In Relation to our Prayers: Answers, 3:19–24

19 And hereby we know that we are of the truth, and shall assure our hearts before him.

20 For if our heart condemn us, God is greater than our heart, and knoweth all things.

3:9 *doth not commit sin.* I.e., cannot sin habitually. Habitual actions indicate one's character. *seed*=the divine nature given the one born of God (John 1:13; 2 Pet. 1:4). This prevents the Christian from habitually sinning.

3:12 *Cain.* See Gen. 4:8.

3:15 *a murderer.* The heart that is full of hate is potentially capable of murder (Matt. 5:21–22).

3:16–17 Self-sacrificing love is required of the believer. However, not many are called on to sacrifice their lives, but all can give sacrificially of their substance. *world's good*=the material necessities of life. *bowels of compassion*=heart. The bowels were considered the seat of tender affections. We today say "heart."

3:20 *God is greater than our heart.* We may be either too strict or too lenient in examining our lives; therefore, John's word of comfort is: God the all-knowing is all-loving also.

21 Beloved, if our heart condemn us not, *then* have we confidence toward God.

22 And whatsoever we ask, we receive of him, because we keep his commandments, and do those things that are pleasing in his sight.

23 And this is his commandment, That we should believe on the name of his Son Jesus Christ, and love one another, as he gave us commandment.

24 And he that keepeth his commandments dwelleth in him, and he in him. And hereby we know that he abideth in us, by the Spirit which he hath given us.

V CAUTIONS OF FELLOWSHIP, 4:1–21

A Concerning False Lying Spirits, 4:1–6

4 Beloved, believe not every spirit, but try the spirits whether they are of God: because many false prophets are gone out into the world.

2 Hereby know ye the Spirit of God: Every spirit that confesseth that Jesus Christ is come in the flesh is of God:

3 And every spirit that confesseth not that Jesus Christ is come in the flesh is not of God: and this is that *spirit* of an'tichrīst, whereof ye have heard that it should come; and even now already is it in the world.

4 Ye are of God, little children, and have overcome them: because greater is he that is in you, than he that is in the world.

5 They are of the world: therefore speak they of the world, and the world heareth them.

6 We are of God: he that knoweth God heareth us; he that is not of God heareth not us. Hereby know we the spirit of truth, and the spirit of error.

3:24 *dwelleth in him.* This is the same word translated "abide" in John 15:1–10. To abide in Christ requires keeping His commandments.

4:1 *believe not every spirit.* Apparently some of John's readers were being lead astray by Gnosticism.

4:3 *spirit of antichrist.* The false prophets were influenced by demonic spirits.

4:4 *he that is in you*=the Holy Spirit (3:24). *he that is in the world*=Satan (John 12:31).

B Concerning a True Loving Spirit, 4:7–21

1 *The ground of brotherly love*, 4:7–10

7 Beloved, let us love one another: for love is of God; and every one that loveth is born of God, and knoweth God.

8 He that loveth not knoweth not God; for God is love.

9 In this was manifested the love of God toward us, because that God sent his only begotten Son into the world, that we might live through him.

10 Herein is love, not that we loved God, but that he loved us, and sent his Son *to be* the propitiation for our sins.

2 *The glories of love*, 4:11–21

11 Beloved, if God so loved us, we ought also to love one another.

12 No man hath seen God at any time. If we love one another, God dwelleth in us, and his love is perfected in us.

13 Hereby know we that we dwell in him, and he in us, because he hath given us of his Spirit.

14 And we have seen and do testify that the Father sent the Son *to be* the Saviour of the world.

15 Whosoever shall confess that Jesus is the Son of God, God dwelleth in him, and he in God.

16 And we have known and believed the love that God hath to us. God is love; and he that dwelleth in love dwelleth in God, and God in him.

17 Herein is our love made perfect, that we may have boldness in the day of judgment: because as he is, so are we in this world.

18 There is no fear in love; but perfect love casteth out fear: because fear hath torment. He that feareth is not made perfect in love.

4:7–12 This is one of John's greatest passages. God is love. This is His supreme quality. God can be known only by those who live in love. Actually we would not have known how to love Him if He had not first loved us. If we love one another, God abides in us and His love is perfected or matured in us (v. 12).

4:16 To live a love-filled life is to be God-filled.

4:17 *boldness in the day of judgment*. The believer who has practiced love during his earthly life will be able to approach the judgment seat of Christ without any shame. Such assurance is not presumption because *as he is, so are we in this world*; i.e., we are like Him in love.

4:18 *fear hath torment*. Lit., fear has punishment.

19 We love him, because he first loved us.

20 If a man say, I love God, and hateth his brother, he is a liar: for he that loveth not his brother whom he hath seen, how can he love God whom he hath not seen?

21 And this commandment have we from him, That he who loveth God love his brother also.

VI CONSEQUENCES OF FELLOWSHIP, 5:1–21

A Love for the Brethren, 5:1–3

5 Whosoever believeth that Jesus is the Christ is born of God: and every one that loveth him that begat loveth him also that is begotten of him.

2 By this we know that we love the children of God, when we love God, and keep his commandments.

3 For this is the love of God, that we keep his commandments: and his commandments are not grievous.

B Victory over the World, 5:4–5

4 For whatsoever is born of God overcometh the world: and this is the victory that overcometh the world, *even* our faith.

5 Who is he that overcometh the world, but he that believeth that Jesus is the Son of God?

C Verification of Christ's Credentials, 5:6–12

6 This is he that came by water and blood, *even* Jesus Christ; not by water only, but by water and blood. And it is the Spirit that beareth witness, because the Spirit is truth.

7 For there are three that bear record in heaven, the Father, the Word, and the Holy Ghost: and these three are one.

8 And there are three that bear witness in earth, the Spirit, and the water, and the blood: and these three agree in one.

4:19 *We love him.* The word *him* is not in the text.

5:6 *by water and blood.* The water refers to the inauguration of Christ's earthly ministry at His baptism by John (Mark (1:9–11) and the blood refers to the close of His earthly life at His crucifixion. Jesus proved Himself to be the Christ at His baptism and by pouring out His soul to death.

5:7 The verse ends with the word *record.* The remainder of v. 7 and half of v. 8 are not in any ancient Greek manuscript, only in later Latin manuscripts.

9 If we receive the witness of men, the witness of God is greater: for this is the witness of God which he hath testified of his Son.

10 He that believeth on the Son of God hath the witness in himself: he that believeth not God hath made him a liar; because he believeth not the record that God gave of his Son.

11 And this is the record, that God hath given to us eternal life, and this life is in his Son.

12 He that hath the Son hath life; *and* he that hath not the Son of God hath not life.

D Assurance of Eternal Life, 5:13

13 These things have I written unto you that believe on the name of the Son of God; that ye may know that ye have eternal life, and that ye may believe on the name of the Son of God.

E Guidance in Prayer, 5:14–17

14 And this is the confidence that we have in him, that, if we ask any thing according to his will, he heareth us:

15 And if we know that he hear us, whatsoever we ask, we know that we have the petitions that we desired of him.

16 If any man see his brother sin a sin *which is* not unto death, he shall ask, and he shall give him life for them that sin not unto death. There is a sin unto death: I do not say that he shall pray for it.

17 All unrighteousness is sin: and there is a sin not unto death.

F Freedom from Habitual Sin, 5:18–21

18 We know that whosoever is born of God sinneth not; but he that is begotten of God keepeth himself, and that wicked one toucheth him not.

19 *And* we know that we are of God, and the whole world lieth in wickedness.

5:11 *record*. Lit., witness.
5:14 *according to his will*. This is a gracious limitation because God's will is always best for His children.
5:16 *sin unto death*. Believers can sin to the point where physical death results as the judgment of God (I Cor. 11:30). The Greek reads *sin*, not *a sin* in vv. 16 and 17.

20 And we know that the Son of God is come, and hath given us an understanding, that we may know him that is true, and we are in him that is true, *even* in his Son Jesus Christ. This is the true God, and eternal life.

21 Little children, keep yourselves from idols. Amen.

5:21 *idols*. An idol is anything that substitutes for God.

INTRODUCTION TO
THE SECOND LETTER OF
John

AUTHOR: John   DATE: 90

The "Elect Lady"   The destination of this second letter is enigmatic. Some believe that the "elect lady" is a figurative way of designating a particular church ("elect sister," v. 13, then, would mean a different church) while others hold that the letter was addressed to an individual lady and her family (in which case her sister would be her natural sister).

The Date   The situation and ideas of this letter indicate that it was written about the same time as the other Johannine letters and from the same place, Ephesus. See the Introduction to 1 John.

The Contents   The main teaching of 1 John is repeated in briefer form in this letter.

OUTLINE OF 2 JOHN

THE SECOND LETTER OF
John

I INTRODUCTION AND GREETING, 1-3

The elder unto the elect lady and her children, whom I love in the truth; and not I only, but also all they that have known the truth;

2 For the truth's sake, which dwelleth in us, and shall be with us for ever.

3 Grace be with you, mercy, *and* peace, from God the Father, and from the Lord Jesus Christ, the Son of the Father, in truth and love.

II COMMENDATION
FOR WALKING IN TRUTH, 4

4 I rejoiced greatly that I found of thy children walking in truth, as we have received a commandment from the Father.

III COMMANDMENT TO LOVE ONE ANOTHER, 5-6

5 And now I beseech thee, lady, not as though I wrote a new commandment unto thee, but that which we had from the beginning, that we love one another.

6 And this is love, that we walk after his commandments. This is the commandment, That, as ye have heard from the beginning, ye should walk in it.

1 *her children.* Either the congregation (if *elect lady* is a church) or her natural offspring (if an individual). *the truth.* I.e., the gospel message; so also in v. 2.

4 *walking in truth.* This means ordering one's life by the Word of God.

6 *Love* is defined as obeying His commandments. *is come.* Lit., coming. This present tense participle seems to include the past coming of Christ in flesh at the incarnation, the present continuance of His risen humanity, as well as His future coming to earth. By contrast the perfect tense participle in 1 John 4:2 emphasizes only His incarnation. *antichrist.* See note at 1 John 2:18.

IV CAUTIONS CONCERNING FALSE TEACHERS, 7–11

7 For many deceivers are entered into the world, who confess not that Jesus Christ is come in the flesh. This is a deceiver and an an'tichrĭst.

8 Look to yourselves, that we lose not those things which we have wrought, but that we receive a full reward.

9 Whosoever transgresseth, and abideth not in the doctrine of Christ, hath not God. He that abideth in the doctrine of Christ, he hath both the Father and the Son.

10 If there come any unto you, and bring not this doctrine, receive him not into *your* house, neither bid him God speed:

11 For he that biddeth him God speed is partaker of his evil deeds.

V CONCLUDING REMARKS AND GREETINGS, 12–13

12 Having many things to write unto you, I would not *write* with paper and ink: but I trust to come unto you, and speak face to face, that our joy may be full.

13 The children of thy elect sister greet thee. Amen.

8 *we*. Better manuscripts read *ye* for all three "we's" in this verse.
10 *receive him not into your house*. Do not give a false teacher hospitality. *God speed*. Do not offer any kind of encouraging greeting.
11 *partaker*. Lit., one who fellowships. He who bids such a person Godspeed actually fellowships in the work of Antichrist.
12 *paper and ink*. The piths of papyrus reeds were cut into strips, laid across each other at right angles, pressed, and pasted together to form sheets of paper. The word *ink* simply means black, for ink in ancient times was compounded of charcoal, gum, and water.

INTRODUCTION TO
THE THIRD LETTER OF
John

AUTHOR: John   DATE: 90

Characteristics of the letter   *This is a very personal letter,
addressed to Gaius, which focuses on an ecclesiastical problem relative to traveling teachers. Gaius had given them
hospitality, while Diotrephes, a self-assertive leader in a
particular church, had refused to receive them. John ex-
hibits his apostolic authority in his rebuke of Diotrephes
(v. 10). Demetrius, who himself may have been a traveling
teacher, probably took the letter to Gaius.*

OUTLINE OF 3 JOHN

706

THE THIRD LETTER OF
John

I OPENING GREETINGS, 1

The elder unto the wellbeloved Gáʹus, whom I love in the truth.

II THE INFLUENCE OF GAIUS, 2–8

A His Godly Life, 2–4

2 Beloved, I wish above all things that thou mayest prosper and be in health, even as thy soul prospereth.

3 For I rejoiced greatly, when the brethren came and testified of the truth that is in thee, even as thou walkest in the truth.

4 I have no greater joy than to hear that my children walk in truth.

B His Generous Treatment of Traveling Ministers, 5–8

5 Beloved, thou doest faithfully whatsoever thou doest to the brethren, and to strangers;

6 Which have borne witness of thy charity before the church: whom if thou bring forward on their journey after a godly sort, thou shalt do well:

7 Because that for his name's sake they went forth, taking nothing of the Gentiles.

1 *elder.* See note at 1 Tim. 3:1.
2 *above all things.* Lit., in all things. *be in health.* I.e., physical health. Perhaps Gaius had been ill.
4 *my children.* I.e., beneficiaries of John's ministry, whom he had probably led to Christ.
5 *to the brethren, and to strangers.* Gaius had aided "brethren" and also "strangers," the latter being the more difficult and therefore the more praiseworthy form of hospitality (Heb. 13:2). Traveling evangelists and teachers were dependent on men like Gaius for shelter and sustenance.
6 *bring forward on their journey.* This means to help on their journey with food, money, arrangements for companions, means of travel, etc.
7 *taking nothing of the Gentiles.* These traveling missionaries declined to receive help from those who were not converted lest they should appear to be selling the gospel.

8 We therefore ought to receive such, that we might be fellowhelpers to the truth.

III THE INDICTMENT OF DIOTREPHES, 9–11

A His Selfish Ambition, 9

9 I wrote unto the church: but Dīot'rephēs, who loveth to have the preeminence among them, receiveth us not.

B His Selfish Activities, 10–11

10 Wherefore, if I come, I will remember his deeds which he doeth, prating against us with malicious words: and not content therewith, neither doth he himself receive the brethren, and forbiddeth them that would, and casteth *them* out of the church.

11 Beloved, follow not that which is evil, but that which is good. He that doeth good is of God: but he that doeth evil hath not seen God.

IV THE INTRODUCTION OF DEMETRIUS, 12

12 Dēmē'trius hath good report of all *men*, and of the truth itself: yea, and we *also* bear record; and ye know that our record is true.

V CONCLUDING REMARKS AND BENEDICTION, 13–14

13 I had many things to write, but I will not with ink and pen write unto thee:

14 But I trust I shall shortly see thee, and we shall speak face to face. Peace *be* to thee. *Our* friends salute thee. Greet the friends by name.

10 *prating.* Lit., talking nonsense. Diotrephes' talk was senseless and malicious (wicked). *casteth them out of the church.* Some sort of exclusion, whether formal excommunication or not.

13 *pen.* The pen was a reed pointed at the end.

14 *Peace be to thee.* In some texts and translations this phrase begins a new verse (15).

INTRODUCTION TO
THE LETTER OF
Jude

AUTHOR: Jude   DATE: 70–80

The Author *Jude identifies himself as the brother of James (v. 1), the leader of the Jerusalem church (Acts 15), and the half-brother of the Lord Jesus. Jude is listed among Christ's half-brothers in Matthew 13:55 and Mark 6:3. Although, by his own statement, he intended to write a doctrinal treatise, pressing circumstances required him to deal instead with the false teachers (v. 3).*

The Purpose *This letter was written to defend the apostolic faith against false teaching which was arising inside the churches. Alarming advances were being made by an incipient Gnosticism—not in this case an ascetic form like that attacked by Paul in Colossians, but an antinomian form. The Gnostics viewed all matter as evil and everything spiritual as good. They therefore cultivated their spiritual lives and allowed their "flesh" to do anything it liked, with the result that they were guilty of lawlessness of all kinds. (See "Gnosticism" in the Introduction to 1 John).*

The Extrabiblical Quotations *In verses 14 and 15 Jude quotes the pseudepigraphal apocalypse of 1 Enoch and in verse 9 he alludes to a reference in another pseudepigraphal book, The Assumption of Moses. This does not mean that he considered these books to be inspired as the canonical Scriptures were. Paul quoted from heathen poets without implying their inspiration (Acts 17:28; 1 Cor. 15:33; Tit. 1:12).*

The Readers *The readers are not identified, but we know that they were beset by false teachers who were immoral, covetous, proud, and divisive.*

The Contents *Condemning the heretics in no uncertain terms, Jude exhorts his readers to "earnestly contend for the faith" (v. 3).*

OUTLINE OF JUDE

I The Salutation and Purpose, 1–4
II Exposure of the False Teachers, 5–16
  A Their Doom, 5–7
  B Their Denunciation, 8–10
  C Their Description, 11–16
III Exhortations to Believers, 17–23
IV The Benediction, 24–25

THE LETTER OF
Jude

I THE SALUTATION AND PURPOSE, 1–4

Jude, the servant of Jesus Christ, and brother of James, to them that are sanctified by God the Father, and preserved in Jesus Christ, *and* called:

2 Mercy unto you, and peace, and love, be multiplied.

3 Beloved, when I gave all diligence to write unto you of the common salvation, it was needful for me to write unto you, and exhort *you* that ye should earnestly contend for the faith which was once delivered unto the saints.

4 For there are certain men crept in unawares, who were before of old ordained to this condemnation, ungodly men, turning the grace of our God into lasciviousness, and denying the only Lord God, and our Lord Jesus Christ.

1 Jude addresses the *called*; i.e., all Christians who have been called to a knowledge of God through Christ. They are beloved by God (*sanctified*; better, beloved) and *preserved in* or, better, kept for Jesus Christ at His second coming.

3 *contend for the faith which was once delivered.* This means: stand for the body of truth once for all given, not to be added to or subtracted from (Gal. 1:23).

4 *denying . . . Christ.* Better, denying our only Master and Lord, Jesus Christ. The word for Master is "despot" as in Acts 4:24, 1 Tim. 6:1, and is applied here to Jesus. To deny Jesus as Lord was to disbelieve the most basic Christian tenet.

II EXPOSURE OF THE FALSE TEACHERS, 5-16

A Their Doom, 5-7

5 I will therefore put you in remembrance, though ye once knew this, how that the Lord, having saved the people out of the land of Egypt, afterward destroyed them that believed not.

6 And the angels which kept not their first estate, but left their own habitation, he hath reserved in everlasting chains under darkness unto the judgment of the great day.

7 Even as Sodom and Gōmor'rha, and the cities about them in like manner, giving themselves over to fornication, and going after strange flesh, are set forth for an example, suffering the vengeance of eternal fire.

B Their Denunciation, 8-10

8 Likewise also these *filthy* dreamers defile the flesh, despise dominion, and speak evil of dignities.

9 Yet Michael the archangel, when contending with the devil he disputed about the body of Moses, durst not bring against him a railing accusation, but said, The Lord rebuke thee.

10 But these speak evil of those things which they know not: but what they know naturally, as brute beasts, in those things they corrupt themselves.

C Their Description, 11-16

11 Woe unto them! for they have gone in the way of Cain, and ran greedily after the error of Bā'lāām for reward, and perished in the gainsaying of Cor'ē.

5 *destroyed them that believed not*. The possibility of lapsing is illustrated by the disbelieving Israelites who were saved out of Egypt but subsequently destroyed.

6 *angels who kept not their first estate*. This is a reference to that group of fallen angels whom Satan persuaded to cohabit with women and who were confined immediately because of the gross nature of that sin (Gen. 6:1-4). In the apocryphal book of Enoch their dramatic end is described. See note at 2 Pet. 2:4.

8 *dignities*. This refers to angels (2 Pet. 2:10) though it may include leaders of the church as well.

11 *the way of Cain*. This is the rejection of God's provision for acceptance with Himself (Gen. 4:1-12). Today, it is the rejection of God's offer of forgiveness through Christ. *the*

12 These are spots in your feasts of charity, when they feast with you, feeding themselves without fear: clouds *they are* without water, carried about of winds; trees whose fruit withereth, without fruit, twice dead, plucked up by the roots;

13 Raging waves of the sea, foaming out their own shame; wandering stars, to whom is reserved the blackness of darkness for ever.

14 And Enoch also, the seventh from Adam, prophesied of these, saying, Behold, the Lord cometh with ten thousands of his saints,

15 To execute judgment upon all, and to convince all that are ungodly among them of all their ungodly deeds which they have ungodly committed, and of all their hard *speeches* which ungodly sinners have spoken against him.

16 These are murmurers, complainers, walking after their own lusts; and their mouth speaketh great swelling *words*, having men's persons in admiration because of advantage.

III EXHORTATIONS TO BELIEVERS, 17–23

17 But, beloved, remember ye the words which were spoken before of the apostles of our Lord Jesus Christ;

18 How that they told you there should be mockers in the last time, who should walk after their own ungodly lusts.

19 These be they who separate themselves, sensual, having not the Spirit.

---

error of Balaam. Balaam hired himself out as a prophet and epitomizes deceit and covetousness (Num. 22–24; 2 Pet. 2:15; Rev. 2:14). *the gainsaying of Core.* The sin of Korah was rebellion against duly constituted authority (Num. 16).
12 *feasts.* Lit. love-feasts. These fellowship meals were eaten in connection with the Lord's Supper (see note at 1 Cor. 11:20). Pride, greed, rebellion—these sins comprise the iniquity of the "ungodly men," v. 4.
14 *Enoch.* See Gen. 5:19–24; Heb. 11:5–6. Though this prophecy is found in the noncanonical book of Enoch (1:9), the original prophecy was uttered by the Enoch of the Bible and was later expanded and incorporated in the book of Enoch.
16 *great swelling words*=arrogant things.
19 *separate themselves*=set up divisions (i.e., heretical groups), *sensual* or, as they are called in 1 Cor. 2:14, "natural." Jude believed that these false teachers were not truly redeemed (Rom. 8:9).

20 But ye, beloved, building up yourselves on your most holy faith, praying in the Holy Ghost,

21 Keep yourselves in the love of God, looking for the mercy of our Lord Jesus Christ unto eternal life.

22 And of some have compassion, making a difference:

23 And others save with fear, pulling *them* out of the fire; hating even the garment spotted by the flesh.

IV THE BENEDICTION, 24–25

24 Now unto him that is able to keep you from falling, and to present *you* faultless before the presence of his glory with exceeding joy,

25 To the only wise God our Saviour, *be* glory and majesty, dominion and power, both now and ever. Amen.

22 have *compassion*. Some manuscripts read "convince." *making a difference*. Lit., who are wavering. Thus the verse says, "Have compassion or convince those who are wavering."

24 *falling*. Lit., stumbling. This is one of the great benedictions of the N.T.

25 *Saviour*. Add "through Jesus Christ our Lord." God is the Savior of the O.T. and in the N.T. that title survives, occurring seven times.

INTRODUCTION TO
The Revelation
TO JOHN

AUTHOR: John   DATE: 90's

The Author   According to the book itself the author's name was John (1:4, 9, 22:8), and he was a prophet (22:9). Traditionally this John has been identified as John the apostle, the son of Zebedee (see the Introduction to 1 John). Although it is true that the style of the Revelation is different from the Gospel and the three epistles of John, this does not necessitate the conclusion that the Revelation was written by a different John. The nature of apocalyptic literature, the ecstatic state in which the vision was received, and the circumstances of being a prisoner could easily account for the different style of the book.

The Date   Clearly the Revelation was written in a period when the Christians were threatened by Rome, undoubtedly by pressure to make them recant and accept the cult of emperor-worship. Some maintain that the book was written during Nero's persecution of Christians after the burning of Rome in A.D. 64. However, the more probable date is during the harsh reign of that warped personality, Domitian (A.D. 81–96). This later date for the book was held by the church father Irenaeus and other early Christian writers, and it agrees better with the picture of complacency and defection of the churches in chapters 2 and 3. This dating is widely accepted by modern scholars, too.

Interpretation of the Book   There are four principal viewpoints concerning the interpretation of this book: (1) The preterist, which sees the prophecies of the book as having been fulfilled in the early history of the church; (2) the historical, which understands the book as portraying a panorama of the history of the church from the days of John to the end of time; (3) the idealist, which considers

714

the book a pictorial unfolding of great principles in constant conflict without reference to actual events; and (4) the futurist, which views most of the book (ch. 4–22) as prophecy which is yet to be fulfilled. This is the viewpoint taken in these notes, and it is based on the principle of interpreting the text plainly.

The book is a revelation (apocalypse, 1:1) and as such is expected to be understood. Much of it is frighteningly clear. Some symbols are explained (1:20; 17:1, 15). It is always important to notice carefully the words "like," "as," and "as it were" (6:1; 9:7), for these words indicate a comparison, not an identification.

The Contents This is the revelation of Jesus Christ, and He is the center of the entire book (1:1). In His risen glory (chapter 1) He directs His churches on earth (2–3). He is the slain and risen Lamb to whom all worship is directed (4–5). The judgments of the coming seven-year period of tribulation on this earth are the display of the wrath of the Lamb (6–19; see especially 6:16–17), and the return of Christ to this earth is described in 19:11–21. The millennial reign of Christ is described in chapter 20, and the new heavens and new earth in 21 and 22.

The outline of the book is indicated in 1:19. The things which John had seen include the vision of the risen Christ in chapter 1. The "things which are" comprise the letters to the seven churches of Asia Minor in chapters 2 and 3. The "things which shall be hereafter" are the prophecies of chapters 4–22.

OUTLINE OF REVELATION

I The Prologue, 1:1–8
  A The Superscription, 1:1–3
  B The Salutation, 1:4–8
II "The Things Which Thou Hast Seen," 1:9–20
  A Circumstances of the Vision, 1:9–11
  B Content of the Vision, 1:12–16
  C Consequences of the Vision, 1:17–20
III "The Things Which Are," 2:1–3:22
  A The Message to Ephesus, 2:1–7
  B The Message to Smyrna, 2:8–11
  C The Message to Pergamum, 2:12–17
  D The Message to Thyatira, 2:18–29
  E The Message to Sardis, 3:1–6
  F The Message to Philadelphia, 3:7–13
  G The Message to Laodicea, 3:14–22

The Revelation

OF ST. JOHN THE DIVINE

I THE PROLOGUE, 1:1–8

A The Superscription, 1:1–3

1 The Revelation of Jesus Christ, which God gave unto him, to shew unto his servants things which must shortly come to pass; and he sent and signified *it* by his angel unto his servant John:

1:1 *of Jesus Christ*=from Jesus Christ. He gave this revelation from God, by means of an angel, to John. *shortly*. This word does not indicate that the events described in this book will

2 Who bare record of the word of God, and of the testimony of Jesus Christ, and of all things that he saw.

3 Blessed *is* he that readeth, and they that hear the words of this prophecy, and keep those things which are written therein: for the time *is* at hand.

B The Salutation, 1:4–8

4 John to the seven churches which are in Asia: Grace *be* unto you, and peace, from him which is, and which was, and which is to come; and from the seven Spirits which are before his throne;

5 And from Jesus Christ, *who is* the faithful witness, *and* the first begotten of the dead, and the prince of the kings of the earth. Unto him that loved us, and washed us from our sins in his own blood,

6 And hath made us kings and priests unto God and his Father; to him *be* glory and dominion for ever and ever. Amen.

7 Behold, he cometh with clouds; and every eye shall see him, and they *also* which pierced him: and all kindreds of the earth shall wail because of him. Even so, Amen.

necessarily occur soon, but that when they do begin to happen they will come to pass swiftly (see the same word in Luke 18:8).

1:3 *Blessed.* There are 7 beatitudes in Revelation. This is the first; the others are found at 14:13; 16:15; 19:9; 20:6; 22:7, 14. John wants the book read at once, and preferably aloud in the churches.

1:4 *seven.* The number 7, occurring 54 times in the book, appears more frequently than any other number. In the Bible it is associated with completion, fulfillment, and perfection (Gen. 2:2; Ex. 20:10; Lev. 14:7; Acts 6:3). In the Revelation there are 7 churches and 7 Spirits (1:4), 7 lampstands (1:12), 7 stars (1:16), 7 seals on the scroll (5:1), 7 horns and 7 eyes of the Lamb (5:6), 7 angels and 7 trumpets (8:2), 7 thunders (10:3), 7 heads of the dragon (12:3), 7 heads of the beast (13:1), 7 golden bowls (15:7), 7 kings (17:10). *the seven Spirits.* Many understand this to refer to the Holy Spirit in His perfect fullness (see Isa. 11:2; Rev. 4:5), though some take this as a reference to 7 angels who are before God's throne.

1:5 *first begotten of the dead.* I.e., Christ was the first to receive a resurrection body which is immortal. See Col. 1:15 where He is designated the firstborn of every creature (Ps. 89:27). *Unto him that loved us, and washed us from our sins.* Some texts read "Unto him who loves us, and who loosed us from our sins."

1:7 See Matt. 24:29–30.

8 I am Alpha and Ōmeg'a, the beginning and the ending, saith the Lord, which is, and which was, and which is to come, the Almighty.

II "THE THINGS WHICH THOU HAST SEEN," 1:9–20

A Circumstances of the Vision, 1:9–11

9 I John, who also am your brother, and companion in tribulation, and in the kingdom and patience of Jesus Christ, was in the isle that is called Patmos, for the word of God, and for the testimony of Jesus Christ.

10 I was in the Spirit on the Lord's day, and heard behind me a great voice, as of a trumpet,

11 Saying, I am Alpha and Ōmeg'a, the first and the last: and, What thou seest, write in a book, and send *it* unto the seven churches which are in Asia; unto Ephesus, and unto Smyrna, and unto Per'gamos, and unto Thȳatī'ra, and unto Sardis, and unto Philadelphia, and unto Lāodicē'a.

B Content of the Vision, 1:12–16

12 And I turned to see the voice that spake with me. And being turned, I saw seven golden candlesticks;

13 And in the midst of the seven candlesticks *one* like unto the Son of man, clothed with a garment down to the foot, and girt about the paps with a golden girdle.

14 His head and *his* hairs *were* white like wool, as white as snow; and his eyes *were* as a flame of fire;

15 And his feet like unto fine brass, as if they burned in a furnace; and his voice as the sound of many waters.

16 And he had in his right hand seven stars: and out

1:8 *Alpha and Omega*. These are the first and last letters of the Greek alphabet, indicating that the Lord God is the beginning and end of all things. The best texts add "God" after the word "Lord."

1:9 *Patmos* is a small island in the Aegean Sea, SW. of Ephesus. *for* (twice)=because of.

1:10 *in the Spirit*. I.e., in a state of spiritual ecstasy.

1:12 *candlesticks*. Better, lampstands. These represent the 7 churches mentiond in v. 11 (see v. 20).

1:13 *paps*=chest. Christ's clothing designates Him as priest and judge. Notice the description in Dan. 7:9.

1:14 *eyes were as a flame of fire*. Compare the figure used in 1 Cor. 3:13 in relation to judgment.

1:16 *in his right hand seven stars*. The right hand is the place of honor (Eph. 1:20). The stars are the "angels of the seven

of his mouth went a sharp twoedged sword: and his countenance *was* as the sun shineth in his strength.

C Consequences of the Vision, 1:17–20

17 And when I saw him, I fell at his feet as dead. And he laid his right hand upon me, saying unto me, Fear not; I am the first and the last:

18 *I am* he that liveth, and was dead; and, behold, I am alive for evermore, Amen; and have the keys of hell and of death.

19 Write the things which thou hast seen, and the things which are, and the things which shall be hereafter;

20 The mystery of the seven stars which thou sawest in my right hand, and the seven golden candlesticks. The seven stars are the angels of the seven churches: and the seven candlesticks which thou sawest are the seven churches.

III "THE THINGS WHICH ARE," 2:1–3:22

A The Message to Ephesus, 2.1–7

2 Unto the angel of the church of Ephesus write; These things saith he that holdeth the seven stars in his right hand, who walketh in the midst of the seven golden candlesticks;

churches" (v. 20). The word "angel" may mean a superhuman being, implying that each church has a special guardian angel, or more likely it refers here to the human leader of each local church (see Luke 9:52 and Jas. 2:25 where the word "angel" translated "messenger," is used of human beings). *sword.* A symbol of the truth and severity of the Word of God (Heb. 4:12).

1:17 *I am the first and the last.* In v. 8 God was the Alpha and Omega. Here Christ gives Himself a similar title.

1:18 *the keys of hell and of death.* The keys denote the authority of Christ over physical death and hell (lit., Hades), the place which temporarily holds the immaterial part of the unbeliever between death and the ultimate casting into the lake of fire (Rev. 20:14).

1:19 Here is the basic outline of the book: (1) Things which John had seen as recorded in chapter 1; (2) things which are; i.e., the present state of the churches (ch. 2–3); (3) things which shall be hereafter. This section clearly begins with 4:1, since the same phrase is used there (translated "hereafter").

2:1 The churches addressed in chapters 2 and 3 were actual churches of John's day. But they also represent churches of all generations. This is supported by the fact that only seven were selected out of the many that existed and flourished in

2 I know thy works, and thy labour, and thy patience, and how thou canst not bear them which are evil: and thou hast tried them which say they are apostles, and are not, and hast found them liars:

3 And hast borne, and hast patience, and for my name's sake hast laboured, and hast not fainted.

4 Nevertheless I have *somewhat* against thee, because thou hast left thy first love.

5 Remember therefore from whence thou art fallen, and repent, and do the first works; or else I will come unto thee quickly, and will remove thy candlestick out of his place, except thou repent.

6 But this thou hast, that thou hatest the deeds of the Nicōlāï'tāns, which I also hate.

7 He that hath an ear, let him hear what the Spirit saith unto the churches; To him that overcometh will I give to eat of the tree of life, which is in the midst of the paradise of God.

B The Message to Smyrna, 2:8–11

8 And unto the angel of the church in Smyrna write; These things saith the first and the last, which was dead, and is alive;

John's time, and by the statement at the close of each letter that the Spirit was speaking to the churches (vv. 7, 11, etc.). *Ephesus.* Under Caesar Augustus, Ephesus became the capital of the Roman province called Asia, which today is the western portion of Turkey (Pergamum had been the capital earlier). It was the residence of the apostle John before and after his exile on Patmos, and it was the site of the great temple of Diana (see the Introduction to Ephesians).

2:3 *fainted*=weary; i.e., have not given up.

2:4 *thou hast left thy first love.* "Left" implies a responsible, not accidental, act. More than 30 years before, the church had been commended for its love (Eph. 1:15–16).

2:5 *remove thy candlestick.* I.e., remove the usefulness of that local church.

2:6 *the Nicolaitanes.* I.e., followers of Nicolas (Acts 6:5) according to early church fathers. These were apparently a sect which advocated license in matters of Christian conduct, including free love, though some understand from the meaning of the word ("conquering of the people") that they were a group which promoted a clerical hierarchy (see 2:15 also).

2:7 *To him that overcometh.* Not a reference to a specially spiritual group among the believers, but including all true Christians (1 John 5:5).

2:8 *Smyrna.* A seaport city about 35 miles N. of Ephesus (called Izmir today). It was a center of the Imperial cult of Rome.

9 I know thy works, and tribulation, and poverty, (but thou art rich) and *I know* the blasphemy of them which say they are Jews, and are not, but *are* the synagogue of Satan.

10 Fear none of those things which thou shalt suffer: behold, the devil shall cast *some* of you into prison, that ye may be tried; and ye shall have tribulation ten days: be thou faithful unto death, and I will give thee a crown of life.

11 He that hath an ear, let him hear what the Spirit saith unto the churches; He that overcometh shall not be hurt of the second death.

C The Message to Pergamum, 2:12–17

12 And to the angel of the church in Per'gamos write; These things saith he which hath the sharp sword with two edges;

13 I know thy works, and where thou dwellest, *even* where Satan's seat *is*: and thou holdest fast my name, and hast not denied my faith, even in those days wherein Antipas *was* my faithful martyr, who was slain among you, where Satan dwelleth.

14 But I have a few things against thee, because thou hast there them that hold the doctrine of Bā'lāam, who taught Balac to cast a stumblingblock before the children of Israel, to eat things sacrificed unto idols, and to commit fornication.

15 So hast thou also them that hold the doctrine of the Nicōlāī'tāns, which thing I hate.

16 Repent; or else I will come unto thee quickly, and will fight against them with the sword of my mouth.

2:10 *ye shall have tribulation ten days.* This may refer to a ten-day period of intense persecution to come, or it may indicate ten periods of persecution from Nero to Diocletian. *crown of life.* The reward of one who is faithful under trial or unto death (see Jas. 1:12 and note at 1 Cor. 3:14).

2:11 *the second death*=eternal separation from God in the lake of fire (see 20:14; also note at Rom. 6:2).

2:12 *Pergamos.* Pergamum, which is about 45 miles N. of Smyrna, boasted one of the finest libraries of antiquity and was the place where parchment was first used. It had once been the capital of the Roman province of Asia.

2:13 *where Satan's seat is.* Lit., where Satan's throne is—a reference to Pergamum's worship either of the Roman emperor or of Zeus at his altar on the local acropolis (or both).

2:14 *the doctrine of Balaam.* See note at Jude 11.

17 He that hath an ear, let him hear what the Spirit saith unto the churches; To him that overcometh will I give to eat of the hidden manna, and will give him a white stone, and in the stone a new name written, which no man knoweth saving he that receiveth *it*.

D The Message to Thyatira, 2:18–29

18 And unto the angel of the church in Thȳatī'ra write; These things saith the Son of God, who hath his eyes like unto a flame of fire, and his feet *are* like fine brass;

19 I know thy works, and charity, and service, and faith, and thy patience, and thy works; and the last *to be* more than the first.

20 Notwithstanding I have a few things against thee, because thou sufferest that woman Jez'ebel, which calleth herself a prophetess, to teach and to seduce my servants to commit fornication, and to eat things sacrificed unto idols.

21 And I gave her space to repent of her fornication; and she repented not.

22 Behold, I will cast her into a bed, and them that commit adultery with her into great tribulation, except they repent of their deeds.

23 And I will kill her children with death; and all the churches shall know that I am he which searcheth the reins and hearts: and I will give unto every one of you according to your works.

24 But unto you I say, and unto the rest in Thȳatī'ra, as many as have not this doctrine, and which have not known the depths of Satan, as they speak; I will put upon you none other burden.

2:17 *hidden manna* refers to the sufficiency of Christ for the believer's needs, as it was for the Hebrews during the wilderness wanderings. The *white stone* may refer to the custom of voting for acquittal by using a white stone (indicating that the believer can be assured of his acquittal before God, Rom. 8:1); or it may refer to the sufficiency of Christ (from the custom of wearing amulets around the neck).

2:18 *Thyatira.* This was a city noted for its numerous trade guilds and for its wool and dyeing industry (Acts 16:14). It was about 35 miles SE. of Pergamum.

2:20 *Jezebel.* This false prophetess may actually have been named Jezebel, or more probably a well-known woman's actions made her a contemporary counterpart of the notorious Jezebel of 1 Kings 16 and 2 Kings 9.

2:24 *the depths of Satan.* Lit., the deep things of Satan. To those of you (John says) who have not been seduced by these doctrines, these deep things of Satan, I say only . . .

25 But that which ye have *already* hold fast till I come.

26 And he that overcometh, and keepest my works unto the end, to him will I give power over the nations:

27 And he shall rule them with a rod of iron; as the vessels of a potter shall they be broken to shivers: even as I received of my Father.

28 And I will give him the morning star.

29 He that hath an ear, let him hear what the Spirit saith unto the churches.

E The Message to Sardis, 3:1-6

3 And unto the angel of the church in Sardis write; These things saith he that hath the seven Spirits of God, and the seven stars; I know thy works, that thou hast a name that thou livest, and art dead.

2 Be watchful, and strengthen the things which remain, that are ready to die: for I have not found thy works perfect before God.

3 Remember therefore how thou hast received and heard, and hold fast, and repent. If therefore thou shalt not watch, I will come on thee as a thief, and thou shalt not know what hour I will come upon thee.

4 Thou hast a few names even in Sardis which have not defiled their garments; and they shall walk with me in white: for they are worthy.

5 He that overcometh, the same shall be clothed in white raiment; and I will not blot out his name out of the book of life, but I will confess his name before my Father, and before his angels.

6 He that hath an ear, let him hear what the Spirit saith unto the churches.

F The Message to Philadelphia, 3:7-13

7 And to the angel of the church in Philadelphia write; These things saith he that is holy, he that is true, he that

---

2:27 *he shall rule them with a rod of iron.* A reference to Christ's reign on earth. See 12:5; 19:15; Ps. 2:9.

2:28 *the morning star.* Probably a reference to Christ Himself (22:16; 2 Pet. 1:19) or, perhaps, the immortal life that one will receive from Christ.

3:1 *Sardis.* The capital of ancient Lydia, situated about 30 miles S. of Thyatira. It was rebuilt by Tiberius in A.D. 17; the imperial cult was strong in it. *and art dead.* I.e., devoid of spiritual life and power.

3:4 *which have not defiled their garments.* I.e., persons who had remained faithful to Christ.

3:7 *Philadelphia.* The word means brotherly love. A lesser city

hath the key of David, he that openeth, and no man shutteth; and shutteth, and no man openeth;

8 I know thy works: behold, I have set before thee an open door, and no man can shut it: for thou hast a little strength, and hast kept my word, and hast not denied my name.

9 Behold, I will make them of the synagogue of Satan, which say they are Jews, and are not, but do lie; behold, I will make them to come and worship before thy feet, and to know that I have loved thee.

10 Because thou hast kept the word of my patience, I also will keep thee from the hour of temptation, which shall come upon all the world, to try them that dwell upon the earth.

11 Behold, I come quickly; hold that fast which thou hast, that no man take thy crown.

12 Him that overcometh will I make a pillar in the temple of my God, and he shall go no more out: and I will write upon him the name of my God, and the name of the city of my God, *which is* new Jerusalem, which cometh down out of heaven from my God: and *I will write upon him* my new name.

13 He that hath an ear, let him hear what the Spirit saith unto the churches.

G The Message to Laodicea, 3:14–22

14 And unto the angel of the church of the Lāodicē′ans write; These things saith the Amen, the faithful and true witness, the beginning of the creation of God;

15 I know thy works, that thou art neither cold nor hot: I would thou wert cold or hot.

than the others addressed, it was located about 38 miles S.E. of Sardis. Its chief deity was Dionysus.

3:7 *the key of David.* A quotation from Isa. 22:22, where it is a symbol of authority. Compare the *keys of hell and of death* (1:18) and the *keys of the kingdom* (Matt. 16:19).

3:10 *I will keep thee from the hour of temptation* (lit., testing). This is a promise that believers will be delivered from the tribulation period which will come upon the entire earth (Matt. 24:14, 21; see note at 1 Thess. 4:17).

3:12 *a pillar in the temple of my God.* This is a promise of honoring believers in the New Jerusalem, referring to the custom of honoring a magistrate by placing a pillar in one of the temples in Philadelphia.

3:14 *Laodiceans.* Inhabitants of a city about 90 miles due E. of Ephesus and 45 miles SE. of Philadelphia. Under Roman rule it was a wealthy city.

16 So then because thou art lukewarm, and neither cold nor hot, I will spue thee out of my mouth.

17 Because thou sayest, I am rich, and increased with goods, and have need of nothing; and knowest not that thou art wretched, and miserable, and poor, and blind, and naked:

18 I counsel thee to buy of me gold tried in the fire, that thou mayest be rich; and white raiment, that thou mayest be clothed, and *that* the shame of thy nakedness do not appear; and anoint thine eyes with eyesalve, that thou mayest see.

19 As many as I love, I rebuke and chasten: be zealous therefore, and repent.

20 Behold, I stand at the door, and knock: if any man hear my voice, and open the door, I will come in to him, and will sup with him, and he with me.

21 To him that overcometh will I grant to sit with me in my throne, even as I also overcame, and am set down with my Father in his throne.

22 He that hath an ear, let him hear what the Spirit saith unto the churches.

IV "THE THINGS
WHICH SHALL BE HEREAFTER," 4:1–22:5

A The Tribulation Period, 4:1–19:21

1 *The throne in heaven,* 4:1–11

a THE THRONE, 4:1–3

4 After this I looked, and, behold, a door *was* opened in heaven: and the first voice which I heard *was* as it were of a trumpet talking with me; which said, Come up hither, and I will shew thee things which must be hereafter.

2 And immediately I was in the spirit: and, behold, a throne was set in heaven, and *one* sat on the throne.

3:16 *I will spue thee out of my mouth.* Lit., I will vomit. . . .

3:18 *eyesalve.* Laodicea was a center for making medicines, including a tablet that was powdered and smeared on the eyes. This verse may make reference to the city's three main sources of wealth (banking, production of wool cloth, and medicines).

3:20 *I stand at the door, and knock.* How incredible that Christ should be kept outside His own church! How gracious that He should still seek entrance!

4:2 *I was in the spirit* as in 1:10.

3 And he that sat was to look upon like a jasper and a sardine stone: and *there was* a rainbow round about the throne, in sight like unto an emerald.

b THE THRONG, 4:4–8

4 And round about the throne *were* four and twenty seats: and upon the seats I saw four and twenty elders sitting, clothed in white raiment; and they had on their heads crowns of gold.

5 And out of the throne proceeded lightnings and thunderings and voices: and *there were* seven lamps of fire burning before the throne, which are the seven Spirits of God.

6 And before the throne *there was* a sea of glass like unto crystal: and in the midst of the throne, and round about the throne, *were* four beasts full of eyes before and behind.

7 And the first beast *was* like a lion, and the second beast like a calf, and the third beast had a face as a man, and the fourth beast *was* like a flying eagle.

8 And the four beasts had each of them six wings about *him*; and *they were* full of eyes within: and they rest not day and night, saying, Holy, holy, holy, Lord God Almighty, which was, and is, and is to come.

c THE THEME, 4:9–11

9 And when those beasts give glory and honour and thanks to him that sat on the throne, who liveth for ever and ever,

10 The four and twenty elders fall down before him that sat on the throne, and worship him that liveth for

---

4:3 *jasper* (clear as crystal, 21:11) *and a sardine* (blood red). *emerald*. Light green.

4:4 *four and twenty elders.* Some understand these to be angelic beings, though it is likely that the 24 elders represent redeemed people who are glorified, crowned, and enthroned (*seats=* thrones).

4:5 *seven Spirits of God.* See note at 1:4.

4:6 *four beasts.* Lit., four living creatures or living ones. These may be angels, probably cherubim (Ezek. 10:15, 20), or they may be representations of the attributes of God Himself (since they are said to be "in the midst of the throne").

4:7 Many see a similarity between the four living ones and the fourfold manner in which Christ is portrayed in the Gospels. In Matthew He appears as the Lion of the tribe of Judah; in Mark as the Servant who became the sacrifice for sin (the calf was a sacrificial animal, Heb. 9:12, 19); Luke's emphasis is on the Son of Man; and "a flying eagle" links Him with heaven, as John does.

ever and ever, and cast their crowns before the throne,
saying,

11 Thou art worthy, O Lord, to receive glory and honour and power: for thou hast created all things, and for
thy pleasure they are and were created.

2 *The scroll in heaven*, 5:1–14

a THE SCROLL, 5:1

5 And I saw in the right hand of him that sat on the
throne a book written within and on the backside,
sealed with seven seals.

b THE SEARCH, 5:2–5

2 And I saw a strong angel proclaiming with a loud
voice, Who is worthy to open the book, and to loose the
seals thereof?

3 And no man in heaven, nor in earth, neither under the
earth, was able to open the book, neither to look thereon.

4 And I wept much, because no man was found worthy
to open and to read the book, neither to look thereon.

5 And one of the elders saith unto me, Weep not:
behold, the Lion of the tribe of Juda, the Root of David,
hath prevailed to open the book, and to loose the seven
seals thereof.

c THE SAVIOR-SOVEREIGN, 5:6–7

6 And I beheld, and, lo, in the midst of the throne and
of the four beasts, and in the midst of the elders, stood a
Lamb as it had been slain, having seven horns and seven
eyes, which are the seven Spirits of God sent forth into all
the earth.

7 And he came and took the book out of the right hand
of him that sat upon the throne.

5:1 *a book.* Lit., a scroll. This may be called the "Book of
Redemption" containing the story of man's fall through sin
and rise through Christ (Heb. 2:5–9).

5:5 *the Lion of the tribe of Juda* (Gen. 49:9); *The Root of
David* (Isa. 11:1, 10). The Messiah, John is assured, is competent and worthy to break the seven seals and open the
scroll to release the plagues.

5:6 *as it had been slain.* Christ, the Lamb, bears the marks of
His death even in His glorified state (Luke 24:40; John 20:20,
27). *horns* are a symbol of strength (1 Kings 22:11; Zech.
1:18).

d THE SONG, 5:8–14

8 And when he had taken the book, the four beasts and four *and* twenty elders fell down before the Lamb, having every one of them harps, and golden vials full of odours, which are the prayers of saints.

9 And they sung a new song, saying, Thou art worthy to take the book, and to open the seals thereof: for thou wast slain, and hast redeemed us to God by thy blood out of every kindred, and tongue, and people, and nation;

10 And hast made us unto our God kings and priests: and we shall reign on the earth.

11 And I beheld, and I heard the voice of many angels round about the throne and the beasts and the elders: and the number of them was ten thousand times ten thousand, and thousands of thousands;

12 Saying with a loud voice, Worthy is the Lamb that was slain to receive power, and riches, and wisdom, and strength, and honour, and glory, and blessing.

13 And every creature which is in heaven, and on the earth, and under the earth, and such as are in the sea, and all that are in them, heard I saying, Blessing, and honour, and glory, and power, *be* unto him that sitteth upon the throne, and unto the Lamb for ever and ever.

14 And the four beasts said, Amen. And the four *and* twenty elders fell down and worshipped him that liveth for ever and ever.

3 *The seal judgments*, 6:1–17

a FIRST SEAL: COLD WAR, 6:1–2

6 And I saw when the Lamb opened one of the seals, and I heard, as it were the noise of thunder, one of the four beasts saying, Come and see.

2 And I saw, and behold a white horse: and he that sat on him had a bow; and a crown was given unto him: and he went forth conquering, and to conquer.

5:8 *vials*. Lit., bowls, like saucers.

5:9–10 Many manuscripts omit "us" in v. 9 and read "them" and "they" instead of "us" and "we" in v. 10. In either case the elders could be singing of their own redemption in either the first or third person.

6:2 *he that sat on him*. Probably a reference to Antichrist (see note at 1 John 2:18). His method of conquest does not seem to include open warfare, since peace is not removed from the earth until the second seal is opened (v. 3). This corresponds to the description of delusion in 1 Thess. 5:3.

b SECOND SEAL: OPEN WAR, 6:3–4

3 And when he had opened the second seal, I heard the second beast say, Come and see.

4 And there went out another horse *that was* red: and *power* was given to him that sat thereon to take peace from the earth, and that they should kill one another: and there was given unto him a great sword.

c THIRD SEAL: FAMINE, 6:5–6

5 And when he had opened the third seal, I heard the third beast say, Come and see. And I beheld, and lo a black horse; and he that sat on him had a pair of balances in his hand.

6 And I heard a voice in the midst of the four beasts say, A measure of wheat for a penny, and three measures of barley for a penny; and *see* thou hurt not the oil and the wine.

d FOURTH SEAL: DEATH, 6:7–8

7 And when he had opened the fourth seal, I heard the voice of the fourth beast say, Come and see.

8 And I looked, and behold a pale horse: and his name that sat on him was Death, and Hell followed with him. And power was given unto them over the fourth part of the earth, to kill with sword, and with hunger, and with death, and with the beasts of the earth.

e FIFTH SEAL: MARTYRDOM, 6:9–11

9 And when he had opened the fifth seal, I saw under the altar the souls of them that were slain for the word of God, and for the testimony which they held:

10 And they cried with a loud voice, saying, How long, O Lord, holy and true, dost thou not judge and avenge our blood on them that dwell on the earth?

11 And white robes were given unto every one of them; and it was said unto them, that they should rest yet for a

6:6 *a penny.* Lit., a denarius, a Roman silver coin worth about 20 cents. It would normally buy 8 measures of wheat or 24 of barley. This will be a severe shortage of food.

6:8 *pale*=a sickly, yellowish-green.   *death.* Probably the inevitable result of disease which accompanies war and famine.

6:9 *the souls of them that were slain.* These are evidently the martyrs of the first months of the tribulation period.

6:11 *rest yet for a little season*=wait a little while. It is difficult for these martyrs to understand why God would allow their murderers to live; yet God asks them to trust Him.

little season, until their fellowservants also and their brethren, that should be killed as they *were*, should be fulfilled.

f SIXTH SEAL: PHYSICAL DISTURBANCES, 6:12–17

12 And I beheld when he had opened the sixth seal, and, lo, there was a great earthquake; and the sun became black as sackcloth of hair, and the moon became as blood;

13 And the stars of heaven fell unto the earth, even as a fig tree casteth her untimely figs, when she is shaken of a mighty wind.

14 And the heaven departed as a scroll when it is rolled together; and every mountain and island were moved out of their places.

15 And the kings of the earth, and the great men, and the rich men, and the chief captains, and the mighty men, and every bondman, and every free man, hid themselves in the dens and in the rocks of the mountains;

16 And said to the mountains and rocks, Fall on us, and hide us from the face of him that sitteth on the throne, and from the wrath of the Lamb:

17 For the great day of his wrath is come; and who shall be able to stand?

4 Interlude: the redeemed of the tribulation, 7:1–17

a THE 144,000 JEWS, 7:1–8

7 And after these things I saw four angels standing on the four corners of the earth, holding the four winds of the earth, that the wind should not blow on the earth, nor on the sea, nor on any tree.

2 And I saw another angel ascending from the east, having the seal of the living God: and he cried with a loud voice to the four angels, to whom it was given to hurt the earth and the sea,

3 Saying, Hurt not the earth, neither the sea, nor the trees, till we have sealed the servants of our God in their foreheads.

4 And I heard the number of them which were sealed: *and there were* sealed an hundred *and* forty *and* four thousand of all the tribes of the children of Israel.

6:12 These cosmic disturbances are predicted elsewhere (Isa. 34:4; Joel 2:30–31; Matt. 24:7).

6:16 When the tribulation comes, men will act as if they believe the end of the world is at hand.

7:4 *sealed an hundred and forty and four thousand.* These are Jews from each of the 12 tribes (12,000×12) who are made secure in order to perform some service for God during these

5 Of the tribe of Juda *were* sealed twelve thousand. Of the tribe of Reuben *were* sealed twelve thousand. Of the tribe of Gad *were* sealed twelve thousand.

6 Of the tribe of Aser *were* sealed twelve thousand. Of the tribe of Nep'thalim *were* sealed twelve thousand. Of the tribe of Manas'sēs *were* sealed twelve thousand.

7 Of the tribe of Simeon *were* sealed twelve thousand. Of the tribe of Levi *were* sealed twelve thousand. Of the tribe of Is'sachar *were* sealed twelve thousand.

8 Of the tribe of Zabū'lon *were* sealed twelve thousand. Of the tribe of Joseph *were* sealed twelve thousand. Of the tribe of Benjamin *were* sealed twelve thousand.

b THE MULTITUDE OF GENTILES, 7:9-17

9 After this I beheld, and, lo, a great multitude, which no man could number, of all nations, and kindreds, and people, and tongues, stood before the throne, and before the Lamb, clothed with white robes, and palms in their hands;

10 And cried with a loud voice, saying, Salvation to our God which sitteth upon the throne, and unto the Lamb.

11 And all the angels stood round about the throne, and *about* the elders and the four beasts, and fell before the throne on their faces, and worshipped God,

12 Saying, Amen: Blessing, and glory, and wisdom, and thanksgiving, and honour, and power, and might, *be* unto our God for ever and ever. Amen.

13 And one of the elders answered, saying unto me, What are these which are arrayed in white robes? and whence came they?

14 And I said unto him, Sir, thou knowest. And he said to me, These are they which came out of great tribulation, and have washed their robes, and made them white in the blood of the Lamb.

15 Therefore are they before the throne of God, and serve him day and night in his temple: and he that sitteth on the throne shall dwell among them.

16 They shall hunger no more, neither thirst any more; neither shall the sun light on them, nor any heat.

days. Perhaps they are evangels. The omission of the tribe of Dan may be because Dan was guilty of idolatry on many occasions (Lev. 24:11; Judg. 18:1–2, 30–31; 1 Kings 12:28).
7:9 *a great multitude*. This multitude is composed of many racial and geographic groups who will be redeemed during the tribulation period (v. 14). In these difficult days, many will find Christ as Savior.

17 For the Lamb which is in the midst of the throne shall feed them, and shall lead them unto living fountains of waters: and God shall wipe away all tears from their eyes.

5 *The six trumpet judgments,* 8:1–9:21

a THE SEVENTH SEAL OPENED, 8:1–6

8 And when he had opened the seventh seal, there was silence in heaven about the space of half an hour.

2 And I saw the seven angels which stood before God; and to them were given seven trumpets.

3 And another angel came and stood at the altar, having a golden censer; and there was given unto him much incense, that he should offer *it* with the prayers of all saints upon the golden altar which was before the throne.

4 And the smoke of the incense, *which came* with the prayers of the saints, ascended up before God out of the angel's hand.

5 And the angel took the censer, and filled it with fire of the altar, and cast *it* into the earth: and there were voices, and thunderings, and lightnings, and an earthquake.

6 And the seven angels which had the seven trumpets prepared themselves to sound.

b FIRST TRUMPET: THE EARTH SMITTEN, 8:7

7 The first angel sounded, and there followed hail and fire mingled with blood, and they were cast upon the earth: and the third part of trees was burnt up, and all green grass was burnt up.

c SECOND TRUMPET: THE SEA SMITTEN, 8:8–9

8 And the second angel sounded, and as it were a great mountain burning with fire was cast into the sea: and the third part of the sea became blood;

9 And the third part of the creatures which were in the sea, and had life, died; and the third part of the ships were destroyed.

8:1 *opened the seventh seal.* Out of the seventh seal comes the second series of judgments—the seven trumpets. Apparently the judgments announced by the trumpets follow chronologically those of the seals.

8:7 Reliable texts insert "and a third part of the earth was burnt up." There is no reason not to understand this and the other judgments plainly, even though the implications are staggering.

d THIRD TRUMPET: THE WATERS SMITTEN, 8:10–11

10 And the third angel sounded, and there fell a great star from heaven, burning as it were a lamp, and it fell upon the third part of the rivers, and upon the fountains of waters;

11 And the name of the star is called Wormwood: and the third part of the waters became wormwood; and many men died of the waters, because they were made bitter.

e FOURTH TRUMPET: THE HEAVENS SMITTEN, 8:12–13

12 And the fourth angel sounded, and the third part of the sun was smitten, and the third part of the moon, and the third part of the stars; so as the third part of them was darkened, and the day shone not for a third part of it, and the night likewise.

13 And I beheld, and heard an angel flying through the midst of heaven, saying with a loud voice, Woe, woe, woe, to the inhabiters of the earth by reason of the other voices of the trumpet of the three angels, which are yet to sound!

f FIFTH TRUMPET: MEN SMITTEN, 9:1–12

9 And the fifth angel sounded, and I saw a star fall from heaven unto the earth: and to him was given the key of the bottomless pit.

2 And he opened the bottomless pit; and there arose a smoke out of the pit, as the smoke of a great furnace; and the sun and the air were darkened by reason of the smoke of the pit.

3 And there came out of the smoke locusts upon the

8:11 *Wormwood.* Though many species of wormwood grow in Palestine, all have a strong, bitter (but not poisonous) taste which causes the plant to be used as a symbol of bitterness, sorrow, and calamity. This plague will make a third part of the fresh water supply of the earth unfit for human consumption.

8:12 Compare Luke 21:25.

8:13 *an angel flying.* Better, an eagle.

9:1 *a star.* This is an intelligent creature, apparently the angel of the bottomless pit (v. 11). Note the "he" in v. 2. *the bottomless pit.* Lit., the shaft of the abyss (for other uses of this phrase see Luke 8:31; Rom. 10:7; Rev. 9:11; 11:7; 17:8; 20:1, 3). Luke 8:31 indicates that this is the abode of the demons.

9:3 *locusts.* The fact that these creatures come from the abyss and their unusual description in vv. 7–11 indicate that they are demonic.

earth: and unto them was given power, as the scorpions of
the earth have power.

4 And it was commanded them that they should not
hurt the grass of the earth, neither any green thing, neither
any tree; but only those men which have not the seal of
God in their foreheads.

5 And to them it was given that they should not kill
them, but that they should be tormented five months: and
their torment *was* as the torment of a scorpion, when he
striketh a man.

6 And in those days shall men seek death, and shall not
find it; and shall desire to die, and death shall flee from
them.

7 And the shapes of the locusts *were* like unto horses
prepared unto battle; and on their heads *were* as it were
crowns like gold, and their faces *were* as the faces of men.

8 And they had hair as the hair of women, and their
teeth were as *the teeth* of lions.

9 And they had breastplates, as it were breastplates of
iron; and the sound of their wings *was* as the sound of
chariots of many horses running to battle.

10 And they had tails like unto scorpions, and there
were stings in their tails: and their power *was* to hurt men
five months.

11 And they had a king over them, *which is* the angel
of the bottomless pit, whose name in the Hebrew tongue
is Abaddon, but in the Greek tongue hath *his* name Apol'-
lyon.

12 One woe is past; *and*, behold, there come two woes
more hereafter.

g SIXTH TRUMPET: MEN KILLED, 9:13–21

13 And the sixth angel sounded, and I heard a voice
from the four horns of the golden altar which is before
God,

14 Saying to the sixth angel which had the trumpet,
Loose the four angels which are bound in the great river
Eûphrā'tēs.

15 And the four angels were loosed, which were prepared
for an hour, and a day, and a month, and a year, for to
slay the third part of men.

9:4–5 The limitations which God places upon the activities of
these creatures show that He is still in full control of these
events.
9:11 *Abaddon . . . Apollyon.* Both words mean destruction.
9:15 *an hour.* Lit., this particular hour.

16 And the number of the army of the horsemen *were* two hundred thousand thousand: and I heard the number of them.

17 And thus I saw the horses in the vision, and them that sat on them, having breastplates of fire, and of jacinth, and brimstone: and the heads of the horses *were* as the heads of lions; and out of their mouths issued fire and smoke and brimstone.

18 By these three was the third part of men killed, by the fire, and by the smoke, and by the brimstone, which issued out of their mouths.

19 For their power is in their mouth, and in their tails: for their tails *were* like unto serpents, and had heads, and with them they do hurt.

20 And the rest of the men which were not killed by these plagues yet repented not of the works of their hands, that they should not worship devils, and idols of gold, and silver, and brass, and stone, and of wood: which neither can see, nor hear, nor walk:

21 Neither repented they of their murders, nor of their sorceries, nor of their fornication, nor of their thefts.

6 *The little scroll*, 10:1-11

10 And I saw another mighty angel come down from heaven, clothed with a cloud: and a rainbow *was* upon his head, and his face *was* as it were the sun, and his feet as pillars of fire:

2 And he had in his hand a little book open: and he set his right foot upon the sea, and *his* left *foot* on the earth,

3 And cried with a loud voice, as *when* a lion roareth: and when he had cried, seven thunders uttered their voices.

4 And when the seven thunders had uttered their voices, I was about to write: and I heard a voice from heaven saying unto me, Seal up those things which the seven thunders uttered, and write them not.

9:16 *the army.* The 200,000,000 creatures who compose this supernatural cavalry may be human beings or demons. For other supernatural armies see 2 Kings 2:11; 6:14-17; Rev. 19:14).

9:18 *By these three*=by these three plagues; i.e., by the fire, smoke, and brimstone.

9:20 The religion of many will involve demon- and idol-worship.

9:21 *sorceries*=magical arts, potions, and poisons (see Gal. 5:20; Rev. 18:23; 21:8; 22:15). This is the word from which we derive the English word "pharmacies."

5 And the angel which I saw stand upon the sea and upon the earth lifted up his hand to heaven,

6 And sware by him that liveth for ever and ever, who created heaven, and the things that therein are, and the earth, and the things that therein are, and the sea, and the things which are therein, that there should be time no longer:

7 But in the days of the voice of the seventh angel, when he shall begin to sound, the mystery of God should be finished, as he hath declared to his servants the prophets.

8 And the voice which I heard from heaven spake unto me again, and said, Go *and* take the little book which is open in the hand of the angel which standeth upon the sea and upon the earth.

9 And I went unto the angel, and said unto him, Give me the little book. And he said unto me, Take *it*, and eat it up; and it shall make thy belly bitter, but it shall be in thy mouth sweet as honey.

10 And I took the little book out of the angel's hand, and ate it up; and it was in my mouth sweet as honey: and as soon as I had eaten it, my belly was bitter.

11 And he said unto me, Thou must prophesy again before many peoples, and nations, and tongues, and kings.

7 *The two witnesses*, 11:1–19

a TEMPLE, 11:1–2

11 And there was given me a reed like unto a rod: and the angel stood, saying, Rise, and measure the temple of God, and the altar, and them that worship therein.

10:6 *there should be time no longer*. Lit., there will be no more delay; i.e., when the seventh angel sounds (11:15), the bowl judgments will be poured out (16:1–21) and the tribulation will come to an end with the return of Christ.

10:7 *the mystery of God*. Truth concerning God Himself which will be not revealed until His kingdom is established on earth.

10:9 The eating of the little scroll was to remind John that although these truths from God may be pleasant to his taste, they were bitter when digested, because they spoke of judgment. The revelation of God's judgment, on second thought, should always bring heaviness of heart to the child of God. Compare Ezek. 2:8–3:3.

10:11 *before*. Better, concerning, about.

11:1 *the temple of God*. This is apparently the temple which will be built during the tribulation days in which Jewish worship will be carried on during the first part of that period and in which at the mid-point of the seven-year period, the man of sin will exalt himself to be worshiped (2 Thess. 2:4).

2 But the court which is without the temple leave out, and measure it not; for it is given unto the Gentiles: and the holy city shall they tread under foot forty *and* two months.

b TIME, 11:3

3 And I will give *power* unto my two witnesses, and they shall prophesy a thousand two hundred *and* threescore days, clothed in sackcloth.

c TRAITS, 11:4–6

4 These are the two olive trees, and the two candlesticks standing before the God of the earth.

5 And if any man will hurt them, fire proceedeth out of their mouth, and devoureth their enemies: and if any man will hurt them, he must in this manner be killed.

6 These have power to shut heaven, that it rain not in the days of their prophecy: and have power over waters to turn them to blood, and to smite the earth with all plagues, as often as they will.

d TERMINATION, 11:7–10

7 And when they shall have finished their testimony, the beast that ascendeth out of the bottomless pit shall make war against them, and shall overcome them, and kill them.

8 And their dead bodies *shall lie* in the street of the great city, which spiritually is called Sodom and Egypt, where also our Lord was crucified.

9 And they of the people and kindreds and tongues and

11:2 *forty and two months.* This equals three and one-half years and probably refers to the last half of the tribulation period.

11:3 *a thousand two hundred and threescore days.* This also equals three and one-half years, and refers to the period of the ministry of the two witnesses.

11:4 *two olive trees.* For the symbolism see Zech. 4:3, 14. *two candlesticks* (lampstands) that give out a witness (v. 3).

11:5–6 The miraculous powers of the two witnesses are reminiscent of those of Elijah and Moses (Ex. 7:20; 8:1–12:29; 1 Kings 17:1; 18:41–45; 2 Kings 1:10–12).

11:7 *the beast.* This is the Antichrist (see note at 1 John 2:18), also called the man of sin (2 Thess. 2:3). The same person is mentioned in Rev. 6:3; 13:1; 14:9, 11; 15:2; 16:2; 17:3, 13; 19:20; 20:10. He cannot kill these two witnesses until God allows him to.

11:8 *the great city*=Jerusalem.

nations shall see their dead bodies three days and an half, and shall not suffer their dead bodies to be put in graves.

10 And they that dwell upon the earth shall rejoice over them, and make merry, and shall send gifts one to another; because these two prophets tormented them that dwelt on the earth.

e TRANSLATION, 11:11–14

11 And after three days and an half the Spirit of life from God entered into them, and they stood upon their feet; and great fear fell upon them which saw them.

12 And they heard a great voice from heaven saying unto them, Come up hither. And they ascended up to heaven in a cloud; and their enemies beheld them.

13 And the same hour was there a great earthquake, and the tenth part of the city fell, and in the earthquake were slain of men seven thousand: and the remnant were affrighted, and gave glory to the God of heaven.

14 The second woe is past; *and*, behold, the third woe cometh quickly.

f SEVENTH TRUMPET, 11:15–19

15 And the seventh angel sounded; and there were great voices in heaven, saying, The kingdoms of this world are become *the kingdoms* of our Lord, and of his Christ; and he shall reign for ever and ever.

16 And the four and twenty elders, which sat before God on their seats, fell upon their faces, and worshipped God,

17 Saying, We give thee thanks, O Lord God Almighty, which art, and wast, and art to come; because thou hast taken to thee thy great power, and hast reigned.

18 And the nations were angry, and thy wrath is come, and the time of the dead, that they should be judged, and that thou shouldest give reward unto thy servants the prophets, and to the saints, and them that fear thy name, small and great; and shouldest destroy them which destroy the earth.

19 And the temple of God was opened in heaven, and there was seen in his temple the ark of his testament: and

11:11 *and they stood upon their feet*. Imagine the effect this resurrection of these two men will have on those who only the moment before were viewing their corpses in the street!
11:13 *the remnant*=the rest who were not killed by the earthquake.

there were lightnings, and voices, and thunderings, and an earthquake, and great hail.

8 War, 12:1–17

a WAR ON EARTH: PHASE I, 12:1–6

12 And there appeared a great wonder in heaven; a woman clothed with the sun, and the moon under her feet, and upon her head a crown of twelve stars:

2 And she being with child cried, travailing in birth, and pained to be delivered.

3 And there appeared another wonder in heaven; and behold a great red dragon, having seven heads and ten horns, and seven crowns upon his heads.

4 And his tail drew the third part of the stars of heaven, and did cast them to the earth: and the dragon stood before the woman which was ready to be delivered, for to devour her child as soon as it was born.

5 And she brought forth a man child, who was to rule all nations with a rod of iron: and her child was caught up unto God, and *to* his throne.

6 And the woman fled into the wilderness, where she hath a place prepared of God, that they should feed her there a thousand two hundred *and* threescore days.

b WAR IN HEAVEN, 12:7–12

7 And there was war in heaven: Michael and his angels fought against the dragon; and the dragon fought and his angels,

12:1 *a woman.* She represents Israel, who gave Christ to the world (v. 5) and who will be persecuted severely during the tribulation days (v. 13).

12:3 *a great red dragon.* This is Satan (v. 9).

12:4 *the third part of the stars of heaven.* This may refer to Satan's past rebellion against God (Ezek. 28:15), in which a third of the angels joined him, or it may indicate a meteor-shower judgment on the earth.

12:5 *her child was caught up unto God.* A reference to the ascension of Christ.

12:6 *a thousand two hundred and threescore days.* The last three and one-half years of the tribulation period will see intense persecution of Israel. Details are given in vv. 13–17. No mention is made of the thousands of years between the ascension (v. 5) and the future tribulation (v. 6). See Dan. 9:27; Matt. 24:14; 1 Thess. 4:17.

12:7 *Michael . . . against the dragon.* This likely will occur at

8 And prevailed not; neither was their place found any more in heaven.

9 And the great dragon was cast out, that old serpent, called the Devil, and Satan, which deceiveth the whole world: he was cast out into the earth, and his angels were cast out with him.

10 And I heard a loud voice saying in heaven, Now is come salvation, and strength, and the kingdom of our God, and the power of his Christ: for the accuser of our brethren is cast down, which accused them before our God day and night.

11 And they overcame him by the blood of the Lamb, and by the word of their testimony; and they loved not their lives unto the death.

12 Therefore rejoice, *ye* heavens, and ye that dwell in them. Woe to the inhabiters of the earth and of the sea! for the devil is come down unto you, having great wrath, because he knoweth that he hath but a short time.

C WAR ON EARTH: PHASE II, 12:13–17

13 And when the dragon saw that he was cast unto the earth, he persecuted the woman which brought forth the man *child*.

14 And to the woman were given two wings of a great eagle, that she might fly into the wilderness, into her place, where she is nourished for a time, and times, and half a time, from the face of the serpent.

15 And the serpent cast out of his mouth water as a flood after the woman, that he might cause her to be carried away of the flood.

16 And the earth helped the woman, and the earth opened her mouth, and swallowed up the flood which the dragon cast out of his mouth.

17 And the dragon was wroth with the woman, and went to make war with the remnant of her seed, which keep the commandments of God, and have the testimony of Jesus Christ.

---

the mid-point of the tribulation. Michael is the only angel designated an archangel in the Bible (Jude 9).

12:9–11 Notice two of Satan's activities in these verses: to deceive the world and to accuse the brethren. The believer's defense against Satan is (1) to bank on the merits of the death of Christ, (2) to be active in witnessing, and (3) to be willing for any sacrifice, including death (v. 11).

12:17 *remnant* = rest.

9 *The beast and his prophet,* 13:1–18

a THE BEAST, 13:1–10

13 And I stood upon the sand of the sea, and saw a beast rise up out of the sea, having seven heads and ten horns, and upon his horns ten crowns, and upon his heads the name of blasphemy.

2 And the beast which I saw was like unto a leopard, and his feet were as *the feet* of a bear, and his mouth as the mouth of a lion: and the dragon gave him his power, and his seat, and great authority.

3 And I saw one of his heads as it were wounded to death; and his deadly wound was healed: and all the world wondered after the beast.

4 And they worshipped the dragon which gave power unto the beast: and they worshipped the beast, saying, Who *is* like unto the beast? who is able to make war with him?

5 And there was given unto him a mouth speaking great things and blasphemies; and power was given unto him to continue forty *and* two months.

6 And he opened his mouth in blasphemy against God, to blaspheme his name, and his tabernacle, and them that dwell in heaven.

7 And it was given unto him to make war with the saints, and to overcome them: and power was given him over all kindreds, and tongues, and nations.

13:1 *And I stood.* Some texts read "he stood" ((referring to the dragon) and continue with "I saw a beast" (the "I" referring to John). *a beast*=the Antichrist. See note at 11:7. *seven heads.* These signify Roman emperors. Five had fallen when John wrote, one was then ruling, and the seventh (Antichrist) is yet to come (17:10). Early emperors of Rome deified themselves; Antichrist will far outstrip all his predecessors in his blasphemous ways. *ten horns.* The ten nations that will give their power and authority to the Antichrist (17:13).

13:2 *the dragon gave him his power.* Satan gives Antichrist his power.

13:3 *his deadly wound was healed.* Apparently Satan will miraculously restore Antichrist to life in imitation of the resurrection of Christ. No wonder the world will acclaim Antichrist.

13:5 *forty and two months.* Apparently the last three and one-half years of the tribulation period during which Antichrist's power is practically unrestrained.

8 And all that dwell upon the earth shall worship him, whose names are not written in the book of life of the Lamb slain from the foundation of the world.

9 If any man have an ear, let him hear.

10 He that leadeth into captivity shall go into captivity: he that killeth with the sword must be killed with the sword. Here is the patience and the faith of the saints.

b THE FALSE PROPHET, 13:11–18

11 And I beheld another beast coming up out of the earth; and he had two horns like a lamb, and he spake as a dragon.

12 And he exerciseth all the power of the first beast before him, and causeth the earth and them which dwell therein to worship the first beast, whose deadly wound was healed.

13 And he doeth great wonders, so that he maketh fire come down from heaven on the earth in the sight of men,

14 And deceiveth them that dwell on the earth by *the means of* those miracles which he had power to do in the sight of the beast; saying to them that dwell on the earth, that they should make an image to the beast, which had the wound by a sword, and did live.

15 And he hath power to give life unto the image of the beast, that the image of the beast should both speak, and cause that as many as would not worship the image of the beast should be killed.

16 And he causeth all, both small and great, rich and poor, free and bond, to receive a mark in their right hand, or in their foreheads:

17 And that no man might buy or sell, save he that had the mark, or the name of the beast, or the number of his name.

18 Here is wisdom. Let him that hath understanding

13:8 Some place the phrase *from the foundation of the world* after *not written.*

13:10 That God will punish evildoers is the faith that sustains those who are persecuted during these days.

13:11 *another beast.* This man is Antichrist's lieutenant, who will enforce the worship of Antichrist by doing miracles (v. 13), by making and animating an image of Antichrist (vv. 14–15), by sentencing to death those who disobey (v. 15), and by requiring a mark on the hand or forehead in order that men may buy and sell (vv. 16–17).

13:18 *his number is Six hundred threescore and six.* Somehow,

count the number of the beast: for it is the number of a man; and his number *is* Six hundred threescore *and* six.

10 *Various announcements,* 14:1–20

a CONCERNING THE 144,000, 14:1–5

14 And I looked, and, lo, a Lamb stood on the mount Sion, and with him an hundred forty *and* four thousand, having his Father's name written in their foreheads.

2 And I heard a voice from heaven, as the voice of many waters, and as the voice of a great thunder: and I heard the voice of harpers harping with their harps:

3 And they sung as it were a new song before the throne, and before the four beasts, and the elders: and no man could learn that song but the hundred *and* forty *and* four thousand, which were redeemed from the earth.

4 These are they which were not defiled with women; for they are virgins. These are they which follow the Lamb whithersoever he goeth. These were redeemed from among men, *being* the firstfruits unto God and to the Lamb.

5 And in their mouth was found no guile: for they are without fault before the throne of God.

b CONCERNING THE EVERLASTING GOSPEL, 14:6–8

6 And I saw another angel fly in the midst of heaven, having the everlasting gospel to preach unto them that dwell on the earth, and to every nation, and kindred, and tongue, and people,

7 Saying with a loud voice, Fear God, and give glory to him; for the hour of his judgment is come; and worship

unknown to us, this number will play an important part in the identification of the Antichrist in a future day.

14:1 *a Lamb*. Lit., the Lamb, i.e., Christ. *an hundred forty and four thousand*. Evidently the same group introduced in 7:4, though now their work on earth is finished and they are in heaven.

14:4 *not defiled with women*. This may mean that the 144,000 were unmarried, or it may indicate their celibate state of separation unto God (2 Cor. 11:2). *firstfruits*. The salvation of the 144,000 indicates that a larger group of Israelites will turn to the Lord at the end of the tribulation (Isa. 2:3; Rom. 16:15).

14:5 *before the throne of God*. Some texts omit this phrase.

14:6 *everlasting gospel*. This is God's last call of grace to the world before the return of Christ in judgment.

him that made heaven, and earth, and the sea, and the fountains of waters.

8 And there followed another angel, saying, Babylon is fallen, is fallen, that great city, because she made all nations drink of the wine of the wrath of her fornication.

c CONCERNING BEAST WORSHIPPERS, 14:9–13

9 And the third angel followed them, saying with a loud voice, If any man worship the beast and his image, and receive *his* mark in his forehead, or in his hand,

10 The same shall drink of the wine of the wrath of God, which is poured out without mixture into the cup of his indignation; and he shall be tormented with fire and brimstone in the presence of the holy angels, and in the presence of the Lamb:

11 And the smoke of their torment ascendeth up for ever and ever: and they have no rest day nor night, who worship the beast and his image, and whosoever receiveth the mark of his name.

12 Here is the patience of the saints: here *are* they that keep the commandments of God, and the faith of Jesus.

13 And I heard a voice from heaven saying unto me, Write, Blessed *are* the dead which die in the Lord from henceforth: Yea, saith the Spirit, that they may rest from their labours; and their works do follow them.

d CONCERNING THE HARVESTING OF THE EARTH, 14:14–20

14 And I looked, and behold a white cloud, and upon the cloud *one* sat like unto the Son of man, having on his head a golden crown, and in his hand a sharp sickle.

15 And another angel came out of the temple, crying with a loud voice to him that sat on the cloud, Thrust in thy sickle, and reap: for the time is come for thee to reap; for the harvest of the earth is ripe.

16 And he that sat on the cloud thrust in his sickle on the earth; and the earth was reaped.

17 And another angel came out of the temple which is in heaven, he also having a sharp sickle.

18 And another angel came out from the altar, which had power over fire; and cried with a loud cry to him that had the sharp sickle, saying, Thrust in thy sharp sickle, and

---

14:8 *Babylon is fallen.* This is described in detail in chapters 17–18. For *Babylon,* see note at 17:5.

14:12 Saints can endure, knowing that God will punish their enemies (vv. 9–11).

gather the clusters of the vine of the earth; for her grapes are fully ripe.

19 And the angel thrust in his sickle into the earth, and gathered the vine of the earth, and cast *it* into the great winepress of the wrath of God.

20 And the winepress was trodden without the city, and blood came out of the winepress, even unto the horse bridles, by the space of a thousand *and* six hundred furlongs.

11 *Prelude to the bowl judgments,* 15:1–8

15 And I saw another sign in heaven, great and marvellous, seven angels having the seven last plagues; for in them is filled up the wrath of God.

2 And I saw as it were a sea of glass mingled with fire: and them that had gotten the victory over the beast, and over his image, and over his mark, *and* over the number of his name, stand on the sea of glass, having the harps of God.

3 And they sing the song of Moses the servant of God, and the song of the Lamb, saying, Great and marvellous *are* thy works, Lord God Almighty; just and true *are* thy ways, thou King of saints.

4 Who shall not fear thee, O Lord, and glorify thy name? for *thou* only *art* holy: for all nations shall come and worship before thee; for thy judgments are made manifest.

5 And after that I looked, and, behold, the temple of the tabernacle of the testimony in heaven was opened:

6 And the seven angels came out of the temple, having the seven plagues, clothed in pure and white linen, and having their breasts girded with golden girdles.

7 And one of the four beasts gave unto the seven angels seven golden vials full of the wrath of God, who liveth for ever and ever.

8 And the temple was filled with smoke from the glory of God, and from his power; and no man was able to enter

14:20 This is apparently a reference to Armageddon (19:17–19), when the blood from the slaughter will flow 180 miles to the depth of about 4½ feet.

15:1 *is filled up*=is finished.

15:3 *King of saints.* Better, King of the nations.

15:5 *the temple of the tabernacle of the testimony*=the Holy of Holies.

15:7 *vials.* Lit., bowls, like saucers.

into the temple, till the seven plagues of the seven angels
were fulfilled.

12 *The bowl judgments,* 16:1–21

a FIRST BOWL: GRIEVOUS SORES, 16:1–2

16 And I heard a great voice out of the temple saying
to the seven angels, Go your ways, and pour out
the vials of the wrath of God upon the earth.

2 And the first went, and poured out his vial upon the
earth; and there fell a noisome and grievous sore upon the
men which had the mark of the beast, and *upon* them
which worshipped his image.

b SECOND BOWL: SEAS SMITTEN, 16:3

3 And the second angel poured out his vial upon the
sea; and it became as the blood of a dead *man*: and every
living soul died in the sea.

c THIRD BOWL: RIVERS SMITTEN, 16:4–7

4 And the third angel poured out his vial upon the
rivers and fountains of waters; and they became blood.

5 And I heard the angel of the waters say, Thou art
righteous, O Lord, which art, and wast, and shalt be, because thou hast judged thus.

6 For they have shed the blood of saints and prophets,
and thou hast given them blood to drink; for they are
worthy.

7 And I heard another out of the altar say, Even so,
Lord God Almighty, true and righteous *are* thy judgments.

d FOURTH BOWL: SCORCHING, 16:8–9

8 And the fourth angel poured out his vial upon the
sun; and power was given unto him to scorch men with fire.

9 And men were scorched with great heat, and blasphemed the name of God, which hath power over these
plagues: and they repented not to give him glory.

16:2 *a noisome and grievous sore.* Lit., foul and evil (possibly
   malignant) sore. A plague of ulcers is probably in view.
16:3 *every living soul died in the sea.* Better, every living thing
   died that was in the sea. See 8:9. Imagine the stench and
   disease that will accompany this.
16:6 *for they are worthy.* I.e., they deserve to drink blood because
   they shed the blood of saints and prophets.
16:9 *they repented not.* See v. 11 and 9:21.

e FIFTH BOWL: DARKNESS, 16:10–11

10 And the fifth angel poured out his vial upon the seat of the beast; and his kingdom was full of darkness; and they gnawed their tongues for pain,

11 And blasphemed the God of heaven because of their pains and their sores, and repented not of their deeds.

f SIXTH BOWL: EUPHRATES DRIED, 16:12–16

12 And the sixth angel poured out his vial upon the great river Eûphrā′tēs; and the water thereof was dried up, that the way of the kings of the east might be prepared.

13 And I saw three unclean spirits like frogs *come* out of the mouth of the dragon, and out of the mouth of the beast, and out of the mouth of the false prophet.

14 For they are the spirits of devils, working miracles, *which* go forth unto the kings of the earth and of the whole world, to gather them to the battle of that great day of God Almighty.

15 Behold, I come as a thief. Blessed *is* he that watcheth, and keepeth his garments, lest he walk naked, and they see his shame.

16 And he gathered them together into a place called in the Hebrew tongue Armaged′don.

g SEVENTH BOWL: WIDESPREAD DESTRUCTION, 16:17–21

17 And the seventh angel poured out his vial into the air; and there came a great voice out of the temple of heaven, from the throne, saying, It is done.

16:11 *their sores.* I.e., those referred to in v. 2. Apparently these seven last judgments will occur in rapid succession.

16:12 *the kings of the east.* Lit., the kings of the rising of the sun. The armies of the nations of the Orient will be aided in their march toward Armageddon by the supernatural drying up of the Euphrates River.

16:13 *the dragon* (Satan) . . . *the beast* (Antichrist, 13:1–10) . . . *the false prophet* (the lieutenant, 13:11–18).

16:14 *the battle of that great day of God Almighty.* Lit., the war of. . . . The war will consist of several battles beginning with Antichrist's campaign into Egypt (Dan. 11:40–45) and including a siege of Jerusalem (Zech. 14:2) as well as the final battle at Armageddon (v. 16).

Megiddo at the head of the plain of Esdraelon. This area was

16:16 *Armageddon.* Lit., Mount of Megiddo, near the city of the scene of many O.T. battles, notably Barak and the Canaanites (Judg. 4) and Gideon and the Midianites (Judg. 7).

18 And there were voices, and thunders, and lightnings; and there was a great earthquake, such as was not since men were upon the earth, so mighty an earthquake, *and* so great.

19 And the great city was divided into three parts, and the cities of the nations fell: and great Babylon came in remembrance before God, to give unto her the cup of the wine of the fierceness of his wrath.

20 And every island fled away, and the mountains were not found.

21 And there fell upon men a great hail out of heaven, *every stone* about the weight of a talent: and men blasphemed God because of the plague of the hail; for the plague thereof was exceeding great.

13 *Religious Babylon,* 17:1–18

a THE DESCRIPTION, 17:1–7

17 And there came one of the seven angels which had the seven vials, and talked with me, saying unto me, Come hither; I will shew unto thee the judgment of the great whore that sitteth upon many waters:

2 With whom the kings of the earth have committed fornication, and the inhabitants of the earth have been made drunk with the wine of her fornication.

3 So he carried me away in the spirit into the wilderness: and I saw a woman sit upon a scarlet coloured beast, full of names of blasphemy, having seven heads and ten horns.

4 And the woman was arrayed in purple and scarlet colour, and decked with gold and precious stones and pearls, having a golden cup in her hand full of abominations and filthiness of her fornication:

5 And upon her forehead *was* a name written, MYSTERY, BABYLON THE GREAT, THE MOTHER OF HARLOTS AND ABOMINATIONS OF THE EARTH.

16:19 *the great city.* Either Jerusalem (11:8; Zech. 14:4) or Babylon (18:2).

16:21 *the weight of a talent.* About 100 pounds.

17:5 *Babylon the Great.* Though there was a city of Babylon on the Euphrates River, this seems to be a symbolic name for Rome (see v. 9 and 1 Pet. 5:13). In chapter 17 Babylon represents the false religious system that will center in Rome during the tribulation period. In ch. 18 it represents more the political and commercial aspect of the revised Roman Empire headed by Antichrist. Thus the term stands both for

6 And I saw the woman drunken with the blood of the saints, and with the blood of the martyrs of Jesus: and when I saw her, I wondered with great admiration.

7 And the angel said unto me, Wherefore didst thou marvel? I will tell thee the mystery of the woman, and of the beast that carrieth her, which hath the seven heads and ten horns.

b THE INTERPRETATION, 17:8–18

8 The beast that thou sawest was, and is not; and shall ascend out of the bottomless pit, and go into perdition: and they that dwell on the earth shall wonder, whose names were not written in the book of life from the foundation of the world, when they behold the beast that was, and is not, and yet is.

9 And here *is* the mind which hath wisdom. The seven heads are seven mountains, on which the woman sitteth.

10 And there are seven kings: five are fallen, and one is, *and* the other is not yet come; and when he cometh, he must continue a short space.

11 And the beast that was, and is not, even he is the eighth, and is of the seven, and goeth into perdition.

12 And the ten horns which thou sawest are ten kings, which have received no kingdom as yet; but receive power as kings one hour with the beast.

13 These have one mind, and shall give their power and strength unto the beast.

14 These shall make war with the Lamb, and the Lamb shall overcome them: for he is Lord of lords, and King of kings: and they that are with him *are* called, and chosen, and faithful.

15 And he saith unto me, The waters which thou sawest,

a city and for a system (religious and commercial) related to the city (much like "Wall Street," which is both a place and a system). For other references to Babylon see Gen. 10:10; 11:9 ("Babel"); Isa. 13:19–20; Jer. 50–51. *mother of harlots.* The false religious system is unfaithful to the Lord and thus is a harlot (vv. 1, 15–16).

17:6 *admiration.* Lit., wonder.

17:8 *shall ascend out of the bottomless pit.* See 11:7. *and go into perdition.* See 19:20.

17:12 *ten kings.* This is the 10-nation federation which will form in the west and will be headed by Antichrist (see Dan. 7:23–24). *one hour.* I.e., for one purpose (as in Luke 22:53).

17:15 The apostate church will be ecumenical or worldwide.

where the whore sitteth, are peoples, and multitudes, and nations, and tongues.

16 And the ten horns which thou sawest upon the beast, these shall hate the whore, and shall make her desolate and naked, and shall eat her flesh, and burn her with fire.

17 For God hath put in their hearts to fulfil his will, and to agree, and give their kingdom unto the beast, until the words of God shall be fulfilled.

18 And the woman which thou sawest is that great city, which reigneth over the kings of the earth.

14 *Commercial Babylon*, 18:1–24

a ANNOUNCEMENT, 18:1–3

18 And after these things I saw another angel come down from heaven, having great power; and the earth was lightened with his glory.

2 And he cried mightily with a strong voice, saying, Babylon the great is fallen, is fallen, and is become the habitation of devils, and the hold of every foul spirit, and a cage of every unclean and hateful bird.

3 For all nations have drunk of the wine of the wrath of her fornication, and the kings of the earth have committed fornication with her, and the merchants of the earth are waxed rich through the abundance of her delicacies.

b APPEAL, 18:4–8

4 And I heard another voice from heaven, saying, Come out of her, my people, that ye be not partakers of her sins, and that ye receive not of her plagues.

5 For her sins have reached unto heaven, and God hath remembered her iniquities.

6 Reward her even as she rewarded you, and double unto her double according to her works: in the cup which she hath filled fill to her double.

7 How much she hath glorified herself, and lived deli-

17:16 *these shall hate the whore.* The political power headed by Antichrist will overthrow the false church organization (probably at the mid-point of the tribulation).

18:2 *the hold . . . and a cage.* These words translate the same Greek word, which means "prison." *the habitation of devils.* Babylon is demonic. See Matt. 13:31–32; Eph. 2:2; 1 John 4:6.

18:4 *my people.* God's people are to separate themselves from the Babylonish system (2 Cor. 6:14–17; 1 John 2:15–17).

ciously, so much torment and sorrow give her: for she saith in her heart, I sit a queen, and am no widow, and shall see no sorrow.

8 Therefore shall her plagues come in one day, death, and mourning, and famine; and she shall be utterly burned with fire: for strong *is* the Lord God who judgeth her.

c ANGUISH, 18:9–19

9 And the kings of the earth, who have committed fornication and lived deliciously with her, shall bewail her, and lament for her, when they shall see the smoke of her burning,

10 Standing afar off for the fear of her torment, saying, Alas, alas, that great city Babylon, that mighty city! for in one hour is thy judgment come.

11 And the merchants of the earth shall weep and mourn over her; for no man buyeth their merchandise any more:

12 The merchandise of gold, and silver, and precious stones, and of pearls, and fine linen, and purple, and silk, and scarlet, and all thyine wood, and all manner vessels of ivory, and all manner vessels of most precious wood, and of brass, and iron, and marble,

13 And cinnamon, and odours, and ointments, and frankincense, and wine, and oil, and fine flour, and wheat, and beasts, and sheep, and horses, and chariots, and slaves, and souls of men.

14 And the fruits that thy soul lusted after are departed from thee, and all things which were dainty and goodly are departed from thee, and thou shalt find them no more at all.

15 The merchants of these things, which were made rich by her, shall stand afar off for the fear of her torment, weeping and wailing,

16 And saying, Alas, alas, that great city, that was clothed in fine linen, and purple, and scarlet, and decked with gold, and precious stones, and pearls!

17 For in one hour so great riches is come to nought. And every shipmaster, and all the company in ships, and sailors, and as many as trade by sea, stood afar off,

---

18:8 *in one day*. The judgment will be consummated in a single day, as happened once before to Babylon, when it was taken by Darius (Dan. 5:1, 3–5, 30).

18:12 *thyine wood*. A dark, hard, and fragrant wood valued by the Greeks and Romans for use in cabinet-making.

18 And cried when they saw the smoke of her burning, saying, What *city is* like unto this great city!

19 And they cast dust on their heads, and cried, weeping and wailing, saying, Alas, alas, that great city, wherein were made rich all that had ships in the sea by reason of her costliness! for in one hour is she made desolate.

d ACCLAIM, 18:20–24

20 Rejoice over her, *thou* heaven, and *ye* holy apostles and prophets; for God hath avenged you on her.

21 And a mighty angel took up a stone like a great millstone, and cast *it* into the sea, saying, Thus with violence shall that great city Babylon be thrown down, and shall be found no more at all.

22 And the voice of harpers, and musicians, and of pipers, and trumpeters, shall be heard no more at all in thee; and no craftsman, of whatsoever craft *he be*, shall be found any more in thee; and the sound of a millstone shall be heard no more at all in thee;

23 And the light of a candle shall shine no more at all in thee; and the voice of the bridegroom and of the bride shall be heard no more at all in thee: for thy merchants were the great men of the earth; for by thy sorceries were all nations deceived.

24 And in her was found the blood of prophets, and of saints, and of all that were slain upon the earth.

15 *The second coming of Christ,* 19:1–21

a ANNOUNCEMENTS, 19:1–10

19 And after these things I heard a great voice of much people in heaven, saying, Alleluia; Salvation, and glory, and honour, and power, unto the Lord our God:

2 For true and righteous *are* his judgments: for he hath judged the great whore, which did corrupt the earth with her fornication, and hath avenged the blood of his servants at her hand.

3 And again they said, Alleluia. And her smoke rose up for ever and ever.

18:20 *for God hath avenged you on her.* I.e., God has judged her for her treatment of you. Heaven and the martyrs may now rejoice.

18:22–23 No music, no worker, no machinery, no light, no happiness shall be found in Babylon any more.

19:3 *Alleluia*=praise ye the Lord. The word occurs only in this chapter in the entire N.T. It does appear as a brief doxology in several Psalms, e.g., Ps. 104.

4 And the four and twenty elders and the four beasts fell down and worshipped God that sat on the throne, saying, Amen; Alleluia.

5 And a voice came out of the throne, saying, Praise our God, all ye his servants, and ye that fear him, both small and great.

6 And I heard as it were the voice of a great multitude, and as the voice of many waters, and as the voice of mighty thunderings, saying, Alleluia: for the Lord God omnipotent reigneth.

7 Let us be glad and rejoice, and give honour to him: for the marriage of the Lamb is come, and his wife hath made herself ready.

8 And to her was granted that she should be arrayed in fine linen, clean and white: for the fine linen is the righteousness of saints.

9 And he saith unto me, Write, Blessed *are* they which are called unto the marriage supper of the Lamb. And he saith unto me, These are the true sayings of God.

10 And I fell at his feet to worship him. And he said unto me, See *thou do it* not: I am thy fellowservant, and of thy brethren that have the testimony of Jesus: worship God: for the testimony of Jesus is the spirit of prophecy.

b ADVENT OF CHRIST, 19:11–16

11 And I saw heaven opened, and behold a white horse; and he that sat upon him *was* called Faithful and True, and in righteousness he doth judge and make war.

12 His eyes *were* as a flame of fire, and on his head *were*

19:8 *the righteousness of saints.* Lit., the righteous deeds of saints; i.e., the good works of believers will constitute the wedding garment when the congregation of the faithful are joined to Him in marriage (2 Cor. 11:2; Eph. 5:26–27).

19:10 *See thou do it not.* Men are not to worship angels, only God. *for the testimony of Jesus is the spirit of prophecy.* This means that prophecy is designed to unfold the loveliness of Jesus.

19:11 *heaven opened.* This is the second coming of Christ to the earth in the midst of the war of Armageddon in which He will be the victor and all who oppose Him will be slain (vv. 19, 21). See notes at 14:20; 16:14, 16. *Faithful and True.* These terms have been used previously of Christ (1:5; 3:7).

19:12 *eyes were as a flame of fire.* See 1:14; 2:18. *a name written that no man knew.* This name is perhaps the same as He will write on the overcomer (2:17; 3:12).

many crowns; and he had a name written, that no man knew, but he himself.

13 And he *was* clothed with a vesture dipped in blood: and his name is called The Word of God.

14 And the armies *which were* in heaven followed him upon white horses, clothed in fine linen, white and clean.

15 And out of his mouth goeth a sharp sword, that with it he should smite the nations: and he shall rule them with a rod of iron: and he treadeth the winepress of the fierceness and wrath of Almighty God.

16 And he hath on *his* vesture and on his thigh a name written, KING OF KINGS, AND LORD OF LORDS.

c ARMAGEDDON, 19:17–21

17 And I saw an angel standing in the sun; and he cried with a loud voice, saying to all the fowls that fly in the midst of heaven, Come and gather yourselves together unto the supper of the great God;

18 That ye may eat the flesh of kings, and the flesh of captains, and the flesh of mighty men, and the flesh of horses, and of them that sit on them, and the flesh of all *men, both* free and bond, both small and great.

19 And I saw the beast, and the kings of the earth, and their armies, gathered together to make war against him that sat on the horse, and against his army.

20 And the beast was taken, and with him the false prophet that wrought miracles before him, with which he deceived them that had received the mark of the beast, and them that worshipped his image. These both were cast alive into a lake of fire burning with brimstone.

21 And the remnant were slain with the sword of him that sat upon the horse, which *sword* proceeded out of his mouth: and all the fowls were filled with their flesh.

19:13 *The Word of God.* This name, applied here to Christ, is found elsewhere in the N.T. only in the writings of John (John 1:1, 14; 1 John 1:1; 5:7).

19:15 *wine press.* It consisted of two receptacles or vats placed at different levels, in the upper one of which the grapes were trodden, while the lower one received the juice (see 14:20).

19:17-18 So great will be the slaughter in the war of Armageddon that an angel calls together the fowls of heaven to eat the flesh of those who fall in battle.

19:21 *the remnant*=the rest.

B The Millennium, 20:1-15

1 *Satan bound*, 20:1-3

20 And I saw an angel come down from heaven, having the key of the bottomless pit and a great chain in his hand.

2 And he laid hold on the dragon, that old serpent, which is the Devil, and Satan, and bound him a thousand years,

3 And cast him into the bottomless pit, and shut him up, and set a seal upon him, that he should deceive the nations no more, till the thousand years should be fulfilled: and after that he must be loosed a little season.

2 *Saints resurrected*, 20:4-6

4 And I saw thrones, and they sat upon them, and judgment was given unto them: and I *saw* the souls of them that were beheaded for the witness of Jesus, and for the word of God, and which had not worshipped the beast, neither his image, neither had received *his* mark upon their foreheads, or in their hands; and they lived and reigned with Christ a thousand years.

5 But the rest of the dead lived not again until the thousand years were finished. This *is* the first resurrection.

6 Blessed and holy *is* he that hath part in the first resurrection: on such the second death hath no power, but they shall be priests of God and of Christ, and shall reign with him a thousand years.

20:2 *a thousand years.* Since the Latin equivalent for these words is "millennium," this period of time is called the millennium. It is the time when Christ shall reign on this earth (Isa. 2:3; Dan. 7:14; Zech. 14:9). Satan will not be free to work (v. 2), righteousness will flourish (Isa. 11:3-5), peace will be universal (Isa. 2:4), and the productivity of the earth will be greatly increased (Isa. 35:1-2). At the conclusion of the time Satan will be loosed to make one final attempt to overthrow Christ, but without success (vv. 7-9).

20:4 *the souls of them that were beheaded for the witness of Jesus.* These are the martyrs of the tribulation days who will share the joys of the millennial kingdom.

20:5 *the first resurrection* includes all the righteous (=the resurrection of life, John 5:29, and resurrection of the just, Luke 14:14) who will be raised before the millennium begins. After the millennium the wicked dead will be raised and judged (*the rest of the dead*).

3 Sinners rebelling, 20:7–9

7 And when the thousand years are expired, Satan shall be loosed out of his prison,

8 And shall go out to deceive the nations which are in the four quarters of the earth, Gog and Magog, to gather them together to battle: the number of whom *is* as the sand of the sea.

9 And they went up on the breadth of the earth, and compassed the camp of the saints about, and the beloved city: and fire came down from God out of heaven, and devoured them.

4 Satan doomed, 20:10

10 And the devil that deceived them was cast into the lake of fire and brimstone, where the beast and the false prophet *are*, and shall be tormented day and night for ever and ever.

5 Sinners judged, 20:11–15

11 And I saw a great white throne, and him that sat on it, from whose face the earth and the heaven fled away; and there was found no place for them.

12 And I saw the dead, small and great, stand before God; and the books were opened: and another book was opened, which is *the book* of life: and the dead were judged out of those things which were written in the books, according to their works.

13 And the sea gave up the dead which were in it; and death and hell delivered up the dead which were in them: and they were judged every man according to their works.

14 And death and hell were cast into the lake of fire. This is the second death.

20:8 *Gog and Magog.* Symbolic names for the worldwide enemies of Christ.

20:11–15 Here is pictured the judgment of the unbelieving dead. It occurs at the close of the millennium; it is based on works in order to show that the punishment is deserved (v. 12, though, of course, these unsaved people are in this judgment because they rejected Christ as Savior during their lifetime); and it results in everyone present in this judgment being cast into the last of fire. This is the resurrection unto condemnation (John 5:29).

20:12 *before God.* Better, before the throne. Christ is the Judge (John 5:22, 27).

15 And whosoever was not found written in the book of life was cast into the lake of fire.

C The Eternal State, 21:1–22:5

1 *Descent of the New Jerusalem*, 21:1–8

21 And I saw a new heaven and a new earth: for the first heaven and the first earth were passed away; and there was no more sea.

2 And I John saw the holy city, new Jerusalem, coming down from God out of heaven, prepared as a bride adorned for her husband.

3 And I heard a great voice out of heaven saying, Behold, the tabernacle of God *is* with men, and he will dwell with them, and they shall be his people, and God himself shall be with them, *and be* their God.

4 And God shall wipe away all tears from their eyes; and there shall be no more death, neither sorrow, nor crying, neither shall there be any more pain: for the former things are passed away.

5 And he that sat upon the throne said, Behold, I make all things new. And he said unto me, Write: for these words are true and faithful.

6 And he said unto me, It is done. I am Alpha and Ōmeg'a, the beginning and the end. I will give unto him that is athirst of the fountain of the water of life freely.

7 He that overcometh shall inherit all things; and I will be his God, and he shall be my son.

8 But the fearful, and unbelieving, and the abominable, and murderers, and whoremongers, and sorcerers, and idolaters, and all liars, shall have their part in the lake which burneth with fire and brimstone: which is the second death.

2 *Description of the New Jerusalem*, 21:9–27

9 And there came unto me one of the seven angels

21:1 *a new heaven and a new earth.* The present creation will be destroyed so that it may be cleansed from all the effects of sin (2 Pet. 3:7, 10, 12).

21:2 *new Jerusalem.* This heavenly city is the abode of the saints (Heb. 12:22–24), the bride of Christ (vv. 9–10), and the place Christ has gone to prepare for his people (John 14:2). During the millennium it will apparently be suspended over the earth (as is described in 21:9–22:5), and it will be the dwelling place of all believers during eternity (as is emphasized in 21:1–8).

21:8 *whoremongers*=fornicators. *brimstone*=sulphur.

which had the seven vials full of the seven last plagues,
and talked with me, saying, Come hither, I will shew
thee the bride, the Lamb's wife.

10 And he carried me away in the spirit to a great and
high mountain, and shewed me that great city, the holy
Jerusalem, descending out of heaven from God,

11 Having the glory of God: and her light *was* like unto
a stone most precious, even like a jasper stone, clear as
crystal;

12 And had a wall great and high, *and* had twelve
gates, and at the gates twelve angels, and names written
thereon, which are *the names* of the twelve tribes of the
children of Israel:

13 On the east three gates; on the north three gates;
on the south three gates; and on the west three gates.

14 And the wall of the city had twelve foundations,
and in them the names of the twelve apostles of the Lamb.

15 And he that talked with me had a golden reed
to measure the city, and the gates thereof, and the wall
thereof.

16 And the city lieth foursquare, and the length is as
large as the breadth: and he measured the city with the
reed, twelve thousand furlongs. The length and the
breath and the height of it are equal.

17 And he measured the wall thereof, an hundred *and*
forty *and* four cubits, *according to* the measure of a man,
that is, of the angel.

18 And the building of the wall of it was *of* jasper: and
the city *was* pure gold, like unto clear glass.

19 And the foundations of the wall of the city *were*
garnished with all manner of precious stones. The first
foundation *was* jasper; the second, sapphire; the third, a
chalcedony; the fourth, an emerald;

20 The fifth, sardonyx; the sixth, sardius; the seventh,
chrysolite; the eighth, beryl; the ninth, a topaz; the tenth,
a chrysoprasus; the eleventh, a jacinth; the twelfth, an
amethyst.

21 And the twelve gates *were* twelve pearls; every

21:11 *jasper*. See note at 4:3.
21:16 *twelve thousand furlongs*=approximately 1500 miles.
21:17 *an hundred and forty and four cubits*=approximately 216
feet.
21:19 *chalcedony*. A greenish-blue agate stone.
21:20 *sardonyx*. Red and white stone. *sardius*. Bright red.
chrysolyte. Golden in color.   *berly*. Sea green.   *topaz*. Yellow-
green.   *chrysoprasus*. Apple-green.   *jacinth*. Blue.   *amethyst*.
Purple.

several gate was of one pearl: and the street of the city *was* pure gold, as it were transparent glass.

22 And I saw no temple therein: for the Lord God Almighty and the Lamb are the temple of it.

23 And the city had no need of the sun, neither of the moon, to shine in it: for the glory of God did lighten it, and the Lamb *is* the light thereof.

24 And the nations of them which are saved shall walk in the light of it: and the kings of the earth do bring their glory and honour into it.

25 And the gates of it shall not be shut at all by day: for there shall be no night there.

26 And they shall bring the glory and honour of the nations into it.

27 And there shall in no wise enter into it any thing that defileth, neither *whatsoever* worketh abomination, or *maketh* a lie: but they which are written in the Lamb's book of life.

3 Delights of the New Jerusalem, 22:1–5

22 And he shewed me a pure river of water of life, clear as crystal, proceeding out of the throne of God and of the Lamb.

2 In the midst of the street of it, and on either side of the river, *was there* the tree of life, which bare twelve *manner of* fruits, *and* yielded her fruit every month: and the leaves of the tree *were* for the healing of the nations.

3 And there shall be no more curse: but the throne of God and of the Lamb shall be in it; and his servants shall serve him:

4 And they shall see his face; and his name *shall be* in their foreheads.

5 And there shall be no night there; and they need no candle, neither light of the sun; for the Lord God giveth them light: and they shall reign for ever and ever.

V EPILOGUE, 22:6–21

A Words of Comfort, 22:6–17

6 And he said unto me, These sayings *are* faithful and true: and the Lord God of the holy prophets sent his angel

---

21:24 *the nations of them which are saved.* Some texts omit "of them which are saved." These are the nations that exist on earth during the millennium.

22:1–2 These descriptive phrases indicate fullness of life and continuous blessing in the new Jerusalem.

to shew unto his servants the things which must shortly be done.

7 Behold, I come quickly: blessed *is* he that keepeth the sayings of the prophecy of this book.

8 And I John saw these things, and heard *them*. And when I had heard and seen, I fell down to worship before the feet of the angel which shewed me these things.

9 Then saith he unto me, See *thou do it* not: for I am thy fellowservant, and of thy brethren the prophets, and of them which keep the sayings of this book: worship God.

10 And he saith unto me, Seal not the sayings of the prophecy of this book: for the time is at hand.

11 He that is unjust, let him be unjust still: and he which is filthy, let him be filthy still: and he that is righteous, let him be righteous still: and he that is holy, let him be holy still.

12 And, behold, I come quickly; and my reward *is* with me, to give every man according as his work shall be.

13 I am Alpha and Ōmeg'a, the beginning and the end, the first and the last.

14 Blessed *are* they that do his commandments, that they may have right to the tree of life, and may enter in through the gates into the city.

15 For without *are* dogs, and sorcerers, and whoremongers, and murderers, and idolaters, and whosoever loveth and maketh a lie.

16 I Jesus have sent mine angel to testify unto you these things in the churches. I am the root and the offspring of David, *and* the bright and morning star.

17 And the Spirit and the bride say, Come. And let him that heareth say, Come. And let him that is athirst come. And whosoever will, let him take the water of life freely.

B Words of Warning, 22:18–19

18 For I testify unto every man that heareth the words

22:8–9 Again John is commanded not to worship angels (see 19:10).

22:11 When Christ comes there will be no more opportunity for man to change his destiny. What he is then he will be forever.

22:14 *Blessed are they that do his commandments*. The better reading is: "Blessed are they who wash their robes," i.e., believers.

22:15 *dogs*. Not animals, but people of low character (Phil. 3:2).

of the prophecy of this book, If any man shall add unto these things, God shall add unto him the plagues that are written in this book:

19 And if any man shall take away from the words of the book of this prophecy, God shall take away his part out of the book of life, and out of the holy city, and *from* the things which are written in this book.

C Closing Benediction, 22:20–21

20 He which testifieth these things saith, Surely I come quickly. Amen. Even so, come, Lord Jesus.

21 The grace of our Lord Jesus Christ *be* with you all. Amen.

22:18 For similar O.T. warnings against additions or omissions see Deut. 4:2; 12:32; Prov. 30:6.

22:19 *God shall take away his part out of the book of life.* The better reading is "from the tree of life," and for *part* read "share."

22:20 *Surely I come quickly.* This is the third occurrence of this promise (vv. 7, 12). The believer's reaction is "Do come, quickly, Lord Jesus!"

THE END

Index

TO THE PRINCIPAL SUBJECTS

IN THE NOTES

HARMONY OF THE GOSPELS*

Based on the harmony of A. R. Fausset.

Contents.

Incidents of the Birth and Boyhood of Jesus Christ Till He was Twelve Years of Age.

Contents.

Contents.	Matt.	Mark.	Luke.	John.
28. John being cast into prison, Jesus leaves Judea for Galilee; John beheaded—not till A.D. 28 (Matt. 14: 12–21), ...	4:12	1:14	4:14,15	4:1-3
29. Passing through Samaria, He converts a woman of Sychar, and through her many of the Samaritans, four months before harvest, ...				4:4-42
30. Commencement of His public ministry in Galilee, ...	4:17	1:14,15	4:14,15	4:43-45
31. Visiting Cana again, He heals a nobleman's son sick at Capernaum, ...				4:46-54
From His Second to His Third Passover.				
32. Returns to Jerusalem at the Passover, *"the feast."* His second Passover. From this to the third, His main Galilean ministry. Jesus cures an infirm man at Bethesda pool on the Sabbath. The Jews seek to kill Him for declaring Himself one with the Father in working, ...				5:1-47
33. Returns to Galilee. A chasm between the earlier visit to Nazareth, while fresh from the Spirit's baptism, and this later visit to Galilee, and His sermon at Nazareth, as Luke 4:23 proves, ...			4:14-30	
34. He settles at Capernaum, and teaches in public, ...	4:13-17	1:21,22	4:31-32	
35. Miraculous catch of fishes; call of Simon, Andrew, James, and John, ...	4:18-22	1:16-20	5:1-11	

Contents.

Contents.

Contents.	Matt.	Mark.	Luke.	John.
62. Jesus visits Nazareth again, when His countrymen disbelieve in Him,	13: 54–58	6: 1–6		
63. Christ teaches throughout Galilee,	9: 35–38	6: 6		
64. Sends forth the Twelve,	10: 1–11: 1	6: 7–13	9: 1–6	
65. Herod, who has murdered John the Baptist, fears that Jesus is John risen from the dead,	14: 1–12	6: 14–29	9: 7–9	
66. The Twelve return to Jesus, telling all they have done and taught. He withdraws with them to a desert on the other side of the Sea of Galilee, and feeds five thousand people,	14: 13–21	6: 30–44	9: 10–17	6: 1–14
67. He sends the disciples across the lake westward to Bethsaida (close to Capernaum, distinct from Bethsaida Julias, northeast of the lake, Luke 9:10), and at night comes walking to them upon the water,	14: 22–33	6: 45–56		6: 15–21
68. The miraculously-fed multitude seek and find Jesus at Capernaum. His discourse in the synagogue and Peter's confession,				6: 22–71

From the Third Passover to the Beginning of the Last Passover Week.

Contents.	Matt.	Mark.	Luke.	John.
69. Healings in the Gennesaret plain for a few days,	14: 34–36	6: 55, 56		
70. Pharisees from Jerusalem object to His neglect of washing hands,	15: 1–20	7: 1–23		
71. Jesus goes northward towards Tyre and Sidon. The Syrophenician woman's faith gains a cure for her daughter,	15: 21–28	7: 24–30		

Contents.

Fifth Day.

	Matt.	Mark.	Luke.	John.
146. Jesus sends two disciples into the city to prepare for the Passover; follows with the rest in the afternoon, ...	26: 17-19	14: 12-16	22: 7-13	
Sixth Day.				
147. *At sunset:* Jesus celebrates the Passover in anticipation, ...	26: 20	14: 17	22: 14	
148. Reproves the ambition of disciples, yet promises the kingdom, ...			22: 24-30	
149. He teaches love and humility by washing disciples' feet, ...				13: 1-20
150. He indicates His betrayer, who, however, did not leave till after the Lord's Supper (Luke 22: 21), ...	26: 21-25	14: 18-21	22: 21-23	13: 21-35
151. He foretells Peter's sifting by Satan, and restoration by His intercession; and scattering of the Twelve,	26: 31-35	14: 27-31	22: 31-38	13: 36-38
152. Ordains the Lord's Supper (1 Cor. 11: 23-25),	26: 26-29	14: 22-25	22: 15-20	
153. Farewell address and intercessory prayer in the paschal chamber, all standing (John 14: 31),				14-17: 26
154. His agony in Gethsemane, ...	[26: 30, 36-46	14: 26, 32-42	22: 39-46	18: 1, 4
155. His betrayal with a kiss, and apprehension. Peter cuts off, and Jesus heals, Malchus' ear, ..	26: 47-56	14: 43-52	22: 47-53	18: 2-12

Contents.	Matt.	Mark.	Luke.	John.
156. He is brought before Annas first at night. Peter's three denials: (1) The *flesh* (Mark 14:54); (2) the *world* (Matt. 26:70—first cock-crowing, Mark 14:68); (3) the *devil* (Mark 14:71, 72—the second cock-crowing; Ps. 1:1), ...	26: 57, 58, 69-75	14: 53, 54, 66-72	22: 54-62	18: 13, 18, 25-27
157. Before Caiaphas, at first dawn, Jesus avows His Messiahship and Godhead. He is condemned for blasphemy and mocked, ...	26: 59-68	14: 55-65	22: 63-71	18: 19-24
158. Brought before Pilate for sentence of crucifixion, ...	27: 1, 2, 11-14	15: 1-5	23: 1-5	18: 28-38
159. Pilate sends Him to Herod; Herod sends Him back to Pilate, ...			23: 6-12	
160. Pilate seeks to release Him, but the Jews demand Barabbas. To appease them, Pilate scourges Him; the Jews clamor for His crucifixion as making Himself a king, Pilate, notwithstanding his wife's warning, sentences Jesus, ...	27: 15-26	15: 6-15	23: 13-25	18: 39, 19: 1-16
161. Jesus mocked by Roman soldiers with scarlet robe, crown of thorns, and reed, ...	27: 27-30	15: 16-19		
162. Judas' remorse; he presumptuously enters the temple, flings down the silver, and hangs himself (Acts 1:18, 19), ...	27: 3-10			
163. Jesus bears His own cross to the city gate, where He is relieved by Simon of Cyrene; refuses stupefying myrrhed wine, ...	27: 31-34	15: 20-23	23: 26-32	19: 16, 17

Contents.

Contents.	Matt.	Mark.	Luke.	John.
164. Crucified at Golgotha, probably outside the Damascus gate. Seven sayings on the cross, *three* relating to *others, four to himself:* (1) For his murderers—*"Father, forgive them,"* etc., ...	27: 35–44	15: 24–32	23: 33–38	19: 18–27
165. (2) The penitent thief promised paradise—*"To-day,"* etc., ...			23: 39–43	
166. His garments divided and vesture cast lots for; (3) commends His mother to the care of John—*"Behold thy son,"* etc., ...				19: 23–27
167. Darkness over the land from sixth to ninth hour. Jesus' loud cry, (4) *"Eli, Eli,"* etc. Says, (5) *"I thirst,"* and receives the vinegar to fulfil Scripture; (6) *"It is finished"*; (7) *"Father, into thy hands I commend my spirit"*; gives up the spirit; the veil of the temple rent. Centurion's testimony, ...	27: 45–54	15: 33–41	23: 44–49	19: 28–30
168. The side pierced by the soldier's spear and the blood and water attest His death and the truth of Scripture (Gen. 2: 21–23; Eph. 5: 30, 32; 1 John 5: 6; Zech. 12: 10). The body, taken down, is wrapped up with Nicodemus' aloes and myrrh, and buried in new tomb of Joseph of Arimathea. *Seventh Day.*	27: 57–61	15: 42–47	23: 50–56	19: 31–42
169. Pilate grants a guard, and they set a seal upon the sepulcher, ...	27: 62–66			

Contents	Matt.	Mark.	Luke.	John.
Subsequent Appearances.				
180. Evening of Sunday after Easter day. Jesus appears to them again, Thomas being present—*Sixth* appearance, ...				20: 24-29
181. The eleven go into Galilee, to a mountain appointed. Jesus appears, and commands them to teach all nations—*Seventh* appearance, ...	28: 16-20	16: 15-18		
182. Jesus shows Himself at the Sea of Tiberias—*Eighth* appearance. Charges Simon to feed His lambs, sheep, and young sheep, ...				21: 1-24
183. Seen of above five hundred brethren at once (1 Cor. 15:6), probably along with the eleven—*Ninth* appearance, ...	28: 16			
184. He is seen by James, then by all the apostles (Acts 1:3-8; 1 Cor. 15:7)—*Tenth* appearance. In all, 538 (549 if the eleven, Matt. 28: 16 be distinct from the 500) persons are *specified* as having seen the risen Saviour; also, after His ascension, St. Paul (1 Cor. 15: 8), ...				
185. The ascension, forty days after Easter (Acts 1: 9-12), ...		16: 19, 20	24: 50-53	
186. Purpose and conclusion, ...				[20: 30, 31, 21: 25]

Dorothy
924 East 20th Street
Baltimore, Maryland 21218
467-2677 10/8/79 received book from Grad. mother book is not for sale. If this book is lost, misplaced or mistaken. You should find it please call above number, or come to above adress when calling or returning ask for Dot

CONTENTS

NOTE: Unless otherwise indicated, Bible quotations in this book are from the modern-language *New World Translation of the Holy Scriptures,* revised edition of 1971.

Will it ever be possible for man to live forever?
Some trees now live for many centuries.

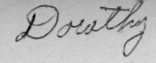
Dorothy

CHAPTER I

You Have Reason to Be Concerned

IS LIFE precious to you? Do you desire life in good health for yourself and your loved ones? Most people will answer, Yes.

But today many things constantly remind us of the uncertainty of life—for ourselves, our mates and our children. Accidents, crimes, riots, wars and famines cut down millions right in the prime of life. Disease takes an appalling toll despite medical advances. Pollution poses a most serious threat.

It is not strange, then, that many persons today ask: 'Is this life all there is? Or can it be that our fondest hope is to be found in a life after death? What actually does happen when a person dies? Does some part of him live on? Is he still conscious, able to see, hear, talk—to do things? Is there such a thing as torment after death? Really, is death a friend or an enemy?' Surely it is to our benefit to know the answers to these questions.

DOES DEATH MOLD OUR LIVES?

You may not have thought about it, but the lives of all of us are molded greatly by the view we hold of death. It affects our enjoyment of life and the way we use our lives far more than most people realize. That is why we need to know the truth about death.

Do you realize, for example, that most of the

world's religions are basically *death-oriented* rather than *life-oriented?* Hundreds of millions of persons have been taught that death will introduce them into another world, 'the world of the dead,' where they face either bliss or torment. Prayers for the dead, costly ceremonies on their behalf and sacrifices to appease them form a vital part of many major religions with vast memberships.

One may say: 'Perhaps so, but I don't spend my time worrying about death or what comes after it. My problem is living and getting as much as I can out of life now while I can.' Yet even that response shows death's molding effect on people's lives. After all, is it not death that determines how long it is before one can no longer get anything out of life?

So, even though we may try to blot the thought of death from our minds, the realization that our life-span is, at best, quite short keeps pressuring us. It may drive a person in a fierce effort to become rich at an early age—'while he can still enjoy things.' The shortness of life makes many people impatient, rude, callous toward others. It moves them to use dishonest ways to reach their goals. They just feel there is not time to do it the right way. Yet, all the while they may claim that death has no part in molding their lives.

What is your own view of death? What part does it play in your thoughts for the future, or, for that matter, the way you are living your life right now?

THE NEED TO BE SURE

The problem is that there is such a wide variation among people's views about life and death.

Often the views are contradictory, exact opposites.

Many people believe that death is the complete end of everything or, at least, that man was made to die. Do you find that acceptable? Does it make sense to you that certain trees can outlive intelligent man by thousands of years? Do you feel that seventy or eighty years of life is long enough for you to do all that you want to do, to learn all that you want to learn, to see all that you want to see and to develop your talents and abilities to the extent you desire?

Then there is the tremendous number of persons who believe that life goes on after death because something—soul or spirit—survives the death of the body. Yet their views also differ greatly. And, of course, their beliefs contradict the idea of those who think that all life ends with death. Contradictory views cannot all be true. Which are right? Does it matter? Yes, very much. Consider why.

For one thing, if the dead can actually benefit from prayers and ceremonies on their behalf, would we not be merciless if we failed to provide these? But what if the dead are really dead, beyond the help of surviving humans? That would necessarily mean that hundreds of millions of persons are victims of a terrible fraud. It would mean that many great religious systems have enriched themselves by deceit, using falsehoods about the dead to exploit the living instead of doing something beneficial for them.

What comfort can we offer when, sooner or later, death invades our family circle, or that of a friend? Does logic support the view that "fate" governs our experiences and the length of our lives? What if the one dying was a small child?

Did God 'take the child to be with Him,' as some would say?

Truly there are many, many things we need to know about death, and the more we love life the more we should want to be sure to get the right answers. But where—especially since there is so much confusion and contradiction?

There are many religious books that discuss life and death, some of them quite ancient. But there is one very ancient book that presents a viewpoint quite different from that of all the others. In fact, the view it presents is surprisingly different from what the great majority of people think it contains. That book is the Bible.

It deals with real people, people who faced the same basic problems that we do today. They, too, pondered the whole purpose of living, asking: "What does a man come to have for all his hard work and for the striving of his heart with which he is working hard under the sun?" "Even supposing that he has lived a thousand years twice over and yet he has not seen what is good, is it not to just one place that everyone is going?" (Ecclesiastes 2:22; 6:6) They, too, raised the question: "If an able-bodied man dies can he live again?" (Job 14:14) Do you know the answers?

In the publication you now hold in your hands you will find discussed, not only the many popular attempts to answer the questions thus far raised, but also the vitally important way the Bible answers each of these. You can learn the unique hope it presents for those facing death or who have come within its grip. The understanding that this information can bring can contribute much to your present and future happiness and peace of mind.

CHAPTER 2

How Death Affects People's Daily Lives

MOST people are very much concerned about what affects their lives and that of their families right now. But few are willing to speak or to think extendedly about death.

True, death is not a bright prospect, but it has a definite effect on one's daily life. Who of us has not experienced the grief and deep sense of loss over the death of a dear friend or beloved relative? A death in a family can change the family's entire pattern of life, destroy a stable income and cause loneliness or depression for the survivors.

Unpleasant though it may be, death is a daily occurrence with which you must reckon. You cannot prolong certain actions indefinitely. Tomorrow may be too late.

How has this affected you? Do you at times feel pressured by the shortness of life to try desperately to get all that you can out of it? Or, do you take the fatalistic view, concluding that, well, what will be will be?

THE FATALISTIC VIEW

Many people today believe that life and death are governed by fate. This is a basic concept of more than 477 million Hindus. In fact, fatalistic views are practically universal. Have you not heard people say, 'It just had to happen,' 'His time was up,' or, 'He escaped because his number wasn't up'? Such statements are frequently made in connection with accidents. Are they true? Consider an example:

During a demonstration flight at the Paris Air Show in 1973 the Soviet Union's supersonic airliner TU-144 exploded, killing its crew. Large sections of the aircraft hurtled down upon the village of Goussainville, France. One woman there had just shut the bedroom door behind her when a part of the wreckage came smashing through the outside wall, completely demolishing the bedroom. She was unharmed.

Others did not escape. The victims included an elderly woman's three grandchildren, but not the grandmother.

Did those children and others die because their "number" or their "time" was up? Were others spared because fate was not due to claim them until later?

Those answering "Yes" to these questions believe that nothing anyone might do can prevent a person's death if his 'time is up.' They feel that, despite any precaution taken, they simply cannot escape what fate dictates. This is a view similar to that of the ancient Greeks who considered man's destiny to be controlled by three goddesses —Clotho, Lachesis and Atropos. Clotho supposedly spun the thread of life, Lachesis determined its length and Atropos cut it off when the time was up.

Is such a fatalistic outlook reasonable? Ask yourself: Why do the number of accidental deaths decrease when safety regulations are obeyed and increase when they are disregarded? Why can the majority of traffic deaths be demonstrated to result from human carelessness, drunkenness, error or lawlessness? Why is it that in countries with high standards of hygiene and good diet people have a far greater average life-span than in countries lacking these things? Why do more smokers than nonsmokers die of lung cancer? How could all of this be due to blind fate over which there is no control? Instead, is it not the case that there are *reasons* for what happens to man?

With many accidental deaths, is it not a matter of a person's just happening to come into a dangerous situation? To illustrate: A man leaves his home at a certain time each workday. One morning, as he passes a neighbor's house, he hears screaming and shouting. He speeds up his walking and, just as he turns the corner, he is hit by a stray bullet. His death is due to his being at the

Does fate control your life, as the ancient Greeks believed?

corner at the wrong time; the circumstance was unforeseen.

Having observed what really happens in everyday life, the wise writer of the Bible book of Ecclesiastes said: "I returned to see under the sun that the swift do not have the race, nor the mighty ones the battle, nor do the wise also have the food, nor do the understanding ones also have the riches, nor do even those having knowledge have the favor; because *time and unforeseen occurrence befall them all.*"—Ecclesiastes 9:11.

The person who appreciates this does not disregard safety regulations and take needless risks, thinking that he is immune to death as long as his "time" is not up. He realizes that a fatalistic view can be dangerous, both to himself and to others. This knowledge, wisely applied, can add years to your life.

On the other hand, a fatalistic outlook can lead to foolhardy actions, and it can also cause a person to be negligent about informing himself as to matters that may deeply affect him and his family.

LIVING ONLY FOR THE PRESENT

Besides the fatalistic outlook, the events of the twentieth century have influenced people's actions.

Consider for a moment what has happened. Millions have perished as victims of war, crime, riots and famine. Life-sustaining air and water are being polluted at an alarming rate. Seemingly from every quarter man's life is being threatened. And there is nothing to give real assurance that mankind will be able to solve its problems in the near future. Life seems so uncertain. What is the result?

Many of earth's inhabitants are living only for the present, to get everything possible out of today. They feel impelled to do so, reasoning that the life they have now is all the life they can ever hope to have. Aptly the Bible describes their attitude: "Let us eat and drink, for tomorrow we are to die."—1 Corinthians 15:32.

In an endeavor to escape the harsh realities of life, they may turn to alcohol or drugs. Others try to find an outlet for their frustrations and concern over the shortness of life by personally indulging in sexual experiences of all kinds— fornication, adultery, homosexuality, lesbianism. Says the book *Death and Its Mysteries:*

> "It seems that more normal people today are affected by this fear of collective death, at least unconsciously. This is at least a partial explanation of the disarray of our times, which is expressed in gratuitous crime, vandalism, eroticism and the accelerated pace of life. Even modern music and dances seem to express the despair of a humanity that no longer believes in its own future."

What has been the effect of all such living for the present as if there may be no tomorrow?

Those given to heavy drinking and drunkenness may temporarily forget their troubles. But they sacrifice their dignity and, while intoxicated, at times injure themselves or others. And the next day they find that they have added an agonizing headache to the troubles that they already had.

Drug addicts, too, pay a high price for their efforts to escape reality. They often experience lasting physical and mental harm. And, to support their costly habit, they may find that they are degrading themselves by engaging in theft or prostitution.

What about promiscuous sex relations? Do they help to improve one's lot in life? To the contrary, the fruitage is frequently a loathsome venereal disease, unwanted pregnancies, illegitimate children, abortions, a broken home, bitter jealousy, fighting and even murder.

Of course, many persons have not succumbed to living a debauched life. Still they have not escaped the pressure that comes from realizing, consciously or subconsciously, that their life will end. Knowing that time is limited, they may seek to get ahead in the world just as quickly as possible. With what result? Their desire for material possessions may prompt them to sacrifice personal honesty. As the Bible proverb truthfully states: "He that is hastening to gain riches will not remain innocent." (Proverbs 28:20) But that is not all.

So much time and energy are used in getting ahead materially that there is little time to enjoy one's family. True, the children may be getting all the material things that they want. But are they getting the guidance and correction they need in order for them to become responsible young men and women? Many parents, while realizing that time spent with their children is somewhat limited, really see no reason for special concern—until it is too late. Yes, it is agonizing to learn that one's own son has been arrested or that one's own teen-age daughter is going to be an unwed mother.

From what is happening today, is it not obvious that, despite the shortness of life, many people need to learn a more satisfying way to live?

The apparent inevitability of death does not make everyone throw moral principles to the wind, nor does it produce a fatalistic apathy in all persons. To the contrary, hundreds of thousands today are enjoying a wholesome way of life because of not being adversely affected by the prospect of death.

A BETTER WAY

Viewed aright, death can teach us something valuable. When death claims victims, we can benefit from thoughtful contemplation about the way we are living our own lives. Some three thousand years ago a careful observer of humanity highlighted this, saying: "A name is better than good oil, and the day of death than the day of one's being born. Better is it to go to the house of mourning than to go to the banquet house, because that is the end of all mankind; and the one alive should take it to his heart. . . . The heart of the wise ones is in the house of mourning, but the heart of the stupid ones is in the house of rejoicing."—Ecclesiastes 7:1-4.

The Bible is not here recommending sadness in preference to rejoicing. Rather, the reference is to the particular time when a household is in mourning over the death of one of its members. It is no time to forget the bereaved and to proceed with one's own feasting and reveling. For, just as death has ended all the plans and activities of the deceased, it can do the same for ours. A person does well to ask himself: What am I doing with my life? Am I building up a fine name or reputation? How much do I contribute to the happiness and well-being of others?

Not at birth, but during the full course of our

life, does our "name" take on real meaning,
identifying us as to what kind of persons we are.
The person whose heart is, as it were, in a "house
of mourning" is one who gives heartfelt consideration to the way he is living his life, regardless of how short it may be. He treats it as something precious. He does not reflect the shallow,
reckless spirit characteristic of a place of revelry.
Rather, he exerts himself to lead a meaningful,
purposeful life and thereby contributes to the
happiness and welfare of fellowmen.

How can anyone determine whether he is now
enjoying the best way of life possible for him,
whether he is truly living a purposeful life? Certainly a standard of judgment is needed. In increasing numbers sincere persons throughout the
earth are coming to the conclusion that the
Bible is that reliable standard. Their examination
of the Bible has enabled them to find real purpose
in life now and it has given them a grand hope
for the future, a hope that involves life under
righteous conditions on this very earth. They
have come to realize that, not death, but life is
God's purpose for mankind.

CHAPTER 3

Man Was Made to Live

GOD made man to live. This is what the Bible
indicates by its description of the provisions
that God made for our first human parents, Adam
and Eve. It informs us that Jehovah God placed
them in a beautiful garden home, a paradise,

occupying a section of the region called "Eden." That paradise contained everything needed for them to continue living. Concerning this, Genesis, the first book of the Bible, says: "Jehovah God made to grow out of the ground every tree desirable to one's sight and good for food and also the tree of life in the middle of the garden and the tree of the knowledge of good and bad." —Genesis 2:9.

Note that there was, not a 'tree of death,' but a "tree of life" in this lovely paradise. That "tree of life" stood as an unchangeable guarantee of continued life to those entitled to partake of it. There was no reason for Adam and Eve to have a morbid fear of the possibility of dying. As long as they continued to be obedient to their Creator in not eating of the forbidden "tree of the knowledge of good and bad" their life would not end. —Genesis 2:16, 17.

But is what the Bible says about man's being made to enjoy an endless life-span in agreement with what we can see of life? Do not the facts show that humans have been dying for thousands of years? Yes, but did you know that right in your own makeup is evidence suggesting that you should have a far longer life-span than is customary in our day?

Consider, for example, the human brain. Is it designed for a lifetime of just seventy or eighty years? Interestingly, biochemist Isaac Asimov, in commenting on the brain's capacity, noted that its filing system is "perfectly capable of handling any load of learning and memory which the human being is likely to put upon it—and a billion times more than that quantity, too."

Is it logical for man's brain to have a storage capacity for information a thousand million times as great as he is able to use during what is today an average life-span? Rather, does this not indicate that man was made to live a lifetime that would require a brain with an infinite capacity for memory?

This is by no means all.

MAN ALONE HAS A CONCEPT OF ETERNITY

A remarkable point to note here is that the Bible sets only before man—not before any of earth's other creatures—the prospect of limitless life. In fact, it says that even the concept of past or future time indefinite or eternity is unique to man. Noted the inspired writer of the Bible book of Ecclesiastes: "I have seen the occupation that God has given to the sons of mankind in which to be occupied. Everything he has made pretty in its time. Even time indefinite he has put in their heart."—Ecclesiastes 3:10, 11.

Now, if what the Bible says about man is true, we should be able to see evidence to this effect. Do we? Does man stand in sharp contrast with the animals? Does man alone think seriously about the future, concern himself with it and work toward it? Does he react to death in a way · different from the animals, showing that he alone has appreciation for what life has meant to him in the past and could mean to him in the future?

There is no denying that all living things cling to life. Instinctively animals that are eaten by other animals seek to escape their predators by flight or concealment. Many creatures will struggle against what appear to be impossible odds to protect their young from death. Rabbits have been known to kick so violently as to send raccoons sprawling. In the western part of the United States a female antelope was observed successfully defending her kid from a timber wolf, her sharp hoofs injuring his hindquarters and knocking out his teeth. As he was seeking to get away, she jumped on top of him and trampled him to death.

Such instinctive reaction to the threat of death plays a vital role in the preservation of creature life. But does this mean that animals have an appreciation for the past and future as does man?

As we know, a man can reflect on the past and can plan for the future. In the privacy of his own home, he can think back to his boyhood days —his pranks, disappointments, failures, successes and joys. He can plan future moves—building a new house, purchasing furniture, determining the kind of education he would like for his children to get, and so forth. But can a dog, for example, meditate about its puppyhood, the children that played with it then, its becoming full grown and then mating? In his book *Animals Are Quite Different,* Hans Bauer shows what research has revealed:

"The dog will always need an actual sense-impression to enable it to conjure up former incidents. He may be taken, let us say, on a certain occasion to an unfamiliar town in which he undergoes some experience or other. After his return home the impressions then received will have been forgotten. But if he goes back to the same spot he will remember them. It is in fact one of the special peculiarities and advantages of the human as compared with the animal psychological structure that the content of human memory is not associated with the needs of every day but embedded in the stream of consciousness as a whole."

Thus, unlike man, animals cannot at will reconstruct events of the past.

But can they plan ahead for the future? Do not hamsters, certain ants, squirrels and other animals store up or hide food supplies for later use? Is not this a planning ahead for the future so as not to suffer want in winter? "No," says the above-mentioned author, and he gives these facts in support:

"They do not know what they are doing or why they do it. They simply proceed in accordance with instinct, the proof being that even animals removed from their parents at a very early age and kept in cages begin 'collecting' in the autumn. Such animals have never known winter conditions and will not be deprived of nourishment in the coming months. Nevertheless, they 'hoard' simply for the sake of 'hoarding.'"

Summing up the contrast between man and animals, he remarks:

"The world of animals is therefore exclusively that of the present moment in the most literal sense of the word. For they can easily be diverted from even the most fascinating objects by others of more immediate appeal at the time and never afterwards return to the former."

Truly, then, man alone has a concept of "time indefinite," the ability to meditate on the past and to look toward the future, planning for it.

It is because animals live only in the present that for them death is clearly not the tragedy it is for humans. Animals seem to react to death as a natural course of events.

Take the case witnessed in Serengeti National Park involving a lioness and her three cubs.

While the lioness was away, the cubs lay hidden in a thicket. Then two male lions from another territory appeared. Finding the hidden cubs, they killed all three. They ate one, carried the other off and left the third behind. What did the lioness do when she returned and saw her remaining dead cub? She displayed no grief, no emotion, but merely sniffed at the carcass of her remaining dead cub—and then devoured it.

It is also noteworthy that animals on which lions prey do not react with terror at seeing a lion some distance away. Once a lion has gotten its meal, herds of animals soon resume their usual routine. In fact, prey animals may come within one hundred and twenty feet of a visible lion.

MAN REACTS TO DEATH AS SOMETHING UNNATURAL

How differently humans react to death! For the majority, the death of a wife, husband or child is the most upsetting experience of a lifetime. Man's entire emotional makeup is jarred for a long time after the death of a person whom he dearly loves.

Even those persons who claim that 'death is natural to humans' find it hard to accept the idea that their own death will mean the end of everything. Observes *The Journal of Legal Medicine:* "Psychiatrists are generally agreed that there is an unconscious denial of death, even when it seems to be imminent." A young avowed atheist, for example, stated before his execution that, from a rational point of view, his death would mean 'nothing more than the definitive termination of a life that had been brief but very intense.' But then he noted that it was difficult, indeed impossible, for him to 'admit that everything would be reduced to nothingness.'

So strong is man's desire to share in future activity that a number of people have arranged to have their bodies frozen at death. The initial cost for this may run as high as $8,500, with an additional $1,000 being paid each year to keep the body frozen. Bodies have been frozen in the hope that scientists will eventually be able to bring them back to life. Of course, at the present time scientists are nowhere even near accomplishing such a thing. Yet the very thought that this might be possible has been enough to move some persons to have their bodies preserved at great cost.

Because humans find it hard to accept death as ending everything, men everywhere have a desire to perpetuate the memory of the dead and to dispose of them ceremoniously. Notes the book *Funeral Customs the World Over:*

> "There is no group, however primitive at the one extreme or civilized at the other, which left freely to itself and within its means does not dispose of the bodies of its members with ceremony. So true is this universal fact of ceremonial funeralization that it seems reasonable to conclude that it flows out of human nature. It is 'natural,' normal, reasonable. It satisfies deep universal urges. To carry it out seems 'right,' and not to carry it out, particularly for those who are closely connected by family, feeling, shared living, common experience or other ties, seems 'wrong,' an unnatural omission, a matter to be apologized for or ashamed of."

What does this work conclude from the universal custom of funerals? It continues:

> "So true is this that to the various definitions of man there might be added another. He is a being that buries his dead with ceremony."

Yet, despite all of this, eventually, as generations come and go, the deceased are totally forgotten. Even those who made a notable name in history centuries ago have, as actual persons, faded from the everyday memory of the living. Their influence on others is gone. For example, such powerful rulers of ancient times as Nebuchadnezzar, Alexander the Great and Julius Caesar do not affect our daily lives now even though they affected the lives of millions of their contemporaries. The hard fact that the dead are in time forgotten was acknowledged by the discerning writer of the Bible book of Ecclesiastes: "There is no remembrance of people of former times, nor will there be of those also who will come to be later. There will prove to be no remembrance even of them among those who will come to be still later on." (Ecclesiastes 1:11) The very fact that man tries everything within his power to be remembered despite his knowing that he will eventually be forgotten shows that his desire to live, if but in memory, is inherent.

MAN'S DEATH DOES NOT SEEM TO MAKE SENSE

In view of man's general reaction to death, his amazing potential as to memory and learning ability, and his inward realization of eternity, is it not clear that he was made to live? Only when we accept the Bible's explanation that man's present dying state was never a part of God's original purpose can we make sense out of things that would otherwise be very puzzling. Take as an example the life-spans of certain plants and animals that far surpass that of man.

A tree may live for hundreds of years; some, such as sequoias and bristlecone pines, for thou-

DOES MAN'S SHORT LIFE-SPAN MAKE SENSE?

Despite their amazing potential for learning, humans live just **70** or **80** years

Even swans are known to live over **80** years

Though unintelligent, tortoises live more than **150** years

Some trees live thousands of years

sands of years. It is not unusual for a giant tortoise to get to be more than 150 years old. Why should this be? Why should mindless trees and unreasoning tortoises outlive intelligent man?

Then, too, is not man's death a terrible waste? While a fraction of a man's knowledge and experience may have been passed on to others, for the most part these things are lost to posterity. To illustrate, a man may be an outstanding scientist, a fine architect or an accomplished musician, painter or sculptor. He may have trained others. But at his death no one has the sum total of his talents and experience. He may even have been in the process of developing something new after having solved many problems. Those who could have benefited from the knowledge and experience he gained may now have to learn through trial and error—and then have their own work cut short by death. Since the field of knowledge is very great, why should man have to labor under the handicap of being deprived of experienced people as they fall victim to death?

Additionally, to say that man was to live just a few years on earth and then to die cannot be reconciled with belief in a loving Creator. Why not? Because this would mean that the Creator cares more about certain unintelligent plants and dumb animals than he does about humans, who can express love and appreciation. It would also mean that he has little compassion for humans, who, of all earthly forms of life, are hurt most deeply by death.

Truly, if this life were all there is, and if God had indeed purposed it this way, how could we really love him? Yes, how could we be drawn to One who made it impossible for us to come to the full realization of our potential? Would it not be an unkindness to be given tremendous potential for gaining knowledge and then to be stifled in one's use of it?

However, if humans were made to continue to live, then they need an answer to the question, Why is it that man dies? And a satisfying answer is needed to help them to understand why God has allowed death to go on claiming human victims for thousands of years. This may well remove a serious obstacle standing in the way of one's coming into a fine relationship with the Creator and finding real meaning and enjoyment in life now.

But how can we be sure about the reason for death?

CHAPTER 4

How Did Old Age and Death Come About?

THOUGH popularly accepted as normal, old age and death still puzzle man. This is evident from the fact that for centuries legends have been handed down attempting to explain why humans grow old and die.

One version of an ancient Greek myth tells of the woman Pandora who opened a box or vase that she had been told to keep closed. This act, it is said, released "Old Age," "Sickness," "Insanity" and other "Spites" that have continued to plague mankind.

In Australia, various aboriginal tribes believe

that humans originally were to live forever. But they were to keep away from a certain hollow tree. When wild bees made this tree their home, the women very much desired their honey. Disregarding the warning of the men, one woman used her tomahawk on the tree. At that, the legend says, a large bat flew out. The bat was "Death." Released from the tree, it proceeded to claim all that it touched with its wings.

It is significant that legends of other, widely scattered peoples similarly attribute death to disobedience, often with a woman initially involved.

WHY THE SIMILARITIES?

When reading such myths, some persons may be inclined to place the Bible's explanation of the cause for old age and death in the same category. They may even point out that in some respects the myths seem to parallel the Bible account. But *why* do these similarities exist? Is it possible that these legends have a factual basis that has simply been distorted?

The Bible itself sheds light on the answers to these questions. It points to ancient Babel in Chaldea as the place from which humans who rebelled against God by defying his command were scattered. (Genesis 11:2-9) Biblical tables of genealogy show that this took place at a time when some men were alive who, as faithful servants of God, knew the truth about life and the reason for death. (Genesis 6:7, 8; 8:20, 21; 9:28; 10:1-9; 11:10-18; 1 Chronicles 1:19) The majority, however, since they themselves were showing disregard for the truth as to God's purpose for man, could hardly be expected to preserve with

accuracy the truth about how death came about.
As they spread out, and with the passage of time,
the facts became distorted and embellished; myths
developed. There is great variety in their mythical
explanations of the cause of aging and death, yet
a common underlying basis is discernible.

This is no mere supposition. Available evidence
clearly shows that religious myths, including
those about death, spring from a common source.
In his book *The Worship of the Dead,* Colonel J.
Garnier observes:

> "Not merely Egyptians, Chaldeans, Phœnicians,
> Greeks and Romans, but also the Hindus, the Bud-
> dhists of China and of Tibet, the Goths, Anglo-
> Saxons, Druids, Mexicans and Peruvians, the Aborig-
> ines of Australia, and even the savages of the South
> Sea Islands, must have all derived their religious
> ideas from a common source and a common centre.
> Everywhere we find the most startling coincidences
> in rites, ceremonies, cus-

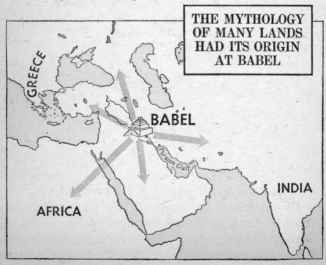

THE MYTHOLOGY
OF MANY LANDS
HAD ITS ORIGIN
AT BABEL

toms, traditions, and in the names and relations of their respective gods and goddesses."

And what place is this common source? Does the evidence point to Chaldea, as the Bible implies? Professor George Rawlinson notes:

"The striking resemblance of the Chaldæan system to that of the Classical [primarily Greek and Roman] Mythology seems worthy of particular attention. This resemblance is too general, and too close in some respects, to allow of the supposition that mere accident has produced the coincidence. In the Pantheons of Greece and Rome, and in that of Chaldæa, the same general grouping [of gods and goddesses] is to be recognized; the same genealogical succession is not unfrequently to be traced; and in some cases even the familiar names and titles of classical divinities admit of the most curious illustration and explanation from Chaldæan sources."

What does he therefore conclude? He says:

"We can scarcely doubt but that, in some way or other, there was a communication of beliefs—a passage in very early times, from the shores of the Persian Gulf [where ancient Babel was] to the lands washed by the Mediterranean, of mythological notions and ideas."

Thus what the Bible indicates as to the development of religious concepts is found to be consistent with other historical evidence. If the Bible really does preserve with accuracy the truth that religious myths later distorted, the Bible account should appeal to our faculties of reason. The account should make sense. Does it?

LIFE DEPENDENT ON OBEDIENCE

In discussing the reasons for aging and death, the first book of the Bible, Genesis, does not deal with some "once-upon-a-time" setting in a "dreamland," but presents a factual account. It deals with an actual place, Eden, its general geographical location being identified by certain rivers. Two of these, the Euphrates and the Tigris (Hiddekel), are known to this day. (Genesis 2:10-14; *New English Bible*) The time can be fixed by Bible chronology as the year 4026 B.C.E. or shortly thereafter. Furthermore, the Bible's reference to a first human pair is scientifically sound. Notes the publication *The Races of Mankind:*

"The Bible story of Adam and Eve, father and mother of the whole human race, told centuries ago the same truth that science has shown today: that all the peoples of the earth are a single family and have a common origin."

After relating the manner in which the first human came to life, the Biblical account shows that the Creator, Jehovah God, started humanity off in a parklike home. He placed before man the prospect of unending life, while at the same time making its enjoyment conditional. God said to the man: "From every tree of the garden you may eat to satisfaction. But as for the tree of the knowledge of good and bad you must not eat from it, for in the day you eat from it you will positively die."—Genesis 2:16, 17.

That was a simple command. Yet is this not what we should expect? The man Adam was alone at the time. Life was simple, uncomplicated. There were no problems in making a living. There were no pressures from a greedy commercial system. Complex laws were not needed to control sinful inclinations within the first man. As a perfect man, Adam had no sinful tendencies.

Simple as this command was, it involved moral issues of serious consequence. Disobedience to God's command on the part of the first humans would have meant rebellion against Him as Ruler. How so?

It was God's prohibition that made partaking of the fruit of the "tree of the knowledge of good and bad" wrong. There were no poisonous properties in it. The fruit was wholesome, literally "good for food." (Genesis 3:6) Hence, God's prohibition regarding the tree simply emphasized man's proper dependence on his Creator as Ruler. By obedience the first man and woman could show that they respected God's right to make known to them what was "good," or divinely approved, and what was "bad," or divinely condemned. Disobedience on their part therefore would mean rebellion against God's sovereignty.

Jehovah God stated the penalty for such rebellion to be death. Was that too severe a penalty? Well, do not many nations of the world consider it within their right to designate certain crimes as capital offenses? Yet these nations cannot give nor indefinitely sustain the life of anyone. But man's Creator can. And it was because of his will that Adam and Eve came into existence. (Revelation 4:11) So was it not right for the Giver and Sustainer of life to designate disobedience to him as worthy of death? Surely! Then, too, he alone fully recognized the seriousness of the damaging effects that would result from disobedience to his law.

By obeying the prohibitive command, that first human pair, Adam and Eve, could have demonstrated their appreciation and gratitude to God for all that he had done for them. Rightly motivated obedience would have prevented them from becoming selfish and ignoring their Benefactor, God.

The Bible says that God gave the first humans the prospect of unending life

The command was of a nature that we would expect from a God of love and justice. It was not unreasonable. He did not deprive them of life's necessities. There were many other trees from which they could satisfy their need for food. Hence, neither Adam nor Eve had any reason to feel a need for the fruit of the "tree of the knowledge of good and bad."

The account shows that one day, however, while not in the company of her husband, Eve fell victim to a deception and partook of the forbidden fruit.* Later she succeeded in persuading her husband to join her in breaking God's law. —Genesis 3:1-6.

Now, it might be argued that God could have taken a permissive attitude toward this rebellion of the first humans. It might be suggested that he could have shut his eyes to their wrongdoing, leaving it unpunished. But would that have been the best course? Is it not true that failure to uphold law among humans today has led to disrespect for just laws and to increasing crime and violence? For God to have left the wrongdoing of Adam and Eve unpunished would have meant emboldening them and their descendants to carry on further lawlessness. This would have made God share responsibility for such acts.

Then, too, permissiveness would have called into question the reliability of God's word. It would have made it appear that he does not mean what he says and that his laws can therefore be violated with impunity.

Thus it becomes clear that it was the only right and just thing for God to uphold his law

---

* The details about this deception and its instigator are discussed in chapter 10.

and to let the first humans suffer the rightful consequences of their willful, deliberate disobedience. Not to be overlooked is that there is no evidence of any repentance on their part. They gave no evidence of a change of heart.

THE BASIC REASON—SIN

By their rebellion against God, Adam and Eve cut themselves off from a good relationship with him. They did not possess an indestructible, immortal life. The Bible says that by means of his power God 'keeps the sun, moon and stars standing forever, to time indefinite.' (Psalm 148:3-6) So, too, with the first human pair. They were dependent upon God for continued life.

By refusing to submit to God's law, Adam and Eve deprived themselves of his sustaining power. Moreover, alienated from God, they were without his divine direction and guidance. In time, then, the sin that had alienated Adam and Eve from God brought about their death.

However, following their transgression against God they still had in themselves tremendous potential for life. This is evident from the historical record, which shows that Adam lived for 930 years. (Genesis 5:5) Yet, fulfilled upon Adam was the warning: "In the day you eat from [the tree of the knowledge of good and bad] you will positively die," for God sentenced Adam to death on that day.—Genesis 2:17.

Through his disobedience, Adam, as the progenitor of the human family, brought death, not only to himself, but also to his unborn offspring. That is why the Bible says: "Through one man sin entered into the world and death through sin, and thus death spread to all men because they had all sinned."—Romans 5:12.

Having forfeited perfection, Adam could not pass it on to his offspring. From the start his children were born with weaknesses. The outworkings of sin in his body made it impossible for him to father offspring without limitations and weaknesses. This harmonizes with the Bible's statement at Job 14:4: "Who can produce someone clean out of someone unclean? There is not one." Hence, the aging and death of humans today can be traced initially to the sin inherited from Adam. As his offspring, they are receiving the wages that sin pays—death.—Romans 6:23.

What does that really mean? Does death mark the end of all one's life processes, or is there some part of man that lives on? Does conscious existence continue after the death of the body?

CHAPTER 5

What Is This Thing Called "Soul"?

WHAT are you? Are you, in effect, two persons in one—a human body with a brain, heart, eyes, ears, tongue, and so forth, but also having within you an invisible spiritual person completely separate from your fleshly organism and that is called the "soul"? If so, what happens when you die? Does just your body die, while the soul continues living? How can you know for sure?

Nearly all religions teach that, in the case of humans, death is not the end of all existence.

This is the case, not just in so-called Christian lands of North and South America, Europe and Australia, but also in non-Christian countries of Asia and Africa. Notes the book *Funeral Customs the World Over:* "People of most cultures believe that at death something which leaves the body has ongoing life."

Belief in the immortality of the soul is very prominent among non-Christian religions. For example, the most esteemed of sacred Hindu writings, *The Bhagavad Gita,* specifically refers to the soul as deathless. It presents this as justification for killing in war, saying:

"These bodies come to an end,
  It is declared, of the eternal embodied (soul),
Which is indestructible and unfathomable.
  Therefore fight, son of Bharata!

Who believes him a slayer,
  And who thinks him slain,
Both these understand not:
  He slays not, is not slain.

He is not born, nor does he ever die;
  Nor, having come to be, will he ever more come not to be.
Unborn, eternal, everlasting, this ancient one
  Is not slain when the body is slain."
—*The Bhagavad Gita*, II, 18-20.

But what is the soul here spoken of? Though strong believers in the immortality of the human soul, Hindus describe its nature in vague terms. Says the publication *Hinduism,* by Swami Vivekananda:

"The Hindu believes that every soul is a circle whose circumference is nowhere, though its centre is located in the body; and that death only means the change of this centre from one body to another. Nor is the soul bound by the conditions of matter. In its very essence, it is free, unbounded, holy, pure, and perfect. But somehow or other it finds itself bound down by matter, and thinks of itself as matter."

What, then, is the general belief among members of Christendom's churches? Professor Cullmann (Theological faculty of the University of Basel and of the Sorbonne in Paris) states:

"If we were to ask an ordinary Christian today (whether well-read Protestant or Catholic, or not) what he conceived to be the New Testament teaching concerning the fate of man after death, with few exceptions we should get the answer: 'The immortality of the soul.'"

When asked about the nature of the "soul," members of Christendom's churches, too, answer in vague, obscure terms. They have no clearer concept of an immortal soul than do adherents of non-Christian religions. This gives rise to the question, Does the Bible teach that the soul is an immortal part of man?

IS THE SOUL IMMORTAL?

In the Bible the word "soul" appears in many translations as a rendering for the Hebrew word *ne'phesh* and the Greek word *psy·khe'*. (See, for example, Ezekiel 18:4 and Matthew 10:28 in the *Authorized Version, New English Bible, Revised Standard Version* and *Douay Version*.) These same Hebrew and Greek terms have also been translated as "being," "creature" and "person." Regardless of whether your Bible consistently renders the original-language words as "soul" (as does the *New World Translation*), an examination of texts where the words *ne'phesh* and *psy·khe'* appear will help you to see what these terms meant to God's people of ancient times. Thus you can determine for yourself the true nature of the soul.

Describing the creation of the first man, Adam, the opening book of the Bible says: "Jehovah God proceeded to form the man out of dust from the ground and to blow into his nostrils the breath of life, and the man came to be a living soul [*ne'phesh*]." (Genesis 2:7) We may note that the Bible does not say that 'man received a soul,' but that "man *came to be* a living soul."

Did first-century Christian teaching differ from this concept of "soul"? No. In what is commonly called the "New Testament," the statement about Adam's creation is quoted as fact: "It is even so written: 'The first man Adam became a living soul.'" (1 Corinthians 15:45) In the original language of this text the word for "soul," *psy·khe'*, appears. Accordingly, in this scripture the Greek word *psy·khe'*, like the Hebrew word *ne'phesh*, designates, not some invisible spirit residing in man, but man himself. Rightly, then, certain Bible translators have chosen to use such words as "being," "creature" and "person" in their renderings of Genesis 2:7 and 1 Corinthians 15:45. —*New English Bible, Young's Literal Translation, Revised Standard Version;* compare *The Bible in Living English*, which uses "person" at Genesis 2:7 but "soul" at 1 Corinthians 15:45.

It is also noteworthy that the terms *ne'phesh* and *psy·khe'* are applied to animals. Concerning the creation of sea and land creatures, the Bible says: "God went on to say: 'Let the waters swarm forth a swarm of living souls ["creatures," *New English Bible*] and let flying creatures fly over the earth' . . . God proceeded to create the great sea monsters and every living soul that moves about . . . 'Let the earth put forth living souls according to their kinds, domestic animal and moving animal and wild beast of the earth according to its kind.' "—Genesis 1:20-24.

Such references to animals as being souls are not limited to the opening book of the Bible. From the first book of the Holy Scriptures to the very last book, animals continue to be designated as souls. It is written: "Take away from the men of war who went out on the expedition one soul [ne'phesh] out of five hundred, of humankind and of the herd and of the asses and of the flock." (Numbers 31:28) "The righteous one is caring for the soul [ne'phesh] of his domestic animal." (Proverbs 12:10) "Every living soul [psy·khe'] died, yes, the things in the sea."—Revelation 16:3.

The application of the word "soul" to animals is very appropriate. It is in agreement with what is thought to be the basic meaning of the Hebrew term ne'phesh. This word is understood to be derived from a root meaning "to breathe." Hence, in a literal sense, a soul is a "breather," and animals are indeed breathers. They are living, breathing creatures.

As to their application to humans, the words ne'phesh and psy·khe' are repeatedly used in such a way as to mean the entire person. We read in the Bible that the human soul is born. (Genesis 46:18) It can eat or fast. (Leviticus 7:20; Psalm 35:13) It can weep and faint. (Jeremiah 13:17; Jonah 2:7) A soul can swear, crave things and give way to fear. (Leviticus 5:4; Deuteronomy 12:20; Acts 2:43) A person might kidnap a soul. (Deuteronomy 24:7) The soul can be pursued and put in irons. (Psalm 7:5; 105:18) Are these not the kind of things done by or to *fleshly* people?

THEY ARE ALL SOULS

Do not such passages of Scripture clearly establish that the human soul is the entire man?

Numerous twentieth-century Bible scholars, Catholic, Protestant and Jewish, have been brought to this conclusion. Note their comments:

"The famous verse in Genesis [2:7] does not say, as is often supposed, that man consists of body and soul; it says that Yahweh shaped man, earth from the ground, and then proceeded to animate the inert figure with living breath blown into his nostrils, so that man became a living *being*, which is all that *nephesh* [soul] here means."—H. Wheeler Robinson of Regent's Park College, London, in *Zeitschrift für die alttestamentliche Wissenschaft* (Journal for the Old Testament Science), Vol. 41 (1923).

"Man must not be thought of as *having* a soul: he *is* a soul."—E. F. Kevan, Principal of the London Bible College, in *The New Bible Commentary* (1965), 2d ed., p. 78.

"The soul in the O[ld] T[estament] means not a part of man, but the whole man—man as a living being. Similarly, in the N[ew] T[estament] it signifies human life: the life of an individual, conscious subject."—*New Catholic Encyclopedia* (1967), Vol. 13, p. 467.

"The Bible does not say we have a soul. 'Nefesh' is the person himself, his need for food, the very blood in his veins, his being."—Dr. H. M. Orlinsky of Hebrew Union College, quoted in New York *Times*, October 12, 1962.

Does it seem strange to you that scholars of various religious persuasions are now saying that the soul is man himself? Is this what you have been taught? Or, have you been taught that the soul is an immortal part of man? If so, what effect has this teaching had on you? Has it moved you to spend money for religious purposes that you would otherwise have used for necessities of life? Could it be that your church has

been dishonest in its teaching? Who is right
—the church or its scholars?

If the scholars are right in saying that the
human soul is the entire person, including his
fleshly body, we should expect the Bible to refer
to the soul as being mortal. Does it? Yes. The
Bible speaks of 'holding back,' 'rescuing' and
'saving' a *ne'phesh* or soul from death. (Psalm
78:50; 116:8; James 5:20) We also read: "Let
us not strike his soul fatally." (Genesis 37:21)
"The manslayer must flee there who fatally strikes
a soul unintentionally." (Numbers 35:11) "Their
soul will die in youth." (Job 36:14) "The soul
that is sinning—it itself will die."—Ezekiel 18:4,
20.

But is it possible that at least in a few Scriptural references the original-language words rendered "soul" designate something that leaves the
body at death and is immortal? What about such
texts as the following? "As her soul was going
out (because she died) she called his name Ben-
oni." (Genesis 35:18) "My God, please, cause the
soul of this child to come back within him."
(1 Kings 17:21) "Stop raising a clamor, for his
soul is in him." (Acts 20:10) Do not these passages indicate that the soul is something that
exists independently of the body?

The text at Job 33:22, written in poetic style,
provides a key to understanding these passages.
There "soul" and "life" are placed in parallel, so
that the two words could be interchanged without
changing the sense of the passage. We read:
"His *soul* draws near to the pit, and his *life* to
those inflicting death." From this parallel we can
see that the word "soul" can mean life as a person
and, therefore, the departure of the soul can be

understood to refer to the end of life as a person.

To illustrate: A man might say that his dog 'lost its life' when it was hit by a truck. Does he mean that this animal's life left the body and continued existing? No, he is simply using a figure of speech indicating that the animal died. The same is true when we speak of a man as 'losing his life.' We do not mean that his life exists independently of the body. Similarly, 'to lose one's soul' means to 'lose one's life as a soul' and carries no meaning of continued existence after death. Recognizing this, *The Interpreter's Dictionary of the Bible* states:

> "The 'departure' of the *nephesh* [soul] must be viewed as a figure of speech, for it does not continue to exist independently of the body, but dies with it (Num. 31:19; Judg. 16:30; Ezek. 13:19). No biblical text authorizes the statement that the 'soul' is separated from the body at the moment of death."

THE SOURCE OF THE BELIEF

The Scriptural evidence is unmistakably clear that man does not have an immortal soul but is himself a soul. How, then, did this belief about an immortal soul find its way into the teachings of Christendom's churches? Today it is frankly acknowledged that this has come about through the influence of pagan Grecian philosophy. Writes Professor Douglas T. Holden in his book *Death Shall Have No Dominion:*

> "Christian theology has become so fused with Greek philosophy that it has reared individuals who are a mixture of nine parts Greek thought to one part Christian thought."

The Catholic magazine *Commonweal,* in its issue of January 15, 1971, confessed that the idea of an immortal soul was a concept that "the late

Jews and early Christians inherited from Athens."

Who is to blame for this mixture of pagan Greek and Christian thought? Is it not the religious clergy? Surely the church members did not on their own come up with this teaching, one that Bible scholars now openly admit to be unscriptural.

But from where did the ancient Greeks get their basic religious foundation? As has already been pointed out, there is strong evidence that the religious concepts of the Greeks and other peoples were influenced by the Babylonians. And as to Babylonian beliefs about the soul note what *The International Standard Bible Encyclopædia* says:

> "After death the souls of men were supposed to continue in existence. . . . The Babylonians . . . placed often with the dead articles which might be used in his future existence. . . . In the future world there seem to have been distinctions made among the dead. Those who fell in battle seem to have had special favor. They received fresh water to drink, while those who had no posterity to put offerings at their graves suffered sore and many deprivations."

So the Greeks could easily have gotten their basic ideas about the immortality of the soul from Babylon, which ideas were then enlarged upon by the Greek philosophers.

Something similar appears to have taken place in connection with the non-Christian religions still in existence today. For example, a comparison of the ancient civilization of the Indus Valley, where Hinduism is the dominant religion, with that of Mesopotamia reveals notable similarities. These include structures like the religious ziggurat platforms of Mesopotamia and pictographic signs bearing a strong resemblance to early Mesopotamian forms. On the basis of his study, the noted Assyriologist Samuel N. Kramer suggested that the Indus Valley was settled by a people who fled from Mesopotamia when the Sumerians took control of the area. It is not difficult to understand, then, where Hinduism got its belief in an undying soul.

The evidence thus points to Babylon as the most ancient source from which belief in the immortality of the human soul radiated to the ends of the earth. And there at Babylon, according to the Bible, a rebellion against God occurred. In itself that would be reason enough to view the doctrine of an immortal soul with reservations. But do not forget that, as we have already seen, this teaching is also in direct conflict with the Bible.

Furthermore, is not the idea that the soul is immortal contrary to what you personally have observed? For example, what happens when a person is knocked unconscious, faints, or is placed under an anesthetic at a hospital? If his "soul" is really something separate from the body and is able to function intelligently apart from the body, so that even death itself does not affect its existence and its functions, why is it that during such period of unconsciousness the person is completely unaware of all activity around him? Why is it that he must be told afterward what happened during that time? If his "soul" can see, hear, feel and think after death, as religions generally teach, why does something far less drastic than death, such as a period of unconsciousness, stop all these functions?

Also, a dead body, whether it be that of a human or of an animal, eventually returns to the elements of the ground. Nothing about death even hints at there being an immortal soul that lives on.

EFFECT OF THE DOCTRINE ABOUT THE SOUL'S IMMORTALITY

What a person believes about the soul is of no little consequence.

The teaching of the immortality of the human soul has been used to override the conscience of people in times of war. Religious leaders have made it appear that taking life is not so bad, as those slain do not really die after all. And those who die in battle against the enemy are promised bliss. Typical are remarks such as those reported on in the New York *Times* of September 11, 1950: "Sorrowing parents whose sons have been drafted or recalled for combat duty were told yesterday in St. Patrick's Cathedral that death in battle was part of God's plan for populating 'the kingdom of Heaven.'" The idea here expressed differs little from the ancient Babylonian teaching that the war dead gained special favors.

Misrepresentations of what the Bible says about the soul have thus contributed toward the placing of a cheapened value on human life and have made people feel dependent on the great religious systems that have falsely claimed to care for their souls.

Knowing these things, what will you do? It is obvious that the true God, who is himself "the God of truth" and who hates lies, will not look with favor on persons who cling to organizations that teach falsehood. (Psalm 31:5; Proverbs 6: 16-19; Revelation 21:8) And, really, would you want to be even associated with a religion that had not been honest with you?

CHAPTER 6

The Spirit That Returns to God

THERE should be no question in the mind of any sincere investigator that what the Bible speaks of as "soul" is not some immortal part of man that continues conscious existence after death. Yet when shown the overwhelming evidence about the true nature of the soul, some persons present other arguments in an effort to support their belief that *something* within man has continued existence after death.

One Biblical text that is often used is Ecclesiastes 12:7, which reads: "The dust returns to the earth just as it happened to be and the spirit itself returns to the true God who gave it." In his *Commentary,* Wesleyan Methodist theologian Adam Clarke writes concerning this verse: "Here the wise man makes a most evident distinction between the body and the soul: they are not the same; they are not both matter. The body, which is matter, returns to dust, its original; but the spirit, which is *immaterial,* returns to God." Similarly, *A Catholic Commentary on Holy Scripture* says: "The soul goes back to God." Thus both commentaries imply that the soul and the spirit are the same.

Interestingly, though, other Roman Catholic and Protestant scholars present an entirely different view. In the "Glossary of Biblical Theology Terms" appearing in the Catholic *New American Bible* (published by P. J. Kenedy & Sons, New

York, 1970), we read: "When 'spirit' is used in contrast with 'flesh,' . . . the aim is not to distinguish a material from an immaterial part of man . . . 'Spirit' does not mean soul." At Ecclesiastes 12:7 this translation uses, not the word "spirit," but the expression "life breath." The Protestant *Interpreter's Bible* observes regarding the writer of Ecclesiastes: "Koheleth does not mean that man's personality continues to exist." In view of such different conclusions, can we be sure just what the spirit is and in what sense it returns to God?

At Ecclesiastes 12:1-7 the effects of old age and death are portrayed in poetic language. After death, the body eventually decomposes and again becomes a part of the dust of the earth. The "spirit," on the other hand, "returns to the true God." So man's death is linked with the spirit's returning to God, this indicating that man's life in some way depends upon that spirit.

In the original-language text of Ecclesiastes 12:7, the Hebrew word translated "spirit" or "life breath" is *ru'ahh*. The corresponding Greek term is *pneu'ma*. While our life does depend on the breathing process, the English word "breath" (as numerous translators often render the words *ru'ahh* and *pneu'ma*) is not always a suitable alternate translation for "spirit." Furthermore, other Hebrew and Greek words, namely, *ne·sha·mah'* (Hebrew) and *pno·e'* (Greek), are also translated as "breath." (See Genesis 2:7 and Acts 17:25.) It is nevertheless noteworthy that, in using "breath" as an alternate rendering for "spirit," translators are showing that the original-language terms apply to something that has no personality but is essential for the continuance of life.

THE SPIRIT IDENTIFIED

That man's life depends on the spirit (*ru'ahh* or *pneu'ma*) is definitely stated in the Bible. We read: "If you [Jehovah] take away their spirit [*ru'ahh*], they expire, and back to their dust they go." (Psalm 104:29) "The body without spirit [*pneu'ma*] is dead." (James 2:26) Hence, the spirit is that which animates the body.

But this animating force is not simply breath. Why not? Because life remains in the body cells for a brief period after breathing stops. For this reason efforts at resuscitation can succeed, also body organs can be transplanted from one person to another. But these things have to be done quickly. Once the life-force is gone from the cells of the body, efforts to prolong life are futile. All the breath in the world could not revive even as much as one cell. Viewed in this light, the "spirit" evidently is an invisible life-force, active in every living cell of man's body.

Is this life-force active only in man? What is stated in the Bible can help us to reach a sound conclusion on this. Regarding the destruction of human and animal life in a global flood, the Bible reports: "Everything in which the breath [*ne·sha·mah'*] of the force [*ru'ahh,* spirit] of life was active in its nostrils, namely, all that were on the dry ground, died." (Genesis 7:22) At Ecclesiastes 3:19 the same basic point is made in connection with death: "There is an eventuality as respects the sons of mankind and an eventuality as respects the beast, and they have the same eventuality. As the one dies, so the other dies;

and they all have but one spirit [ru'ahh], so that there is no superiority of the man over the beast." Accordingly, man is not superior to animals when it comes to the spirit animating his body. The same invisible spirit or life-force is common to both.

In a sense, the spirit or life-force active in both animals and man might be compared to a flow of electrons or electricity through a machine or an appliance. The invisible electricity may be used to perform various functions, depending upon the type of machine or appliance being energized. Stoves can be made to produce heat, fans to produce wind, computers to solve problems, and television sets to reproduce figures, voices and other sounds. The same invisible force that produces sound in one appliance can produce heat in another, mathematical computations in another. But does the electric current ever take on the often complex characteristics of the machines or appliances in which it functions or is active? No, it remains simply electricity—a mere force or form of energy.

Similarly, both humans and animals "have but one spirit," one activating force. The spirit or life-force that enables man to carry out functions of life in no way differs from the spirit that makes it possible for animals to do so. That spirit does not retain the characteristics of the dead body's cells. For example, in the case of brain cells, the spirit does not retain the information stored there and continue thought processes apart from these cells. The Bible tells us: "His spirit [ru'ahh] goes out, he goes back to his ground; in that day his thoughts do perish."—Psalm 146:4.

This being the case, the return of the ru'ahh

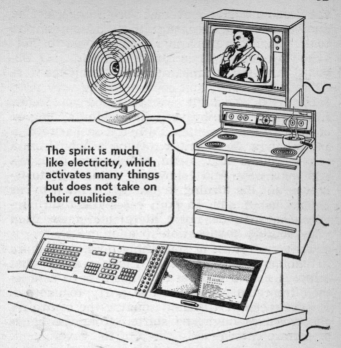

The spirit is much like electricity, which activates many things but does not take on their qualities

or spirit to God simply could not mean the continuance of conscious existence. The spirit does not continue human thought processes. It is only a life-force that has no conscious existence apart from a body.

HOW THE SPIRIT RETURNS TO GOD

How, then, does this invisible, impersonal force or spirit return to God? Does it return to his literal presence in heaven?

The way in which the Bible uses the word "return" does not require that we, in each case, think of an actual movement from one place to another. For instance, unfaithful Israelites were told: " 'Return to me, and I will return to you,' Jehovah of armies has said." (Malachi 3:7) Obviously this did not mean that the Israelites were to leave the earth and come into the very presence of God. Nor did it mean that God would leave his position in the heavens and begin dwelling on earth with the Israelites. Rather, Israel's "returning" to Jehovah meant a turning around from a wrong course and again conforming to God's righteous way. And Jehovah's "returning" to Israel meant his turning favorable attention to his people once again. In both cases the return involved an attitude, not a literal movement from one geographical location to another.

That the return of something does not require actual movement might be illustrated by what happens in a transferal of a business or a property from the control of one party to another. For example, in a certain country the control of the railroads might be shifted from the hands of private enterprise to those of the government. When such a transferal takes place, the railroad equipment and even all the records may remain where they are. It is the *authority* over them that changes hands.

So it is in the case of the spirit or life-force. At death no actual movement from the earth to the heavenly realm need occur for it to 'return to God.' But the gift or grant of existence as an intelligent creature, as enjoyed once by the dead person, now reverts to God. That which is needed to animate the person, namely, the spirit or life-force, is in God's hands.—Psalm 31:5; Luke 23:46.

The situation might be compared to that of an

accused man who says to a judge, 'My life is in your hands.' He means that what will become of his life rests with the judge. The accused has no choice in the matter. It is out of his hands.

Similarly, in the case of a dead man, he does not have control over his spirit or life-force. It has returned to God in the sense that he controls the future life prospects of the individual. It is up to God to decide as to whether he will restore the spirit or life-force to the deceased.

But does this necessarily shut out all possibility of life after death? Is there not something else to consider?

WHAT ABOUT REBIRTH OR REINCARNATION?

Millions of persons of various religious persuasions, whether called Christian or non-Christian, believe that humans had an existence prior to their present life and will continue to live after they die. Though their concepts vary greatly, they share in common the conviction that some part of man is reborn or reincarnated in another body.

Presenting one line of argument in favor of the belief in rebirth, *A Manual of Buddhism* states: "Sometimes we get strange experiences which cannot be explained but by rebirth. How often do we meet persons whom we have never before met and yet inwardly feel that they are quite familiar to us? How often do we visit places and yet feel impressed that we are perfectly acquainted with their surroundings?"

Have you ever experienced such things? After meeting a person, have you ever had the feeling that you have known him for a long time? What accounts for such an experience?

There are many similarities in people. Perhaps, after some thought, you yourself realized that the person had personality traits and physical features resembling those of a relative or a friend.

Likewise you may have lived in a particular city or seen pictures of it. Then, when visiting another city, you may note certain similarities so that you feel that you are not really amid strange and unfamiliar surroundings.

So, then, is it not reasonable to conclude that feelings of familiarity about previously unknown people and places are, not the product of some past life, but a result of experiences in the present life? Really, if all people had actually had previous existences, should they not all be aware of this? Why, then, do millions not even have the slightest sense or thought of having lived an earlier life? Furthermore, how can a person avoid the mistakes of his earlier lives if he cannot even recall them? Of what benefit would such previous lives be?

Some may offer the explanation that 'life would be a burden if people knew the details of their previous existences.' That is the way Mohandas K. Gandhi expressed it, saying: "It is nature's kindness that we do not remember past births. Where is the good either of knowing in detail the numberless births we have gone through? Life would be a burden if we carried such a tremendous load of memories. A wise man deliberately forgets many things, even as a lawyer forgets the cases and their details as soon as they are disposed of." That is an interesting explanation, but does it rest on a solid foundation?

While our ability to recall many things that we have experienced may be limited, our minds are certainly not *totally blank* respecting them. A lawyer may forget the precise details of certain cases, but the experience gained in handling them becomes part of his fund of knowledge. He would indeed be at a great disadvantage if he actually forgot everything. Then, too, which causes people greater disturbance—a poor memory or a good memory? Is not an old man who has a good recall of his fund of knowledge and experience far better off than an old man who has practically forgotten everything?

Really, what "kindness" would there be in having to learn all over again things that one had already learned during a previous existence? Would you consider it "nature's kindness" if every ten years of your life you forgot practically everything you knew and had to start learning a language again and then begin building up a fund of knowledge and experience, only to have it eradicated? Would this not be frustrating? Would this not result in terrible setbacks? Why, then, imagine that it happens every seventy or eighty years? Can you feature that a loving God could have made such rebirth part of his purpose for mankind?

Many who accept the doctrine of rebirth believe that those leading a bad life will be reborn in a lower caste or as insects, birds or beasts. Yet why is it, then, that there is a big *human* population explosion at a time when crime and violence are increasing on an unprecedented scale? Also, why can even those in the lowest caste excel when given educational opportunities? For example, the New York *Times* of October 26, 1973, reported that a sixteen-year-old girl of low caste was the brightest girl in the school at Kallipashim,

India. She was smarter than a girl of the highest caste, a Brahman. How might this be explained? Is it not true that the doctrine of rebirth or reincarnation cannot provide satisfying explanations for such things?

Think, too, of the fruitage that such teaching has produced. Has it not deprived many humans of a dignified standing, forcing them to take menial jobs under poor working conditions, with little possibility of improving their lot in life through education?

DOES THE BIBLE TEACH REBIRTH?

Of course, some persons might point out that logical deductions do not necessarily rule out the possibility of rebirth. Their reply to the aforementioned arguments might be: 'Even the Bible teaches rebirth. This is just one of many things that humans cannot fully explain.'

Since believers in rebirth do bring the Bible into the discussion, we should want to consider what it does say. Just what Biblical evidence is there for the belief in rebirth? The book *What Is Buddhism?* answers: "For the Christian reader we would point out that [the doctrine of rebirth] is clearly present in such mutilated fragments of Christ's teachings as are still extant. Consider, for example, the widely current rumours that he was John the Baptist, Jeremiah or Elijah come again (Matt. xvi, 13-16). Even Herod seemed to think that he was 'John the Baptist risen from the dead.' "

What about such arguments? Did Jesus Christ himself claim to be John the Baptist, Jeremiah or Elijah? No, these claims were made by persons who did not accept Jesus for what he really was, namely, the promised Messiah or Christ. Jesus simply could not have been John the Baptist, for when about thirty years of age the younger man, Jesus, was baptized by John, who was older. (Matthew 3:13-17; Luke 3:21-23) King Herod came up with the unreasoning conclusion that Jesus was John raised from the dead, because of his feelings of extreme guilt for having executed John.

But are there not direct statements of Jesus Christ that are viewed as supporting belief in rebirth or reincarnation? Yes, there is one. On one occasion Jesus Christ linked John the Baptist with the ancient Hebrew prophet Elijah, saying: "Elijah has already come and they did not recognize him but did with him the things they wanted. . . . Then the disciples perceived that he spoke to them about John the Baptist." (Matthew 17:12, 13) In stating, "Elijah has already come," did Jesus mean that John the Baptist was Elijah reborn?

The answer to this question must be determined on the basis of what the Bible says as a whole. Many Jews back in the time of Jesus' earthly ministry did think that Elijah would come back literally. And the prophecy of Malachi pointed forward to the time when Jehovah God would send the prophet Elijah. (Malachi 4:5) John the Baptist, however, did not view himself as Elijah in person or as a reincarnation of that Hebrew prophet. On one occasion certain Jews asked him, "Are you Elijah?" John replied, "I am not." (John 1:21) It had, however, been foretold that John would prepare the way before the Messiah "with Elijah's spirit and power." (Luke 1:17) Accordingly, when Jesus linked John the Baptist with Elijah he was merely showing how the prophecy was fulfilled in John who did a *work like that* of Elijah of old.

Another passage of Scripture appealed to by believers in reincarnation is Romans 9:11-13: "When [Esau and Jacob] had not yet been born nor had practiced anything good or vile, in order that the purpose of God respecting the choosing might continue dependent, not upon works, but upon the One who calls, it was said to [Rebekah]: 'The older will be the slave of the younger.' Just as it is written [at Malachi 1:2, 3]: 'I loved Jacob, but Esau I hated.'" Does this passage not show that God's choosing was based on what Jacob and Esau had done during lives prior to their being born to Rebekah?

Why not reread it? Note that it specifically says that God's choosing was made *before* either one had practiced good or bad. So God's choice did not depend upon a record of past works in some earlier life.

On what basis, then, could God make a choice before the birth of the boys? The Bible reveals that God is able to see the embryo and, therefore, knows the genetic makeup of humans before birth. (Psalm 139:16) Exercising his foreknowledge, God perceived how the two boys would be basically as to temperament and personality and thus he could make a choice of the one who might be more suitable for the superior blessing. The record made by the two boys in life confirms the wisdom of God's choice. While Jacob demonstrated spiritual interests and faith in God's promises, Esau manifested a materialistic bent and lack of appreciation for sacred things.—Hebrews 11:21; 12:16, 17.

As to the apostle Paul's quotation from Malachi about God's 'loving Jacob' and 'hating Esau,' this, too, relates to Jehovah's view of them based on their genetic makeup. While recorded by Malachi many centuries after their lifetime, the statement confirmed what God had indicated about the boys before their birth.

A question raised by Jesus' disciples is yet another example cited by some in support of reincarnation. Regarding a man blind from birth, the disciples asked: "Who sinned, this man or his parents, so that he was born blind?" (John 9:2) Do these words not reveal that the man must have had a previous existence?

No! Jesus Christ did not go along with any suggestion that the child developing in the womb of its mother had sinned of itself before birth. Jesus said: "Neither this man sinned nor his parents, but it was in order that the works of God might be made manifest in his case." (John 9:3) That is to say, human imperfections and defects such as this man's blindness provided the opportunity for the works of God to become manifest in the form of a miraculous cure. Had no one ever been born blind, humans would not have come to know that God can give sight to one born blind. Jehovah God, in allowing a sinful human race to come into existence, has used their imperfections and defects to show what he can do for them.

So while there may be Bible texts that some persons think support the concept of rebirth, closer examination indicates otherwise. In fact, nowhere in the Bible do we find any mention of the rebirth or transmigration of a soul, spirit or something else that survives the death of the body. Some have tried to 'read into' the Holy Scriptures the idea of rebirth or reincarnation. It is not a Bible doctrine.

The Bible clearly shows that conscious existence does not continue by means of a soul or spirit that leaves the body at death. When sentencing the first man to death for disobedience, God did not set before him any prospect of rebirth or reincarnation. Adam was told: "In the sweat of your face you will eat bread until you return to the ground, for out of it you were taken. For dust you are and to dust you will return." (Genesis 3:19) Yes, the man was to return to the lifeless dust of the ground.

Are we, then, to understand that this life is all there is? Or, is there a provision for future life that is available in some other way? Might this provision make it necessary for the living to help the dead, or are the dead beyond any help from the living?

CHAPTER 7

Do the Dead Need Your Help?

"TO SERVE those now dead as if they were living," says an old Chinese proverb, "is the highest achievement of true filial piety." If the dead truly exist in another realm and can benefit from the services of those remaining on earth, it would be a loving thing to show concern for them.

Of course, many people simply go through the motions of observing ancient traditions, though not really being firm believers in continued existence after death. But others are convinced that the dead need their help.

Millions of persons throughout most of Asia and parts of Africa believe that they must pay homage to dead ancestors all their life. Before the ancestral tablets of their deceased relatives, they burn incense, pray, place flowers and even offer food. It is thought that such veneration will help the dead to enjoy a pleasant existence in the next life and prevent them from becoming hostile spirits.

Especially in connection with mourning and the funeral do the survivors put forth costly efforts to help the deceased. Consider the following traditional practices that were carried out in the Orient upon the death of a prominent governmental adviser:

Buddhist priests handled the rites. Firecrackers were set off to chase away evil spirits. Rice paper containing prayers was burned, in the belief that this would benefit the spirit of the dead man. Food, drink and tobacco were placed near the corpse so that the spirit could refresh itself whenever it chose to do so.

Thereafter the body was placed in a casket, which remained in a room of the funeral home for forty-nine days. For six days the eldest son mourned there. On the seventh day he returned home to sleep, bathe and change clothes. The cycle of six days of mourning and one day of rest was then repeated for the full course of the forty-nine days. Practically without any break in the entire period, firecrackers were set off, while flutes, drums and crashing cymbals resounded around the clock.

The forty-ninth day witnessed the impressive funeral march. Bands played. Along the route firecrackers strung on telephone poles, lampposts and trees were set off. Food, drink and tobacco were put on the altar tables, and paper containing prayers, as well as joss sticks, was burned in the little shrines set up all along the route. Attractive floats of paper, gold leaf and bamboo added to the colorfulness of the funeral march. Many of the mourners carried lanterns, the purpose of such lanterns being to light the way for the spirit of the dead man. At the graveside the beautiful floats, representing palaces, airplanes, ships, armies, servants and other things, were burned.

In the case of persons having lesser means and prominence, similar procedures are followed but on a much smaller scale. For example, fewer and less elaborate paper items are burned.

Belief in a purgatory is the underlying basis for such burning of paper items. After a person's death, the spirit is believed to wander in purgatory for two years, but needing help to enter heaven. The offerings made in the form of paper items are designed to show that the dead man lived a good life and has everything needed to function in the next world. This being the case, many Chinese believe, his spirit should be freed from purgatory sooner.

How do you react to such elaborate and costly ceremonies? Would you share in similar practices? If so, why?

If you believe that the dead need your help, what positive evidence do you have that something conscious survives the death of the body? What makes you sure that the means used to help the dead are effective? How, for example, could one prove that lanterns light the way for a spirit, that firecrackers chase away evil spirits and that burned paper items can help the spirit of the deceased to enter celestial bliss? What basis is there for claiming that such things are effective means for helping the spirits of the dead?

While religious ceremonies to help the dead may be quite different in your area, could anyone prove to your satisfaction that what is done brings beneficial results?

It is worth while, too, to consider how much justice and fairness are found in these efforts to help the dead. Those having great wealth naturally can buy far more firecrackers, paper items or other things supposed to aid the dead. What, then, of the poor person? Though he might have lived a good life, he would be at a disadvantage if no one did anything after his death. Also, the poor person who buys things to aid the dead labors under a great financial burden, while the rich person is only slightly affected.

How do you feel about such obvious partiality? Would you be drawn to a god that would favor the rich over the poor without consideration for what they are as persons? The God of the Bible shows no such partiality. Of him, the Holy Scriptures say: "There is no partiality with God." —Romans 2:11.

Now suppose a person realized that religious ceremonies in behalf of the dead were valueless, completely out of harmony with the will of the impartial God. Would it be reasonable for him to engage in them just for the sake of tradition and to avoid being different from his neighbors?

Is it logical to support religious ceremonies that one considers to be a falsehood? Is it right to go along with something that favors the rich and puts a hardship on the poor?

CHRISTENDOM'S BELIEF IN PURGATORY

The belief that the dead need help to get out of purgatory is not limited to non-Christian religions. The *New Catholic Encyclopedia* states:

> "The souls in purgatory can be helped by works of piety, such as prayer, indulgences, alms, fasting, and sacrifices. . . . While one cannot dictate that God apply the satisfactory value of his works to the poor souls, he may certainly hope that God will hear his petitions and help the members of the Church suffering."

How strong a guarantee is offered that such

Taoist rites, said to release a soul from purgatory

Catholic rites, said to aid souls in purgatory

efforts will bring benefit? The *Encyclopedia* continues:

"Because the application of these good works depends on one's petition to God, there is no infallible assurance that one's prayers help an individual soul in purgatory, or any one of them, here and now. But the mercy and love of God for the souls in purgatory, who are already so close to Him, surely prompt Him to speed their release from the period of purification when the faithful on earth direct their prayers to this purpose."

Thus no genuine assurance is given that the things done in behalf of those believed to be in purgatory really accomplish something. And there is no basis for giving such assurance, for the Bible does not do so. It does not even contain the word "purgatory." The *New Catholic En-*

cyclopedia acknowledges: "In the final analysis, the Catholic doctrine on purgatory is based on tradition, not Sacred Scripture."—Vol. 11, p. 1034.

Granted, tradition is not necessarily bad. But this particular tradition is out of harmony with God's Word. The Scriptures do not teach that the "soul" survives the death of the body. Obviously, then, it cannot be subjected to a period of purification in purgatory. Hence, the words of Jesus Christ to the Jewish religious leaders could rightly be directed to those teaching the purgatory doctrine: "You have made the word of God invalid because of your tradition. You hypocrites, Isaiah aptly prophesied about you, when he said, 'This people honors me with their lips, yet their heart is far removed from me. It is in vain that they keep worshiping me, because they teach commands of men as doctrines.' "—Matthew 15:6-9.

Consider also the means for helping those in purgatory, in the light of what is taught in the Holy Scriptures. As noted in the *New Catholic Encyclopedia,* prayer is one of the works of piety that supposedly can help the souls in purgatory. Concerning such prayers, the booklet *Assist the Souls in Purgatory* (published by the Benedictine Convent of Perpetual Adoration) says:

"A short but fervent prayer is often of greater benefit to the poor souls than a prolonged form of devotion which is wanting in attention. Innumerable are the short ejaculatory prayers to which the Church has granted indulgences, all of which are applicable to the poor souls. . . . How easily we can multiply these little fiery darts of prayer during the day as we go from task to task, and even while our hands are busy with some occupation! . . . How many souls could we not relieve or release from purgatory if frequently during the day we offered this short indulgenced prayer of the Church for the departed: 'Eternal rest give unto them, O Lord, and let perpetual light shine upon them. May they rest in peace. Amen.' (Ind[ulgence] of 300 days each time. 'Manual of Indulgences,' 582.) If we repeat with fervent devotion the holy names of 'Jesus, Mary, Joseph' an indulgence of seven years may be gained each time."

Does it not seem strange to you that the repetition of three names would be eight times as effective as a considerably longer, twenty-word prayer? Is repetition of a prayer over and over again what God approves? Concerning this, Jesus Christ said: "When praying, do not say the same things over and over again, just as the people of the nations do, for they imagine they will get a hearing for their use of many words. So, do not make yourselves like them."—Matthew 6:7, 8.

Rather than your saying memorized phrases over and over again, the Bible encourages heartfelt expressions in prayer.

Not to be overlooked is the role that money has had in relation to the purgatory doctrine. Of course, it might be argued that interest in gaining money for the church is not the reason for that teaching. But this does not change the fact that the religious organizations adhering to the purgatory doctrine are pleased to receive material offerings. No one is ever censured by the church for trying to buy his or someone else's way out of purgatory. No one is ever advised by the church that it would be better for him to use his limited material assets for necessities of life. For centuries rich and poor alike have been filling the coffers of religious organizations in the hope of reducing the time they or their loved ones are in purgatory. Observes author Corliss Lamont, in his book *The Illusion of Immortality:*

"The religious ceremonies connected with the departed have meant untold wealth for the Church. Particularly has this been true in the Roman Catholic and Eastern Orthodox faiths where much stress is laid upon masses, prayers and other good offices on behalf of the dead, the dying and all those in any way concerned over their future state.

"Since the early Middle Ages the Catholic Church has obtained, through the granting of indulgences alone, huge sums from rich and poor alike. These indulgences, given in return for money payments, almsgiving or other kinds of offerings, provide that one's own soul or the soul of a deceased relative or friend be spared all or part of its destined punishment in purgatory. . . . In Russia the Orthodox Church accumulated enormous wealth through similar intercessions on behalf of the dead. Besides the steady income from workers and peasants anxious to mitigate divine retribution, many members of the nobility and upper class endowed monasteries and churches on condition that daily prayers be said for their departed souls."

If it were true that such material offerings did benefit the dead, this would mean that God is interested in money. But he does not need anyone's money or material possessions. Speaking through the inspired psalmist, God declares: "I will not take out of your house a bull, out of your pens he-goats. For to me belongs every wild animal of the forest, the beasts upon a thousand mountains. I well know every winged creature of the mountains, and the animal throngs of the open field are with me. If I were hungry, I would not say it to you; for to me the productive land and its fullness belong."—Psalm 50:9-12.

Really, all the riches in the world cannot help a dead man. Money and material possessions cannot even save him from dying. As the Bible says: "Those who are trusting in their means of maintenance, and who keep boasting about the abundance of their riches, not one of them can by any means redeem even a brother, nor give to God a ransom for him; (and the redemption price of their soul is so precious that it has ceased to time indefinite) that he should still live forever and not see the pit."—Psalm 49:6-9.

There can be no question that efforts to help the dead are unscriptural. The teaching that the dead can be aided by the living has only put a heavy burden on people. Knowledge of God's Word, however, frees one from this false idea. This can provide for us real incentive to do our best while our family members are still alive to make them feel that they are needed, loved and appreciated. After their death it is too late for anyone to make up for neglected acts of kindness and consideration.

CHAPTER 8

Should You Fear the Dead?

NOT everyone views the dead as the ones who are in need of help. Even more widespread is the belief that the living are the ones who need help—to safeguard them from the dead. At night, cemeteries are often avoided. Strangely, even relatives and friends who were loved while living, after death may come to be viewed as a source of dread and terror.

Among the Indians inhabiting the hills of Central Chiapas, Mexico, red pepper is burned on the day of the burial. This is done in the hope that the unpleasant smoke will drive the soul of the deceased out of the house.

In some parts of Europe, people quickly open all doors and windows as soon as a death occurs. This is done with a view to "liberating" the soul. So that no spell might be cast on anyone, a member of the family places the dead man's hands over his heart and closes the man's eyes with coins.

When a Buddhist of Mongolia dies in a tent, his body is not taken out through the regular opening. Another opening may be made in the tent and, when the body is removed, this opening is closed. Or a masking of straw may be placed in front of the regular door. After the body is carried out, the masking of straw is burned. The purpose of such action is to prevent the spirit of the dead man from coming back into the dwelling and harming the living.

In many parts of Africa, when sickness strikes a family, when a child dies, when a business fails or any other kind of misfortune occurs, a man will quickly consult a juju priest. Usually the priest tells him that a dead family member has been offended. The oracle is consulted and sacrifices are prescribed. The priest charges much money for this and also gets the meat of whatever animal is offered in sacrifice.

Should humans be in such fear of the dead, even going to considerable expense to protect themselves?

The Bible says of the dead: "Their love and their hate and their jealousy have already perished, and they have no portion anymore to time indefinite in anything that has to be done under the sun." (Ecclesiastes 9:6) So there is no harm that can come to you from the dead. And no one can disprove this Bible statement.

True, people may attribute certain manifestations to the spirits of the dead. They may claim that they gained relief from sickness, economic reverses and the like after the spirits of the dead were pacified. But might there not be another source for such trouble and apparent relief from adversity?

Is it not strange that people are unaware of having offended a dead relative until their consulting a juju priest or someone occupying a comparable position? And why should it be that the "spirit" of a dead father, mother, son or daughter would threaten the happiness and welfare of those who, in the past, were deeply loved? What would cause the "spirit" of a dead man to be vengeful when that was not a trait

Fear of the dead moves many to consult juju priests

of the man when alive? Since what is attributed
to the deceased is often so contrary to that one's
personality when alive, would this not lend strong
support to the conclusion that the "spirits" of the
dead are not involved? Most assuredly. The Bible
is indeed right when it says that the dead have
'no portion in anything that is to be done under
the sun.'

Consider also the damaging effect that fear
of the dead has on the living. Many have been
brought into slavery to juju priests or other religious leaders who claim that the fortunes or
misfortunes of a man or woman are largely controlled by the "spirits" of the dead. These men
have set themselves up as the ones who can rectify
matters with the offended dead. Believing their
claims, many people have spent much money
on costly ceremonies, money that they might
otherwise have used for needed things of life.
Even though some maintain that they definitely
have been helped through such ceremonies, has
their experience produced within them real joy in
having had the privilege of doing something to
heal a breach with a dead loved one? Rather, do
they not act much like a person from whom something has been extorted?

Then, too, think of the deceptive methods that
are frequently employed—burning red pepper,
taking the deceased through another tent opening and the like—to prevent the "spirit" of
the dead from returning and disturbing the living.
Would you want to be deceived in this way during
your lifetime? Is it reasonable for a person to
try to deceive dead persons whom he would never
have wanted to deceive while they were alive?

The very practice of resorting to deception can

also have an unwholesome effect on a person. Once a person approves of deceiving the dead whom he views as continuing in conscious existence, will he not weaken his conscience to the point of attempting to deceive the living when that appears to be advantageous?

The One who identifies himself in the Bible as the true God could never approve of the practices that have come about because of people's fear of the dead. Why not? Because those practices, in addition to being based on a false idea, are completely out of harmony with His personality, ways and dealings. "God is not a man that he should tell lies." (Numbers 23:19) He does not approve of deception resorted to for selfish gain. The Bible says: "A man of . . . deception Jehovah detests."—Psalm 5:6.

Since the Bible reveals that the dead are unconscious, why should you fear them? (Psalm 146:4) They can neither help you nor harm you. You now know from the Bible that the "soul" dies and that the "spirit" has no conscious existence apart from the body. Whatever manifestations have given rise to fear of the dead must therefore be from another source. Since in some cases persons claim to gain some improvement in their problems as a result of engaging in acts of appeasement for the dead, this source would have to be one that is willing to bring such temporary relief, but for a wrong motive. What is its aim? To keep people in bondage and blinded to the way to a life free from fear and dread.

It is important to identify this source.

CHAPTER 9

Can You Talk with the Dead?

IN LIFE, we humans keenly sense a need to talk with those whom we love. We want to know that our loved ones are well and happy. When things go well for them, we are encouraged. But when we learn that they face grave danger due to a "natural" disaster or some other calamity, we begin to worry. We anxiously wait to hear from them. As soon as we have word that they are safe we are relieved.

The desire to know about the welfare of loved ones has prompted many to want to talk with the dead. They want to know whether their deceased loved ones are happy 'in the beyond.' But is it possible to talk with the dead?

Some maintain that they have periodically felt the presence of a deceased relative or friend and have heard his voice. Others have had like experiences with the help of spirit mediums. Through these mediums they believe that they have heard voices from 'the beyond.' What are they told by such voices? Basically this: 'The dead are very happy and contented. They continue to take a real interest in the life of their surviving loved ones and can see and hear everything they do.'

Regarding such messages, François Grégoire, in his book *L'au-delà* (The Hereafter), observes: "What do these Spirits have to say to us? 'Above all, they appear to be anxious to prove their identity and that they still exist' . . . but on the nature of the other world, nothing essential, not even the smallest revelation."

What do you think about these messages? Do you believe that the dead are actually talking? Since, as the Bible shows, no soul or spirit survives the death of the body to continue conscious existence, could these voices really be the voices of the dead?

THE CASE OF KING SAUL

Some among those believing that the dead can give messages to the living point to the Holy Bible as confirming their view. One example they cite is an incident involving King Saul of ancient Israel.

Because of his unfaithfulness to Jehovah God, King Saul was cut off from divine direction for carrying out his responsibilities. Therefore, when the Philistines came to wage war against him, in desperation he sought help from a spirit medium. He asked her to bring up the dead prophet Samuel. As to what happened thereafter, the Bible relates:

"When the woman [the medium] saw 'Samuel' she began crying out at the top of her voice; and the woman went on to say to Saul: 'Why did you trick me, when you yourself are Saul?' But the king said to her: 'Do not be afraid, but what did you see?' And the woman went on to say to Saul: 'A god I saw coming up out of the earth.' At once he said to her: 'What is his form?' to which she said: 'It is an old man coming up, and he has himself covered with a sleeveless coat.' At that Saul recognized that it was 'Samuel,' and he proceeded to bow low with his face to the earth and to prostrate himself. And 'Samuel' began to say to Saul: 'Why have you disturbed me by having me brought up?' "—1 Samuel 28:12-15.

Was Saul, in this case, actually brought in touch with the dead prophet Samuel? How could this be, for the Bible links *silence,* not talking, with death? We read: "The dead themselves do not praise Jah [Jehovah], nor do any going down into *silence*."—Psalm 115:17.

Other passages of the Holy Scriptures shed light on the matter. First, it is clear that what Saul did in consulting a spirit medium was a violation of God's law. Both spirit mediums and those consulting them were judged guilty of a capital offense. (Leviticus 20:6, 27) God's law to Israel stated: "Do not turn yourselves to the spirit mediums, and do not consult professional foretellers of events, so as to become unclean by them." (Leviticus 19:31) "When you are entered into the land that Jehovah your God is giving you, you must not learn to do according to the detestable things of those nations. There should not be found in you . . . anyone who consults a spirit medium or a professional foreteller of events or anyone who inquires of the dead."—Deuteronomy 18:9-11; Isaiah 8:19, 20.

If spirit mediums could actually get in touch with the dead, why, then, did God's law label their practice as something "unclean," "detestable" and deserving of death? If the communication were with dead loved ones, for example, why would a God of love designate this as a terrible crime? Why would he want to deprive the living of getting some comforting messages from the dead? Does not God's view indicate that people are not really talking to the dead but that a terrible deception must be involved? Scriptural evidence shows that is the case.

Against this background, consider the case of Saul. Regarding divine communication with him, Saul acknowledged: "God himself has departed from me and has answered me no more, either by means of the prophets or by dreams; so that I am calling you [Samuel] to let me know what I shall do." (1 Samuel 28:15) Obviously, God would not allow a spirit medium to get around this divine cutoff of communication by getting in touch with a dead prophet and having him deliver a message from God to Saul. Then, too, during the latter part of his life, Samuel himself, a faithful prophet of God, had ceased to have any dealings whatsoever with Saul. Would it not be unreasonable, therefore, to conclude that Samuel was willing to speak with Saul by means of a spirit medium, an arrangement that was condemned by God?

Manifestly, there must have been deception involved, something so unclean that spirit mediums

Who was it that spoke to Saul by means of the spirit medium at En-dor?

and those consulting them merited the death sentence. That same deception must be behind claimed communication with the dead today.

Indicating this is the fact that, under the influence of supposed "voices" from the beyond, many persons have committed suicide. They have given up their most precious possession—life—in an effort to join dead loved ones. Others have begun to dread such voices, as the messages have been gloomy, telling of some terrible accident or death about to occur. How could such voices possibly come from a good source? Who or what might be behind these voices?

CHAPTER 10

Could It Be a Masterful Deception?

OVER the centuries humans have witnessed the strangest of happenings. Rocks, water glasses and the like have been seen sailing through the air as if moved by invisible hands. Voices, rappings and other noises have been heard even though there was no apparent source or cause for them. Shadowy figures have appeared and then quickly disappeared. At times such happenings have been so well attested to that there is little room for doubt.

Many people consider manifestations of this kind to be evidence that death does not end conscious existence. Some believe that departed spirits are trying in some way to get the attention of the living and to communicate with them.

But one might ask: If these are truly deceased loved ones who are trying to get in touch with the living, why do their manifestations generally frighten observers? What, really, is behind such things?

The Bible clearly shows that death ends all conscious existence. (Ecclesiastes 9:5) Hence, there must be other forces responsible for things that are often attributed to the spirits of the dead. What might those forces be? Could they be intelligent? If so, could they be guilty of perpetrating a masterful deception on humankind?

Surely we do not want to be deceived. To be deceived would mean loss to us and, perhaps, cause us even to come into a position of grave danger. That is why we have good reason to examine the available evidence, reasoning on it, to be sure that we have not fallen victim to a masterful deception. We should be willing to go back as far as possible in human history in an effort to get at the truth of the matter.

The Bible enables us to do that. It takes us back to the time when the first human pair came into existence. In the third chapter of Genesis the Bible relates a conversation that may sound unbelievable to many today. Yet it is not fiction. This conversation provides a clue as to whether a masterful deceiver is at work in human affairs.

THE START OF DECEPTION

One day, while not in the company of her husband, the first woman, Eve, heard a voice. From all appearances it was the voice of a serpent. Regarding the conversation, the Bible reports:

"Now the serpent proved to be the most cautious

of all the wild beasts of the field that Jehovah God had made. So it began to say to the woman: 'Is it really so that God said you must not eat from every tree of the garden?' At this the woman said to the serpent: 'Of the fruit of the trees of the garden we may eat. But as for eating of the fruit of the tree that is in the middle of the garden, God has said, "You must not eat from it, no, you must not touch it that you do not die."' At this the serpent said to the woman: 'You positively will not die. For God knows that in the very day of your eating from it your eyes are bound to be opened and you are bound to be like God, knowing good and bad.' Consequently the woman saw that the tree was good for food and that it was something to be longed for to the eyes, yes, the tree was desirable to look upon." —Genesis 3:1-6.

The message transmitted by the serpent was a lie. That lie was the first one on record. Accordingly, its source must be the originator or father of lies. Since the lie led to death-dealing consequences, the liar was also a murderer. Obviously this liar was not the literal serpent, a creature that is not endowed with the power of speech. But there must have been someone behind the serpent, someone who, by what might be called ventriloquism, made it appear that the serpent was talking. That should not seem so strange to us in this twentieth century when a cone in the speaker of a radio or a television set can be made to vibrate in such a way as to reproduce the human voice. But who was the speaker behind the serpent?

AN INVISIBLE DECEIVER

He is identified by Jesus Christ, who himself had come from the heavens and knew what went on in the invisible realm. (John 3:13; 8:58) When certain religious leaders were seeking to kill him, Jesus said to them: "You are from your father the Devil, and you wish to do the desires of your father. That one was a manslayer when he began, and he did not stand fast in the truth, because truth is not in him. When he speaks the lie, he speaks according to his own disposition, because he is a liar and the father of the lie." —John 8:44.

Being a liar and a manslayer, the Devil is obviously someone who possesses intelligence. This gives rise to the question, How did he come into existence?

The Bible reveals that even before the earth came to be, invisible, spirit persons were enjoying life. Job 38:7 speaks of these spirit persons, "sons of God," as "shouting in applause" when the earth was created. As "sons of God," they received their life from him.—Psalm 90:2.

Hence, the one who deceived Eve by means of the serpent must have been one of these spirit sons, one of God's intelligent creatures. In contradicting God's warning about the tree of the knowledge of good and bad, this one slandered his Creator, making God appear to be a liar. He is therefore rightly called the "Devil," as that word is drawn from the Greek term *di·a′bo·los*, meaning "false accuser, misrepresenter, slanderer." By his course of action this creature set himself in resistance to God and thereby made himself Satan (Hebrew, *sa·tan′*; Greek, *sa·ta·nas′*), which means "resister."

Jehovah God cannot be blamed for what this creature did. "Perfect is his activity," says the Bible concerning God, "for all his ways are justice. A God of faithfulness, with whom there is no injustice; righteous and upright is he." (Deuteronomy 32:4) He created his intelligent sons, spirit and human, with the capacity of free will. He did not force them to serve him but wanted them to do so willingly, out of love. He endowed them with the capacity to develop ever greater love for him as their God and Father.

The spirit creature who made himself a resister and a slanderer of God, however, did not choose to perfect his love for his Creator. He allowed selfish ambitions to take root in his heart. (Compare 1 Timothy 3:6.) This is reflected in the conduct of the "king of Tyre" over whom a dirge was rendered in the prophecy of Ezekiel. In the dirge, it is said to the king of Tyre who turned traitor to the kingdom of Israel:

"You are sealing up a pattern, full of wisdom and perfect in beauty. In Eden, the garden of God, you proved to be. . . . You are the anointed cherub that is covering, and I have set you. On the holy mountain of God you proved to be. In the midst of fiery stones you walked about. You were faultless in your ways from the day of your being created until unrighteousness was found in you. . . . Your heart became haughty because of your beauty. You brought your wisdom to ruin on account of your beaming splendor."—Ezekiel 28:12-17.

The rebellious spirit son of God, similar to the traitorous "king of Tyre," thought too highly of himself. Pride caused him to want to control the human race, and he sought to gain his ends through deception. To this day the majority of humankind are still victims of this deception. By refusing to do God's will as set forth in his Word, the Bible, they actually align themselves with Satan. In so doing, they accept the same lie that Eve did, namely, that choosing to act contrary to God's will can bring real gain.

Since God's Word condemns communication

with the dead, those who try to speak with the dead put themselves on Satan's side. While they may think that they are talking with the dead, they have become the victims of a hoax. Just as Satan made it appear to Eve that a serpent was talking, so he can just as easily make it appear that the dead are talking through mediums. Does this mean that Satan is directly responsible for all the strange phenomena that are often attributed to the spirits of the dead? Or, are others also involved?

OTHER INVISIBLE DECEIVERS

The Bible reveals that Satan is not the only rebellious spirit creature. Revelation 12:3, 4, 9 shows that there are others. In this Scripture passage Satan the Devil is symbolically depicted as a "great fiery-colored dragon" having a "tail" that "drags a third of the stars of heaven." Yes, Satan was able to use his influence, like a tail, to get other "stars," spirit sons of God, to join him in a rebellious course. (Compare Job 38:7, where spirit sons of God are called "morning stars.") This happened before the global deluge in the days of Noah. Numerous angels, contrary to God's purpose, "forsook their own proper dwelling place" in the heavens, materialized human bodies, lived as husbands with women and fathered hybrid offspring known as Nephilim. Of this, we are told:

"Now it came about that when men started to grow in numbers on the surface of the ground and daughters were born to them, then the sons of the true God began to notice the daughters of men, that they were good-looking; and they went taking wives for themselves, namely, all whom they chose. . . . The Nephilim proved to be in the earth in those days, and also after that, when the sons of the true

God continued to have relations with the daughters of men and they bore sons to them, they were the mighty ones who were of old, the men of fame." —Genesis 6:1-4.

During the Flood these sons of God lost their wives and their hybrid offspring. They themselves had to dematerialize. Respecting what happened to them thereafter, the Bible reports: "God did not hold back from punishing the angels that sinned, but, by throwing them into Tartarus, delivered them to pits of dense darkness to be reserved for judgment." (2 Peter 2:4) And at Jude 6 it adds: "The angels that did not keep their original position but forsook their own proper dwelling place he has reserved with eternal bonds under dense darkness for the judgment of the great day."

As these descriptions relate to spirit creatures, it is evident that the "pits of dense darkness" and "eternal bonds" are not literal. These expressions simply convey to us a picture of restraint, a condition of debasement separated from all divine enlightenment.

There is no Scriptural basis for concluding that these disobedient angels are in a place like the mythological Tartarus of Homer's *Iliad,* that is, in the lowest prison where Cronus and the other Titan spirits were said to be confined. The apostle Peter did not believe in any such mythological gods. So there is no reason to conclude that his use of the Greek expression 'throwing into Tartarus' even hinted at the existence of the mythological place referred to by Homer some nine centuries earlier. In fact, in Greek the expression 'throwing into Tartarus' is only one word, a verb, *tar·ta·ro'o.* It is also used to mean debasing to the lowest degree.

To illustrate, the English word "debase" contains the noun "base." Yet our use of the word does not mean that a *literal base* in some geographical location is involved in the act of debasement. Likewise the Greek verb rendered 'throwing into Tartarus' need not be viewed as suggesting the existence of an actual place, but as suggesting a condition.

At 1 Peter 3:19, 20 the debased spirit creatures are referred to as "spirits in prison, who had once been disobedient when the patience of God was waiting in Noah's days, while the ark was being constructed." Thus the Bible makes it plain that after the Flood the "angels that sinned" came under a form of restraint. There is no Biblical indication that they were able to materialize and take up visible activity on earth after the Flood. So it logically follows that the restraint under which they came made it impossible for them to take on flesh again.

BEWARE OF DEMON INFLUENCE

It should be noted, however, that the disobedient angels, who now came to be known as demons, had a strong desire to be in close association with humans. They were willing to abandon their heavenly position for the pleasure of living as husbands with women. Scriptural evidence shows that, though restrained from such physical contact now, they have not changed their desires. They seek every means open to them to be in touch with humans and even to control them. Jesus Christ referred to this, using figurative speech in saying:

"When an unclean spirit comes out of a man, it passes through parched places in search of a resting-place, and finds none. Then it says, 'I will go back to my house out of which I moved'; and on arriving it finds it unoccupied but swept clean and adorned. Then it goes its way and takes along with it seven different spirits more wicked than itself, and, after getting inside, they dwell there; and the final circumstances of that man become worse than the first." —Matthew 12:43-45.

It is vital therefore to be on guard lest a person yield himself to demon influence. He may be very uncertain about himself and his future. He may desperately want some assurance that things will go well for him. Or he may find a certain fascination in the weird and frightening manifestations of occult practices. He may hear about someone who reportedly can accurately predict the future. Or he may learn about the various means of divination used—Ouija boards, ESP (extrasensory perception), patterns of tea leaves in cups, oil configurations on water, divining rods, pendulums, the position and movement of stars and planets (astrology), the howling of dogs, the flight of birds, the movement of snakes, crystal-ball gazing and the like. His situation may appear so desperate or his fascination be so great that he may decide to consult a fortune-teller or a medium or to resort to some form of divination. He might be willing to try anything just once.

Is that wise? Definitely not. His curiosity can lead to his coming under demon control. Rather than such a course's bringing him relief and comfort, his situation may only worsen. Supernatural disturbances may rob him of sleep and fill even daylight hours with dread. He may begin to hear strange voices, suggesting that he kill himself or someone else.

Is it not wise therefore to avoid such a risk

and to shun all forms of divination? Jehovah God does not view this matter lightly. To protect the Israelites from being deceived and harmed by wicked spirits, he made the practice of divination a capital offense, saying in the Law: "As for a man or woman in whom there proves to be a mediumistic spirit or spirit of prediction, they should be put to death without fail."—Leviticus 20:27.

God's view of spirit mediums, sorcerers and divination has not changed. A divine decree still stands against all practicers of spiritism.—Revelation 21:8.

Therefore exert yourself to resist being deceived by wicked spirit creatures. Should you ever hear a strange voice, perhaps suggesting that it is that of a deceased friend or relative, do not pay any attention. Call upon the name of the true God, Jehovah, to help you to resist coming under demon influence. As God's own Son advised, make your prayerful petition: 'Deliver me from the wicked one.' (Matthew 6:13) As to items associated with divination, imitate the example of those who accepted true worship in ancient Ephesus. "Quite a number of those who practiced magical arts [there] brought their books together and burned them up before everybody." Expensive as these items were, they did not hold back from destroying them.—Acts 19:19.

In view of this example, do you think that it would be right to associate deliberately with those known to dabble in the occult and to accept gifts from them? Might they not become the instrumentalities by means of which you could come under demon influence?

Our recognizing that wicked spirits are often

responsible for causing people to see or hear weird and frightening manifestations—voices, rappings and shadowy figures for which there are no apparent causes—is a major factor in safeguarding us from being deceived. This knowledge will free us from fearing the dead and from engaging in valueless rites in their behalf. It will also help to prevent our being victimized by wicked spirits.

But if we are to be protected from every aspect of the deception that Satan and his demons have perpetrated in connection with the dead, we must believe and act in harmony with the entire Bible. This is because all of it is the inspired Word of God.

CHAPTER 11

Is Hell Hot?

IS IT NOT a fact that many translations of the Bible refer to a place called "hell"? Yes, many translations of the Holy Scriptures use that expression. But the question is whether the things that the clergy have taught about the place called "hell" have come from the Holy Bible or from some other source.

Did you know that, not only members of Christendom's churches, but many non-Christians as well, have been taught to believe in a hell of torment? It is revealing to read from a variety of sources what is said about the torments of those confined in hell.

A non-Christian "holy book" of the seventh century C.E. says the following:

"Hell!—they will burn therein,—an evil bed (indeed, to lie on)!—Yea, such!—Then shall they taste it,—a boiling fluid, and a fluid dark, murky, intensely cold! . . . (They will be) in the midst of a fierce Blast of Fire and in Boiling Water, and in the shades of Black Smoke: Nothing (will there be) to refresh, nor to please."

Buddhism, which got started in about the sixth century B.C.E., provides this description of one of the "hells" about which it teaches:

"Here there is no interval of cessation either of the flames or of the pain of the beings."

A Roman Catholic *Catechism of Christian Doctrine* (published in 1949) states:

"They are deprived of the vision of God and suffer dreadful torments, especially that of fire, for all eternity. . . . The privation of the beatific vision is called the pain of loss; the torment inflicted by created means on the soul, and on the body after its resurrection, is called the pain of sense."

Also among the Protestant clergy in some places there are those who paint vivid verbal pictures of the horrors of hell. Even their church members at times claim to have had visions of its torments. One man described what he envisioned as follows: 'As far as my eyes could reach there were only burning fire and human beings to be seen. What pain and suffering! Some people screamed, others wailed and begged for water, water! Some rent their hair, others gnashed their teeth; still others bit themselves in the arms and hands.'

The claim is often made that the threatened punishments of hell are a strong force in moving people to do what is right. But do the facts of history bear this out? Have not some of the greatest cruelties been perpetrated by believers in the doctrine of hellfire? Are not the horrible inquisitions and blood-spilling crusades of Christendom examples of this?

So it should come as no surprise that a growing number of people do not really believe in the existence of a hell of torment nor do they view

Scenes from Buddhist pictures of hell

its punishments as a deterrent to wrongdoing. Though not having actually disproved this teaching, they are simply not inclined to believe what does not appeal to them as reasonable and true. Still they may be members of a church that teaches this doctrine and, by supporting it, share responsibility for propagating the teaching of hellfire.

But just what does the Bible say about torment after death? If you have read earlier chapters of this book, you know that many common beliefs about the dead are false. You know, according to the Bible, that no soul or spirit separates from the body at death and continues conscious exis-

Scenes from the "Inferno"
of Catholic Dante

tence. Hence, there is no Scriptural foundation for the doctrine of eternal torment after death, for nothing survives that can be subjected to literal torment. What, then, is the place that various Bible translations refer to as "hell"?

"SHEOL" IDENTIFIED

In the Catholic *Douay Version,* the first mention of "hell" is found at Genesis 37:35, which quotes the patriarch Jacob as saying respecting Joseph, whom he believed to be dead: "I will go down to my son into hell, mourning." Clearly Jacob was not expressing the idea of joining his son in a place of torment. Even the footnote on this verse in the *Douay Version* (published by the Douay Bible House, New York, 1941) does not put such an interpretation on the text. It says:

"Into hell. That is, into *limbo,* the place where the souls of the just were received before the death of

our Redeemer. . . . [It] certainly meant the place of rest where he believed his soul to be."

However, nowhere does the Bible itself refer to such a place as "limbo." Nor does it support the idea of a special resting-place for the soul as something distinctly separate from the body. As acknowledged in the glossary of a modern Catholic translation, *The New American Bible* (published by P. J. Kenedy & Sons, New York, 1970): "There is no opposition or difference between soul and body; they are merely different ways of describing the one, concrete reality."

What, then, is the "hell" in which Jacob thought he would join his son? The correct answer to this question lies in getting the proper sense of the original-language word for "hell," namely, *she'ohl'*, which is transliterated "Sheol." This term, also translated as "grave," "pit," "abode of the dead" and "nether world," appears sixty-six times* (in the *New World Translation*) in the thirty-nine books of the Hebrew Scriptures (commonly called the "Old Testament"), but it is never associated with life, activity or torment. To the contrary, it is often linked with death and inactivity. A few examples are:

"For in death there is no mention of you [Jehovah]; in Sheol [the grave, *Authorized Version;* hell, *Douay Version*] who will laud you?"—Psalm 6:5 (6:6, *Douay Version*).

---

* Genesis 37:35; 42:38; 44:29, 31; Numbers 16:30, 33; Deuteronomy 32:22; 1 Samuel 2:6; 2 Samuel 22:6; 1 Kings 2:6, 9; Job 7:9; 11:8; 14:13; 17:13, 16; 21:13; 24:19; 26:6; Psalms 6:5; 9:17; 16:10; 18:5; 30:3; 31:17; 49:14, 15; 55:15; 86:13; 88:3; 89:48; 116:3; 139:8; 141:7; Proverbs 1:12; 5:5; 7:27; 9:18; 15:11, 24; 23:14; 27:20; 30:16; Ecclesiastes 9:10; Song of Solomon 8:6; Isaiah 5:14; 7:11; 14:9, 11; 15; 28:15, 18; 38:10, 18; 57:9; Ezekiel 31:15-17; 32:21, 27; Hosea 13:14; Amos 9:2; Jonah 2:2; Habakkuk 2:5.

"All that your hand finds to do, do with your very power, for there is no work nor devising nor knowledge nor wisdom in Sheol [the grave, *Authorized Version;* hell, *Douay Version*], the place to which you are going."—Ecclesiastes 9:10.

"For it is not Sheol [the grave, *Authorized Version;* hell, *Douay Version*] that can laud you [Jehovah]; death itself cannot praise you. Those going down into the pit cannot look hopefully to your trueness. The living, the living, he is the one that can laud you, just as I can this day."—Isaiah 38:18, 19.

Hence, Sheol is obviously the place to which the dead go. It is not an individual grave but the common grave of dead mankind in general, where all conscious activity ceases. This is also what the *New Catholic Encyclopedia* acknowledges to be the Biblical significance of Sheol, saying:

"In the Bible it designates the place of complete inertia that one goes down to when one dies whether one be just or wicked, rich or poor." —Vol. 13, p. 170.

That no place of fiery torment existed during the entire Hebrew Scripture period is also confirmed by the fact that torment is never set forth as the penalty for disobedience. The choice that was put before the nation of Israel was, not life or torment, but life or death. Moses told the nation: "I have put life and death before you, the blessing and the malediction; and you must choose life in order that you may keep alive, you and your offspring, by loving Jehovah your God, by listening to his voice and by sticking to him."—Deuteronomy 30:19, 20.

Similarly, God's later appeals for unfaithful Israelites to repent served to encourage them to avoid experiencing, not torment, but an untimely death. Through his prophet Ezekiel, Jehovah declared: "I take delight, not in the death of the wicked one, but in that someone wicked turns back from his way and actually keeps living. Turn back, turn back from your bad ways, for why is it that you should die, O house of Israel?"—Ezekiel 33:11.

HADES THE SAME AS SHEOL

Yet someone might ask, Did not the coming of Jesus Christ to this earth change matters? No, God does not change his personality or his righteous standards. By means of his prophet Malachi, he stated: "I am Jehovah; I have not changed." (Malachi 3:6) Jehovah has not changed the penalty for disobedience. He is patient with people so that they might be able to escape, not torment, but destruction. As the apostle Peter wrote to fellow believers: "Jehovah is not slow respecting his promise, as some people consider slowness, but he is patient with you because he does not desire any to be destroyed but desires all to attain to repentance."—2 Peter 3:9.

In keeping with the fact that the penalty for disobedience has continued to be death, the place to which the Christian Greek Scriptures (commonly called the "New Testament") describe the dead as going does not differ from the Sheol of the Hebrew Scriptures. (Romans 6:23) This is evident from a comparison of the Hebrew Scriptures with the Christian Greek Scriptures. In its ten occurrences, the Greek word *hai'des,* which is transliterated "Hades," basically conveys the same meaning as the Hebrew word *she'ohl'.* (Matthew 11:23; 16:18; Luke 10:15; 16:23;* Acts 2:27, 31; Revelation 1:18; 6:8; 20:13, 14

---

* Luke 16:23 is discussed in detail in the next chapter.

[If the translation you are using does not read "hell" or "Hades" in all these texts, you will, nevertheless, note that the terms used instead give no hint of a place of torment.]) Consider the following example:

At Psalm 16:10 (15:10, *Douay Version*) we read: "For you [Jehovah] will not leave my soul in Sheol [hell]. You will not allow your loyal one to see the pit." In a discourse given by the apostle Peter, this psalm was shown to have a prophetic application. Said Peter: "Because [David] was a prophet and knew that God had sworn to him with an oath that he would seat one from the fruitage of his loins upon his throne, he saw beforehand and spoke concerning the resurrection of the Christ, that neither was he forsaken in Hades [hell] nor did his flesh see corruption." (Acts 2:30, 31) Note that the Greek word *hai'des* was used for the Hebrew word *she'ohl'*. Thus Sheol and Hades are seen to be corresponding terms.

Observes the glossary of the French Bible Society's *Nouvelle Version,* under the expression "Abode of the dead":

> "This expression translates the Greek word *Hades,* which corresponds to the Hebrew *Sheol.* It is the place where the dead are located between [the time of] their decease and their resurrection (Luke 16:23; Acts 2:27, 31; Rev. 20:13, 14). Certain translations have wrongly rendered this word as *hell.*"

THE SOURCE OF THE HELLFIRE TEACHING

Clearly, references to Sheol and Hades in the Scriptures do not support the doctrine of a fiery hell. Admitting that it is not Christian and even contradicts the spirit of Christianity, the Catholic periodical *Commonweal* (January 15, 1971) notes:

"For many people, some philosophers included, hell answers a need of the human imagination—a sort of Santa Claus in reverse. . . . Who among the righteous doesn't like to see the unjust get punished with some equity? And if not in this life, why not in the next? Such a view, however, is not compatible with the New Testament, which invites man to life and to love."

Then this magazine goes on to show probable sources of this doctrine, saying:

"Another element that might have contributed to the traditional Christian concept of hell can be found in the Roman world. Just as intrinsic immortality was a premise in a major part of Greek philosophy, justice was a primary virtue among the Romans, particularly when Christianity began to thrive. . . . The wedding of these two minds—the philosophical Greek and judicial Roman—might well have brought about the theological symmetry of heaven and hell: if the good soul is rewarded, then the bad soul is punished. To confirm their belief in justice for the unjust, the Romans merely had to pick up Virgil's *Aeneid* and read about the blessed in Elysium and the damned in Tartarus, which was surrounded by fire and overflowing with the panic of punishment."

The teaching about a fiery hell is thus acknowledged to be a belief shared by persons alienated from God. It can rightly be designated as a 'teaching of demons.' (1 Timothy 4:1) This is so because it has its source in the falsehood that man does not really die, and it mirrors the morbid, vicious and cruel disposition of the demons. (Compare Mark 5:2-13.) Has not this doctrine needlessly filled people with dread and horror? Has it not grossly misrepresented God? In his Word, Jehovah reveals himself to be a God of love. (1 John 4:8) But the teaching about a fiery hell slanders him, falsely accusing him of the worst cruelties imaginable.

Those teaching the hellfire doctrine are therefore saying blasphemous things against God. While some clergymen may not be familiar with the Biblical evidence, they should be. They represent themselves as speaking God's message and therefore are under obligation to know what the Bible says. They certainly know full well that what they do and say can deeply affect the lives of those who look to them for instruction. That should cause them to be careful in making sure of their teaching. Any misrepresentation of God can turn people away from true worship, to their injury.

There can be no question that Jehovah God does not look with approval upon false teachers. To unfaithful religious leaders of ancient Israel, he pronounced the following judgment: "I . . . for my part, shall certainly make you to be despised and low to all the people, according as you were not keeping my ways." (Malachi 2:9) We can be sure that like judgment will come upon false religious teachers of our time. The Bible indicates that they will soon be stripped of their position and influence by the political elements of the world. (Revelation 17:15-18) As for those who continue to support religious systems teaching lies, they will fare no better. Jesus Christ said: "If . . . a blind man guides a blind man, both will fall into a pit."—Matthew 15:14.

That being the case, would you want to continue supporting any religious system that teaches a fiery hell? How would you feel if your father had been maliciously slandered? Would you continue to accept the slanderers as your friends? Would you not, rather, cut off all association with them? Should we not likewise want to break off all association with those who have slandered our heavenly Father?

Fear of torment is not the proper motivation for serving God. He desires that our worship be motivated by love. This should appeal to our hearts. Our realizing that the dead are not in a place filled with screaming anguish in blazing fires, but, rather, are unconscious in the silent and lifeless common grave of dead mankind can remove a barrier to our expressing such love for God.

CHAPTER 12

A Rich Man in Hades

SINCE Hades is just the common grave of dead mankind, why does the Bible speak of a rich man as undergoing torments in the fire of Hades? Does this show that Hades, or at least a part of it, is a place of fiery torment?

Teachers of hellfire eagerly point to this account as definite proof that there is indeed a hell of torment that awaits the wicked. But, in so doing, they disregard such clear and repeated Biblical statements as: "The soul that is sinning —it itself will die." (Ezekiel 18:4, 20) And: "As for the dead, they are conscious of nothing at all." (Ecclesiastes 9:5) Clearly these statements do not support the idea of torment for "lost souls" in a fiery hell.

The Bible's teaching about the condition of the dead therefore leaves many of Christendom's clergymen in an awkward position. The very book on which they claim to base their teachings, the Bible, conflicts with their doctrines. Yet, consciously or subconsciously, they feel impelled to reach into the Bible to seize on something to prove their point, thereby blinding themselves and others to the truth. Often this is done deliberately.

On the other hand, sincere seekers for the truth want to know what is right. They realize that they would only be fooling themselves if they rejected portions of God's Word while claiming to base their beliefs on other parts. They want to know what the Bible actually says about the condition of the dead. And, to fill out the picture, they want to know the meaning of what is said about the rich man who experienced torment in Hades, and how that fits in with the rest of the Bible.

It was Jesus Christ who spoke about a certain rich man and also a beggar named Lazarus. His words are found at Luke 16:19-31 and read:

"A certain man was rich, and he used to deck himself with purple and linen, enjoying himself from day to day with magnificence. But a certain beggar named Lazarus used to be put at his gate, full of ulcers and desiring to be filled with the things dropping from the table of the rich man. Yes, too, the dogs would come and lick his ulcers. Now in course of time the beggar died and he was carried off by the angels to the bosom position of Abraham.

"Also, the rich man died and was buried. And in Hades he lifted up his eyes, he existing in torments, and he saw Abraham afar off and Lazarus in the bosom position with him. So he called and said, 'Father Abraham, have mercy on me and send Lazarus to dip the tip of his finger in water and cool my tongue, because I am in anguish in this blazing fire.' But Abraham said, 'Child, remember that you received in full your good things in your lifetime, but Lazarus correspondingly the injurious things. Now, however, he is having comfort here but you are in anguish. And besides all these things, a great chasm has been fixed between us and you people, so that those wanting to go over from here to you people cannot, neither may people cross over from there to us.' Then he said, 'In that event I ask you, father, to send him to the house of my father, for I have five brothers, in order that he may give them a thorough witness, that they also should not get into this place of torment.' But Abraham said, 'They have Moses and the Prophets; let them listen to these.' Then he said, 'No, indeed, father Abraham, but if someone from the dead goes to them they will repent.' But he said to him, 'If they do not listen to Moses and the Prophets, neither will they be persuaded if someone rises from the dead.' "

Note what is said about the rich man. Why was he tormented in Hades? What had he done? Jesus did not say that the rich man led a degraded life, did he? All that Jesus said was that the man

was rich, dressed well and feasted sumptuously.
Does such conduct of itself merit punishment
by torment? True, a serious failing is implied
in the attitude of the rich man toward the beggar Lazarus. The rich man lacked compassion
for him. But did that failing distinguish him sufficiently from Lazarus?

Think about what Jesus said concerning Lazarus. Is there anything in the account to lead us
to conclude that, if the situation had been reversed, Lazarus would have been a compassionate
man? Do we read that Lazarus built up a record
of fine works with God, leading to his coming
into the "bosom position of Abraham," that is,
a position of divine favor? Jesus did not say
that. He merely described Lazarus as a sickly
beggar.

So is it logical to conclude that all sickly beg-
gars will receive divine blessings at death, whereas
all rich men will go to a place of conscious torment? Not at all. Begging is of itself no mark of
God's favor. To the contrary, the Bible contains
the prayerful expression:
"Give me neither poverty
nor riches." (Proverbs
30:8) And of his time,
King David wrote: "I
have not seen
anyone righ-
teous left en-
tirely, nor his
offspring look-
ing for bread."
—Psalm 37:25.

If we take Jesus' words literally, we would have to draw still other conclusions that would make the illustration strange indeed. These include: That those enjoying celestial happiness are in position to see and speak to those suffering torment in Hades. That the water adhering to one's fingertip is not evaporated by the fire of Hades. And, that, although the torment of Hades is great, a mere drop of water would bring relief to the sufferer.

Taken literally, do these things sound reasonable to you? Or, do you feel, instead, that what Jesus said was not meant to be taken literally? Is there any way to be sure?

THE "RICH MAN" AND "LAZARUS" IDENTIFIED

Examine the context. To whom was Jesus talking? At Luke 16:14 we are told: "Now the Pharisees, who were money lovers, were listening to all these things, and they began to sneer at him."

Since Jesus spoke in the hearing of the Pharisees, was he relating an actual case or was he simply using an illustration? Concerning Jesus' method of teaching the crowds, we read: "Indeed, without an illustration he would not speak to them." (Matthew 13:34) Accordingly, the account about the rich man and Lazarus must be an illustration.

This illustration was evidently directed to the Pharisees. As a class they were like the rich man. They loved money, as well as prominence and flattering titles. Jesus said of them: "All the works they do they do to be viewed by men; for they broaden the scripture-containing cases that they wear as safeguards, and enlarge the fringes of their garments. They like the most

prominent place at evening meals and the front
seats in the synagogues, and the greetings in the
marketplaces and to be called Rabbi by men."
—Matthew 23:5-7.

The Pharisees looked down on others, especially
on tax collectors, harlots and others having the
reputation of being sinners. (Luke 18:11, 12)
On one occasion when officers, sent to arrest
Jesus, came back empty-handed because of having
been impressed by his teaching, the Pharisees
spoke up: "You have not been misled also, have
you? Not one of the rulers or of the Pharisees
has put faith in him, has he? But this crowd
that does not know the Law are accursed people."
—John 7:47-49.

Hence, in the parable the beggar Lazarus well
represents those humble persons whom the Pharisees despised but who repented and became followers of Jesus Christ. Jesus showed that these
despised sinners, upon repenting, would gain a
position of divine favor, whereas the Pharisees
and other prominent religious leaders as a class
would lose out. He said: "Truly I say to you that
the tax collectors and the harlots are going ahead
of you into the kingdom of God. For John came
to you in a way of righteousness, but you did
not believe him. However, the tax collectors and
the harlots believed him, and you, although you
saw this, did not feel regret afterwards so as to
believe him."—Matthew 21:31, 32.

DEATH OF THE "RICH MAN"
AND OF "LAZARUS"

What, then, is signified by the death of the
"rich man" and of "Lazarus"? We do not need

to conclude that it refers to actual death. As used in the Bible, death can also represent a great change in the condition of individuals. For example: Persons pursuing a course of life contrary to God's will are spoken of as being 'dead in trespasses and sins.' But when they come into an approved standing before God as disciples of Jesus Christ they are referred to as coming "alive." (Ephesians 2:1, 5; Colossians 2:13) At the same time such living persons become "dead" to sin. We read: "Reckon yourselves to be dead indeed with reference to sin but living with reference to God by Christ Jesus."—Romans 6:11.

Since both the "rich man" and "Lazarus" of Jesus' parable are clearly symbolic, logically their deaths are also symbolic. But in what sense do they die?

The key to answering this question lies in what Jesus said just before introducing the illustration: "Everyone that divorces his wife and marries another commits adultery, and he that marries a woman divorced from a husband commits adultery." (Luke 16:18) This statement may appear to be completely unrelated to the illustration. But this is not the case.

By reason of the Mosaic law the nation of Israel was in a covenant relationship with God and therefore could be spoken of as being a wife to him. At Jeremiah 3:14, for example, God refers to the nation as an unfaithful wife: " 'Return, O you renegade sons,' is the utterance of Jehovah. 'For I myself have become the husbandly owner of you people.' " Then, with the coming of Jesus, an opportunity was extended to the Jews to become part of his "bride." That is why John the Baptist said to his disciples: "You yourselves bear me witness that I said, I am not the Christ, but, I have been sent forth in advance of that one. He that has the bride is the bridegroom. However, the friend of the bridegroom, when he stands and hears him, has a great deal of joy on account of the voice of the bridegroom. Therefore this joy of mine has been made full. That one [Jesus] must go on increasing, but I must go on decreasing."—John 3:28-30.

In order to become part of Christ's "bride," the Jews had to be released from the Law that made them, figuratively speaking, a wife to God. Without such release, they could not come into a wifely relationship with Christ, as that would be an adulterous relationship. The words of Romans 7:1-6 confirm this:

> "Can it be that you do not know, brothers, (for I am speaking to those who know law,) that the Law is master over a man as long as he lives? For instance, a married woman is bound by law to her husband while he is alive; but if her husband dies, she is discharged from the law of her husband. So, then, while her husband is living, she would be styled an adulteress if she became another man's. But if her husband dies, she is free from his law, so that she is not an adulteress if she becomes another man's.
>
> "So, my brothers, *you also were made dead to the Law* through the body of the Christ, that you might become another's, the one's who was raised up from the dead, that we should bear fruit to God. . . . Now we have been discharged from the Law, because we have died to that by which we were being held fast, that we might be slaves in a new sense by the spirit, and not in the old sense by the written code."

While the death of Jesus Christ was the basis for releasing the Jews from the Law, even before his death repentant ones could come into a favored position with God as disciples of his Son.

The message and work of John the Baptist and of Jesus Christ opened the door for the Jews to seize the opportunity to gain divine favor and put themselves in line for a heavenly inheritance as members of Christ's bride. As Jesus himself expressed it: "From the days of John the Baptist until now the kingdom of the heavens is the goal toward which men press, and those pressing forward are seizing it."—Matthew 11:12.

Hence, the work and message of John the Baptist and of Jesus Christ began to lead toward a complete change in the condition of the symbolic "rich man" and "Lazarus." Both classes died to their former condition. The repentant "Lazarus" class came into a position of divine favor, whereas the "rich man" class came under divine disfavor because of persisting in unrepentance. At one time the "Lazarus" class had looked to the Pharisees and other religious leaders of Judaism for spiritual "crumbs." But Jesus' imparting the truth to them filled their spiritual needs. Contrasting the spiritual feeding provided by Jesus with that of the religious leaders, the Bible reports: "The crowds were astounded at his way of teaching; for he was teaching them as a person having authority, and not as their scribes." (Matthew 7:28, 29) Truly a complete reversal had taken place. The religious leaders of Judaism were shown up as having nothing to offer to the "Lazarus" class.

On the day of Pentecost of the year 33 C.E. the change in conditions was accomplished. At that time the new covenant replaced the old Law covenant. Those who had repented and accepted Jesus were then fully released from the old Law covenant. They died to it. On that day of Pentecost there was also unmistakable evidence that

the disciples of Jesus Christ had been exalted
far above the Pharisees and other prominent religious leaders. Not the religious leaders of Judaism, but these disciples received God's spirit,
enabling them to speak about "the magnificent
things of God" in the native languages of people
from widely scattered places. (Acts 2:5-11) What
a marvelous manifestation this was of their having God's blessing and approval! The "Lazarus"
class had indeed come into the favored situation
by becoming the spiritual seed of the Greater
Abraham, Jehovah. This was pictured as the
"bosom position."—Compare John 1:18.

As for the unrepentant Pharisees and other
prominent religious leaders, they were dead to
their former position of seeming favor. They were
in "Hades." Remaining unrepentant, they were
separated from the faithful disciples of Jesus as
if by a "great chasm." This was a "chasm" of
God's unchangeable, righteous judgment. Of this,
we read in Scripture: "Your judicial decision is
a vast watery deep."—Psalm 36:6.

THE "RICH MAN'S" TORMENT

The "rich man" class was also tormented. How?
By the fiery judgment messages of God being
proclaimed by Jesus' disciples.—Compare Revelation 14:10.

That the religious leaders were tormented by
the message proclaimed by Jesus' disciples there
can be no question. They tried desperately to stop
the proclamation. When the apostles of Jesus
Christ made their defense before the Jewish
supreme court composed of prominent religious
men, the judges "felt deeply cut and were wanting
to do away with them." (Acts 5:33) Later, the

disciple Stephen's defense had a like tormenting
effect upon the members of that court. "They
felt cut to their hearts and began to gnash their
teeth at him."—Acts 7:54.

These religious leaders wanted the disciples
of Jesus to come and 'cool their tongue.' They
wanted the "Lazarus" class to leave the "bosom
position" of God's favor and present his message
in such a way as not to cause them discomfort.
Similarly, they wanted the "Lazarus" class to
water down God's message so as not to put their
"five brothers," their religious allies, in a "place
of torment." Yes, they did not want any of their
associates to be tormented by judgment messages.

But, as indicated by Jesus' illustration, neither
the "rich man" class nor his religious allies would
be freed from the tormenting effects of the message proclaimed by the "Lazarus" class. The
apostles of the Lord Jesus Christ refused to water
down the message. They refused to stop teaching
on the basis of Jesus' name. Their reply to the
Jewish supreme court was: "We must obey God
as ruler rather than men."—Acts 5:29.

If the religious allies of the "rich man" wanted
to escape that torment, they could do so. They
had "Moses and the Prophets," that is, they had
the inspired Holy Scriptures written by Moses and
other ancient prophets. Not once did those inspired Scriptures point to any literal place of
torment after death, but they did contain all that
was necessary to identify Jesus as the promised
Messiah or Christ. (Deuteronomy 18:15, 18, 19;
1 Peter 1:10, 11) Hence, if the "rich man" class
and his "five brothers" had paid attention to
"Moses and the Prophets," they would have accepted Jesus as the Messiah. That would have

brought them in line for divine favor and shielded them from the tormenting effects of God's judgment message.

CHRISTENDOM SHOULD KNOW

There is little reason for Christendom's clergymen not to be familiar with this understanding of Jesus' parable. A leading Protestant commentary, *The Interpreter's Bible,* calls attention to a similar explanation. It points out that many interpreters believe Jesus' words to be "an allegorical appendix that presupposes the conflict between early Christianity and orthodox Judaism. The rich man and his brothers represent the unbelieving Jews. Jesus is made to assert that they have stubbornly refused to repent in spite of the obvious testimony to himself in Scripture and to predict that they will fail to be impressed by his resurrection. It is conceivable that Luke and his readers imposed some such interpretation on these verses." And, in a footnote on Luke chapter 16, the Catholic *Jerusalem Bible* acknowledges that this is a "parable in story form without reference to any historical personage."

In view of this, we can rightly ask: Why have Christendom's clergymen not at least acknowledged to their church people that this is a parable? Why do those who know that the Bible does not teach the immortality of the human soul continue to put a literal application on an obvious parable? Is this not dishonest? Are they not showing disregard for the Word of God, deliberately hiding the facts?

The illustration of the rich man and Lazarus contains vital lessons for us today. Are we paying attention to the inspired Word of God? Do we

desire to follow it as devoted disciples of Jesus
Christ? Those who refuse to do so, like the Jewish
Pharisees, will not escape the tormenting effects
of God's judgment message against them. His
loyal servants will keep right on declaring the
truth, fearlessly exposing religious error.

Where do you stand in this matter? Do you
believe there should be a letup on such an exposure, feeling that there is good in all religions?
Or, do you feel indignant about Christendom's
misrepresenting God by its false doctrines about
the dead? Do you want to see God's name cleared
of the reproach brought upon it through the
teaching of false doctrines? Do you desire to see
no effort spared in freeing honest-hearted ones
from bondage to religious falsehoods? If you do,
you will find God's purpose concerning the dead
and the living most comforting.

CHAPTER 13

What About
the Fire of Gehenna?

'GRANTED,' someone might say, 'Hades is
never used in the Bible to refer to a place
of fiery torment. But does not the Bible speak
of "hell fire"?'

True, numerous translations of the Christian
Greek Scriptures (commonly called the "New
Testament") use the expression "hell fire" or
"fires of hell." In this case the Greek term rendered "hell" is ge'en·na (Gehenna). But is Gehenna the name of a place of fiery torment? Yes,

say many of Christendom's commentators. Yet they well know that the soul is not immortal. They also know that the Scriptures show that immortality is bestowed as a reward only upon those whom God designates as worthy of receiving it, and not as a curse on the wicked so that they might be tormented everlastingly.—Romans 2:6, 7; 1 Corinthians 15:53, 54.

Other commentators of Christendom acknowledge that Gehenna is not a place of eternal fiery torment. Says *The New Bible Commentary* (page 779): "Gehenna was the Hellenized form of the name of the valley of Hinnom at Jerusalem in which fires were kept constantly burning to consume the refuse of the city. This is a powerful picture of final destruction."

What is the truth of the matter? The best way to find out is to examine what the Bible itself says.

The term "Gehenna" is found twelve times in the Christian Greek Scriptures. Once it is used by the disciple James, and eleven times it appears in statements attributed to Jesus Christ and relates to a condemnatory judgment. These texts read:

"I say to you that everyone who continues wrathful with his brother will be accountable to the court of justice; but whoever addresses his brother with an unspeakable word of contempt will be accountable to the Supreme Court; whereas whoever says, 'You despicable fool!' [thereby wrongly judging and condemning his brother as morally worthless] will be liable to the fiery Gehenna."—Matthew 5:22.

"Do not become fearful of those who kill the body but cannot kill the soul; but rather be in fear of him that can destroy both soul and body in Gehenna."—Matthew 10:28.

"I will indicate to you whom to fear: Fear him who after killing has authority to throw into Gehenna. Yes, I tell you, fear this One."—Luke 12:5.

"Woe to you, scribes and Pharisees, hypocrites! because you traverse sea and dry land to make one proselyte, and when he becomes one you make him a subject for Gehenna twice as much so as yourselves. Serpents, offspring of vipers, how are you to flee from the judgment of Gehenna?"—Matthew 23:15, 33.

"If ever your hand makes you stumble, cut it off; it is finer for you to enter into life maimed than with two hands to go off into Gehenna, into the fire that cannot be put out. And if your foot makes you stumble, cut it off; it is finer for you to enter into life lame than with two feet to be pitched into Gehenna. And if your eye makes you stumble, throw it away; it is finer for you to enter one-eyed into the kingdom of God than with two eyes to be pitched into Gehenna, where their maggot does not die and the fire is not put out."—Mark 9:43-48; see also the similarly worded passages at Matthew 5:29, 30; 18:8, 9.

"Well, the tongue is a fire. The tongue is constituted a world of unrighteousness among our members, for it spots up all the body and sets the wheel of natural life aflame and it is set aflame by Gehenna [that is, improper use of the tongue is as destructive as Gehenna; it can so affect the whole round of life into which a person comes by birth that it can lead to his meriting the judgment of Gehenna]."—James 3:6.

Note that, while these texts associate fire with Gehenna, none of them speak of any conscious existence, any suffering, after death. Rather, as shown at Matthew 10:28, Jesus pointed out that God can "destroy," not merely the body, but the entire person, the soul, in Gehenna. Just what is the nature of this destruction? An understanding of this is gleaned from a closer examination of the word "Gehenna."

GEHENNA—THE VALLEY OF HINNOM

Though found in the Christian Greek Scriptures, "Gehenna" is drawn from two Hebrew words, *Ga'i* and *Hin·nom'*, meaning Valley of Hinnom. This valley lay south and southwest of Jerusalem. In the days of faithless Judean Kings Ahaz and Manasseh the Valley of Hinnom served as a place for idolatrous religious rites, including the abhorrent practice of child sacrifice. (2 Chronicles 28:1, 3; 33:1, 6; Jeremiah 7:31; 19:2, 6) Later, good King Josiah put a stop to the idolatrous worship carried on there and made the valley unfit to use for worship.—2 Kings 23:10.

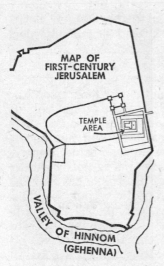

MAP OF FIRST-CENTURY JERUSALEM

TEMPLE AREA

VALLEY OF HINNOM (GEHENNA)

Tradition relates that the Valley of Hinnom thereafter became a place for the disposal of garbage. And the Bible provides confirmation for this. At Jeremiah 31:40, for example, the Valley of Hinnom is evidently called the "low plain of the carcasses and of the fatty ashes." There was also the "Gate of the Ash-heaps," a gate that seems to have opened out onto the eastern extremity of the Valley of Hinnom at its juncture with the Kidron Valley.—Nehemiah 3:13, 14.

That Gehenna should be linked with the destructive aspects of a city dump is in full agreement with the words of Jesus Christ. With reference to Gehenna, he said, "their maggot does not die and the fire is not put out." (Mark 9:48) His words evidently allude to the fact that fires burned continually at the city dump, perhaps being intensified by the addition of sulfur. Where the fire did not reach, worms or maggots would breed and feed on what was not consumed by fire.

It should also be observed that Jesus, in speaking of Gehenna in this way, did not introduce a concept completely foreign to the Hebrew Scriptures. In those earlier Scriptures practically identical wording appears in references to what will befall the ungodly.

Isaiah 66:24 foretells that persons having God's favor "will actually go forth and look upon the carcasses of the men that were transgressing against [God]; for the very worms upon them will not die and their fire itself will not be extinguished, and they must become something repulsive to all flesh." Clearly this is not a picture of conscious torment but of a terrible destruction. What are left are, not conscious souls or "disembodied spirits," but dead "carcasses." The scripture shows that it is, not the humans, but the maggots or worms upon them that are alive. No mention is made here of any "immortal soul."

In the prophecy of Jeremiah the Valley of Hinnom is similarly linked with a destruction of faithless humans. " 'Look! there are days coming,' is the utterance of Jehovah, 'when this place will be called no more Topheth and the valley of the son of Hinnom, but the valley of the killing. And I will make void the counsel of Judah and of Jerusalem in this place, and I will cause them to fall by the sword before their enemies and by the hand of those seeking for their soul. And I will give their dead bodies as food to the flying creatures of the heavens and to the beasts of the earth.' "—Jeremiah 19:6, 7.

Note that Jeremiah's reference to the Valley of Hinnom contains no hint of conscious torment after death. The picture drawn is one of total destruction, the "dead bodies" being consumed by scavenger birds and beasts.

A SYMBOL OF DESTRUCTION

In keeping with the Biblical evidence, then, Gehenna or the Valley of Hinnom could appropriately serve as a symbol of destruction but not of conscious fiery torment. Joseph E. Kokjohn, in the Catholic periodical *Commonweal,* acknowledges this, saying:

> "The final place of punishment, evidently, is Gehenna, the Valley of Hinno[m], which at one time had been a place where human sacrifice was offered to pagan gods, but in biblical times had already become the city dump, a refuse heap on the outskirts of Jerusalem. Here the stench and smoke and fire were a constant reminder to the inhabitants of what happened to things that had served their purpose—they were destroyed."

That the destruction symbolized by Gehenna is a lasting one is shown elsewhere in the Holy Scriptures. The apostle Paul, when writing to Christians at Thessalonica, said that those causing them tribulation would "undergo the judicial punishment of *everlasting destruction* from before the Lord and from the glory of his strength." —2 Thessalonians 1:6-9.

Biblical evidence thus makes it plain that those whom God judges as undeserving of life will experience, not eternal torment in a literal fire, but "everlasting destruction." They will not be preserved alive anywhere. The fire of Gehenna is therefore but a symbol of the totality and thoroughness of that destruction.

It is noteworthy that, in addressing the religious leaders of his day, Jesus Christ said: "Serpents, offspring of vipers, how are you to flee from the judgment of Gehenna?" (Matthew 23:33) Why was this? It was because those religious leaders were hypocrites. They desired to be looked up to and addressed with high-sounding titles, but they had no regard for those whom they were to help spiritually. They burdened others down with traditional regulations, and disregarded justice, mercy and faithfulness. They were false teachers, placing human traditions above the authority of God's Word.—Matthew 15:3-6; 23:1-32.

Have you noticed like things among the religious leaders of today, particularly in Christendom? Will they fare any better than the religious leaders of Judaism in the days of Jesus' earthly ministry? Not in the least, for Christendom's religious leaders have disobediently misrepresented God and the "good news about our Lord Jesus." So as long as they persist in teaching false doctrines they stand in danger of undergoing the "judicial punishment of everlasting destruction."

The truth about Gehenna therefore should help us to appreciate the importance of avoiding association with false religion. Not only the leaders but, as Jesus showed, also those who support the false religious teachers are in danger. Jesus Christ, in fact, spoke of a proselyte of the scribes and Pharisees as becoming a 'subject for Gehenna twice as much so as they were.' (Matthew 23:

15) Hence, people who blindly continue to follow false religious teaching today cannot hope to escape God's adverse judgment.

While making us think seriously about our own position, this can also be a comforting assurance to us. How so? In that we can be sure that Jehovah God will not leave serious wrongdoing unpunished. If people do not want to conform to his righteous laws and deliberately persist in a course of wickedness, he will not allow them much longer to continue to disrupt the peace of righteous people.

CHAPTER 14

What 'Torment in the Lake of Fire' Means

HOW would you react if, now that you know what the Bible says about the unconscious condition of the dead, you were to find a Bible text mentioning a place of torment? Would you reason that this justifies ignoring all the other scriptures and holding onto the idea that there may still be a possibility of conscious existence continuing after death? Or, would you undertake a careful examination of the context to determine just what the text might really mean and how it harmonizes with the rest of the Bible?

The reason for considering this is that the Bible book of Revelation does speak of "torment" in a "lake of fire." Revelation 20:10 states: "The Devil who was misleading them was hurled into the lake of fire and sulphur, where both the wild beast and the false prophet already were; and they will be tormented day and night forever and ever."—See also Revelation 19:20.

How are those cast into the "lake of fire" tormented? That we should not be hasty in taking this expression as literal is evident from the nature of the book of Revelation. The opening words of the book read: "A revelation by Jesus Christ, which God gave him, to show his slaves the things that must shortly take place. And he sent forth his angel and presented it in signs through him to his slave John."—Revelation 1:1.

As there stated, this revelation was presented "in signs." What, then, of the "lake of fire" and the "torment" there? Are they literal or are they also "signs" or symbols?

Additional information as to what is cast into the lake of fire, besides the Devil, the "wild beast" and the "false prophet," sheds light on the matter. Note the words of Revelation 20:14, 15: "Death and Hades were hurled into the lake of fire. This means the second death, the lake of fire. Furthermore, whoever was not found written in the book of life was hurled into the lake of fire."

Now, is it possible for death and Hades to be hurled into a literal lake of fire? Obviously not, for they are not objects, animals or persons. Death is a state or condition. How could it be tossed into a literal lake of fire? As for Hades, it is the common grave of mankind. What kind of a lake could hold it?

Then, too, Revelation 20:14, 15 does not say that the lake is literal. Rather, we read that the "lake of fire" is itself a sign or symbol of "second death." The same point is made at Revelation 21:8: "As for the cowards and those without faith and those who are disgusting in their filth and murderers and fornicators and those practicing spiritism and idolaters and all the liars, their portion will be in the lake that burns with fire and sulphur. *This means the second death.*"

Since the lake of fire is a symbol of second death, the casting of death and Hades into it is simply a symbolic way of saying that these will be forever destroyed. This agrees with the Bible's statement that 'the last enemy, death, is to be brought to nothing.' (1 Corinthians 15:26) And, since Hades, the common grave of mankind in general, is emptied and "death will be no more," that means that Hades ceases to function, passes out of existence.—Revelation 20:13; 21:4.

FIGURATIVE TORMENT

What, then, is the "torment" experienced by wicked humans and others that are thrown into the "lake of fire"? Without conscious existence, they could not experience *literal* torment, could they? And there is nothing in the Holy Scriptures to show that they will have any conscious existence. So why does the Bible speak of eternal torment in the "lake of fire"?

Since the "lake of fire" is symbolic, the torment associated with it must also be symbolic or figurative. This can be better appreciated in the light of what the Bible says about the things that are pitched into the "lake of fire." What we should observe is that the "second death" is what is symbolized by the "lake of fire." The Adamic death, that is, the death that all born humankind inherited from Adam and Eve after they had sinned, is never likened to such a fearful thing, even though death is "the wages sin pays."—Romans 6:23.

Jesus Christ likened the death state of those who die because of inherited sin to a sleep. For instance, he said of Lazarus, who lay dead for parts of four days, "Lazarus our friend has gone to rest, but I am journeying there to awaken him from sleep." (John 11:11) Later on, even Jesus slept the sleep of death for parts of three days. "Now Christ has been raised up from the dead, the firstfruits of those who have fallen asleep in death." (1 Corinthians 15:20) Death is like a sleep, as it ends in an awakening.

However, those who must undergo the "second death" do not have the comfort of a resurrection hope. Theirs is not a sleep. They never awaken from destruction in second death. As this hopeless state keeps hold of them, they are 'tormented forever' in the sense of being eternally restrained from having any conscious existence or activity. That their restraint in "second death" is compared to torture by being confined in prison is shown by Jesus in his parable of the ungrateful, merciless slave. Concerning the action his master took against him, Jesus said: "And in his anger the master handed him over to the torturers till he should pay all his debt." (Matthew 18:34, *Jerusalem Bible*) The *New World Translation* shows who these tormentors are by reading: "With that his master, provoked to wrath, delivered him to the jailers [*marginal reading:* tormentors], until he should pay back all that was owing."

The very fact that the "lake of fire" is a symbol

of "second death" rules out the idea of its being a place of conscious torment. Nowhere does the Bible even suggest that the dead can experience conscious torment, but the dead have lost all sensations. Of those dead in the common grave of mankind, the Bible says: "There the wicked themselves have ceased from agitation, and there those weary in power are at rest. Together prisoners themselves are at ease; they actually do not hear the voice of one driving them to work. Small and great are there the same, and the slave is set free from his master."—Job 3:17-19.

Just as the death to which humans in general continue to be subject ends all sensations and feeling, so does the "second death." However, no forgiveness of sins or ransoming is possible for those punished with "second death." That reproachful state is their lot forever. Memory of them is as rotten.—Isaiah 66:24; Proverbs 10:7.

Yet even before wicked ones are plunged into total annihilation, "second death," they experience torment. This is referred to symbolically at Revelation 14:9-11: "If anyone worships the wild beast and its image, and receives a mark on his forehead or upon his hand, he will also drink of the wine of the anger of God that is poured out undiluted into the cup of his wrath, and he shall be tormented with fire and sulphur in the sight of the holy angels and in the sight of the Lamb. And the smoke of their torment ascends forever and ever, and day and night they have no rest, those who worship the wild beast and its image, and whoever receives the mark of its name." By what means are the worshipers of the "wild beast" and its "image" tormented? The words of Revelation that follow immediately thereafter provide the clue: "Here is where it means endurance for the holy ones, those who observe the commandments of God and the faith of Jesus."—Revelation 14:12.

There would be no need for endurance on the part of the holy ones if the worshipers of the "wild beast" and its "image" were confined to a literal place of torment. Those false worshipers would then be stripped of all power to do harm to God's faithful servants. But as long as they are alive and free they can engage in hateful, vicious acts against the "holy ones."

The fact that the "holy ones" are brought into the picture indicates that they are the instrumentalities for bringing torment on the wicked. How could this be? Well, they proclaim the message that points to the eternal destruction awaiting the worshipers of the "wild beast" and its "image." This message puts these false worshipers in torment, giving them no rest day or night. That is why they try everything within their power to silence God's servants. The resulting persecution calls for endurance on the part of the "holy ones." Finally, when the worshipers of the "wild beast" and its "image" are destroyed as by "fire and sulphur," the evidence of that total destruction will, like smoke, ascend for all time to come.

The completeness of that destruction might be illustrated by what befell the cities of Sodom and Gomorrah. The disciple Jude wrote: "Sodom and Gomorrah and the cities about them . . . are placed before us as a warning example by undergoing the judicial punishment of everlasting fire." (Jude 7) The fire that destroyed those cities had stopped burning long before Jude wrote his letter. But the permanent, "everlasting" evidence of that fire's destructiveness remained, for those cities continued nonexistent.

ETERNAL TORMENT DOES NOT HARMONIZE WITH GOD'S PERSONALITY

That total destruction, not conscious torment for all eternity, is the punishment meted out to those persisting in rebellion also agrees with what God reveals about himself in his Word the Bible. Jehovah God has tender feelings toward his human creation as well as his animal creation.

Consider for a moment God's law about a working bull: "You must not muzzle a bull while it is threshing." (Deuteronomy 25:4) This law reflected God's compassionate concern and care for unreasoning animals. The bull was not to be tormented by being forcibly prevented from satisfying its desire to feed on some of the grain it was threshing.

Far greater is God's concern and love for humankind than for the unreasoning animals. As Jesus Christ reminded his disciples: "Five sparrows sell for two coins of small value, do they not? Yet not one of them goes forgotten before God. But even the hairs of your heads are all numbered. Have no fear; you are worth more than many sparrows."—Luke 12:6, 7.

Would it not be totally inconsistent, then, for anyone to claim that a God with such tender feelings would literally torment some humans for all eternity? Who of us would want to see someone undergoing the most horrible torture for even an hour? Is it not true that only fiendish persons would delight in seeing others suffer? Does not our inward sense of love and justice go into a state of revolt when we hear that a father tortured his child nearly to the point of death for some act of disobedience? Regardless of how bad the child may have been, we find it impossible to have any tender feelings for such a father.

God's compassionate dealing with imperfect mankind, however, does appeal to our moral sense. It warms our hearts and draws us closer to our Creator. Just think of it: Even when people deserve punishment, God has no pleasure in having to administer it. As the prophet Jeremiah exclaimed with reference to God's judgment that befell unfaithful Jerusalem: "Although he has caused grief, he will also certainly show mercy according to the abundance of his loving-kindness. For not out of his own heart has he afflicted or does he grieve the sons of men."—Lamentations 3:32, 33.

If it is not in his heart to afflict or to grieve humans who deserve punishment, how could Jehovah God for all eternity look approvingly upon the anguish of wicked ones? Furthermore, what purpose would it serve? According to the clergy's unscriptural "hell fire" theory, even if those experiencing the torment wanted to change, they could not do so, nor could they improve their situation. God's Word, however, shows unmistakably that total destruction, not torment, is the punishment for all who persist in wickedness.

Appreciating that Jehovah is a loving and just God, we can rest assured that his purpose for those who want to serve him is grand indeed. With eager anticipation, then, let us examine the Scriptures to learn of the loving provisions that he has made to deliver mankind from bondage to disease and death.

CHAPTER 15

A Government That Will Conquer Man's Enemy Death

GOD'S original purpose for man was that he might live and enjoy life on a paradise earth. We can have confidence that this purpose will be realized. It is backed by God's dependable promise that man's enemy death will be conquered, destroyed.—1 Corinthians 15:26.

A life-span of but seventy or eighty years is not all there is. If that were the full extent of what even lovers of God could hope for, their situation would differ little from that of those who have no regard for God or his Word. But this is not the case. The Bible says: "God is not unrighteous so as to forget your work and the love you showed for his name."—Hebrews 6:10; 11:6.

What is the reward for those who are serving Jehovah God because of their deep love for him and his righteous ways? There is both a present and a future reward. The apostle Paul wrote: "Godly devotion is beneficial for all things, as it holds promise of the life now and that which is to come." (1 Timothy 4:8) Even now obedience to God's law leads to enjoying a contented, happy life. As to the life "which is to come," Romans 6:23 says: "The gift God gives is everlasting life."

Under present conditions, of course, everlasting life may appear undesirable. But it is eternal life under a righteous administration that God has promised. For that promise to become reality, humans must first be freed from the cause of death. What is that cause? The inspired apostle Paul answers: "The sting producing death is sin."—1 Corinthians 15:56.

Already at the time of pronouncing judgment on the rebellious human pair, Adam and Eve, and upon the instigator of rebellion, Jehovah God pointed to the means by which humans would be freed from sin and death. Not to the unreasoning snake used in the deception, but to Satan himself as the "original serpent" God's words were directed: "I shall put enmity between you and the woman and between your seed and her seed. He will bruise you in the head and you will bruise him in the heel." This judgment, recorded at Genesis 3:15, provided the basis for hope for the future offspring of Adam and Eve. It indicated that man's enemy would be conquered. —Revelation 12:9.

Of course, the mere killing of the "original serpent," Satan the Devil, would not be enough to undo all the injury that he caused by influencing the first humans to rebel against God. But just how the undoing would come about remained a secret until such time as God chose to reveal it. —1 John 3:8.

With the aid of the complete Bible, we today can unravel this sacred secret. The "woman" referred to at Genesis 3:15 could not have been Eve. Eve, by her course of rebellion, aligned herself with the "original serpent," thus making herself a part of his "seed." Then, too, no female descendant of Adam and Eve could be that woman. Why not? Because the 'seed of the woman' had to possess power far greater than that of a mere man in order to crush the "original serpent," the invisible spirit person Satan the Devil. To produce such a mighty "seed," the "woman" would have to be, not human, but spiritual.

At Galatians 4:26 this "woman" is identified as "Jerusalem above." This is very significant. How so?

The ancient city of Jerusalem was the capital of the kingdom of Judah. Because the first Judean king, David, established his seat of government there, Jerusalem from his time onward produced the kings for the nation. Therefore it would only be natural to expect that the "Jerusalem above" would produce a king. This factor pointed to a heavenly government, with a heavenly king, as the agency for putting an end to sin and death.

The "Jerusalem above" is no literal woman or city. It is a symbolic, spiritual city. Being heavenly, it is composed of mighty spirit persons, angels. So, then, for one from among these spirit persons to be designated as king would mean that the "Jerusalem above" had produced an heir to a kingdom. Did such a thing happen?

THE KING IS BROUGHT FORTH

That is exactly what happened in the year 29 C.E. At that time the man Jesus was anointed by God's holy spirit to become King-Designate. This occurred at the time he presented himself to John the Baptist for immersion in water. As to what took place, the Bible reports: "After being baptized Jesus immediately came up from the water; and, look! the heavens were opened up, and he saw descending like a dove God's spirit coming upon him. Look! Also, there was a voice from the heavens that said: 'This is my Son, the beloved, whom I have approved.' "—Matthew 3:16, 17.

Some months later Jesus began proclaiming: "Repent, you people, for the kingdom of the heavens has drawn near." (Matthew 4:17) Yes, the kingdom had drawn near in the person of the King-Designate.

Though born as a man on earth, Jesus had had a prehuman existence. He himself said: "No man has ascended into heaven but he that descended from heaven, the Son of man." (John 3:13) In calling attention to Jesus' outstanding example of humility, the inspired apostle Paul wrote: "He emptied himself and took a slave's form and came to be in the likeness of men." (Philippians 2:5-7) As to how this transferal from heavenly to earthly life came about, we have the recorded conversation of the angel Gabriel with the virgin Mary:

"The angel said to her: 'Have no fear, Mary, for you have found favor with God; and, look! you will conceive in your womb and give birth to a son, and you are to call his name Jesus. This one will be great and will be called Son of the Most High; and Jehovah God will give him the throne of David his father, and he will rule as king over the house of Jacob forever, and there will be no end of his kingdom.'

"But Mary said to the angel: 'How is this to be, since I am having no intercourse with a man?' In answer the angel said to her: 'Holy spirit will come upon you, and power of the Most High will overshadow you. For that reason also what is born will be called holy, God's Son.' "—Luke 1:30-35.

Thus, as one of the sons of God making up the "Jerusalem above," Jesus had his life transferred from heaven to the womb of the virgin Mary and was born a perfect human baby. Such a miracle may sound unbelievable to some, yet that casts no valid doubt on the actuality of the event. Surely the One who made it possible for a complete person to develop from an egg cell that is smaller than the period at the end of this sentence could, by means of his spirit or active force, transfer life from the heavens to the earth. And since Jesus' life had been transferred in this way in order for him to become the permanent heir of King David, he actually came forth from the "Jerusalem above."

As foretold in God's prophecy of Genesis 3:15, Jesus experienced a 'heel wound' from the "original serpent" when he was nailed to an executional stake on Nisan 14 of the year 33 C.E. Unlike a crushing in the head from which there is no recovery, that 'heel wound' was but temporary. On the third day God raised Jesus up from the dead, granting him the "power of an indestructible life." (Acts 10:40; Hebrews 7:16) As an immortal spirit person, the King Jesus Christ is in position to crush the "original serpent" in the head and undo all the damage that that one has caused.

ASSOCIATE RULERS

Jesus Christ is the main one of that composite "seed." By means of him Almighty God will crush Satan the Devil under the feet of Jesus' associates in the heavenly kingdom. (Revelation 20:1-3) Writing to those in line for rulership, the Christian apostle Paul stated: "The God who gives peace will crush Satan under your feet shortly." (Romans 16:20) Who are these associate rulers?

In the last book of the Bible, Revelation, the

number is given as 144,000. Describing what he saw in vision, the writer of Revelation, the apostle John, says: "Look! the Lamb [Jesus Christ, who died a death like a sacrificial lamb] standing upon the Mount Zion, and with him a hundred and forty-four thousand having his name and the name of his Father written on their foreheads. . . . These are the ones that keep following the Lamb no matter where he goes. These were bought from among mankind [not just one nation of people like the Israelites] as firstfruits to God and to the Lamb."—Revelation 14:1-4.

It is indeed appropriate that the 144,000 are depicted as being with the Lamb on Mount Zion. Mount Zion of the ancient city of Jerusalem was the place from which the kings of Judah ruled, the site of the royal palace. It was also at Mount Zion that David pitched a tent for the sacred ark (chest) of the covenant in which were placed the two tablets of stone inscribed with the Ten Commandments. Later that ark was transferred to the innermost compartment of the temple built by David's son Solomon a short distance away on Mount Moriah. The term Zion, in time, came to include Moriah. Thus Zion had prominent association with kingship as well as priesthood. —2 Samuel 6:12, 17; 1 Kings 8:1; Isaiah 8:18.

This agrees with the fact that Jesus is both King and Priest, combining both offices as did Melchizedek of ancient Salem. Therefore Hebrews 6:20 speaks of Jesus as having "become a high priest according to the manner of Melchizedek forever." In the capacity of King-Priest, Jesus rules from heavenly Mount Zion.

His fellow rulers are also priests. As a body they are called a "royal priesthood." (1 Peter

2:9) Of their function, Revelation 5:10 tells us: "You [Christ] made them to be a kingdom and priests to our God, and they are to rule as kings over the earth."

PURPOSE OF THE ADMINISTRATION

A principal concern of the King-Priest Jesus Christ and his associate priestly rulers is to bring all humankind into unity with Jehovah God. This means the removal of all traces of sin and imperfection, for only those who reflect God's image perfectly can stand on their own merit before him. That the administrative Kingdom is part of God's administration of affairs for bringing this about is indicated at Ephesians 1:9-12:

"[God] made known to us the sacred secret of his will. It is according to his good pleasure which he purposed in himself for an administration at the full limit of the appointed times, namely, to gather all things together again in the Christ, the things in the heavens and the things on the earth. Yes, in him, in union with whom we were also assigned as heirs, in that we were foreordained according to the purpose of him who operates all things according to the way his will counsels, that we should serve for the praise of his glory."

Since Jesus Christ is sinless and in perfect harmony with Jehovah God, the bringing of all things into unity with him results in mankind's being brought into unity with Jehovah God. This is clear from the fact that after this aspect of the Kingdom's work is completed, the Bible says that Jesus Christ "hands over the kingdom to his God and Father."—1 Corinthians 15:24.

To accomplish the tremendous task of per-

fecting humankind, the heavenly rulers will also
be using earthly representatives, men of outstanding devotion to righteousness. (Psalm 45:16;
Isaiah 32:1, 2) These men will have to meet
the qualifications the King Jesus Christ looks for
in those whom he entrusts with responsibility.
Two basic qualifications are humility and self-
sacrificing love. Said Jesus: "You know that the
rulers of the nations lord it over them and the
great men wield authority over them. This is not
the way among you; but whoever wants to become great among you must be your minister,
and whoever wants to be first among you must
be your slave." (Matthew 20:25-27) He also said:
"This is my commandment, that you love one
another just as I have loved you. No one has love
greater than this, that someone should surrender
his soul in behalf of his friends."—John 15:12, 13.

Would you not feel secure under Kingdom
representatives who reflect such love and humility, who would genuinely care for you?

There will be no problems in communication
between the heavenly government and the earthly
representatives of the King Jesus Christ. In times
past Jehovah God transmitted messages to his
servants on earth by means of angels and his invisible active force. (Daniel 10:12-14; 2 Peter
1:21) Why, even men have been able to transmit
and receive messages to and from capsules and
space stations circling far above the earth. If
imperfect men can do such things, why should
anyone think that this would be too difficult for
perfect heavenly rulers?

However, before the Kingdom administration
of Jesus Christ and his fellow rulers can proceed
with the work of bringing mankind into unity

with God, all opposing forces must be removed. There is not the slightest indication that those governing mankind today are willing to hand over their sovereignty to Jesus Christ and his associate rulers. They scoff at the idea that a heavenly government will take full control over earth's affairs. That is why they will have to be forced to recognize the authority of God's kingdom by his Christ. This will be at the cost of their ruling positions as well as their lives. As the Bible tells us: "In the days of those kings the God of heaven will set up a kingdom that will never be brought to ruin. And the kingdom itself will not be passed on to any other people. It will crush and put an end to all these kingdoms, and it itself will stand to times indefinite."—Daniel 2:44.

After clearing out all opposition, the Kingdom administration will set itself to the task of liberating humans from sickness and death. How will this be accomplished?

CHAPTER 16

An Earth Free from Sickness and Death

WHAT grand relief an earth forever free from sickness and death would mean for us humans! It would put an end to the bitter tears shed in expression of grief and suffering. Gone would be the excruciating pain and horrible deformities that sickness can bring. No longer would the ravages of old age weaken humans, often bringing them to a state of hopeless despair and helplessness. People everywhere would be enjoying youthful strength and vigor. Not a single mournful sound would ever come forth from their lips!

This is not based on idle imagination. It is what Jehovah God has purposed. He has far more in mind for mankind than just a few years of life filled with problems and suffering.—Revelation 21:3, 4.

COULD IT LEAD TO TREMENDOUS PROBLEMS?

But would an earth free from sickness and death give rise to other serious problems? Do you wonder: Where would all the people live? Would not the end of sickness and death quickly bring about crowded conditions, making life unpleasant, and leading to great food shortage?

It was never God's purpose to overpopulate the earth. To the perfect Adam and Eve, God said: "Be fruitful and become many and fill the earth." (Genesis 1:28) There is quite a difference between 'filling' the earth and overpopulating it. If someone asked you to fill a glass with juice, you would not keep on pouring until the glass overflowed. Once the glass was sufficiently filled, you would stop pouring. Similarly, once the earth was comfortably filled with humankind, God would see to it that further population growth stopped on this planet.

Moreover, we should not, on the basis of what we see or hear today, misjudge earth's ability to provide a home for us and to sustain human and animal life. While large populations are jammed together in cities, vast regions of the earth are sparsely populated. If the present population were evenly distributed, there would be about six acres of fertile land for every man, woman and child. This would be more than ample room indeed!

The hunger that so many humans must endure in various parts of the earth is not because the full capability of the soil to produce has been reached. Rather, widespread food shortage stems mainly from an unequal distribution of food supplies. Whereas much is produced in certain areas and surpluses exist, in other places there are extreme shortages. Actually, the earth could produce much more than it does at present. Back in 1970 the United Nations Food and Agriculture Organization estimated the world's agricultural potential to be great enough to feed about forty-two times as many people as the present world population.

What man has already done in some regions of the earth gives some indication of what great possibilities there are for increasing earth's productivity.

The Imperial Valley of California was once an inhospitable, uncultivated desert. But irrigation of the mineral-rich desert soil has made this valley one of the richest agricultural regions in the United States.

With about half the farmland, Europe, through more intensive cultivation, produces about as much food as North America.

Truly there can be no question that more land could be brought under more intensive cultivation, and that without spoiling the beauty of forests and meadows.

There is yet another factor that will assure an ample food supply for an earth comfortably filled with animal and human life. What is that? It is the divine help and direction that will then be given to mankind under the administration of God's kingdom by his Son Jesus Christ. No one knows the earth better than does God, for he is its Creator. And under the wise administration of his kingdom the land will yield abundantly. As was the experience of ancient Israel when faithful, so it will be then: "The earth itself will certainly give its produce; God, our God, will bless us."—Psalm 67:6.

Dry deserts and other unproductive areas, occupying millions of acres, will doubtless be reclaimed on a large scale. Receiving divine help in getting needed water is not without historical parallel. Back in the sixth century B.C.E., in fulfillment of God's prophetic promises, thousands of Jewish exiles returned to Jerusalem from Babylon. (Ezra 2:64-70) They evidently took a direct route through the inhospitable Syrian Desert. Yet God provided what they needed to keep alive. Even regarding their homeland he had predicted: "In the wilderness waters will have burst out, and torrents in the desert plain."—Isaiah 35:6.

Since God did this in the past, we have good reason to expect that under the administration of his kingdom by Christ this will be done on a far grander scale.

We need not fear that the ushering in of an earth free from sickness and death will give rise to unpleasant conditions. Not only will there be no overcrowding, but everyone will be able to eat food to satisfaction.

The administration in the hands of God's appointed King, Jesus Christ, and his 144,000 fellow rulers will see to it that earth's inhabitants are well cared for. Pointing to the abundance of wholesome food to be enjoyed, the prophecy of Isaiah states: "Jehovah of armies will certainly make for all the peoples, in this mountain, a banquet . . . of well-oiled dishes filled with marrow, of wine kept on the dregs, filtered."—Isaiah 25:6.

We can have confidence in Jehovah God, the One of whom the Bible declares: "You are opening your hand and satisfying the desire of every living thing." (Psalm 145:16) Never has he failed to fulfill his promises. As the Scriptures say of ancient Israel: "Not a promise failed out of all the good promise that Jehovah had made to the house of Israel; it all came true."—Joshua 21:45.

HOW SICKNESS AND DEATH WILL PASS AWAY

Besides promising to provide the material things that humans need in order to enjoy life, Jehovah God has promised something worth much more. What is that? Relief from sickness and death. His declared purpose about the grand banquet mentioned in Isaiah is, in fact, followed up by the promise: "He will actually swallow up death forever, and the Sovereign Lord Jehovah will certainly wipe the tears from all faces." —Isaiah 25:8.

In harmony with God's promise here expressed, the Kingdom administration in the hands of Jesus Christ and his associate rulers will be working toward bringing about the liberation of humankind from death. As sickness and death have come about through our being born imperfect sinners due to inheritance from the first man Adam, the death-dealing effects of sin must be counteracted. How?

The basis for doing so must be an arrangement that satisfies justice. Logically it must be an arrangement that offsets the damage caused by the rebellion of Adam. What Adam lost must be regained. The price would have to be a ransom having the exact value of what Adam lost, namely, perfect human life with all its rights and prospects.

None of Adam's sinful descendants could provide such a ransom. This is made clear at Psalm 49:7: "Not one of them can by any means redeem even a brother, nor give to God a ransom for him." But Christ Jesus could do so, for he was a perfect man, and he willingly laid down his life, thereby giving "his soul a ransom in exchange for many."—Matthew 20:28.

On the basis of his sacrificing his own perfect human life, Jesus Christ is in position to apply the benefits of his atoning sacrifice for the uplift of mankind from enslavement to sin. As sinful tendencies have become part of the human make-up, it will take time and help to overcome these. Under the Kingdom in the hands of Jesus Christ, all its human subjects will receive training in the way of righteousness.—Revelation 20:12; Isaiah 26:9.

However, this does not necessarily mean that those suffering from a serious physical disability or deformity are going to have to wait a long period of time during which they will finally recover from their affliction. When Jesus Christ was here on the earth, he healed the sick and afflicted instantly, miraculously. A number of cures he performed from a distance, while he was unseen by the afflicted ones and not in immediate touch with them. (Matthew 8:5-13; 15:21-28; Luke 7:1-10) Therefore any seriously handicapped persons, like a person with one leg or one arm, living when the Kingdom begins administering all of earth's affairs can hope for miraculous, instantaneous healing at God's appointed time. Marvelous indeed it will be to see sight restored to the blind, hearing to the deaf and soundness of body to the disfigured, maimed and deformed!

The bringing of humans to full perfection in body and mind, however, will be a gradual process, requiring the application of Jesus' atoning sacrifice and obedience to the direction of the Kingdom administration. What will take place might be compared to rehabilitating a disabled person under the guidance of a skilled therapist. During the course of his training the disabled person may make many mistakes but eventually he may come to the point where he is able to live a useful life without having to depend on others. The progress he makes depends on his response to the help given.

QUALIFICATIONS OF THOSE REHABILITATING IMPERFECT HUMANS

In rehabilitating the human race, Jesus Christ has all the needed qualifications. Having lived as a man on earth, he has personal acquaintance with the problems of imperfect humans. Though perfect, he, nevertheless, experienced suffering and sorrow, to the point of shedding tears. The Bible record tells us: "In the days of his flesh Christ offered up supplications and also petitions to the One who was able to save him out of death, with strong outcries and tears, and he was favorably heard for his godly fear. Although he was a Son, he learned obedience from the things he suffered."—Hebrews 5:7, 8.

As a result of what Jesus Christ experienced on earth, we can have confidence that he will be an understanding ruler. He will not deal harshly with his subjects, for he willingly laid down his life for mankind. (1 John 3:16) Then, too, since he is also the High Priest, Jesus will deal compassionately in freeing from sin those who respect his direction. He will not become impatient with them nor make them feel crushed because of their slipping into an act that does not perfectly reflect the personality of God. With reference to Jesus' priestly service, Hebrews 4:15, 16 says: "We have as high priest, not one who cannot sympathize with our weaknesses, but one who has been tested in all respects like ourselves, but without sin. Let us, therefore, approach with freeness of speech to the throne of undeserved kindness, that we may obtain mercy and find undeserved kindness for help at the right time."

While growing to perfection, humans will still be committing sins unintentionally. But by repenting and asking for forgiveness of God through their High Priest Jesus Christ, they will be forgiven and will continue to receive help in overcoming their weaknesses. Depicting the divine provisions for life and healing, Revelation 22:1, 2 speaks of "a river of water of life, clear as crystal, flowing out from the throne of God and of the Lamb down the middle of its broad way. And on this side of the river and on that side there were trees of life producing twelve crops of fruit, yielding their fruits each month. And the leaves of the trees were for the curing of the nations."

Those associated with Jesus Christ in rulership are likewise well qualified to help humankind.

These fellow rulers include both men and women from a great variety of walks of life. (Galatians 3:28) Some of them came from backgrounds that had involved them in such conduct as fornication, adultery, homosexuality, stealing, drunkenness, extortion and the like. But they repented, turned around and began living a clean life, to the praise and honor of God. (1 Corinthians 6:9-11) At the time of their death all who become associate king-priests of Jesus Christ must be found to be lovers and practicers of righteousness, haters of bad, and persons who unselfishly devoted themselves to further the welfare of fellowmen. —Romans 12:9; James 1:27; 1 John 3:15-17; Jude 23.

Maintaining a clean standing before God has not been easy for them. They have been subjected to tremendous pressures to adopt the world's selfish ways. Many have had to face external pressures in the form of reproach, physical abuse and general dislike and scorn. As to what they should expect, Jesus Christ told them: "People will deliver you up to tribulation and will kill you, and you will be objects of hatred by all the nations." (Matthew 24:9) Additionally, all during the course of their life they have had to struggle to combat their own sinful tendencies. One of them, the apostle Paul, said of himself: "I pummel my body and lead it as a slave, that, after I have preached to others, I myself should not become disapproved somehow."—1 Corinthians 9:27.

Truly, then, this body of 144,000 king-priests can sympathize with the problems of the Kingdom's human subjects. They themselves had to contend with them and proved themselves loyal to God despite great difficulties.

IDEAL CONDITIONS ON EARTH

On earth, too, everything will be just right for assisting humans to grow to perfection. Only those who have shown themselves to be desirous of doing the divine will with a complete heart will remain after the Kingdom destroys its enemies. This means that the human greed and selfishness that have largely been responsible for polluting the food we eat, the water we drink and the air we breathe will be things of the past. The survivors will not be plagued by divisive racial and national barriers. United in the worship of Jehovah God, all will act as brothers and pursue peace. Even the wild animals will do no harm to man or his domestic animals. The prophetic words of Isaiah 11:6-9 will then go beyond a spiritual fulfillment and witness a physical fulfillment:

> "The wolf will actually reside for a while with the male lamb, and with the kid the leopard itself will lie down, and the calf and the maned young lion and the well-fed animal all together; and a mere little boy will be leader over them. And the cow and the bear themselves will feed; together their young ones will lie down. And even the lion will eat straw just like the bull. And the sucking child will certainly play upon the hole of the cobra; and upon the light aperture of a poisonous snake will a weaned child actually put his own hand. They will not do any harm or cause any ruin in all my holy mountain; because the earth will certainly be filled with the knowledge of Jehovah as the waters are covering the very sea."

Through the Kingdom administration Jehovah God will be turning his attention to humans in a special way. This is portrayed in a prophetic vision recorded in the Bible book of Revelation. After comparing the extension of the Kingdom's power to the coming down of New Jerusalem out of heaven, the account tells us: "[God] will wipe out every tear from their eyes, and death will be no more, neither will mourning nor outcry nor pain be anymore. The former things have passed away."—Revelation 21:2-4.

Think of what that means. This present life with its pains and sorrows is definitely not all there is. Humankind will be freed from all mental, emotional and physical pain resulting from imperfection. Mental anguish over uncertainties or grave calamities and dangers will be a thing of the past. The depression, emptiness and loneliness associated with emotional pain will be no more. Never again will people cry out or groan due to severe physical pain. Bitter tears will no longer fill their eyes and stream down their cheeks. There will be no reason for anyone to give way to expressions of grief. Restored to perfection of mind and body, humans will find real pleasure in life for all eternity. Would you not want to be among those to enjoy these blessings from God?

CHAPTER 17

What Everlasting Life on Earth Offers Us

LIFE in good health and under pleasant conditions for more than seventy or eighty years is certainly a desirable thing. In fact, scientists have devoted scores of years to research ways to combat aging and disease. They often express the view that an average life-span of a hundred years is a goal to be worked toward.

However, the thought of a never-ending life-span does not seem to have the same appeal. Many persons are inclined to argue: 'Without sickness, death and some troubles we would lose appreciation for good things. Everlasting life on earth would be boring. We would run out of things to do.' Perhaps you have heard people express such thoughts, but is that the way you personally view life? Really, is that kind of reasoning sound?

Do we, for example, need sickness so as not to become bored with good health? People do not lose joy in living because they feel well. Security, pleasant surroundings, interesting and productive work, and wholesome food do not cause people to tire of life. Is it not, rather, a lack of food, unpleasant surroundings, trouble and friction that make life disagreeable? A man does not have to cut off one hand to appreciate the other one, does he? We can enjoy and appreciate good things without experiencing bad.

Life in human perfection does not mean that everyone will be doing all things equally well and with the same intense interest. What the Bible holds forth is the promise of life without sickness and death. (Revelation 21:3, 4) Healthy people today are not all alike, so why should anyone conclude that bodily and mental perfection would make people virtual copies of one another? People will still vary as to personality. They will have varying preferences as to work, building, home decoration, landscaping, food and drink, entertainment, the fine arts and the like. Their personal likes and preferences will have a strong bearing on the skills and fields of activity for which they will show a preference.

But is there really enough for humans to do on earth to keep them active for an eternity? Would not increase in knowledge eventually come to a standstill because we would have done everything?

MUCH CAN BE DONE

Reflect on your own life now. Do you feel that your capabilities are being used to the full or ever will be? How many things are there that you feel capable of doing and would like to accomplish —if only you had the time and needed assets?

Perhaps you would like to develop some talent, in music, painting, sculpture or carving, or to learn something about woodworking, mechanics, designing or architecture, or to study history, biology, astronomy or mathematics, or to take up the cultivation of certain plants or the breeding of animals, birds or fish. Possibly you would like to travel, to see new lands. Many would like to do, not just one, but a number of these things. But even if you had the needed assets, time would simply not permit you to do all the things you would like to do.

Furthermore, does not limited time also subject you to a certain degree of pressure to get things done? Would it not be a delight to do things without having to feel rushed?

Little danger exists of running out of things to do. Our home, this earth, is filled with such a great variety of plant and creature life that there is limitless potential for learning new things and putting our acquired knowledge to use. Many are the secrets that are just begging to be discovered. Think of it: There are over 30,000 varieties of fish, about 3,000 types of amphibians, about 5,000 sorts of mammals and more than

9,000 kinds of birds. Insects, the most numerous of earth's living creatures, number about 800,000 varieties. Scientists believe that between one and ten million varieties may still remain to be discovered. Added to this are hundreds of thousands of varieties of plants.

How many of us know even the barest fraction of earth's living things by name? Still more limited is our knowledge of their interesting habits and the vital role each plays in the continuance of life on earth. The potential for increased knowledge is stupendous.

You may have never heard of the tropical freshwater fish known as the cichlid. Yet one scientist remarked regarding his study of them: "For me, cichlids have proved an absorbing 14-year study." Think how many years it would take to study thousands of living creatures and plants—and with real benefit.

Take as an example the lowly barnacle. This creature gives man considerable trouble when it attaches itself to ships. Barnacles have to be scraped off the ships, as their presence in great number causes considerable drag and may increase fuel consumption as much as 40 percent. One might be inclined to think that little could be learned from a creature that seemingly makes such a nuisance of itself. But not so.

The cement by means of which the barnacle becomes firmly attached is about 3/10,000 of an inch thick. Yet its resistance to being sheared from the surface exceeds 7,000 pounds per square inch. This is twice the strength of the epoxy glues that have been used in recent years for spacecraft. When subjected by researchers to a temperature of 662 degrees Fahrenheit, barnacle cement did not melt, and it withstood a temperature of 383 degrees Fahrenheit below zero without cracking or peeling. Barnacle cement was also found to be resistant to most solvents. Its outstanding properties have incited researchers to try to produce an artificial barnacle cement, a "Superglue."

Thus, knowledge gained through research can bring benefits to man. Today there is no way of knowing just how many things done by earth's living things could be utilized or duplicated by man for his use. What has been learned is enough to show that the reservoir of knowledge has barely been tapped.

Even in areas where man has done considerable research much remains to be discovered. For example, one of the amazing things done by green plants is changing water and carbon dioxide into sugar. This process, known as photosynthesis, still baffles man despite some two centuries of research. Laurence C. Walker, a plant physiologist, noted that "if the secret unfolded, man could probably feed the world—using a factory the size of a common school building."

All mankind could benefit tremendously by learning more about plant and creature life. By understanding the interdependency of living things and their needs, man could avoid unknowingly upsetting the balance of life. Accurate knowledge would help him to avoid injuring himself and other living things.

For instance, if the harmful effects of DDT had been fully understood and man had acted in harmony with his knowledge, widespread pollution could have been avoided. But, sadly, man made indiscriminate use of DDT. What has been the result? Dr. Lorenzo Tomatis of the International Agency for Research on Cancer in France states: "There is no animal, no water, no soil on this earth which at present is not contaminated with DDT." In some cases DDT contamination has built up in animals and birds to the point of killing them. Truly, accurate knowledge could have prevented this tragic contamination.

Man could also continue to learn about sound, light, chemical reactions, electronics, minerals and a host of other inanimate things. And that still leaves the vast reaches of outer space largely unexplored. What a field for investigation this is! The universe contains billions of galaxies or star systems, and these galaxies may embrace billions of stars.—Psalm 8:3, 4.

Not to be overlooked is the fact that, even without long years of study, animate and inanimate things can stir human creativity and imagination. The colors and designs found among plants, animals and inanimate things not only delight the eye but provide a limitless source of ideas for the decorative arts. There is no reason to fear that human creativity would eventually cease to be stimulated and that life would become drab and uninteresting.

But even if there were a remote possibility of reaching the point of attaining complete knowledge of the earth and all life on it, would that in itself make life boring? Consider: In a year a person may eat more than a thousand meals. At forty years of age a man might have eaten well over forty thousand meals. But does eating become more boring with the passing of each year? Does the man who has eaten forty thousand meals feel more bored than the one who has eaten about half that number?

There can be true enjoyment even in things that are repeated. Who of us is bored by feeling gentle breezes, by the touch of those whom we love, by the sound of babbling brooks, waves crashing against the shore, birds chirping or singing, by seeing gorgeous sunsets, winding rivers, clear lakes, cascading waterfalls, lush meadows, towering mountains or palm-lined beaches, and by catching the scent of sweet-smelling flowers? —Compare Song of Solomon 2:11-13.

OPPORTUNITIES TO EXPRESS LOVE

Of course, just learning and applying what we learn would not be enough to make everlasting life rich and meaningful. We humans have an inherent need to love and to be loved. When we feel that others need, appreciate and love us, we want life to continue. It warms our hearts to know that others miss us when we are away, that they long to see us again. Association with dear relatives and friends is upbuilding and encouraging. We find happiness in being able to do things for those whom we love, to look out for their welfare.

Everlasting life would set before us endless opportunities to express love and to benefit from the love of others. It would give us the needed time to get to know fellow humans, to come to appreciate their fine qualities and to cultivate intense love for them. Earth's inhabitants are indeed varied—varied in personality, styles of dress, preferences in food, in architecture, in music and other arts. The time it would take to get to know and appreciate billions of humans and to learn from their experience and talents staggers the imagination. But would it not be a pleasure to know the entire human family and to be able to accept each member thereof as a very dear friend?

What everlasting life on earth could offer us is rich and rewarding. How could we possibly be bored when there is so much that we could learn and apply beneficially? How could we possibly tire of expressing love for others to the full? Observed Doctor Ignace Lepp in his book *Death and Its Mysteries:*

> "Those who have experienced authentic love and intellectual achievement know well that they can never reach a saturation point. The scientist who consecrates all of his time and energy to research knows that the more he learns, the more there is to learn and the more his appetite for knowledge increases. Likewise, those who love truly know that there is no imaginable limit to the growth of their love."

But when will those opportunities afforded by eternal life become ours? When will God's kingdom by Christ make it possible? And if we should die before that time comes, is there any possibility of our being restored to life?

CHAPTER 18

Why Many Now Living Have Opportunity Never to Die

THE time for God's kingdom to begin administering all earth's affairs is at hand. You may be among those to witness the grand blessings it will bring to mankind. That is no unfounded assertion. There is much evidence to back it up, including evidence that you have personally seen.

Many centuries ago Jehovah God revealed the specific time for the conferring of rulership upon the one whom he would designate to be king over the world of mankind. He used symbols to do so and transmitted some of the information by means of a dream.

That such means of communication were used by God to convey this vital information to men should not give rise to doubts. Consider what modern men now do in transmitting information. Cryptic messages are sent in code through space. Thereafter these coded messages are "unscrambled" by either men or machines. This manner of conveying information is purposeful. It conceals the meaning of the information from those not entitled to it.

Similarly, God's use of symbolisms has not been without purpose. The understanding of such symbolisms requires diligent study. But many people are unwilling to take the time to understand, because of having no real love for God and truth. Hence, the "sacred secrets of the kingdom" remain hidden to them.—Matthew 13:11-15.

AN ANCIENT PROPHETIC DREAM

One of those "sacred secrets" is contained in the Bible book of Daniel. That book provides essentials for determining the time for the giving of royal authority to God's appointed king. In the fourth chapter of that book you will find narrated a divinely sent dream of King Nebuchadnezzar of Babylon. What was the intent or purpose of this dream and its fulfillment? The record states:

"That people living may know that the Most High is Ruler in the kingdom of mankind and that to the one whom he wants to, he gives it and he sets up over it even the lowliest one of mankind."—Daniel 4:17.

The content of the dream was basically this: An immense tree was seen being chopped down at the command of a "holy one," an angel. The stump of the tree was then banded to prevent it from sprouting. It was to remain thus banded amid the "grass of the field" for "seven times." —Daniel 4:13-16.

What was the meaning of this dream? The inspired explanation of the prophet Daniel to Nebuchadnezzar was:

"The tree that you beheld, . . . it is you, O king, because you have grown great and become strong, and your grandeur has grown great and reached to the heavens, and your rulership to the extremity of the earth.

"And because the king beheld a watcher, even a holy one, coming down from the heavens, who was also saying: 'Chop the tree down, and ruin it. However, leave its rootstock itself in the earth, but with a banding of iron and of copper, among the grass of the field, and with the dew of the heavens let it become wet, and with the beasts of the field let its portion be until seven times themselves pass over it,' this is the interpretation, O king, and the decree of the Most High is that which must befall my lord the king. And you they will be driving away from men, and with the beasts of the field your dwelling will come to be, and the vegetation is what they will give even to you to eat just like bulls; and with the dew of the heavens you yourself will be getting wet, and seven times themselves will pass over you, until you know that the Most High is Ruler in the kingdom of mankind, and that to the one whom he wants to he gives it.

"And because they said to leave the rootstock of the tree, your kingdom will be sure to you after you know that the heavens are ruling."—Daniel 4:20-26.

So this dream had an initial fulfillment upon King Nebuchadnezzar. For "seven times," or seven literal years, Nebuchadnezzar was insane. His kingdom, however, was held secure for him so that, upon regaining soundness of mind, he again assumed his royal office.—Daniel 4:29-37.

KINGSHIP OF "THE LOWLIEST ONE OF MANKIND"

But this detailed account about the chopped-down tree was not limited in its fulfillment to King Nebuchadnezzar. How do we know this? Because, as stated in the vision itself, it relates to God's kingdom and rulership by the one whom he designates. And who is God's choice for the kingship? The answer given to King Nebuchadnezzar was: "the lowliest one of mankind." —Daniel 4:17.

The facts of history prove undeniably that lowliness has not been displayed by human political rulers. Human governments and their rulers have exalted themselves and they have made a beastly record for themselves, waging sanguinary wars against one another. It should therefore come as no surprise that the Bible compares imperfect human governments or kingdoms to beasts and shows that all of them will eventually be deprived of their rulership. (Daniel 7:2-8) As to who will replace them, the Bible records these words of the prophet Daniel:

"I kept on beholding in the visions of the night, and, see there! with the clouds of the heavens some-one like a son of man happened to be coming; and to the Ancient of Days he gained access, and they brought him up close even before that One. And to him there were given rulership and dignity and king-dom, that the peoples, national groups and languages should all serve even him. His rulership is an indefi-nitely lasting rulership that will not pass away, and his kingdom one that will not be brought to ruin." —Daniel 7:13, 14.

The one here described is none other than Jesus Christ, who is designated in the Scriptures as both the "Son of man" and as the "King of kings and Lord of lords." (Matthew 25:31; Reve-lation 19:16) He willingly gave up his superior position in the heavens and became a man, a "little lower than angels." (Hebrews 2:9; Philip-pians 2:6-8) As a man, Jesus Christ, even under extreme provocation, proved himself to be "mild-tempered and lowly in heart." (Matthew 11:29) "When he was being reviled, he did not go reviling in return. When he was suffering, he did not go threatening, but kept on committing himself to the one who judges righteously."—1 Peter 2:23.

The world of mankind viewed Jesus Christ as being of no account, refusing to accord him the honor he rightfully deserved. The situation was as had been foretold by the prophet Isaiah: "He was despised and was avoided by men, a man meant for pains and for having acquaintance with sickness. And there was as if the concealing of one's face from us. He was despised, and we held him as of no account."—Isaiah 53:3.

There can be no question that Jesus fits the description of "the lowliest one of mankind." Hence, the prophetic dream about the chopped-down tree must point to the time when he would receive rulership over the world of mankind. This would be at the end of "seven times." How long are these "times"? When do they start? When do they end?

THE LENGTH OF THE "SEVEN TIMES"

More than six centuries after Nebuchadnezzar's dream, Jesus Christ appeared on the scene, declaring that "the kingdom of the heavens has drawn near." (Matthew 4:17) He could say this because he, as King-Designate, was present. But he did not at that time receive kingship over the world of mankind. Thus, on one occasion when others wrongly concluded that "the kingdom of God was going to display itself instantly," Jesus Christ gave an illustration showing that a long period of time would be involved before his gaining such kingly power. (Luke 19:11-27) It is, therefore, clear that in the larger fulfillment of Daniel's prophecy the "seven times" cover a period, not of just seven years, but of many centuries.

The evidence is that these "seven times" amounted to 2,520 days, that is, seven prophetic years of 360 days each. This is confirmed in other parts of the Bible that mention "times," "months" and "days." For example, Revelation 11:2 speaks of a period of "forty-two months," or three and a half years. In the next verse the same period is mentioned as being "a thousand two hundred and sixty days." Now, if you were to divide 1,260 days by 42 months, you would get 30 days for each month. A year of 12 months would therefore be 360 days long. On this basis, "seven times," or seven years, would be 2,520 days long (7 x 360).

The correctness of this computation is verified by Revelation 12:6, 14, where 1,260 days are spoken of as "a time and times and half a time," or 'three and a half times' ("three years and a half," *The New English Bible*). Seven being the double of three and a half, "seven times" would equal 2,520 days (2 x 1,260).

Of course, as they relate to Jesus' receiving the kingship over the world of mankind, the "seven times" of Daniel's prophecy span a period of far more than 2,520 twenty-four-hour days. Is there any way to ascertain the length of each of these "days"? Yes, the Bible's formula for prophetic days is: "A day for a year." (Numbers 14:34; Ezekiel 4:6) Applying this to the "seven times," we see that they amount to 2,520 years.

THE START OF THE "SEVEN TIMES"

Knowing the length of the "seven times," we are now in position to investigate when they began. Again we direct our attention to what happened to Nebuchadnezzar in fulfillment of the prophetic dream about the chopped-down tree. Consider his situation:

At the time that Nebuchadnezzar lost his sanity he was exercising world domination, for Babylon was then the number one power on earth. In Nebuchadnezzar's case the cutting down of the symbolic tree meant a temporary break in his rule as a world sovereign.

The whole intent of what God did in Nebuchadnezzar's case involved rule by the king of God's own choice. Nebuchadnezzar's losing his throne for "seven times" must therefore have been symbolic. Of what? Of a temporary break in rulership or sovereignty by God's arrangement, since, in Nebuchadnezzar's case, Jehovah God was the one who had permitted him to attain the position of world ruler and thereafter took that position away from him temporarily, as the king himself acknowledged. (Daniel 4:34-37) So what befell Nebuchadnezzar must have been symbolic of the removal of sovereignty from a kingdom of God. Hence, the tree itself represented world domination as regards the earth.

At one time the government that had its seat in Jerusalem was a kingdom of God. The rulers of the royal line of David were said to sit upon "Jehovah's throne" and were under command to reign according to his law. (1 Chronicles 29:23) Jerusalem was therefore the seat of God's government in a representative sense.

So when the Babylonians under Nebuchadnezzar destroyed Jerusalem, and the land of its dominion was completely desolated, world rulership passed into Gentile hands without any interference from a kingdom representing Jehovah's sovereignty. The Supreme Sovereign restrained himself from exercising his rulership in this way. This restraining of himself from wielding sovereignty over the earth by a kingdom of his is likened to the banding of the remaining tree stump. At the time of its destruction and total desolation Jerusalem, as the capital city representing the governmental expression of Jehovah's sovereignty, began to be "trampled on." That means, therefore, that the "seven times" had their start at the time that Nebuchadnezzar destroyed Jerusalem and the land of Judah was completely desolated. When did that event occur?

The Bible and secular history can be used to establish 607 B.C.E. as the date for this event.* The evidence is as follows:

Secular historians are in agreement that Babylon fell to Cyrus the Persian in the year 539 B.C.E. This date is substantiated by all available historical records of ancient times. The Bible reveals that in his first year of rule, Cyrus issued a decree permitting the exiled Israelites to return to Jerusalem and rebuild the temple. There being first the brief rule of Darius the Mede over Babylon, Cyrus' first year of rule toward Babylon evidently extended from 538 to 537 B.C.E. (Daniel 5:30, 31) As considerable distance in traveling was involved, it must have been by the "seventh month" of 537 B.C.E. (rather than 538 B.C.E.) that the Israelites were back in their cities, ending the desolation of Jerusalem and the land of Judah. (Ezra 3:1, 6) Nevertheless, they remained under Gentile domination, and therefore spoke of themselves as 'slaves upon their own land.'—Nehemiah 9:36, 37.

The Bible book of Second Chronicles (36:19-21) shows that a period of seventy years passed from

---

* Modern secular historians do not generally present 607 B.C.E. as the date for this event, but they are dependent on the writings of men who lived centuries after it happened. On the other hand, the Bible contains testimony from eyewitnesses, and it sets out factors that are ignored by secular writers. Furthermore, the fulfillment of Bible prophecy at the end of the "seven times" establishes the date beyond doubt. As to why the Bible's chronological data is more reliable than secular history, see the book *Aid to Bible Understanding*, pp. 322-348.

the time of the destruction of Jerusalem and the desolation of its domain until the restoration. It says:

> "He [Nebuchadnezzar] proceeded to burn the house of the true God and pull down the wall of Jerusalem; and all its dwelling towers they burned with fire and also all its desirable articles, so as to cause ruin. Furthermore, he carried off those remaining from the sword captive to Babylon, and they came to be servants to him and his sons until the royalty of Persia began to reign; to fulfill Jehovah's word by the mouth of Jeremiah, until the land had paid off its sabbaths. All the days of lying desolated it kept sabbath, to fulfill seventy years."

Counting back seventy years from the time the Israelites arrived back in their cities, that is, in 537 B.C.E., brings us to 607 B.C.E. It was in that year, therefore, that Jerusalem, the seat of God's government in a representative sense, began to be trampled on by Gentile nations.

THE END OF THE "SEVEN TIMES"

Jesus Christ referred to this trampling on Jerusalem when he said to his disciples: "Jerusalem will be trampled on by the nations, until the appointed times of the nations are fulfilled." (Luke 21:24) Those "appointed times" were to end 2,520 years after 607 B.C.E. This would be in the year 1914 C.E. Did the trampling on Jerusalem cease then?

True, the earthly city of Jerusalem did not witness the restoration of a king in the royal line of David in 1914 C.E. But such a thing was not to be expected. Why not? The earthly city of Jerusalem no longer had any holy significance from God's viewpoint. While on earth, Jesus Christ stated: "Jerusalem, Jerusalem, the killer of the prophets and stoner of those sent forth to her—how often I wanted to gather your children together in the manner that a hen gathers her brood of chicks under her wings, but you people did not want it! Look! Your house is abandoned to you." (Luke 13:34, 35) Moreover, the kingdom in the hands of Jesus Christ is not an earthly government with Jerusalem or any other city as its capital. It is a heavenly kingdom.

Hence, it was in the invisible heavens that the year 1914 C.E. witnessed the fulfillment of Revelation 11:15: "The kingdom of the world did become the kingdom of our Lord and of his Christ, and he will rule as king forever and ever." What Jerusalem *represented,* that is, the Messianic government ruling with divine approval, was then no longer being trampled on. Once again there was a king of the Davidic dynasty who, by divine appointment, exercised rulership over the affairs of mankind. The visible events that have taken place here on earth in fulfillment of Bible prophecy since 1914 C.E. prove that this is the case.

One of these prophecies is found in the sixth chapter of the Bible book of Revelation. There the giving of royal authority to Jesus Christ and the events following it are described in symbolic terms.

Of Jesus' receiving the kingship the account says: "Look! a white horse; and the one seated upon it had a bow; and a crown was given him, and he went forth conquering and to complete his conquest." (Revelation 6:2) Later on, the book of Revelation unmistakably identifies the rider on that horse, saying: "Look! a white horse. And the one seated upon it is called Faithful and True, and he judges and carries on war in righteousness. . . . And upon his outer garment, even upon his thigh, he has a name written, King of kings and Lord of lords."—Revelation 19:11-16.

As to what would happen here on earth after Jesus' receiving the "crown" of active kingship over the world of mankind, Revelation chapter 6 continues:

"Another came forth, a fiery-colored horse; and to the one seated upon it there was granted to take peace away from the earth so that they should slaughter one another; and a great sword was given him. And when he opened the third seal, I heard the third living creature say: 'Come!' And I saw, and, look! a black horse; and the one seated upon it had a pair of scales in his hand. . . . And when he opened the fourth seal, I heard the voice of the fourth living creature say: 'Come!' And I saw, and, look! a pale horse; and the one seated upon it had the name Death. And Hades was closely following him. And authority was given them over the fourth part of the earth, to kill with a long sword and with food shortage and with deadly plague and by the wild beasts of the earth."—Vss. 4-8.

Have not these words been fulfilled? Did not the sword of global warfare rage from 1914 onward? Indeed! World War I witnessed the slaughter of humans on a scale never known before. Over nine million combatants died from wounds, disease and other causes. Civilian deaths directly or indirectly resulting from the war also ran into the millions. The second world war snuffed out an even greater number of lives. It claimed an estimated fifty-five million civilians and combatants.

Did not food shortage, like a black horse, stalk through the earth? Yes, in many parts of Europe there was famine during and after the World War I period. In Russia millions died. After the second world war came what *The World Book Encyclopedia* (1973) describes as "the greatest world-wide shortage of food in history." And today the grim fact is that one out of every three people on earth is slowly starving or suffering from malnutrition.

Deadly plague also took its toll. In a matter of months, during 1918-1919, the Spanish influenza epidemic alone killed about 20,000,000. No single disaster had ever before caused such a mammoth destruction of life among mankind.

Truly these things have been too big to escape notice. Says Joseph Carter, in his book *1918 Year of Crisis, Year of Change:* "In that autumn [of 1918], horror was piled on horror, for three of the Four Horsemen of the Apocalypse—war, famine, and pestilence—were indeed abroad." To this day the symbolic horsemen have not stopped their ride.

Thus there exists visible evidence that in 1914

C.E. the restraining bands were removed from the symbolic tree stump of Nebuchadnezzar's dream. Jehovah God began exercising authority through the kingdom of his Son, the Lord Jesus Christ. But why did this not improve conditions on earth? Why has the time of Christ's being given ruling authority over mankind been associated with trouble?

This is because Satan the Devil is against God's kingdom by Christ. He fought against it at the time of its being given authority over mankind. But he lost the battle and was ousted along with his demons from the holy heavens. Enraged, he and his demons are stirring up all the trouble they can among mankind to bring everyone and everything to ruin. That is why, after describing the war in heaven and its outcome, the Bible account continues: "Be glad, you heavens and you who reside in them! Woe for the earth and for the sea, because the Devil has come down to you, having great anger, knowing he has a short period of time."—Revelation 12:7-12.

How short is that period of time remaining to the Kingdom's adversary? Jesus Christ revealed that the time of his coming in Kingdom glory and the removal of the ungodly system of things would fall within the lifetime of one generation of people. He said: "Truly I say to you that this generation will by no means pass away until all these things occur."—Matthew 24:3-42.

Hence, some of the generation alive in 1914 C.E. must be among the people to witness Jesus' completing his conquest and taking full control of earth's affairs. That also means that many now living have the opportunity never to die. How so?

WHY MANY NOW LIVING WILL NOT
EXPERIENCE DEATH

In completing his conquest, Jesus Christ as king will take action only against those who refuse to submit to his rulership. When comforting fellow believers who were suffering persecution, the inspired apostle Paul wrote of this, saying: "It is righteous on God's part to repay tribulation to those who make tribulation for you, but, to you who suffer tribulation, relief along with us at the revelation of the Lord Jesus from heaven with his powerful angels in a flaming fire, as he brings vengeance upon those who do not know God and those who do not obey the good news about our Lord Jesus. These very ones will undergo the judicial punishment of everlasting destruction from before the Lord and from the glory of his strength."—2 Thessalonians 1:6-9.

Certainly not all persons refuse to "know" or recognize God's authority in their lives. Not all are disobedient to the 'good news about Jesus Christ.' Though few, when compared with the world's population, there is a body of Christians who are striving hard to prove themselves to be devoted servants of God and loyal disciples of Jesus Christ. Those whom the day of divine execution finds exclusively devoted to Jehovah God can rest assured that they will not be swept away by that judgment. The Bible says:

"These are the ones that come out of the great tribulation, and they have washed their robes and made them white in the blood of the Lamb. That is why they are before the throne of God; and they are rendering him sacred service day and night in his temple; and the One seated on the throne will spread his tent over them. They will hunger no more nor thirst anymore, neither will the sun beat down upon them nor any scorching heat, because the Lamb, who is in the midst of the throne, will shepherd them, and will guide them to fountains of waters of life. And God will wipe out every tear from their eyes." —Revelation 7:14-17.

The prospect before the great crowd of "tribulation" survivors is, not death, but life. The "Lamb," that is, the Lord Jesus Christ, will be guiding them to "fountains of waters of life." This is not life for merely seventy or eighty years, but forever. He will be applying to them the benefits of his sin-atoning sacrifice, liberating them from sin and its death-dealing effects. As they obediently respond to his help, they will attain to human perfection, with no need to die.

There will be no interference from Satan and his demonic horde to hinder their progress. After the "great tribulation" has brought an end to the earthly wicked system of things, Satan will be abyssed for a thousand years. The Bible's symbolic description of this event reads: "I saw an angel coming down out of heaven with the key of the abyss and a great chain in his hand. And he seized the dragon, the original serpent, who is the Devil and Satan, and bound him for a thousand years. And he hurled him into the abyss and shut it and sealed it over him, that he might not mislead the nations." (Revelation 20:1-3) Thus, as if dead, Satan and his demons will be in no position to cause trouble for humankind.

The Bible clearly pinpoints the generation alive in 1914 C.E. as the one that will yet witness the ushering in of Kingdom rule free from Satanic interference. Hence, many living today will have the opportunity never to die. They will survive the destruction of the present ungodly system and thereafter gradually be freed from sin and brought to human perfection. As sinless humans they will then be exempt from sin's wages—death. —Romans 6:23.

This makes it urgent for you to place yourself on the side of the King Jesus Christ, if you have not already done so, and to live now as one of his loyal subjects. That is what Jehovah's Christian witnesses are endeavoring to do, and they are eager to assist others to do the same.

CHAPTER 19

Billions Now Dead Will Soon Live Again

THE Kingdom administration in the hands of Jesus Christ and his 144,000 associate rulers will indeed bestow grand blessings upon the survivors of the "great tribulation." At that time the damaging effects of Adam's plunging himself and his unborn offspring into sin will not be recalled in such a way as to be mentally and emotionally painful. The inspired words of the prophet Isaiah promise: "The former things will not be called to mind, neither will they come up into the heart."—Isaiah 65:17.

For that to be the case, the pain and sorrow resulting from the death-dealing effects of sin must be completely undone. This would include raising to life billions of people now dead. Why?

Well, if you were to survive the "great tribulation," would you be truly happy knowing that dear friends and relatives who had died in years past were still deprived of life and its blessings? Would this not bring pain of heart and mind to you? To remove any possibility of such pain, the dead must be raised. Only if they can be restored to life and be assisted to attain perfection in body and mind will the damaging effects of sin be fully erased.

The Holy Scriptures assure us that the dead in general will live again. They will be given the opportunity to have more than the short life-span that ended at their death. Jehovah God has empowered his Son Jesus Christ to resurrect them. (John 5:26-28) Jesus' being empowered to raise the dead agrees with the fact that he is prophetically referred to in the Bible as the "Eternal Father." (Isaiah 9:6) By raising to life those sleeping in death, Jesus becomes their Father.—Compare Psalm 45:16.

BASIS FOR BELIEF

For one who accepts the existence of God, there should be no problem in having a firm belief in the resurrection. Is it not reasonable that the One who originally started off human life is also wise enough to restore life to the dead, to re-create dead humans? Jehovah God has personally promised that the dead will live again. He has also performed powerful works that strengthen one's confidence in this promise.

Jehovah God empowered some of his faithful servants actually to raise the dead. At Zarephath, not far from the eastern shore of the Mediterranean Sea, Elijah the prophet resurrected the only son of a widow. (1 Kings 17:21-23) His successor Elisha raised the only son of a prominent, hospitable woman at Shunem, in the northern part of Israel. (2 Kings 4:8, 32-37) Jesus Christ resurrected the daughter of Jairus, a presiding officer of a synagogue near the Sea of Galilee; the only son of a widow at Nain, to the southwest of the Sea of Galilee; and his dear friend Lazarus, who had been dead four days and was buried not far from Jerusalem. (Mark 5:22, 35, 41-43; Luke 7:11-17; John 11:38-45) At Joppa, on the Mediterranean coast, the apostle Peter raised Dorcas (Tabitha) from the dead. (Acts 9:36-42) And the apostle Paul, on a stopover in the Roman province of Asia, resurrected Eutychus after he had tumbled to his death from a third-story window.—Acts 20:7-12.

The most remarkable resurrection was that of Jesus Christ himself. This well-attested historical event provides the strongest proof for there being a resurrection. That is what the apostle Paul pointed out to those assembled at the Areopagus in Athens, Greece: "[God] purposes to judge the inhabited earth in righteousness by a man whom he has appointed, and he has furnished a guarantee to all men in that he has resurrected him from the dead."—Acts 17:31.

Jesus' resurrection was a fact established beyond a shadow of doubt. There were far more than two or three witnesses who could testify to it. Why, on one occasion the resurrected Jesus Christ appeared to upward of five hundred disciples. So well confirmed was his resurrection that the apostle Paul could say that denial of the resurrection meant denial of Christian faith as a whole. He wrote: "If, indeed, there is no resurrection of the dead, neither has Christ been raised up. But if Christ has not been raised up, our preaching is certainly in vain, and our faith is in vain.

Moreover, we are also found false witnesses of God, because we have borne witness against God that he raised up the Christ, but whom he did not raise up if the dead are really not to be raised up."—1 Corinthians 15:13-15.

Early Christians, like the apostle Paul, knew for a certainty that Jesus had been raised from the dead. So powerful was their conviction of being rewarded in the resurrection that they were willing to face severe persecution, even death itself.

RESURRECTION TO SPIRIT LIFE

The resurrection of Jesus Christ shows that raising the dead does not mean bringing back to life the identical body. Jesus was raised, not to human life, but to spirit life. With reference to this, the apostle Peter wrote: "Why, even Christ died once for all time concerning sins, a righteous person for unrighteous ones, that he might lead you to God, he being put to death in the flesh, but being made alive in the spirit." (1 Peter 3:18) At his resurrection Jesus received a body, not of flesh and blood, but one suitable for heavenly life.—1 Corinthians 15:40, 50.

That spirit body was, of course, invisible to human eyes. Hence, for his disciples to see him after his resurrection, Jesus had to take on flesh. It should be noted that Jesus was not buried with clothing but was wrapped up in fine linen bandages. After his resurrection the bandages remained in the tomb. So, just as Jesus had to materialize clothing, he also took on flesh to make himself visible to his disciples. (Luke 23: 53; John 19:40; 20:6, 7) Strange? No, this was exactly what angels had done prior to this time when they appeared to humans. The fact that Jesus materialized a body of flesh explains why his disciples did not always recognize him at first and why he could appear and disappear suddenly.—Luke 24:15-31; John 20:13-16, 20.

Only the 144,000 joint heirs who are associated with Jesus Christ in rulership will experience a resurrection like his. Discussing that resurrection to spirit life, the Bible tells us:

"What you sow is not made alive unless first it dies; and as for what you sow, you sow, not the body that will develop, but a bare grain, it may be, of wheat or any one of the rest; but God gives it a body just as it has pleased him, and to each of the seeds its own body. . . .

"So also is the resurrection of the dead. It is sown in corruption, it is raised up in incorruption. It is sown in dishonor, it is raised up in glory. It is sown in weakness, it is raised up in power. It is sown a physical body, it is raised up a spiritual body. If there is a physical body, there is also a spiritual one. It is even so written: 'The first man Adam became a living soul.' The last Adam became a life-giving spirit. Nevertheless, the first is, not that which is spiritual, but that which is physical, afterward that which is spiritual. The first man is out of the earth and made of dust; the second man is out of heaven. As the one made of dust is, so those made of dust are also; and as the heavenly one is, so those who are heavenly are also. And just as we have borne the image of the one made of dust, we shall bear also the image of the heavenly one." —1 Corinthians 15:36-49.

RESURRECTION TO LIFE ON EARTH

But what of those who, unlike Jesus Christ and his 144,000 fellow rulers, will be resurrected to earthly life? Since they have 'returned to the dust,' will God have to reassemble all the atoms that once formed their bodies so that their bodies are identical in every respect to what they were at the moment of death?

No, that simply could not be. Why not? First of all, because this would mean that they would be brought back to life in a condition on the verge of death. Persons resurrected in the past were not brought back in the identical sickly condition that preceded their death. Though not perfect at the time of their resurrection, they had a whole, reasonably sound body.

Moreover, it would not be reasonable to insist that precisely the same atoms be regathered to form their restored body. After death, and through the process of decay, the human body is converted into other organic chemicals. These may be absorbed by plants, and people may eat these plants or their fruit. Thus the atomic elements making up the deceased person can eventually come to be in other people. Obviously, at the time of the resurrection the identical atoms cannot be reassembled in every person brought back from the dead.

What, then, does resurrection mean for the individual? It means his being brought back to life as the same *person*. And what makes an individual the person he is? Is it the chemical substance making up his body? No, inasmuch as the molecules in the body are regularly being replaced. What really distinguishes him from other people, then, is his general physical appearance, his voice, his personality, his experiences, mental growth and memory. So when Jehovah God, by means of his Son Jesus Christ, raises a person from the dead, he evidently will provide that person with a body having the same traits as previously. The resurrected person will have the same memory that he had acquired during his lifetime and he will have the full awareness of that memory. The person will be able to identify himself, and those who knew him will also be able to do so.

'But if a person is thus re-created,' someone may say, 'is he really the same person? Is he not just a copy?' No, for this reasoning overlooks the fact earlier mentioned that even in life our bodies are constantly undergoing change. About seven years ago the molecules making up our bodies were different from the molecules forming them today. We even differ in appearance as the years go by. Yet, do we not have the same fingerprints? Are we not the same persons? Most certainly.

Those to whom the resurrection seems almost unbelievable should reflect on a similarly marvelous process that takes place at the time of human conception. The tiny cell that is formed by the uniting of the sperm and the egg has within it the potential for becoming a person different from any other person that has ever lived. Within this cell there are the factors that direct the

Is it not possible for the one who makes a baby grow in its mother's womb also to resurrect the dead?

building of the individual and the forming of the basic personality he inherits from his parents. Then, of course, his life experiences thereafter add to that personality. Similar to what happens at the time of conception, at the time of the resurrection or re-creation the deceased person will have his personality and life record restored to him, every cell of his body being impressed with the characteristics that make him different from all other persons. And his heart, mind and body will have impressed within them the added qualities, traits and abilities that he developed during his former lifetime.

Regarding the Creator, the inspired psalmist noted: "Your eyes saw even the embryo of me, and in your book all its parts were down in writing, as regards the days when they were formed and there was not yet one among them." (Psalm 139:16) Accordingly, as soon as the genetic combinations are formed at the time of conception, Jehovah God is capable of perceiving and having a record of a child's basic traits. So it is wholly logical that he is capable of having an accurate record by which to re-create one who has died.

We can have confidence in Jehovah's perfect memory. Why, even imperfect humans, by means of videotape, can preserve and construct visible and audible reproductions of persons. Far greater is God's ability to keep such records, for he calls all the numberless stars by name!—Psalm 147:4.

It can be seen, therefore, that resurrection or re-creation is possible because the deceased individual lives in God's memory. Because of his perfect memory of life patterns and his purpose to resurrect the dead, Jehovah God could count deceased men of faith like Abraham, Isaac and Jacob as being alive. That is what Jesus Christ called to the attention of unbelieving Sadducees, saying: "That the dead are raised up even Moses disclosed, in the account about the thornbush, when he calls Jehovah 'the God of Abraham and God of Isaac and God of Jacob.' He is a God, not of the dead, but of the living, for they are all living to him."—Luke 20:37, 38.

There is indeed ample basis for believing in the resurrection or re-creation. True, some may reject the idea. But would you be better off to close your eyes and mind to the evidence and refuse to believe in the resurrection? Would it make it easier for you to lose a dear relative or friend in death? Would you be better prepared to face the grim prospect of your own death?

Knowing that this life is not all there is frees one from the fear of having it cut off prematurely by violent means. This fear has been exploited by Satan the Devil in holding people in slavery, maneuvering them through his earthly agents to do his bidding. (Matthew 10:28; Hebrews 2:14) Afraid of the possibility of being executed, many have failed to follow the dictates of their conscience and have committed dastardly crimes against humanity, as was done in the concentration camps of Nazi Germany.

The person with strong faith in the resurrection, however, is strengthened in his determination to do what is right even if that might mean death for him. To him the life that he will enjoy upon being raised from the dead is far more precious than a few years of life now. He does not want to jeopardize his opportunity to gain everlasting life for what, by comparison, could hardly be called a lengthening of his life. He is like the men of ancient times of whom the Bible book of Hebrews reports: "[They] were tortured because they would not accept release by some ransom [some compromise of what is right], in order that they might attain a better resurrection."—Hebrews 11:35.

Certainly those who have confidence in God's promise to raise the dead are far better off than those who do not have the resurrection hope. They can look to the future without fear.

Biblical evidence shows that this system will soon come to its end, within this generation, and be replaced by a righteous administration in the hands of Jesus Christ and his associate rulers. That is why billions now dead will soon live again and begin to benefit from Kingdom rule. How grand it will be for the "tribulation" survivors to welcome back the dead! Think of the joy of once again being able to have the encouraging companionship of dear friends and beloved relatives, to hear their familiar voices and to see them in good health.

What effect should this have on you? Should it not prompt you to thank God for the marvelous resurrection hope? Should not your gratitude move you to do all that you can to learn about him and then to serve him faithfully?

CHAPTER 20

For Whom Will Resurrection Bring Benefits?

MANY questions come up about the resurrection of the dead. Who will be resurrected? Infants? Children? Both the righteous and the wicked? Will those who were married be reunited with their former mates?

The Bible does not go into every detail about the resurrection. However, it contains the marvelous promise that the dead will be raised to life and it gives enough particulars to establish faith in that promise. Should its silence about certain matters keep us from appreciating the soundness of that promise?

In our dealings with fellowmen we do not expect every detail to be spelled out, do we? For example, if you were invited to a banquet, you would not ask the one extending the invitation: 'Where will all the people sit? Are you prepared to cook for so many people? How can I be sure you will have enough serving utensils and dishes?' To ask such questions would be an insult, would it not? No one would think of saying to a host: 'First convince me that I will enjoy myself.' Having the invitation and knowing its source should be sufficient for one to be confident that things will go well.

Really, no one would appreciate being called upon to explain or prove each statement that he makes. Let us say that an acquaintance described an experience in saving a person from drowning. If he was a respected friend, we would not ask him to prove that he actually did the things he described. To require this would show lack of confidence and trust. It would be no basis for building and maintaining a friendship. Obviously, then, one who would not accept God's promise of a resurrection without first having every detail clarified could never be counted as His friend. God accepts as his friends only those who exercise faith, who trust his word. (Hebrews 11:6) He provides abundant evidence on which to base such faith, but he does not force people to believe by providing and proving every single detail so that faith is unnecessary.

Thus the absence of certain details serves to test people as to what they are at heart. There are those who have a high opinion of themselves and their own pet ideas, and who follow a course of independence. They do not want to be accountable to anyone. Belief in the resurrection would require them to acknowledge a need to live in harmony with God's will. But this they do not want to do. Hence, due to the absence of certain details about the resurrection, they may find what they consider to be justification for their disbelief. They are much like the Sadducees in the time of Jesus' earthly ministry. The Sadducees refused to believe in the resurrection and pointed to what they thought to be an insurmountable problem. They said to Jesus:

"Teacher, Moses wrote us, 'If a man's brother dies having a wife, but this one remained childless, his brother should take the wife and raise up offspring from her for his brother.' Accordingly there were seven brothers; and the first took a wife and died

childless. So the second, and the third took her. Likewise even the seven: they did not leave children behind, but died off. Lastly, the woman also died. Consequently, in the resurrection, of which one of them
does she become the wife? For the seven got her as
wife."—Luke 20:28-33.

In answering their question, Jesus Christ exposed the wrongness of the Sadducees' reasoning
and emphasized the surety of the resurrection
promise. He replied:

"The children of this system of things marry and
are given in marriage, but those who have been
counted worthy of gaining that system of things and
the resurrection from the dead neither marry nor
are given in marriage. . . . But that the dead are
raised up even Moses disclosed, in the account about
the thornbush, when he calls Jehovah 'the God of
Abraham and God of Isaac and God of Jacob.' He is
a God, not of the dead, but of the living, for they
are all living to him."—Luke 20:34-38.

WHY RESURRECTION HOLDS FORTH
NO PROMISE OF MARRIAGE

On the basis of Jesus' answer to the Sadducees,
some may be disturbed about his saying that
there will be no marrying among those raised
from the dead. They may even think that without
marriage the resurrection is something undesirable, that it would not benefit them.

However, when reasoning on Jesus' reply, we
do well to remember that we are imperfect. Our
likes and dislikes are largely conditioned by the
things to which we have become accustomed. So
no one really has any basis for being sure that
he would not like the future provisions that God
will make for the resurrected ones. Then, too,
not all the details have been provided. This has
really been a kindness on God's part. Why, as

imperfect humans, we might at first react unfavorably to things that would actually fill our life with joy in a perfect state. Such details therefore might be beyond our present ability to receive. Christ Jesus showed awareness and consideration of the limitations of imperfect humans, as evident from what he said to his disciples on one occasion: "I have many things yet to say to you, but you are not able to bear them at present."—John 16:12.

Those who will attain a resurrection to immortal spirit life in the heavens have no concept of what it will be like. They cannot compare it with anything they know on earth. Their bodies will be completely different. All sex distinctions belonging to humans will be things of the past for them. So there can be no marrying among those raised to spirit life in the heavens because they all together as a body become the "bride" of Christ.

But what about those who are brought back from the dead to live on earth? Will they be reunited with former marriage mates? No statement in the Bible indicates that this will be the case. The Scriptures definitely show that death dissolves the marriage. Romans 7:2, 3 reads: "A married woman is bound by law to her husband while he is alive; but if her husband dies, she is discharged from the law of her husband . . . so that she is not an adulteress if she becomes another man's."

Hence, if a person chooses to remarry now, he does not have to worry about the effect this might have on a resurrected mate in the future. If singleness is not for him, he does not have to struggle to maintain it in the hope of being re-

united in marriage with his former mate in the
resurrection. Surely, then, it was a kindness on
God's part not to require former marriage relationships to be in force at the time of a person's resurrection, as the Sadducees erroneously
thought.

While we do not know where on earth or with
whom the resurrected ones will live, we can
rest assured that whatever arrangement exists
will contribute to the happiness of the resurrected
ones. God's gifts, including the resurrection, will
wholly satisfy the desires and needs of obedient
mankind. His gifts are perfect, flawless. (James
1:17) The generous gifts that we have already
received as expressions of his love convince us
of that.

CHILDREN AND OTHERS TO BE RAISED

What of children who die? Will they too return
to life when righteousness prevails on this earth?
Surely that is what loving parents would want
for any children that they may have lost in
death. And there is solid basis for entertaining
such a hope.

Among those reported in the Bible as having
been resurrected were children. The daughter of
Jairus, who lived in Galilee, was about twelve
years of age; Jesus brought her back to life.
(Luke 8:42, 54, 55) The boys who were raised
from the dead by the prophets Elijah and Elisha
may have been older or younger. (1 Kings 17:
20-23; 2 Kings 4:32-37) In view of these past
resurrections of children, is it not right to expect that a large-scale resurrection of children
will take place during Jesus' rule as king? Most
assuredly! We can be certain that whatever

Jehovah God has purposed in this regard will be the just, wise and loving thing for all concerned.

The Bible reveals that by far the majority of mankind—men, women and children—will be raised from the dead. As the apostle Paul affirmed in his defense before Governor Felix: "I have hope toward God . . . that there is going to be a resurrection of both the righteous and the unrighteous." (Acts 24:15) The "righteous" are those who lived in God's favor. The "unrighteous" are the rest of mankind. But does that mean that every dead individual will have a resurrection? No, it does not.

THOSE WHO WILL NOT BE RESURRECTED

Certain ones have been judged by God as undeserving of a resurrection. Regarding those who in the present time refuse to submit to Christ's rulership and fail to do good to his "brothers" on earth, the Bible says: "These will depart into everlasting cutting-off." (Matthew 25:46) They will experience this everlasting cutting-off when Jesus Christ, along with his angelic forces, destroys all opposers of his righteous rule in the "great tribulation," now near.

As to any in line for the kingdom of the heavens who prove unfaithful to God, we are told: "There is no longer any sacrifice for sins left, but there is a certain fearful expectation of judgment and there is a fiery jealousy that is going to consume those in opposition."—Hebrews 10:26, 27.

Also, there are classes of people who are spoken of as experiencing an eternal destruction. Jesus Christ indicated that the unrepentant Pharisees and other religious leaders of his day as a class had sinned against the holy spirit. He said of such sin: "Every sort of sin and blasphemy will be forgiven men, but the blasphemy against the spirit will not be forgiven. For example, whoever speaks a word against the Son of man, it will be forgiven him; but whoever speaks against the holy spirit, it will not be forgiven him, no, not in this system of things nor in that to come." (Matthew 12:31, 32) There being no forgiveness for such sin, all guilty of denying obvious manifestations of God's spirit pay the penalty for such unforgivable sin by remaining dead forever.

Aside from what the Bible says specifically about those who have perished everlastingly, we are in no position to say that particular individuals will not be raised from the dead. The fact that some will not be, however, should serve as a warning to us to avoid a course leading to divine disapproval.

A RESURRECTION OF JUDGMENT

The fact that the majority of mankind will be raised from the dead is truly an undeserved kindness on God's part. It is something that God does not have to do, but his love and compassion for humankind moved him to lay the basis for it by providing his Son as a ransom. (John 3:16) That any humans would fail to appreciate their being raised from the dead with the prospect of eternal life is, therefore, hard to imagine. Yet there will be some who will not develop full, unbreakable, loyal attachment to Jehovah God. They will therefore lose out on the lasting blessings that being brought back to life will offer them.

Jesus Christ called attention to this when he spoke of a "resurrection of judgment" and set it in contrast with the "resurrection of life." (John 5:29) The fact that life is here contrasted with judgment makes it clear that a condemnatory judgment is involved. What is this condemnation?

To understand this, contrast first the situation of those resurrected to earthly life with that of those resurrected to heavenly life. The Bible says of those sharing in the "first resurrection": "Happy and holy is anyone having part in the first resurrection; over these the second death has no authority." (Revelation 20:6) Raised to immortal life in the heavens, the 144,000 joint heirs of Christ *cannot die*. Their loyalty to God is so certain that he can entrust them with an indestructible life. But this is not the case with all those raised to life on earth. There will be some of these latter ones who will become disloyal to God. The condemnatory judgment passed on them for unfaithfulness will be "second death," a death from the "authority" of which no recovery is possible.

Yet why would anyone end up following a course leading to condemnatory judgment when he has been granted the undeserved favor of being raised from the dead?

The answer to this question can be better understood in the light of what Jesus Christ said about people who would be resurrected. Addressing his unbelieving fellow countrymen, Jesus said:

"Men of Nineveh will rise up in the judgment with this generation and will condemn it; because they repented at what Jonah preached, but, look! some-

thing more than Jonah is here. The queen of the
south will be raised up in the judgment with this
generation and will condemn it; because she came
from the ends of the earth to hear the wisdom of
Solomon, but, look! something more than Solomon is
here."—Matthew 12:41, 42; Luke 11:31, 32.

With reference to a city that would stubbornly
refuse to listen to the message of truth, Jesus
noted:

"It will be more endurable for the land of Sodom
and Gomorrah on Judgment Day than for that city."
—Matthew 10:15; see also Matthew 11:21-24.

How would it be more endurable on Judgment
Day for Sodom and Gomorrah? How would the
"queen of the south" and the Ninevites who
responded to Jonah's preaching condemn the
generation of Jesus' fellow countrymen?

This will be in the way such resurrected ones
respond to the help given during the reign of
Jesus Christ and his 144,000 associate king-
priests. That period of rulership will be a "Judgment Day" in that it will provide all persons
opportunity to demonstrate whether they want
to submit to God's arrangements. In the case of
those like the unbelieving inhabitants of cities
who witnessed the powerful works of Jesus
Christ, this is not going to be easy.

It is going to be hard for them to recognize
humbly that they were wrong in rejecting Jesus
as the Messiah and then to have to submit themselves to him as their King. Pride and stubborn-
ness will make submission more difficult for them
than for the inhabitants of Sodom and Gomorrah,
who, while sinful, never rejected grand opportunities like those set before persons who witnessed
the works of Jesus Christ. The better response

of the resurrected Ninevites and that of the queen of Sheba will serve as a reproof to the resurrected generation of Jesus' fellow country-men living in the time of his earthly ministry. It will be much easier for these Ninevites and similar ones to accept the rule of someone toward whom they had never been prejudiced.

Those who positively refuse to make progress in the way of righteousness under Christ's king-dom will experience the condemnatory judgment of "second death." In certain cases this will happen before they reach human perfection.

Furthermore, others, after having been brought to human perfection, will unappreciatively fail to demonstrate loyal devotion to Jehovah God when put to the test. Following the thousand-year reign of Christ, Satan the Devil will be released for a short time from his confinement in the abyss. As he attacked God's sovereignty to seduce Eve, who then persuaded Adam, he will again seek to get perfect humans to rebel against God's rulership. Of Satan's attempt and its outcome, Revelation 20:7-10, 14, 15 says:

"As soon as the thousand years have been ended, Satan will be let loose out of his prison, and he will go out to mislead those nations in the four corners of the earth, Gog and Magog, to gather them together for the war. The number of these is as the sand of the sea. And they advanced over the breadth of the earth and en-circled the camp of the holy ones and the beloved city. But fire came down out of heaven and de-voured them. And the Devil who was misleading them was hurled into the lake of fire and sulphur . . . This means the second death, the lake of fire. Furthermore, whoever was not found written in the book of life was hurled into the lake of fire." This signifies their unending destruction or annihilation. Thus these unfaithful ones will have what Jesus called "a resurrection of judgment," a condemnatory judgment.

On the other hand, those who refuse to join Satan in rebellion will be judged worthy of receiving everlasting life. They will forever rejoice in having life as perfect humans, expressing love and being loved for all eternity. Theirs will prove to be a "resurrection of life."

Even now we can start to develop the qualities that God looks for in those whom he recognizes as his approved servants. If we show ourselves appreciative for all that he has done and get an advance start in the way of righteousness, we can have the wonderful prospect of having far more than the present life. Yes, we can have life everlasting in perfection, free from all sorrow and pain!

CHAPTER 21

How Can You Have More than This Life?

FROM all the foregoing information it is abundantly clear that there is much, much more to life than what we now experience. Just think of it—Jehovah God has set before mankind the grand prospect of life here on earth under righteous conditions, with freedom from sickness and death! It can be yours to enjoy, not just for a hundred years or a thousand years, but forever.

And the time when this will become reality is so near at hand!

Will you be among those to benefit from the realization of God's glorious purpose for man and his home, the earth? You definitely can be. But you need to act without delay. We are now living at the time when the Bible's warning takes on great urgency: "Before there comes upon you people the burning anger of Jehovah, before there comes upon you the day of Jehovah's anger, seek Jehovah, all you meek ones of the earth, who have practiced His own judicial decision. Seek righteousness, seek meekness. Probably you may be concealed in the day of Jehovah's anger." —Zephaniah 2:2, 3.

The "burning anger of Jehovah" is against all who have misled their fellowmen by lying about God and his purpose. And he does not hold guiltless those who support such men by attending their religious services or being members of their organizations. The time left before the execution of divine judgment is short. If you are a lover of righteousness you need to act quickly to obey the Scriptural command to break all ties with the world empire of false religion. Take seriously the urging of God's Word, which says: "Get out of her, my people, if you do not want to share with her in her sins, and if you do not want to receive part of her plagues." —Revelation 18:4.

But it is not enough simply to break off one's connections with organizations that have tolerated and encouraged unrighteousness. The Bible puts us on notice that God's "wrath is being revealed from heaven against all ungodliness and unrighteousness," yes, against the practices themselves and those who continue to indulge in them. (Romans 1:18) It does not leave us in any doubt as to what those practices are. It clearly identifies them and urges all who would have Jehovah's approval to clean such things out of their lives. Love for Jehovah and gratitude for his goodness can make such a change possible. —Ephesians 4:25–5:6; Colossians 3:5, 6.

This is no time to seek to justify oneself, presuming that the good deeds that one does from day to day more than offset one's shortcomings. Setting their own standards of good and bad led to calamity in the case of Adam and Eve. And even in our day the Bible proverb is true that says: "There exists a way that is upright before a man, but the ways of death are the end of it afterward." (Proverbs 16:25) Now is the time, then, to learn Jehovah's ways, to seek his "righteousness." This is also the time to "seek meekness," that is, to be submissive to God's judgment and humbly to accept his correction and discipline, conforming to his will. Only by doing this will it be possible for you to be "concealed in the day of Jehovah's anger."

Do not conclude, as some have, that your way of life has been too bad for God to forgive you. Rather, take comfort from the words addressed to unfaithful Israelites of old: "Let the wicked man leave his way, and the harmful man his thoughts; and let him return to Jehovah, who will have mercy upon him, and to our God, for he will forgive in a large way." (Isaiah 55:7) Also, find encouragement in his promise that says: "Though the sins of you people should prove to be as scarlet, they will be made white just like snow; though they should be red like crimson cloth, they will become even like wool."—Isaiah 1:18.

Jehovah God has no pleasure in executing judgment against anyone but wants all to enjoy life. (2 Peter 3:9) Still, Jehovah cannot and will not condone unrighteousness. Hence, it is necessary for all who would have his approval to repent of their former way of life and to change their ways to conform to his righteous will.—Isaiah 55:6.

The thing to do now is to start to learn what God requires of you, to take in the vital knowledge contained in his Word, and then to act in harmony with it. This is the way that leads to eternal life. (John 17:3) Jehovah's Christian witnesses will gladly give you personal help in acquiring an accurate knowledge of the Bible, free of charge. They also welcome you to their Kingdom Halls, where they regularly discuss God's Word.

A TRULY BENEFICIAL WAY

By responding to the things you learn from the Bible, you will experience beneficial changes in your life. You will find that the application of Bible principles will improve relationships at home, at work and in your daily contacts with fellowmen. (Romans 12:17-21; 13:8-10; Ephesians 5:22–6:4; 1 Peter 3:1-7) This will contribute much toward making your life happier, more contented and meaningful even now.

Of course, this does not mean that you will be immune from the problems and pressures of the world. You are still going to be living among people who have no love of righteousness, and some of them will no doubt endeavor to discourage you from learning and applying the

Bible in your life. (2 Timothy 3:12; 1 Peter 4:4) But, as you grow in knowledge of God's Word, you will find that you are able to cope with the problems of life far more effectively than do those who rely on mere human reasoning. Instead of becoming bitter because of injustices that you may suffer, you will know the reason for them and will have the firm conviction that God's kingdom by Christ will soon put an end to all these things that detract from full enjoyment of life.—2 Peter 3:11-13.

As you acquire faith in God's loving provisions for eternal life, you will gain freedom from the oppressive influence that the prospect of death has had on all mankind. No longer will the falsehoods that have been taught concerning death mar your enjoyment of life. The shortsighted view that this life is all there is will lose any influence that it may have had toward tempting you to sacrifice right principles and a good conscience in an effort to get ahead in the world. The conviction that God can and will bring the dead back to life will enable you to gain freedom from the fear of death itself. Faith based on an accurate knowledge of God's Word will make it possible for you to enjoy life now as never before and to rejoice in the grand prospect of the future—everlasting life in God's righteous new order.

May appreciation for the loving provisions that God has made for mankind kindle in you a burning desire to know and to do his will. May it move you, with a sincere heart, to join with the psalmist who said: "Make me know your own ways, O Jehovah; teach me your own paths. Make me walk in your truth and teach me, for you are my God of salvation."—Psalm 25:4, 5.

THE FUTURE FOR MANKIND
Is Connected with Its Past

♦ Is man's past connected with mindless evolution and thus governed by chance? If it is, what future does humanity have? On the other hand, if man originally was created by God, then the purpose of God determines what the future holds for mankind.

But what about the evidence that scientists give on behalf of evolution? This is discussed in the thoroughly documented 192-page book **Did Man Get Here by Evolution or by Creation?** Examine that evidence and see for yourself which is most reasonable—a popular theory or the Bible's account of man's origin and his future.

DID MAN GET HERE BY EVOLUTION OR BY CREATION?

♦ But how can a person be sure that the Bible truly is from God? Read the 192-page book **Is the Bible Really the Word of God?**

To obtain either of these attractive hardbound books postpaid, just send 25c, or 50c for both.

Write to **Watchtower**, using an address from the next page.

WHAT WAS FORETOLD ABOUT OUR DAY AND THE FUTURE

Events foretold by the Bible for our day have come to pass. This gives you a basis for strong confidence in what the Holy Scriptures say about the future. Did you know that the Bible foretells a thousand years of peace? Would you like to have thrilling details about this thousand-year reign of Jesus Christ? Do you want a preview of the blessings it will bring? Then obtain and read the book **God's Kingdom of a Thousand Years Has Approached.**

This volume also discusses the amazing events foretold for our day, as found in the Bible at Matthew chapters twenty-four and twenty-five. Explained are Jesus Christ's prophetic parables of the ten virgins, the talents, and the sheep and goats. How they relate to your future is made clear. This hard-covered 416-page book will be sent to you postpaid for just 50c.

If you would like to have someone visit your home to discuss Bible questions with you, write to **Watchtower** at an address given below.

ALASKA 99507: 2552 East 48th Ave., Anchorage. AUSTRALIA: 11 Beresford Road, Strathfield, N.S.W. 2135. BAHAMAS: Box N-1247, Nassau, N.P. BARBADOS, W.I.: Fontabelle Rd., Bridgetown. BELIZE: Box 257, Belize City. BRAZIL: Rue Guaíra, 216, Bosque da Saúde, 04142 São Paulo, SP. CANADA: 150 Bridgeland Ave., Toronto, Ont. M6A 1Z5. CONGO REPUBLIC: B.P. 2.114, Brazzaville. ENGLAND: Watch Tower House, The Ridgeway, London NW7 1RN. FIJI: Box 23, Suva. FRANCE: 81 rue du Point-du-Jour, 92100 Boulogne-Billancourt. GERMANY (WESTERN): Postfach 13025, 62 Wiesbaden-Dotzheim. GHANA: Box 760, Accra. GUYANA: 50 Brickdam, Georgetown 16. HAWAII 96814: 1228 Pensacola St., Honolulu. HONG KONG: 312 Prince Edward Rd., Second Floor, Kowloon. INDIA: South Avenue, Santa Cruz, Bombay 400054. INDONESIA: Jl Batuceper 47, Jakarta Pusat, DKI. IRELAND: 86 Lindsay Rd., Glasnevin, Dublin 9. JAMAICA, W.I.: 41 Trafalgar Rd., Kingston 10. KENYA: Box 47788, Nairobi. LEEWARD ISLANDS, W.I.: Box 119, St. Johns, Antigua. LIBERIA: P.O. Box 171, Monrovia. MALAYSIA: 20 Scotland Close, Penang. NEWFOUNDLAND, CANADA A1C 2M1: 239 Pennywell Rd., St. John's. NEW ZEALAND: 6-A Western Springs Rd., Auckland 3. NIGERIA: P.O. Box 194, Yaba, Lagos State. PAKISTAN: 8-E Habibullah Rd., Lahore 3. PANAMA: Apartado 1386, Panama 1. PAPUA NEW GUINEA: Box 113, Port Moresby. PHILIPPINE REPUBLIC: 186 Roosevelt Ave., San Francisco del Monte, Quezon City D-503. RHODESIA: P.O. Box 1462, Salisbury. SIERRA LEONE: Box 136, Freetown. SOUTH AFRICA: Private Bag 2, P.O. Elandsfontein 1406. SRI LANKA, REP. OF: 62 Layard's Road, Colombo 5. SWITZERLAND: Ulmenweg 45, P.O. Box 477, CH-3601 Thun. TRINIDAD, W.I.: 2 La Seiva Road, Maraval, Port of Spain. UNITED STATES OF AMERICA: 117 Adams St., Brooklyn, N.Y. 11201.